Time Out

San Francisco

timeout.com/sanfrancisco

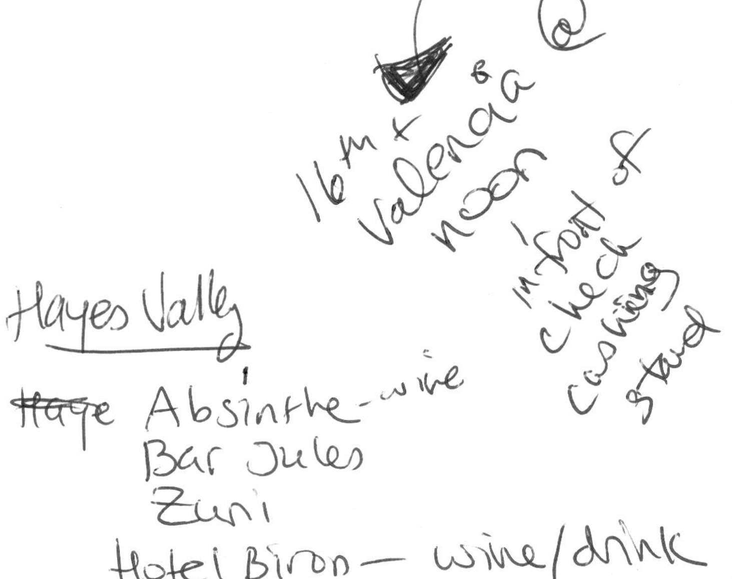

Time Out Guides Ltd
Universal House
251 Tottenham Court Road
London W1T 7AB
United Kingdom
Tel: +44 (0)20 7813 3000
Fax: +44 (0)20 7813 6001
Email: guides@timeout.com
www.timeout.com

Published by Time Out Guides Ltd, a wholly owned subsidiary of Time Out Group Ltd.
Time Out and the Time Out logo are trademarks of Time Out Group Ltd.

10 9 8 7 6 5 4 3 2 1

This edition first published in Great Britain in 2011 by Ebury Publishing.
A Random House Group Company
20 Vauxhall Bridge Road, London SW1V 2SA

Random House Australia Pty Ltd 20 Alfred Street, Milsons Point, Sydney, New South Wales 2061, Australia

Random House New Zealand Ltd 18 Poland Road, Glenfield, Auckland 10, New Zealand

Random House South Africa (Pty) Ltd Isle of Houghton, Corner Boundary Road & Carse O'Gowrie, Houghton 2198, South Africa

Random House UK Limited Reg. No. 954009

Distributed in the US and Latin America by Publishers Group West (1-510-809-3700)
Distributed in Canada by Publishers Group Canada (1-800-747-8147)

For further distribution details, see www.timeout.com.

ISBN: 978-1-84670-220-4

A CIP catalogue record for this book is available from the British Library.

Printed and bound in Great Britain by Butler Tanner & Dennis, Frome, Somerset.

The Random House Group Limited supports the Forest Stewardship Council® (FSC®), the leading international forest certification organisation. All our titles that are printed on Greenpeace approved FSC® certified paper carry the FSC® logo. Our paper procurement policy can be found at www.randomhouse.co.uk/environment.

Time Out carbon-offsets its flights with Trees for Cities (www.treesforcities.org).

Contents

Introduction

San Francisco is a city of happy contradictions. Growing up almost overnight in the din and mercurial heat of the Gold Rush, it turned around a century later and launched a decade of 'free love'. It's made millionaires out of teenage technowizards, but also leads the nation in numbers of charitable and nonprofit organizations. It's got a reputation for tolerance that's legendary, but cuts scofflaws no slack when it comes to enforcing composting and recycling rules.

Somehow, San Francisco finds a way to make all these seemingly dissonant impulses work together in harmony. Maybe in part because people can afford to be gracious in a town where you can play Frisbee on the beach in the middle of February, and where, when you ask how fresh the crab is, the waiter looks at his watch. One thing is certain: San Francisco is never dull.

For visitors – and some 16 million descend here every year – the drama begins with geography. On the city's precipitous slopes, little cable cars climb halfway to the stars, giving a nod to dolled-up Painted Lady Victorians before plunging down to Fisherman's Wharf, as ominous Alcatraz Island and the fog-shrouded Golden Gate Bridge dance in the background. In myriad iconic neighborhoods, amazing views trade off with hidden nooks and crannies, windswept ocean bluffs give way to serene pocket gardens crammed with every vegetable imaginable – and the weather often varies from block to block.

From the wall-to-wall murals of the Mission District to the peekaboo stairways of Twin Peaks, the adorned alleyways of Chinatown to the sidewalk cafes of North Beach – San Francisco invites exploration with a sense of wonder and discovery that's as irresistible to locals as it is to visitors.

It's why you'll find even long-time residents tromping up the steps to Coit Tower, snaking their cars down windy Lombard Street, shopping for arugula at the Ferry Plaza Farmer's Market, and nibbling on crab cocktails from Wharf street vendors. We invite you to use this book as your local tour guide and join in the adventure. Happy trails! *Bonnie Wach, Editor.*

Supperclub
S
amuse

San Francisco in Brief

IN CONTEXT

An overview of the city's past, present and future reveals a picture of San Francisco that is equal parts nostalgia and progress. An indefatigable survivor of disasters both natural and manmade, the City by the Bay continues to march to the distinctive beat of its own drummer, blazing new trails in everything from architecture and urban planning to environmental policy and social networking.

▶ *For more, see pp15-41.*

SIGHTS

A big city sandwiched into a seven-square-mile package, San Francisco is one of America's most accessible cities. Major attractions – museums and monuments, bridges and beaches – are sprinkled throughout its neighborhoods, and all are easily reached by public transportation or on foot. Our Sights section gives you the flavor and highlights of each district, as well as offering our picks of must-see attractions.

▶ *For more, see pp43-110.*

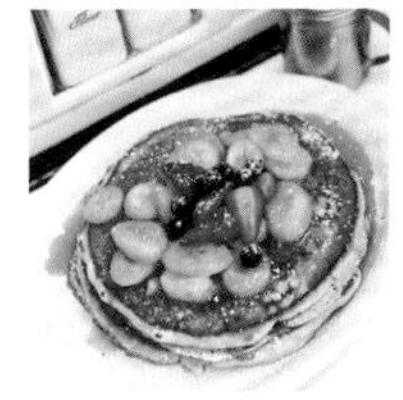

CONSUME

With more than 3,500 restaurants, San Francisco is undoubtedly one of the world's best restaurant cities, a pioneer in farm-to-table and sustainable dining practices that draw on the incredible bounty of the region. These days, the fresh, seasonal, local mantra extends to beverages as well, with bars and lounges offering cocktail menus that rival the food options.

▶ *For more, see pp111-200.*

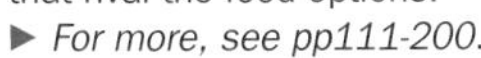

ARTS & ENTERTAINMENT

San Francisco is an incubator for the arts, whether it's breaking new ground in theatrical genres, supporting controversial artistic expression, or developing its own San Francisco sound. You'll also find a healthy share of big-city crowd-pleasing fare, including Broadway blockbusters, international touring acts and major traveling exhibitions from around the globe.

▶ *For more, see pp201-262.*

ESCAPES & EXCURSIONS

Travel less than an hour in any direction from San Francisco and you'll find wine country to rival Tuscany, breathtaking beaches and dramatic coastal landscapes, dreamy harbor villages, and buzzing university towns. Even better, many of these places are accessible by ferry, train, or on a bicycle, making the journey as enjoyable as the destination.

▶ *For more, see pp263-284.*

San Francisco in 48 Hrs

Day 1 Cable Cars and Chocolate Bars

9AM Start your tour aboard San Francisco's world-famous cable cars. The intersection of Powell and Market streets is the Downtown terminus for Fisherman's Wharf lines, but if you don't want to wait in the long queue, head up the hill to any of the cable car stops along Powell Street and hop aboard.

11AM Jump off at the **Cable Car Museum** (*see p62*) on Mason Street. Inside the powerhouse, you can view the giant pulleys and gears that haul the 140-year-old cars up and down the city's steep slopes on a constantly moving cable beneath the street.

NOON By the time you reach the north end of the line at **Fisherman's Wharf**, you'll be ready for lunch. Pick up a crab cocktail at **Alioto's** (*see p148)* or any of the sidewalk stands along Jefferson Street, and a loaf of sourdough bread at **Boudin Bakery** (*see p148*). Next, head over to the **Musée Mécanique** at Pier 45 (*see p73*), home to dozens of vintage arcade games.

2PM If you're hankering for dessert, your next stop has to be **Ghirardelli Square** (*see p72*), site of Domingo Ghirardelli's famous chocolate factory. Here you can sample Ghirardelli hot-fudge sundaes and shop for giant one-pound chocolate bars.

4PM Walk off the calories with a stroll down to **Hyde Street Pier & Maritime National Historical Park** (*see p73*), home to a fleet of restored historic ships. Then hit happy hour at the legendary **Buena Vista Café** (*see p72*), where Irish coffee was first introduced to America in 1952. The bar serves up more than 2,000 glasses of it every day.

7PM Make your way over to **Columbus Avenue**, the main artery of North Beach, San Francisco's Little Italy. Sit at a sidewalk café for a glass of vino and a hearty Italian dinner. Or for something more intimate, try tiny **L'Osteria del Forno** (*see p147*), where locals flock for oven-roasted specialties and thin-crust pizza.

NAVIGATING THE CITY

While San Francisco's steep slopes may seem daunting to some, 'The City that Knows How' has never met a mountain it couldn't conquer. In 1873, Andrew Hallidie's cable cars met the challenge of Nob Hill and defeated it. Today, cable cars are still the best way to scale many of Downtown's precipitous peaks, other than walking or cycling.

In fact, there is almost no part of San Francisco that isn't served by reliable, inexpensive public transportation. Parking fees, on the other hand, are prohibitive, the city's ticket-toting meter maids are vigilant, and traffic is constant – making driving your least best option. Muni buses and Metro streetcars operate day and night (most until 1am); BART (Bay Area Rapid Transit) trains run until midnight from San Francisco International Airport through the Mission District and Downtown to the East Bay. Your best value is probably a monthly Muni Fast Pass or a Muni Passport, good

Day 2 Exploring the Golden Gate

10AM Head down to **Golden Gate Park**, the city's communal backyard (*see p92-94*) and spend the morning at the **de Young Museum** and the **California Academy of Sciences**. Considered the world's greenest museum, the Academy features an aquarium, planetarium, indoor rainforest, and a living roof covered with native plants.

1PM After lunch at either the de Young or Academy cafés (both of which offer excellent menus featuring local, organic and sustainably farmed ingredients), wander through the **Japanese Tea Garden** past manicured bonsai and cherry trees, ornate pagodas, and then go to the teahouse for traditional Japanese tea and snacks. If it's Sunday, rent skates or a bike from a nearby shop (*see p252*) and cruise John F Kennedy Drive (it's closed to cars on Sundays), past the **Conservatory of Flowers**, **Stow Lake**, and the **buffalo paddock**, all the way to the **Dutch Windmill**.

2PM Stop for a house-brewed beer on the Adirondack chairs at the grassy **Park Chalet**, or head upstairs to the **Beach Chalet** (for both, *see p93*) for spectacular views of the Pacific Ocean.

3PM If you still have a craving for art and ocean vistas, make your way along Ocean Beach and the Great Highway to the **California Palace of the Legion of Honor** (*see p96*). Modeled on the Palais de la Légion d'Honneur in Paris, the museum houses an outstanding collection of Rodin sculpture and works by Monet, Matisse and Picasso.

5.30PM When the sun starts to set, head down Lincoln Boulevard to take in views of the **Golden Gate Bridge** (*see p104*). You can walk or bike across the bridge during daylight hours (it's 1.7 miles), but the parking area on the east side affords equally fine vantage points.

7PM For dinner, try **Epic Roasthouse** (*see p137*) or **Waterbar** (*see p139*) on the Embarcadero waterfront; both feature outstanding fresh, seasonal menus and amazing Bay views.

for three to seven consecutive days of unlimited rides on Muni buses and cable cars; see www.sfmta.com.

Be aware that taxis are not plentiful outside the airport and major downtown hotels and you will likely have to call one if heading home late at night from a club or bar. For more on transport, *see p286-288*.

PACKAGE DEALS

Admission prices to the big museums can be expensive, but several companies offer discounted rates on multi-day museum/sightseeing packages, including Go San Francisco Card, Explorer Pass (www.smartdestinations.com) and San Francisco CityPass (www.citypass.com/san-francisco), which combines Muni and cable car Passports with admission to five attractions for about $69 ($39 for kids). If that's too much of a commitment, look online at individual museums, which often offer reduced admission once a week, or free admission once a month.

San Francisco in Profile

DOWNTOWN

Union Square anchors the center of Downtown, a bustling quadrant surrounded by designer boutiques, department stores, and high-end shopping centers. From here, it's easy walking distance to other major visitor destinations.
► *For more, see pp44-56.*

SOMA & SOUTH BEACH

A former industrial wasteland, **SoMa** has undergone massive regeneration over the last 20 years, and is now one of the city's hippest urban enclaves, with a vibrant arts district around **Yerba Buena Gardens**. **South Beach** is bookended on one side by the Embarcadero and **AT&T baseball park**, and on the other by the sprawling **Mission Bay** complex.
► *For more, see pp57-61.*

NOB HILL & CHINATOWN

The mansions of the wealthy 'nabobs' who once populated **Nob Hill** are long gone, but their legacy lives on in stately **Grace Cathedral**, the grand hotels and elegant residences. Far below, the colorful streets of **Chinatown** teem with ornate temples, dim sum restaurants, and shops.
► *For more, see pp62-67.*

NORTH BEACH & FISHERMAN'S WHARF

Bisected by **Columbus Avenue**, **North Beach** is the heart of San Francisco's Little Italy, and the birthplace of the Beat Generation. Italian restaurants and sidewalk cafés represent the former; the legendary **City Lights** bookstore, **Vesuvio** bar and the **Beat Museum** the latter. The honky-tonk charms of **Fisherman's Wharf** are targeted at tourists, but you'll also find street vendors offering fresh Dungeness crab.
► *For more, see pp68-75.*

THE MISSION & THE CASTRO

Urban hipsters blend with Latino culture in the diverse and artistically vibrant **Mission** neighborhood. From the trendy shops, restaurants, and indie galleries along **Valencia Street** to the taco stands, *panaderias*, and murals of lower Mission – it's a tasty melting pot. Uptown in the **Castro**, the rainbow flag of gay pride flies high and proud, festooning everything from restored Victorians to cruiser bars.
► *For more, see pp76-82*

THE HAIGHT

The former '60s hippie enclave still boasts its fair share of anarchist bookstores and Grateful Dead paraphernalia. Down on Lower Haight though, funky bars, and progressive politics are more the norm. To the north lies the up-and-coming **Western Addition** and **Alamo Square**, home of the famous 'painted lady' Victorians. East is hip **Hayes Valley**.
► *For more, see pp83-88.*

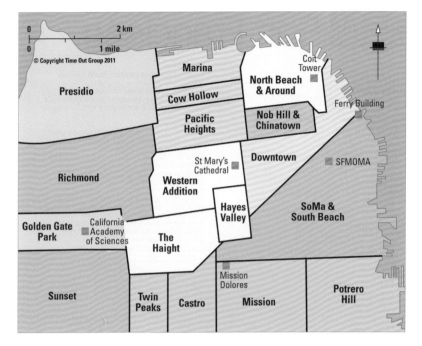

0 2 km
0 1 mile

Presidio
Marina
Cow Hollow
Pacific Heights
Coit Tower
North Beach & Around
Nob Hill & Chinatown
Ferry Building
Richmond
St Mary's Cathedral
Western Addition
Downtown
SFMOMA
Hayes Valley
SoMa & South Beach
Golden Gate Park
California Academy of Sciences
The Haight
Mission Dolores
Sunset
Twin Peaks
Castro
Mission
Potrero Hill

SUNSET, RICHMOND & GOLDEN GATE PARK

A mix of immigrant communities, families, students, and surfers, along with a perennial fogbank, keep these largely residential districts from getting too touristy. This is where you'll find some of the city's best ethnic eateries. In the middle is **Golden Gate Park**; to the west, the wild windswept shores of the **Pacific Ocean**.

► *For more, see pp89-96.*

PACIFIC HEIGHTS & THE MARINA

Pacific and **Presidio Heights** are neighborhoods of mansions, with enviable views of the Golden Gate. Down the hill is the more youthful but equally well-heeled **Cow Hollow**. To the north, the **Marina District** beckons with waterfront parks, posh restaurants and upscale bars, leading up to the huge green space of the **Presidio**; at its northern tip is **Golden Gate Bridge**.

► *For more, see pp97-104.*

EAST BAY: BERKELEY & OAKLAND

Cross the Bay Bridge or take BART to leave San Francisco for **Berkeley**, centered on its famous (and beautiful) university campus, and also a gourmet center, and a resurgent **Oakland**, now home to some of the Bay Area's hottest restaurants.

► *For more, see pp105-110.*

Time Out San Francisco

Contributors
History Michael Ansaldo. *Profile: Mark Twain* Jonathan Derbyshire. *The Social Network* Matt Markovich. **San Francisco Today** Bonnie Wach. **Architecture** Matt Markovich. **San Francisco on Screen** Matt Markovich. **Downtown** Bonnie Wach. *Uphill Journeys* Will Fulford-Jones. **SoMa & South Beach** Bonnie Wach. **Nob Hill & Chinatown** Bonnie Wach. *Profile: Portsmouth Square* Matt Markovich. **North Beach & Fisherman's Wharf** Bonnie Wach. *Walk: On the Beat-en Track* Jake Bumgardner. **The Mission & the Castro** Bonnie Wach. *Mission Murals, Streets of San Francisco: Castro* Matt Markovich. **The Haight & Around** Bonnie Wach. *Streets of San Francisco: Haight* Matt Markovich. **Sunset, Richmond & Golden Gate Park** Bonnie Wach. *Walk: Panhandle to the Pacific* Matt Markovich. **Pacific Heights to the Golden Gate Bridge** Bonnie Wach. *Life's a Beach* Matt Markovich. **East Bay: Oakland & Berkeley** Elaine Proulx. *Oakland on the Front Burner; Streets of San Francisco: Telegraph Avenue, Berkeley* Matt Markovich. **Hotels** Bonnie Wach, Jeanne Cooper. *Ralston's Crowning Achievement; Sleep Well, Do Good* Bonnie Wach. **Restaurants** Bonnie Wach, Robert Farmer. *Frisco Foraging; Grounds Control; Viva la Tortilla; Taking it to the Street* Matt Markovich. **Bars** Matt Markovich. **Shops & Services** Kimberly Chun. *Knocked Down & Up* Again Bonnie Wach. **Calendar** Tony Hayes. *Burn Baby Burn!* Miranda Morton. **Children** Bonnie Wach. *Story Time With a Twist* Matt Markovich. **Film** Elise Proulx. *Film Festivals* Matt Markovich. **Galleries** Mark Taylor. **Gay & Lesbian** Marke Bieschke. *'I Do' Blues* Matt Markovich. **Music** Matt Markovich. *And the Band Played On* Kimberly Chun. **Nightclubs** Marke Bieschke. **Sport & Fitness** Bonnie Wach. *Freaks & Geeks: The 2010 World Champions* Matt Markovich. **Theater & Dance** Robert Avila. *Pretty Sketchy* Matt Markovich. **Heading North** Elise Proulx. *A Whale of a Time* Bonnie Wach. **Heading South** Bonnie Wach. **Wine Country** Lesley McCave. *Grape Expectations* Matt Markovich.

Maps john@jsgraphics.co.uk

Front Cover Photography Corbis
Back Cover Photography Elan Fleisher and Hans Kwiotek

Photography by Hans Kwiotek; except pages 3, 5, 7, 8, 9, 10 (middle and bottom left), 11 (top), 15, 39, 48, 49 (top right), 52, 73, 87, 130, 136, 146, 147, 153, 195, 211, 226, 241, 249, 251, 255, 265, 266, 305 Elan Fleisher; page 7 (bottom left) Toni Gauthier; page 7 (right) Brandon Bourdagas; page 10 (top left) Tomas Sereda; page 11 (bottom) Jim Feliciano; page 16 Getty Images; page 20 Corbis; page 25 Allen Ginsberg/CORBIS; pages 31, 47, 51, 75, 82, 111, 139, 166, 185, 188, 191, 252 Barry J. Holmes; page 32 Caltrans; page 40 SFMOMA / Chrysler Museum of Art; page 43 Dibrova; page 59 Bruce Damonte; page 61 Scott Chernis; page 72 San Francisco Art Institute; page 80 Eric Nielson; page 84 Oksana Perkins/Shutterstock; page 95 Chee-Onn Leong/Shutterstock.com; page 133 Laurie Levefeld/Zoom Photography; page 143 Aubrie Pick; page 144 Paul Dyer; page 148 (bottom) Hardy Wilson; pages 150, 154, 157 (bottom) Naseema Khan; page 157 (top) Henrik Kam; page 161 Alex Farnum; page 172 Jennifer Yin; page 175 Thomas Winz; page 177 Cesar Rubio; pages 196, 197 Jessica Watson; page 205 Laura Dittmann/Burning Man; page 209 (top left) Rachel Tom; page 209 (right) Chris Picon; page 209 (bottom left) Winnie Wintermeyer; pages 217, 218 Ren Dodge; page 223 GLBT Historical Society; page 228 ArrowStudio, LCC/Shutterstock; pages 257, 262 Erik Tomasson; page 258 Jennifer Reiley; page 261 Toni Gauthier; page 263 Harris Shiffman; page 264 Rebecca Photography/Shutterstock; page 270 John Silva/Shutterstock; page 275 Mike Brake/Shutterstock; page 276 Cedric Weber/Shutterstock; page 279 Rachael Towne/Shutterstock.

The following images were supplied by the featured establishments/artists: pages 107, 114, 117, 119, 123, 125, 129, 143 (top), 202, 203, 235, 237, 246, 247.

About the Guide

GETTING AROUND

The back of the book contains street maps of San Francisco, as well as overview maps of the city and its surroundings. The maps start on page 305; on them are marked the locations of hotels (❶), restaurants and cafés (❶), and pubs and bars (❶). The majority of businesses listed in this guide are located in the areas we've mapped; the grid-square references in the listings refer to these maps.

THE ESSENTIALS

For practical information, including visas, disabled access, emergency numbers, lost property, useful websites and local transport, please see the Directory. It begins on page 285.

THE LISTINGS

Addresses, phone numbers, websites, transport information, hours and prices are all included in our listings, as are selected other facilities. All were checked and correct at press time. However, business owners can alter their arrangements at any time, and fluctuating economic conditions can cause prices to change rapidly.

The very best venues in the city, the must-sees and must-dos in every category, have been marked with a red star (★). In the Sights chapters, we've also marked venues with free admission with a FREE symbol.

PHONE NUMBERS

The area code for San Francisco (and Marin County) is 415. You don't need to use the code when calling from within the area: simply dial the seven-digit number as listed in this guide. There are various other codes for other parts of the Bay Area. If you're dialing outside the area code you'll need to add the initial 1 (1-510 and so on).

From outside the US, dial your country's international access code or a plus symbol, followed by the US country code (1), the area code and the seven-digit number as listed. So to reach SFMOMA, dial +1 415 357 4000. For more on phones, *see p293*.

FEEDBACK

We welcome feedback on this guide, both on the venues we've included and on any other locations that you'd like to see featured in future editions. Please email us at guides@timeout.com.

Time Out Guides

Founded in 1968, Time Out has grown from humble beginnings into the leading resource for anyone wanting to know what's happening in the world's greatest cities. Alongside our influential weeklies in London, New York and Chicago, we publish more than 20 magazines in cities as varied as Beijing and Beirut; a range of travel books, with the City Guides now joined by the newer Shortlist series; and an information-packed website. The company remains proudly independent, still owned by Tony Elliott four decades after he launched *Time Out London*.

Written by local experts and illustrated with original photography, our books also retain their independence. No business has been featured because it has advertised, and all restaurants and bars are visited and reviewed anonymously.

ABOUT THE EDITOR

San Francisco native **Bonnie Wach** is a former columnist for the *San Francisco Chronicle* and former editor of *WHERE* magazine. A freelance travel and food writer, she is the author of *San Francisco As You Like It* and has covered the Bay Area in publications including *Travel + Leisure*, the *Los Angeles Times* and *Via*.

A full list of the book's contributors can be found opposite.

In Context

Alamo Square. *See p87.*

History

Built on gold, nourished on non-conformity.

TEXT: MICHAEL ANSALDO

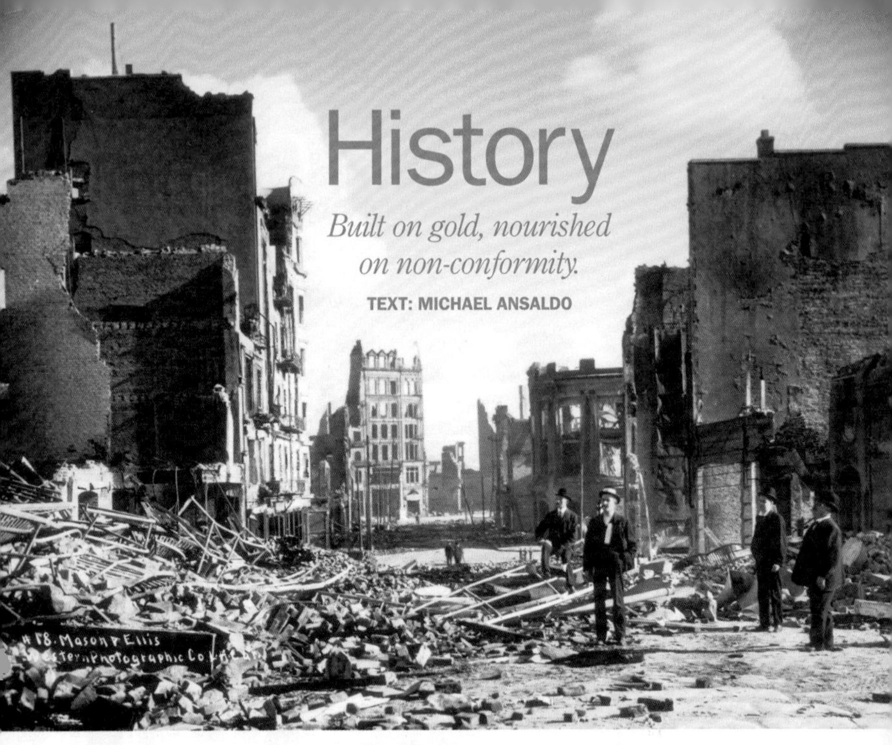

When excavation began in 1969 for BART's Civic Center station, workers uncovered the body of a young woman. Experts dated the remains to approximately 2,950 BC, the city's earliest known burial. It was a glimpse into the rich indigenous culture of the Bay Area. During the last Ice Age, 15,000 years ago, nomadic tribes migrated across the Bering Strait from Asia and eventually settled along the shores of the Bay. Despite its name, the San Francisco Bay is actually an estuary, mixing the cold Pacific Ocean with fresh Sierra Nevada snowmelt that flows down the San Joaquin and Sacramento rivers. Ringed by hills covered with pastures, the Bay Area sustained more than 10,000 Northern Californian natives of different tribes, later collectively dubbed Costanoans ('coast dwellers') by the Spanish. At first, the Ohlone people lived here in harmony both with their Miwok neighbors and the land, which provided them with rich pickings of game, fish, shellfish, fruit and nuts (it was, in the words of a later French explorer, a land of 'inexpressible fertility'). They lived a successful hunter-gatherer existence until the arrival of Spanish missionaries. Their previous contacts with Europeans had been friendly, but the Spanish brought with them the dubious gifts of Christianity, hard labor and diseases such as smallpox, which eventually annihilated half the native population of California in 75 years.

THEY CAME, THEY SAW

Looking at the Golden Gate today, it's not hard to imagine how early navigators missed the mile-wide opening. The Bay and its native peoples were hidden by 'stynkinge fogges' (as Francis Drake later complained), which prevented numerous explorers over a period of 200 years from discovering the harbor entrance.

An early series of Spanish missions sent up the coast by Hernán Cortés, notorious conqueror of Mexico and the Aztecs, never got as far as Upper California. In 1542, under the flag of Cortés's successor, Antonio de Mendoza, Portuguese explorer Juan Rodríguez Cabrillo became the first European to visit the area. Inspired by a popular 16th-century novel, the Spanish named their new-found land California. Cabrillo passed the Bay's entrance on his way north and on his way back again, but failed to discover its large natural harbor.

An Englishman got even closer, yet still managed to miss it. In 1579, during a foraging and spoiling mission in the name of the Virgin Queen, Elizabeth I, the then-unknighted Francis Drake landed in Miwok Indian territory just north of the Bay. With one ship, the *Golden Hind*, and a crew in dire need of rest and recreation, he put in for a six-week berth on the Marin coastline, probably near Point Reyes. Long before the Pilgrims landed at Plymouth Rock or the English settled Cupid's Cove at Newfoundland, Drake claimed California for Elizabeth I as 'Nova Albion' or 'New Britain'.

It would be 190 years before another white man set eyes on the Bay. Spurred on by the pressure of British colonial ambitions in America, the Spanish sent northbound missions to stake out their own territories, intent on converting the *bestias* and claiming land for the Spanish crown. Sailing under the Spanish flag in 1595, Portuguese explorer Sebastian Rodríguez Cermeno was shipwrecked just north of the Golden Gate at what is now known as Drake's Bay. Before he made his way back to Mexico in a small boat saved from the ship, he named the protected cove Bahia de San Francisco.

In 1769 came the 'sacred expedition' of Gaspar de Pórtola, a Spanish aristocrat who would later become the first governor of California, and the Franciscan priest Father Junípero Serra, who set off with 60 men on a grueling march across the Mexican desert with the aim of establishing a mission at San Diego. Once they'd done so, the party worked its way north to Monterey, building missions and baptizing Indians as they went. During the expedition, an advance party discovered an unexpectedly long bay 100 miles further up the coast. They mistook it for Cermeno's Bahia de San Francisco and, since the expedition's brief was only to claim Monterey, returned to San Diego.

It was not until August 1775 that the *San Carlos*, a Spanish supply vessel, became the first ship to sail into the Bay. Meanwhile, a mission set off to establish a safer land route to what would eventually become San Francisco. Roughly concurrent with the signing of the American Declaration of Independence, Captain Juan Bautista de Anza led an advance party to the southern point of the Golden Gate, which he declared a perfect location for a Spanish military garrison, or *presidio*. Three miles inland to the south-east, a suitable site was found for a mission. Before the year was out, the *presidio* was erected, and the mission – named Misión San Francisco de Asís after the holy order operating in Upper California, but popularly known as Mission Dolores – was established by the indefatigable Serra.

FOLLOW THE BEAR

A mix of favoritism, authoritarianism and religious fervor eventually helped sow the seeds of resentment and resistance in territories colonized by Spain. The country's hold on its American empires first began to crumble in Mexico, which declared itself a republic in 1821. The Mexican annexation of California in the same year opened up the area to foreign settlers, among them American pioneers such as fur trapper Jedediah Smith, who in 1828 became the first white American to reach California over the Sierra

Nevada mountain range. His feat was impressive, but a more sedate arrival by a whaler ship had more lasting impact. Englishman Captain William Richardson, who in 1835 built the first dwelling on the site of the future San Francisco, is credited with giving the city its first name: Yerba Buena, named after the sweet mint (literally 'good herb') the Spanish used for tea.

That same year, the US tried unsuccessfully to buy the whole of the Bay Area from the Mexicans. In the long run, though, they got California for free: the declaration of independence of the territory of Texas, and its subsequent annexation by the US, triggered the Mexican-American war in June 1846. The resulting Guadalupe-Hidalgo Treaty of 1848 officially granted the Union all the land from Texas to California and from the Rio Grande to Oregon. But before the treaty could be nailed down, a few hotheads decided to 'liberate' the territory from Mexico themselves.

The short-lived Mexican rule of California coincided with the era of idealistic frontiersmen such as Kit Carson and Captain John Fremont, who, in June 1846, convinced a motley crew to take over the abandoned *presidio* to the north of Yerba Buena in Sonoma. Fremont proclaimed his new state the 'Bear Flag Republic', after the ragged banner he raised over Sonoma's square (the design was eventually adopted as the state flag), and he named the mouth of San Francisco Bay the 'Golden Gate' after Istanbul's Golden Horn. A few weeks after the Bear Flaggers annexed Sonoma, the US Navy captured Yerba Buena without a struggle and the whole of California became US territory.

The infant Yerba Buena was a sleepy trading post of 500 people. The newly appointed mayor, Lieutenant Washington A Bartlett, officially renamed it San Francisco on 30 January 1847. But unbeknownst to its residents, the tiny settlement was about to change dramatically.

ALL THAT GLITTERS

Californians have the eagle eye of one James Marshall to thank for their current prosperity. While building a mill on the American River near Sacramento in January 1848, Marshall spotted gold in a sawmill ditch. Along with John Sutter, the Swiss-born rancher who was Marshall's landlord, he attempted to keep his findings secret, but when newspaper publisher Sam Brannan got word, he marched down to San Francisco's Portsmouth Square, waved a bottle of gold dust, and the Gold Rush was on.

The news brought droves of drifters and fortune-seekers to the Bay Area, their fever fanned by people like Brannan, whose *California Star* newspaper told of men digging up a fortune in an hour (Brannan eventually became California's first millionaire by selling goods to gold prospectors). Many never made it: by land, the journey meant months of exposure to blizzards, mountains, deserts and hostile tribes; by sea, they faced disease, starvation or brutal weather. Still, more than 90,000 prospectors appeared in California in the first two years after gold was discovered, and 300,000 had arrived in the state by 1854 – one out of every 90 people then living in the US. Though they called themselves the Argonauts (after the mythical sailors who accompanied Jason in search of the Golden Fleece), locals named them after the year the Rush began: the Forty-Niners.

The port town in which they arrived was one without structure, government, or even a name (to many, it was still Yerba Buena). They found more hardship than gold: on their way to the mines, predatory merchants fleeced them; when they returned, broke, they were left to grub mean existences from the city streets, seeking refuge in brothels, gambling dens and bars. Within two years of Marshall's discovery, nearly 100,000 men had passed through the city; the population grew from 600 in 1848 to 25,000 in 1849, swelling the tiny community into a giant, muddy campsite. Despite a fire that levelled the settlement on Christmas Eve 1849, a new town rose up to take its place and the population exploded. Still, this brave new boomtown was not a place for the faint-hearted. Lawlessness and arson ruled; frontier justice was common.

The opening of a post office marked the city's first optimistic stab at improving links with the rest of the continent. John White Geary, appointed postmaster by President James Knox Polk, rented a room at the corner of Montgomery and Washington Streets, where he marked out a series of squares for each letter of the alphabet and began filing letters. This crude set-up was San Francisco's first postal system. In April 1850, the year California became the Union's 31st state, San Francisco's city charter was approved; the city elected Geary its first mayor.

Geary's council later bought the ship *Euphemia* to serve as San Francisco's first jail. It proved a sound investment. Gangs of hoodlums controlled certain districts: the Ducks, led by Australian convicts, lived at a spot known as Sydney Town and, together with New York toughs the Hounds, roamed Telegraph Hill, raping and pillaging the orderly community of Chilean merchants who occupied Little Chile. Eventually, right-minded citizens decided to take the law into their own hands. Whipped into a fury by rabble-rouser Brannan, vigilantes lynched their first victim, John Jenkins, at Portsmouth Square in June 1851. They strung up three more thieves during the following weeks; the other Ducks and Hounds wisely cut out for the Sierras.

By 1853, the riverbed gold started running dry and boom had turned to bust. The resulting depression set a cyclical pattern oft-repeated through the city's history. Then, in 1859, a second boom arrived. Henry Comstock's discovery of a rich blue vein of silver (the 'Comstock Lode') in western Nevada triggered another invasion by fortune-seekers, nicknamed the Silver Rush. This time the ore's nature demanded more elaborate methods of extraction, with high yields going to a small number of companies and tycoons rather than individual prospectors. Before the supply had been exhausted, silver barons had made enough money to transform San Francisco, establishing a nouveaux riches neighborhood atop Nob Hill (the name was adapted from the word 'nabob').

Mission Dolores. *See p17.*

Profile Mark Twain

Tales of the city.

When Samuel Clemens arrived in San Francisco in May 1864, he'd been 'Mark Twain' for a little over a year. He first adopted the pseudonym in Virginia City, Nevada, where he worked as city editor on the local newspaper. But it wasn't until he settled in San Francisco that Twain began to treat that name as if it were his own.

Twain found a room on California Street and a job as a reporter on the *Call*. He was dazzled by the city, which was then in the grip of an extraordinary share-dealing boom. San Francisco was a 'gambling carnival', Twain wrote, simply the 'liveliest, heartiest community on our continent' – compensation, it seems, for the frequent earthquakes, which he never got used to. He complained that when he 'contracted to report for this newspaper, the important matter of two earthquakes a month was not considered in the salary'.

He needn't have worried: the job on the *Call* didn't last long. Twain was soon contributing essays, criticism and society gossip to a number of other publications. Indeed, it was in San Francisco that Twain first properly acknowledged that his vocation was writing. And it wasn't long before he was at the center of a literary circle known as the 'Bohemians'.

Twain wrote vividly about the city, not least about earthquakes. The most powerful struck on October 8, 1865, with Twain noting that 'such another destruction of mantel ornaments and toilet bottles as the earthquake created, San Francisco never saw before'.

He left San Francisco in December 1866. In the last piece he ever wrote in the city, Twain looked to the future. 'This straggling town shall be a vast metropolis: this sparsely populated land shall become a crowded hive of busy men. Its estate will be brighter, happier and prouder a hundred fold than it is this day. This is its destiny, and in all sincerity I can say, So mote it be!

WEATHER WATCH

It's doubtful that Mark Twain really uttered his often-quoted comment on the city's weather: 'the coldest winter I ever spent was summer in San Francisco'.

IN CONTEXT

If the nabobs took the geographical and moral high ground, those on the waterfront were busy legitimizing their reputation as occupants of the 'Barbary Coast'. Naïve newcomers and drunken sailors were seen as fair game by gamblers and hoods waiting to 'shanghai' them (shanghai, like 'hoodlum', is a San Francisco expression), as were the immigrant women who found themselves trapped into lives of prostitution or slavery. At one low point, the female population numbered just 22; many a madam made fortune enough to buy her way on to Nob Hill.

COME ONE, COME ALL

The seeds of San Francisco's present-day multiculturalism were sown during this period, when a deluge of immigrants poured in from all over the world. French immigrants vying with Italians to make the best bread started baking sourdough in North Beach. A young German garment-maker named Levi Strauss started using rivets to strengthen the jeans he made for miners. In Chinatown, *tongs* (Mafia-like gangs) controlled the opium dens and other rackets; a Chinese immigrant, Wah Lee, opened the city's first laundry. The building in the 1860s of the transcontinental railroad, which employed thousands of Chinese laborers at low pay rates, led to further expansion of Chinatown. Still, despite their usefulness as cheap labor, the Chinese became the targets of racist anti-immigrant activity; indeed, proscriptive anti-Chinese legislation persisted until 1938.

Even in those days, entertainment was high on the agenda for San Franciscans. By 1853, the city boasted five theaters and some 600 saloons and taverns serving 42,000 customers. Locals downed seven bottles of champagne for every bottle swallowed in Boston (San Francisco still leads the US in alcohol consumption per capita). Lola Montez, entertainer to European monarchs and thieves, arrived on a paddle-steamer from Panama in 1853; her 'spider dance' became an instant hit at the American Theater.

San Francisco's relative isolation from the rest of the continent meant the city was hardly affected by the Civil War that devastated the American South in the early 1860s. The rest of the country seemed remote; mail sometimes took six months to arrive. However, communications were slowly improving. Telegraph wires were being strung across the continent; where telegraph poles ran out, the Pony Express picked up messages, relaying up to 75 riders across the West to the Pacific coast.

The completion of the Central Pacific Railroad in 1869 was the signal for runaway consumption in the city. The biggest spenders were the 'Big Four' – Charles Crocker, Collis P Huntington, Mark Hopkins and Leland Stanford – brutally competitive millionaires who were the powerful principal investors behind the Central Pacific. Their eagerness to impress the West with their flamboyantly successful business practices manifested itself in the mansions they built on Nob Hill. By 1871, 121 businessmen controlled $146 million, according to one newspaper – but others got in on the act. In particular, four Irishmen – the 'Bonanza Kings': James Flood, William O'Brien, James Fair and John Mackay – made the ascent to Nob Hill, having started out as rough-hewn miners and bartenders chipping out their fortunes from the Comstock Lode.

A Scottish-Irish banker, William Ralston, opened the Bank of California on Sansome Street in 1864. Partnered with Prussian engineer Adolph Sutro, later famous for building the first Cliff House and the Sutro Baths, Ralston was determined to extract every last ounce of silver from the Comstock's Sun Mountain. Unfortunately, he did so too quickly: the ore ran out before he could recoup his investment, and his bank collapsed. Ralston drowned himself, leaving behind the luxurious Palace Hotel (*see p118* **Ralston's Crowning Achievement**) and a lasting contribution towards San Francisco's new civic pride: Golden Gate Park. Ralston's company provided the water for William Hammond Hall's audacious project, which transformed a barren area of sand dunes into a magnificent expanse of trees, flowers and lakes.

THE BIG ONE

The city continued to grow, and by 1900 its population had reached more than a third of a million, making it the ninth-largest city in the Union. But shortly after 5am on April 18, 1906, dogs began howling and horses whinnying – noises that, along with glasses tinkling and windows rattling, marked the unnerving moments before an earthquake.

When the quake hit – a rending in the tectonic plates 25 miles beneath the ocean bed that triggered the shifting of billions of tons of rock – it generated more energy than all the explosives used in World War II. The rip snaked inland, tearing a gash now known as the San Andreas Fault down the coastline. Cliffs appeared from nowhere, cracks yawned, ancient redwoods toppled and part of the newly built City Hall tumbled down. A second tremor struck, ripping the walls out of buildings, destroying the city alarms and disrupting the water pipes that fed the fire hydrants, leaving the city's firefighters helpless. The blaze that followed did most of the damage; it only ceased when, in desperation, Mayor Eugene Schmitz and General Frederick Funston blew up the mansions along Van Ness Avenue, creating a firebreak.

The earthquake and three-day inferno probably killed several thousand. Around 250,000 people were left homeless and thousands of acres of buildings were destroyed; on Schmitz's orders, anyone suspected of looting in the ensuing chaos was shot dead. On the third day of the catastrophe, the wind changed direction, bringing rain. By April 21, the fire was out.

ONWARDS AND UPWARDS

Before the ashes had cooled, undaunted citizens set about rebuilding, and within 10 years, San Francisco had risen from the ruins. Some claimed that in the rush to rebuild, planners passed up the chance to replace the city's grid street system with a more sensible one that followed the area's natural contours. But there's no doubt San Francisco was reborn as a cleaner, more attractive city – within three years of the fire, it could boast half of the nation's concrete and steel buildings. Such statistical pride was not out of keeping with the boosterism that accelerated San Francisco's post-Gold Rush growth into a large, modern city. The most potent symbol of restored civic pride was the new City Hall (*see p56*), the construction of which was secured by an $8 million city bond. Completed in 1915, it rose 14 inches higher than its model, the US Capitol in Washington, DC.

In the years following the catastrophe, two waterways opened that would prove critical to California's economic vitality. The Los Angeles aqueduct was completed in 1913, beginning the transformation of a sleepy Southern California cowtown into the urban sprawl of modern LA. Then, in 1915, the opening of the Panama Canal considerably shortened shipping times between the Atlantic and Pacific coasts, an achievement celebrated in San Francisco by the Panama-Pacific Exposition. Not even the outbreak of World War I in Europe could dampen the city's high spirits. Its optimism was well founded: the war provided a boost to California's mining and manufacturing industries. But, as elsewhere in America, the good times were quickly swallowed up by the Wall Street Crash of 1929 and the Great Depression.

The crisis hit the port of San Francisco especially badly; half the workforce was laid off. On May 9, 1934, under the leadership of Harry Bridges, the International Longshoremen's Association declared a coast-wide strike. Other unions, including the powerful Teamsters, came out in sympathy, shutting down West Coast ports for three months. Blackleg workers managed to break through the picket on July 5 – Bloody Thursday – but with disastrous results. As violence escalated, police opened fire, killing two strikers and wounding 30. A general strike was called for July 14, when 150,000 people stopped work and brought San Francisco to a standstill for three days. The strike fizzled, but the action wasn't completely futile: the longshoremen won a wage increase and control of the hiring halls.

'The immediate post-war period was colored by the return of the demobilized GIs, among them Lawrence Ferlinghetti.'

At the same time, San Francisco managed an amazing amount of construction. The Opera House was completed in 1932; the following year, the island of Alcatraz was transferred from the army to the Federal Bureau of Prisons, which set about building a high-security lock-up. The San Francisco Museum of Modern Art, the first West Coast museum to feature exclusively 20th century works, opened in 1935. The same decade saw the completion of the San Francisco–Oakland Bay Bridge – six months before work started on the Golden Gate Bridge's revolutionary design. In 1939, on manmade Treasure Island, the city hosted another fair: the Golden Gate International Exposition, described as a 'pageant of the Pacific'. Those who attended were dubbed 'the Thirty-Niners' by local wits. It was to be San Francisco's last big celebration for a while: in 1941 the Japanese attacked Pearl Harbor, and America entered World War II.

The war changed the city almost as much as the Gold Rush or the Great Quake. More than 1.5 million men and thousands of tons of material were shipped to the Pacific from the Presidio, Travis Air Force Base and Treasure Island. Between 1941 and 1945, almost the entire Pacific war effort passed under the Golden Gate. The massed ranks of troops, not to mention some half a million civilian workers who flooded into San Francisco, turned the city into a milling party town hellbent on sending its boys into battle with smiles on their faces.

Towards the end of the war in Europe, in April 1945, representatives of 50 nations met at the San Francisco Opera House to draft the United Nations Charter. It was signed on June 26, 1945 and formally ratified in October at the General Organisation of the United Nations in London. Many people felt that San Francisco would be the ideal location for the UN's headquarters, but the British and French thought it too far to travel. To the city's great disappointment, the UN moved to New York.

BEATNIK BLUES AND HIPPIE HIGHS

The immediate post-war period was colored by the return of the demobilized GIs, among them Lawrence Ferlinghetti. While studying at the Sorbonne in the early 1950s, the poet had discovered Penguin paperbacks, which inspired him to open his tiny, wedge-shaped bookshop at 261 Columbus Avenue. Called City Lights, the shop became a mecca for the bohemians later dubbed the Beat Generation by Jack Kerouac.

The Beats reflected the angst and ambition of a post-war generation attempting to escape both the shadow of the Bomb and the rampant consumerism of ultra-conformist 1950s America. In Kerouac's definition, Beat could stand for either beatific or beat – exhausted. The condition is best explained in his novel *On the Road*, which charts the coast-to-coast odysseys of San Francisco-based Beat saint Neal Cassady (thinly disguised as Dean Moriarty), poet Allen Ginsberg and Kerouac himself (named Sal Paradise).

'The emergence of the Beat Generation made North Beach the literary center of San Francisco and nurtured a new vision that would spread far beyond its bounds,' reflected Ferlinghetti 40 years on. 'The Beats prefigured the New Left evolution and the impulse for change that swept eastward from San Francisco.' The attention of the world might have been on the beret-clad artists and poets populating North Beach cafés, but an event in Anaheim, 500 miles to the south, was more reflective of mainstream America. In 1955, Disneyland opened its gates.

'Combined with the sun, drugs and a psychedelic music explosion, the local laissez-faire attitude gave rise to the Summer of Love.'

Despite the imaginary world portrayed by Disney, the media exposure received by Kerouac and Ginsberg established the Bay Area as a center for the burgeoning counterculture, generating mainstream America's suspicions that San Francisco was the fruit-and-nut capital of the US. Its fears were about to be confirmed by the hippie explosion of the 1960s. The Beats and hippies might have shared a love of marijuana and a common distaste for 'the system', but Kerouac – now an embittered alcoholic – abhorred what he saw as the hippies' anti-Americanism. (It was, in fact, the Beats who coined the term 'hippie' to refer to those they saw as second rate, lightweight hipsters.) Kerouac's distaste for these new bohemians was shared by John Steinbeck, who shied away from the recognition he received in the streets.

The original Beats had no interest in political action, but the newer generation embraced it. A sit-in protest against a closed session of the House of Representatives Un-American Activities Committee (HUAC) at the City Hall in 1961 drew protesters from San Francisco State University and the University of California's Berkeley campus. It quickly degenerated into a riot, establishing the pattern for later protests and police responses. In 1964 Berkeley students, returning from a summer of civil rights protests in the South, butted heads with university officials over the right to use campus facilities for their campaigns. The conflict signalled the beginning of the 'free speech movement', led by student activist Mario Savio; it marked the split between the politically conscious and those who chose to opt out of the system altogether. America's escalating involvement in the Vietnam War added urgency to the voices of dissent; Berkeley students remained at the forefront of protests on campuses around the country.

The availability of LSD, its popularity boosted in San Francisco by such events as the Human Be-In and the Acid Tests overseen by Owsley Stanley and the Grateful Dead, helped draw an estimated 8,000 hippies from across America. Over half stayed, occupying the cheap Victorian houses around the Haight-Ashbury district (dubbed 'the Hashbury'). Combined with the sun, drugs and a psychedelic music explosion, the local laissez-faire attitude gave rise to the famous Summer of Love. By 1968, however, the spread of hard drugs, notably heroin, had taken the shine off the hippie movement; the fatal stabbing by Hell's Angels of a Rolling Stones fan at the Altamont Speedway during the band's 1969 concert there signaled that darker times were ahead.

Like its drugs, the city's politics were getting harder. Members of the Black Panther movement, a radical black organization founded across the Bay in Oakland by Huey Newton and Bobby Seale, asked themselves why they should ship out to shoot the Vietnamese when the real enemy was at home. Around Oakland, the Panthers took to exercising the American right to bear arms. Gunfights inevitably followed: Panther leader Eldridge Cleaver was wounded and 17-year-old Bobby Hutton killed in a shoot-out with Oakland police in April 1968. The Black Panther movement had petered out by the early 1970s, its leaders either dead, imprisoned or, like Cleaver, on the run. The kidnapping in 1974 of Patty Hearst, heir to the Hearst newspaper fortune, was the point at which the 1960s revolution turned into deadly farce. When she was captured, along with the other members of the tiny Symbionese Liberation Army, Hearst seemed to have been brainwashed into joining the cause.

Despite the violence that characterized the student and anti-war protests, however, black radicalism and failed revolutions, the enduring memory of 1960s San Francisco is as the host city to the Summer of Love. The music of the Grateful Dead, Janis

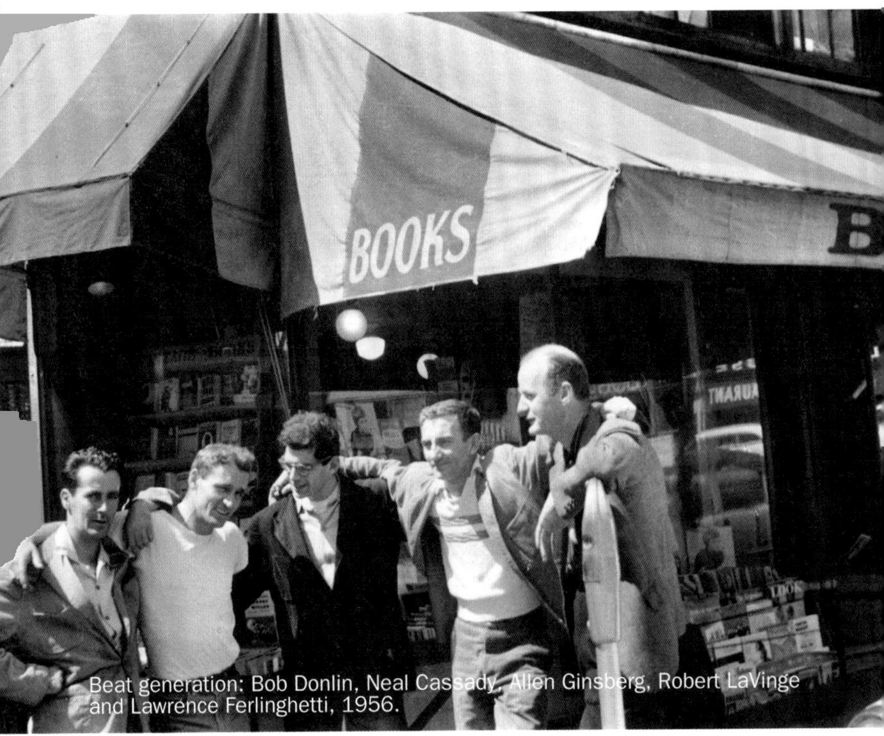

Beat generation: Bob Donlin, Neal Cassady, Allen Ginsberg, Robert LaVinge and Lawrence Ferlinghetti, 1956.

Joplin,Country Joe and the Fish and Jefferson Airplane defined both the San Francisco sound and its countercultural attitude. Berkeley student Jann Wenner founded *Rolling Stone* magazine in 1967 to explain and advance the cause, helping to invent New Journalism in the process.

THE RAINBOW REVOLUTION

San Francisco's radical baton was taken up in the 1970s by the gay liberation movement. Local activists insisted that gay traditions had always existed in the city, first among the Ohlone and later during the 1849 Gold Rush, when women in the West were more scarce than gold. Early groups such as the Daughters of Bilitis, the Mattachine Society and the Society for Individual Rights (SIR) paved the way for more radical new political movements. Gay activists made successful forays into mainstream politics in 1977: SIR's Jim Foster became the first openly gay delegate at a Democratic Convention, and Harvey Milk was elected to the city's Board of Supervisors.

Then Dan White changed everything. A former policeman, White had run for supervisor as an angry, young, blue-collar populist – and won. He suffered poor mental health and had to resign under the strain of office, but quickly changed his mind and asked Mayor George Moscone to reinstate him. When Moscone refused, White assassinated him along with Harvey Milk. The killings stunned the city, but the slap-on-the-wrist verdict outraged its citizenry, resulting in the White Night Riot. *See p81* **Streets of San Francisco**. White committed suicide not long after his release.

Gay life and politics changed radically and irrevocably with the onset of AIDS, which tore the gay community apart. There was controversy when the city's bathhouses, a symbol of gay liberation and promiscuity, closed in a panic over the spread of the disease. Gay radicals branded *Chronicle* writer Randy Shilts a 'fascist Nazi, traitor and homophobe' when he criticized bathhouse owners who refused to post safe-sex warnings. However, his book, *And the Band Played On,* is still the definitive account of the period.

COLLAPSE AND RECOVERY

Because of its location on the San Andreas Fault, San Francisco has always lived in anticipation of a major earthquake to rival the 1906 disaster. It came in October 1989: the Loma Prieta quake, named after the ridge of mountains at its epicenter, registered 7.1 on the Richter scale (the 1906 quake was an estimated 7.8). Part of the West Oakland Freeway collapsed, crushing drivers; the Marina district was devastated by fires; and 50 feet (15 meters) of the Bay Bridge's upper deck collapsed. In just 15 seconds, more than 19,000 homes were damaged or destroyed; 62 people were killed and 12,000 were displaced.

As the 1990s progressed, changes in the city reflected those in the world beyond. The end of the Cold War meant cuts in military spending, and the Presidio – which operated as a US military base for almost 150 years – was closed in 1994. As part of the Base Closure and Realignment Act, the land was transferred to the National Park Service. The collapse of the Soviet Union also brought in a wave of Russian immigrants, many of them settling in the ethnically diverse Richmond district.

San Francisco also experienced a remarkable renaissance. Its proximity to Silicon Valley's economic boom rejuvenated the city's business structure and reshaped the skyline. In the wake of the Loma Prieta earthquake, the Embarcadero Freeway was torn down and the city's historic bayside boulevard turned into a palm-tree-lined haven for

The Social Network

The rise, fall and rise again of a revolutionary technology.

At its peak in 2001, the internet economy had produced what one Silicon Valley venture capitalist called 'the largest legal accumulation of wealth in the history of the world'. Two years later it tanked. Companies such as San Francisco's Pets.com, which went from an IPO (Initial Public Offering) on the stock exchange to liquidation in just 268 days – in between spending an estimated $1.2 million to feature its sock puppet in a 2000 Super Bowl ad – seemed like a textbook example of hubris. Many looked on the much-ballyhooed Death of the Internet with no small amount of glee – amazingly, no one started schadenfreude.com. Yet, while there was no shortage of Pets.coms, reports of the demise of the internet were greatly exaggerated. The people that had built the true internet, the young tinkerers and coders in dorm rooms, garages and their parent's basements, apparently failed to heed the voices of doom.

One year to the month after the financial bellwether of the internet economy, the NASDAQ stock index, bottomed out, the man who would become the world's youngest billionaire began a small internet group called Facemash. Nineteen-year-old Harvard University freshman Mark Zuckerberg and his company, **Facebook**, would eventually count over 600 million users worldwide, with approximately 100 million users signing up every 160 days. Social Media Today, an online community itself, estimates that 41.9% of US citizens now have a Facebook account.

The speed with which these mega companies have been created, and their technologies universally adopted, walkers, joggers, in-line skaters and cyclists. Numerous major projects were brought to completion and others begun: in 1995, the San Francisco Museum of Modern Art moved into a new building in burgeoning SoMa, and voters passed a bond allowing for the restoration of City Hall. Five years later, Pac Bell Park (now AT&T Park), the first privately funded Major League Baseball park in nearly 40 years, opened its gates. The Yerba Buena Center and Zeum children's museum also opened their doors during this time.

As the 20th century rolled into the 21st, San Francisco suffered from many of the same social problems that plagued other major US cities. Homelessness was particularly severe, with up to 14,000 destitute men and women sleeping without nightly shelter. The late '90s internet boom brought workers from around the world into an increasingly tight housing market and gentrified working-class neighborhoods.

But by the end of the decade, the dotcom bubble had burst. What no one could have predicted was that within a few years there would be another tech boom. By 2008, technology companies were on the move again, followed on their heels by the phenomena of social networking. With feet firmly planted in the San Francisco area and profits soaring, Google, Facebook, YouTube, and Twitter are paving the way for the next gold rush. *See below* **The Social Network**. A collection of new skyscrapers, all exceeding height limits set in the previous century, are perhaps the most obvious manifestation of the once-again burgeoning economy.

San Francisco also continues to maintain its best-of-the-West-Coast reputation for magnificent food, stylish design, charming architecture and an ideas-driven population. In 1889, Rudyard Kipling described San Francisco as a 'mad city inhabited for the most part by perfectly insane people'. His conclusion is one shared by many residents even today: 'Tis hard to leave.'

is as surprising as the relative proximity of their headquarters from each other. Of Facebook, **YouTube** and San Francisco-based **Twitter**, the oldest (Facebook) was founded as recently as 2004. The top three most trafficked Internet sites in the world at the time of writing – **Google** (located in nearby Mountain View), Palo Alto's Facebook, and San Bruno-based YouTube – are all located within 30 miles of each other. Add in networking and software powerhouses such as Cisco and Oracle, and comeback kid Apple Computers (now the world's second most highly valued company), and one quickly realizes that the Bay Area hasn't missed a step in maintaining its status as the nexus of the Information Age.

Today, sites like these are no longer just about socializing and navel gazing. The region's social networking sites and services have gone well beyond electronic yearbooks and places to gawk at videos of celebrity wardrobe malfunctions. Wael Ghonim, an internet activist, computer engineer and Google executive created the Facebook page for Egypt's preeminent dissident Mohammed El-Baradei, and helped launch the demonstrations that toppled the Egyptian government. It wasn't the first time social networking sites have inspired uprisings. From the Ukraine to Bahrain, Iran to Serbia, Facebook and Twitter have been instrumental in turning the democratization of information into real-time democratic movements. On February 21, 2011, Egyptian protester Jamal Ibrahim named his newborn daughter 'Facebook' in honor of the site he credited with making Egypt's January 25th Movement possible.

San Francisco Today

A city that likes to lead, not follow.

TEXT: BONNIE WACH

San Francisco is a city that doesn't like to be told what to do. Take the current grim economic picture. While pundits around the country continue to shake their heads and predict several more years of recession, San Francisco just shrugs its shoulders and gears up for what looks to be another Gold Rush. Glancing back at the city's history, it has always been thus. Stubborn, trend-bucking, and unconventional, San Francisco marches to the beat of its own drum and makes fools out of those who try to prophesize its fortunes.

Everywhere you look these days, internet and multimedia companies are blossoming again, though this time around with actual paths to profitability versus the virtual reality of the last dotcom boom. South of Market Street, where the first internet Gold Rush began back in the 1990s, new tech companies are gobbling up office space once more. According to a recent survey, SoMa vacancy rates have dropped from 20 per cent at the end of 2009 to just 9.5 per cent in 2011.

Led by a coterie of mega companies like Twitter, YouTube and Google, Web 2.0, as it's being called, is also seeing a new wave of up-and-comers such as Zynga and Qwiki expand and thrive – fueled by an abundance of cash-rich venture capitalists and a seemingly unlimited braintrust of innovating engineers. And it's not just South of Market Street. Internet wildfires have also spread to less likely areas, including Union Square, the Financial District, and the ever-downtrodden mid-Market Street corridor. In a move bound to boost an area dominated for decades by empty storefronts, indigents, and drug-related crime, Black Rock Arts Foundation, the organization that puts on the annual Burning Man arts extravaganza, has struck a deal to move their headquarters to Sixth and Market Streets. Likewise, microblogging behemoth Twitter has announced plans to open offices in an old furniture warehouse at 10th and Market streets, and the San Francisco Film Commission has opened a 10,000-square-foot incubator for local independent filmmakers on Golden Gate Avenue just above 6th and Market streets. Nearby on Mint Plaza, a former wino alley abutting the historic Old Mint and across from the Westfield Shopping Centre, a lovely pedestrian-only plaza has sprouted and is now populated by several good restaurants, and the cult-coffee purveyor Blue Bottle.

BUILDING BOOM

Perhaps the most telltale sign of the warming economic temperatures of the last few years has been the rapidly changing skyline. The Transamerica Pyramid, once the definitive exclamation point in a city fairly devoid of looming skyscrapers, is rapidly being eclipsed by a series of larger, imposing structures that were begun during the last big boom, and will finally see completion with the next one. The obelisk-like One Rincon Hill condominium tower – initially the first of two skyscrapers to be constructed next to the Bay Bridge (the recession has put the kibosh on a second tower, at least for now) – looms some 641 feet (195 meters) above the Bay. Recently approved plans for the massive Transbay Center, a regional transit hub for buses, light rail and high-speed trains, will include a 1,200-foot (365-metre) tower and a rooftop park the length of five football fields, and will give San Francisco the dubious distinction of having the tallest building on the West Coast. Just across the street, Millennium Tower, a 60-story, 645-foot (197-metre) residential condo complex with $12 million penthouse units and a swanky restaurant, has recently been completed. A half-dozen other buildings have also been proposed, ranging in height from 600 to 800 feet (183 to 244 metres).

Further south, the sprawling Mission Bay area, which includes 303 acres (123 hectares) of research, retail, office, residential and recreation space, as well as a large biotech and research campus for the University of California, continues to expand with high-end lofts and trendy restaurants, as well as upscale shops, and the big lure – AT&T ballpark, where the World Series champion San Francisco Giants baseball team brings in sell-out crowds. It's a transformation made all the more remarkable when you consider that the neighborhood was an industrial wasteland for upwards of half a century.

South of China Basin, the debut of the Third Street light-rail line has also brought gentrification to the formerly scruffy quadrant known as Dogpatch (off 3rd Street, roughly between Pennsylvania and 22nd Street). For decades, the area's claim to fame was a commuter train stop and a hard-drinking saloon; these days, you'll find lovingly restored Victorian houses, homey cafés, chic-trendy restaurants, artisan shops, and even an all-organic wine bar and a microbrewery.

POLITICS AS UNUSUAL

Politics continues to make waves on the wild West Coast as well. In the wake of a contentious, back-biting, and downright vicious gubernatorial election, ex-eBay CEO Meg Whitman went down in flames, after having outspent her opponent, the former California Governor 'Moonbeam' Jerry Brown, by more than $140 million—the most expensive campaign for state office in the nation's history. Brown, who was California's governor back in the free-to-be 1970s and early '80s, has adopted a new pragmatic,

'After a lull, residents' devotion to cultural pastimes seems back on track.'

no-nonsense style that's found appeal among both Democrats and Republicans, though his austere measures to deal with the state's dire budget shortfalls may test his popularity in the coming years. Meanwhile, San Francisco's other heir apparent, the former dashing boy-mayor Gavin Newsom, who made headlines when he legalized gay marriage back in 2004, has moved up to be Brown's lieutenent governor – his aspirations for even higher office not-so-thinly disguised. Newsom leaves behind a temporary mayor and a vow to make city government carbon-neutral by 2020 – a goal his successor might yet accomplish (*see right* **Going Green**).

ALMIGHTY TOURIST DOLLARS

Nearly 16 million visitors left their hearts and wallets in San Francisco in 2010, an increase of 3.1 per cent from 2009 that translated to $8.34 billion in the city's pocketbook. Among the benefactors have been dining establishments, which had seen a downturn in the last few years due to high local unemployment rates and a law forcing them to offer paid sick leave and health insurance to employees. But appetites and growing paychecks have prevailed in this town of fanatical foodies, and San Francisco's restaurant scene is by all accounts bustling again, with new hotspots opening all around town – many of whom pay as much attention to their cocktail menu and wine lists as their dining menus. In a recent survey by the San Francisco Travel Association, 30.7 per cent of tourists polled said San Francisco's restaurants and cuisine were the most important factor in visiting the city; almost 91 per cent claimed dining in restaurants as their prime activity. The economic picture looks equally bright for San Francisco's convention bookings, which are 109 per cent ahead of goal for the upcoming years. Perhaps the only sectors not looking so prosperous are the housing and retail markets. While San Francisco wasn't plagued by the volume of home foreclosures that have decimated the rest of the country, it's still smarting from a drop in prices and lethargic sales, neither of which have picked up since 2008. Meanwhile with the free-spending days of the dotcom boom just a fond memory, independent retailers have been hit especially hard, undermined by big-box stores such as Target, which can continue to pay the high rents many landlords still demand.

CULTURE CRAVINGS

After a lull, residents' devotion to cultural pastimes seems back on track. The opening of the state-of-the-art California Academy of Sciences – the greenest museum in the world – in 2008 has drawn record crowds. The natural science museum, aquarium and all-digital planetarium, designed by Italian architect Renzo Piano, is housed in an environmentally sustainable building that boasts a living rainforest, the world's largest living coral reef display, and a roof that supports some 1.7 million native plants.

In Yerba Buena, the Museum of the African Diaspora and the Museum of Craft and Folk Art joined the Museum of Modern Art and the Yerba Buena Center for the Arts in the rapidly expanding arts district, followed in short order by the über-modern Contemporary Jewish Museum, designed by famed New York architect Daniel Libeskind. The tranformation of this formerly down-and-out warehouse district into one of the city's most vibrant arts enclaves (now increasingly attracting high-end residential developments as well), surprises only those who don't know San Francisco – and San Franciscans – all that well. Reinvention is second nature in a city where earthquakes, fires, economic booms and busts are as common as fog in July. It's a resilience that continues to make San Francisco relevant, vital and, above all, interesting – for both residents and visitors.

Going Green

Turning eco-dreams into green reality

San Francisco has long had a reputation as a city of tree huggers and whale savers – a place where school children know the 'reduce, re-use, recycle' song as well as 'The Wheels on the Bus'. But in the fat, comfortable 1990s that image got a bit muddied in the stampede for the almighty dotcom dollar. These days, green – the leafy kind – is back with a vengeance and is once again putting the city and the state at the forefront of the environmental movement.

It goes much further than tossing expensive bottles of wine into the recycling bin or driving a hybrid SUV. This year, barring legal roadblocks, California will implement the nation's first country's first cap and trade system to curb greenhouse gas emissions. At restaurants, where the terms 'sustainable', 'local' and 'organic' have long been the rule, used french-fry oil now powers the city's buses. Add to that mandatory composting laws, bans on plastic bags, water bottles, Styrofoam, and smoking, and the Bay Area has become, as one newspaper editorial put it, 'the world's last, best hope against climate change'. Small wonder that Nobel Prize winner Al 'An Inconvenient Truth' Gore owns a home in the city and based his venture, CurrentTV, here.

To get a sense of how committed San Francisco is to conservation, consider that in 2010 the city recycled 77 per cent of its waste – the highest recycling rate in the nation – with a goal to reach zero waste by 2020. A staggering number of healthy green initiatives have been passed in the last few years. Among the more controversial:

- A ban on plastic shopping bags in large supermarkets and drugstores, the first city in the US to impose one.
- A ban on the use of Styrofoam in local restaurants.
- Mandatory composting and recycling for all city residents.
- A ban on city departments buying single-serving bottled water.
- City-sponsored collection of used cooking oil for conversion into biodiesel.
- A commitment to make all city buses emission-free by 2020, and to convert all taxis to alternative fuels by 2011.
- Bans on smoking that include bars, restaurants, office building doorways, apartment building public areas, ATM lines, sporting events, and cars with minor passengers.

Restaurants all over town continue to ride the momentum of the sustainable 'farm to table' movement, betting that the way to the public's heart is through its stomach. And hotels have jumped on the bandwagon, increasingly building to LEED (Leadership in Energy and Environmental Design) specs, and using environmentally friendly products. While some grumble, most residents are happily embracing the wave, banking on the idea that being green will translate into seeing green – the dollar kind – in the not-too-distant future.

Architecture

Building on the edge.

TEXT: MATT MARKOVICH

Building in San Francisco has always been a challenge. At times, due to technological constraints, it has been literally impossible, and even when possible, it has been unadvisable. Why? Three words: quakes, water and hills. Packed into San Francisco's tiny 47-square-mile area are more than 70 hills, ranging in height from 100 feet to 927 feet (30 to 283 meters). Add to this the fact that it's surrounded on three sides by water and is located in one of the nation's most populous and seismically active regions. As a result, San Francisco has had to build and rebuild itself many times over. These challenges haven't prevented architects from wanting to put their stamp on the city. The risks, it seems, are worth it.

A MISSIONARY POSITION

It was the establishment of **Mission Dolores** (*see p79*), an adobe chapel built on swampland, that initially drew settlers to the city; the first Mass was celebrated on June 29, 1776. The simple chapel, with its thick adobe walls, sits beside a cemetery where Native Americans, outlaws, and the city's first Irish and Hispanic mayors are buried. The mission was one of 21 built in California by the Spanish; only Carmel and Monterey rival it for authentic atmosphere. Along with a portion of the walls of the Officers' Club in the Presidio, the mission is the sole piece of colonial architecture to have outlived the city's progress from hamlet to metropolis.

The town inhabited by Gold Rush immigrants known as the Forty-Niners suffered a series of fires. The heart of the outpost was **Portsmouth Square** (*see p63* **Profile**), located in present-day Chinatown. It was incinerated by two blazes; the surrounding streets perished in the fire following the 1906 earthquake. The most impressive buildings from the Gold Rush era are in the **Jackson Square Historical District** (*see p50*; best viewed on Jackson between Montgomery and Sansome Streets).

THE BOOM YEARS: PART ONE

Although precious metals flooded the town, the big Gold Rush money actually came from outfitting the legions of fortune-seekers. A burst of prosperity in the 19th century quickly filled San Francisco's once-empty sloping streets with what have become its signature Victorian terraced houses. Built by middle-class tradesmen in the Mission, Castro and Haight districts, and by rich merchants in Presidio Heights and around **Alamo Square**, these famous 'Painted Ladies' provide San Francisco's most characteristic architectural face. One of the most popular views of the city is framed by a row of six painted Victorians along Steiner Street between Hayes and Grove Streets ('**Postcard Row**'), but there are more than 14,000 examples of this eye-catching vernacular, some even more fanciful.

The wooden frames and elaborate woodwork of San Francisco's Victorians come in four distinct styles: Gothic Revival, Italianate, Stick-Eastlake and Queen Anne. The earliest Gothic Revival houses have pointed arches over their windows and were often painted white, rather than in the bright colours of the later styles. The Italianate style, with tall cornices, neo-classical elements and add-on porches, are best exemplified in the Lower Haight, notably on Grove Street near Webster Street, but there are other examples at **1900 Sacramento Street** (near Lafayette Park) and at 1818 California Street in the shape of the **Lilienthal-Pratt House**, built in 1876.

The Italianate was succeeded by the Stick-Eastlake style, named after furniture designer Charles Eastlake and characterized by square bay windows framed with angular, carved ornamentation. The 'Sticks' are the most common of the Victorian houses left in the city; a shining example is the over-the-top extravaganza at **1057 Steiner Street**, on the corner of Golden Gate Avenue.

With its turrets, towers and curvaceous corner bay windows, the Queen Anne style is amply demonstrated by the **Wormser-Coleman House** in Pacific Heights (1834 California Street, at Franklin Street). However, the most extravagant example is the **Haas-Lilienthal House** (*see p98*); it was built in 1886 by Bavarian grocer William Haas, who treated himself to a home with 28 rooms and six bathrooms. Now a museum, the house is one of the few such examples of Victorian architecture open to the public.

TAKING A BATH

Engineer Adolph Sutro came to own most of the western side of the city, including the sandy wasteland on its westerly edge, which he bought in 1881 for his **Sutro Baths**. Annexed by the new Golden Gate Park, the therapeutic baths were the most elaborate in the western world. Much in need of repair by the 1960s, and badly burned in a fire, they were sold to developers for high-rise apartments that remained unbuilt, and are now San Franciscans' favorite ruins. The adjoining **Cliff House** (*see p96*) burned twice,

'Angular in shape, the museum's helix-like viewing tower rises high above the park.'

rebuilt first in the fashion of a grand French chateau and later in neoclassical style. It underwent further cannibalization over the years before the owners gave it an extreme makeover in 2004 that brought it back to its neo-classical roots.

Closer to Downtown, San Francisco's 'Big Four' railroad barons – Mark Hopkins, Leland Stanford, Collis P Huntington and Charles Crocker – made their architectural mark in the late 19th century by building grand edifices. Their mining investments funded railroads, banks and businesses, but also paid for their baronial mansions on Nob Hill. Many were destroyed in the 1906 fire, but their sites have since been filled in suitably grand fashion. Two old mansions have been replaced by hotels: the **Stanford Court Renaissance** (905 California Street, at Powell Street) and the **Mark Hopkins Inter-Continental** (1 Nob Hill, at California & Mason Streets; *see p124*), while the site of the former **Crocker Mansion**, a Queen Anne manor built in 1888, is now occupied by gothic **Grace Cathedral** (*see p65*), itself a stunning addition to San Francisco's architectural heritage.

However, the nearby **Flood Mansion** (1000 California Street, at Mason Street) survived the blaze and remains a brilliant example of the grandeur of the homes that once perched on Nob Hill. Believed to be the first brownstone west of the Mississippi River, the 42-room sandstone marvel was built in 1886 by silver baron James C Flood and now houses a private club. Another grand old survivor, albeit one that post-dates the quake, is the **Spreckels Mansion**, an impressive Beaux Arts building in Pacific Heights (2080 Washington Street, at Octavia Street). Built in 1912 for sugar baron Adolph Spreckels, it's now owned by mega-selling novelist Danielle Steel.

Unsurprisingly, this most curious of cities boasts many architectural curiosities. Perhaps chief among them is the **Octagon House** (*see p100*). Built in 1861 during a city-wide craze for eight-sided buildings (they were considered healthier because they let in more light), it's one of just two octagonal buildings left in the city. Furnished in early colonial style, the upper floors have now been fully restored, with a central staircase leading to a domed skylight.

Another oddity is the **Columbarium** (*see p96*), a neo-classical temple built in 1898 that holds the ashes of thousands of city residents. Its interior is decorated with mosaic tiling and elaborate urns in imaginatively bedecked niches. Oriental promise meets occidental vulgarity at the **Vedanta Temple** (*see p99*), an eccentricity built in 1905 for the Hindu Vedanta Society. Its bizarre mix of styles includes a Russian Orthodox onion-shaped dome, a Hindu cupola, castle-like crenellations, and Moorish arches.

FROM BOOMTOWN TO METROPOLIS

When the growing city began to burst at its peninsula seams, a ferry network evolved to carry passengers to and from other parts of the Bay Area. Intended as a symbol of civic pride for the young city, with a clock tower inspired by the Moorish campanile of Seville Cathedral, the **Ferry Building** was built on the Embarcadero in 1896. Its impeccably restored Great Nave, a 660-foot-long steel-framed, two-story interior now houses everything from office space to the wildly popular farmers' market (*see p192*).

After the 1906 earthquake, a passion for engineering spurred an interest in Chicago architect Daniel Burnham's City Beautiful project. Arising from it was a proposal for a heroic new Civic Center planted below a terraced Telegraph Hill, laced with tree-lined boulevards that would trace the city's contours. The plan was the result of Burnham's two-year consultations with leading city architects Bernard Maybeck and Willis Polk (the latter designed the wonderful **Hobart Building** at Market and Montgomery Streets; the former the just-restored **Palace of Fine Arts**, *see p101*), and countered the city's impractical grid street pattern. But it never came to fruition.

Under Mayor 'Sunny Jim' Rolph, the thrust of the 1915 Civic Center complex eventually came from public contests; many were won by Arthur Brown, architect of the mighty domed **City Hall** (*see p56*). Several other Civic Center buildings date back to this era, among them Brown's **War Memorial Opera House**, completed in 1932, and the **Bill Graham Civic Auditorium** (for both, *see p55*). All reflect the Imperial, Parisian Beaux Arts style, sometimes described as French Renaissance or classical baroque, with grandiose proportions and ornamentation, as well as theatrical halls and stairways. The former main library, built by George Kelham in 1915, was redesigned by Italian architect Gae Aulenti, best known for her transformation of Paris's Musée d'Orsay; it now offers a spectacularly modern experience as the **Asian Art Museum** (*see p56*).

It was largely Rolph's idea to host the huge Panama-Pacific Exposition in 1915, for which he commissioned Bernard Maybeck to build the **Palace of Fine Arts** and its myriad pavilions. The only building left from the Exposition, the Palace was originally made of wood and plaster and rebuilt using reinforced concrete in the 1960s. It underwent a complete restoration 2011. Around the same time in the '60s, Julia Morgan, another Arts and Crafts architect, was designing buildings around the East Bay, at least when she wasn't working for San Francisco newspaper magnate William Randolph Hearst on the extravagant Hearst Castle. In San Francisco, she designed the old Chinese YMCA building, now home to the **Chinese American National Museum & Learning Center** (*see p67*).

Passionate rebuilding continued during the Depression, with two staggering landmarks leading the way. The **Golden Gate Bridge** (*see p104*) opened to traffic in 1937, a year after the completion of the **San Francisco-Oakland Bay Bridge**; the latter is currently undergoing extensive retrofitting and the construction of a new east span that is scheduled to be completed in 2013.

The Works Progress Administration (WPA), part of President Roosevelt's New Deal job-creation scheme, was responsible for many structures, such as **Coit Tower** (*see p70*), designed by Arthur Brown in 1932, and the prison buildings on **Alcatraz** island (*see p73*). Other examples from this period include the 1932 **Herbst Theatre** (with murals by Frank Brangwyn; *see p257*), the 1930 **Pacific Coast Stock Exchange** (complete with mural by Diego Rivera; *see p50*) and the Rincon Annex Post Office Building, built in 1940 to include Anton Refregier's murals and now part of the **Rincon Center** (*see p53*).

While Frank Lloyd Wright's **Marin Civic Center**, located north of the city in San Rafael and completed after his death in 1972, is his most stunning civic work, there is one other Lloyd Wright building in the city, at 140 Maiden Lane. Wright designed the edifice in 1948, originally a gift store, as a prototype Guggenheim (notice the winding, circular stair). It now houses a tribal- and folk-art gallery, and is open to the public as the **Xanadu Gallery** (*see p47*).

Bay Bridge.

CONTEMPORARY CLASSICS

The 1970s saw a small wave of construction that had a big impact on the city's image. Pietro Belluschi and Pier Luigi Nervi completed the **Cathedral of St Mary of the Assumption** (*see p88*) in 1972; a 255-foot (78-meter) concrete structure supporting a cross-shaped, stained-glass ceiling, it's a 1970s symbol of anti-quake defiance. The same year saw the completion of the 853-foot (260-meter) **Transamerica Pyramid** (*see p48*), one of San Francisco's most iconic buildings. The $34-million structure has an internal suspension system, which served to protect its 48 stories and 212-foot (65-meter) spire in the 1989 quake. At first unpopular, the pyramid now has few detractors: for many it's become a symbol for the city itself.

Following a relatively restrained period, the last decade has seen a flurry of construction. Unlike Los Angeles, San Francisco has always taken a quiet approach to building, zealously protecting its past and begrudgingly embracing its future. However, recently, world-renowned architects are being selected for some of its defining projects.

THE BOOM YEARS: PART TWO

During the second Bay Area boom of the mid to late 1990s, there was not only a renewed interest in development, but deeper pockets to fund it. Designed by architects James Ingo Freed of Pei Cobb Freed and Cathy Simon of Simon Martin-Vegue Winkelstein Moris, the **San Francisco Main Library** (*see p56*) is a marriage of Beaux Arts and more recent styles. One side links the building to the more contemporary Marshall Plaza; the other echoes the old library to the north, with grandiose neo-classical columns. The dramatic interior centers around a five-story atrium below a domed skylight designed to let natural light filter throughout the building.

However, it's SoMa that has really been transformed, most dramatically with the **San Francisco Museum of Modern Art** (*see p60*). Designed by Mario Botta and opened in 1995, it features a series of stepped boxes and a striped cylindrical facade. Just

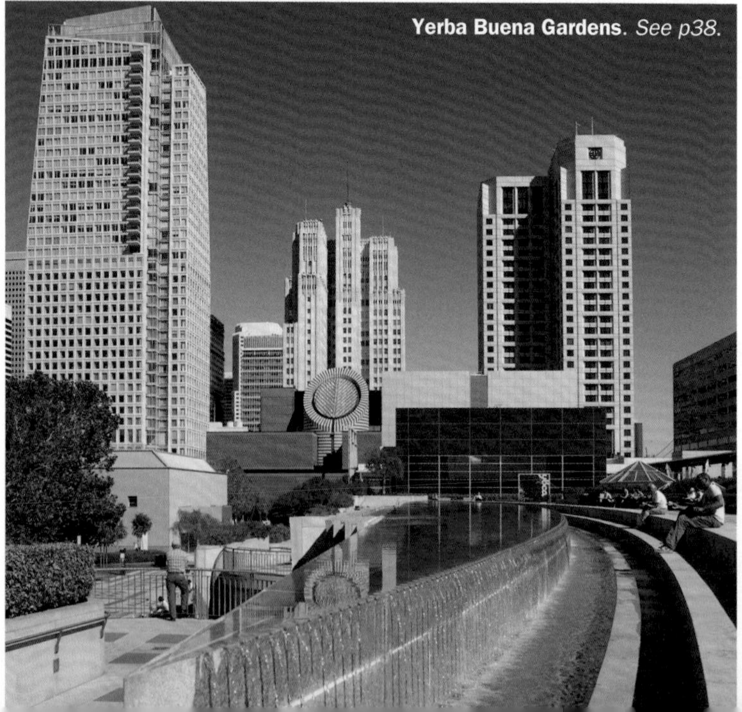

Yerba Buena Gardens. *See p38.*

Can You Top That?

Building skywards.

In 1896, the man who would be elected mayor that year, James Phelan, outlined his vision of San Francisco: 'On the map of the world the great bay and harbor opening to 76,000,000 miles of ocean was stamped by the hand of Fate and destined for Empire.'

Only one thing stood in the way of his grand scheme: reality. Although not fully appreciated at the time, the challenges of building upwards in earthquake country quickly became understood. In 1906, the great earthquake, and the fire that followed, leveled the city and much of its imperial ambitions. It became clear that if the city was to grow, it had to build outwards. And so it did. Past its boundaries and even deep into the Bay, a significant portion of 'land' was added to Downtown. Today, almost everything beyond Montgomery Street, including the Embarcadero and the Marina district, is constructed on landfill.

In the last decade, however, a new generation of developers has emerged. Citing modern urban planning models and green architecture technology, their proposals encouraged high-density urban areas designed to reduce suburban sprawl and the waste and pollution associated with it. A relatively undeveloped area set on bedrock in the south-west section of the city, known as Rincon Hill, provided the right location.

The project that best exemplifies this new model is the gargantuan Transbay Center, which officially broke ground on August 11, 2010. The centerpiece is the 1,200 foot (3,658-meter) Transbay Tower, a structure that will dwarf the city's tallest building, the 853-foot Transamerica building. Plans are to include 11 regional transit operators, the northern terminus for a yet-unbuilt rail system, and a roof park the length of several football fields. Estimated to cost $4.2 billion, the development will entirely reconfigure a significant portion of Downtown San Francisco. At least six other buildings are proposed, ranging from 600 to 800 feet tall.

Rincon Hill.

The Transbay Tower won't be alone up there. Just across the street is the recently completed Millennium Tower, a 60-story, 645-foot (197-meter) residential condominium complex. Nearby, One Rincon Hill's South Tower, a 641-foot (195-meter) all-residential building, was completed in 2008. The recession put plans for a second tower 'indefinitely on hold'. But, meanwhile, an additional four skyscrapers, each more than 400 feet tall, have been approved by the city, and proposals for an additional 19 towers are in the works.

The development blitz doesn't stop at the shoreline. The city recently gave a nod to a complex on manmade Treasure Island in San Francisco Bay that is likely to include a 450 foot-tall tower.

Some may never reach completion, but the eagerness of developers to create such massive plans clearly heralds a new era – not only for San Francisco architecture, but also for the very spirit of San Francisco.

west of SFMOMA is a great triumph of recent urban planning: **Yerba Buena Gardens** (*see p57*), a beautiful urban park framed by museums, theaters and shops and replete with lush greenery, fountains, sculptures, cafés and the **Metreon** (*see p57*), a hyper-modern urban mall. Directly opposite is **Moscone West**, the latest addition to the **Moscone Convention Center** (*see p57*). The stunning glass structure incorporates a graphic display screen designed by New York artists/architects Elizabeth Diller and Ricardo Scofidio. Perhaps the most dramatic of the new SoMa projects is the **San Francisco Federal Building** at 7th and Mission streets. Designed by Thom Mayne, the structure's perforated metal façade plays on the idea of government transparency and promises to reduce energy use. Daniel Libeskind's **Contemporary Jewish Museum** (*see p60*) is a strikingly modern update of a 1907 Willis Polk substation. A blue steel cube – symbolic of the Hebrew letters for 'chai' (life) – is attached to the original brick facade, marrying the old with the new. Nearby, in Mission Bay, Ricardo Legorreta's **UCSF Community Center** at the University of California campus is a building that echoes the architect's Mexican roots with its brilliant-red clay and fuchsia-toned palette.

There has been plenty of activity across town at Golden Gate Park, too. The old **de Young Museum** (*see p94*) was replaced in 2005 after suffering structural damage in the Loma Prieta earthquake. The ultra-modern design by Swiss architects Herzog & de Meuron caused huge controversy when it was first unveiled. Angular in shape, the museum's helix-like viewing tower rises high above the park; the dappled, copper façade, which will develop a patina over time, offers a burst of color in the otherwise mild-mannered park setting.

Across from the de Young, the **California Academy of Sciences** (*see p94*) received a similar makeover in 2008. Architect Renzo Piano transformed the 155-year-old institution into the world's 'greenest' museum, featuring a digital planetarium, indoor rainforest, aquarium with an active coral reef, and a 'living' roof that recycles rainwater and provides insulation for the museum. The park's oldest building, the whimsical **San Francisco Conservatory of Flowers**, was fully restored following the 1989 quake.

The Presidio has also seen action over the last few years, as work continues on converting and upgrading the old army properties on the site for public habitation. The decision to allow filmmaker George Lucas to build the $350-million **Letterman Digital Arts Center** on a plot at the eastern edge of the park was not without controversy, but the beautiful whitewashed campus blends in seamlessly with its surroundings, and has won over most of its critics.

The 2005 unveiling of the **St Regis Hotel** (*see p123*) announced the city's first new luxury hotel in four years. Designed by Skidmore, Owings & Merrill architect Craig Hartman, who also lent his touch to the sparkling International Terminal at **San Francisco International Airport**, the building is also home to the three-story **Museum of the African Diaspora** (*see p60*).

FUTURE SHOCK

The most notable signs of new development in the city are the high-rise 'multi-use' and luxury condominium buildings increasingly taking up sky space in the **SoMa** and **Rincon Hill** area. One of the few parts of the city suitable for tall buildings because of its bedrock foundation, the area is slated to become home to around a dozen buildings in the next few years, with new One Rincon Hill towering at 641 feet (195 meters), making it the city's fourth tallest building (*see p37* **Can You Top That?**). To many San Franciscans, the prospect of towering structures that seem so antithetical to the city's overall vibe is, to put it mildly, disturbing. In 2010, the city broke ground on a sweeping structure to replace the dilapidated **Transbay Terminal**. Dubbed the 'Grand Central Station of the West', the $4 billion project by Hines and Pelli Clarke Pelli Architects will connect eight Bay Area counties and the State of California through 11 transit systems, and will feature a 1,200-foot (3,658-meter) office tower – the tallest building on the West Coast – smack in the middle of the most earthquake-prone region in the country.

San Francisco on Screen

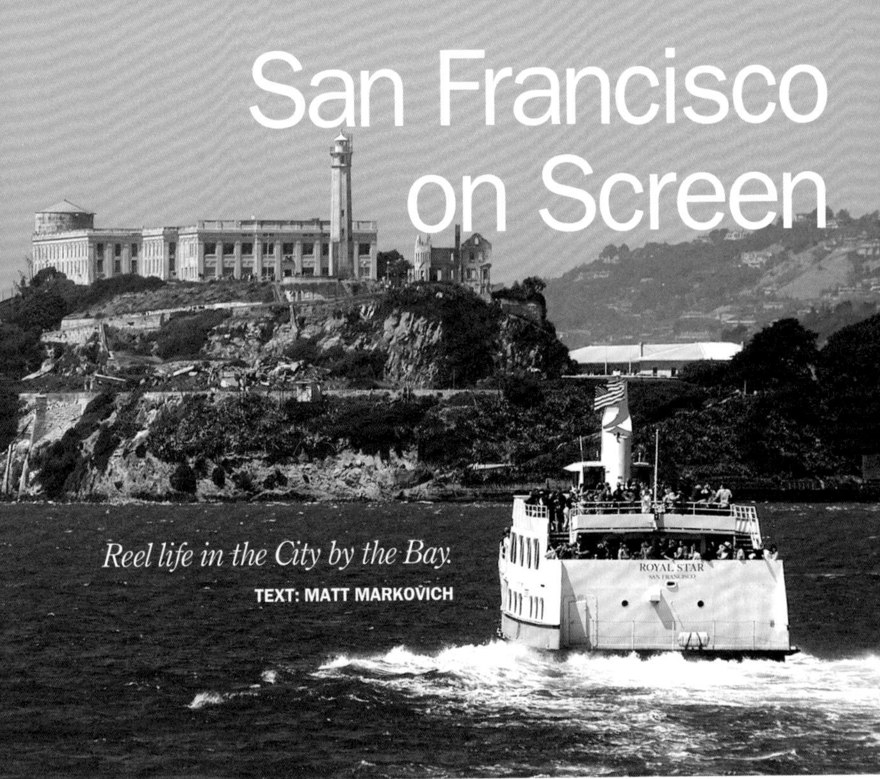

Reel life in the City by the Bay.

TEXT: MATT MARKOVICH

If geological and geopolitical events hadn't conspired against it, San Francisco may have become the center of the cinematic world and a desert town named Hollywoodland would have remained a parched backwater in Southern California. The truth is that cinematic history has indeed been made in the Bay Area, but aside from film buffs, trivia hounds and tech geeks, San Francisco's status as filmmaking's leading lady has been largely overlooked.

The very first moving image on film was created 30 miles south of San Francisco at a Palo Alto horse track. It all began as a bet that Leland Stanford, former California governor, railroad tycoon, and founder of Stanford University, was convinced he would win. In the late 1800s, a vigorous debate existed about the gait of galloping horses. Stanford contended that all four hooves left the ground simultaneously, and to prove his point, he enlisted the help of Eadweard Muybridge, a photographer whose nature photography would later inspire Ansel Adams. Muybridge developed a device that allowed multiple cameras to capture several successive images. Dubbed the Zoopraxiscope, Muybridge proved his patron's point in 1878 – and in the process made him the world's first film producer.

MAKING MOVIES

The pair also created the first movie star, William Lawton, a gymnast at San Francisco's Olympic Club, who was the first human subject to be captured in a moving picture. At a screening, held in 1880 at the San Francisco Art Association (later the site of the Bank of America, 555 California Street, the building featured in the 1970s disaster epic *The Towering Inferno*), the pair charged the public 50 cents ($11 in today's dollars) to view their collection of zoopraxography – proving ticket prices have remained more or less constant.

More than a century later, Muybridge's innovations are credited with techniques used in *The Matrix* (whose last two installments were filmed across the Bay in Oakland). As Philip Brookman, curator of the Muybridge retrospective (at SFMOMA, *see p60*, through June 2011) put it: 'The breaking down of motion that you see in *The Matrix* comes directly from the [Muybridge] animal locomotion project, where you see one moment in time depicted from all these different angles.'

CELLULOID CITY

Motion picture technology quickly evolved in the 20th century. Equipment became less cumbersome, more affordable and easy to operate, and the technology increasingly turned towards storytelling and entertainment. Within 20 years, the Bay Area was dotted with movie studios. Stars of the era, including Charlie Chaplin, Buster Keaton, Gilbert M 'Broncho Billy' Anderson, Douglas Fairbanks, and Mary Pickford worked for companies such as Essanay Studios West in Niles, north-east of San Francisco, and for the California Motion Picture Company in San Rafael – the town now home to George Lucas' Skywalker Ranch.

San Francisco also became the location of one of the first movie-star scandals in 1921 when comedian Fatty Arbuckle, who had just landed the world's first million-dollar film contract, visited the city to celebrate his windfall with a party at the St Francis Hotel just off Union Square. Festivities were cut short by the collapse of 26-year-old actress Virginia Rappe, who subsequently died. Arbuckle was accused of her rape and murder. Guests can still stay in rooms 1219, 1220 and 1221 – the rooms rented by Arbuckle that fateful weekend.

Other Bay Area innovations included the first color film, *Cupid Angling*, which was shot using techniques patented by Leon F Douglass in 1917. Douglass went on to

Studies of foreshortenings. Horses. Running. Eadweard Muybridge, 1879.

'To date, more than 3,000 films and television shows have been shot in San Francisco.'

invent zoom lenses, wide-angle film photography, early special-effects techniques and underwater photography at his lab in Menlo Park, just south of the city. A decade later, Al Jolson's landmark 1927 film, *The Jazz Singer*, the nation's first 'talkie', was filmed in San Francisco, with scenes shot at Coffee Dan's, a speakeasy that is now Slide (*see p166*), a basement bar that patrons enter via a 15-foot slide, as seen in the film.

A small laboratory at 200 Green Street (a plaque marks the spot) holds the distinction of being the place where inventor Philo T Farnsworth invented television. A polymath with over 300 patents to his name at the time of his death, Farnsworth began creating the technology behind television when he was only 15 years old. Following years of development, Farnsworth's backers became impatient and demanded results. Farnsworth provided them on September 7, 1927. The first television image he broadcast? A dollar sign.

LUCAS AND LASSETER

In 1975, George Lucas, the man behind *Star Wars*, who revolutionized the world of special effects, founded his Industrial Light and Magic (ILM) studio in San Rafael, moving film production into the computer age. ILM still operates from across the Golden Gate, but Lucas's Letterman Digital Arts Center in the Presidio (*see p101*) is arguably the world's most advanced film production center (video game fans will note that it's also the site of the headquarters of *Star Trek: Starfleet Command*). The facility is responsible for the technologies behind virtually all the latest generation of computer special effects – from the first digital editing facilities to bluescreen techniques.

Just across the Bay from ILM is Emeryville's Pixar Studios, headed up by animation wizard John Lasseter. Acquired by Apple Computers CEO Steve Jobs in 1996 and later purchased by Disney, Pixar is an animated film empire, producing blockbusters that include *Toy Story*, *Monsters, Inc.*, *A Bug's Life*, *Cars*, and *Finding Nemo*.

LOCATION, LOCATION, LOCATION

The Bay area's contribution to the film world is not solely based on technology. The region is also home to numerous film luminaries, including Francis Ford Coppola (whose American Zoetrope studios is at 916 Kearny Street), Saul Zaentz, Clint Eastwood, Sean Penn, Chris Columbus, Danny Glover, Robin Williams, and Amy Tan. The 2007 documentary *Fog City Mavericks* chronicles the rise of San Francisco filmmakers and the movies they made here, among them *American Graffiti*, *Star Wars*, the Indiana Jones series, the *Godfather* trilogy, *Apocalypse Now*, *One Flew Over the Cuckoo's Nest*, *Amadeus*, *Lost in Translation*, *Flags of Our Fathers*, and many more.

And, of course, the city itself has starred in countless films as well, from vintage classics like *The Maltese Falcon* and *Vertigo* to modern offerings such as *Interview with the Vampire*, *The Hulk*, *The Conversation*, *Milk*, *Bullitt*, *Dirty Harry*, *Invasion of the Body Snatchers*, and *Star Trek IV*. Cinema's attraction to Alcatraz Island (*see p73*) has been especially strong, with the former prison featured in everything from *Escape from Alcatraz* and *The Rock* to *X-Men: The Last Stand*.

To date, more than 3,000 films and television shows have been shot in San Francisco – more than 60 in the 21st century alone. And judging by the number currently in production (including Steven Soderbergh's *Contagion* and *Hemingway & Gellhorn*, starring Nicole Kidman and Clive Owen), Hollywood's fascination with the City by the Bay shows no signs of abating.

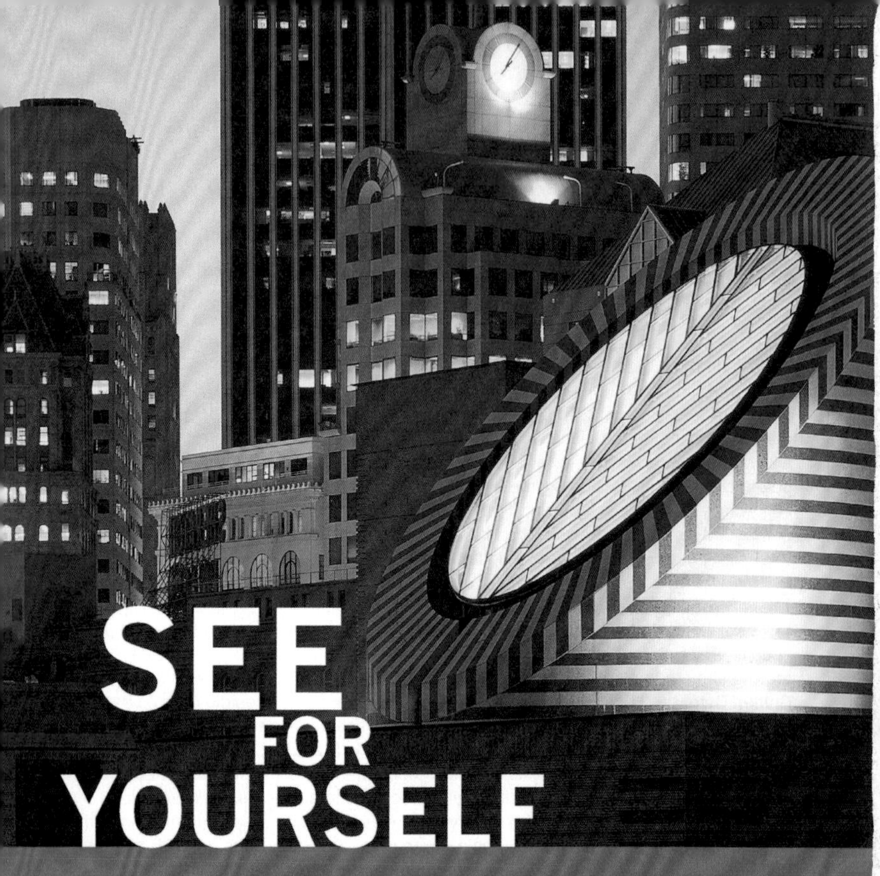
SEE
FOR
YOURSELF

Sights

Golden Gate Bridge. *See p104.*

Downtown

The heart of the city.

San Francisco's Downtown area may be the hub that saves the city from being seen simply as a series of villages. With its myriad cultural attractions and stellar shopping – including outposts representing virtually every significant international luxury brand – it lends the city a cosmopolitanism that exceeds its modest size. Luckily, Downtown's compactness means it's a breeze to navigate on foot. And if you don't want to climb its daunting hills, there are always the famous cable cars.

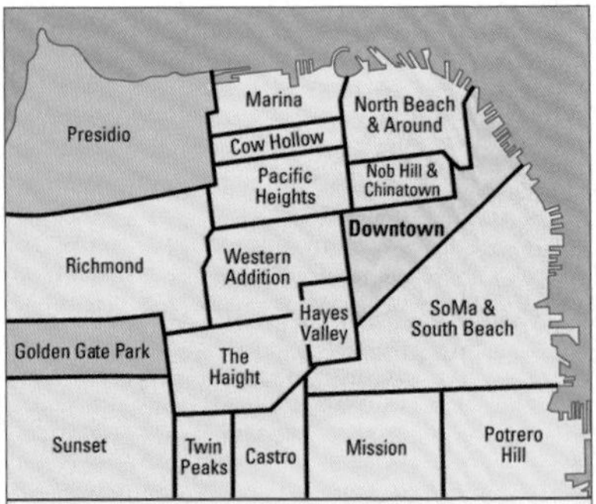

Map p315, p318
Hotels p112
Restaurants & Cafés p133
Bars p165

The center of the action is **Union Square**, a handsome public space ringed with shops and hotels. East of here sits the **Financial District**, one of the few places where one can see northern Californians in business attire; beyond it is the elegant **Embarcadero**, which meanders towards the Bay. To the west is the **Tenderloin**, a gritty area defined by dive bars, ethnic restaurants and homeless panhandlers; and beyond that the **Civic Center**, the stately seat of city government and home to cultural heavyweights that include the War Memorial Opera House, Louise M Davies Symphony Hall, and Asian Art Museum.

UNION SQUARE & AROUND

The best place to begin an exploration of Union Square is at the corner of Post and Stockton Streets, where a timeline of its history is etched into the granite. This little patch of the city was destined to be common ground from an early date. In 1839, Jean Vioget laid out a park in the location when designing Yerba Buena, the city that would become San Francisco. In 1850, Colonel John Geary (who would give his name to Geary Boulevard, west of the square) deeded the land to the city for use as a public space.

The square's name harkens back to its use in 1861 as a pro-Union rallying point on the eve of the Civil War. The 97-foot (30-meter) Corinthian column that rises from the middle of the square was designed by Robert Aitken to commemorate Admiral Dewey's 1898 victory at Manila during the Spanish-American War.

In 1941, the square was rebuilt according to a somewhat severe design by Timothy Pflueger. Pflueger's vision can still be seen in the early Francis Ford Coppola film *The Conversation*, and it acts as a counterpoint to some of his more characteristic art deco designs – notably the stunning Castro Theatre (*see p213*). In 1997, a competition was held to create a new Union Square. After much wrangling, April Phillips and Michael Fotheringham's winning design was unveiled in 2002. Conceived to encourage use by shoppers and lunchtime throngs, yet maintain its vast central area, the new layout altered the character of the area overnight, with a more open design and plenty of benches.

Once a major hangout of San Francisco's homeless, Union Square is now a lively gathering place in the center of Downtown. Tourists and locals sprawl on the strips of lawn along the southern edge of the square, taking a break from shopping, connecting to the square's free WiFi network, or just enjoying a bit of sun and some live music.

At the south-west corner of the square is a **TIX Bay Area** kiosk, offering half-price

Union Square.

tickets for shows, tours and events throughout the city. Diagonally across the square is a branch of **Emporio Rulli** café, with sandwiches, strong espressos and frosty-mugged beers. However, the real commerce is around the outside: the square is ringed by upscale stores and hotels. At no.335, facing right on the square, the still-glamorous **Westin St Francis Hotel** is where silent-era film star Fatty Arbuckle's lethal libido ignited Hollywood's first sex scandal in 1921.

At the opposite corner, the Rotunda restaurant at **Neiman Marcus** (150 Stockton Street, 362 4777, www.neimanmarcus.com) has a breathtaking stained-glass dome – drop in for a lobster club sandwich and a glass of chardonnay for a good view. Built in 1909 for the City of Paris department store that first occupied this site, the dome was shipped across the country for repair when Neiman Marcus took over the building; each of its 26,000 pieces was individually cleaned and restored. There's more history at nearby jeweler **Shreve & Co** (200 Post Street, 421 2600, www.shreve.com): founded in 1852, four years after the discovery of gold in California, it remains the city's oldest retail store.

The stretch of **Powell Street** that links Union Square to Market Street is among the city's busiest thoroughfares. Watching the cable cars clatter past, as the cables that pull them hum beneath your feet, is a quintessential San Francisco experience. At the foot of Powell, huge queues wait to catch a cable car at the roundabout, where conductors manually rotate the cars on a giant turntable for the return journey up the hill.

The once-grand **Market Street** has not aged well, though recent revitalization proposals are giving San Franciscans renewed hope. Lined with offices at its northern end and dilapidated storefronts in its midsection, the street improves rapidly as you move north to the Ferry Building. At 5th Street, the crowds come for the big chain stores: Old Navy looms large on the south side of Market, flanked by Bloomingdale's (*see p178*) and Nordstrom (*see p179*), part of the posh Westfield San Francisco Centre. The most handsome building in the area is arguably the triangular **Phelan Building**, on the north side of Market Street, between Stockton and O'Farrell Streets. Built in 1908 as part of Mayor James Phelan's post-quake reconstruction programme, it's the largest of San Francisco's 'flat-iron' structures, similar to the notable **Flood Building** just down the street (870 Market Street, between 4th & 5th Streets). Across the street, levity is provided at the historic **Mechanics' Institute** (57 Post Street, 393 0101, www.milibrary.org), home to the nation's oldest chess club and a 150-year-old private library that contains more than 160,000 books. Free tours are offered every Wednesday at noon and author events, monthly film series and special exhibitions are ongoing.

The streets north of Market Street and east of Union Square are home to several handsome little alleyways, missed by most tourists but treasured by locals for the relative peace and quiet they afford. **Maiden Lane**, adjoining the square to the east, was once a notorious thoroughfare where randy residents headed to pick up cheap prostitutes. Now gated by day, it's considerably more handsome, awash with chic boutiques and one-off stores such as **Xanadu Gallery** (no.140, 392 9999, www.folkartintl.com). The swooping circular interior of

INSIDE TRACK
VINTAGE MODERN

You can shell out the big bucks for a bus tour to see the city. Alternatively, hop on one of San Francisco's vintage F-Line streetcars and get a grand tour of Downtown for $2, as well as a rolling lesson in mass-transit history. The historic fleet that rumbles up and down Market Street originally hailed from places like Hamburg, Blackpool, Milan, Philly, and Paris. The cars were exported and lovingly restored over the years, and each still bear the markings of its native city.

SIGHTS

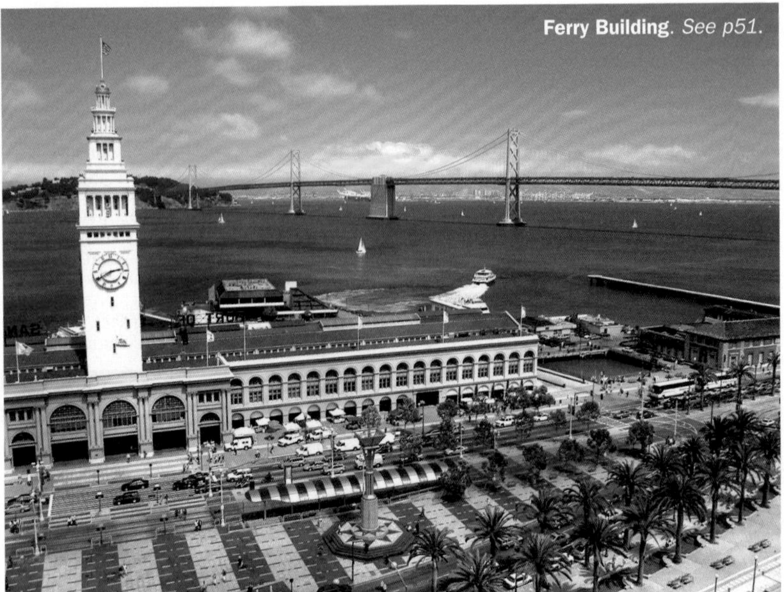
Ferry Building. *See p51.*

the building, designed in 1948 by Frank Lloyd Wright, is filled with wonderful and exotic merchandise – everything from coffee-table books on South Seas art to nandi masks from 17th-century India.

Further north sit two more notable alleys. **Belden Place**, a small street between Kearny and Montgomery Streets, is the main artery of Downtown's unofficial French Quarter, offering dining both fine and casual, plus the most enthusiastic Bastille Day celebrations (July 14) in the city. Nearby **Mark Lane**, another tiny road just off Bush Street, forgoes the red, blue and white in favor of green: it's home to the Irish Bank, an old-school Irish pub. Post-work revelers spill out into the alley clutching pints of the black, and the annual St Patrick's Day celebrations (March 17) are the stuff of legend.

The other streets surrounding Union Square are dominated by shops and hotels, although there are a handful of landmarks that may please literary buffs. Head two blocks north of Union Square up Stockton Street, take a left down Bush Street, and you'll come to **Burritt Street**. In this alley, the byzantine plot of Dashiell Hammett's *The Maltese Falcon* begins with the murder of Sam Spade's partner, Miles Archer. The street opposite is even named after the author, who, like his fictional alter ego Sam Spade, used to regularly visit the century-old **John's Grill** (63 Ellis Street, between Market & Powell Streets, 986 0069, www.johnsgrill.com).

THE FINANCIAL DISTRICT

Bounded by Market, Kearny and Jackson Streets, and the Embarcadero to the east, the Financial District has been the business and banking hub of San Francisco, and the West at large, since the 1849 Gold Rush. Its northern edge is overlooked by the **Transamerica Pyramid**, (600 Montgomery Street, between Washington & Clay streets). Built on the site of the Montgomery Block, a four-story office building that formerly housed writers, artists and radicals including Rudyard Kipling and Mark Twain, the structure provoked public outrage when William Pereira's design was unveiled. However, since its completion in 1972, the 853-foot (260-meter) building has become an iconic spike that defines the city's skyline. The pyramid sits on giant rollers that allow it to rock safely in the event of an earthquake. It sounds a little wacky, but it works: the building came out unscathed by the 7.1 Loma Prieta earthquake in 1989. Sadly, the only people who get to access the observation deck on top are those who work in the building.

On the pyramid's east side, tiny **Redwood Park** is a cool refuge that lunching workers share with majestic trees and bronze sculptures of frogs that are frozen mid-leap in the pond. Across from the Transamerica, in front of the California Pacific Bank, a plaque marks another classic piece of vanished Americana: the Western Headquarters of **Russell, Majors & Waddell**,

founders and operators of the Pony Express (1860-61), whose riders tore across the West at breakneck speeds delivering messages over the 1,966 miles from St Joseph, Missouri, to Sacramento, California. The fastest run on record took seven days and 17 hours, with riders averaging 10.6mph over some of the world's most rugged and dangerous terrain and carrying packages of real import – not least among them, President Abraham Lincoln's first inaugural address. Further south, on nearby Commercial Street, in the city's former mint, the modest **Pacific Heritage Museum** (*see p50*) holds an art collection that's small but worth a peek.

Continuing south from the Transamerica, the area's history as the financial heart of the American West reveals itself further in its architecture. The **Omni Hotel** (500 California Street, at Montgomery Street) was built in 1926 as a bank and wears its origins proudly; just up the road is the small but nonetheless enjoyable **Wells Fargo History Museum** (*see p50*). However, both are dwarfed by the nearby **Bank of America Center**, now officially known as 555 California Street, which towers over the Financial District. The skyscraper is 75 feet (23 meters), shorter than the Transamerica, but feels more massive thanks to its larger girth and its carnelian granite zigzag frame, often seen disappearing into the clouds. At its entrance, the 200-ton black granite sculpture by Masayuki Nagare titled *Transcendence* is appropriately known locally as 'The Banker's Heart'.

A block east of the Bank of America Center sits the **Merchant's Exchange** (465 California Street, between Sansome & Montgomery Streets, 421 7730). The building is no longer used by share traders, but its historic spaces illustrate the important role it once played in the financial life of the city. The lavish trading hall, designed by Julia Morgan, is now the lobby of the California Bank & Trust offices and home to a rather impressive collection of William Coulter seascapes.

There's further financial heritage close by at the Union Bank of California's **Museum of the Money of the American West** (400 California Street, at Sansome Street, no phone). The bank's doors and imposing columns may seem massive next to the museum's modest Wild West collection, but the collection actually includes a variety of fascinating artifacts. Among them is a hyper-rare three-dollar bill signed by the founder of Mormonism, Joseph Smith, and a pair of dueling pistols used in a fateful 1859 duel between a former Chief Justice of the California Supreme Court and a US Senator, which came to be known as 'the duel that ended duels'. The museum also reveals a little about William Chapman Ralston, the bank's founder, a major figure in the development of the city and the man responsible for the lavish Palace Hotel (*see p118* **Ralston's Crowning Achievement**.

INSIDE TRACK
NOT SO DAINTY DAMSEL

While the small alleyway delicately named Maiden Lane (between Stockton, Geary, Post and Kearny streets) is today one of Downtown's most refined shopping streets – home to Marc Jacobs, Chanel, and other big-name designers – its origins are far more nefarious. Known in the Barbary Coast days as Morton Street, it was home to the city's sleaziest brothels, where hookers enticed customers by standing naked to the waist behind small barred windows that fronted 'cribs' – tiny rooms in which they peformed all manner of sexually depraved acts.

A block east, at the intersection of Market, Kearny and Geary Streets, a uniquely San Franciscan ritual is played out every year. At 5.13am on April 18, the last survivors of the 1906 earthquake and their descendants gather around the ornate lion-headed **Lotta's Fountain** (named after the popular vaudevillian Lotta Crabtree, who donated it to the city), just as they did a century ago when families separated by the huge quake used the fountain as a meeting point. On the 104th anniversary in 2010, one survivor was still able to attend the commemoration – 104-year-old William Del Monte.

FREE Pacific Coast Stock Exchange

155 Sansome Street, at Pine Street (421 9939, tours 202 9700 ext 72). Bus 1, 10, 12, 15, 41/cable car California. **Map** p315 N5.

The Exchange was modernized in 1928 by architect Timothy Pflueger, who believed art should be an integral part of architecture. He commissioned sculptor Ralph Stackpole to create the two granite statues outside, which represent Agriculture and Industry (the twin sources of wealth), while above the entrance is a figure called *Progress of Man* with arms outstretched. The stock exchange trading floor closed in 2002 and the building now houses an Equinox fitness center. The main attraction however, Diego Rivera's 1930 mural *Allegory of California,* can still be viewed on the 10th floor of the building inside the City Club (tours are available by appointment only, www.cityclubsf.com). It is richly ironic that Rivera, a committed communist, should have been allowed to create such a magnificent work within the heart of capitalism; Stackpole, an old friend of Rivera, had recommended him for the job. The mural shows Bay Area industries, including aviation and oil, with Mother Earth in the center and the emphasis firmly on workers rather than bosses, highlighting Rivera's socialist penchant for sticking it to the authorities.

FREE Pacific Heritage Museum

608 Commercial Street, at Montgomery Street (399 1124, www.ibankunited.com/phm). Bus 1, 10, 12, 15, 41/cable car California. **Open** 10am-4pm Tue-Sat. **Admission** free. **Map** p315 N4.

Once the city's mint, this structure is now a Bank of Canton and also a museum. Emphasizing San Francisco's connections with the Pacific Rim, the museum features changing exhibits of contemporary artists from countries such as China, Taiwan, Japan and Thailand. Much of what is displayed here is on loan from private collections rarely seen elsewhere.

FREE Wells Fargo History Museum

420 Montgomery Street, at California Street (396 2619, www.wellsfargohistory.com/museums/museum_sf.htm). Bus 1, 10, 30, 41/cable car California. **Open** 9am-5pm Mon-Fri. **Admission** free. **Map** p315 N4.

Wells Fargo is California's oldest bank, and this collection of Gold Rush memorabilia gives a good history of banking in California. You'll find gold nuggets, an old telegraph machine and a Concord stagecoach, built in 1867, plus historical photos.

JACKSON SQUARE

The northern edge of the Financial District is marked by the **Jackson Square Historical District** (bounded by Washington, Kearny and Sansome Streets, and Pacific Avenue).

It's the last vestige of San Francisco's notorious Barbary Coast, once a seething mass of low-life bars and 19th-century sex clubs, the floor shows of which made modern-day Tijuana seem like an ice-cream social. Today, the few blocks of 1850s-era brick buildings that once stood on the shoreline house upmarket antiques shops and lovingly restored offices now far from the waterfront. Many of their foundations are made from the hulls of ships abandoned by eager gold-seekers that eventually filled in the bay.

Stroll along Jackson Street (between Sansome & Montgomery Streets) and Hotaling Street to see the only neighborhood left in San Francisco that pre-dates the ubiquitous Victorian style. It was spared during the 1906 quake and the subsequent fire, not least because several of the buildings were liquor warehouses that had been built of stone to protect the precious booze. By the 1930s, Jackson Square was popular with a number of bohemian artists and writers; John Steinbeck and William Saroyan, among others, used to drink at the now long-vanished Black Cat Café (710 Montgomery Street). For a bit of the maritime history of these few blocks, duck into the **Old Ship Saloon** (298 Pacific Avenue, at Battery Street, 788 2222, www.oldshipsaloon.com). A ship that ran aground on Alcatraz Island, the *Arkansas,* was towed to the corner where the bar now resides – the original proprietor simply cut a door in the hull to allow access. Over the past century, the boat has morphed into a fairly conventional bar, but the story holds water: the remains of ships are still regularly unearthed in the area as crews excavate for new constructions.

THE EMBARCADERO

For decades, San Franciscans old enough to recall the majesty of the original Embarcadero became misty-eyed for the old days when it was a palm-lined thoroughfare as opposed to a double-decker freeway with all the charm of Chicago's Lower Wacker Drive. Then came the devastating 1989 Loma Prieta earthquake. Although the quake wreaked havoc throughout the region, it also felled the Embarcadero's ill-considered upper deck, returning it to its former glory. Today, refurbished antique streetcars from around the world – Moscow, Milan, Oporto, Japan, and even a roofless number from the English resort town of Blackpool – ply the ribbon of road that unfurls along the Bay.

At the foot of Market Street stands the centerpiece of the Embarcadero: the beautifully restored **Ferry Building**, which divides even-numbered piers (to the south) from odd (to the north). Major renovations to this California landmark, originally completed in 1898, were unveiled in 2003; the building now bustles with the unmatched **Ferry Plaza Farmers' Market** (*see p192*), where stall holders sell organic produce, artisan breads and chocolate, cheeses, and many other gourmet delicacies. The 660-foot (201-meter) Grand Nave gets packed with foodies as daytrippers pile out of the back, laden with picnic supplies, to hop on ferries to Sausalito, Tiburon, or the East Bay.

Opposite the Ferry Building is Justin Herman Plaza, where you'll be confronted by Benicia-born artist Robert Arneson's bronze sculpture *Yin and Yang*. Looming behind it is a mysteriously dry series of square pipes that together make up a much-criticized fountain created by French-Canadian artist Armand Vaillancourt; at the foot of the Hyatt Regency hotel is Jean Dubuffet's *La Chiffonière*, a stainless steel sculpture of a larger-than-life figure.

The phalanx of towers behind the plaza, at the foot of Sacramento Street, comprises the **Embarcadero Center** (*see p137*), a labyrinthine shopping, dining and theatre complex. The **Embarcadero Cinema** (*see p212*) screens art house movies.

Walk south from the Ferry Building along the Embarcadero to Howard Street, and you'll see low cement walls where bronze starfish, turtles and octopi have been 'washed up' on the shore. Nearby, and easy to miss, is the small sign that marks **Herb Caen Way**, named after the late and ever-popular *San Francisco Chronicle* columnist. Lovers who come down this way may feel they've walked into their destiny when they spy an immense Cupid's bow in gold, complete with a silver and red arrow. This is Claes Oldenburg and Coosje van Bruggen's *Cupid's Span*, installed in 2002 in a field of native grass.

After taking in the wonderful views of the Bay Bridge, and perhaps also stopping for a spot of lunch at the Hotel Vitale's **Americano** restaurant (*see p137*), continue south to **Red's Java House** (Pier 30, 777 5626), a small and quirky snack shack that has been a favorite for coffee and burgers since it opened in 1912, when workers constructing the original Bay Bridge would drop in for meals.

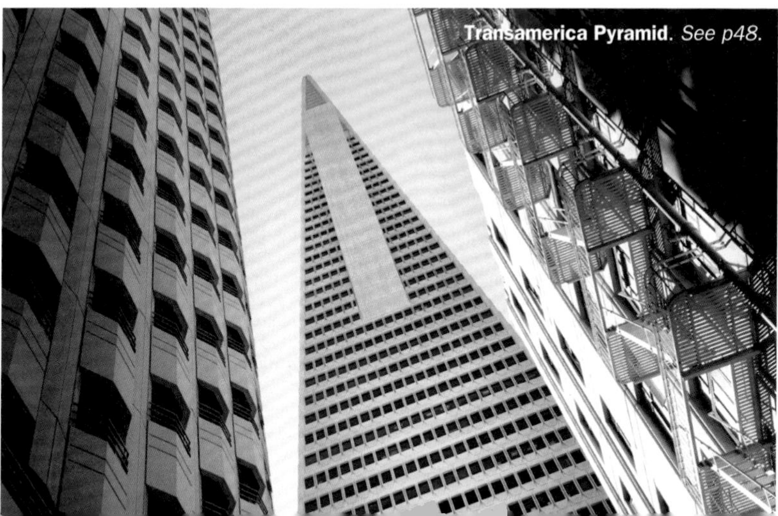

Transamerica Pyramid. *See p48.*

Uphill Journeys

San Francisco just wouldn't be the same without its historic cable cars.

Installed in 1873 by wily Scotsman Andrew Hallidie, cable cars were an ingenious solution to San Francisco's eternal problem: how to get up the damn hills. Nob Hill and Russian Hill in particular were tempting morsels of real estate, yet they remained mostly undeveloped. Horse-drawn carriages could barely make the climb, and Victorian gentlefolk were unwilling to exhaust themselves by slogging up and down on foot.

Enter Hallidie and his idea of introducing cable-drawn transport to the city streets, a method he had first used hauling ore carts in California's gold mines. When, to everyone's amazement, his first cars worked flawlessly, imitators sprang up overnight. Soon, more than 100 miles of tracks criss-crossed the city, operated by seven cable car companies.

It didn't last. Earthquakes, fires and the advent of cars and electric trolleys spelled doom for most of the cable car lines; by 1947, the city had proposed tearing up the last lines and replacing them with buses. Happily, the outraged citizenry stopped the plan. Since then, the government has declared the system a National Historic Landmark, which means the cars are here to stay. Three lines survive: the Powell-Mason and Powell-Hyde lines, both of which depart from Powell Street turnaround (where Powell meets Market Street) and run to, respectively, North Beach and Fisherman's Wharf; and the California line, which runs along California Street between Market Street and Van Ness Avenue.

If you're expecting to see a network of cable cars dangling in the air above the city, think again. San Francisco cable cars remain firmly grounded. First-timers are often surprised to learn that cable cars have no engine or other means of propulsion. All they need is a 'grip', a steel clamp that grabs on to a subterranean cable, running under the streets at a constant 9.5mph. The cables never stop moving: you can hear them humming even when there are no cable cars in sight. Every car has two operators: a gripman, who works the cranks and levers that grab on to and release the underground cable; and a conductor, who takes fares and somehow manages to cram 90-plus passengers, many of them hanging off the running boards, on to a single vehicle. Visit the **Cable Car Museum** (*see p62*) to inspect the system's inner workings: as well as Hallidie's original 1873 car, you'll get to see the immense winding turbines that pull the cables. From the balcony you can watch the ten-foot (three-meter) wheels spinning, as gears and pulleys whir and hum.

While the cable cars are a legendary part of San Francisco history, so is the hassle of waiting for one at Powell Street turnaround. So don't. Instead, walk up Powell a few blocks and board the car at O'Farrell or Union Square. Or, if you aren't going anywhere in particular, take the rarely crowded California line. The views aren't as good as on the Powell lines, but it's still a cable car.

Cars run every 12-15 minutes from 6.30am to midnight; the Powell Street ticket booth is open from 8.30am until 8pm. And if you are tired of forking over the $5 fare, cable car rides are included in the price of various travel passes (*see p286*).

Between Brannan and Townsend Streets, you'll see a cement marker reading 'Great Seawall'. This is exactly what the Embarcadero was built to be. It is entirely man-made, neatly rounding off the treacherous crags and coves that had been the end of many ships plying the San Francisco shores. Work on the sea wall started in 1878 and continued for nearly five decades, adding another 800 acres to the city and an additional 18 miles of useable dock space. Today, a push to revitalize the vacant waterfront areas sees new stores, restaurants and public spaces emerging from the timber skeletons of the old docks.

Once you've had your fill of the waterside views, head inland to the **Rincon Center**, at the intersection of Mission and Spear Streets. This former main post office, now containing a number of impressive art pieces and historic murals, is clear of San Franciscans at weekends, except for the dim sum crowd at **Yank Sing** (49 Stevenson Street, between 1st & 2nd Streets).

Alternatively, head north. From the Ferry Building, the Embarcadero evolves into a long, gently curving promenade along the waterfront, extending all the way to the confounding tourist magnet of **Fisherman's Wharf**. Skaters meet at 9pm each Friday for the Midnight Rollers, a 12-mile skate through the city (www.cora.org). Pier 7, a wide-open public pier jutting out into the Bay, offers lovely views of **Treasure Island** (*see below*). North and a little inland, where Green and Sansome Streets meet, you'll find the former laboratory of boy-genius Philo T Farnsworth. Here, in 1927, Farnsworth invented the current system of TV transmission; a small plaque marks the achievement.

FREE Rincon Center

101 Spear Street, at Mission Street (243 0473). BART & Metro to Embarcadero/bus 1, 12, 20, 30, 41 & Market Street routes. **Open** 24hrs daily. **Admission** free. **Map** p315 O4.

The lobby (facing Mission Street) of this art deco post office-cum-residential and office tower has intriguing WPA-style murals. Painted in 1941 by the Russian Social Realist painter Anton Refregier, this luscious historical panorama was hugely controversial at the time of its unveiling, not only because it was the most expensive of the WPA mural projects, but also because it included many dark moments from California's past. The central atrium has a unique all-water sculpture by Doug Hollis, dubbed *Rain Column*. The sculpture's 50-plus gallons of recycled water fall 85ft (26m) into a central pool every minute.

Treasure Island

Bus 108.

Flat-as-a-griddle Treasure Island, built on the shoals of neighboring Yerba Buena Island, is entirely man-made from boulders and sand. Originally constructed as a site for 1939's Golden Gate International Exposition, the island was requisitioned by the US Navy in 1942. It served as a troop deployment staging area for many years, until it was returned to the city in 1997. At around this time it was determined that the entire island sinks a bit deeper into the Bay each year. Despite this, it now functions as a sort of mid-Bay suburb, with some lucky San Franciscans moving into the former military housing. Why lucky? The views are spectacular, as many Hollywood location scouts and city planners have realized. Recently, long-awaited revitalization plans have gained momentum, with builders poised for final approval on a grand scheme that will include 8,000 housing units and a 450-foot high-rise tower, a ferry terminal, pollution-absorbing wetlands, and a working farm.

Neighboring Yerba Buena Island – literally, 'Good Herb Island' (the Yerba Buena referred to is actually an aromatic perennial from the mint family used in medicinal tea by Native Americans) – is an important Coast Guard station. You can drive on the island's one road, but there's nowhere to stop.

THE TENDERLOIN

There are two competing stories as to how the Tenderloin got its name. The first is that police who worked the beat here in the 19th century were paid extra for taking on such a tough neighborhood, and could therefore afford to buy better cuts of meat. The second is similar, but with one key change: the cops got their extra cash not from police chiefs in the form of wages, but from local hoods in the form of bribes. No one is sure which tale is correct, but neither reflects especially well on an area that's always lived on the wild side.

The Tenderloin is a far cry from the retail mecca of Union Square a few blocks to the east. The area is home to a spirited community and its reputation shouldn't put people off visiting the local theaters, staying in one of its stylish hotels or checking out its myriad cool dive bars. That said, there's not much reason to visit the area during the day, when the only streetlife comes courtesy of the panhandlers and drug addicts who cluster on corners. Depending on where you're planning to walk (Geary Street and points north are usually safe; streets south of it can get a bit sketchy), it may be best to hail a cab at night.

While the city struggles with the question of how best to care for the Tenderloin's dissolute souls (it's been a key issue in every mayoral contest for at least two decades), soup kitchens provide a partial solution. In particular, one pair of churches share a long and compassionate history. **St Boniface Catholic Church** (*see p54*) hosts dozens of benefit programs and has a dining room that serves food to the

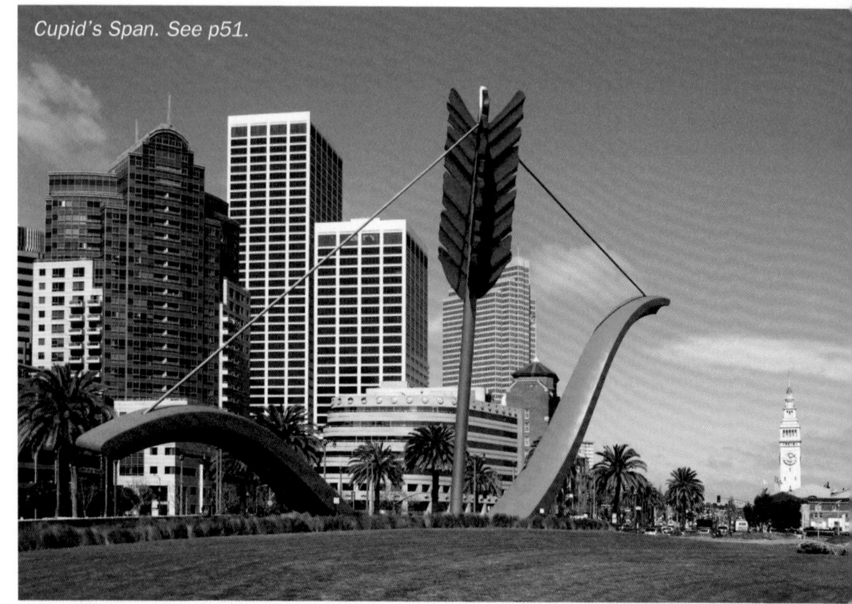
Cupid's Span. See p51.

needy, while the Free Meals program at **Glide Memorial Church** (330 Ellis Street, at Taylor Street), started back in 1969, offers similar sustenance. Both, of course, also cater to the religious: St Boniface offers Mass in English, Spanish, Tagalog and Vietnamese, while at Glide on Sundays, ecstatic gospel singing drags an amazingly diverse congregation to its feet. Glide runs services at 9am and 11am; get there early, as the place is usually packed.

Outside of Sundays, the main attractions in the Tenderloin are nocturnal. Dinner (as well as lunch) is served by aspiring chefs at the California Culinary Academy's **Carême Room** (625 Polk Street, at Turk Street, 292 8229, www.baychef.com/restaurants.asp). The area is also known as the Tandoor-loin because of the surprising profusion of good and affordable Indian restaurants on or near O'Farrell Street: try **Shalimar** (532 Jones Street, at O'Farrell Street, 928 0333, www.shalimarsf.com), which serves up inexpensive Pakistani and Indian food, or **Naan 'n' Curry** (690 Van Ness Avenue, at Turk Street, 775 1349, or 336 O'Farrell Street, near Mason Street, 346 1443). Wherever you eat, wash your dinner down with a beer or a cocktail at one of countless bars in the locale, which range from spit 'n' sawdust dives to wannabe-swank lounges. However, the joint most characteristic of the area's reputation is the landmark **Mitchell Brothers O'Farrell Theatre** (895 O'Farrell Street), a huge strip club that started life as a porn cinema, with a colorful and murderous history (in 1991 one brother, Jim, shot the other, Artie). Just down the street is the **Great American Music Hall** (859 O'Farrell Street, between Polk & Larkin Streets), said to be the oldest nightclub in San Francisco and now a beautiful music venue whose interior evokes Versailles' Hall of Mirrors. However, even this grand space is not as virtuous as it looks: although it's now unimpeachably respectable, it spent a number of its early years as a bordello.

St Boniface Catholic Church

133 Golden Gate Avenue, at Leavenworth Street (863 7515). BART & Metro to Civic Center/bus 19, 31 & Market Street routes. **Open** hours vary. **Map** p318 L7.

St Boniface's Romanesque interior, restored in the 1980s, has some impeccable stencilling and a beautifully gilded apse topped by a four-storey cupola. Outside Mass times, you'll find the church is gated, so ring the buzzer to get in. Be sure to get there before 1.30pm during the week, when the church closes for cleaning until the next morning.

CIVIC CENTER

Southwest of the Tenderloin and north of Market Street, San Francisco's Civic Center is a complex of imposing government buildings and immense performance halls centered on the Civic Center Plaza, an expansive and well-tended lawn. By day, it's populated by an extreme spread of locals, from smartly turned-out officials and dignitaries who work within the buildings, to the homeless folk who hang around outside them. At night, the worker bees are replaced by culture vultures, here to take in a concert, ballet, lecture or opera at one of the area's several venues.

Facing the plaza, and dominating the area, is the stunning Beaux Arts **City Hall**, a glory both inside and out. Across the four lanes of traffic on Van Ness Avenue is a trio of grand edifices. The multistory curved-glass façade of the **Louise M Davies Symphony Hall** (201 Van Ness Avenue, at Hayes Street; *see p234*) would be unforgettable even without the reclining Henry Moore bronzes in front, while just north of Grove Street sits the **War Memorial Opera House** (301 Van Ness Avenue, at Grove Street; *see p233*), directly behind City Hall. In many ways the City Hall's companion piece, the Opera House was also designed by architect Arthur Brown.

The last of the triumvirate of buildings is the **Veterans' Memorial Building** (Van Ness Avenue, at McAllister Street), the various spaces of which hold offices, performance theaters, and even galleries. On its main floor sits the tiny **San Francisco Arts Commission Gallery** (*see p221*), which specializes in politically or sociologically driven art. Take the elevator to the fourth floor and you'll find the **Museum of Performance & Design** (*see p56*); also here is the beautiful **Herbst Theatre** (*see p256*). It is a little-known but proud part of San Francisco history that the UN Charter was drafted and signed by 51 nations in what is now the Herbst Theatre on June 26, 1945.

In the south-east corner of Civic Center Plaza are two further landmark buildings. Named after the promoter who almost single-handedly created the musical juggernaut that was San Francisco in the 1960s, the 7,000-capacity **Bill Graham Civic Auditorium** (99 Grove Street, at Polk Street) now stages gigs by big names. The nearby **Main Library** (*see p56*) is a six-story building mixing Beaux Arts elements with modernism; the old library is now home to the world-class collections of art and antiquities at the **Asian Art Museum** (*see p56*).

On the edge of the Civic Center is the **United Nations Plaza**. A farmers' market operates here on Wednesdays and Sundays, with gourmet food truck coalition Off the Grid moving in on Friday afternoons

Bridge of Sighs

Rebuilding bridges takes engineering genius and money – lots of it.

In 1936, a tourist booklet heralded the opening of the **San Francisco-Oakland Bay Bridge**: 'It will be the greatest bridge in the world for its cost, length, quantities of steel and concrete, weight, depth and number of piers, the bore of its island tunnel, and versatility of its engineering.' At the then-astronomical cost of $77,600,000, the Bay Bridge was the largest and most expensive bridge of its time, expected to 'stand as the largest bridge in the world for probably 1,000 years'.

Then, in 1989, the Loma Prieta earthquake cut its life expectancy short. It shook loose a large section of the eastern span, and suddenly, the Oakland half of the Bay Bridge was in need of an extreme makeover. Civic planners and designers, who had long seen it as a utilitarian eyesore, were giddy over the prospects. Politicians and bean counters were less enthused, pushing for a swift, cheap retrofit. Bureaucratic bickering, budget overruns, design debates, and a nasty squabble involving ex-Mayor Willie Brown ensued, stalling plans for more than a decade. Finally, the city agreed to move forward on a graceful, single-span suspension bridge by TY Lin International/ Moffat & Nichol.

But the bridge's troubles weren't over. In 2004, ex-governor Arnold Schwarzenegger once again threatened to scupper plans, citing the high cost and slow construction of the chosen design. Billions of tax dollars later, a compromise was finally reached, and the soaring skyway finally got under way.

If the bridge's initial cost seems astounding, the current bill is truly mind-boggling – $6.3 billion at last tally. Equally exasperating for the 280,000 cars that cross it daily, is that while the first bridge took just three years to complete, the completion of the updated eastern span is pushing 25 – its opening date is now scheduled for late 2013. That and the fact that despite state-of-the-art seismic features designed to prevent damage in the event of an earthquake, builders estimate the city will have to replace the bridge again in 150 years.

(*see p141* **Taking it to the Streets**). The action takes place under the approving gaze of a mounted statue of Simón Bolívar, the great liberator of Central America.

There's not much in the way of restaurants, bars or shops in this corner of the city. One of the few good bets for eating is the great little café-restaurant in the Asian Art Museum. Alternatively, if you can successfully negotiate the legions of homeless, head across Market Street to **Tu Lan** (8 6th Street, at Market Street; *see p141*). While this hole-in-the-wall diner may look like nothing to write home about (and there really are holes in its walls), it's widely considered to serve some of the best Vietnamese cuisine in the city.

★ Asian Art Museum

200 Larkin Street, at Fulton Street (581 3500, www.asianart.org). BART & Metro to Civic Center/streetcar F/bus 5, 19, 21, 47, 49 & Market Street routes. **Open** 10am-5pm Tue, Wed, Fri-Sun; 10am-9pm Thur. **Admission** $12; $7-$8 reductions. **Credit** AmEx, Disc, MC, V. **Map** p318 K7.

This popular museum has one of the world's most comprehensive collections of Asian art, spanning 6,000 years of Asian history and with more than 15,000 objects on display. Artifacts range from Japanese Buddhas and sacred texts to items from the Ming Dynasty. The outdoor café is a great place to enjoy American- and Asian-inspired dishes on sunny days, and the gift shop is well stocked with high-quality stationery, decorative items and a handsome selection of coffee-table books. The museum once resided in Golden Gate Park, but in 2003 it reopened in this building, former home of the San Francisco Public Library. Extensively and beautifully redesigned by Gae Aulenti, the architect responsible for the heralded Musée d'Orsay conversion in Paris, the museum retains remnants of its previous role, including bookish quotes etched into the fabric of the building.

★ City Hall

1 Dr Carlton B Goodlett Place (Polk Street), between McAllister & Grove Streets (554 4933, tours 554 6023). BART & Metro to Civic Center/streetcar F/bus 19, 21, 47, 49 & Market Street routes. **Open** 8am-8pm daily. *Tours* 10am, noon, 2pm Mon-Fri. **Admission** free. **Map** p318 K7.

Built in 1915 to designs by Arthur Brown and John Bakewell, City Hall is the epitome of the Beaux Arts style visible across the whole Civic Center. The building has lots of ornamental ironwork, elaborate plasterwork and a dome – modeled on the one at St Peter's in Rome – that is higher than the one on the nation's Capitol. The central rotunda, with its sweeping staircase, is a magnificent space and the dome overlooks a five-story colonnade, limestone and granite masonry, regal lighting and majestic marble floors. Dubbed 'the most significant interior space in the United States' by a New York architectural critic, City Hall inspires a marked feeling of municipal awe.

Beneath its neo-classical exterior, the building hums with modern technology. After it was damaged in the 1989 earthquake, city planners spent $300 million protecting it against future shocks and restoring it to its original grandeur (that's real gold atop its dome). A system of rubber-and-steel 'base isolators' now allows the structure to move a meter in any direction. Its 600 rooms have seen plenty of history: Joe DiMaggio got hitched to Marilyn Monroe on the third floor in 1954, although nobody knows in which office; on a more somber note, it was here that Dan White assassinated Mayor George Moscone and City Supervisor Harvey Milk in 1978. Today, the building houses the legislative and executive branches of both city and county government. Free tours offering behind the scenes views of the Board of Supervisors' chambers (paneled in hand-carved Manchurian oak) are available Monday to Friday. There's a small café for the weary of feet, and the basement contains exhibits sponsored by the San Francisco Arts Commission.

San Francisco Main Library

100 Larkin Street, between Grove & Fulton Streets (library 557 4400, history room 557 4567, www.sfpl.org). BART & Metro to Civic Center/bus 5, 21, 47, 49 & Market Street routes. **Open** *Library* 10am-6pm Mon, Sat; 9am-8pm Tue-Thur; noon-6pm Fri; noon-5pm Sun. *History Room* 10am-6pm Tue-Thur, Sat; noon-6pm Fri; noon-5pm Sun. *Tours* 2.30pm Wed, Fri. **Admission** free. **Map** p318 L7.

Built in 1996 by the architectural firm Pei Cobb Freed & Partners, San Francisco's public library is beautifully designed, though locals still complain about the number of missing and lost books. On the top floor, the San Francisco History Room hosts changing exhibitions, a large photo archive and knowledgeable, friendly staff. The basement café is mediocre, but the small shop on the main floor has bargains on local titles. Readings by big-name and up and coming authors are held here on a regular basis.

FREE Museum of Performance & Design

4th floor, Veterans' Memorial Building, 401 Van Ness Avenue, at McAllister Street (255 4800, www.mpdsf.org). BART & Metro to Civic Center/bus 21, 47, 49 & Market Street routes. **Open** noon-5pm Wed-Sat. **Admission** $5 suggested donation. **Map** p318 K7.

Exhibitions at this enjoyable museum relate to every one of the performing arts, from puppet shows to operas, but the principal attraction for scholars is the prodigious amount of resource material: thousands of books, musical scores and programs from the worlds of design, fashion, music, theater, opera and other art forms.

SIGHTS

SoMa & South Beach

It burned, it boomed, it tanked, now SoMa is soaring again.

Following devastation in the 1906 fire, the streets south of Market Street became an industrial wasteland of warehouses and sweatshops, and stayed that way for much of the 20th century. With the dotcom boom came rapid regeneration: warehouses were converted into high-end loft apartments, bars opened to serve the new locals, and SoMa ('South of Market') took off. The dotcom implosion of the early 2000s saw vacancy signs everywhere, but with new technologies emerging, and construction of a satellite campus of the University of California San Francisco and the 3rd Street light-rail line, SoMa is on the rise again.

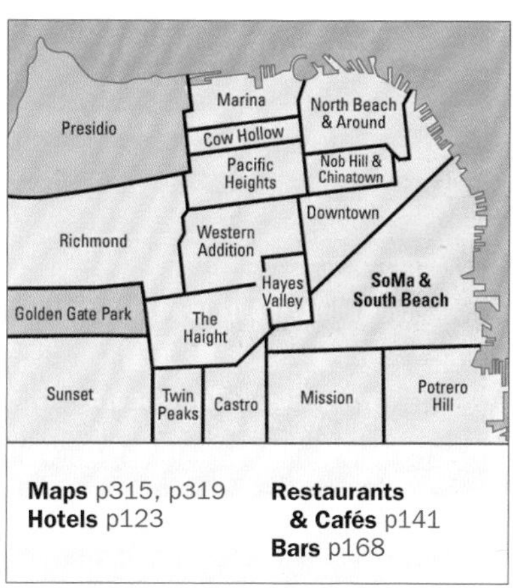

Maps p315, p319
Hotels p123
Restaurants & Cafés p141
Bars p168

In South Beach, the primary draw remains the San Francisco Giants baseball team, fresh off their 2010 World Series win. Their stadium, AT&T Park, draws huge crowds for its 81 home games each spring and summer, packing the surrounding hip bars and restaurants – many housed in former industrial warehouses.

YERBA BUENA GARDENS & AROUND

Bounded by Mission, 3rd, Folsom and 4th Streets, the Yerba Buena Gardens complex was renovated as part of a city-funded project in the 1980s and '90s. Attractions and businesses are housed in a series of structures that is half above ground and half below it. Within the Gardens, **Esplanade** is an urban park with sculpture walks, shady trees and the *Revelations* waterfall, constructed in 1993 in memory of Martin Luther King Jr. A selection of Dr King's quotes is inscribed beneath the waterfall in various languages. On one side of the block sits the **Yerba Buena Center for the Arts** (*see p61*), an architectural beauty in itself. Filling the other half of the block (4th Street, from Howard to Mission Streets) is **Metreon**, a four-story futuristic mall where 16 cinema screens (including a giant-screen IMAX) are backed up by shops, restaurants, video-game rooms and the Island Earth indoor organic farmer's market (open daily).

Across 3rd Street from Yerba Buena Gardens sits the **San Francisco Museum of Modern Art** (*see p60*), where the permanent collection and temporary exhibits are supplemented by a top-quality shop and a somewhat pricey café. Next door is the staggering **St Regis Museum Tower**, a luxury hotel that also houses the **Museum of the African Diaspora** (*see p60*). The **Moscone Convention Center** (747 Howard Street, between 3rd & 4th Streets), named after assassinated mayor George Moscone, is a similarly daunting building. Most of it is of little interest to casual visitors, but the Rooftop at Yerba Buena Gardens,

THE Storytelling CAR
GPS GUIDED TOUR
GOCAR
TOURS

To advertise in the
next edition of...
TimeOut
SAN FRANCISCO
Eat | Drink | Shop | Sleep | Explore | Enjoy

Easy to learn... fun to ride!
SEGWAY TOURS
San Francisco Sausalito
"The best part of our family vacation!"
"it was a blast!"

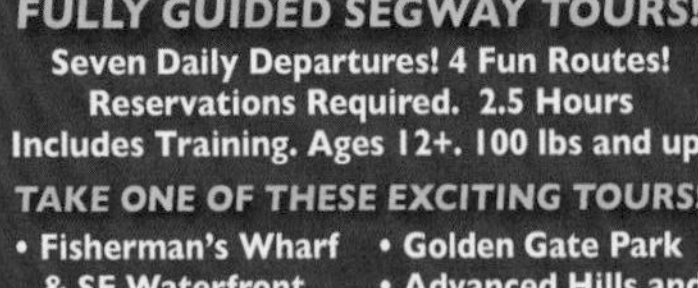
FULLY GUIDED SEGWAY TOURS!
Seven Daily Departures! 4 Fun Routes!
Reservations Required. 2.5 Hours
Includes Training. Ages 12+. 100 lbs and up.
TAKE ONE OF THESE EXCITING TOURS!
• Fisherman's Wharf & SF Waterfront
• Sausalito Waterfront
• Golden Gate Park
• Advanced Hills and Crookedest Street
Call: 415-474-3130
ElectricTourCompany.com

Good for two days
San Francisco Wharf pass
CITY TOUR
BAY CRUISE
ATTRACTIONS
The Best of Fisherman's Wharf for One Low Price!
A Great City Tour!
An Exciting SF Bay Cruise!
Choose 4 More Top Attractions!
Save $36.99!
Choice of 6 of 20 Tours, Bay Cruises, & Attractions Plus 47 Discount Coupons!
$67.00 Adult $41.00 Child (5-11)
Buy Online, or Purchase at Attractions!
(415) 440-4474 • WharfPass.com

ingeniously covering the top of the Moscone Center on the south side of Howard Street, offers the child-friendly attractions of the **Children's Creativity Museum** (221 4th Street, at Howard Street, 820 3320, www.zeum.org). Also here are a delightful carousel, hand-carved by Charles Looff in 1906, an ice rink, a bowling alley and an ultra-cool interactive sculpture by Chico Macmurtrie: sit on the middle pink bench and your weight moves the metal figure up and down on top of its globe. Attempt this only before lunch.

Contrasting with all this modernity is the high-ceilinged **St Patrick's Church** (756 Mission Street, between 3rd & 4th Streets, 421 3730, www.stpatricksf.org). Built in 1851, the church ministered to the growing Irish population brought to the city by the Gold Rush. It was destroyed by the 1872 earthquake but subsequently restored to its original state; it now hosts both services and concerts (*see p233*). Nearby is a quintet of other museums: the **Cartoon Art Museum**, the **Museum of Craft and Folk Art**, the **Contemporary Jewish Museum**, **California Historical Society** and the **Society of California Pioneers**.

Several blocks southwest of Yerba Buena, **Folsom Street** savors its kinky reputation each autumn during the annual Folsom Street Fair, but the Cake Gallery (290 9th Street, at Folsom Street, 861 2253, www.thecakegallerysf.com) is a year-round thrill: with a nod to the legendary Magnolia Thunderpussy, it's the only bakery in the city that sells pornographic cakes. Nearby are many good restaurants catering to the young and hip, and the **BrainWash Café** (1122 Folsom Street, between 7th & 8th Streets, www.brainwash.com), a spot about which weary travelers have fantasized for generations: a combo bar/music venue/restaurant/laundromat, where you can sip some suds while your duds get their suds.

California Historical Society

678 Mission Street, between 3rd & New Montgomery Streets (357 1848, www.calhist.org). BART & Metro to Montgomery/bus 9, 9X, 10, 14, 30, 45, 71. **Open** noon-4.30pm Wed-Sat. **Admission** $3; $1 reductions. **Credit** (bookstore only) AmEx, DC, Disc, MC, V. **Map** p315 N6.

The state's official history group has focused its efforts on assembling this impressive collection of Californiana. The vaults hold half a million photographs and thousands of books, magazines and paintings, as well as an extensive Gold Rush collection; selections are presented as changing displays on the state's history. The gift shop has an excellent little bookshop and a selection of souvenirs, including one of the best: the California Republic T-shirt.

★ Cartoon Art Museum

655 Mission Street, between 3rd & New Montgomery Streets (227 8666, www.cartoonart.org). BART & Metro to Montgomery/bus 9, 10, 14, 30, 45, 71. **Open** 11am-5pm Tue-Sun. **Admission** $7; $3-$5 reductions; free under-6s. **Credit** DC, MC, V. **Map** p315 N6.

The camera that was used to create the first animation for television (called *Crusader Rabbit* and produced from 1949 to 1951) graces the lobby of this museum. Boasting more than 5,000 pieces of cartoon and animation art, as well as a research library, this is the only museum in the western US dedicated to the form. The bookstore contains a large and eclectic selection of books, 'zines, periodicals and coffee-table

Contemporary Jewish Museum. *See p60.*

tomes covering everything from erotic photography to Asterix books. The first Tuesday of each month is 'Pay What You Wish Day'.

Contemporary Jewish Museum

736 Mission Street, between 3rd & 4th Streets (655 7800/www.thecjm.org). BART & Metro to Montgomery/bus 9, 9X, 10, 14, 30, 45, 71. **Open** 11am-5pm Mon, Tue, Fri-Sun; 1-8pm Thur. **Admission** $10; $8 reductions; $5 Thur after 5pm. **Credit** AmEx, DC, Disc, MC, V. **Map** p315 M6.

Opened in 2008 across from Yerba Buena Gardens, the Contemporary Jewish Museum is devoted to linking the art of the Jewish community with the community at large. Maybe the best reason to visit is the building – carved out of a 1907 Willis Polk power substation, New York architect Daniel Libeskind married the old brick façade to an ultra-modern blue-steel cube that looks like something out of a sci-fi movie. Inside, there are soaring skylights and enormous windows that shed light on exhibits about Jewish culture, history, art, and ideas. The café offers traditional dishes such as matzo ball soup, latkes, and bagels with lox. *Photos p59.*

Museum of the African Diaspora

685 Mission Street, at 3rd Street (358 7200, www.moadsf.org). BART & Metro to Montgomery/bus 9, 9X, 10, 14, 30, 45, 71. **Open** 11am-6pm Wed-Sat; noon-5pm Sun. **Admission** $10; $5 reductions; free under-12s. **Credit** AmEx, DC, MC, V. **Map** p315 N5.

Located on the first three floors of the St Regis Museum Tower, the Museum of the African Diaspora (MoAD) is the world's first museum dedicated to exploring the international impact of the diaspora of African peoples across the globe. Rotating exhibitions highlight the art and culture of the continent, with multimedia exhibits and moving first-person accounts.

INSIDE TRACK ONE FOR THE FANS

Home of the World Champion San Francisco Giants, **AT&T Park** (*see p250*) is roundly acknowledged to be one of the best stadiums in baseball. Designed to be sheltered from Bay winds, there's not a bad seat in the park, with even upper decks enjoying unobstructed views of the entire field and the Bay. If the game drags, ride the slides inside the 80-foot (24-meter) Coke bottle, and admire the huge sculpture of a baseball mitt. Cheapskates can duck inside the archway along the right-field waterfront wall and catch a few innings for free through the field-level windows. You might even see a home run land in the Bay at McCovey Cove, where die-hard fans in boats paddle around trying to find the balls that make a 'splash landing'.

Museum of Craft & Folk Art

51 Yerba Buena Lane, at Mission between Third & Fourth Streets (227 4888, www.mocfa.org). BART & Metro to Montgomery/bus 9, 9X, 10, 14, 30, 45, 71. **Open** 11am-6pm Wed-Sat. **Admission** $5; $4 reductions; free under-18s. **Credit** AmEx, DC, MC, V. **Map** p315 N5.

Housed in a refurbished pathway, this jewel-box museum features traditional and contemporary folk art and craft from around the world and exhibits on cultural traditions, coupled with educational programs.

★ San Francisco Museum of Modern Art (SFMOMA)

151 3rd Street, between Mission & Howard Streets (357 4000, www.sfmoma.org). BART & Metro to Montgomery/bus 9, 9X, 10, 14, 30, 45, 71. **Open** *Memorial Day-Labor Day* 10am-5.45pm Mon, Tue, Fri-Sun; 10am-8.45pm Thur. *Labor Day-Memorial Day* 11am-5.45pm Mon, Tue, Fri-Sun; 11am-8.45pm Thur. **Admission** $18; $9-$12 reductions; free under-12s. Half price 6-8.45pm Thur; free 1st Tue of mth. **Credit** AmEx, DC, Disc, MC, V. **Map** p315 N6.

The second-largest US museum devoted to modern art, SFMOMA reaps enthusiastic approval as much for its design as for its collections. Swiss architect Mario Botta's red-brick building, with its huge, circular skylight, is as dramatic from the outside as within. Don't miss the spectacular catwalk beneath the skylight, accessible from the top-floor galleries. The museum's holdings received an enormous boost with the Doris and Donald Fisher collection, bringing the couple's world-renowned modern art collection of some 1,100 works by the likes of Alexander Calder, Willem de Kooning, Richard Diebenkorn, and Roy Lichtenstein, to public view for the first time. To accommodate, the museum is planning a major expansion that will triple its gallery space.

The four floors of galleries that rise above the stark black-marble reception area house a solid permanent collection, with some 15,000 paintings, sculptures and works on paper, as well as thousands of photographs and a range of works related to the media arts. The collection includes works by artists as varied as René Magritte, Jeff Koons, Piet Mondrian, and Marcel Duchamp.

Society of California Pioneers Seymour Pioneer Museum

300 4th Street, at Folsom Street (957 1849, www.californiapioneers.org). BART & Metro to Montgomery/bus 9X, 12, 27, 30, 45. **Open** 10am-4pm Wed-Fri, 1st Sat of mth. *Library* by

Yerba Buena Center for the Arts.

appointment. **Admission** $5; $2.50 reductions. **Credit** (bookstore only) DC, MC, V. **Map** p319 N7.
Operated by descendants of the state's first settlers, this small museum, a treasure trove for the historically inclined, has occasional intriguing displays on California's past, alongside 10,000 books, 50,000 prints and all kinds of other ephemera, such as 19th-century paintings, sculpture and furniture.

Yerba Buena Center for the Arts

701 Mission Street, at 3rd Street (978 2787, www.ybca.org). BART & Metro to Montgomery/bus 9, 9X, 10, 14, 30, 45, 71. **Open** noon-5pm Tue, Wed, Fri-Sun; noon-8pm Thur. **Admission** $7; $5 reductions. Free 1st Tue of mth. **Credit** AmEx, DC, MC, V. **Map** p315 N6.
Yerba Buena stands opposite SFMOMA and is somewhat in its shadow, yet it seems unintimidated, tugging at the modern art scene's shirttails with a scrappy itinerary and great attitude. Housed in Fumihiko Maki's futuristic-looking building, it contains four changing galleries and a 96-seat theater. The focus is on the contemporary and the challenging (installation and video art, outsider art); exhibitions have included work by such diverse names as Henry Darger, Fred Thomaselli, Anna Halprin and Kumi Yamashita.
▶ *For theater at Yerba Buena, see p260.*

SOUTH PARK & SOUTH BEACH

If any one area in San Francisco embodies the dotcom rollercoaster ride, it's this one. A few years ago, finding a clear space in the green oval of **South Park**, the original 'Multimedia Gulch', took more time and moxie than snagging one of the coveted parking spaces. Techies would duck out to grab a burrito and end up never returning to the office: they'd been poached by a rival offering an extra 20k a year. Then, for a while after the dotcom bust, it returned to being a serene oasis of green. Today, it's back to a pleasant buzz, with new cafés and restaurants feeding the new wave of digerati.

South Park was San Francisco's first gated community, until it suffered from a string of misfortunes. Getting burned to the ground early in the 20th century may have been careless, but it was pure bad luck that the invention of the cable car caused the local millionaires to abscond to Nob Hill. The building of the Bay Bridge separated the haves and the have-nots even further. After World War II, the area became an African-American enclave, falling into neglect until a tornado of young men both fueled by and fluent in Java arrived in the 1990s.

Establishments that represent the new tenor of South Park include the **American Grilled Cheese Kitchen** (1 South Park Avenue, 243 0107, www.theamericansf.com) and the ridiculously popular **Caffe Centro** (102 South Park Avenue, 882.1500, www.caffecentro.com), which serves soups, salads and sandwiches to hungry lunchtime workers.

A few blocks south, **AT&T Park** (24 Willie Mays Plaza, at 3rd & King Streets) is home to the San Francisco Giants baseball team. Instantly hailed as a classic when it opened in 2000, the Bayside ballpark is a wonderful place to catch a game: with striking views of the Bay and a design that shelters from the blustery breezes.

Close by stands an intriguing architectural gem: the **Francis 'Lefty' O'Doul Bridge** (3rd Street, near Berry Street), the only working drawbridge in the city. A charming antique, it was designed by JB Strauss, better known for designing the Golden Gate Bridge. Born in San Francisco, 'Lefty' started out as a pitcher but made his name as a hitter in New York and Philadelphia, before eventually returning home to manage the minor league San Francisco Seals. The eponymous restaurant and bar he opened just steps from Downtown's Union Square in 1958 (333 Geary Street, at Powell Street, 982 8900, www.leftyodouls.biz) remains in business to this day.

Nob Hill & Chinatown

Cable cars, mansions and Taoist temples.

Sitting on a perch looking down, literally and figuratively, over San Francisco's teeming masses, Nob Hill is home to grand dame hotels and the social elite, exuding an air of Old World formality and elegance all but forgotten in this determinedly casual city. Historic hotel bars, mansion gawking and visiting stately Grace Cathedral are the main draws.

Down the hill, Chinatown is the antidote to Nob Hill's stiff reserve, a cultural mecca of fragrant herbalists, hole-in-the-wall restaurants serving unusual Chinese specialties, knick-knack shops, and markets selling everything from live fish and chickens to wind gongs.

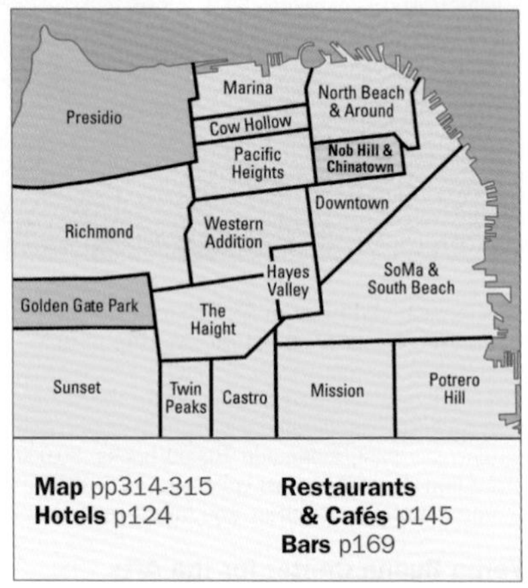

Map pp314-315
Hotels p124
Restaurants & Cafés p145
Bars p169

SIGHTS

NOB HILL

Overlooking the Tenderloin and Union Square, the Nob Hill neighborhood was named after the wealthy nabobs – as they were known – who built their mansions in the area; Robert Louis Stevenson, who lived briefly on its lower flank, described it as 'the hill of palaces'. A short but incredibly steep walk up from Union Square, the summit stands 338 feet (103 meters) above the Bay. Both the houses and their residents retain an appropriately haughty grandeur.

After the cable car started running up the hill in the 1870s, the area began to attract wealthy folk, among them the 'Big Four' railroad tycoons: Charles Crocker, Mark Hopkins, Leland Stanford and Collis P Huntington. Their grand mansions perished in the fire that followed the 1906 earthquake – in fact, only the 1886 mansion belonging to millionaire silver baron James C. Flood survived. Later remodeled by Willis Polk, the brownstone is now the site of the private **Pacific-Union Club** (1000 California Street, at Mason Street). Next to it, at the corner of California and Taylor Streets, is the public but prissy **Huntington Park**, with a fountain modeled on Rome's Fontana delle Tartarughe. Across the park, **Grace Cathedral** (*see p65*) is a Gothic landmark. Midnight Mass here, sung by the celebrated boys' choir, is a marvelous Christmas tradition; evensong with the choir is at 3pm most Sundays.

Elegant hotels surround the park and the club. The **Fairmont Hotel** (950 Mason Street, at California Street; *see p124*) has a plush marble lobby and the fabulously tacky **Tonga Room** (*see p169*), complete with regularly scheduled monsoons. The quieter **Huntington Hotel** (1075 California Street, at Taylor Street; *see p124*) is known as a royals' hideaway, but you don't have to stay there to use its luxurious Nob Hill Spa (345 2888) or cozy up next to the fireplace with a cognac at the wood-paneled bar of the Big Four restaurant. Nearby, the **Top of the Mark** bar (*see p170*), on the 19th floor of the **Mark Hopkins Inter-Continental Hotel**, has terrific views over the city. Moving down the hill, the free **Cable Car Museum** (*see below*) displays antique cable cars and the mighty turbines that power the cables that run beneath the city's streets.

★ FREE Cable Car Museum

1201 Mason Street, at Washington Street (474 1887, www.cablecarmuseum.org). Bus 1, 9, 12, 30, 45/cable car Powell-Hyde or Powell-Mason. **Open** *Oct-Mar* 10am-5pm daily. *Apr-Sept* 10am-6pm daily. **Admission** free. **Map** p314 L4.

Profile Portsmouth Square

Setting for key events that shaped the city, and the state.

Even some longtime residents are unaware that Portsmouth Square can lay claim to being the true birthplace of San Francisco, if not California. It was in this unassuming plaza (on the corner of Clay and Kearny streets) that Captain John B Montgomery first hoisted the US flag in California. Montgomery captured the city – then known as Yerba Buena – from Mexico on July 9, 1846, and the plaza is named in honor of his ship, the USS *Portsmouth*.

Just two years later, newspaper boss Sam Brannan stood on this same spot and announced that gold had been discovered at Sutter's Mill, sparking the Gold Rush and his own meteoric rise to fame and riches. In addition to founding San Francisco's first newspaper, Brannan owned a number of stores that sold goods and supplies to the throngs of hopeful prospectors. If records are to be believed, just one of Brannan's stores in Sutter Fort cleared $150,000 a month in 1849. The state's first millionaire, Brannan was also a state senator, founder of the Society of California Pioneers, and builder of the first Cliff House (it burned down twice; for the current structure, *see p96*). In the years following the gold rush, however, Brannan lost much of his fortune in a divorce settlement. He moved south to San Diego where he became a brewer and, later, a land speculator along the Mexican border. He was eventually reduced to selling pencils door to door and did not leave enough cash to pay his funeral expenses.

By the 1850s, Chinese immigrants had settled in Portsmouth Square, and today, the plaza is known as the Heart of Chinatown. Other notable monuments include one to Robert Louis Stevenson, shaped like the galleon *Hispaniola* from his novel *Treasure Island*. Stevenson used to relax here when he lived nearby at 608 Bush Street in 1879. The south-west corner was also home to the first public school in California. Flanking the square at 743 Washington Street, the Bank of Canton is one of the most photographed structures in Chinatown. The pagoda-like structure was built in 1909 for the Chinese American Telephone Exchange, where for four decades, multilingual phone operators routed calls throughout Chinatown by memory alone. Today, elderly residents congregate to practice t'ai chi, argue politics, play cards and kibbitz over games of Go.

BIRTH OF CHINATOWN

For more on the development of Chinatown, *see p23*.

FISHERMANS WHARF
OF SAN FRANCISCO

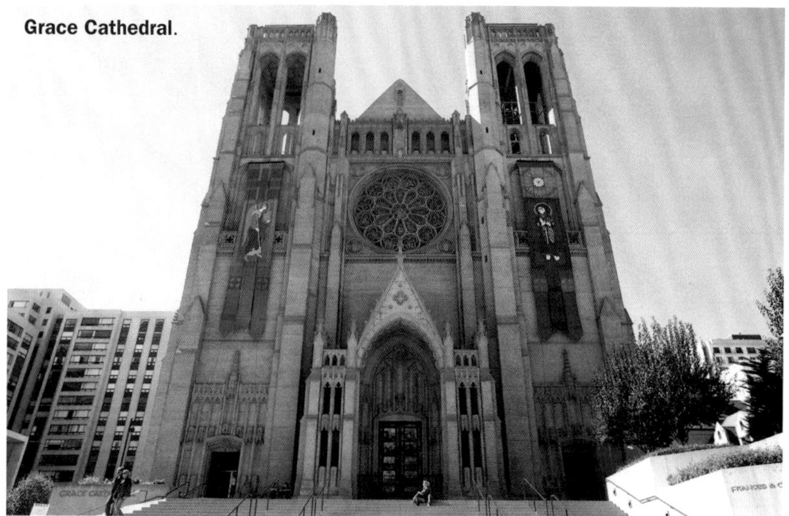
Grace Cathedral.

The sight most often associated with San Francisco is its cable cars. The best way to study them is to ride one, but at this entertaining museum you can find out how the cars work, as well as view the cable-winding machinery that actually powers them. You'll also learn about emergency procedures, bell-ringing competitions and the workmanship that goes into each car. Vintage cable cars, associated artifacts and dozens of old photos complete matters.

Grace Cathedral

1100 California Street, at Taylor Street (749 6300, www.gracecathedral.org). Bus 1, 2, 3, 4, 27/cable car California. **Open** 7am-6pm Mon-Fri, Sun; 8am-6pm Sat. *Tours* 1-3pm Mon-Fri; 11.30am-1.30pm Sat; 12.30-2pm Sun. **Admission** donation requested. **Map** p314 L5.

Begun in 1928, this Episcopalian cathedral was once a private mansion. It was later taken over by the church and is, by the standards of most cathedrals in the US, an architectural extravaganza, with a façade modeled on Paris's Notre Dame. There's a fine rose window, a magnificent organ and gilded bronze portals made from casts of the Doors of Paradise in Florence's Baptistery. Murals depict the founding of the United Nations and the burning of Grace's predecessor; the AIDS Interfaith Chapel has an altarpiece by Keith Haring. Two massive labyrinths, based on the 13th-century labyrinth at Chartres, allow visitors to wander in a contemplative manner.

CHINATOWN

The 1849 Gold Rush and its promise of untold prosperity drew shiploads of Cantonese to California. The excitement didn't last, but many immigrants decided to stay, finding work on the railroads or the farms of the San Joaquin Valley. Californians both feared and loathed the Chinese, and were enthusiastic about the federal Chinese Exclusion Act of 1882, which halted the immigration of anyone of Chinese origin. Only officially repealed in 1943, the act also effectively made existing Chinese immigrants permanent aliens, with no hope of gaining citizenship. However, famine and unrest across China gave the immigrants little incentive to return home, and their understandable need for a strong community led to a 20-block area of central San Francisco becoming a focal point for Chinese immigrants of every stripe.

The Chinatown that arose in San Francisco soon developed a reputation for vice; curious Caucasians were lured here round the clock by cheap hookers, well-stocked opium dens and all-hours gambling.

After the 1906 earthquake and fire devastated the district, the city fathers tried to clean up the neighborhood and, crucially, appropriate what had become prime real estate. However, not only did the illicit activity continue, but the Chinese held fast and rebuilt their community.

The crowded streets and dark alleys of Chinatown – bordered today by **Bush Street** to the south, **Broadway** to the north, and **Powell** and **Kearny streets** from west to east – evoke an earlier era. There are nearly 100 restaurants, some serving exotic specialties. Elsewhere, herbalists prepare natural remedies and laundry flutters from windows above the streets. Many wealthier Chinese immigrants have moved out

Chinatown.

to the Richmond, Sunset and even other Bay Area towns, but some 10,000 Chinese still live in Chinatown, lending it one of the largest Asian populations outside Asia itself.

Today, Chinatown also feels like two distinct neighborhoods. Along **Grant Avenue**, one of the two main north–south drags, store owners target tourists with plastic Buddhas and bright fabrics; conversely, little English is spoken at the ornate temples and food stalls on and near **Stockton Street**.

Stockton Street & around

You'll see very few tourists among the throngs of customers that pack the grocery stores of Stockton Street. It's easy to understand why, especially if you contrast it with the shops on adjacent Grant Avenue (*see right*), which offer an anaesthetised version of Chinese culture, and fill daily with gift-hunting visitors. However, whether selling medicines or turtles (many of the markets here are 'live', with fish and animals on display in tanks and cages), the enterprises on Stockton cater to locals, who conduct their business in a range of dialects. In much the same way, the restaurants on Stockton have a more authentic feel than those on Grant; indeed, for many, Stockton Street constitutes the 'real' Chinatown.

One of the oldest religious structures in San Francisco, the **Kong Chow Temple**, stands on Stockton Street (no.855, between Sacramento & Clay Streets). Established in 1857, it was moved to its present home on the fourth floor of the Chinatown Post Office in 1977. Divination sticks, red satin banners and flowers flank a fabulous altar from which a statue of the god Kuan Ti has a keen view of the Bay. Nearby, the façade of the photogenic **Chinese Six Companies Building** (no.843) sports stone lions, ceramic carp and colored tiles.

Perhaps the truest taste of Chinatown can be found in the alleys a half-block east of Stockton Street, sprouting off Jackson and Washington Streets. In cozy **Ross Alley**, you can watch cookies being made by hand at the **Golden Gate Fortune Cookie Factory** (no.56, 781 3956), or have a trim at **Jun Yu's Barber Shop** (no.32), which, since opening in 1966, has reputedly sheared celebrities including Michael Douglas and Clint Eastwood. Sweet **Waverly Place**, just to the south, was the scene of a famous 1879 battle between two *tongs* (local organized crime gangs that ran gambling and prostitution) over the ownership of a prostitute – at least four men are believed to have been hacked to death by cleavers during the skirmish. These days, it's best visited for the historic **Tien Hau Temple** (no.125). Another kind of history was made in adjacent **Spofford Street**, where between 1904 and 1910 Sun Yat-sen launched a revolution against the Manchu Dynasty from the **Ghee Kung Tong Building** (no.36).

An intriguing landmark stands just south of here, at 920 Sacramento Street. Named after Donaldina Cameron, the New Zealander who devoted her life to saving San Francisco's Chinese girls from prostitution and slavery, **Cameron House** today provides help to low-income Asian immigrants and residents. However, it's also just about the only place in the city where you can still see traces of the great 1906 fire: misshapen 'clinker' bricks, melted by the intense heat, protrude from the walls.

Chinese Historical Society of America Museum

965 Clay Street, between Stockton & Powell Streets (391 1188, www.chsa.org). Bus 1, 9, 12, 30, 45/ cable car Powell-Hyde or Powell-Mason. **Open** noon-5pm Tue-Fri; 11am-4pm Sat. **Admission** $5; $2-$3 reductions; free 1st Thur of month. **Credit** DC, MC, V. **Map** p315 M4.

Founded in 1963 and re-opened in 2001 in the historic Chinese YWCA building designed by renowned local architect Julia Morgan, CHSA is the oldest and largest organization in the country dedicated to the documentation, study, and presentation of Chinese American history. Since moving to the Morgan building, the museum has expanded its exhibits and public programming, with displays in English and Chinese that follow California's Chinese population from the frontier years to the Gold Rush, through the building of the railroads and the Barbary Coast.

Grant Avenue & around

A few blocks from Union Square, at Grant Avenue and Bush Street, the dragon-topped **Chinatown Gate** heralds the southern entrance to Chinatown. A gift from Taiwan in 1970, the green-tiled portal is made to a traditional design, and comes complete with a quotation from Confucius that urges passers-by to work for the common good.

Grant Avenue itself is Chinatown's main thoroughfare and arguably the oldest street in the city. In the 1870s and '80s, when it was called Dupont Street (it was renamed in honor of President Ulysses Grant after the 1906 earthquake), it was controlled by *tongs*. These days, however, the cash-grabbing is more obvious: almost as far as the eye can see, souvenir shops sell T-shirts, toys, ceramics and jewelry, the genuine mixed with the junk.

Although most buildings on Grant have been built in undistinguished American styles, a few structures stand out. The **Ying On Labor Association** building (nos.745-747) is a gaudy study in chinoiserie; across the street, the **Sai Gai Yat Bo Company** building (no.736) features ornate balconies and a pagoda-style roof. Slightly more kitsch – check the circular gold entrance – is the **Li Po** dive bar (no.916, *see venue index*), named after the great drunken poet of the T'ang Dynasty. Even the street lamps are sculpted in the likeness of golden dragons, created during the tourist boom of the 1920s at the behest of the Chinese Chamber of Commerce. The shops are a mixed bunch, but one popular stop is the **Ten Ren Tea Company** (no.949, 362 0656, www.tenren.com), which offers free samples to help its patrons choose. On the corner of Grant and California Streets, meanwhile, is the Roman Catholic **Old St Mary's Cathedral**, a sturdy 1854 edifice made of granite imported from China.

> **INSIDE TRACK**
> **THE OTHER NEW YEAR**
>
> The annual Chinese Lunar New Year Festival is San Francisco's answer – in size, color, and pageantry – to Mardis Gras, with a parade that attracts more than three million spectators, live and on TV. Held every year in January or February (according to the Chinese lunar calendar), it features two weeks of celebrations, including a community festival, the Miss Chinatown USA pageant, and a parade of dazzling floats, costumes, exploding firecrackers, and a 250-foot Golden Dragon that requires a team of over 100 men and women to carry it through the streets of San Francisco. Best viewing is at the beginning or end of the parade route (Market & 2nd Streets, or Kearny Street near Columbus Avenue).

★ FREE Old St Mary's Cathedral

660 California Street, at Grant Avenue (288 3800, www.oldsaintmarys.org). Bus 1, 9X, 30, 45/cable car California. **Open** 7am-4.30pm Mon-Fri; 10am-6pm Sat; 7.30am-3pm Sun. **Map** p315 M5.

Much early missionary work, and the city's first English lessons for Chinese immigrants, took place under this 19th-century building's foreboding clock tower: 'Son, observe the time and fly from evil', it warns. Observe your time at lunchtime concerts staged in the cathedral's dainty yet glorious interior.

FREE Chinese Culture Center

3rd floor, Hilton Hotel, 750 Kearny Street, at Washington Street (986 1822, www.c-c-c.org). Bus 1, 9X, 12, 20, 41/cable car California. **Open** 10am-4pm Tue-Sat. **Admission** free. **Map** p315 M4.

Linked to Portsmouth Square by a footbridge and located on the third floor of a Hilton hotel, the Center hosts a variety of events, including Asian-themed art exhibitions and performances, as well as workshops and walking tours. There's also an annual festival to celebrate Chinese New Year.

North Beach to Fisherman's Wharf

Birthplace of the Beats.

Among San Francisco's many notable neighborhoods, North Beach is one of the best known, a popular destination for tourists, beloved by locals and an integral part of the old Barbary Coast. Grant Avenue, which runs through the middle of the area, is San Francisco's oldest street. Along with the North Point docks, the century-old ethnic neighborhoods of Chinatown and Little Italy are reminders that San Francisco once served as the gateway to the west. With the legendary City Lights bookstore and a variety of cafés, the area is also bound to the Beat movement of the 1950s (*see p71* **Walk**).

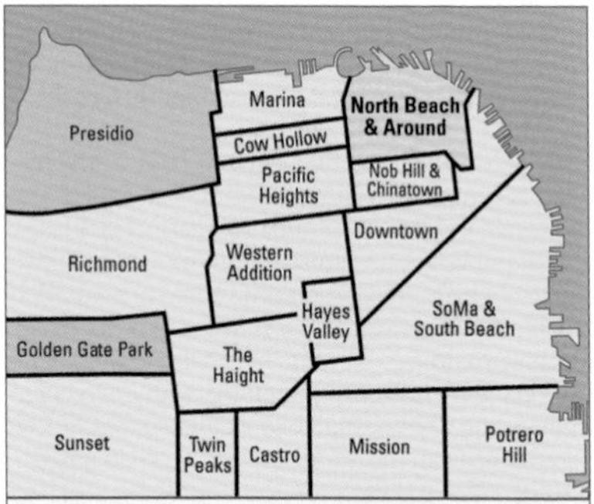

To the north of North Beach is the dreary tourist trap of **Fisherman's Wharf**, its theme park vibe fed by T-shirt stalls, tacky museums and overpriced restaurants. Looking down on all this tomfoolery are the residents of **Russian Hill**, one of the city's richest neighborhoods and also, it stands to reason, among its nicest. Bisected by tiny alleyways and pretty pocket gardens, it draws tourists for its most unique feature: zigzagging Lombard Street.

Map p314-315
Hotels p127
Restaurants & Cafés p147
Bars p170

NORTH BEACH

North Beach, north and east of Columbus Avenue, was the place that turned San Francisco into the counterculture capital of the US. Established at the turn of the century by the city's Italian community, it came to attract leagues of writers and artists, drawn not only by the European aura but by the low rents. The Beat Generation reigned here in the 1950s, and later their trailblazing path of individualism and artistic endeavor carried into the early 1960s, when nightclubs such as the Purple Onion and the Hungry i showcased an array of boundary-pushing comedians such as Woody Allen and Lenny Bruce. Later, punk venues solidified the indelible stamp of hipness. Today, North Beach has avoided falling victim to homogeny. The mellow streets, with their famously lambent light on sunny days, are still home to elderly Italians playing *bocce*, reading Neapolitan newspapers and nibbling *cannoli* at sidewalk cafes.

The brash strip joints along Broadway are another tourist draw, whether locals like it or not. But time hasn't stood still here. Amid the long-standing strip clubs and vintage cafés, now sit shops offering handmade goods, restaurants serving all manner of classic, contemporary and international cuisine, and a slew of lively – or, if you prefer, noisy – bars and nightclubs. North Beach's secret, it seems, is that it has figured out that with a little effort, it is possible to be all things to all people.

City Lights & around

Much of North Beach's history and many of its treasures lie along **Columbus Avenue**, especially close to the three-way junction of Columbus, Broadway and Grant Avenue that represents North Beach's beating heart.

To get up to speed on the Beats and their legacy, check out the **Beat Museum** (540 Broadway, at Columbus Avenue, 399 9626, www.thebeatmuseum.org) before heading over to what was both the head and the heart of the Beat movement, **City Lights** bookstore (261 Columbus Avenue, at Broadway; *see p181*). Still presided over by the original owner, 92-year-old poet Lawrence Ferlinghetti, City Lights has grown to occupy an entire building. Ferlinghetti began his shop with the then-radical concept of selling only paperbacks, believing that the best books should be available to as many people as possible, in an economical form. To this day, City Lights stocks not only books published in-house, but a variety of the finest world literature, political thinking and small-circulation periodicals. The upper floor houses the shop's considerable Beat collection.

Step across Jack Kerouac Alley just next door to **Vesuvio** (255 Columbus Avenue, at Broadway; *see p171*), which welcomes mad poets and tourists in equal measure, much as it did when Kerouac and crew drank here in the 1950s (*see p168* **One More for the Road**). **Tosca Café** (242 Columbus Avenue, between Broadway Street & Pacific Avenue) was another favorite watering hole of the Beats, and today attracts actors and filmmakers.

The copper-sheathed **Columbus Tower** at the corner of Columbus and Kearny Streets, purchased by film director Francis Ford Coppola following the resounding success of *The Godfather*, houses his American Zoetrope Studios, as well as office space for a number of independent film producers. On the ground floor is charming **Café Zoetrope** (916 Kearny Street, at Jackson Street, 291 1700, www.cafecoppola.com), which also sells wines from the director's own Napa Valley vineyard.

East of here is **Broadway**, a boulevard lined with nightclubs featuring strippers and sexy floorshows. History was made at the **Condor Club** (300 Columbus Avenue, at Broadway, 781 8222, www.condorsf.com) in 1964 when a buxom waitress named Carol Doda went topless for the first time. Just down the street, the **Hungry i** (546 Broadway, at Columbus Avenue), once a nightclub that launched the careers of luminaries such as Barbra Streisand and Woody Allen, is now a strip club. A new culture of a slightly different stripe was forged in the **Mabuhay Gardens** at 443 Broadway, a punk mecca where the Dead Kennedys got their start. The area's bohemian history is remembered in the **Beat Museum** (*see below*), also on Broadway.

Just down on Kearny Street are two newer adult hangouts, which represent a pair of contradictory extremes. Larry Flynt's **Hustler Club** (No.1031) is about as crude and modern as they come, every bit the reflection of its famous owner's proudly crass image. Next door sits the **Lusty Lady** (No.1033), a pretty scruffy-looking peep show notable for being the first unionized strip joint in the US, and, since 2003, for being the only place of its type to be owned and operated by the women who work in it. The club was the subject of a 2000 documentary, *Live Nude Girls Unite*.

Beat Museum

540 Broadway, at Columbus Avenue (1-800 537 6822, 1-831 372 4911, www.thebeatmuseum.org) Bus 9X, 12, 20, 30, 41, 45. **Open** 10am-7pm daily. **Admission** $5. **Map** p315 M3.

Formerly located down the coast near Big Sur, the Beat Museum houses an impressive archive of letters, magazines, pictures, first editions and artifacts that explore the lives of beat figures such as Jack Kerouac, Lawrence Ferlinghetti, Allen Ginsberg, and Neal Cassady. The gift shop and bookstore are free. The museum also offers a walking tour of North Beach with curator Jerry Cimimo.

▶ *For more on the Beats, see p23. For the meeting that never happened between Jack Kerouac and Henry Miller, see p168* **One More for the Road**.

Washington Square & around

Molinari Delicatessen (373 Columbus Avenue, at Vallejo Street; *see p192*), one of San Francisco's most beloved institutions, boasts

INSIDE TRACK WHERE'S THE BEACH?

The perennial question of tourists walking past the Italian cafés, shops, and pretty Victorians in North Beach – where's the actual beach? In the early 1800s, the city's shoreline reached all the way to Taylor and Francisco Streets, what is today the northern boundary of Fisherman's Wharf, and North Beach was in fact, a beach. The hulls of abandoned Gold Rush ships began filling in the waterfront in the 1850s (one of which was converted into a saloon that still operates today at Pacific and Battery Streets). Gradually the shoreline receded and was topped with landfill, upon which warehouses, wharves, and docks were built. To find what's left of the beach today, head to Aquatic Park, located at the end of Hyde and Jefferson Streets.

a cameo role in *Babycakes*, one of Armistead Maupin's Tales of the City series. Pick up a *sopressata* sandwich on a hard roll and take it just up the road to Washington Square, a lovely patch of greenery that really comes into its own at the height of summer. Alternatively, walk up **Grant Avenue** and browse blocks of one-of-a-kind boutiques, antiques and curiosity shops. From luxury lingerie to Asian antiquities, Grant Avenue is entertaining in itself, but perhaps the best place to stop for a bit of history is **Schein and Schein** (No.1435, 339 8882, www.scheinandschein.com), a miscellany of antique maps and prints, and also home to a fascinating collection of vintage photographs. Just down the street is **Savoy Tivoli** (No.1434, *see p170*), a bar that has been in operation since 1907, and a great place to stop for a drink on the patio.

Washington Square is overlooked by the white stucco Romanesque **Church of St Peter and St Paul**, where Marilyn Monroe and local hero Joe DiMaggio had their wedding photos taken. Since both were divorced and Joe was a Catholic, the couple were married in a civil ceremony at City Hall. An 1879 statue of Benjamin Franklin stands in the park on a granite-encased time capsule – it's scheduled to be reopened in 2079.

At **Caffe Roma** (526 Columbus Avenue, *see p146*), coffee is freshly roasted on the premises, while at **Liguria** (1700 Stockton Street, at Filbert Street, 421 3786), the locals stand in line for foccacia made in-house, baked by members of the same family since 1911.

The district of **Telegraph Hill**, bordered by Grant Avenue and Green, Bay and Sansome Streets, was so named as the site of the West Coast's first telegraph. The landmark **Coit Tower** sits on top. Two nearby hotels neatly sum up the area. The **Hotel Bohème** (444 Columbus Avenue, between Vallejo & Green Streets, *see p127*) celebrates Beat heritage with framed snapshots of life in bohemian North Beach in the 1950s and '60s, while the *pensione*-like **San Remo Hotel** (2337 Mason Street, at Chestnut Street, *see p128*), a pretty Italianate Victorian, is an ideal base for soaking up the area's Italian ambience.

Coit Tower

Peak of Telegraph Hill, at the end of Telegraph Hill Boulevard (362 0808). Bus 39. **Open** 10am-6pm daily. **Admission** *Elevator* $5. **No credit cards. Map** p315 M3.

This 210ft (64m) concrete turret, built by City Hall architect Arthur Brown in 1933, was a gift to the city from the eccentric Lillie Hitchcock Coit, famed for her love of firemen. Legend has it that as a schoolgirl, Coit happened upon the Knickerbocker #5 Volunteer Fire Company attempting to haul their fire engine up steep Telegraph Hill. As their energy flagged, she grabbed the rope and exhorted the men to pull on. From that day on, she became the mascot of the #5s. Upon her death, she bequeathed a massive sum to the city. A memorial to her beloved Knickerbockers was erected in Washington Square, and Coit Tower was built to fulfil her wish to 'add to the beauty of the city I have always loved'. While most assume that the tower represents the nozzle of a fire hose, the architects always denied it. The spectacular views from the top aren't the tower's only attraction. Under the supervision of Diego Rivera, some wonderful murals were created here, a series of socialist-realist images so subversive that, when they were completed in 1934, delayed the opening so that an errant hammer and sickle could be erased.

FISHERMAN'S WHARF

Fisherman's Wharf dates back to the Gold Rush, when Italian and Chinese immigrants plied the Bay for crab and other seafood and sold it right off their boats. Famous families included the DiMaggios (kin of late baseball great Joe DiMaggio) and the Alioto clan (who own an eponymous restaurant on the Wharf, *see p148*). Alas, there is little evidence of that historic past today: the wharf, roughly bounded by Jefferson, North Point and Kearny Streets and Fort Mason, is little more than a conglomeration of novelty attractions, tacky shops and heavy pedestrian traffic. In surveys, Fisherman's Wharf routinely ranks as the No.1 destination for visitors, despite the fact that its main attractions were built in the late 1960s and '70s. Still, those with a few hours to kill can find some inexpensive entertainment here, along with unrivaled views of the Bay.

Jefferson Street, the wharf's main drag, is a fairly undignified spectacle. The **Wax Museum** (No.145, 1-800 439 4305, www.waxmuseum.com) and **Ripley's Believe It Or Not! Museum** (No.175, 202 9850, www.ripleys.com) are clichéd dockside diversions; elsewhere, sidewalk crab stalls and seafood restaurants thrive. For the only remaining glimpse of Fisherman's Wharf as it once was, turn towards the water off Jefferson and on to Leavenworth Street, then slip into **Fish Alley**. There, you will find real fishing boats and real fishermen. Although it's within shouting distance of Jefferson, it feels like miles away. Another nipper of the fishing life can be hooked at **Frank's Fisherman** (366 Jefferson Street, between Leavenworth Street & Al Scoma Way, 775 1165, www.franksfisherman.com), which sells everything from silk yachting shirts to antique scrimshaw tusks.

At the eastern end, **Pier 39** is a sprawling prefab array of seafront shops, attractions and arcade games patently designed to separate

Walk On the Beat-en Track

Follow in the footsteps of Jack Kerouac and friends.

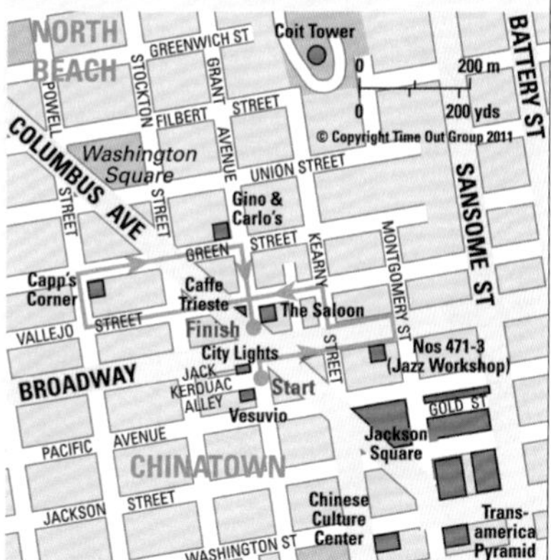

Our walk starts on Columbus Avenue and Broadway in North Beach, where the literary spirits are packed so tightly you practically have to step into the road to avoid them. First, have a peek into **Vesuvio** (No.255, *see p171*); the jaunty multicolored sign has welcomed poets and artists since it opened in 1948. Neither Dylan Thomas nor Jack Kerouac could resist when they were in town, nor can the dipsomaniacal poets and poetical dipsomaniacs of today. To the right of Vesuvio is Jack Kerouac Alley, renamed by the city in 1988, and the world-famous **City Lights** bookstore (No.261, *see p181*).

Cross Columbus heading east along Broadway. **Tosca** (No.242, *see p171*) can lay proud claim to having ejected Bob Dylan one boisterous evening, and it was at **Spec's** (12 William Saroyan Place, *see p170)* columnist Herb Caen coined the derogatory term 'Beatnik' to describe the increasingly large numbers of youths heading to North Beach in search of jazz, sex and poetry. They found the former, at least, just away from City Lights along the righthand side of Broadway: at nos.471-3, the Jazz Workshop once hosted the likes of Miles Davis, John Coltrane, Sonny Rollins and Ornette Coleman; it was also here that Lenny Bruce was first arrested for obscenity in 1961.

Head up Montgomery Street for a great view of the Bay Bridge, then cross Broadway. Allen Ginsberg lived at 1010 Montgomery with Peter Orlovsky, and probably conceived his epochal poem *Howl* here. The site is now an old folks' home. Heading back along Broadway you will pass the Green Tortoise Hostel at No.494. It may not look like much now, but this was once the chic El Matador, where Frank Sinatra and Duke Ellington performed for Marlon Brando's Hollywood set.

Cafe Trieste.

Turn right on to Kearny and you're facing more than 100 pretty steps. Locals call them the Kearny Steps, but the official title is the Macchiarini Steps – named for a local artisan family that's been making jewelry here since 1948 (at 1544 Grant Avenue, www.macreativedesign.com). From the top, it's downhill again for a break at **Caffe Trieste** (601 Vallejo Street, *see p146*), the coffee house where Francis Ford Coppola is said to have penned *The Godfather*.

Turn right down Green Street. If it's sunny, turn left and head up to Washington Square for a glorious mix of tatty old bohemians, wannabe alternative types and discreet Chinese ladies doing t'ai chi. Otherwise, zigzag across the intersection between Green, Columbus and Stockton. Stick on Green Street, passing **Caffè Sport** at No.574. When this was the Cellar, Kenneth Rexroth and Ruth Weiss read to improvised accompaniment here, a first foray into jazz poetry. Turn right on to Grant Avenue and head past the **Grant & Green Saloon** (No.1371), until you reach the plain old **Saloon** (No.1232). This is San Francisco's oldest bar, open since 1861. There's no smoky jazz, but there is live blues.

The Making of Fresco Showing the Building of San Francisco.

INSIDE TRACK
DIEGO RIVERA WAS HERE

Mexican muralist Diego Rivera was at the peak of his powers when he created his three San Francisco murals, painting dominantly political works that make them some of the most significant surviving pieces of his career. *The Making of a Fresco Showing the Building of San Francisco* (1931) at the **San Francisco Art Institute** (*see p74*) was his first truly public piece in the US, drawing vast crowds at its unveiling. Featuring workers bent to their tasks and a rear view of the artist himself, it's inconspicuously tucked into a classroom off the courtyard. Rivera's ambitious *Pan American Unity Mural* resides across town at **City College of San Francisco** (50 Phelan Avenue, www.riveramural.com). Made up of five massive panels spanning 1,800 square feet, it traces the history of the North American continent from early Mexico to the Industrial Age, and the labors of various American inventors. *The Allegory of California* at the **City Club** (inside the Pacific Coast Stock Exchange, *see p50*) is the most moderate in tone, depicting a large figure of Califia, the spirit of California, as well as gold miners, farmers, and industrialists.

you from your money. Luckily, crowds of sea lions barking and belching on nearby pontoons provide a natural respite. Offshore from H Dock on Pier 39, **Forbes Island** (951 4900, www.forbesisland.com) is 700 tons of manmade, engine-propelled, floating lighthouse and restaurant. Further west, at Pier 45, the **USS Pampanito** (*see p74*) World War II submarine is open to the public for self-guided tours.

A reminder of the area's former industrial life is the **Cannery** (2801 Leavenworth Street, enter on Jefferson or Beach Streets, 771 3112, www.delmontesquare.com). Built in 1907 as a fruit-canning factory, it's now really just another mall. The red-brick **Ghirardelli Square** (at North Point & Larkin Streets, *see p179*) dates to the 19th century and housed a chocolate factory until the 1960s; the namesake chocolate is still sold, but the building itself is now a complex of shops and restaurants. The newest addition is theconversion of part of the structure into luxurycondominiums. Despite all this, the **Ghirardelli Ice Cream & Chocolate Shop** (900 North Point Street, 474 1414, www.ghirardelli.com) on the southern edge of the square is the place to get some of the best hot fudge sundaes on earth. The lovely *Mermaid Fountain* in the square's central plaza was sculpted by local artist Ruth Asawa. There's more refreshment nearby at the famous **Buena Vista Café** (2765 Hyde Street, at Beach Street, 474 5044, www.thebuenavista.com), where Irish coffee was introduced to the US in 1952.

There's more to enjoy to the west. The shores of **Aquatic Park** (between Hyde Street & Van Ness Avenue) offer one of the best strolls in the city, with a panorama of the Golden Gate Bridge, Alcatraz, windsurfers, sailing boats, wildly colored kites and dogs catching frisbees. Along the **Municipal Pier** (access from the northern end of Van Ness), fisherm en try their luck; at **Hyde Street Pier** (*see right*), a fleet of carefully restored historic ships is docked permanently and open to the public; the **San Francisco Maritime Museum** opposite Ghirardelli Square is currently closed for a major refurbishment, but the lobby, with its gorgeous WPA murals, is open for viewing.

The **Golden Gate Promenade** begins here, continuing for three miles along the shoreline to **Fort Point** (*see p103*). The entire stretch of waterfront from Aquatic Park to Ocean Beach was incorporated into the Golden Gate National Recreation Area in 1972, with the authorities thankfully arresting Fisherman's Wharf-style tourist kitsch spreading any further along one of the most scenic bits of coast in the region.

★ Alcatraz

Alcatraz Island, San Francisco Bay (www.nps.gov/alcatraz). Alcatraz Cruises ferry from Pier 33, Embarcadero (981 7625, www.alcatrazcruises.com).

Streetcar F. **Tickets** (incl audio guide) $26-$33; $16-$30.50 reductions. **Credit** AmEx, Disc, MC, V. **Map** p315 M1.

'Alcatraz' is Spanish for pelican, but to its inmates it was simply known as 'the Rock'. The West Coast's first lighthouse was built here in 1854, but it was soon decided that the island's isolated setting made it perfect for a prison. It became a military jail in the 1870s, but it wasn't until it was converted into a high-security federal penitentiary in 1934 that the name Alcatraz became an international symbol of punishment. Despite being in operation for less than 30 years, Alcatraz remains fixed in the popular imagination as the ultimate penal colony. Today, its ominous prison buildings are no longer used (its last inmates left in 1963), but the craggy outcrop, now a National Park, lures over a million visitors each year.

Despite what you might expect, Alcatraz is far from being a tourist trap. The audio tour, which features actual interviews from a variety of former prisoners and guards, is powerful, chilling and evocative, and the buildings retain an eerie and fascinating appeal. Departure times for both the day tours and the far less frequent (and wildly oversubscribed) evening jaunts vary by season: check the website for details. One word of warning: capacity on the tours is limited, and those who don't book ahead of time may find the only views they get of the island are from the shore.

Angel Island

Angel Island State Park, San Francisco Bay (435 1915/www.angelisland.org). Blue & Gold ferry from Pier 41, Embarcadero (705 5555, www.blueandgoldfleet.com). Streetcar F. **Tickets** $16; $9 reductions. **Credit** AmEx, MC, V. **Map** p314 L1.

Blue & Gold runs a ferry service to Angel Island; times vary with the season, so check online or call before setting out. Boats arrive at the Ayala Cove visitors' center, where there are maps, bikes to rent and picnic tables. Views from the island are unrivalled. At its peak, there are 360-degree views of the entire Bay Area – one of the primary reasons the top was sheared off and replaced with a gun bunker as a part of the Bay's coastal defenses. Luckily, they replaced the top but the bunkers are still scattered around the island, whose history dates back before the Civil War. Richard Henry Dana recounts in his *Two Years Before the Mast* (1840) how he collected a year's supply of wood for his ship *Alert* when it stopped here in the winter of 1835-36. Later it acted as 'the Ellis Island of the West' serving as one of America's busiest immigration ports. In its darkest chapter, it was as an internment camp for Japanese-Americans during World War II.

Alcatraz.

FREE Hyde Street Pier

Foot of Hyde Street (561 7000, www.maritime.org). Streetcar F/bus 19, 30, 47, 90/cable car Powell-Hyde. **Open** 9.30am-5pm daily. **Admission** free ($5 for vessels). **No credit cards. Map** p314 K1.

Maritime fans, students of history, and children will love the historic vessels permanently docked here. Typical of the ships that would have been common here in the 19th and early 20th centuries, they include the 1886 full-rigged *Balclutha*, built to carry grain from California to Europe; the *CA Thayer*, an 1895 sailing ship that carried timber along the West Coast; the *Alma*, an 1891 scow schooner that hauled cargo throughout the Bay Area; *Hercules*, a 1907 ocean tugboat; and the 1890 commuter ferry *Eureka*.

Along with the San Francisco Maritime Museum, the set-up is the highlight of what is officially designated as the San Francisco Maritime National Historic Park. The park's lovely visitors' center, at the corner of Jefferson and Hyde Streets (June-Sept 9.30am-7pm daily; Oct-May 9.30am-5pm daily), contains fascinating displays on the area's seafaring history. For more on the park and its various services and attractions, call 447 5000 or visit www.nps.gov/safr. *Photo p74.*

★ FREE Musée Mécanique

Pier 45, at the end of Taylor Street (346 2000, www.museemecanique.org). Streetcar F/bus 19, 30, 47, 90/cable car Powell-Mason. **Open** 11am-7pm Mon-Fri; 10am-8pm Sat, Sun. **Admission** free. **Map** p314 K1.

Pack a pocketful of quarters before you visit this wonderful museum, a vintage arcade housing more than 170 old-fashioned coin-operated gizmos dating from the 1880s, ranging from fortune-telling machines to player pianos. Best of all is Laffing Sal, a somewhat scary relic from Whitney's Playland at the Beach, San Francisco's long-defunct coastside amusement park. It's an enormous mechanical figure with a crazy laugh that sends little kids running for their parents.

FREE San Francisco Maritime Museum

900 Beach Street, at Polk Street (561 7100, www.maritime.org). Streetcar F/bus 19, 30, 47, 90/cable car Powell-Hyde. **Open** 10am-4pm daily. **Admission** free. **Map** p314 J2.

The streamline moderne cruiseliner that houses the museum is closed for major refurbishment, but visitors can view the lobby and the fantastic Atlantis murals by Hilaire Hiler.

USS Pampanito

Pier 45 (775 1943, www.maritime.org). Streetcar F/bus 10, 19, 30, 47/cable car Powell-Hyde. **Open** *Mid Oct-late May* 9am-6pm Mon-Thur, Sun; 9am-8pm Fri, Sat. *Late May-mid Oct* 9am-8pm Mon, Tue, Thur-Sun; 9am-6pm Wed. **Admission** $10; $4-$6 reductions; $20 family. **Credit** AmEx, MC, V. **Map** p314 K1.

The *Pampanito* is a World War II, Balao-class Fleet submarine with an impressive record: it made six patrols in the Pacific at the height of the war, sinking six Japanese ships and damaging four others. The vessel has been restored to look much as it would have in its prime in 1945. The sub is still seaworthy: in 1995 it sailed under the Golden Gate Bridge for the first time in 50 years.

RUSSIAN HILL

Russian Hill got its name when several Cyrillic-inscribed gravestones were discovered here during the Gold Rush. Local lore has it that a Russian warship put into the harbor of San Francisco in the early 1840s, and a number of the disease-stricken crew died while ashore. As they belonged to the Orthodox Church, they couldn't be buried in any of the existing Protestant or Catholic cemeteries, so one was created for them in this area. By the late 1800s, the gravestones had disappeared; along with them went any trace of Russian influence.

Today, Russian Hill is a quiet, residential and pricey neighborhood roughly bordered by Larkin and North Point Streets, Columbus Avenue, Powell Street and Pacific Avenue. Its most notorious landmark is the world's 'crookedest' street (though technically the 'real' crookedest street lies on the back side of Potrero Hill, *see p79*). **Lombard Street**, which snakes steeply down from Hyde Street to Leavenworth, packs nine hairpin bends into one brick-paved and over-landscaped block. In summer, tourists queue for the thrill of driving down its hazardous 27 per cent gradient at 5mph, much to the annoyance of local residents. Arrive early or late to avoid the throng. For further thrills, test your skills behind the wheel on the steepest street in the city: Filbert Street between Hyde and Leavenworth descends at a whopping 31.5 percent gradient. Also up on Russian Hill is the **San Francisco Art Institute** (*see below*), housed in an attractive 1920s Spanish Revival building on Chestnut Street and containing a wonderful Diego Rivera mural.

Struggle up Vallejo Street to Taylor Street to take in the views from **Ina Coolbrith Park**, little more than a narrow ledge with benches. Arrive early in the morning, and you'll catch elderly Chinese practising t'ai chi. Up from the park, the top of the **Vallejo Street Stairway**, designed by Willis Polk and surrounded on each side by landscaped gardens, is the apex of the neighborhood. Laura Ingalls Wilder, author of *Little House on the Prairie*, lived here (at 1019 Vallejo). Indeed, Russian Hill is riven with quaint stairs and alleyways: if you don't mind the ups and downs, it can be fun to prowl the neighborhood for secret passages.

Other landmark addresses in the district include **29 Russell Street**, off Hyde Street, where Jack Kerouac lived with Neal and Carolyn Cassady during his most creative period in the 1950s; and the **Feusier Octagon House**, one of the city's oldest dwellings, at 1067 Green Street, near Leavenworth. Best viewed from across the street to appreciate its odd shape, the pastel structure is one of only two survivors of the 19th-century octagonal-house craze (the other is in Pacific Heights).

Hyde Street Pier. *See p73.*

★ FREE San Francisco Art Institute

800 Chestnut Street, between Leavenworth & Jones Streets (771 7020, www.sfai.edu). Bus 30, 47, 91/cable car Powell-Hyde or Powell-Mason. **Open** *Diego Rivera Gallery* 9am-5pm daily. *Walter McBean Gallery* 11am-6pm Tue-Sat. **Admission** free. **No credit cards. Map** p314 K2.

This hip and prestigious art school offers the full spectrum of fine arts, including painting, film, photography, sculpture and new media. Its student shows are legendary. Most people visit to see Diego Rivera's mural *The Making of a Fresco*, one of various works he completed in San Francisco in the 1930s. If you're worn out from climbing all those hills, have a rest in the pretty open-air courtyard, or grab a cheap snack in the cafeteria and soak up the views.

Secret Stairways to Heaven

Step up for some of the best city views.

Coit Tower.

Often overgrown with foliage and unmarked, San Francisco's network of stairways are some of the city's most untraveled byways – and many of them have outstanding views. Nearly 400 different stairways connect the city's 42 hills.

Leafy **Macondray Lane** (off Leavenworth Street, between Union and Green Streets), was the inspiration for Armistead Maupin's Barbary Lane in *Tales of the City*. Idiosyncratic houses line one side, through which you can catch tantalizing glimpses of the Bay beyond. The signpost for the steps is hard to spot – look for the name imprinted in the concrete of the curb.

The architect-designed steps on **Vallejo Street** (between Jones and Mason Streets) have breathtaking views and arum lilies growing in adjacent flowerbeds. Try walking east from Jones and Vallejo Streets (uphill) for a block, admiring the collision of architecture at the peak of Nob Hill. Take the stairs to the right of the overlook and, winding past landscaped backyards and friendly cats, descend slowly to Ina Coolbrith Park a block down. Continue down the steps for showstopping views of the Bay Bridge, the piers and Treasure Island.

Tucked between North Beach and the Embarcadero, the glorious **Filbert Street** steps take you from the bottom of Sansome Street and Filbert up to Coit Tower, along the way passing through the lovely, rambling Grace Marchant gardens with their famous flocks of wild parrots.

The steps along **Broadway** between Taylor and Jones Streets lead to a perch where you can take in vistas of the Bay Bridge with the Transamerica Pyramid and the Financial District spread out below. Over in Twin Peaks, the spectacular panoramic views from Tank Hill are your reward for climbing the steep **Pemberton Steps**, accessed at the intersection of Corbett and Clay streets.

Arguably the grandest stairway is on **Lyon Street**, between Green Street and Broadway, a stairway 'street' built in 1916 to connect Cow Hollow with Pacific Heights. Four sets of stairs, totaling 288 steps, take you past manicured hedges and flower gardens to an iron gate that marks the entrance to the Presidio. From the top, there are views of Alcatraz, the Palace of Fine Arts, and the Golden Gate Bridge.

For more stairways, consult Adah Bakalinsky's exhaustive (and exhausting) guide, *Stairway Walks in San Francisco*.

The Mission & the Castro

Quintessential San Francisco.

The heady cultural mix of the Mission, the Castro and Noe Valley makes for a uniquely San Franciscan kind of melting pot. The Mission is San Francisco's centre of Latin life, while Castro is the gay hub of what many think of as the gayest city on earth. Here, rainbow-swathed muscle shirt boutiques rub shoulders with beautifully renovated Victorian homes; temples to pristine gastronomy give way to burritos the size of a baby's arm. These close-knit enclaves of all things queer, yuppie, hip and Latino provide a colorful snapshot of the city's remarkably diverse charm.

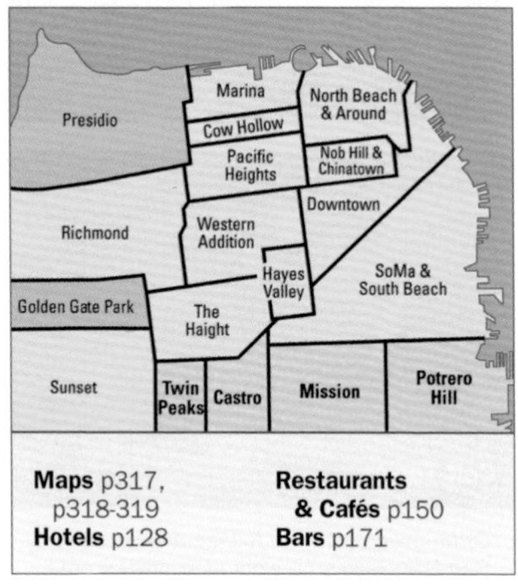

Maps p317, p318-319
Hotels p128
Restaurants & Cafés p150
Bars p171

THE MISSION

First settled by the Spanish in the 1770s and later home to Irish, German, Italian and Asian immigrants, the Mission today is the center of Latin culture in San Francisco. A steady influx of families and workers from Mexico and South and Central America lends the neighborhood its distinctive character, especially on **Mission Street** between 14th and Cesar Chavez Streets, the area's main drag. Along here, the scents and sights are plentiful: the mix of sidewalk sausage stands, bootleg DVD vendors, dollar stores and *taquerías* colorfully paints the strip of one of the city's tightest ethnic communities.

However, walk a couple of blocks west to **Valencia Street** and you'll see evidence of the area's other main occupants: San Francisco's creative classes. The invasion of *nouveau riche* techies during the dotcom boom drove some rents sky-high, sending many locals on a scramble to find cheaper quarters, but the musicians and artists who colonized the area in the 1990s remain in situ, and despite fears that the area would gentrify beyond recognition, it seems to have regained its equilibrium. Trendy Valencia Street hasn't yet overwhelmed the throbbing pulse of blue-collar Mission Street, and the two coexist in relative harmony.

A quick practical note: unlike Downtown and SoMa, the street numbering along Mission and Valencia Streets doesn't correspond to the numbered streets that cross them. For example, 2000 Mission Street is not at the junction of 20th Street, as you might expect, but of 16th Street; similarly, 2800 Mission is actually at 24th Street. It's a similar story two blocks away: 500 Valencia Street sits at the junction with 16th Street, while 1300 Valencia is at 24th Street. Still, while the numbering doesn't match the streets, it does at least increase at the standard rate of 100 per block, which makes it easy to figure out how far you have to walk.

Mission Street & East

Mission Street is the main thoroughfare of the Latino quarter. Cheque-cashing operations, bargain shops, taco stands and grocery stores (selling such exotica as sugar cane and prickly pears – the fruit borne by the cactus of the same name) conduct brisk business, while Banda (the

Mexican music descended from the oompah bands of German immigrants) drifts out of open doors and windows. In a few places, the narrow, crowded sidewalks are a scene straight out of Guadalajara; it's especially eye-catching in autumn, when Mexican-run shops and art galleries fill with traditional ghoulish items in advance of Día de los Muertos (Day of the Dead) in November.

The neighborhood can feel a little shady east of Mission Street in the inner Mission, particularly north of 19th Street and its environs. The *barrio* has its share of prostitutes, drug addicts and gangs, and doorway drug-deals around the scruffy junction of 16th and Mission Streets are usually enough to scare off the timid. However, it's safer than it once was, and 24th Street is undergoing a transformation that celebrates the personality of the Mission with a more business-savvy outlook.

Tourist buses tend to limit their explorations to the admittedly fascinating Mission Dolores, but there are other worthwhile stops. On Mission Street, the **Mission Cultural Center** (No.2868, at 25th Street, 821 1155, www.missioncultural center.org) hosts a theater and a gallery displaying works by under-the-radar artists. It's also a terrific resource for the area's wealth of public art, as is the **Precita Eyes Mural Arts & Visitor Center** on 24th Street.

At this juncture it's important to acknowledge the centrality of food to the Mission experience. It's one of the area's main attractions, and no discussion of Mission food would be complete without mentioning the mythical creation that is the Mission burrito: a glory to behold, this steamed tortilla is an object of fanatical devotion. Packed with meat, cheese, rice, beans, guacamole and spicy, peppery salsa, it is perhaps the ultimate food for the new millennium. It's fast, cheap and portable, takes under five minutes to prepare and costs about $5. Needless to say, competition is fierce. A quick course in the fundamentals of what makes a good burrito can be found at www.burritoeater.com. Some of the area's best are **Taqueria San Francisco** (2794 24th Street, at York Street, 641 1770), **La Taqueria** (2889 Mission Street, 285 7117), **Taqueria Cancun** (2288 Mission Street, 252 9560) and the place that lays claim to creating the original Mission burrito, **Taqueria La Cumbre** (515 Valencia Street, 863 8205). **Casa Sanchez** (2278 24th Street, 695 0700, www.casasanchezfoods.com), which makes and sells its own line of salsas, once offered free burritos for life to anyone who would get a tattoo of its logo; it had to cancel the offer after several regulars tookup the challenge. At **Pancho Villa** (3071 16th Street, at Valencia Street, 864 8840, www.sfpanchovilla.com) rocker Beck has been spotted sitting in for the *taqueria*'s regular serenading mariachi.

Valencia Street & west

While Mission Street retains a headily Latino feel, Valencia Street, parallel to Mission and just two blocks west, is an altogether different kettle of fish. The occasional Mexican business remains, but many of the storefronts have been taken over by boho types, who occupy bar stools, dine on gourmet pizzettas, and fill seats at the **Roxie Theater** (3117 16th Street, 863 1087, www.roxie.com), the neighborhood movie house and one of a handful of independent cinemas left in San Francisco.

Lined with boutiques, with nary a chain store in sight, Valencia Street is a shopaholics' paradise. Within a four-block stretch, book-lovers get to sift through the shelves of **Dog-Eared Books** (No.900, 282 1901, www.dogearedbooks.com) and **Modern Times Bookstore** (No.888, 282 9246, www.mtbs.com), a trove of new and second-hand literary treasures that comes in handy for students of the über-liberal New College of California, just blocks away, and the City College of San Francisco. **Aquarius Records** (No.1055, between 21st & 22nd Streets, 647 2272, www.aquariusrecords.org) satisfies the area's vinyl junkies.

Local designers also have a presence here, at shops such as **Dema** (No.1038, at 21st Street, 206 0500, www.godemago.com). At **Paxton Gate** (No.824, between 19th & 20th Streets; *see p196*), a cadre of creative landscapers and taxidermists sells gardening equipment and stuffed vampire mice. However, the most notable commercial landmark is the pirate supply store

INSIDE TRACK THE REAL 'CROOKEDEST' STREET

Ask where America's crookedest street is, and you'll undoubtedly be directed to world-famous Lombard Street on Russian Hill. Unbeknown to most tourists (and even many locals) however, the real crookedest street lies south of Lombard on the back side of Potrero Hill. While not nearly as splashy or scenic, the end of Vermont Street, between 20th and 22nd Streets, packs seven tightly twisting switchbacks at a 14.3 per cent gradient, compared to Lombard's eight. To its credit, at a 27 per cent gradient, Lombard is considerably steeper and thus a bit more hair-raising.

Mission Murals

A slice of Latino culture.

A blend of Mexican, Cuban, Salvadoran, Guatemalan and American, 24th Street east of Mission Street is the Mission District in microcosm, with a profusion of murals and tasty places to stop for a snack. Begin your walk west of Mission Street at **Casa Bonampak** (1051 Valencia Street, 1-888 722 4264, www.casabonampak.com), a must-see shop where you can pick up all your Día de los Muertos (Day of the Dead) supplies. It also sells excellent compilation CDs and fair trade apparel, as well as postcards of such figures as Che Guevara and Mexico's masked revolutionary, Subcomandante Marcos. Heading back east across Mission, you'll encounter colorful murals everywhere – even the local McDonald's on the corner of Mission and 24th has a technicolor coat. The vivid public art that graces the area's alleys is here largely thanks to the vision of one woman, Susan Cervantes, founder of **Precita Eyes Mural Arts & Visitors Center** (No.2981, at Harrison Street, 285 2287, www.precitaeyes.org), which celebrated its 30th birthday in 2007. The center has a shop that carries mural T-shirts, mural maps and mural postcards as well as general art supplies. For the best overview, Precita Eyes runs walking tours: the Mission Trail Mural Walk runs every Saturday and Sunday at 1.30pm ($15); other slightly shorter walks are held at 11am at weekends; private tours are available by appointment.

If you can't take the tour, be sure to double back to check out the murals along **Balmy Alley**. Back on 24th Street, at the corner of Florida Street, St Peter's Church is similarly adorned. And don't miss the hilarious mural on the **Mr Burbujas** (Mr Bubbles) laundromat, just across the street. By now it's probably lunchtime, and food is a big part of what's good about this part of the Mission. Don't let the humble appearance of many of the restaurants put you off. There's some great Mexican food to be had, at **Restaurente El Delfin** (no.3066, 643 7955) or **Tortas Los Picudos** (no.2969, 824 4199), for example, both within easy reach of Balmy Alley and St Peter's Church. To follow your burrito with something sweet, check out one of the many Mexican bakeries or panaderías. At **La Victoria** (no.2937, 642 7120), customers can pick up a tray and tongs and choose from a selection of crazy-colored sugar cookies, quivering flan and pan de muerto, the Bread of the Dead, a traditional sweet bun made for the Día de los Muertos festivals in late October and early November.

SIGHTS

at **826 Valencia** (*see p211*). It's said that owner Dave Eggers, bestselling author and the brains behind publishing house McSweeny's, opened the shop to meet a commercial storefront zoning code: in reality, its main purpose is as a support for the center for young writers located inside.

The Mission's reputation as a kind of art colony-cum-neighborhood is evident in the numerous galleries and performance stages in the area, the majority either on Valencia Street or just off it. The **Women's Building** (3543 18th Street, between Valencia & Guerrero Streets, 431 1180, www.womensbuilding.org) is home to a dozen feminist non-profit groups. Meanwhile, three groups on Valencia Street – **Artists' Television Access** (no.992, 824 3890, www.atasite.org), the **Marsh** (no.1062, 826 5750, www.themarsh.org) and **Intersection for the Arts** (no.446, 626 2787, www.theintersection.org) – offer a forum for genre-smashing filmmakers, actors, playwrights, artists and musicians.

The three-block stretch of 16th Street between Mission and Dolores Streets is packed with colorful hangouts, although most are a bit heavier on bohemian atmosphere than they are on taste. Still, a walk along 16th will lead you to the building that gave the city its name: the 225-year-old Misión San Francisco de Asís, better known as **Mission Dolores** (*see below*).

Just south of here, bordered by Dolores, Church, 18th and 20th Streets, is **Mission Dolores Park**. There's great people- and dog-watching during the day; when it's warm, sunbathers line the park's upper end, earning it the nickname Dolores Beach. Summer evenings offer free film screenings (www.sfntf.org; *see also p216* **Films alfresco**), often of classic, SF-centric flicks, but bring a sensible coat and blanket: contrary to Eric Burdon of the Animals' experience, there's no such thing as 'a warm San Franciscan night'.

★ Mission Dolores

3321 16th Street, at Dolores Street (621 8203, www.missiondolores.org). BART 16th Street/Metro J to Church/bus 22, 33. **Open** 9am-5pm daily. **Admission** $3-$5. **Credit** (groups only) AmEx, MC, V. **Map** p318 J10.

Founded by a tiny band of Spanish missionaries and soldiers in 1776, and completed 15 years later, Mission Dolores is the oldest structure in the city and San Francisco's Registered Landmark No.1. The building was originally called the Misión San Francisco de Asís (after St Francis of Assisi), and provided the town with its name. However, it takes its common name from Laguna de los Dolores, the long-gone lagoon on the shores of which it was allegedly built. Although the original mission became an expansive outpost, housing over 4,000 monks and converts, today only the tiny old church remains. The adobe structure, constructed from 16,000 earthen bricks and 4ft (1.2m) thick (a display at the back offers a peek inside the walls), survived the 1906 and 1989 earthquakes unscathed, while the new church next door crumbled. Small wonder that the cool, dim interior looks and feels authentic: almost everything about it is unreconstructed and original, from the redwood logs holding up the roof to the ornate altars brought from Mexico centuries ago. (The modern-day church next door is a 20th-century basilica with no real architectural significance; it does, however, handle all the mission's religious services.) A small museum on the mission premises offers volunteer-led tours. The picturesque, flower-filled cemetery contains the remains of California's first governor and the city's first mayor, as well as assorted Spanish settlers and the mass grave of 5,000 Costanoan Indians who died in their service. Film buffs may recall that in Hitchcock's *Vertigo*, an entranced Kim Novak led Jimmy Stewart to the gravestone of the mysterious Carlotta Valdes in this very cemetery. You won't find Carlotta's stone, though: it was a prop and was removed after filming.

► *For more about the founding of Mission Dolores, see p17.*

POTRERO HILL & BERNAL HEIGHTS

On the outskirts of the Mission, the quiet neighborhoods of **Potrero Hill** (loosely bordered by 16th Street, I-280, Cesar Chavez Avenue and Potrero Avenue) and **Bernal Heights** (south of the Mission) are often sunny, even when the rest of San Francisco is shrouded in fog. Home to a mix of young families, dog-walking lesbians and hipsters who've fled the Mission, both areas are a little off the beaten track, but boast compact, lively commercial districts.

On 18th Street at the peak of Potrero Hill, upscale yet friendly **Chez Papa Bistrot** (No.1401, 824 8210, www.chezpapasf.com) leads a small cadre of good neighborhood eateries that includes new locavore breakfast/lunch spot **Plow** (No.1299, 821 7569, www.eatatplow.com), and **Farley's** (No.1315 648 1545, www.farleys coffee.com), one of the city's most iconic coffeehouses. Meanwhile, local bar **Bloom's Saloon,** (no.1318, 552 6707) is a low-key place to knock back a drink while drinking in the panoramic views from its back deck. Heading down the hill, the aptly named **Bottom of the Hill** (1233 17th Street, at Missouri Street; *see p241*) is the place to go for punk, metal and rockabilly bands and/or a seat on the patio, while the beautiful **Anchor Brewery** (1705 Mariposa Street, between Carolina & De Haro Streets, 863 8350, www.anchorbrewing.com) has an illustrious history as a pioneer of the American craft brewing movement. It created its first brew in 1896, and bottled its first 200 cases of Anchor

Harvey's.

Steam beer in 1971. Today, it produces various beers and spirits, including the much-admired Junipero Gin and Old Potrero Whiskey. Informative tours (ending in the tasting room, of course) take place twice a day, by reservation only (call four to six weeks in advance).

Bernal Heights, meanwhile, boasts an eclectic mix of bars, restaurants and shops on and around Cortland Avenue, including attitude-free lesbian spot **Wild Side West** (No.424, at Bennington Street, 647 3099), which welcomes patrons of all genders and proclivities. Those with energy to burn can hike up the hill to **Bernal Park**, a car-free stretch that affords spectacular 360° views of the city and Bay.

THE CASTRO

The Castro is an international gay center. Being gay is the norm here; straights are welcome, but, for once, they're in the minority. Along this rainbow-flag-festooned stretch of trendy shops and see-and-be-seen cafés and bars, most of them gay-owned, a predominantly male populace enjoys a hard-won social and political influence.

A working-class Irish-Catholic stronghold for nearly a century, the Castro changed rapidly in the 1970s, when gay residents began buying businesses and battered Victorian and Edwardian properties at rock-bottom prices, renovating them into what's now some of the city's prettiest and priciest real estate. No place exemplifies the change more than the landmark **Twin Peaks Tavern** (401 Castro Street, at Market Street, 864 9470, www.twinpeakstavern.com): its 1973 metamorphosis from traditional pub to gathering place for a mostly male and conspicuously gay clientele began just as the Castro was, so to speak, coming out. The bar's location on what was fast becoming the gayest corner of the gayest street in the country drew an ever-larger crowd, and socializing unashamedly behind its daring, pavement-fronting windows became more of a political act than a mere evening's entertainment. So strong was the sense of community in the area that the AIDS crisis of the 1980s and '90s proved to be a force as socially galvanizing as it was locally disastrous.

During the week, the Castro is a relatively quiet, cheerful neighborhood. On weekends, however (and, of course, during Pride Week), the area around Castro and 18th Streets is overrun with visitors and locals who come to mix it up at **Harvey's** (500 Castro Street, at 18th Street, 431 4278, www.harveyssf.com) or **Moby Dick's** (4049 18th Street, at Harford Street, 861 1199, www.mobydicksf.com), and revel in the exuberantly queer party atmosphere.

A huge rainbow flag flies over **Harvey Milk Plaza** (the Muni stop at the corner of Market and Castro Streets), named after the camera-shop owner and activist who, in 1977, became San Francisco's city supervisor and the first openly gay elected official in the US, but was assassinated the following year. The **GLBT History Museum**, the first of its kind in the US, opened in 2011 near the site of Milk's old camera shop at 575 Castro Street. He is also remembered around the area in the names of a school, a library and a community center. *See also right* **Streets of San Francisco**.

The other must-see local landmark is the dazzling art deco **Castro Theatre** (*see p213*). Constructed in 1922, it's one of the few American movie palaces that has remained in constant operation. It was designed by noted Bay Area architect Timothy L Pflueger, and became the 100th structure to be designated a US National Historic Landmark, 55 years after its completion. The theater (motto: an acre of seats in a palace of dreams) has retained its original vibe, with an organist hunched over the mighty Wurlitzer pipe organ banging out show tunes before each night's screening. Programming includes large-scale film festivals, premières, themed film series and new prints of classic movies.

For a great view of the Castro from above, get lunch to go and wander up to **Corona Heights** – walk all the way up 16th Street to Flint Street, then take a right; the bare red rock of Corona will loom overhead. Along with beautiful vistas, you'll see plenty of Castro pooches out with their humans. And if you've got tinies in tow, you can also check out the animal exhibits and miniature railroad at the **Randall Museum** (199 Museum Way, 554 9609, www.randallmuseum.org).

Streets of San Francisco Castro

The hub of the city's gay life.

If everyone didn't know that San Francisco was the capital of the gay world, and that Castro Street was the capital of gay San Francisco, they'd take the hint when they saw the massive rainbow flag – symbol of gay pride – cracking in the breeze above the corner of Market and Castro Streets. It was here, on 25 June 1978, that the prototype of the flag, hand-dyed by San Francisco artist Gilbert Baker, was first flown. It marked not only the heart of the neighborhood, but the center of a community that has given San Francisco a large part of its identity.

Castro's transformation into a gay hub, begun in the 1960s, really became visible in the '70s. Among those buying homes and businesses in the area was Harvey Milk, who moved to San Francisco in 1972 with his partner, Scott Smith, and opened a camera store on Castro Street. Over the next few years Milk became active in the gay rights movement and in local politics, running for the San Francisco Board of Supervisors. Despite being defeated twice, Milk became a prominent voice of the gay community, known as the 'Mayor of Castro Street'. It was at his third attempt, in 1977, that Milk finally became what *Time* magazine referred to as 'the first openly gay man elected to any substantial political office in the history of the planet'. Castro Street politics were now mainstream politics.

Tragically, the victory was short-lived. Dan White, a former member of the Board, approached San Francisco mayor George Moscone on 27 November 1978 with a plea to be reinstated. When his request was denied, White shot and killed the mayor. He reloaded, went to Milk's office and shot him five times. At trial, White's lawyers contended that his severe depression – as evidenced by increased consumption of Twinkies and Coca-Cola – meant he had diminished responsibility for his actions. The 'Twinkie defense', as the press went dubbed it, appeared to work. White was found guilty of manslaughter rather than murder, and sentenced to just seven years. Outraged, members of the gay community marched on City Hall, igniting the White Night Riots. Later that same evening, the police came to Castro Street to carry on the fight, storming the Elephant Walk bar at Castro and 18th Streets (now Harvey's) and beating up patrons.

Milk's shop premises at 575 Castro Street have been restored, and there's a plaque in front, as well as a mural honoring Milk, completed in September 2007. Fearful of assassination, Milk had recorded audiotapes outlining his political stance and how he wished to be remembered if he met a violent death. In the mural, a pistol is aimed at Milk's head and appears to fire the words of his eerily prescient statement: 'If a bullet should enter my brain, let the bullet destroy every closet door.'

NOE VALLEY

Quaint **Noe Valley**, roughly bordered by 20th, Dolores, 30th and Douglass Streets, is a self-contained village cut off from the rest of the city by steep hills on every side. In the 1970s it housed a fairly bohemian mix of straight, gay, working-class and white-collar residents, before growing more family-oriented in the 1980s and '90s – a place to which well-paid young couples could retreat to raise a family away from the chaos of the rest of the city. **Twin Peaks** overlooks the area from the west and its flanks offer attractive views of the East Bay.

Noe's main shopping strip, 24th Street, is substantially different from its funky brother that stretches east of Mission Street. This part of 24th is outfitted with all the amenities you might expect: streetside cafés, romantic restaurants and boutiques where owners and regulars are on first-name terms. The **24th Street Cheese Company** (No.3893, 821 6658) has a massive selection of cheeses, both local and international, along with a variety of snacks and charcuterie. For mystery buffs, a stop at the **San Francisco Mystery Book Store** (No.4175, at Castro Street, 282 7444, www.sfmysterybooks.com) is a must. Selling nothing but mystery and true crime books for more than 30 years, the staff have an encyclopaedic grasp of the genre. Just across the street is the cozy **Firefly** (no.4288, at Douglass Street, 821 7652, www.fireflyrestaurant.com), whose warm atmosphere, carefully chosen wine list and amazingly affordable three-course prix fixe menu make it the perfect place for a romantic end to the day. A few blocks off the main drag, **Lovejoy's Antiques & Tea Room** (1351 Church Street, at Clipper Street, 648 5895, www.lovejoystearoom.com) seems to think it's in the Lake District, complete with Victorian high teas. It's a little bit out of the way, but **Mitchell's Ice Cream** (688 San José Street, at 29th Street, 648 2300, www.mitchellsicecream.com) arguably serves the city's best.

DOGPATCH

Located on the east side of Potrero Hill along 22nd and Third Streets, Dogpatch is a formerly industrial neighborhood of dry docks and steel mills that escaped the rampages of the 1906 earthquake with most of its gorgeous Victorians intact. In recent years, an influx of artists and entrepreneurs, attracted by low rents, live-work lofts, and a new light-rail line, has transformed the district into something of a boho Bowery, with a rapidly growing cache of hip restaurants and bars, local cottage industries, design studios, chocolatiers, and even a brewery. Stop in at **Piccino** (1001 Minnesota Street at 22nd Street, 824 4224, www.piccinocafe.com) for exquisitely thin pizzettas topped with seasonal ingredients; **Serpentine** (2495 Third Street, 252 2000, www.serpentinesf.com) champions the farm-to-table movement with offerings such as a housemade charcuterie platter and gnocchi with baby fava leaves, hedgehog mushrooms, and English peas. Across the street, **Yield Wine Bar** (2490 Third Street, 401 8984, www.yieldsf.com) serves a fantastic selection of organic and biodynamic wines by the glass. Or if you prefer beer, the yet-to-be-formally-named **Magnolia Brewery** (www.magnoliapub.com), an outpost of the beloved Haight Street brewpub, is set to open on Third Street, next to artisanal ice-cream shop **Mr & Mrs Miscellaneous** (699 22nd Street, at 3rd Street) in 2011.

Dogpatch.

The Haight & Around

Once hippie central, today just a few traces of a radical past remain.

Mention the words Haight-Ashbury, or even just 'the Haight', and members of a certain generation will either sigh with nostalgic longing or groan in exasperation, depending on their political persuasion and/or their psychological or physical proximity to 1967's legendary Summer of Love. However, once the crowds had tuned out, turned off and dropped back in again, the neighborhood resumed duty as one of the most liveable in San Francisco.

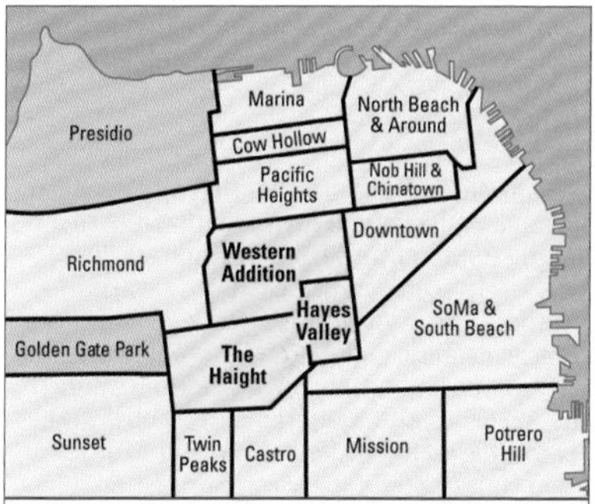

Bordering the Haight, the Western Addition has alternately been the heart of the West Coast jazz scene and the center of its Japanese community, while Hayes Valley has emerged as an enclave of considerable hipness.

Map p317, p318
Hotels p129
Restaurants & Cafés p155
Bars p173

THE HAIGHT

The Haight's history is written in its Victorian buildings, many of them painstakingly restored and elaborately painted. Despite being three miles from the ocean, the neighborhood was considered a beach town in the mid 19th century and many wealthy families from Nob Hill kept vacation homes here. In 1870, the first San Francisco Park Commission was appointed. As development began on Golden Gate Park, the neighboring Haight began to expand, and it was to thrive still further in the years following the 1906 earthquake, from which it emerged relatively unscathed.

As the 1950s phenomenon of 'white flight' swept through urban areas, families left for the suburbs, and the Victorian houses of the Haight were increasingly left both vacant and affordable. Inevitably, the city's students and post-war bohemian culture kids moved in. An offshoot of the North Beach beat scene of the late 1950s, the Haight went on to become the epicenter of hippie culture, the most famous youth movement in history. The beats, however, were scornful of the monied, pleasure-seeking hippies, considering them a kind of 'beatnik-lite': the word 'hippie' is itself said to have derived from a derogatory beatnik term meaning 'little hipster'.

In Berkeley and Oakland, the Free Speech and Black Power movements were already bringing a new political consciousness to the Bay Area. Duly inspired, the hippies were the driving force behind the anti-Vietnam War protests in San Francisco in the 1960s, and a new counterculture emerged. In January 1967, 25,000 gathered for the Human Be-In, a proto-hippie get-together that was the precursor to the Summer of Love. Yet after speed and heroin replaced marijuana and LSD as the drugs of choice, and free love turned into grim disaffection, unsavory sorts such as Charles Manson (who lived at 636 Cole Street) emerged as gurus to the impressionable youth, counteracting the work of idealistic political groups such as the Diggers, and guerrilla theater pioneers the San Francisco Mime Troupe, who still perform today and whose anti-war message has regained currency with the conflicts in Iraq and Afghanistan.

Just as the bold and the beautiful still flock to Hollywood from all over the world hoping to be 'discovered', so teenage runaways still gravitate to **Haight Street** looking for peace, love and understanding. Traces of the radical past linger at anarchist-run bookshop **Bound Together** (1369 Haight Street, at Masonic Avenue, 431 8355) and the **Haight-Ashbury Free Clinic**

(558 Clayton Street, at Haight Street), while the mellow coffeehouses hark back decades. Famous for its vehement anti-corporate stance (attempts to build a chain drugstore in 1988 were met with an arsonist's firebomb), the Haight appears to be turning over a new leaf with the opening of a **Whole Foods** at the corner of Haight and Stanyan streets, and the likely closure of a recycling center that has long served as an ersatz homeless hangout.

Haight-Ashbury

The stretch of Haight Street that sits between Masonic and Stanyan Streets, known both as Haight-Ashbury and Upper Haight, makes for a lively scene on weekends and warm-weather days. Stores hawk new age and Eastern esoterica, elaborate hand-blown glass smoking paraphernalia, edgy clothing, high-fashion shoes and mountains of records and CDs, not least at the vast **Amoeba Music** (1855 Haight Street, between Shrader & Stanyan Streets, *see p200*). Shoppers also have to duck the buskers and bums, who add more local flavor than some tourists were expecting. Just west of Amoeba, across Stanyan Street, is **Golden Gate Park**. A couple of blocks north is the **Panhandle**, the park's grand entrance; at the height of the hippie era, local bands that went on to fill stadiums (the Grateful Dead, Janis Joplin *et al*) played free shows here.

More evidence of the neighborhood's past can be found at the charming **Red Victorian B&B** (1665 Haight Street, between Clayton & Cole Streets, *see p130*), which not long ago added a coffee shop and retail space; the independent **Red Vic Movie House** (1727 Haight Street, at Cole Street, *see p213*); the groovy tie-dye shop **Positively Haight Street** (1427 Haight Street, 252 8747), and the **Magnolia** brewpub (1398 Haight Street, at Masonic Avenue, *see p174*). This former pharmacy served as a hippie haven called the Drogstore Café [sic] back in the 1960s, before becoming the base for Magnolia Thunderpussy and her erotically themed desserts. The new owners named their brewpub in her honor and covered the walls in psychedelic 1960s murals.

At the corner of Haight Street and Central Avenue is the aptly named, beautifully wooded **Buena Vista Park**, the oldest designated park in the city and the unofficial eastern terminus of Upper Haight. In 1867, when the land was still known as Hill Park, the city paid squatters $88,250 (equivalent to around $1.1 million today) to gain rights to the park. It was a wise investment, not only for the city, but in terms of the example it set for the zealous culture of land preservation that still flourishes today across northern California. The paths on the west side of the park are lined with marble gutters and a retaining wall built by WPA workers using Victorian headstones, some laid face up with their inscriptions visible. The walk to the park's 589-foot (180-meter) peak is worth the effort: the views over the city and (on clear days) out to the Golden Gate Bridge and Marin Headlands are commanding.

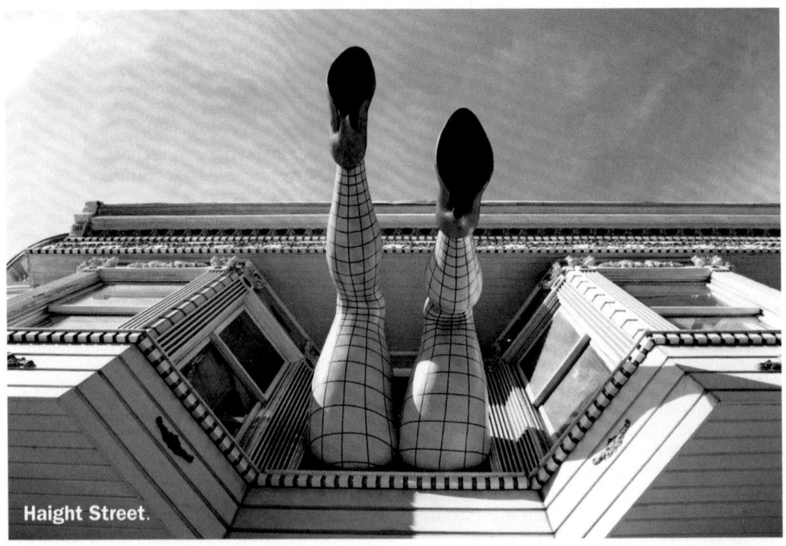

Haight Street.

Cole Valley

It's only a few blocks from the bustle of Haight-Ashbury, but the cozy enclave of Cole Valley is a different world altogether: low-key, smart and upscale. The businesses here are all clustered around a two-block area of Cole and Carl Streets. **Zazie** (941 Cole Street, at Carl Street, 564 5332, www.zaziesf.com) is a great spot for brunch or lunch; **Le Boulange de Cole** (1000 Cole Street, at Parnassus Street, 242 2442) serves own-made pastries, breads and small baguette sandwiches.

Alternatively, you can pick up supplies from **Say Cheese** (856 Cole Street, at Carl Street, 665 5020), which sells vast selections of gourmet cheeses, meats and wines, and enjoy a picnic on **Tank Hill**. Head one block west from Cole Street to Shrader Street and continue south up the hill until you reach Belgrave Street; turn left (east) on to Belgrave and take the rustic stairway at the end of the street to the top of the hill. It's a bit of a slog, but worth the effort. Once home to a water tank (hence the name), the 650-foot (200-meter) peak offers some of the city's best views.

LOWER HAIGHT

While Upper Haight still clings dreamily to its political past, the young, the disenchanted and the progressive have migrated down the hill to Lower Haight, on and around Haight Street between Divisadero and Octavia Streets. The area's main intersection is at Haight and Fillmore Streets, from which fashion shops, tattoo parlors, funky bars, and ethnic eateries radiate in all directions. Beer-lovers would do well to try **Toronado** (547 Haight Street, between Fillmore & Steiner Streets, *p174*). It doesn't serve food, but you can get gourmet sausages next door at the Rosamunde Sausage Grill (545 Haight Street, 437 6851) and take them to the bar.

The **Western Addition** was not only the city's first suburb, but also its first multicultural neighborhood. Mapped out in the 1860s to accommodate the post-Gold Rush population boom, the area was home to a thriving Jewish community in the 1890s. After the 1906 earthquake, the Fillmore District, the area's heart, sprang to life as displaced residents, many of them Japanese, began arriving.

After the Japanese had been sent to internment camps following Pearl Harbor, thousands of black Southerners, who had come west for work, moved into their houses. Because the area didn't observe the racial covenant laws that prevented African Americans from owning land elsewhere in the city, the Western Addition soon developed into what became known as the 'Harlem of the West'.

Today, it still has a very distinct character, with a mix of African Americans, Russian seniors, immigrants from other countries and UCSF students who live in everything from amazing Victorians – some of the oldest in the city – to bland highrises. Gentrification is slowly creeping in, but the area's shopping

Streets of San Francisco Haight

They were going to remake the world, starting here.

For most people, the Haight-Ashbury didn't exist before the Summer of Love. But in reality, it was in the years just prior to that vaunted summer of '67 that the Haight truly shone – a magnet for many talents that combined to produce an unprecedented explosion in virtually all forms of art, political discourse, and even healthcare. The trouble was that as word spread about the new world of the Haight, people started to pour in – mainly to drop out – and Haight Street and the area surrounding it, arguably the world's most fecund artists' colony, turned into a kind of hippie refugee camp virtually overnight.

To hear it told by the people who lived through it, being a part of the Haight scene prior to the invasion was the closest thing to bathing in a primordial ooze of creativity (not to mention LSD). What really made the time and place unique, though, was how those many strands of creativity were fused together by a shared pursuit – re-imagining what society could be.

Legions of people who are now household names lived in close proximity. Walking down Haight Street, one might encounter the likes of the **Grateful Dead**, **Jefferson Airplane**, or **Janis Joplin**. The father of underground comics, **Robert Crumb**, might be scribbling away somewhere, while visionary musician **Frank Zappa** was hunched over a score with collaborator **Captain Beefheart**. Howl poet **Allen Ginsberg** (who once lived at 1360 Fell Street) might be found wandering the park in a trance. One might bump into **Steve Miller** (in his pre-Steve Miller Band days), or **Jimi Hendrix** (he lived at 1524A Haight Street), **Sly and the Family Stone**, **Carlos Santana**, or **Crosby, Stills and Nash**.

Those strapped for cash could visit the Free Store run by the **Diggers**, a semi-anarchic group dedicated to turning the Haight into a barter society, or get medical help at the **Haight-Ashbury Free Clinic**. The Hell's Angels' clubhouse, meanwhile, was located across the street from the Grateful Dead's residence. (Although the Angels no longer own the building, the gang still starts its annual Thanksgiving run from the People's Café on Haight Street).

In his seminal *Fear and Loathing in Las Vegas*, **Hunter S Thompson**, who lived at 318 Parnassus Street, delivered a eulogy to the San Francisco of the '60s: 'There was a fantastic universal sense that whatever we were doing was right, that we were winning,' he wrote. 'And that, I think, was the handle – that sense of inevitable victory over the forces of Old and Evil... Our energy would simply prevail... We had all the momentum; we were riding on the crest of a high and beautiful wave...'

remains mostly chain-free. The stretch of Divisadero Street between Page and Fulton Streets holds a number of notable stops, including the **Independent** club (no.628, at Hayes Street) and the bar-restaurant **Club Waziema** (no.543, at Fell Street, 346 6641), which offers honey wine, Harar beer and Ethiopian food. The most notable addition to the area, meanwhile, is **Nopa** (no.560, 864 8643; *see p156*), shorthand for North of the Panhandle and one of the hottest restaurants in town, with a cuisine and a clientele that embodies a whole new neighborhood aesthetic.

At the corner of Divisadero and Fulton, past the incense emporiums and African American barbershops, sit yet more notable businesses, including **Café Abir** (No.1300, *see p156*; beer and magazines),**Tsunami** (No.1306, 567 7664; sushi and saké) and, serving some of the best pizza in the city, **Little Star Pizza** (846 Divisadero Street, 441 1118, www.littlestarpizza.com).

Alamo Square

San Francisco is crammed full of handsome Victorian-era houses (commonly known as 'Victorians'). However, most tourists choose not to roam the city and discover them at random; instead, they head to the 'Postcard Row' of tidy pastel Victorians on the east side of Alamo Square, which are juxtaposed wonderfully against the sweeping view of Downtown behind them. While these 'Painted Ladies' are certainly the most famous (they're featured in numerous films and TV shows), there are other fine Victorians nearby to visit, chiefly the ornate Italianate **Westerfeld House**, at the corner of Fulton and Scott Streets, which dates back to 1882; and the **Chateau Tivoli** (1057 Steiner Street at Golden Gate Avenue), an opulent 1892 Victorian mansion that is now a bed and breakfast inn.

The Fillmore District

The Fillmore neighborhood was a mecca for jazz and blues musicians in the 1940s and '50s. Several albums, among them Miles Davis's 1961 *In Person* recordings at the Blackhawk club, are testament to its pedigree. However, the locale was declared a slum by the San Francisco Redevelopment Agency in the 1960s and torn apart under the guise of urban renewal.

Happily, new life is being slowly and steadily breathed into the area. In 2007, the San Francisco branch of the much-loved Oakland-based **Yoshi's Jazz Club** (1330 Fillmore Street, at Eddy Street, *see p228*) opened here with a 400-seat venue and trademark sushi restaurant, followed a year later by jazz/R&B club and Ethiopian restaurant, **Rasselas** (647 Valencia Street, at Geary Boulevard, *see p238*).

The legendary **Fillmore Auditorium** (1805 Geary Boulevard, at Fillmore Street, *see p239*) is still going strong, booking top-flight rock and independent acts. So close you can almost hear the ghosts is the now-defunct Winterland (formerly at the north-west corner of Post and Steiner Streets), where The Band filmed *The Last Waltz* and Johnny Rotten asked the audience 'Ever get the feeling you've been cheated?' at the final Sex Pistols show in 1978 (Sid Vicious endured a non-fatal overdose at the Haight's 32 Delmar Street following the show).

Yards away, on the wall of the **Hamilton Recreation Center** at the corner of Post and Steiner, is a huge musical mural, created by local musician and painter Santie Huckaby. The mural features dozens of musicians with an SF connection: some lived here, some simply played here, and one, bluesman John Lee Hooker, even opened his own club here. Hooker died in 2001, but the **Boom Boom Room** (1601 Fillmore Street, at Geary Boulevard, *see p237*) lives on. Next to the Fillmore Auditorium, at 1849 Geary Boulevard, is an eerier landmark. A post office has stood here in recent years, but from 1971 to

Alamo Square.

1977 this site was the home of the notorious Jim Jones and his People's Temple. Despite running his own legendarily cultish church, Jones was a respectable citizen. However, when reports emerged of physical and sexual abuse within the church, he moved it from here to a settlement he named Jonestown located in French Guyana. The following year, Jones and almost 1,000 disciples, the majority former Fillmorites, committed mass suicide or were murdered in the now-infamous Jonestown Massacre.

JAPANTOWN

Three commercial blocks and a compound-like shopping mall are all that remains of what once may have been the US's largest Japanese community. Devastated by the forced relocation of Japanese Americans to internment camps during World War II, the community is now home to only a tiny percentage of the city's 12,000 Japanese Americans. But the locale still provides support for the elderly, history lessons for the young, and a banquet of aesthetic and pop-culture delights for anyone interested.

At the heart of Japantown is the **Japan Center**, a mostly underground maze of shops, restaurants and unique businesses that cater to Japanese residents. The **Kinokuniya Bookstore** (1581 Webster Street, 567 7625) is a fascinating clearing-house of J-pop culture, comics and Japanese-language books, while **Paper Tree** (1743 Buchanan Mall, 921 7100, www.paper-tree.com) specializes in origami supplies. The **Sundance Kabuki Theater** (1881 Post Street, at Fillmore Street, 929 4650, www.sundancecinemas.com), is the flagship cinema of actor/activist Robert Redford's film company. Seven screens with stadium seating feature the latest independent films and the winners of Redford's renowned Sundance Film Festival. There are two bars inside; the one at the top offers wine, beer, and a light fare menu, which you can bring on to the theater balcony.

To gain a bit of cultural context on the area, visit the **National Japanese American Historical Society** (684 Post Street, between Buchanan & Laguna Streets, 921 5007, www.nikkeiheritage.org) or the nearby **Japanese American Community Center** (1840 Sutter Street, at Webster Street, 567 5505, www.jcccnc.org), which hosts exhibitions on the Japanese-American way of life. To the east of the Japan Center, meanwhile, is the impressively modern Cathedral of St Mary of the Assumption.

FREE Cathedral of St Mary of the Assumption

1111 Gough Street, at Geary Boulevard (567 2020, www.stmarycathedralsf.org). Bus 2, 3, 4, 38. **Open** 6.45am-4pm Mon-Fri, Sun; 6.45am-5.30pm Sat. **Admission** free.

Dominating the skyline, the exterior of this 1970 cathedral is stark, a flowing, sculptural structure (some say it resembles the blades of a washing machine) reaching 198ft (60m) into the sky. The four corner pylons were designed to support millions of pounds of pressure and extend 90ft (27m) down to the bedrock beneath the church. Inside, the staggering structure of the cupola is revealed in 1,500 triangular coffers, in over 128 sizes, meant to distribute the weight of the roof. The trumpets of the huge organ, on a raised pedestal that floats above the congregation, appear capable of blasting down the walls of Jericho. Large corner windows allow views of the city.

HAYES VALLEY

Hayes Valley, just west of the Civic Center, was literally overshadowed by the Central Freeway for years. But when the 1989 earthquake irreparably damaged the roadway, its demolition transformed the area from a drug- and prostitution-riddled slum to perhaps the hippest urban shopping area in town (*see p185* **Knocked Down & Up Again**). Streets that once sat under a tangle of concrete overpasses now have sidewalk cafés, boutiques, galleries and even **True Sake** (560 Hayes Street, at Laguna Street, *see p194*), a specialist saké shop.

The locals know how good they've got it. The community association is active here, and gets results: it has fought to keep out the chains (current score: Hayes Valley 1, Starbucks 0), won the battle to close the major Fell Street highway off-ramp, and established a little tree-lined boulevard along Street that features rotating sculpture exhibits. During the day, Hayes Street gets busy with well-dressed couples shopping for modernist furniture and Italian shoes, and brunching on champagne and oysters at **Absinthe** (no.388, at Gough Street, *see p157*), a belle époque French restaurant with tables spilling on to the pavement. Don't miss the stretch of Market Street between Gough Street and Van Ness Avenue, a shopping hub for deco antiques and upmarket accessories. But be wary of walking west of Laguna Street at night: the area changes abruptly and can occasionally feel a bit dicey.

Based in the city for three decades, the **African Orthodox Church of St John Coltrane** at 1286 Fillmore Street (at Eddy Street, 673 7144, www.coltranechurch.org) continues to hold jazz-driven services – Coltrane's seminal invocation of the divine, 'A Love Supreme', is the key work – every Sunday at noon.

Sunset, Golden Gate Park & Richmond

Fog, forest, ethnic food and ocean waves.

To many visitors, and some San Franciscans, the Richmond and Sunset districts are largely unexplored areas that sandwich the verdant expanse of Golden Gate Park, one of San Francisco's greatest attractions. And that's fine with the residents, who tend to be a bit more unassuming, a bit less concerned with appearances and a bit more welcoming than those in other neighborhoods. This happy melange of active immigrant communities, students, families, working-class folk and, by the ocean, surfers, also enjoys the city's very best coastal trails. Less touristy, less flashy and more foggy: for some, this is the real San Francisco.

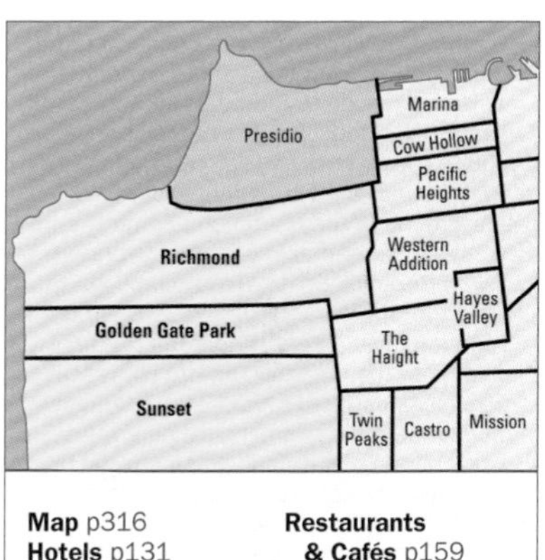

Map p316
Hotels p131
Restaurants & Cafés p159
Bars p174

SIGHTS

SUNSET & FURTHER SOUTH

This large southern neighborhood, west of the Haight and south of Golden Gate Park, usually belies its own name. The sunsets in the Sunset are more often than not swathed in fog from June to September, and often in other months too. But if you are able to catch a fair day, they can be spectacular.

The stretch of **Irving Street** between 5th and 10th Avenues, in an area informally known as the **Inner Sunset**, is the area's shopping corridor. Just off Irving on 9th Avenue sit two fine eateries: sushi stop **Ebisu** (no.1283, 566 1770, www.ebisusushi.com), and **Park Chow** (no.1240, 665 9912, www.chowrestaurant.com). However, the Sunset's main attractions are way out west, where the turf meets the surf. Perhaps chief among them is thin, sandy **Ocean Beach** (*see p102* **Life's a Beach**), which runs for three and a half miles south from the **Cliff House** (*see p96*). It's a good spot for a contemplative wander, to spend time watching the surfers (who sometimes count Sunset homeowner and rocker Chris Isaak among their number) battling strong rip tides and chilly water. Take a warming break either over coffee at the **Java Beach Café** (*see p159*) or with a garlic whole-roasted crab at Vietnamese restaurant **Thanh Long** (4101 Judah Street, at 46th Avenue, 665 1146, www.anfamily.com).

The southernmost point of Ocean Beach is marked by **Fort Funston**, a large natural area in the far south-west of the city. The reservation is criss-crossed with hiking trails, promontories and jagged beaches, and is both a favorite place for local dog-walkers and a point from which hang gliders launch themselves above the waves.

Just over a mile north of Fort Funston is **San Francisco Zoo** (*see p208*), one of very few zoos to house koalas. Beyond the zoo is refurbished **Harding Municipal Park**

Walk Panhandle to the Pacific

Cultural meets pastoral in Golden Gate Park.

Start your tour of Golden Gate Park at the **McLaren Lodge** (John F Kennedy Drive, 831 2700). Once the residence of John McLaren, the lodge is now the site of the park offices and visitors' center (open 8am-5pm Mon-Fri). Strike out south from the lodge down the tree-lined path running parallel to Stanyan Street, bearing right until you come to **Alvord Lake**. Keep right by the lake and pass under Alvord Lake Bridge, which dates to 1889. It was the first reinforced concrete bridge in the US and one of few bridges to survive the 1906 earthquake, vindicating its builder's then-controversial faith in concrete construction.

Head through to Mothers' Meadow until you reach a fork. The left branch brings you to the inventively restored **Children's Playground**, the oldest municipal playground in the nation and home to the 62 hand-painted animals of the wonderful 1912 Herschel-Spillman Carousel. North, past the Sharon Art Building, is Sharon Meadow. You'll hear **Hippie Hill**, in the middle of the meadow, before you see it. The hill became the heart of the Summer of Love; the never-ending pick-up drum jams on the hill are still going strong.

Follow the path north to the tennis courts and continue round their right-hand side. Cross John F Kennedy Drive after you emerge from the trees to take in the gleaming, white-domed **Conservatory of Flowers** up to your left. Badly damaged by a storm in 1995, it reopened to considerable excitement in 2003 after an eight-year $25-million restoration. The oldest glass-and-wood Victorian greenhouse in the western hemisphere, it's home to more than 10,000 plants.

Take the stairs up to JFK Drive and head along Middle East Drive. On your left is the 7.5-acre **National AIDS Memorial Grove**. It bears the names of some of the city's nearly 20,000 dead engraved in stone amid redwoods, oaks and maples. (For a guided tour, call 750 8340.) Opposite, a path leads north to the lovely **Lily Pond**. Follow it round the west side to the crossroads. On the right, a grove of ferns dates to 1898. Head straight on, taking the footpath to your left that parallels JFK Drive, to another botanical delight: the **John McLaren Rhododendron Dell**. Lovingly restored following the same storm that damaged the Conservatory of Flowers, it holds a statue of McLaren himself.

Here you have a choice: carry on west towards the **De Young Museum** (*see p94*) before heading south, or amble south along leafy walkways to the **California Academy of Sciences** complex (*see p94*). From either venue, walk across the Music Concourse (free concerts Sunday afternoons Apr-Sept) to reach the **Japanese Tea Garden** (752 1171, $3.50). Built in 1893 for the Exposition, the landmark garden – ironically, the spot where the Chinese fortune cookie is said to have been invented – still delights visitors with its steep bridges, bonsai, huge

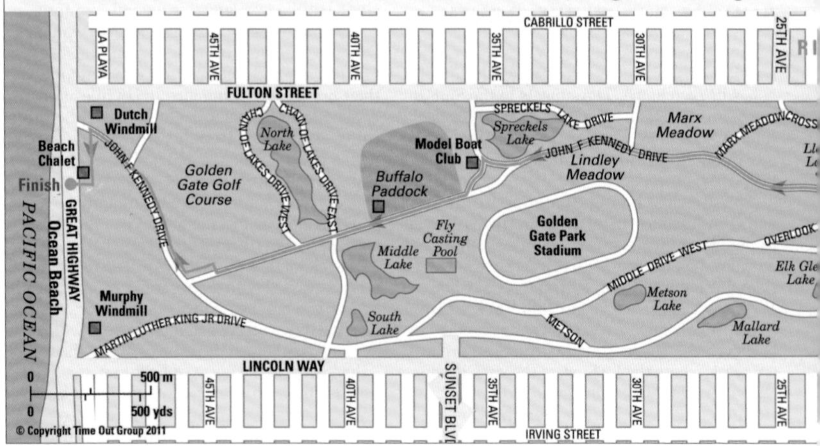

bronze Buddha and outdoor tearoom with kimono-clad servers. Another nice stopping-off point is the **Strybing Arboretum & Botanical Gardens** (661 1316), which house some 7,000 species from diverse climates. There's a fragrant garden designed for the visually impaired and a particularly appealing moon-viewing garden.

Return to MLK Drive, head west up the hill and take the stairs to **Stow Lake**. Wandering along the broad path on the south side of the lake, you'll come to the Rustic Bridge: cross here to explore **Strawberry Hill** island and its **Chinese pavilion**. A gift from the people of Taipei, it was shipped in 6,000 pieces and reassembled here in 1981. Head round the lake to the **Boathouse**, where paddle boats, canoes and bicycles are available for rent.

From the Boathouse walk north. Pick up the path to the left of the restrooms across the parking lot, and you'll come out opposite **Rainbow Falls** and the **Prayer Book Cross**, which commemorates Sir Francis Drake's chaplain offering up prayers during a brief stay in the Bay Area in 1579. Follow the little waterway west under Cross Over Drive Bridge and across Transverse Drive to Lloyd Lake and the **Portals of the Past**, the only memorial in the city devoted to the 1906 earthquake and fire. The ornate marble archway that now stands here was once the front entrance to the Towne Mansion at 1101 California Street; it was the last structure left standing in Nob Hill following the great fire. From there JFK Drive takes you through meadows offering plenty of picnicking opportunities. After about half a mile, you'll come to **Spreckels Lake**, with its ducks and model sailing boats.

When you're ready, get back on to JFK (passing the San Francisco Model Yacht Club on your right) and press ever west. Almost immediately, on your right, you'll pass the large **Buffalo Paddock**, where a small herd of bison roams on a 'prairie.' Pass Chain of Lakes Drive West on your right and keep going for about five minutes. Just past the golf course, you'll find a pleasant tree-lined pedestrian path that will take you round to the north, and soon to **Queen Wilhelmina's Tulip Gardens**. A gift from the eponymous Dutch monarch in 1902, the garden is shaded by the commanding **Dutch Windmill**, which boasts the world's largest windmill wings. It functioned as a huge pump, feeding water to the verdant urban wonderland that is now Golden Gate Park but was once only sand dunes. The windmill underwent a $6.4-million restoration a few years ago that had it turning once more, but has since stopped again.

Head through the tunnel or across the road on one of the wooded paths and you'll shortly arrive at journey's end: the 80-year-old **Beach Chalet** and the new **Park Chalet** (*see p93*). Bus 5 will take you back to civilization.

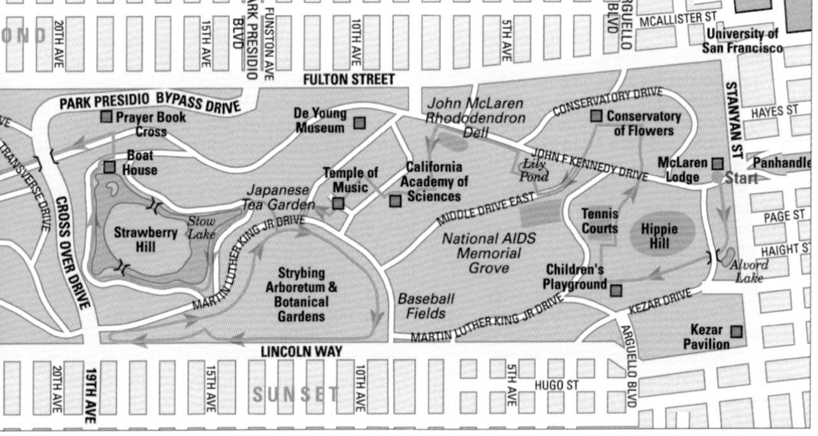

Ocean Beach. *See p89.*

& Golf Course (*see p252*). Cradled by picturesque Lake Merced and encircled by biking and jogging trails, the public course played host to the 2009 President's Cup. North of the lake is Stern Grove, just over 60 acres of eucalyptus and redwood that hosts the annual free **Stern Grove Festival** (*see p239*). Slightly further inland is **Mount Davidson**, which at 927 feet (283 metres) is the highest point in San Francisco. If you can ignore the enormous cross at its apex, the views are terrific. If you can't, you are not alone: the cross has been a source of controversy since it was first erected in 1923.

GOLDEN GATE PARK

Roughly three miles in length and half a mile wide, **Golden Gate Park** is one of the largest manmade parks in the world and a testament to human dominion over nature – or, put another way, a gargantuan project that introduced non-native species and used vast resources in ways that would never have been approved in modern day San Francisco. The ambitious task of creating this pastoral loveliness – a thousand acres of landscaped gardens, forests and meadows – from barren sand dunes began in 1870 in an attempt to solidify San Francisco's position as a modern urban center, to meet the growing public demand for a city park, and, on the part of the wealthy land speculators in the area, to stimulate property values.

William Ralston, founder of the Bank of California and builder of the Palace Hotel, first approached Frederick Law Olmsted, the visionary behind Manhattan's Central Park, to design the project. Believing that the arid landscape of the Outside Lands, as the virtually uninhabited area was then known, was a barren wasteland that could never support a park, Olmsted's original design instead proposed a green stretch that would take advantage of the large natural valley that ran through the city. However, once Olmsted left town, his plan was shelved; the valley is now Van Ness Avenue.

The project was next awarded to a young civil engineer named William Hammond Hall. The park's wealthy patrons, whose motives were more fiscal- than civic-minded, saw Hall as a sympathetic individual who would accede to their plans for the land development, and they were right. Hall's family was hooked into every level of government and industry, and many felt that he had been handed an impossible task. Olmsted even wrote to Hall, telling him that he 'did not believe it practicable to meet the natural but senseless demand of unreflecting people bred in the Atlantic states and the North of Europe for what is technically termed a park under the climatic conditions of San Francisco'.

Work continued, however, and while it cost the surrounding environment dearly, the result

INSIDE TRACK FREE MUSEUM DAYS

If you time it right, or happen to get lucky, you may be able to get into the city's five major museums for free: all offer free admission days once a month. In Golden Gate Park, the **De Young Museum** (*see p94*) and the **California Academy of Sciences** (*see p94*) are free the first Tuesday and third Wednesday every month, respectively. On the western edge of town, the **Legion of Honor** (*see p96*) offers free admission every first Tuesday. The **Asian Art Museum** (*see p56*) in Civic Center is free the first Sunday of every month. And south of Market Street, the **Museum of Modern Art** (*see p60*) is free the first Tuesday of the month, as well as offering half-price admission every Thursday evening, 6-8.45pm.

was clearly a marvel. Still, it wasn't until eccentric Scottish-born John McLaren took over stewardship in 1890 that the park finally came together. McLaren spent more than 50 years as park superintendent, expanding on Hall's innovations and planting by stages, to allow what are now the lakes, meadows and forests of the park to evolve in ways that would allow the substrate to sustain them. In the process, he was responsible for planting more than a million trees.

The park's public debut occurred in 1894, when more than 1.3 million people visited for the Midwinter International Exposition. Covering 200 acres, the six-month fair filled more than 100 temporary buildings. Two still remain: the **Japanese Tea Garden** and the **Music Concourse**. As the park's fame spread, horticulturalists from all over the world sent in seeds and cuttings. Today, a rose garden, a Shakespeare garden, a rhododendron dell and a tulip garden are among the living delights.

Sampling all that the park has to offer, from the assorted natural attractions to the violently modern new **De Young Museum** (*see p94*), would take days. The prospect is even more daunting when one adds in the natural history museum, the **California Academy of Sciences** (*see p94*), which was transformed in 2008 into the world's greenest museum.

However, one great way to see it over the course of a single afternoon is to stroll all the way from the entrance of the park along the pedestrian footpaths beside John F Kennedy Drive, the park's main east–west artery, to the ocean. It takes a few hours if you stop along the way, but your reward will be the crashing waves of the Pacific. If you prefer to travel on wheels, then bikes and in-line skates can be hired from various locations. Indeed, if you join the throngs of locals biking, walking, jogging and in-line skating along JFK Drive on a Sunday afternoon, when the road is closed to traffic, you'll soon understand why the park is known as San Francisco's collective backyard.

If you're planning on entering Golden Gate Park from Haight-Ashbury, you can do so at the west end of Haight Street by crossing Stanyan Street. Otherwise, come in via the Panhandle, a couple of blocks north. This was once the grand entrance to the park, with paths wide enough to accommodate carriages. It brings you out next to the park headquarters in McLaren Lodge, where you can pick up information. For a self-guided tour of the park, *see p90* **Walk**.

Beach Chalet & Park Chalet

1000 Great Highway (visitor center 751 2766, restaurant 386 8439, www.beachchalet.com). Bus 5, 18. **Open** *Visitor center & Beach Chalet* 9am-10.30pm daily. *Park Chalet* noon-10.30pm daily. **Credit** AmEx, DC, MC, V.

A perfect spot for sunset cocktails, the Beach Chalet, a historic Willis Polk-designed building on the coast, is home to a fine restaurant and brewpub. The ground-floor walls are awash in WPA (Works Progress Administration) frescoes by Lucien Labaudt depicting notable San Franciscans, among them sculptor Benny Bufano and John McLaren. The views of the ocean from upstairs are stupendous.

The newer Park Chalet, which faces Golden Gate Park, doesn't have the views of the Beach Chalet. But the mellow atmosphere makes it ideal for whiling away a sunny afternoon on the lawn in one of the Adirondack chairs. In the summer, the restaurant offers live music and an outdoor BBQ.

SIGHTS

Beach Chalet.

★ California Academy of Sciences

55 Concourse Drive (321 8000, www.cal academy.org). Bus 5, 44. **Open** 9.30am-5pm Mon-Sat; 11am-5pm Sun. **Admission** $29.95; $19.95-$24.95 reductions; free under-4s. Free 3rd Wed of mth. **Credit** AmEx, DC, MC, V. **Map** p316 B9.

The architecturally stunning natural history museum – the world's largest public LEED Platinum-rated building and its greenest museum – debuted in 2008 after a $500 million remodel. Renzo Piano's design, clearly inspired by the natural world, doesn't disappoint. The organically shaped living roof – a vast expanse of green, undulating domes – accommodates 1.7 million native flowers and plants that reduce energy needs for heating and cooling, convert carbon dioxide into oxygen, capture rainwater, and provide a habitat for dozens of species of birds and insects.

Inside, exhibits cover a huge spectrum of life on our planet – and worlds beyond. They include the country's largest planetarium; its 90ft-tall (27m) domed screen allows visitors to watch real-time NASA feeds. Elsewhere, the 212,000-gallon tank of the Steinhart Aquarium is home to 4,000 fish and 1,500 colonies of living coral. The four-story indoor rainforest takes visitors on a spiral walkway from ground level to above the tree canopy, where birds and butterflies fly free, then drops them via an elevator to the Amazon flooded basin, home to anacondas, piranhas and giant catfish, and to the aquarium. Other exhibits recreate an American subtropical swamp, with a rare albino alligator, and a zoological landscape of Africa with traditional dioramas and a live penguin display. The museum has an excellent café, with menus designed by renowned local chefs Charles Phan and Loretta Keller serving a variety of multicultural food options. The upscale Moss Room restaurant downstairs features a living, dripping moss wall and an all-organic and sustainable menu.

De Young Museum

50 Hagiwara Tea Garden Drive (863 3330, www.deyoung.famsf.org). Bus 5, 44. **Open** 9.30am-5.15pm Tue-Thur, Sat, Sun; 9.30am-8.45pm Fri. **Admission** $10; $6-$7 reductions; free under-12s. **Credit** AmEx, DC, MC, V. **Map** p316 B9.

The most prominent feature of this controversial future-primitive building, designed by Herzog & de Meuron, is the massive tower that emerges from the surrounding canopy of trees, making all those who approach from the 10th Avenue entrance to Golden Gate Park feel like the vanguard of an expedition that's just stumbled across an ancient lost city – or an abandoned mothership. Most people would agree that the design – seemingly a combination of extraterrestrial metals wedded to sharp angles and organic forms found in ancient structures – is at once overwhelming and electrifying. The exterior walls are made from patterned copper, designed to take on the color of the surrounding greenery as it oxidizes. Along with its vast collections of American art from the 17th to 20th centuries, the museum showcases an extensive collection from New Guinea and Oceania, as well as contemporary crafts and textiles. There's also an excellent store and café with outdoor seating areas in a delightful sculpture garden. With commanding views over the park, the soaring observation tower is worth the trip alone. The courtyard, café, store, sculpture garden and tower can be entered without paying the admission fee.

RICHMOND

Bordering the northern edge of Golden Gate Park, from beyond Arguello Boulevard to the Pacific Ocean, and from Fulton to California Streets, the largely residential neighborhood of Richmond is a highly flavored cultural mix, predominantly but not exclusively made up of Russian, Chinese and Irish immigrants. Once a sandy waterfront wasteland, the region was developed after the construction of the Geary Boulevard tramway in 1906. Eastern European Jews formed a strong community after World War I, and many of their synagogues and delicatessens still thrive.

The **University of San Francisco** and the peculiar **Columbarium** (*see p96*) hover at the easterly edge of the area, but **Clement Street** is the district's primary commercial center. Stretching from 2nd Avenue all the way to 34th Avenue, the area between Arguello and Park Presidio Boulevards arguably offers a more accessible Chinatown than the more famous one in the center of the city. Literary types have long been enamored of **Green Apple Books** (506 Clement Street, at 6th Avenue; *see p181*). Just a block north is **the Antique Traders** (4300 California Street, at 5th Avenue, 668 4444, www.theantiquetraders.com), whose breathtaking collection of stained-glass windows, salvaged from the city's many Victorians, has countless out-of-town shoppers calculating shipping costs. Tucked away behind the misleadingly tiny shopfront, **6th Ave Aquarium & Flowers** (425 Clement Street, between 5th & 6th Avenues, 668 7190, www.6thaveaquarium.com) is a store that offers a selection of sea creatures, among them dwarf jellyfish and bioluminescent shrimp, which swim through the cumulative 13,000 gallons of water in their tanks.

Speaking of shrimp, the takeout dumplings from **Good Luck Dim Sum** (no.736, at 8th Avenue, 386 3388) are authentic and cheap (you can get stuffed for under $5). Super-funky **Q Restaurant** (no.225, at 3rd Avenue; *see p160*) serves up American comfort food in a mildly surreal setting; the Burmese specialities at **Burma Superstar** (no.309, at 4th Avenue, 387 2147, www.burmasuperstar.com) are

Profile John McLaren

The quirky Scotsman who planted Golden Gate Park.

When Scottish horticulturalist John McLaren came to San Francisco in 1870, much of the land that would later become Golden Gate Park was a barren wasteland of sand dunes that few believed could ever sustain a single tree, let alone an entire park. Indeed, when civic leaders had asked landscape designer Frederick Law Olmsted (of Central Park fame) several years earlier to design a park on this stretch, he scoffed and said it couldn't be done. But the park's first superintendent, engineer William Hammond Hall, had faith. He hired McLaren as his assistant and within a few short years, McLaren had built two Dutch windmills near the ocean to pump water for irrigation. Slowly, a glorious greenbelt arose stretching from the Panhandle to the Pacific Ocean. McLaren had an uncanny instinct for cultivating plants that would thrive in the cool, damp local climate, as well as a strong belief that parks were places where people should freely mingle with nature, unencumbered by 'Keep off the grass' signs and imposing statuary. During his 53-year tenure as gardener and superintendent, 'Uncle John' managed to dispose of dozens of statues – or 'stookies' as he called them – stowing them away in wooded glens, stashing them behind buildings and shrubbery, and surrounding them with dense plantings chosen for their rapid growth.

Golden Gate Park.

McLaren died in 1943 at the ripe age of 96; in a rare honor, his casket lay in state in City Hall and was driven through Golden Gate Park on its way to burial in nearby Colma. Given his hatred of statuary, it's no small irony that today a lifesize 'stookie' bearing McLaren's likeness presides over the restored rhododendron dell named in his honor. One can only imagine how he would have cringed at the looming contemplative figure in bronze, which was actually crafted in 1911 by sculptor and Park Commissioner M Earl Cumming. Mysteriously, the statue remained hidden for years and wasn't unearthed until after McClaren's death. Lore has it that McLaren hid the monument under an old mattress in the horse stables, until park workers discovered it and resurrected it for public display.

WALK IN THE PARK

Find the rhododendron dell with McLaren's statue by following our Golden Gate Park walk, *see p90*.

SIGHTS

inspired; and **Chapeau!** (no.1408, at 15th Avenue, 750 9787) offers more upscale ambience, highlighting Provençal cuisine. One block south of Clement is **Geary Boulevard**, Richmond's main thoroughfare. Fine home-made ice-cream can be found at **Joe's** (no.5351, between 17th & 18th Avenues, 751 1950). Heading deeper into the avenues you will stumble across **Tommy's Mexican Restaurant** (no.5929, at 23rd Avenue), with 250 pure agave tequilas on offer. The much-admired 'free wine while you wait' policy is an added bonus at **Pacific Café** (no.7000, at 34th Avenue, 387 7091), which serves fresh seafood.

Out at 34th Avenue, turn north back over Clement into Lincoln Park and you'll find the **California Palace of the Legion of Honor** (*see below*), built by George Applegarth to pay homage to the Palais de la Legion d'Honneur in Paris. Just north of the car park is the haunting **Jewish Holocaust Memorial**, created by George Segal. The surrounding park contains the 18-hole **Lincoln Park Golf Course** (*see p252*) and a number of well-maintained hiking trails, shaded by twisted cypresses that meander along the spectacular cliffs of Land's End.

At the westerly end of the Richmond, **Sutro Heights Park** is a tiny idyll, virtually empty except for a few Russians walking their dogs or playing chess. A statue of the goddess Diana is often decorated with flowers by local pagans. In the nearby garden, enjoy a secluded picnic and marvel at the view of the Pacific. If the weather's not good enough, head across the street below Sutro Heights Park to **Louis' Restaurant** (902 Point Lobos Avenue, 387 6330), a 74-year-old diner serving milkshakes and ham steaks (set to reopen spring of 2011 following an extensive remodel). The views of the ocean rival those from the somewhat touristy and pricey **Cliff House** (*see below*) down the road; both perch on the very edge of the city.

The Cliff House was the brainchild of silver baron and former mayor Adolph Sutro, who owned most of the land on the western side of the city. The remains of Sutro's own mansion are at the western edge of Sutro Heights Park; below the Cliff House to the north are the ruins of Sutro Baths, built by the man himself in 1896 and once the world's biggest swimming baths. Fed by the Pacific, seven pools holding more than 1.5 million gallons of water could be filled by the tides in one hour. The baths were destroyed by fire in 1966, but the ruins are strangely photogenic. A windswept three-mile coastal path winds north towards the Golden Gate Bridge.

California Palace of the Legion of Honor

Lincoln Park, at 34th Avenue & Clement Street (750 3600, www.thinker.org). Bus 1, 2, 18, 38. **Open** 9.30am-5.15pm Tue-Sun. **Admission** $10; $6-$7 reductions; free under-12s. Free 1st Tue of mth. **Credit** AmEx, DC, MC, V.

Built as a memorial to the Californians who died in World War I, and set in a wooded spot overlooking the Pacific Ocean, the Palace of the Legion of Honor is San Francisco's most beautiful museum, its neo-classical façade and Beaux Arts interior virtually unchanged since it was completed in 1924. A cast of Rodin's *The Thinker* dominates the entrance; the French sculptor was the personal passion of Alma Spreckels, the museum's founder, and the collection of his work here is second only to that of the Musée Rodin in Paris. A glass pyramid acts as a skylight for galleries containing more than 87,000 works of art, spanning 4,000 years but with the emphasis on European painting and decorative art (El Greco, Rembrandt, Monet). An expanded garden level houses temporary exhibitions, the Achenbach Foundation for Graphic Arts and the Bowles Collection of porcelain.

Cliff House

1090 Point Lobos Avenue, at the Great Highway (386 3330, www.cliffhouse.com). Bus 18, 38. **Open** *Bar/restaurant* 11.30am-3.30pm, 5-9.30pm daily. *Bistro* 9am-9.30pm Mon-Sat; 8.30am-9.30pm Sun. *Walkways* 24hrs daily. **Credit** AmEx, DC, MC, V.

After a fire in 1894, a magnificent, eight-story Victorian turreted palace replaced the original 1860s house on this site. However, only a year after surviving the 1906 earthquake, the second building also burned. Its subsequent 'restorations' involved more demolition and rebuilding; the current neo-classical structure, completed in 2004, includes an upscale restaurant and bar with floor-to-ceiling glass walls that make the most of its breathtaking Pacific views. Public walkways allow the less well-heeled to amble around the building. The whimsical camera obscura, a 19th-century optical marvel, was saved after a public outcry halted its demolition and is still accessible on the walkway; it projects an image of the outside world, including a large stretch of Ocean Beach, on to a giant parabolic screen using mirrors and lenses.

FREE Columbarium

1 Loraine Court, off Anza Street (752 7891). Bus 31, 33, 38. **Open** 9am-5pm Mon-Fri; 10am-3pm Sat, Sun. **Admission** free. **Map** p316 D7.

This round, domed neo-classical rotunda is honeycombed with hundreds of niches, all filled with lavishly decorated cremation urns. Among them are the remains of many of the city's first families, such as the Folgers (of coffee fame), the Magnins and the Kaisers. With the exception of the Presidio's military cemetery, it's the only active burial site in the city: a 1901 law made burial illegal within San Francisco, and all graves were moved south to the town of Colma. Indeed, most Richmond residents are unaware that their homes were built on a massive 167-acre cemetery now known as the Richmond district, which centered around the Columbarium.

SIGHTS

Pacific Heights to the Golden Gate Bridge

There's a lot to see en route to that iconic San Francisco landmark.

If there's one classic San Francisco view – in a city with a multitude – it's the vista across the Bay from Pacific Heights and the northern waterfront. What sets this view apart from all the others is the presence of the iconic Golden Gate Bridge. It's hard to imagine the view without the bridge, but the very wealthy had already staked their claim to these hills well before its construction began in 1933.

The area covered in this chapter spans Bush Street to the Bay and from Van Ness Avenue to the Presidio, and it has much to offer beyond the engineering marvel that grabs all the attention. The Pacific Heights mansions overlook some of the most beautiful coastline in the United States, while the vast expanses of wooded trails and cliffs in the former military base of the Presidio run up against the well-scrubbed opulence of the Marina.

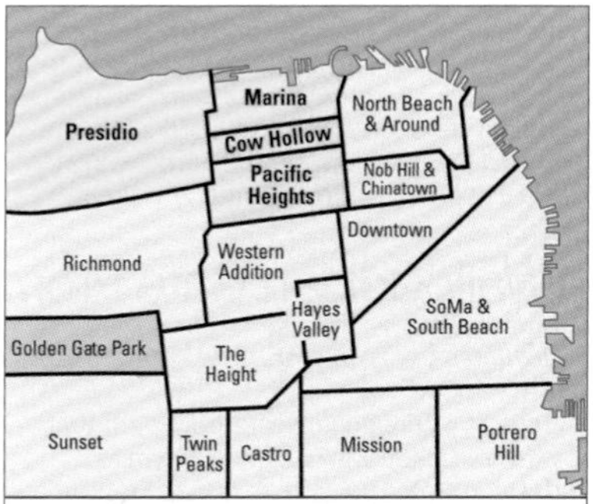

Maps p312-313, p314
Hotels p131
Restaurants & Cafés p160
Bars p176

PACIFIC HEIGHTS

True to its name, **Pacific Heights** peers over the Pacific from on high, its mansions home to the cream of San Francisco's high society for generations. The Casebolt house at 2727 Pierce Street was built in 1866, the Burr mansion at 1772 Vallejo Street in 1878 and the Flood mansion (which now operates as a school) at 2222 Broadway was completed in 1901. One of the newest mansions in the neighborhood is a little way down the road at 2845 Broadway: construction on this Frankenstein's monster of a home was only 40 percent complete when it sold in 2002 for $32 million – the most ever paid for a home in San Francisco at the time. The new owner spent the next five years pumping an additional $18 million into the house and to date no one has ever lived in the building. You need to be a millionaire to buy around here; normal people, meanwhile, can get a taste of the Heights life at the **Hotel Drisco** (*see p131*), housed in a grand building constructed in 1903.

As if anyone needed further proof of the neighborhood's cup running over, billionaire socialites Gordon and Ann Getty and Oracle billionaire Larry Ellison have houses here, as do many of the famous 'old' families of San Francisco (the Floods, the Bechtels and others).

The eastern edge of the neighborhood contains some beautiful Victorian houses. The blue-and-white **Octagon House** (*see p99*) is perhaps the most famous, but there are also rich pickings to the south: the **Haas-Lilienthal House** (*see below*), for example, which offers visitors a rare chance to see inside a grand old Queen Anne. Nearby is the ornate **Spreckels Mansion**, which spans the entire block between Jackson, Gough, Washington and Octavia Streets. Built by sugar heir Adolph Spreckels for his young wife Alma (the model for the statue that adorns the top of the Dewey Monument in Union Square), the 'Parthenon of the West' has been used as a location in several films, most notably Steve McQueen's *Bullitt*. It's now home to the novelist Danielle Steel.

Wander west from here, perhaps stopping in **Lafayette Park** (Washington & Gough Streets) to watch pedigree dogs walking their pedigree owners, to the stretch of **Fillmore Street** between Bush and Jackson Streets. This is the main shopping hub of the area, lined with smart shops and restaurants. A few blocks west, elegant antiques shops, ateliers and boutiques sit on **Sacramento Street** between Presidio Avenue and Spruce Street; **George** (2411 California Street, at Fillmore Street, 441 0564, www.georgesf.com) sells gourmet confections and couture canine sweaters to what must be the most spoiled dogs on the West Coast; and nearby charity shops stock the cast-offs of the rich and famous.

It may come as some surprise to learn that it was from this now-highfalutin neighborhood that poet Allen Ginsberg launched a cultural renaissance in 1955, when he gave the first public reading of *Howl* at the long-vanished Six Gallery, (3115 Fillmore Street, at Filbert Street). North-west of here, past **Alta Plaza Park** (Jackson & Steiner Streets), things grow even more handsome: the stretch of **Broadway** between Divisadero Street and the Presidio holds some of the best architecture in the city.

Haas-Lilienthal House

2007 Franklin Street, between Washington & Jackson Streets (441 3000, www.sfheritage.org/haas-lilienthal-house). Bus 1, 10, 12, 19, 27, 47, 49, 90. **Open** noon-3pm Wed, Sat; 11am-4pm Sun. **Admission** $8; $5 reductions. **Credit** AmEx, MC, V. **Map** p314 J4.

Walk Golden Gate Promenade

Follow this trail for some classic San Francisco scenery.

Part of a contiguous waterfront path that makes up the Bay Trail, the 3.5-mile Golden Gate Promenade is San Francisco's most scenic biking, jogging and walking path. Beginning at Aquatic Park, follow the path around the tip of the promontory to **Fort Mason** (*see p100*), the former military base that now houses several small museums and theaters, Greens Restaurant, the Museum of Modern Art rental gallery, and the Readers Café Bookstore, where you can get old library books at bargain prices. From here, stroll the path past the sailboat marina until you hit **Marina Green**, a curious and blissful cross-section of sunbathers in Speedos, volleyball players, rollerbladers, cyclists, and wealthy boat owners who have vessels parked at the St Francis Yacht Club. To the west is **Crissy Field**, the restored wetlands recreation area that once served as an army airfield. Today, it's populated by weekend windsurfers, strollers, joggers, beach-goers, and picnickers who hang out

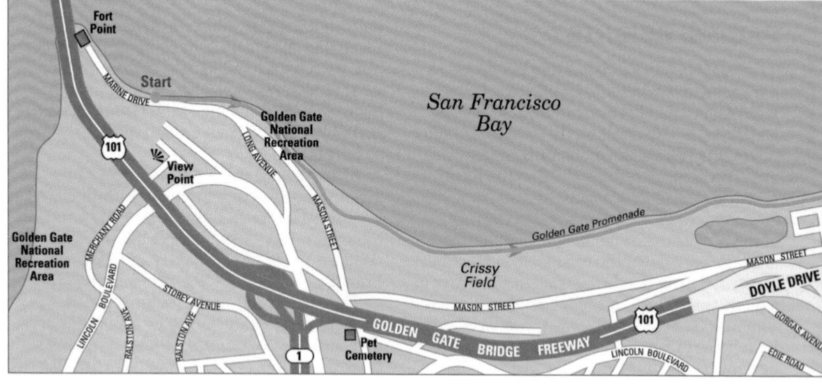

Built in 1886 by Bavarian immigrant William Haas, this 28-room house has elaborate wooden gables and a circular tower, clearly delineating the Queen Anne style. Fully restored and filled with period furniture, it also has photos documenting its history and that of the family that lived in it until 1972. It's maintained by San Francisco Architectural Heritage, which also organizes walking tours.

COW HOLLOW

From Pacific Heights, it's only a few blocks downhill towards the Bay to Cow Hollow. Once a dairy pasture, the area is still serene, but its grazers are now of the well-heeled, two-legged kind. The activity is centered on **Union Street** between Broderick and Buchanan Streets, a chic and bijou stretch of bars, restaurants (among them **Betelnut** at No.2030, 929 8855, www.betelnutrestaurant.com) and boutiques (including wonderful antiques store **Past Perfect** at No.2224, 929 7651). Hiding in an alleyway is **Carol Doda's Champagne & Lace Lingerie Boutique** (No.1850, 776 6900); Doda, who owns the store, found fame in the mid 1960s when, while as a waitress at the Condor Club in North Beach, she became the city's first-ever topless dancer.

Perhaps even more impressive than Carol's fabled domes are those atop the nearby **Vedanta Temple** (2963 Webster Street, at Filbert Street), former headquarters of the Vedanta Society. Dating back to 1905, the temple is dedicated to an ancient strain of Hinduism that holds all religions to be viable paths to spiritual awareness. Accordingly, each of its six domes represents a different architectural style, with elaborate Moorish arches, a Saracenic crescent, a Russian onion-style dome and a Victorian gingerbread trim.

FREE Octagon House

2645 Gough Street, at Union Street (441 7512). Bus 41, 45. **Open** noon-3pm 2nd & 4th Thur, 2nd Sun of mth. **Admission** free. **Map** p314 J4.

The 1861 Octagon House is home to the small Museum of Colonial and Federal Decorative Arts, but is most notable as one of two surviving examples

on the grassy expanse that skirts the shoreline. Two good stops for refueling are the **Crissy Field Center**, which houses a cafe, education center, and shop, and the locals' favorite, **Warming Hut**, which offers organic soups, sandwiches, and espresso, as well as a terrific book and gift shop. Lying between the two inside former military buildings are the **Gulf of the Farallones Marine Sanctuary**, a small museum with displays on local marine life that's great for young kids; the **Planet Granite** rock-climbing gym (www.planetgranite.com); and **House of Air** (www.houseofair.com), an enormous indoor trampoline park. At the western end of the promenade, **Fort Point**, a military fortification built between 1853 and 1861 to protect San Francisco from an attack by sea that never came, affords awe-inspiring views of the tremendous underbelly of the Golden Gate Bridge. You can view a film about the construction of the bridge daily inside the Fort Point bookstore.

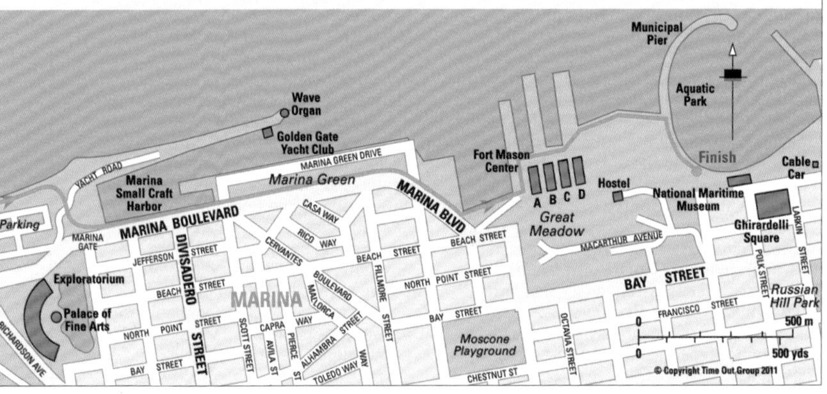

of eight-sided homes in the city. Across the nation, 700 such houses were built in the belief that they improved their occupants' health by letting in more natural light. Once owned by a wealthy dairyman named Charles Gough (back when nearby Cow Hollow still contained cows), the Octagon House stands on the street to which he magnanimously gave his name while on the city's naming commission; he also named an adjacent street 'Octavia' in honor of his sister.

THE MARINA & THE WATERFRONT

Built on soft rubble from the 1906 earthquake, the Marina, between the Fort Mason Center and the Presidio, shook harder than any other part of San Francisco in 1989's Loma Prieta quake. Buildings collapsed hither and thither, but the only reminders of the damage are the renovated pavements and suspiciously new structures among the otherwise staid townhouses.

In a city famous for its gay scene, the pastel-painted Marina is conspicuously straight. It's also one big pick-up joint. By night, its bars fill with twentysomethings sipping cocktails and making eye contact; for decades, even the local **Safeway** (15 Marina Boulevard, at Laguna Street) was a pulling spot – featured in Armistead Maupin's *Tales of the City*. The main commercial drag is **Chestnut Street**. The stretch between Fillmore and Divisadero Streets is a shrine to self-indulgence, with clothing boutiques and beauty salons seeming to occupy half the shopfronts. The renovated **Presidio Theatre** (No.2340, at Scott Street, 776 2388, www.lntsf.com/presidio_theatre) lends the place a little culture. The **Grove** (No.2250, at Avila Street) is a woodsy café where it is said that San Francisco resident and author of the *Tapestry* series, Henry Neff, wrote much of the first installment (there is even a café called the Grove in the book). It's also a good stopping point to watch the preened denizens of the area 'fabu-lapping'.

A little more levity is provided at the eastern edge of the Marina waterfront. The **Fort Mason Center** (*see right*) started out as a US Army command post in the 1850s, and its reconditioned military buildings retain a forbidding mien, but these days they house some fine little museums and exhibitions, as well as the **Magic Theatre** (*see p258*). For the 1915 Panama-Pacific Exposition, a mile-long swath of temporary structures was erected all the way from here to **Fort Point** (*see p103*). This fantastical city-within-a-city was torn down to make way for the houses we see today, but a small part of the fantasy-scape survived in the shape of the **Palace of Fine Arts**. The original plaster edifice, set in a little park at the western edge of the Marina, was recently restored (*see below* **Inside Track**). The adjacent **Exploratorium** (*see p208*), which opened in 1969, was one of the world's first (and is arguably still among the finest) hands-on science museums; it's scheduled to move to a grand new facility on Piers 15 and 17 in 2013.

The vast, sloping lawns of the **Marina Green** (Marina Boulevard, between Scott and Webster Streets) are the locals' favorite place to fly kites, jog or picnic, with dizzying views of the Golden Gate Bridge and the Bay. At the far west side of the green, a path leads past the **Cavern on the Green**, a small stone snack hut perched above a large pool just past the boat marina but before Crissy Field. Stop in for an It's It (a delicious Bay Area-made ice-cream treat) on a warm afternoon.

From here, head west along the edge of Marina Boulevard and around the harbor. Either continue west to the fascinating **Crissy Field** to explore a model of wetlands restoration, or follow the signs to the **Golden Gate Yacht Club**, along a kind of expansive promontory. Keep going past the boats and the boaters and, when you can go no further, you'll get to Peter Richards's amazing **Wave Organ**. Part artwork, part musical instrument, this mostly underwater structure is made up of pipes and benches built from San Francisco's dismantled cemeteries; the tubes make eerie music with the ebb and flow of the Bay.

★ FREE Fort Mason Center

Marina Boulevard, at Buchanan Street (441 3400, www.fortmason.org). Bus 22, 28. **Map** p314 H2.

INSIDE TRACK
PALACE OF FINE ARTS

Once the crowning jewel of the 1915 Panama Pacific Exposition, Bernard Maybeck's **Palace of Fine Arts** (*see right*) had fallen into ruin, its graceful rotunda and colonnades crumbling and its stagnant lagoon creating an inhospitable environment for resident swans, ducks, and birds. But a massive seven-year, $21 million, restoration has given the nearly century-old Palace a new lease on life. The grime is gone from the weeping maidens that top the 45-foot columns, and grit has been scrubbed from the hexagonal tapestry inside the rotunda dome – even the lagoon has been dredged and once again offers a pristine backdrop for wedding photos and visitors in search of a tranquil isle of contemplation.

SIGHTS

This collection of ex-military buildings features various cultural institutions, including the Museo ItaloAmericano (Building C, 673 2200, www.museo italoamericano.org) and the airy SFMOMA Artists' Gallery (Building A, 441 4777, www.sfmoma.org), the latter selling and renting out contemporary works by northern Californians. Both museums are closed on Mondays and admission is free. Other enterprises here include the Readers Café Bookstore (Building C, 771 1011, www.readerscafe.org), which sells rejected stock from the public library, as well as LPs and art. Over in Building D is the Magic Theatre (441 8822, www.magictheatre.org), which stages works by a mix of emerging and established playwrights in its two performance spaces. Before the performance, have dinner at Greens (Building A, 771 6222, www. greensrestaurant.com), one of the city's best vegetarian eateries. An array of changing displays is on view at two waterside pavilions (reconstituted shipbuilding bays); concerts, art shows, and book sales. On Sundays, Fort Mason hosts a farmer's market (9.30am-1.30pm, www.fortmason.org/farmersmarket).

FREE Palace of Fine Arts

Lyon Street, at Bay Street (563 6504, www.palace offinearts.org). Bus 28, 30, 43, 91. **Map** p313 F2.

Local architect Bernard Maybeck's *pièce de résistance*, the Palace is a neo-classical domed rotunda supported by a curved colonnade topped with friezes and statues of weeping women, and flanked by a pond alive with ducks, swans and lily pads. Initially designed as a temporary structure, the original building was demolished in 1964, leaving only the shell of the rotunda intact, then reconstructed at ten times the original cost. The Palace has been repeatedly saved by generations of San Franciscans – most recently with a splendid $21 million restoration.

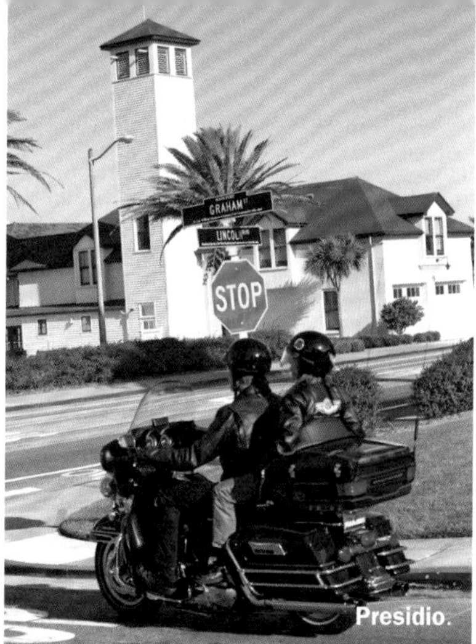

Presidio.

THE PRESIDIO

The Presidio is sometimes called 'the prettiest piece of real estate in America'; it's certainly among the most valuable. At the northern tip of the city, overlooking the Bay, the Pacific and the Golden Gate Bridge, its location could hardly be more stunning, but for centuries it endured a workaday existence as a military base, closed to the public. Now completely demilitarized and amazingly revitalized, it has become a national park, complete with 11 miles of hiking trails, 14 miles of bicycle routes and three miles of beaches, and with the more recent addition of residential housing and several fine restaurants.

The tip of the San Francisco Peninsula was first established as a military outpost in 1776, when a group led by Captain Juan Bautista de Anza planted the Spanish flag here to protect the newly discovered San Francisco Bay. The site was claimed as a garrison first for Spain (*presidio* means fortress in Spanish) and then for Mexico, but the US took it over, along with the rest of California, in 1848. The US military embarked on a huge landscaping project that converted hundreds of acres of windswept, sandy moors into a tree-lined garden. However, by 1994 they'd had enough. After 220 years, the US Army handed the Presidio over to the Park Service, claiming it could no longer afford the upkeep. The dramatic changeover, from army base to national park, followed soon after.

The switch hasn't been without its controversies. The Presidio Trust, charged with the unenviable task of making the Presidio self-sustaining by 2013, hopes to accomplish this by renting some buildings as private residences, renting others to businesses, and even allowing new construction. Among the arguable success stories so far is George Lucas's Industrial Light & Magic film company, which spent $350 million to transform the 24-acre plot at the former Letterman Hospital into the **Letterman Digital Arts Center**. The state-of-the-art complex of offices and studios features white-washed buildings that blend into their bucolic surroundings, criss-crossed by paths and grassy expanses, with views of the Golden Gate Bridge. The public can visit the lobby of Building B during business hours to view a gallery of Lucasfilm memorabilia that includes props and costumes from the *Star Wars* film series.

Both the Letterman complex and nearby park also now boast a variety of dining options to suit all tastes and budgets. **Dish Café** (San Francisco Film Center, 39 Mesa Street, 561 2336, www.sffilmcentre.com/dishcafe) offers good picnicking fare, while the alfresco tables at French bistro **La Terrasse** (215 Lincoln Boulevard, 922 3463, www.laterrasse presidio.com) boast spectacular views of the bridge. Upscale **Presidio Social Club** (563 Ruger Street, 885 1888, www.presidiosocialclub.com), housed in beautifully restored barracks, serves up gourmet versions of San Franciscan and American favorites.

The sheer size of the park, not to mention its inevitably hilly nature, makes exploring it purely on foot something of an adventure, and it's definitely worth considering hiring a bike from one of the rental firms at Fisherman's Wharf. While getting lost in this curious environment is something of a pleasure, maps are available at several information points: the **Crissy Field Center** on Mason Boulevard (enter the Presidio at Marina Boulevard, in its northeast corner, and carry on down the road for around half a mile); the **Visitor Center** in the old Officers' Club at the Main Post, close to the center of the park (easily accessible from any entrance, but coming in via the Presidio Boulevard Gate at Presidio and Pacific Avenues will take you through fairytale woods, often shrouded in mist); and at the **Battery East Overlook** close to the Golden Gate Bridge.

Life's a Beach

Sun, sea and sand on the city's stunning shoreline.

Unlike in Southern California, the majority of beaches in and around San Francisco aren't great for swimming. As if the locals care: between cavorting families, picnicking couples, idle promenaders and – on one or two beaches – clothes-free pick-up artists, visitors to beaches in San Francisco aren't short of activities.

Most visitors start with the **East Beach**, up close to the Marina in the Presidio. During the week, it can be very pleasant, with dog-walking women, jogging men and cyclists of both sexes (including many tourists bound for the Golden Gate Bridge, *see p104*) passing the time of day along the edge. However, on weekends, it gets a little busier, and space is at a premium. Many people head further west to **Crissy Field**, where there's a lagoon popular with kiddies, and a lovely (if unofficial) beach that's part of the protected shoreline along Golden Gate Promenade.

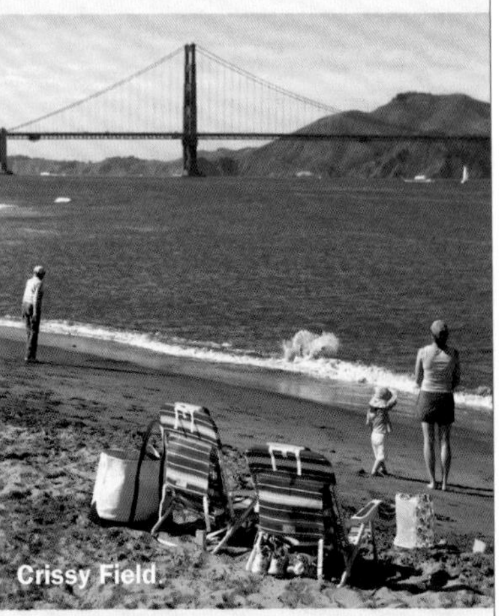
Crissy Field

Running for almost a mile along the craggy western Presidio shoreline, **Baker Beach** is a better bet. It's accessible, for one thing, and offers both great views and easy access to the city's most popular nude beach, the north end of the same stretch. In 1905 the US Army decided to use Baker as the hiding place for a huge 95,000-pound (43,000-kilogram) cannon. The naval invasion it was built to repel never came, but a replica of the original has been installed for the curious.

Hidden between Baker Beach and Lincoln Park, in the exclusive Seacliff neighborhood, you'll find the exquisitely sheltered James D Phelan Beach. Better known as **China Beach** (Seacliff Avenue, off 26th Avenue), it takes its nickname from the settlement of Chinese fishermen who camped here in the 19th century. There's plenty of parking and a pleasant hike down to the sand, then a free sundeck, showers and changing rooms once you get there. It's the favorite beach of many locals; should you be there at sunset, with Marin Headlands opposite, the Golden Gate Bridge to your right and sea lions in the ocean ahead of you, you may well agree.

Extending from Cliff House (*see p96*) south towards the city limits, **Ocean Beach** (Great Highway, between Balboa Street & Sloat Boulevard) is San Francisco's biggest beach: a three-mile sandy strip along the Pacific. Widening into dunes and plateaus at the end of the fog-bound Sunset District, it's a fine place for strolling, dog-walking and the odd illicit midnight ritual and bonfire. But look, don't taste: tremendous waves come thundering ashore when the weather's up, and even on seemingly calm days the tides and currents can be lethal.

The grassy area and bucolic wetlands area on the northern Presidio shoreline has a military past as an army airfield. Since its return to the city it has been restored to its original state, planted with over 100,000 native plants: a pristine tidal marshland home for hundreds of migrating bird species. The shoreline promenade now lures walkers and joggers, daredevil kiteboarders, and windsurfers who challenge the notorious waters. For more on Crissy Field and the Bay Trail that runs along the northern waterfront, *see p98* **Walk**.

The center of the Presidio is the **Main Post**, a complex of old buildings arrayed along parallel streets on the site of the original Spanish fort. Along with the main **Visitors' Center** located in the Officers' Club (Building 50 Moraga Avenue, 561 4323), home to a well-stocked shop selling maps, books and gifts – you'll also find the **Walt Disney Family Museum** (*see below*), a fascinating museum on the life and work of Walt Disney opened by members of his family. Follow Sheridan Avenue west from the Main Post and you'll soon arrive at the **San Francisco National Cemetery**. Among the army officers (and their family members) laid here in hauntingly straightforward fashion are more than 450 'Buffalo Soldiers'. African-American servicemen known to many simply as the subject of the eponymous Bob Marley song, they served not only alongside future president Theodore Roosevelt at the Battle of San Juan Hill (the battle namechecked by Marley), but also throughout the Civil War, the Indian Wars, the Spanish-American War and virtually every conflict up to the Korean War, after which the US armed services became officially integrated.

Continuing along Lincoln and taking the first right (McDowell Avenue), you'll soon stumble upon the **Pet Cemetery**. While its human counterpart sits high on a hill, its gravestones gleaming and its grass immaculately tidy, the cemetery in which servicemen buried their beloved animals sits directly under the Route 101 overpass, its markers made by hand and its grass unkempt. Still, there's something touching about these crumbling memorials, some of which – complete with poems and drawings – almost constitute folk art.

Much of the rest of the Presidio is a jumble of former servicemen's quarters, now converted into private homes. Around 500 structures from the former military base remain, ranging from Civil War mansions to simple barracks. Some are utilitarian, but others, such as **Pilot's Row** on Lincoln Boulevard near the Golden Gate Bridge toll plaza, are truly delightful. In between these sometimes melancholic clusters run numerous hiking and cycling paths, all marked on the maps available from the visitors' centers. Taking one – or more – is the best way to really get a feel for the Presidio. The hilly, unpaved **Coastal Trail** runs out past the Golden Gate Bridge to the beginning of the Pacific, with spectacular views of the Marin Headlands. The **Ecology Trail** begins directly behind the Officers' Club and follows a pastoral path on to **Inspiration Point**, which affords terrific views, and picturesque **El Polin Spring**.

A number of haunting old coastal batteries that once held guns capable of shooting 15 miles out to sea – thankfully never fired in anything other than practice – sit along the western edge of the park. **Batteries Godfrey** and **Crosby** are both easily accessible on foot. The last pictures taken by photographer Ansel Adams were of these concrete bunkers and they offer stunning views of the Golden Gate Bridge, making them the perfect place to enjoy a romantic bottle of wine at sunset. Below them is **Baker Beach** (*see left* **Life's a Beach**), a favorite getaway among locals where, in 1986, the first 'Burning Man' was the spark that began one of the biggest festivals in the country. To the south of the Presidio sits the relaxing idyll of **Mountain Lake Park** (access at Lake Street and Funston Avenue). Just next to it is the public **Presidio Golf Course**, formerly a private club favored by presidents and generals.

FREE Fort Point

Marine Drive, beneath Golden Gate Bridge (556 1693, www.nps.gov/fopo). Bus 28. **Open** 10am-5pm Fri-Sun. **Admission** free. **Map** p312 A1.

The spectacular brick-built Fort Point was built between 1853 and 1861 to protect the city from a sea attack. The assault never came; the 126 cannons remained idle, and the fort was closed in 1900. Today the four-story, open-roofed building houses various military exhibitions; children love to scamper among the battlements and passageways. Climb on to the roof for a fabulous view of the underbelly of the Golden Gate Bridge, which was built more than seven decades after the fort was completed.

The fort's pier is famous as the spot where Kim Novak's character attempts suicide in Hitchcock's *Vertigo*. While Novak was only pretending, onlookers might think the surfers plying the point break as it wraps around the fort are actually suicidal. They're certainly daredevils, but they're not dumb: many wear helmets to guard against the hazards of a wipeout on the jagged, rocky shoreline.

★ Walt Disney Family Museum

Presidio Main Post, 104 Montgomery Street at Sheridan Avenue (345 6800, www.waltdisney.org). Bus 28 or 43. **Open** 10am-6pm Mon, Wed-Sun. **Admission** $20 adults; $12-$15 reductions; free under 6s (with adult admission). **Map** p312 D3.

Opened in 2009 by the Walt Disney Family Foundation, the museum is geared as much to adults as to kids, offering a fascinating, in-depth look at Disney's life, career, and art. Housed in beautifully repurposed brick army barracks, its galleries follow a chronological history, from Walt's early attempts at cartooning to his death in 1966. Along the way, there's an interactive gallery showing Disney's innovations in sound, where kids can add sound effects to a *Steamboat Willie* cartoon; absorbing audio stations that recount tales of brothers Roy and Walt's early successes and the swindlers who tried to cash in on them; an original multiplane camera that shows how Disney developed dimensional animation; and a look at the financing and making of Disney's first full-length feature, *Snow White and the Seven Dwarfs*.

THE GOLDEN GATE BRIDGE

Few cities need bridges like this one. Without the **Golden Gate Bridge** connecting it to the northern half of the state and the **Bay Bridge** linking it to the rest of the country, the city would be isolated at the tip of a mountainous peninsula. Sure, it thrived that way for almost a century, but the rise of the automobile meant that ferries and ocean liners were no longer sufficient. Bridges were built, and now, for $6 (charged only on southbound journeys), motorists can exult in crossing one of the greatest bridges in the world.

Luminous symbol of San Francisco and of California itself, the Golden Gate Bridge (linking the Presidio to Marin County, 921 5858, www.goldengatebridge.org) may not be the longest bridge in the world, but it's among the most beautiful and may well be the most famous. Completed in 1937, it's truly immense: the towers are 746 feet (227 meters) high, the roadway runs for 1.75 miles, and enough cable was used in its construction to encircle the globe three times. However, raw statistics can't convey the sense of awe the bridge inspires, and no trip to the city is complete without walking across it. Drive, walk, ride a bike or take a bus to the toll plaza, and head out on foot along the walkway. Once you feel it thrumming beneath your feet, you'll understand even more why people feel such a strong connection to the span.

The man mainly responsible for making the bridge a reality was Joseph Strauss, a pugnacious Chicagoan engineer. Strauss spent over a decade lobbying to build a bridge, circumventing innumerable financial and legal hurdles in the process. But it was a little-known freelance architect named Irwin F Morrow who eventually designed it, his brilliantly simple pitch selected in preference to Strauss's hideous and complicated cantilever plans.

The bridge's name has nothing to do with its color, and everything to do with the name of the strait it spans. The Golden Gate strait was named by Captain John Fremont – not after the Gold Rush (Fremont came up with the name in 1846, more than two years before gold was discovered), as many believe, but after Istanbul's Golden Horn, the geologically similar channel that links the Black Sea to the Mediterranean. The bridge's stroke-of-genius orange color was also an accident of fate: San Franciscans were so delighted by the reddish tint of the bridge's primer paint that the builders decided to stick with it, rather than paint the whole bridge in the traditional grey or silver. The bridge has been totally repainted only once, a project completed in 1995 using 2,206 gallons (8,350 litres) of primer and topcoat designed to withstand the corrosive salt and fog that continually bathe it. However, it's constantly being repaired and touched up by a 55-strong team of ironworkers and painters.

Reputedly five times stronger than it needs to be, the bridge has survived hurricane-force winds, earthquakes and over 65 years of abuse without the slightest sign of damage. Built to flex under pressure, it can sway 21 feet (6.4 meters) and sag ten feet while withstanding 100mph winds, and can support the weight of bumper-to-bumper traffic across all six lanes at the same time as shoulder-to-shoulder pedestrians cover the walkways. Although large portions of the Marina were totally devastated by the 1989 earthquake, the bridge survived unscathed. But the virtual certainty of another earthquake of a similar (if not greater) magnitude prompted officials to undertake a seismic refitting project. Vehicle tolls were hiked to help pay for the reinforcements, which will require around 22 million pounds (10 million kilograms) of structural steel and 24,000 cubic yards (18,000 cubic meters) of concrete.

It's estimated that around 1,200 people have committed suicide by plunging the 250 feet (76 meters) or more into the water below, although countless more are never found, swept out to sea by the intense currents. For years debate has raged about erecting a suicide barrier beneath the bridge, but opponents fear such an addition would ruin its aesthetic appeal. City newspapers stopped publishing a running tally of suicide figures years ago at the request of the authorities, leaving it a topic rarely discussed by locals, albeit one that was brought back into the spotlight when filmmaker Eric Steel released *The Bridge*, a documentary highlighting bridge suicides and including actual footage of jumpers plunging to their deaths. Although many San Franciscans are reluctant to discuss the bridge's status as the world's most popular suicide spot, it nevertheless engenders a solemn respect as both a monument to the triumph of the human spirit and a memorial to its fragility.

East Bay: Oakland & Berkeley

Eastern promise.

There's so much to see and do in San Francisco that many visitors miss the less well-known opportunities lying just across the Bay. Reached by BART, trans-Bay bus (with free Wi-Fi), car, or even ferry with a full cocktail bar, Oakland and Berkeley are home to fine museums, a world-renowned university, miles of parkland, some of the region's newest and best restaurants and music venues, tons of shops and three professional sports teams. Need another reason to visit? The temperatures in East Bay run an average 10°F higher than in San Francisco and it is almost entirely outside the fog belt. There's a reason they call it the 'Sunny Side of the Bay'.

Map p109
Restaurants & Cafés p164
Bars p177

Oakland

Once the gateway to the interior of California, Oakland's Broadway Street has always been a main thoroughfare – beginning when it was a footpath used by Native Americans leading up from Bay. Later, the town became the western terminus of the 3,000-mile transcontinental railway, and is currently the West Coast's second most bustling port. Today, Oakland is, demographically, the most ethnically diverse city in America and the mix of cultures, cuisines and curiosities means that it's a great place to explore. Oakland's rennaissance has gained notice from travel magazines, newspapers and food-focused magazines around the world – its restaurant scene alone has put it on the map (*see p107* **Oakland: On the Front Burner**).

The 1960s ushered in an era of upheaval – both in terms of violence and social change – with the once-notorious Black Panthers leaving their imprint, along with hippies, yippies, Merry Pranksters and mob-handed, crystal-meth-snorting Hell's Angels. Today, parts of Oakland (specifically the more industrial regions of West Oakland) still have a high crime rate, but much of the city is on the rise, with luxurious hillside mansions, swanky live-work lofts and hip shopping districts. Check out the city with eight free walking tours from May to October (1-510 238 3234, www.oaklandnet.com/government/cmo/walkingtours), covering everything from churches to the spiffed-up 1930s shopping district.

Oakland is easily accessible from San Francisco. At off-peak times it's a 15-minute drive over the Bay Bridge or a BART ride to City Center/12th Street or 19th Street, both handy for central Oakland. There's also a regular ferry service from the Ferry Building (*see p51*) and Pier 41 in San Francisco to Oakland's Clay Street Ferry Terminal, near Jack London Square (1-510 522 3300, www.eastbayferry.com).

On the waterfront lies one of Oakland's main tourist hives: **Jack London Square** (Broadway & Embarcadero), named after the noted local author who used to carouse at **Heinold's First & Last Chance** (*see p177*), a funky bar in a little wooden shack. The square also offers a newly rejuvenated farmers' market, held from 10am to 2pm on Sundays. Franklin Delano Roosevelt's 'floating White House', the *USS Potomac*, is docked to the west; its visitors' center (540 Water Street, 1-510 627 1215, www.usspotomac.org) arranges tours and Bay cruises. At night, the lowing of the foghorn coming in across the Bay from the Marin headlands plays call-and-response with the horns of the trains rumbling past the square as patrons pack the Oakland location of **Yoshi's** (*see p238*), a world-renowned jazz club drawing top names.

Chinatown, which covers the few blocks south of Broadway around 7th, 8th and 9th Streets, is less tourist-focused than its San Francisco counterpart, but still packed with places to eat and shop. Grab a Vietnamese sandwich, dim sum or Thai barbecue while you're there: all can be found within a few steps of the corner of 9th and Franklin Streets. Across Broadway, check out **Swan's Marketplace** (907 Washington Street, at 9th Street, 1-510 444 1935), a renovated 1917 brick building filled with food and wine vendors, and the adjoining **Oakland Museum of Children's Art** (538 9th Street, at Washington Street, 1-510 465 8770, www.mocha.org, closed Mon), which has a wealth of hands-on activities for kids. For adults, Old Oakland's the **Trappist** (*see p177*) and **Beer Revolution** (*see p177*) are some of the top beer-centric spots in the Bay Area.

Next stop: the **Oakland Museum of California** (*see p108*). Recently the recipient of a $27 million renovation, it's a great place to learn about the history, art and culture of California; it's also well worth negotiating the arduous road that separates it from the lovely Lake Merritt, where you can catch a ride in a Venetian-style gondola at the end of Bellevue Avenue (1-510 737 8494, www.gondolaservizio.com). Down the road is the charming **Children's Fairyland** (699 Bellevue Avenue, at Grand Avenue, 1-510 452 2259, www.fairyland.org), full of sets and characters from classic nursery rhymes; Walt Disney allegedly used it as inspiration for Disneyland. Nearby, the Lake Chalet restaurant offers visitors a chance to enjoy the East Bay weather with outdoor seating on a pier extending into the lake, along with burgers and seafood. Other notable attractions, a short ride away in East Oakland, include the **Chabot Space & Science Center** (*see p108*), **Oakland Zoo** (*see p108*) and **Redwood Regional Park** (7867 Redwood Road, 1-510 562 7275, www.ebparks.org), the latter being almost three square miles of partially wild parkland, with horse riding, 150-foot (45-meter) redwoods and hiking trails.

When the dotcom boom of the late '90s priced musicians and artists out of San Francisco, Oakland developed strong arts scenes. West of Lake Merritt is the **Paramount Theatre** (2025 Broadway, between 20th & 21st Streets, 1-510 465 6400, www.paramounttheatre.com), a fabulous art deco movie house built by renowned Bay Area architect Timothy L Pflueger in 1931. Complete with a Mighty Wurlitzer organ and full bar in the lobby, the theater is home to the Oakland East Bay Symphony (1-510 444 0801, www.oebs.org), and also features rock, blues, soul and comedy shows. The newly renovated **Fox Theater** (1807 Telegraph Avenue, 1-510 302 2277, www.thefoxoakland.com) is yet another spectacular restoration project that now draws some of the top names in the indie scene. For punk and hardcore rock, try the **Stork Club** (2330 Telegraph Avenue, at 23rd Street, 1-510 444 6174, www.storkcluboakland.com), where you can hear local favorites letting rip in a suitably grubby corner of the neighborhood.

The best corner for shoppers is the stretch of College Avenue in the ritzy Rockridge district to the north (served by its own BART station). As well as high-end home accessories, pricey children's boutiques and French bistros, you'll find the **Market Hall** (5665 College Avenue, 1-510 652 4680, www.rockridgemarkethall.com), with a butcher, fishmonger, wine shop, bakery, pasta shop, cheese shop, florist and café. Another shopping destination is the Temescal district, along Telegraph Avenue at 51st Street. A weekly farmers' market (5300 Claremont Avenue, at Telegraph Avenue, 1-510 745 7100, www.urbanvillageonline.com, 9am-1pm Sun) is a major draw. Just a bit further down Telegraph is Oakland's Koreatown, well known for its restaurants. A favorite with local critics is **Koryo Wooden Charcoal BBQ** (Suite J, 4390 Telegraph Avenue, at 44th Street, 1-510 652 6007), where barbecue feasts are cooked at your own tabletop *hibachi*.

The nearby city of **Alameda**, accessible by car from downtown Oakland through the Webster Street Tube or by ferry from San Francisco's Ferry Building or Pier 41, is a charming blast from the past. Once the railroads' Western Terminus (before Oakland took away that honor), then home to a naval air station, Alameda – along its main drags of Webster Street and Park Street – is now a good destination for shopping, eating and… pinball. Visit **Lucky Ju Ju** (713 Santa Clara Avenue, at Webster Street, 1-510 205 9793, www.ujuju.com) for hours of fun with vintage pinball games from the 1960s to the '80s. You can also catch some rays or learn to windsurf at Alameda's **Crown Memorial Beach** (Boardsports School, Westline Drive, at Otis Drive, 385 1224, www.boardsportsschool.com).

Oakland On the Front Burner

The hottest new restaurants are opening here.

Hibiscus.

Of the 160 new businesses that have opened on downtown Oakland in the past six years, 65 have been restaurants. Superstar chefs from around the Bay Area and the country are converging here – attracted by low overheads and by a savvy and adventurous dining public. With proximity to fresh, regional produce – pasture-raised and free-range meats and dairy products, sustainable seafood, and locally made beer, wine and spirits – everything has converged to make Oakland the new culinary hotspot.

Among the recent transplants is Michelin-starred **Commis** (1-510 653 3902, www.commisresturant.com), whose chef, James Syhabout, left his plum gig at four-star Manresa to start a place in Oakland. A few blocks away, **Adesso** (1-510 601 0305, www.dopoadesso.com/adesso) boasts one of the region's best happy hours and a minimum of 30 – yes, 30 – kinds of house made salumi and charcuterie. San Francisco star chef Daniel Patterson, who gained acclaim with his four-star Coi in San Francisco's North Beach, has added a more casual spot in Oakland: the Uptown District's **Plum** (1-510 444 7586, www.plumoakland.com). Next door, 'natural wine bar' **Punchdown** (1-510 251 0100, www.puchdownwine.com) offers wines made using only sustainable, organic methods. Patterson has plans to add another Oakland destination, Bracina, in the newly built Jack London Market.

Also in the Uptown District is **Flora** (1-510 286 0100, www.floraoakland.com), housed in a stunning art deco building and boasting some of the Bay's best cocktails (try a Carter Beats the Devil), as well as a wide-ranging menu. The owners plan to add an upscale taqueria, Xolo, as well as a 2,000sq ft bar space next door. A few blocks over, Sarah Kirnon mans the kitchen at the inventive **Hibiscus** (1-510 444 2626, www.hibiscusoakland.com), a modern take on Caribbean cuisine, inspired by her childhood in Barbados. With dishes such as a molasses-brined pork chop and Miss Ollie's fried chicken, along with an excellent cocktail selection, Hibiscus is a great place to start or end an evening. Upscale sushi and Japanese cuisine complement one of the region's most well-tended saké lists at the Oakland outpost of **Ozumo** (1-510 286 9866, www.ozumo.com), while just next door, Pican (1-510 834 1000, www.picanrestaurant.com) offers gourmet Southern fare paired with the best Bourbon and rye whiskey selections this side of the Mississippi (don't miss the fried chicken with truffle-honey drizzle).

The Temescal District is home to Chez Panisse alumnus Charlie Hallowell's **Pizzaiolo** (1-510 652 4888, www.pizzaiolooakland.com), whose wood oven-baked pizza Napoletano is topped with fresh, seasonal ingredients and house-made charcuterie. The Lakeshore District's justly acclaimed **Camino** (1-510 547 5035, www.caminorestaurant.com) was opened by Russell Moore, another member of the Chez Panisse diaspora. Moore's menus are focused on dishes cooked in a massive, open fireplace at the rear of the restaurant.

The smart Rockridge neighborhood is home to several notable restaurants, including the granddaddy of Oakland's fine dining scene, **Oliveto** (1-510 547 5365, www.oliveto.com). Steps from the BART station, Oliveto's housemade pastas, salumi, and whole hog dinners are the reason it has remained a destination dining spot for 25 years.

Chabot Space & Science Center

10000 Skyline Boulevard (1-510 336 7300, www.chabotspace.org). **Open** 10am-5pm Wed, Thur; 10am-10pm Fri, Sat; 11am-5pm Sun. **Admission** (incl Planetarium and Megadome theater) $14.95; $10.95 3-12s. **Credit** DC, MC, V.

High in the Oakland Hills, the Chabot combines a superbly equipped, state-of-the-art planetarium with an observatory and film theater; the latter runs 70mm projections of the internal workings of the human body or the cosmos, seen at both the largest scale and the submolecular level. The three telescopes include a 36in reflector telescope that is housed in the rotating roof observatory; you can look through all three most Fridays and Saturdays, depending on the weather.

★ Oakland Museum of California

1000 Oak Street, at 10th Street (1-510 238 2200, www.museumca.org). **Open** 10am-5pm Wed-Sat; noon-5pm Sun. **Admission** $12; $6-$9 reductions; free under-8s. Free 2nd Sun of mth. **Credit** AmEx, DC, MC, V.

A $27 million renovation has helped reinvigorate the OMCA. With updated exhibit spaces, a new restaurant and café, new landscaping and refreshed sculpture gardens, the museum has come alive. Art collections include sketches by early explorers and genre pictures from the Gold Rush, along with sculpture, landscapes and Bay Area figurative, pop and funk works, and contemporary exhibits such as a celebration of Pixar computer animation. Events blend music, food, and cultural themes, such as the annual Day of the Dead celebrations. The collection of Chinese artifacts includes some stunning pieces.

Oakland Zoo

9777 Golf Links Road, off I-580 (1-510 632 9525, www.oaklandzoo.org). **Open** 10am-4pm daily. **Admission** $9.50; $6 2-12s, reductions; free under-2s. **Credit** DC, MC, V.

Over the last few years the once-cramped Oakland Zoo in Knowland Park has created a beautifully landscaped and maintained parkland that is home to natural, largely cage-free habitats for its 400-plus species. Other zoo attractions include the CP Huntington miniature train, a carousel and the Sky Ride, a children's petting zoo and a chair lift that takes you over the bison and elk on the 'North American Range'.

Berkeley

Berkeley worked hard to earn a reputation for its avant-garde arts, leftist politics and marvelous food. Over the decades, it has shown proper dedication to maintaining all three. It remains a fascinating and wonderfully contradictory place, where gourmet eating is accepted as a form of radical liberalism.. Relying on public transport? Downtown Berkeley BART station is convenient for all attractions.

UNIVERSITY OF CALIFORNIA

To suggest that Berkeley is slightly in thrall to its university is like hinting that San Francisco gets a little foggy from time to time – the University of California campus here, known locally just as 'Cal', is the straw that stirs the

Streets of San Francisco Telegraph Avenue, Berkeley

You can't fool the children of the Revolution.

As the student activism and radical politics of the 1960s heated up, many believed that revolution was imminent. And if there was going to be a revolution, it was probably going to happen at Berkeley. Young people on the campus were in the vanguard of the student movement. Always focused on opposition to the Vietnam War, the movement had become increasingly radicalized until, for many, the ultimate aim was nothing less than bringing down the state.

By 1969, demonstrations against the war and the establishment had escalated. Clashes with police took place regularly along Telegraph Avenue, the most violent and notorious of which centered around a piece of unused university property that had been claimed by students and local residents, planted with trees, and turned

Berkeley cocktail, and it has lent the place a countrywide reputation for its erudite, progressive liberalism. The university was the birthplace of America's youth revolution over 40 years ago, with student protests against campus rules and the Vietnam War inspiring a nation of youthful rebels.

It's very easy to idle away a few hours just wandering the campus. However, it's worth heading first to the Sather Tower (known simply as 'the Campanile'); for great views of the campus and the surrounding area, take the elevator to the 200-foot (60-meter) level observation deck (open 10am-4pm Mon-Fri, 10am-5pm Sat, 10am-1.30pm, 3-5pm Sun, $2). Elsewhere on the campus are museums dedicated to art, anthropology, paleontology and plenty of other disciplines. Some operate set hours, while others are open by appointment only; see www.berkeley.edu/libraries for information. However, at the head of the pack are the **Berkeley Art Museum** (*see p110*) and, across the street, the **Pacific Film Archive** (2575 Bancroft Way, between Telegraph Avenue & Bowditch Street, 1-510 642 1412). On the peak above the campus, but still run by the university, is the **Lawrence Hall of Science** (*see p110*), a fascinating science museum aimed at children, with views over the entire Bay Area. Cal also operates a handful of excellent outdoor swimming pools, lovely on summer days, including two pools (one a wading pool for the kids) at **Strawberry Canyon Recreation Area** (Centennial Drive, at Memorial Stadium, 1-510 642 6400).

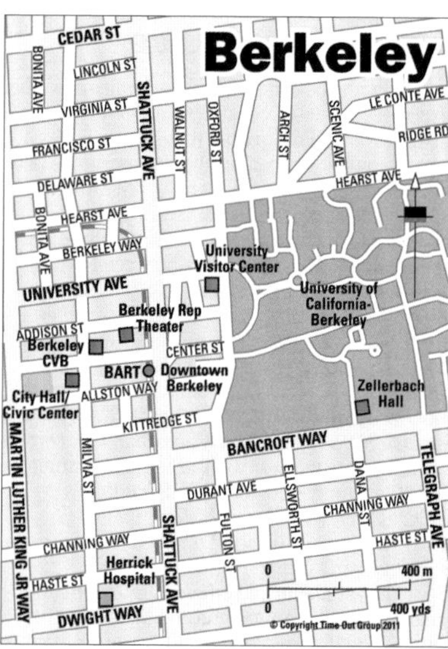

For more information, drop in on the campus **Visitors' Center** (University Hall, 2200 University Avenue, at Oxford Street, 1-510 642 5215, www.berkeley.edu/visitors). If you've time, take a 90-minute campus tour; they leave from the Visitors' Center (10am Mon-Sat) and from the Campanile (10am Sat, 1pm Sun). Bookings are only needed for groups of ten or more.

into a People's Park. Governor Ronald Reagan, hardly a friend of the students (he called Berkeley 'a haven for communist sympathizers, protesters and sex deviants'), decided to make an issue of it. He sent in the police to reclaim the park on 15 May 1969. Plants were destroyed and a fence put up to keep people out. Later that day a huge crowd gathered on Sproul Plaza at the north end of Telegraph Avenue. Angry demonstrators set off down the avenue shouting 'We want the park'. After local police failed to quell the demonstration, officers from other districts entered the fray. They chased the crowd down Telegraph Avenue, firing buckshot that caused serious injuries and one death. Reagan declared a state of emergency and sent in the National Guard – it would remain for two weeks. During a peaceful memorial for the slain student at Sproul Plaza, National Guardsmen surrounded the plaza, put on gas masks, and then CS gas was let loose from helicopters. Many were injured in the ensuing panic. For a while it seemed as if war had been declared and the battle lines firmly drawn between old and young, left and right.

There never was a war, of course, and today street vendors and hippie clothes are the most obvious references to Telegraph's past. The park survived, though. Hardly the beating heart of a radical community as '60s idealists had envisioned, it is inhabited largely by the homeless, but it also features organic demonstration gardens popular with kids and, more recently, basketball courts that cater to students – an egalitarian distribution that seems to satisfy the people and the establishment alike.

BEYOND THE COLLEGE

Even outside the campus, a liberal collegiate vibe dominates Berkeley. Spiking southwards from the university, **Telegraph Avenue** provides a home for street-vendor jewelry, crafts stands and hippyish clothes shops. Woefully, the world-famous Cody's Books has shut down, citing increasing rents in the area, but bibliophiles can still check out Moe's (No.2476, between Dwight Way & Haste Street, 1-510 849 2087) for a huge selection of both new and used books. Further south along Telegraph are two huge record stores: **Rasputin** (No.2401, at Channing Way, 1-800 350 8700, www.rasputinmusic.com) and the superior **Amoeba Records** (No.2455, at Haste Street, 1-510 549 1125, www.amoebamusic.com). Cafés line the university's southern limit, among them the mainly outdoor **Café Strada** (2300 College Avenue, at Bancroft Way, 1-510 843 5282) and **Café Milano** (2522 Bancroft Way, at Telegraph Avenue, 1-510 644 3100). At weekends, students and others loiter around on the corner of Ashby Avenue and Martin Luther King Jr Way for the Berkeley Flea Market.

Northwest of campus sits the culinary hot zone known as the Gourmet Ghetto, which runs along Shattuck Avenue between Delaware and Rose Streets. It's more popular with professors and tutors than with their students, on the whole, but the restaurants are still very egalitarian. The star of the show is undeniably **Chez Panisse** (*see p164*), set up back in the 1970s by Alice Waters, the elfin leader of the revolution in California cuisine. It's hardly the only option, though. Next door is **César** (1515 Shattuck Avenue, 1-510 883 0222, www.barcesar.com), which serves an enticing array of cultured tapas; more or less opposite is **Cheese Board Collective** (No.1512, 1-510 549 3055, www.cheeseboardcollective.coop), an employee-owned collective bakery that offers heavenly breads, cheeses, and a daily pizza. **Juice Bar Collective** (2114 Vine Street, between Shattuck Avenue & Walnut Street, 1-510 548 8473, www.thejuicebar.org), just around the corner, is another co-operative featuring inexpensive organic comfort food. A few doors away is **Peet's Coffee & Tea** (2124 Vine Street, at Walnut Street, 1-510 841 0564, www.peets.com). Opened in 1966, this branch of the coffee chain was where Jerry Baldwin, one of the founders of Starbucks, got his training – and where the chain got its beans for its first year of operation. So now you know who to blame.

Other areas of Berkeley hold different fascinations. Trendy 4th Street, between Hearst Avenue and Virginia Street, near the waterfront, is home to numerous exclusive and stylish shops. On the food front, there's great fish at century-old **Spenger's** (1919 4th Street, at University Avenue, 1-510 845 7771) and hearty fare at **Brennan's** (4th Street & University Avenue, 1-510 841 0960), a cavernous, old-fashioned Irish pub and cafeteria. Residential South Berkeley, meanwhile, has many California Craftsman-style homes, plus the **Judah L Magnes Museum** (2911 Russell Street, between Claremont & College Avenues, 1-510 549 6950, www.magnes.org), a large mansion that bursts at the seams with Jewish history and culture.

Many people visit the area just for its hills. The lovely and magnificently wild **Tilden Regional Park** (1-510 562 7275) offers hiking, nature trails and pony rides, a botanical garden containing the world's most complete collection of native California plants, a children's carousel, an amazing steam train that wows children and adults alike with rides through the wooded hilltops, and Lake Anza, a great spot for taking a dip on hot days. Those who manage the trek up to Inspiration Point or Wildcat Peak are rewarded with 180° views. For a more leisurely take on nature, the **UC Berkeley Botanical Garden** (200 Centennial Drive, 1-510 643 2755, www.botanicalgarden.berkeley.edu), below Tilden Park, has cacti, orchids and an abundance of native California flora.

Berkeley Art Museum

2626 Bancroft Way, at Telegraph Avenue (1-510 642 0808, www.bampfa.berkeley.edu). **Open** 11am-5pm Wed, Fri-Sun; 11am-7pm Thur. **Admission** $10; $7 reductions; free under-12s. Free 1st Thur of mth. **Credit** AmEx, DC, MC, V.

Opened in 1970, this dramatic exhibition space is arranged in terraces so visitors can see the works from various vantage points. The collection's strength is 20th-century art – sculpture, painting, photography and conceptual work, as well as a good collection of Asian pieces. The affiliated Pacific Film Archive (2575 Bancroft Way, between College and Telegraph) is a treasure trove of cinema, with a permanent collection of over 10,000 films and videos, some 7,600 books on film history, theory, criticism, and more than 7,500 posters. Its film schedule runs the gamut from avant-garde and experimental film, to westerns, classic Hollywood, international cinema, and silent film.

★ Lawrence Hall of Science

Centennial Drive, nr Grizzly Peak Boulevard (1-510 642 5132, www.lhs.berkeley.edu). **Open** 10am-5pm daily. **Admission** $10; $5.50-$8 reductions; free under-3s. **Credit** DC, Disc, MC, V.

Perched on the hills facing the Bay, this kids' science museum has computers to explore the inside of your brain, a Young Explorers Area and a huge DNA model to scramble over. It's also a great spot for day-time views and evening stargazing. Don't miss the telescope, earthquake simulator, and wind-driven organ pipes at the back.

Consume

Propellor. *See p185.*

Hotels

Budget, boutique or blow out: San Francisco has all bases covered.

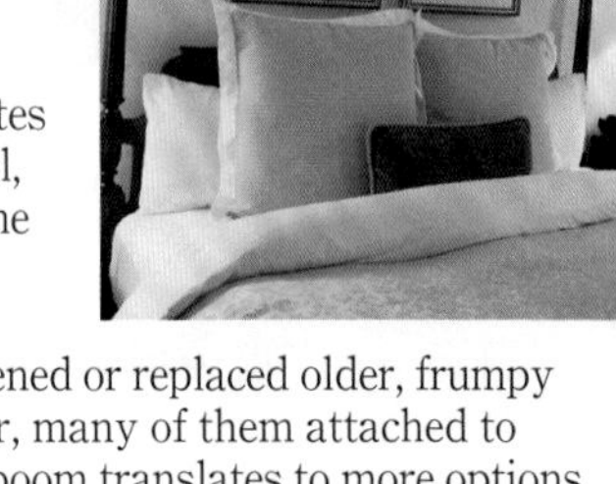

Contradicting the current economic malaise, San Francisco has seen more large and lavish hotels debut in the last few years then almost any time in the past two decades. For many, the operative word is 'green': from the luxury **Intercontinental San Francisco** (*see p124*), recently awarded LEED Gold certification, to Union Square's **Orchard Garden** (*see p127*), which incorporates sustainable design into every aspect of the hotel, environmentally conscious features have become the preferred and prevailing norm.

In addition, a number of smaller, personality driven, chic-boutique properties have either opened or replaced older, frumpy hotels on the fringes of the Downtown corridor, many of them attached to trendy restaurants. For travelers, the building boom translates to more options in more price ranges, with properties willing to bargain as they vie for the almighty tourist dollar.

INFORMATION & PRICES

Accommodation prices vary wildly in San Francisco. From hotel to hotel, sure, but also for the same room within a single property, which might double in price from a dreary midwinter Tuesday to a July weekend or even during a big convention. Financial District hotels tend to offer the best deals on Friday and Saturday nights, when the suits have gone home. The rates given here reflect this disparity: always shop around. Bear in mind, too, that quoted rates exclude a gasp-inducing 14 per cent room tax. Parking fees can be exorbitant, too ($20-$55), and in-room internet charges can also add up (although there are plenty of hotels and other sites in the city with free Wi-Fi access). Many hotels offer internet-only deals and special packages, but if those prices aren't low enough, check reservation systems such as hotels.com, expedia.com and priceline.com. Always ask about cancellation policies when booking, so you don't get stuck paying for a room you can't use. Most hotels require notice of cancellations at least 24 hours in advance; however, this may not be the case if you booked via an outside website, or with a service such as San Francisco Reservations (1-800 737 2060, www.hotelres.com).

In our listings, 'Wi-Fi' denotes a hotel that has a wireless connection throughout; 'DSL' is used for hotels where a high-speed connection is available only via a cable; and 'shared terminal' refers to a computer in the hotel's lobby or business center that offers high-speed net access. All hotels are required by law to provide accommodation for disabled visitors and, thanks to California's strict anti-smoking policies, all hotels have no-smoking rooms. Indeed, many hotels are now completely non-smoking, so we've made special note of hotels that still offer rooms for smokers.

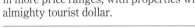

> ❶ Red numbers in this chapter correspond to the location of each hotel as marked on the street maps. *See pp312-319.*

Downtown

UNION SQUARE & AROUND

Expensive

Four Seasons
757 Market Street, between 3rd & 4th Streets, CA 94103 (633 3000, www.fourseasons.com). BART & Metro to Powell/bus 2, 3, 5, 6, 9, 14, 21, 27, 30, 38, 45, 71, 91 & Market Street routes/cable car Powell-Hyde or Powell-Mason.
Rates $395-$590 double. **Credit** AmEx, Disc, JCB, MC, V. **Map** p315 M6 ❶

The sleek 36-story Four Seasons is situated nicely on the south side of Market Street, convenient for both Union Square and SoMa. Its 277 rooms and suites, 142 residential condos, high-end shops and upscale restaurant create the feeling of a city unto itself. The general design and ambience are pretty similar to other Four Seasons around the world: as you might expect, the amply sized rooms (the smallest are 460sq ft/43sq m) are sumptuously appointed, with no corner-cutting. The list of on-site amenities is lengthy and all-encompassing; perhaps the jewel is the health club, with spa, pool and jacuzzi.
Bar. Business center. Concierge. Gym. Internet ($14.95, Wi-Fi & high-speed). Parking ($51). Pool (indoor). Restaurant. Room service. Smoking rooms. Spa. TV: pay movies.

Hotel Nikko

222 Mason Street, between Ellis & O'Farrell Streets, CA 94102 (1-800 248 3308, 394 1111, www.hotelnikkosf.com). BART & Metro to Powell/ bus 2, 3, 5, 6, 9, 21, 27, 30, 38, 45, 71, 91 & Market Street routes/cable car Powell-Hyde or Powell-Mason. **Rates** $270-$595 double. **Credit** AmEx, Disc, JCB, MC, V. **Map** p315 M6 ❷
Part of the Japan Airlines hotel chain, the 25-story Nikko is incredibly popular with Japanese visitors but welcoming to all. Rooms are large, bright and reasonably attractive, furnished with Frette linens, pillow-top beds and pale furniture. Elsewhere, the design is clean with Asian touches throughout. There's an indoor pool that lets in light through a glass ceiling, plus a gym and a *kamaburo* (dry Japanese sauna). The Anzu sushi bar and steakhouse isn't a bad place to eat, and the Rrazz Room, the city's newest cabaret, features big-name headliners from Chita Rivera to Mary Wilson of the Supremes (*see p245*).
Bar. Business center. Concierge. Gym. Internet ($15.95, Wi-Fi). Parking ($45). Pool (indoor). Restaurant. Room service. Spa. TV: pay movies.

JW Marriott San Francisco

500 Post Street, at Mason Street, CA 94102 (1-800 605 6568, 771 8600, www.marriott.com). Bus 2, 3, 4, 27, 30, 38, 45, 91/cable car Powell-Hyde or Powell-Mason. **Rates** $299-$429 double. **Credit** AmEx, Disc, MC, V. **Map** p314 L5 ❸
The former Pan Pacific hotel is far enough from Union Square so guests can avoid the crush, but close enough for the shops to be mere steps away. The dazzling third-floor lobby, with its soaring 18-story ceiling, offers a coffee kiosk, bar and American restaurant. Guest rooms include flat-screen TVs, sophisticated lighting, and updated decor.
Bar. Business center. Concierge. Gym. Internet ($12.95, Wi-Fi & high-speed). Parking ($49). Restaurant. Room service. TV: pay movies.

Taj Campton Place Hotel

340 Stockton Street, between Post & Sutter Streets, CA 94108 (781 5555, www.tajhotels.com). BART & Metro to Montgomery/bus 2, 3, 30, 38, 45, 91 & Market Street routes/cable car Powell-Hyde or Powell-Mason. **Rates** $275-$375 double. **Credit** AmEx, Disc, JCB, MC, V. **Map** p315 M5 ❹
Although it's just half a block from Union Square, this refined hotel attracts a very discreet and wealthy following. Neatly tucked into a small space on Stockton Street, it offers exceptional service, including valet-assisted packing and unpacking. Campton Place was acquired by luxury brand Taj Hotels in 2007. Since then, pets are only allowed to stay with their owners after a $100 non-refundable pet fee. Room amenities remain excellent, and there's an elegant restaurant downstairs, plus a handsome cocktail lounge.
Bar. Business center. Concierge. Gym. Internet (free Wi-Fi in business centers, $12.50 high-speed in rooms). Parking ($50). Restaurant. Room service. TV: pay movies.

THE BEST HOTELS

For all-out luxury
Four Seasons (*see p112*), **Huntington Hotel** (*see p124*), **Mandarin Oriental** (*see p115*), **Ritz-Carlton** (*see p125*), **St Regis Hotel** (*see p123*).

For eco friendliness
Hotel Triton (*see p115*), **Orchard Garden Hotel** (*see p127*).

For wallet friendliness
Edwardian Inn (*see p123*), **Hotel Metropolis** (*see p121*), **Seal Rock Inn** (*see p131*).

For on-site entertainment
Hotel Bijou (*see p121*), **Hotel Rex** (*see p115*).

For views with a room
Argonaut Hotel (*see p128*), **Hotel Vitale** (*see p119*), **HI-Fisherman's Wharf** (*see p132*), **Mandarin Oriental** (*see p115*).

Moderate

The smart **Hotel Union Square** (114 Powell Street, CA 94102, 1-800 553 1900, 397 3000, www.hotelunionsquare.com, $139-$239 double) and the modern **Orchard Hotel**, (665 Bush Street, CA 94108, 1-888 717 2881, 362 8878, www.theorchardhotel.com, $139-$379 double), with spacious rooms, are also recommended.

Crescent San Francisco

417 Stockton Street at Sutter Street, CA 94108 (1-888 817-9050, 400 0500, www.crescentsf.com).

Hotel Rex.

Bus 1, 2, 3, 30, 38, 45, 76, 91. **Rates** $129-$200 double. **Credit** AmEx, Disc, MC, V. **Map** p315 M5 ❺

One of the city's newest boutique offerings, the Crescent SF (the other location is in Beverly Hills) is a sleek and stylish overhaul of a down-and-out Victorian in a prime Union Square location. Brick walls and Victorian columns have been integrated into a clean, modern design awash in black leather settees, white marble bathrooms, and amenities ranging from 400-thread-count Sateen sheets to flat-screen TVs and iPod docking stations. Probably the biggest draw, though, is the noir-cool Burritt Room, where artisan cocktails are crafted at a long wooden bar under crystal chandeliers. A free continental breakfast is provided.

Bar. Business center. Concierge. Internet (free Wi-Fi). Parking (off-site, $28). Room service. Spa.

► *For the Burritt Room bar, see p165.*

Hotel des Arts

447 Bush Street, between Grant & Kearny Streets, CA 94108 (1-800 956 4322/3232, www.sfhoteldesarts.com). Bus 1, 2, 3, 30,45, 91/cable car California. **Rates** $79-$199 double. **Credit** AmEx, Disc, MC, V. **Map** p315 M5 ❻

Once a Victorian boarding house, this small hotel has been dramatically altered by local cutting-edge artists over the last few years. An aggressive, urban aesthetic dominates (spray paint is popular), while furnishings are in the minimalist IKEA vein. Bathrooms are on the small side, like the guest rooms – but then a two-room suite isn't much more expensive than the regular rate. Stairs are steep, and opening the windows will let in street noise, but pluses at this price range include flat-panel cable TV, mini-fridge, a basic but free breakfast and complimentary wireless internet access. Since art is subjective, it pays to peruse the differing decors online first. Beware of the three-day cancellation/date change policy.

Concierge. Internet (free Wi-Fi). Parking (off-site, $30). TV.

Hotel Diva

440 Geary Street, between Mason & Taylor Streets, CA 94102 (1-800 553 1900, 885 0200, www.hoteldiva.com). Bus 2, 3, 27, 30, 31, 38, 45, 91/cable car Powell-Hyde or Powell-Mason. **Rates** $139-$399 double. **Credit** AmEx, Disc, JCB, MC, V. **Map** p314 L5 ❼

Located in the heart of the city's Theater District, just a block from Union Square, the Diva has a dressy look, with deluxe bedding, as well as designer lounges by local artists. High tech complements the high style: there are CD players and 36in flat-screen TVs in the rooms, while the Little Divas suite for children comes with an iPod Shuffle, a karaoke machine and a costume trunk. The hotel is part of the local Personality Hotels chain, which includes the Hotel Union Square (*see p113*).

Business center. Concierge. Gym. Internet (free Wi-Fi). Parking ($36). TV: pay movies.

Hotel Frank

386 Geary Street at Mason Street, CA 94102 (986 2000, www.hotelfranksf.com). Bus 2, 3, 4, 30, 38, or 45/cable car Powell-Hyde or Powell-Mason. **Rates** $169-$399 double. **Credit** AmEx, DC, Disc, MC, V. **Map** p315 M5 ❽

Formerly the Maxwell Hotel, the boutique Frank received an extreme makeover in 2009 with a design by Thomas Schoos, and emerged as one of the hippest hotels in the Union Square area. Located a block from the theater district and shops, it caters to both business and pleasure with 32-inch flat-screen TVs, iPod docking stations, free Wi-Fi, and guestroom interiors that include standing full-length mirrors, houndstooth carpeting, turquoise crocodile headboards, and white leather couches. Max's on the Square restaurant anchors the bottom floor – it's the place to go for enormous deli sandwiches, meatloaf, and desserts bigger than your head.

Concierge. Internet (free Wi-Fi). Room service. TV: pay movies. Parking ($35).

Hotel Milano

55 5th Street, between Market & Mission Streets, CA 94103 (543 8555, www.hotelmilanosf.com). BART & Metro to Powell/bus 5, 6, 14, 21, 27, 30, 45, 71, 91 & Market Street routes. **Rates** $99-$209 double. **Credit** AmEx, Disc, MC, V. **Map** p315 M6 ❾

The Milano boasts some of the best-value rooms in Downtown, and one of the best locations: right next door to the San Francisco Shopping Centre, a block from Yerba Buena and five minutes' walk from Union Square. The neo-classical façade dates from 1913, while guest rooms are modern, featuring Italian decor (blond wood, black accents). A two-story fitness center with a steam room, a sauna and a jacuzzi, plus a well-priced Thai restaurant with a bar that stays open late put this a cut above the average business hotel.

Gym. Internet ($9.95, Wi-Fi). Parking ($30). Restaurant. Smoking rooms. TV: pay movies.

★ Hotel Rex

562 Sutter Street, between Powell & Mason Streets, CA 94102 (1-800 433 4434, www.thehotelrex.com). Bus 5, 6, 9, 14, 21, 27, 30, 31, 38, 45, 71, 91/cable car Powell-Hyde or Powell-Mason. **Rates** $149-$349 double. **Credit** AmEx, Disc, MC, V. **Map** p314 L5 ❿

Named after Kenneth Rexroth, MC for the fabled Six Gallery reading that provided a launchpad for the Beat Generation, the Rex is one of the city's most appealing small hotels, taking 20th-century literary salons for inspiration. There are books scattered throughout, and the walls are adorned with caricatures of writers with local ties. Literary events are often held in the back salon, and the modern business center even has a few antique typewriters. Local artists' work decorates the guest rooms, and guests have access to a spacious gym near the hotel. The tiny Café Andrée serves seasonal cuisine; hotel guests receive a free glass of wine at cocktail hour.

Bar. Business center. Concierge. Internet (free Wi-Fi). Parking ($38). Restaurant. Room service. TV: pay movies.

Hotel Triton

342 Grant Avenue, between Bush & Sutter Streets, CA 94108 (1-800 800 1299, 394 0500, www.hoteltriton.com). Bus 1, 2, 3, 30, 38, 45, 76, 91. **Rates** $169-$299 double. **Credit** AmEx, Disc, MC, V. **Map** p315 M5 ⓫

This colorful hotel, across from the ornate Chinatown gate, succeeds in being both fun and funky. Part of the Kimpton chain, it's a leader in 'green hotel' practices. Rooms have Frette linens and 'Earthly Beds' made entirely of recycled materials; the seventh-story 'Eco-Floor' has special water- and air-filtration systems and water-saving devices. Also on the hotel's eclectic menu are nightly tarot readings, fresh cookies and free drinks in the lobby. Much of the joy, though, is in the design quirks: the small 'Zen Dens' have incense, books on Buddhism and daybeds, and there are celebrity suites designed by Jerry Garcia, Carlos Santana and even comedienne Kathy Griffin.

Business center. Concierge. Gym. Internet (free Wi-Fi with Kimpton InTouch membership). Parking ($38). Restaurant. Room service. TV: pay movies.

Sir Francis Drake Hotel

450 Powell Street, between Post & Sutter Streets, CA 94102 (1-800 795 7129, 392 7755, www.sirfrancisdrake.com). Bus 2, 3, 27, 30, 38. 45, 76, 91/cable car Powell & Mason, Powell & Hyde. **Rates** $159-$179 double. **Credit** AmEx, Disc, MC, V. **Map** p315 M5 ⓬

Named for the Elizabethan explorer whose near-discovery of San Francisco is celebrated in vintage murals in the lobby, the venerable 1930s hotel plays up its heritage with Beefeater-costumed doormen (its most famous, Tom Sweeney, has served more than three decades as a greeter here), an over-the-top ornate lobby and tours of the subterranean speakeasy that once occupied a hidden space beneath the street. The rooms are more up to date, with flatscreen TVs and DVD players, and smart baths done in black tile and stainless steel. At the top, Harry Denton's Starlight Room entertains thirtysomething crowds with panoramic city views and dancing, while downstairs, a morning café and Scala's Bistro offers much better than average hotel dining options.

Bar. Business center. Concierge. Gym. Internet (free WiFi with Kimpton InTouch membership). Parking ($48). Restaurants (2). Room service. Spa. TV: DVD & pay movies.

▶ *For Harry Denton's Starlight Room, see p244.*

THE FINANCIAL DISTRICT

Expensive

Mandarin Oriental

222 Sansome Street, between Pine & California Streets, CA 94104 (1-800 622 0404, 276 988, www.mandarinoriental.com). Bus 1, 10, 12, 15, 41/cable car California. **Rates** $265-$3,000 double. **Credit** AmEx, Disc, MC, V. **Map** p315 N4 ⓭

Few hotels in the world can boast such extraordinary views, or such decadent means of enjoying them, as the Mandarin Oriental. Its lobby is on the ground floor of the 48-story First Interstate Building, but all of the rooms and suites are on the top 11 floors, affording breathtaking vistas of the city and the Bay. Rooms contain Asian artwork and plush furnishings in sumptuous, bold red and blue fabrics, along with iPod docking stations and big flat-screen plasma TVs. All have binoculars, and some have glass-walled bathtubs beside the windows. Service is exemplary, while the lobby-level Silks Asian fusion restaurant continues to receive high acclaim.

Bar. Business center. Concierge. Gym. Internet ($15 wi-fi). Parking ($57). Restaurant. Room service. TV: DVD.

CONSUME

Omni San Francisco

500 California Street, at Montgomery Street, CA 94104 (1-888 444 6664, 677 9494, www.omnihotels.com). BART & Metro to Montgomery/bus 1, 9X, 10, 12, 41/cable car California. **Rates** $242-$389 double. **Credit** AmEx, Disc, MC, V. **Map** p315 N4 ⓮

With a great central location right on the cable car line, this business-friendly hotel is relatively new, but feels as though it's been part of the landscape for years. That's partly because it has been built into a historic structure, with decor inspired by the 1920s and '30s, but it's also due to the exceptional service. The rooms are larger than you might expect and are appointed with comfortable amenities, including upscale bath accessories, plush robes and large work desks. The ground-floor restaurant, Bob's Steaks & Chops, is one of the better steakhouses in town.

Bar. Business center. Concierge. Gym. Internet ($9.95, Wi-Fi). Parking ($26 weekends, $48 weekdays). Restaurant. Room service. TV: pay movies.

★ Palace Hotel

2 New Montgomery Street, at Market Street, CA 94105 (1-800 325 3589, 512 1111, www.sfpalace.com). BART & Metro to Montgomery/bus 2, 3, 4, 30, 45 & Market Street routes. **Rates** $259-$499 double. **Credit** AmEx, Disc, MC, V. **Map** p315 N5 ⓯

See p118 **Ralston's Crowning Achievement**.

Bar. Business center. Concierge. Gym. Internet ($15, Wi-Fi). Parking ($48). Pool (indoor). Restaurants (3). Room service. Spa. TV: pay movies.

Moderate

Two chain favourites here are the **Hyatt Regency** (5 Embarcadero Center, CA 94111, 1-866 716 8145, 788 1234, http://sanfranciscoregency.hyatt.com) and the polished **Le Méridien** (333 Battery Street, CA 94111, 1-888 591 1234, 296 2900, www.lemeridien.com).

Galleria Park Hotel

191 Sutter Street, at Kearny Street, CA 94104 (1-800 792 9639, 781 3060, www.jdvhotels.com/galleria_park). Bus 1, 9X, 30, 31, 38, 45. **Rates** $139-$179 double. **Credit** AmEx, Disc, MC, V. **Map** p315 M5 ⓰

Next to the Crocker Galleria mall, this boutique hotel was looking a bit frayed until the Joie de Vivre chain snapped it up some years ago and poured in $7 million of updates. Now its rooms provide pillow-top bedding with Frette linens, flat-panel TVs and DVD players, and free internet access and office supplies. The endearingly snug lobby, with its elegant art nouveau fireplace and evening wine reception, is the hotel's showcase of charm. Newly opened Hecho serves sushi with a fine range of tequila for those tempted.

Concierge. Gym. Internet (free Wi-Fi). Parking ($35). Restaurant. Room service. TV: pay movies.

CONSUME

Harbor Court Hotel. *See p119.*

Ralston's Crowning Achievement

The rise, fall and rise of a landmark hotel.

One of San Francisco's most storied hotels, the **Palace** (*see p122*) was the vision of financier William Ralston, whose meteoric rise and tragic fall are as steeped in San Francisco lore as the hotel itself. Ralston began work on the hotel in 1873, part of his grand vision to make San Francisco a world-class metropolis. Two years later, just days before his dream was to become reality, Ralston was found floating in the bay. William Sharon, one of his partners, had created a run on the Bank of California, which Ralston had co-founded in 1864, by selling massive portions of his holdings. As depositors panicked and attempted to withdraw their money, it was found that Ralston had been using the bank's capital to fund his private investments. Early on the morning of August 27, 1875, Ralston resigned and went to take his daily swim off North Beach; his body was recovered later that day.

Barely five weeks later, on October 2, 1875, the Bank of California reopened its doors. On the same day, right on schedule despite its owner's death, the Palace Hotel welcomed the first members of the public as the largest and most lavish hotel in the country, offering modern innovations that included electric call buttons in each room, plumbing and private toilets, and the first hydraulic elevators in the West.

The hotel survived the 1906 earthquake, but not the fire that followed. When the blaze threatened to destroy Market Street, firemen tapped the Palace's massive reservoir system to fight the flames. But after the hotel's emergency tanks were exhausted, the 'Grande Dame of the West' was left defenseless. The building burned and had to be demolished, a Herculean task taking 18 months.

A very different Palace soon rose in its place. American illustrator Maxfield Parrish was commissioned to paint a mural for the hotel's 1909 opening; the result was the 7x16-foot *Pied Piper of Hamelin*, which still hangs behind the bar in Maxfield's, the hotel's watering hole. On the opposite wall are photos of the hotel's many famous guests, who have have included Thomas Edison, Winston Churchill, Charlie Chaplin, Oscar Wilde and US president Ulysses S Grant. In fact, the Palace was the site of perhaps the most mysterious presidential death in American history: Warren G Harding passed away in the hotel's Presidential Suite in August 1923, though no one has been able to say for sure whether he died of a heart attack, a stroke, a cerebral hemorrhage, food poisoning or even suicide.

The hotel also suffered the effects of the Loma Prieta earthquake in 1989. While the damage wasn't extensive, the hotel's owners took the opportunity to close it for restoration. The renovated Palace dining rooms and public spaces are simply breathtaking, with a spectacular 80,000 panes of stained glass in the Garden Court's ceiling dome (high tea here is a longstanding tradition) and a covered swimming pool that is by far the finest in the city. Free tours of the hotel are offered on Saturday mornings through San Francisco City Guides (www.sfcityguides.org).

THE EMBARCADERO

Expensive

★ Hotel Vitale
8 Mission Street, at Embarcadero, CA 94105 (1-888 890 8688, 278 3700, www.hotelvitale.com). BART & Metro to Montgomery/bus 2, 14, 31 & Market Street routes. **Rates** $399-$499 double. **Credit** AmEx, Disc, MC, V. **Map** p315 O4 ⑰

Blessed with a truly dramatic location on the Embarcadero (many of the rooms have great views of the Bay Bridge, and the spa is atop a penthouse suite), Joie de Vivre's Hotel Vitale is otherwise discreet in its stylishness. The capacious rooms are done out in pale colors, all the better to reflect the light, with super-comfortable beds and excellent amenities – including wall-mounted LCD flat-screen TVs. The huge but inviting bathrooms have a sliding door that allows some sounds to waft through; you can also soak in the spa's deep tubs on the rooftop. Downstairs is a bar and restaurant (the Americano) that conforms immaculately to the comfortably chic ambience.
Bar. Business centre. Concierge. Gym. Internet (free Wi-Fi). Parking ($48). Restaurant. Room service. Spa. TV: pay movies.

▶ *For the Americano restaurant, see p137.*

Moderate

★ Harbor Court Hotel
165 Steuart Street, between Mission & Howard Streets, CA 94105 (1-866 792 6283/882 1300, www.harborcourthotel.com). BART & Metro to Embarcadero/bus 12, 14, 20, 38, 41 & Market Street routes. **Rates** $159-$309 double. **Credit** AmEx, Disc, MC, V. **Map** p315 O4 ⑱

On the Embarcadero waterfront, Harbor Court is something of an undiscovered treat. The stylishly cozy rooms look out to San Francisco Bay and the bridge; in addition to niceties such as bathrobes, guests enjoy freebies such as WiFi and a weekday morning in-town car service, as well as use of the adjacent fitness club (a top-quality facility with pool, sauna and steam room) at a discounted fee. The on-site Japanese restaurant, Ozumo, is one of a half-dozen excellent dining options on this block. *Photo p117.*
Business center. Concierge. Internet (free Wi-Fi). Parking ($40). Restaurant. Room service. TV: DVD & pay movies.

THE TENDERLOIN

Expensive

Clift Hotel
495 Geary Street, at Taylor Street, CA 94102 (1-800 697 1791, 775 4700, www.clifthotel.com). Bus 2, 3, 27, 31, 38/cable car Powell-Hyde or Powell-Mason. **Rates** $285-$370 double. **Credit** AmEx, Disc, MC, V. **Map** p314 L6 ⑲

Hotel Monaco. *See p121.*

CONSUME

This Schrager-Starck property is oh-so-hip – and doesn't it know it. Staff range from cooler-than-thou to ultra-friendly (thankfully, there are more of the latter), and there's no denying the beauty of the public spaces – from the striking lobby with oversized bronze chair to the gorgeous Redwood Room bar and classy Velvet Room restaurant. The minimalist rooms are on the right side of comfortable, with easy-on-the eye grey, tangerine and lavender decor, but standard rooms lack the 'wow' factor, and the bathrooms are poky. Snag a heavily discounted rate on the website and it'll feel like value for money.
Bar. Business centre. Concierge. Gym. Internet ($14.95 Wi-Fi). Parking ($45). Restaurant. Room service. Spa. TV: pay movies.

Hotel Monaco

501 Geary Street, at Taylor Street, CA 94102 (1-866 622 5284/292 0100, www.monaco-sf.com). Bus 2, 3, 27, 31, 38/cable car Powell-Hyde or Powell-Mason. **Rates** $219-$349 double. **Credit** AmEx, Disc, MC, V. **Map** p314 L6 ⑳

Part of the Kimpton group, the Monaco is much more down to earth than its swanky neighbor, the Clift. But that doesn't mean it's boring: rooms feature striped wallpaper, huge mirrors and beds with silk canopies, and there are funky touches such as animal-print robes, iHomes and flat-screen TVs. Thoughtful extras include complimentary WiFi, and free wine and cheese receptions every night. It's also a pet-friendly hotel: you can even request a goldfish for your room. The location is great, right near Union Square and the entertainment district, but with the Grand Café and bar (open late for post-theater dining), and the spa within the hotel, you need never set foot outside the door. *Photo p119.*
Bar. Business center. Concierge. Gym. Internet (free Wi-Fi with Kimpton InTouch membership). Parking ($49). Restaurants. Room service. Spa. TV: pay movies & DVD.

Moderate

In addition to the hotels listed below, the old-fashioned **Best Western Hotel California** (580 Geary Street, CA 94102, 1-800 227 4223, 441 2700, http://book.bestwestern.com, $119-$219 double) is good value.

★ Hotel Adagio

550 Geary Street, between Taylor & Jones Streets, CA 94102 (1-800 228 8830/775 5000, www.thehoteladagio.com). Bus 2, 3, 27, 31, 38/cable car Powell-Hyde or Powell-Mason. **Rates** $109-$329 double. **Credit** AmEx, Disc, MC, V. **Map** p314 L5 ㉑

The Adagio has been in town in one incarnation or another since 1929. Its current version is the best yet: the casual, mellow decor combines deserty muted colors and 1920s arty decor, making the 171-room hotel feel both languidly chic and up-to-the-moment modern. Lather bathroom products, high-definition TVs and on-the-spot room service help guests feel pampered. Bar Adagio serves affordable American classics from grilled prawns to gourmet burgers and pizzettas.
Bar. Business center. Concierge. Gym. Internet (free Wi-Fi). Parking ($39). Restaurant. Room service. TV: pay movies.

Hotel Bijou

111 Mason Street, at Eddy Street, CA 94102 (771 1200, www.hotelbijou.com). BART & Metro to Powell/bus 14, 27, 30, 31, 38 & Market Street routes/cable car Powell-Hyde or Powell-Mason. **Rates** $109-$199 double. **Credit** AmEx, Disc, MC, V. **Map** p315 M6 ㉒

If you're happy in this slightly edgy pocket of the Tenderloin, you'll appreciate this hotel's proximity to Market Street. Cinephiles will love the cleverly executed homage to 1930s movie houses: walls are covered in black and white images of old cinema marquees and local film schedules are posted on a board. Best of all, there's a mini-theater, with real vintage cinema seating, in which guests can enjoy nightly viewings (albeit on a TV). All of the comfortably stylish rooms are named after a movie shot in the city. Free pastries, coffee and tea in the morning will help you face the all-too-real world outside.
Concierge. Internet (free Wi-Fi). Parking ($36). TV.

Hotel Metropolis

25 Mason Street, at Turk Street, CA 94102 (1-800 553 1900, 775 4600, www.hotelmetropolis.com). BART & Metro to Powell/bus 14, 27, 30, 31 & Market Street routes/cable car Powell-Hyde. **Rates** $109-$179 double. **Credit** AmEx, DC, Disc, MC, V. **Map** p315 M6 ㉓

An oasis where Market Street turns dodgy (especially at night), the Metropolis is eco-friendly yin meets mid-priced yang, with each floor color-coded in shades of olive green (earth), taupe (wind), yellow (fire) and aquamarine (water). The compact rooms have nicely understated furnishings: one of the suites, specially designed for kids, has bunk beds, a blackboard and toys. Cable TV and better-than-average toiletries complete the comforts. From the tenth floor, where some rooms have balconies, there are splendid views to the Oakland hills. Facilities include a small library, tiny workout room (ask for the discounted passes to a nearby gym) and small meditation space. You can expect some street noise at night, but bargain hunters will be happy. *Photo p122.*
Business centre. Concierge. Gym. Internet (free Wi-Fi). Parking ($30). TV: pay movies.

Hotel Serrano

405 Taylor Street, at O'Farrell Street, CA 94102 (1-866 289 6561, 885 2500, www.serranohotel.com). Bus 2, 3, 27, 31, 38/cable car Powell-Hyde. **Rates** $119-$259 double. **Credit** AmEx, Disc, MC, V. **Map** p314 L6 ㉔

Hotel Metropolis. *See p121.*

Right next door to the more lavish and expensive Monaco (*see p121*), this 17-story Spanish Revival building turned hotel is no less decoratively daring. The lobby is in a Moorish style – jewel tones, rich dark woods and high, elaborately painted ceilings – but the rooms are cozier, with buttery yellow damask walls, cherrywood furniture and warm red-striped curtains. The upper floors have good city views too. Pet- and child-friendly, the Serrano has a games library; at check-in guests are invited to play a round of blackjack for prizes. Ponzu, the hotel's hip Asian-fusion restaurant, is a popular place for dinner.
Bar. Business center. Concierge. Gym. Internet (free Wi-Fi & shared terminal). Parking ($40). Restaurant. Room service. Spa. TV: DVD & pay movies.

Phoenix Hotel

601 Eddy Street, at Larkin Street, CA 94109 (1-800 248 9466, 776 1380, www.thephoenixhotel.com). Bus 19, 31, 38. **Rates** $109-$349 double. **Credit** AmEx, DC, Disc, MC, V.
Map p314 K6 ㉕
Add funky styling to affordable rates and parking for tour buses in a 'gritty' neighborhood, and then sit back and watch the hipsters roll in. That's certainly the way things have worked at the Phoenix, which has housed a who's who of upcoming musical talent on tour – everyone from Red Hot Chili Peppers to the Killers. Rooms are bright and casual, but they're not the main draw. Chambers Eat and Drink serves New American style tapas within a rock 'n roll frenzy. The heated courtyard swimming pool is a bonus, where free continental breakfast is also served.
Bar. Concierge. Internet (free Wi-Fi). Parking (free). Pool. Restaurant.

Budget

The **Adelaide Hostel** (*see p132*) also has 20 private rooms, some with en suite bathrooms.

Touchstone Hotel

480 Geary Street, between Mason & Taylor Streets, CA 94102 (1-800 620 5889, 771 1600, www.thetouchstone.com). BART & Metro to Powell/bus 2, 3, 27, 31, 38/cable car Powell-Hyde or Powell-Mason. **Rates** $89-$169 double. **Credit** AmEx, MC, V.
Map p314 L5 ㉖
This family-run hotel offers good-value basic accommodation in an excellent location (it's two blocks from Union Square and virtually next door to the pricier Clift). Rooms are small and come with few frills, but they're all clean and nicely appointed, with complimentary water and organic toiletries. The Jewish deli downstairs is a local institution, popular with theatergoers for the pastrami on rye, and with guests for the made-to-order breakfasts with organic coffee.
Internet (free Wi-Fi). Parking ($30). Restaurant. TV.

CIVIC CENTER

Moderate

★ Inn at the Opera
333 Fulton Street, between Gough & Franklin Streets, CA 94102 (1-800 325 2708, 863 8400, www.shellhospitality.com/hotels/inn_at_the_opera/). BART & Metro to Civic Center/bus 5, 21, 47, 49, 90. **Rates** $129-$189 double. **Credit** AmEx, Disc, MC, V. **Map** p318 J7 ㉗
Tagged by crooner Tony Bennett as the 'best romantic hotel I know', this charmer is popular with a culturally motivated older crowd, thanks to its handy location near the Opera House, Davies Symphony Hall and the shops of Hayes Valley. Framed portraits of composers hang on the walls, and the sound systems in every room are tuned to classical stations. Rooms are fairly handsome and spacious, and most have kitchenettes (a continental breakfast buffet is complimentary). The restaurant, Ovation at the Opera, gets busy before and after performances.
Bar. Concierge. Internet (free Wi-Fi). Parking ($28.50 including tax). Restaurant. Room service. TV.

Budget

Edwardian Inn
1668 Market Street, between Rose & Haight Streets, CA 94102 (1-888 864 8070, 864 1271, www.edwardiansfhotel.com). Metro to Van Ness/bus 6, 9, 14, 47, 49, 71, 90. **Rates** $119-$189 double. **Credit** AmEx, MC, V. **Map** p318 K8 ㉘
This European-style hotel is one of the best bargains in the area, offering charm and tidiness for a relative song. The location is a plus: it's close to various performing arts venues and with easy access to Market Street transportation. Some rooms are small, but all offer private bathrooms (some with jetted tubs), and all are warmly appointed with good-quality bedlinens and nice touches such as freshly cut flowers.
Bar. Concierge. Internet (free Wi-Fi). Parking ($15). TV.

SoMa & South Beach

SOMA

Expensive

St Regis Hotel
125 3rd Street, at Mission Street, CA 94103 (1-877 787 3447, 284 4000, www.stregis.com). BART & Metro to Montgomery/bus 12, 30, 38, 45 & Market Street routes. **Rates** $649-$799 double. **Credit** AmEx, Disc, MC, V. **Map** p315 N6 ㉙
The pinnacle of SoMa's museum district and a worthy rival to the nearby Four Seasons, this 40-story hotel and condominium tower seemed to take

Sleep Well, Do Good

Eco all the way.

Going beyond flat-screen TVs and iPod docks, San Francisco hotels these days offer amenities to soothe your social and environmental conscience too. At the **Good Hotel** in SoMa (112 Seventh Street, 621 7001, www.thegoodhotel.com, rates $89-$129), you can fight global warming by borrowing a bicycle for touring around town, partner with a nonprofit to be a 'voluntourist' during your stay, and get free parking if you rent a hybrid car. Rooms feature bedframes made from recycled wood, bathroom sinks with foot pedals, recycled glass water bottles, and vending machines in the lobby featuring ReadyMade items such as emergency modular dwellings and wallets made from FedEx envelopes. At the budget-priced **Mosser** (*see p124*), you'll feel better about cozying under your Frette linens knowing that a portion of your room fee is going to support international reforestation projects. The **Hotel Triton** (*see p115*) takes its environmental mission seriously, even if its decor feels like the court jester on steroids. Energy efficient lighting, low-flow showers, recycling bins, organic linens, and biodegradable soaps and shampoos are just a few of the eco-minded amenities. The **Orchard Garden** (*see p127*) brings earth-friendly to another level entirely. The first hotel in California built from scratch to LEED standards, the downtown hotel features everything from in-room recycling and organic cleaning products, to keycards that turn off lights when you leave the room.

Good Hotel.

forever to open, but now that it's here it has redefined luxury (and how much people are willing to pay for it). Guest rooms come with butler service, limestone baths, high-end finishings and high-tech fixtures; rooms on the sixth floor and above have the best city views. A combination of new and old construction, the property includes sprawling spa facilities with a heated indoor lap pool, the new Museum of the African Diaspora and two restaurants patronized by the city's elite, Ame and Vitrine.
Bar. Business center. Concierge. Gym. Internet ($14.95 Wi-Fi). Parking ($50). Restaurant. Room service. Spa.

W Hotel

181 3rd Street, at Howard Street, CA 94103 (1-888 625 5144, 777 5300, www.whotels.com). BART & Metro to Montgomery/bus 12, 30, 38, 45 & Market Street routes. **Rates** $169-$520 double. **Credit** AmEx, Disc, MC, V. **Map** p315 N6 ㉚
This trailblazing, chic urban hotel chain continues to expand around the country, but it hasn't yet reached the point at which hip and fashionable turns to yesterday's thing. For that, full credit goes to the design, which eschews grand flourishes in favor of a simple, unobtrusive stylishness in both the rooms and the public spaces. Immediately on entering the hotel, you'll find yourself in a buzzing lobby bar, crowded with visitors and after-work locals making the scene. The rooms are modern and loaded up with indulgences: CD players, keyboards, goosedown duvets. The Bliss Spa includes manicures with movies, and men's and women's lounges.
Bar. Business center. Concierge. Gym. Internet (free Wi-Fi in lobby, $14.95 high-speed). Parking ($48). Pool (indoor). Restaurant. Room service. Spa. TV: DVD & pay movies.

Moderate

Courtyard San Francisco Downtown

229 2nd Street, between Howard & Folsom Streets, CA 94105 (1-800 321 2211, 947 0700, www.marriott.com/courtyard). BART & Metro to Montgomery/bus 12, 30, 38, 45 & Market Street routes. **Rates** $189-$269 double. **Credit** AmEx, Disc, MC, V. **Map** p315 N6 ㉛
Although it's run by Marriott, this comfortable, modern hotel with artful touches feels like a one-off. Service is friendly and professional, and amenities are far nicer than those of most hotels of this caliber. Rooms include 37in flat-screen TVs, and plenty of accessories (big desks, free internet) designed to cater to business travelers. The location, close to the ballpark and within walking distance of Yerba Buena and the Financial District, is also a selling point. Coffee addicts will appreciate the on-site Starbucks.
Bar. Business center. Concierge. Gym. Internet (free Wi-Fi in lobby, free high-speed internet in rooms). Parking ($43). Pool (indoor). Restaurant. Room service. TV: pay movies.

★ Mosser

54 4th Street, between Market & Mission Streets (1-800 227 3804, 986 4400, www.themosser.com). BART & Metro to Powell/bus 14, 30, 38, 45 and Market Street routes/cable car Powell-Hyde & Powell-Mason. **Rates** $59-$279. **Credit** AmEx, DC, Disc, MC, V. **Map** p315 M6 ㉜
A gem of a smart, eco-friendly, and value-priced hotel. A distinguished-looking Victorian lobby leads up to spruced-up modern rooms that are not large, but chic and comfortable, with clever use of space. Palettes are fuschia and brown with bright white walls: simple but effective. All rooms come with CD players. A few rooms are available without bath, hence the very reasonable charges at the lower end of the price scale. The location is ideal: a block from Yerba Buena Center and the Westfield Shopping Centre.
Bar. Concierge. Internet (free Wi-Fi). Parking ($33). Restaurant. TV: pay movies.

Nob Hill & Chinatown

NOB HILL

Expensive

The imposingly swanky **Fairmont Hotel & Tower** (950 Mason Street, CA 94108, 1-800 527 4727, 772 5000, www.fairmont.com); the similarly moneyed **Mark Hopkins InterContinental** (1 Nob Hill, CA 94108, 1-800 662 4455, 392 3434, www.san-francisco.intercontinental.com); and the **Renaissance Stanford Court Hotel** (905 California Street, CA 94108, 1-800 236 2427, 989 3500, www.marriott.com) are also recommended.

★ Huntington Hotel

1075 California Street, at Taylor Street, CA 94108 (1-800 227 4683, 474 5400, www.huntingtonhotel.com). Bus 1, 2, 3, 27/cable car California, Powell-Hyde or Powell-Mason. **Rates** $195-$399 double. **Credit** AmEx, Disc, MC, V. **Map** p314 L5 ㉝
One of San Francisco's grand dame hotels, this old-world, family-owned and -operated property exemplifies understated luxury. The hotel is perched high on Nob Hill, and features lovely, well-appointed rooms and suites, offering Irish linens, iPod clock radios and eye-popping views of the city. What could be better than a swimming pool overlooking Union Square or indulgent treatments at the lush Nob Hill Spa (345 2888)? Of course, you'll pay for the privilege: if you have to check the rates before booking, you're probably in the wrong place. The California cable car line rattles past the front door.
Bar. Business center. Concierge. Gym. Internet ($9.95 Wi-Fi). Parking ($39). Pool (indoor). Restaurant. Room service. Spa. TV: DVD & pay movies.

Ritz-Carlton

600 Stockton Street, at California Street, CA 94108 (1-800 241 3333, 296 7465, www.ritzcarlton.com). Bus 1, 2, 3, 30, 45, 91/cable car California, Powell-Hyde or Powell-Mason. **Rates** $389-$629 double. **Credit** AmEx, Disc, MC, V. **Map** p315 M4 ㉞

The Ritz-Carlton has been the de facto choice for dignitaries and heads of state for years. As you might expect, then, the rooms and suites are sumptuously appointed, immaculately clean, stocked with luxurious treats and new gadgets like 32in LCD flat-panel TVs and iPod docking stations. Amenities include an indoor spa with gym, swimming pool, whirlpool and sauna; the Dining Room, a top-class French restaurant helmed by one of the city's best chefs; daily piano performances in the Lobby Lounge; and an armada of valets to meet your every need. Mere mortals can pop in for the lavish Sunday Jazz Brunch, held on a sunken roof terrace.

Bars (3). Business center. Concierge. Gym. Internet ($14.95, Wi-Fi & high speed). Parking ($62). Pool. Restaurants (3). Room service. Spa. TV: DVD, pay movies.

Moderate

The century-old, 21-room **Nob Hill Inn** (1000 Pine Street, CA 94109, 673 6080, www.nobhillinn.com) is another Nob Hill option.

Executive Hotel Vintage Court

650 Bush Street, at Powell Street, CA 94108 (1-800 654 1100, 392 4666, www.executivehotels.net/vintagecourt). Bus 1, 2, 3, 30, 38, 45, 91/cable car Powell-Hyde or Powell-Mason. **Rates** $160-$309 double. **Credit** AmEx, Disc, MC, V. **Map** p315 M5 ㉟

Despite the uninspiring name, this elegant, relaxed hotel gives guests a taste of Wine Country within a stroll of both Union Square and Chinatown. Every room is named after a Californian winery, and there are daily tastings beside the grand marble fireplace in the lobby. Rooms have bay windows with venetian blinds, handsome writing desks and green-striped, padded headboards. But the best reason to bunk here is that guests get guaranteed reservations at Masa's, the hotel's exclusive, well known and notoriously hard-to-access French restaurant.

Concierge. Gym. Internet (free Wi-Fi). Parking ($38). Restaurant. TV: pay movies.

► *For Masa's restaurant, see p134.*

White Swan Inn

845 Bush Street, between Taylor & Mason Streets, CA 94108 (1-800 999 9570, 775 1755, www.whiteswaninnsf.com). Bus 2, 3, 27, 38/cable car Powell-Hyde or Powell-Mason. **Rates** $179-$229 double. **Credit** AmEx, Disc, MC, V. **Map** p314 L5 ㊱

Essentially, California's version of an English B&B, and how you just reacted to that sentence will be pretty much how you react to the inn itself. Some will find its lodgings quaint and delightful, while others will take one look, throw both hands in the air, holler 'Chintz!' and run screaming from the premises. Either way, the early-evening wine receptions and the breakfast buffet with freshly baked bread are a nice touch (as are fireplaces in all the rooms) and the staff are charmers. Next door, the Petite Auberge (www.petiteaubergesf.com) is a cheaper, country-French version of the Swan, with many of the same amenities.

Concierge. Gym. Internet (free Wi-Fi). Parking ($32). TV.

Hotel Vertigo. *See p127.*

Budget

In addition, try the cheap but nicely located **Hotel Astoria** (510 Bush Street, CA 94108, 1-800 666 6696, 545 8889, www.hotelastoria-sf.com), the no-frills but good-value **Dakota** (606 Post Street, at Taylor Street, CA 94109, 931 7475, www.hotelsanfrancisco.com). **USA Hostels** has private rooms, some with en suite baths (711 Post Street, CA 94109, 1-877-483-2950, 440-5600, www.usahostels.com,).

Andrews Hotel

624 Post Street, between Jones & Taylor Streets, CA 94109 (1-800 926 3739, 563 6877, www.andrewshotel.com). BART & Metro to Powell/bus 2, 3, 4, 27, 38, 76/cable car Powell-Hyde or Powell-Mason. **Rates** $109-$169 double. **Credit** AmEx, MC, V. **Map** p314 L5 37

It's something of a lingering mystery as to why American hotels continue to describe themselves as 'European-style' when seasoned travelers are aware that, in Europe itself, that often means creaky bedsprings, rude staff and a toilet several miles down the corridor. Fortunately, however, this handsome old Queen Anne structure, which was formerly the opulent Sultan Turkish Baths, isn't on that particular radar. Guest rooms are well kept, if hardly stylish, while the public spaces are considerably more charming and Fino, the hotel's restaurant, is a pretty decent spot. The main drawback: walls are on the thin side – but that's true of many vintage buildings.

Bar. Concierge. Internet (free Wi-Fi). Parking ($33). Restaurant. Room service (evenings). TV: DVD.

Cornell Hotel de France

715 Bush Street, between Powell & Mason Streets, CA 94108 (1-800 232 9698/421 3154, www.cornellhotel.com). Bus 2, 3, 27, 38/cable car Powell-Hyde or Powell-Mason. **Rates** $80-$170 double. **Credit** AmEx, DC, Disc, MC, V. **Map** p315 M5 38

One of a number of small hotels and B&Bs along Bush Street, the Cornell makes no secret of its origins: the Lamberts, who've run the Cornell for decades, are French imports. Downstairs is a restaurant, Jeanne d'Arc, serving complimentary breakfast and non-complimentary dinners; the place is a blast on Bastille Day. Rooms are attractive; the smallest ones have just a shower in the bath, but lower rates to match.

Internet (free Wi-Fi in lobby, $6 in rooms, $1/15 mins shared terminal). Parking ($20). Restaurant. TV.

Golden Gate Hotel

775 Bush Street, between Powell & Mason Streets, CA 94108 (1-800 835 1118, 392 3702, www.goldengatehotel.com). Bus 2, 3, 27, 38/

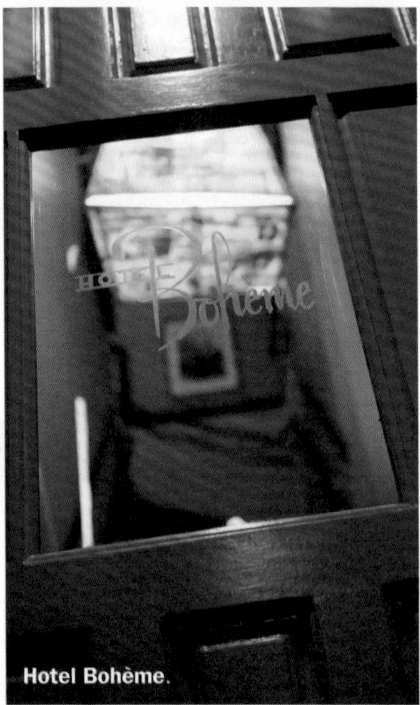

Hotel Bohème.

cable car Powell-Hyde or Powell-Mason. **Rates** $80-$150 double. **Credit** AmEx, DC, MC, V. **Map** p314 L5 ❸❾

This 1913 Edwardian hotel is a real charmer; a little creaky in places, certainly, but generally delightful. Rooms vary in style a fair bit, thanks to the presence throughout of one-of-a-kind antiques, but the majority are cozy and easy on the eye; many have claw-foot tubs. The welcome from owners John and Renate Kenaston, not to mention the hotel dog and cat, couldn't be warmer (or the oatmeal cookies fresher). The traffic noise from busy Bush Street isn't as bad as you might expect, but light sleepers should ask for a room in the back.

Internet (free Wi-Fi & shared terminal). Parking ($20). TV.

Hotel Vertigo

940 Sutter Street, between Leavenworth & Hyde Streets, CA 94109 (1-800 553 1900, 885 6800, www.hotelvertigosf.com). Bus 2, 3, 19, 27, 38. **Rates** $169-$269 double. **Credit** AmEx, Disc, MC, V. **Map** p314 K5 ❹⓿

LA designer Thomas Schoos was responsible for this hotel's identity shift from the York to the Hotel Vertigo some years ago, going for a bold effect with plenty of color and bold patterns. Rooms here are larger than many in the city. *Photo p125.*

Bar. Business center. Concierge. Internet (free Wi-Fi). Parking ($35). Restaurant. Room service.

CHINATOWN

Moderate

The sweepingly remodeled, choicely located **Hilton San Francisco Financial District** (750 Kearny Street, CA 94108, 1-800 445 8667, 483 1498, www.sanfranciscohiltonhotel.com, $185-$325 double) is another reliable option in Chinatown.

Orchard Garden Hotel

466 Bush Street, between Grant & Kearny Streets, CA 94108 (1-888 717 2881, 399 9807, www.theorchardgardenhotel.com). Bus 1, 2, 3, 30, 38, 45, 91/cable car Powell-Hyde or Powell-Market. **Rates** $179-$289 double. **Credit** AmEx, Disc, MC, V. **Map** p315 M5 ❹❶

Opened in 2007, the Orchard Garden was only the fourth hotel in the world to win LEED (Leadership in Energy & Environmental Design) certification, meaning it was designed according to strict environmental standards. Chemical-free cleaning products are used in its energy-saving rooms (the lights go off when you're not there), which are large by boutique hotel standards (and surprisingly quiet); furnishings sport a pale green and light wood palette. The lobby-level restaurant relies on organic, seasonal ingredients. The fitness center is petite, but discounted day passes are available to larger gyms nearby; the rooftop garden beckons in fair weather. A few blocks away on Bush Street, between Stockton and Powell, is its sister operation, the similarly pleasant and modern – though not as 'green' – Orchard Hotel (*see p113*).

Bar. Business center. Concierge. Gym. Internet (free Wi-Fi & high-speed). Parking ($45.60 incl tax). Restaurant. Room service. TV: DVD & pay movies.

Budget

Grant Plaza Hotel

465 Grant Avenue, at Pine Street, CA 94108 (1-800 472 6899, 434 3883, www.grantplaza.com). BART & Metro to Montgomery/bus 1, 2, 3, 30, 45, 91/cable car California. **Rates** $69-$139 double. **Credit** AmEx, DC, Disc, MC, V. **Map** p315 M5 ❹❷

As long as you don't need to find somewhere to park, the Grant Plaza Hotel, located right in the middle of busy Chinatown, is an excellent deal. The immaculately clean (if rather small) rooms are hardly stacked with amenities (there's basically a bath, a TV, a clock radio and a phone), but it's all about the location, location, location for most people who stay here.

Internet (free Wi-Fi). TV.

North Beach to Fisherman's Wharf

NORTH BEACH

Moderate

★ Hotel Bohème

444 Columbus Avenue, between Vallejo & Green Streets, CA 94133 (433 9111, www.hotelboheme.com). Bus 10, 12, 30, 39, 41, 45, 91. **Rates** $174-$194 double. **Credit** AmEx, Disc, MC, V. **Map** p315 M3 ❹❸

First set up after the 1906 earthquake by an Italian immigrant family and reopened as the Hotel Bohème in 1995, this hotel positively brims with North Beach Beat-era history. The walls are lined with smoky black and white photos of 1950s jazz luminaries, fragments of poetry turn up everywhere and you may even sleep in Allen Ginsberg's room (no.204): in his last years he was often seen here, looking out of the bay window, tapping away on his laptop (Wi-Fi access is free). The rooms are pretty tiny, on the whole, but at least you're surrounded by cafés and restaurants. For quieter nights, request a room that is not facing bustling Columbus Avenue.

Concierge. Internet (free Wi-Fi). TV.

▶ *The famous City Lights bookstore (see p181) is just across the street.*

Washington Square Inn

1660 Stockton Street, between Union & Filbert Streets, CA 94133 (1-800 388 0220, 981 4220, www.wsisf.com). Bus 10, 12, 30, 39, 41, 45, 91. **Rates** $209-$279 double. **Credit** AmEx, Disc, MC, V. **Map** p315 M3 ㊹

Close to one of San Francisco's prettiest urban parks, in a quiet part of North Beach, this is a convivial little inn, beautifully decorated with large gilt mirrors, pots of exotic orchids and lots of character. Each of the smallish rooms is furnished with antiques and luxurious fabrics, and the modern touch of free Wi-Fi. A couple of rooms' private baths are across the hall. The service is excellent: guests are provided with tea, wine and hors d'oeuvres every afternoon. The rates also include a decent continental breakfast, though it's a foolish soul who forgoes getting in line early for the outstanding breakfasts served at Mama's across the square.

Concierge. Internet (free Wi-Fi). Parking ($20-$35). Room service. TV.

Budget

San Remo Hotel

2337 Mason Street, at Bay Street, CA 94133 (1-800 352 7366, 776 8688, www.sanremohotel.com). Bus 30, 39, 47, 91/cable car Powell-Mason. **Rates** $69-$99 double. **Credit** AmEx, MC, V. **Map** p314 L2 ㊺

It's difficult to imagine this meticulously restored Italianate Edwardian serving time as a boarding house for dockworkers displaced by the Great Fire. Although the rooms are on the small side and the spotless shower rooms are shared (there's also one bath), you would be hard-pressed to find a finer hotel in San Francisco at this price. The rooms have either brass or cast-iron beds, wicker furniture and antique armoires, but otherwise are fairly basic. Ask for a room on the upper floor facing Mason Street or, if the penthouse is free, book it: it's so lovely you'll never want to leave.

Bar. Concierge. Internet (free Wi-Fi). Parking ($16). Restaurant.

FISHERMAN'S WHARF

Expensive

Argonaut Hotel

495 Jefferson Street, at Hyde Street, CA 94109 (1-866 415 0704, 563 0800, www.argonauthotel.com). Streetcar F/bus 19, 30, 47, 91/cable car Powell-Hyde. **Rates** $315-$449 double. **Credit** AmEx, Disc, MC, V. **Map** p314 K2 ㊻

Built into a historic fruit-packing warehouse, this beautiful luxury hotel is the best in the area by far. Located directly opposite Hyde Street Pier, the property celebrates the city's seafaring past, evidenced in the blue and yellow maritime decor and the abundant nautical props. The carefully furnished regular rooms have all the mod cons you might need (flat-screen TVs, Aveda bath products), but it's in the suites that the hotel excels itself: hot tub with a view of the ocean, tripod telescope in the lounge by the dining table. Breakfast is served in the Blue Mermaid (*see p150*) on the ground floor. If you want a sea view, ask for a north-facing room on the third floor or above. There's a small nautical museum off the lobby.

Bar. Business center. Concierge. Gym. Internet (free Wi-Fi). Parking ($45). Restaurant. Room service. TV: DVD & pay movies.

Moderate

There are also two big-chain favorites of tour groups and meeting planners in the area: the lively, brightly renovated 529-room **Sheraton Fisherman's Wharf** (2500 Mason Street, CA 94133, 1-877 271 2018, 362 5500, www.sheratonatthewharf.com) and the 313-room, family-friendly **Hyatt Fisherman's Wharf** (555 North Point Street, CA 94133, 1-888 591 1234, 563 1234, http://fishermanswharf.hyatt.com).

Wharf Inn

2601 Mason Street, at Beach Street, CA 94133 (1-800 548 9918, 673 7411, www.wharfinn.com). Streetcar F/bus 39, 47/cable car Powell-Mason. **Rates** $135-$215 double. **Credit** AmEx, Disc, MC, V. **Map** p314 L2 ㊼

This little hotel doesn't look like much from the outside. And, if we're being totally honest, it doesn't look like much from the inside, either. However, the location is perfect for those traveling with children, the rates are decent (the free parking is a real bonus). The service is friendly, and most of the rooms – which are done out with a playful retro beach motel theme – have balconies, some overlooking Pier 39.

Concierge. Internet (free Wi-Fi). Parking (free). TV.

The Mission & the Castro

THE MISSION

Moderate

Inn San Francisco

943 S Van Ness Avenue, between 20th & 21st Streets, CA 94110 (1-800 359 0913, 641 0188, www.innsf.com). BART to 24th Street Mission/bus 12, 14, 49. **Rates** $120-$245 double. **Credit** AmEx, Disc, MC, V. **Map** p318 K11 ㊽

This friendly Italianate Victorian, built in 1872, invites you to sprawl about in its beautifully restored sitting rooms, rather than just admire them. You can also take advantage of the garden hot tub or the

panoramic city views from its rooftop if your antiques-bedecked room starts to feel a bit too cozy. All but two rooms have private baths; thick rugs and carpets help dampen the noise common to older hotels. In any case, you'll probably use this location to explore the still-gentrifying neighborhood. The ample breakfast buffet is served until 11am, allowing late sleepers a chance to restore themselves completely before hitting the streets of the Mission again.
Internet (free Wi-Fi). Parking ($18). TV.

Parker House

520 Church Street, between 17th & 18th Streets, CA 94114 (1-888 520 7275, www.parkerguesthouse.com). Metro to Castro & Church & 18th Street/bus 22, 33. **Rates** $139-$229 double. **Credit** AmEx, Disc, MC, V. **Map** p318 J10 ㊾
A couple of blocks from the heart of the Castro, this smartly renovated Victorian (with an Edwardian annex) caters to gay and lesbian travelers, but everyone is welcome. Most rooms have private baths, and all have homey, contemporary decor. There are slight variations in amenities (dataports, desk sizes, shower versus bath), so let the hotel know if you have special requests. On sunny days the English gardens provide a nice respite from the bustling street scene, which also spills over into nearby Dolores Park (best avoided at night). Continental breakfast, free internet access and a wine social are included.
Concierge. Internet (free Wi-Fi & high speed terminal). Parking ($20). TV.

The Haight & Around

HAIGHT-ASHBURY

Moderate

Stanyan Park Hotel

750 Stanyan Street, at Waller Street, CA 94117 (751 1000, www.stanyanpark.com). Metro to Cole & Carl/bus 6, 33, 37, 43, 66, 71. **Rates** $155-$225 double. **Credit** AmEx, Disc, MC, V. **Map** p317 E9 ㊿
This beautifully maintained, three-story Victorian building on the edge of Golden Gate Park has been accommodating travelers in fine style since 1904; it's even listed on the National Register of Historic Places. The handsome rooms, of varying sizes and views, are filled with authentic Victorian antiques, right down to the drapes and quilts. Large groups may be attracted to the six big suites with full kitchens, dining rooms and living spaces – great for extended stays. Rates include free WiFi, breakfast and afternoon tea.
Internet (free Wi-Fi & shared terminal). TV.

Red Victorian

1665 Haight Street, between Belvedere & Cole Streets, CA 94117 (864 1978, www.redvic.com). Metro to Cole & Carl/bus 6, 33, 37, 43, 66, 71. **Rates** $129-$229 double. **Credit** AmEx, DC, Disc, MC, V. **Map** p317 E9 51

Hotel Kabuki. *See p130.*

Still basking in the Summer of Love, the hotel wears its hippie heart on its sleeve: wildly colorful rooms revel in names such as Flower Child and Rainbow, there's a Peace Café downstairs, and the eccentric, septuagenarian artist-owner goes by the name Sami Sunchild. Rooms have no TVs; only six have private baths; some of the furnishings are looking rather tatty, but neatness wasn't exactly what the '60s were about. A continental breakfast is included. No smoking – tobacco or grass – throughout the hotel, despite what the decor may lead you to believe.
Internet (shared terminal). Restaurant.

LOWER HAIGHT

Budget

Metro Hotel

319 Divisadero Street, between Oak & Page Streets, CA 94117 (861 5364, www.metrohotelsf.com). Bus 6, 21, 24, 71. **Rates** $76-$130 double. **Credit** AmEx, Disc, MC, V. **Map** p317 G8 ㊷

The 24-room Metro is cheap, convenient and a good base for exploring neighborhoods somewhat off the tourist track. The decor is bare-bones, the walls are a little thin, and the street-side rooms are noisy at night; all rooms have shower stalls only. Still, at these prices, complaining seems a little churlish. Request a room overlooking the back garden. Around the corner, and under the same ownership, is a two-room apartment, which is available for about $100 a night.
Concierge. Internet (free Wi-Fi). TV.

THE WESTERN ADDITION

Moderate

★ Hotel Kabuki

1625 Post Street, at Laguna Street, CA 94115 (1-800 533 4567, 922 3200, www.hotelkabuki.com). Bus 2, 3, 38. **Rates** $159-$199 double. **Credit** AmEx, DC, Disc, MC, V. **Map** p314 J6 ㊸

Unveiled in 2007, the former Miyako is still Japonesque, but will appeal to both eastern and western sensibilities, with sophisticated, modern design and plush American comforts. (For a budget, postmod version, inspired by the Japanese comic book art of anime, stay at the nearby Best Western Hotel Tomo, also managed by Joie de Vivre). The rooms include 26in flat-panel TVs, iPod docking stations, and new marble and tile baths (some with Japanese-style soaking tubs). Other touches: Asian tea kettles in the rooms, traditional welcome tea service, and J-Pop restaurant and bar that shows Japanese baseball on TV. Overlooking the Peace Pagoda, the Kabuki is just steps from dozens of sushi restaurants, shops and a Japanese spa and bathhouse (hotel guests receive a free pass). *Photo p129.*
Bar. Business center. Gym. Internet (free Wi-Fi & high-speed). Parking ($40). Restaurant. Room service. TV: pay movies.

Queen Anne Hotel

1590 Sutter Street, at Octavia Street, CA 94109 (1-800 227 3970, 441 2828, www.queenanne.com). Bus 2, 3, 38, 47, 49, 90. **Rates** $129-$199 double. **Credit** AmEx, Disc, MC, V. **Map** p314 J6 ㊹

One of the more successful olde-worlde hotel operations in San Francisco, the Queen Anne is, as its name suggests, housed in an extremely handsome old Victorian property. Having begun life as a finishing school for the city's posh young debs (the headmistress, Mary Lake, is rumored to haunt her former office, now Room 410), it was converted into a hotel in the 1980s. Each of the individually decorated rooms contains Victorian antiques, and the lobby area is a splendid space. Continental breakfast, afternoon tea and sherry, and a weekday morning car service to Downtown are all included in the rate, and guests also receive a discounted rate on day passes to the posh Plaza Athletic Club two blocks away.
Business center. Concierge. Internet (free Wi-Fi, high speed). Parking ($16). Room service. TV: pay movies.

HI-Fisherman's Wharf. *See p132.*

CONSUME

Sunset, Golden Gate Park & Richmond

RICHMOND

Budget

Seal Rock Inn
545 Point Lobos Avenue, at 48th Avenue, CA 94121 (1-888 732 5762, 752 8000, www.sealrockinn.com). Bus 38. **Rates** $129-$167 double. **Credit** AmEx, MC, V. 55

San Francisco doesn't really do beach motels, but this 1960s motor lodge comes pretty close. Most of the large and spotless rooms have at least partial ocean views and, at night you can fall asleep to the sound of distant foghorns. Furnishings won't win any awards, but most third-floor rooms have wood-burning fireplaces (in this foggy part of town, these book up early). Family-sized rooms come with a folding vinyl wall for visual privacy; some rooms have kitchenettes, the rest have mini-fridges and microwaves. Seal Rock is across from the Cliff House, perched on the Pacific's edge, and has free covered parking, a patio and, for the thick of skin, a heated outdoor pool.
Internet (free high-speed). Parking (free). Pool (outdoor). Restaurant. TV.

Pacific Heights to the Golden Gate Bridge

PACIFIC HEIGHTS

Expensive

Hotel Drisco
2901 Pacific Avenue, at Broderick Street, CA 94115 (1-800 634 7277, 346 2880, www.hoteldrisco.com). Bus 3, 24. **Rates** $209-$299 double. **Credit** AmEx, DC, Disc, MC, V. **Map** p313 F5 55

The hotel has actually been in business for over a century, but these days, the rooms only pay gentle homage to the hotel's history: the decor is a crisp, modern update of past fashions, the various fittings as handsome and refined as the environs. (Note that a few rooms have private but detached baths down a hall.) Business travelers will be grateful for the morning town car service to the Financial District (weekdays only). The complimentary breakfast buffet includes espresso drinks, while evenings bring free wine and cheese. (And you can work off indulgences with a free pass to the Presidio YMCA.)
Business center. Concierge. Internet (free Wi-Fi). Gym. Room service. TV: DVD.

Moderate

Jackson Court
2198 Jackson Street, at Buchanan Street, CA 94115 (929 7670, www.jacksoncourt.com). Bus 1, 3, 10, 22, 24. **Rates** $170-$235 double. **Credit** AmEx, MC, V. **Map** p314 H4 56

This fantastic neighborhood B&B is still, happily, flying under most visitors' radar. Located on a calm residential stretch of tony Pacific Heights, Jackson Court is built into a beautiful 19th-century brownstone mansion and is as quiet as a church. Each of the eight rooms and two suites is furnished with a soothing combination of antiques and tasteful contemporary pieces; all have private baths. Some have working fireplaces; ask for the Library Room, which boasts a hearth and a brass bed. Rates include continental breakfast and afternoon tea.
Internet (free Wi-Fi). TV.

Laurel Inn
444 Presidio Avenue, between California & Sacramento Streets, CA 94115 (1-800 552 8735, 567 8467, www.thelaurelinn.com). Bus 1, 2, 3, 43. **Rates** $149-$189 double. **Credit** AmEx, DC,Disc, MC, V. **Map** p313 F5 57

A motor inn renovated in mid-century modern style, this gem packs plenty of hip into a modest shell. The rooms are chicly appointed, with great bathroom amenities and modern accessories; some have kitchenettes and city views. Located well off the Downtown path, the Laurel nonetheless has easy transport options just out front. The lobby level is home to the popular Swank Cocktail Club (*see p176*), which brings in the scenesters on weekend nights. Service is excellent, continental breakfast is included, and there are great restaurants close at hand.
Bar. CD. Concierge. DVD. Internet (Wi-Fi, DSL, shared terminal). Parking (free).

COW HOLLOW

Moderate

Hotel Del Sol
3100 Webster Street, at Greenwich Street, CA 94123 (1-877 433 5765, 921 5520, www.thehoteldelsol.com). Bus 22, 28, 30, 41, 43, 45, 91. **Rates** $119-$189 double. **Credit** AmEx, Disc, MC, V. **Map** p313 H3 58

This former 1950s motel was made over with a splashy tropical palette and hip décor that separates it from the many no-tell motels along the Lombard strip. A (very rare) outdoor pool gives it another edge. The 47 rooms and 10 suites (three with kitchenettes, two with fireplaces) are decorated with bright crayon colors; cool details include clock radios that wake guests to the sound of rain or waves. The family suite has bunkbeds, toys, books and games, and guests can go to the quirky Pillow Library to choose their own headrests. Complimentary coffee, tea and muffins

CONSUME

are served by the pool each morning, and the free parking is a valuable commodity in these parts.
Concierge. Internet (Wi-Fi). Parking (free). Pool (outdoor).

Union Street Inn

2229 Union Street, between Fillmore & Steiner Streets, CA 94123 (346 0424, www.unionstreet inn.com). Bus 22, 28, 41, 43, 45, 91. **Rates** $189-$329 double. **Credit** AmEx, Disc, MC, V. **Map** p313 G4 59

Rooms at this B&B are furnished in traditional style, with canopied or brass beds, feather duvets and fresh flowers. All have private bathrooms, some of them with jacuzzi tubs. The English Garden room has a private deck, while the Carriage House behind the inn has its own garden. An extended continental breakfast can be taken in the parlour, in your room or on a terrace overlooking the hotel garden. Evening pampering is available in the form of hors d'oeuvres and cocktails, included in the room price.
Concierge. Internet (Wi-Fi). Parking ($15).

THE MARINA & THE WATERFRONT

Budget

The **HI-Fisherman's Wharf** hostel (*see right*) also has some private rooms. The **Marina Motel** (2576 Lombard Street, CA 94123, 1-800 346 6118, 921 9406, www.marinamotel.com, $149-$169 double) is another basic but affordable option.

Marina Inn

3110 Octavia Street, at Lombard Street, CA 94123 (1-800 274 1420, 928 1000, www.marinainn.com). Bus 28, 30, 91.
Rates $75-$125 double. **Credit** AmEx, DC, Disc, MC, V. **Map** p314 H3 60

Spread over four stories of this quiet Victorian-style inn (it actually dates to 1924), rooms are all furnished with floral wallpaper, pine fittings and four-poster beds. Continental breakfast included.
Internet (free Wi-Fi). TV.

INSIDE TRACK HAUTE HOSTELS

San Francisco is no longer America's crash pad, as it was in the '60s,but there are several solid, low-cost options for travelers on a budget. **USA Hostels San Francisco** (*see right*) was named the best hostel in the US for 2010, and, with eight cooking stations, a video game lounge, and a 50-seat theater it's easy to understand why. And there are plenty of other hostel choices in the city; for some of the best, *see right*.

Hostels

San Francisco Hostels (www.sfhostels.com) has three locations: the City Center hostel is a converted boutique hotel, the Downtown branch is one block from Union Square, and the Fisherman's Wharf outpost at Fort Mason sits on a slice of San Francisco real estate that many would pay millions for.

There are around 20 hostels in the city. For full listings, go to www.hostels.com/us.ca.sf.html.

Adelaide Hostel

5 Isadora Duncan Lane, off Taylor Street, between Post & Geary Streets, Tenderloin, CA 94102 (1-877 359 1915, 359 1915, www.adelaidehostel.com). Bus 2, 3, 27, 31, 38/cable car Powell-Hyde or Powell-Mason. **Rates** $23 dorm bed; rooms from $60. **Credit** AmEx, Disc, MC, V. **Map** p314 L5 61

Until 2003, the Adelaide was a friendly, old-fashioned pension, but the owners expanded the 18 rooms to add six en suites and two 12-bed dormitories, and for a mere $23, you also get continental breakfast and free internet.

HI-Downtown

312 Mason Street, at O'Farrell Street, Union Square & around, CA 94102 (1-888 464 4872, 788 5604, www.sfhostels.com). BART & Metro to Powell/bus 2, 3, 4, 30, 38, 76 & Market Street routes/cable car Powell-Hyde or Powell-Mason. **Rates** $25-29.75 dorm bed; $79-99 room. **Credit** AmEx, Disc, MC, V. **Map** p315 M6 62

Make your reservation at least five weeks in advance during high season to stay at this popular 260-bed hostel. It prides itself on its privacy and security, with guests accommodated in small single-sex rooms; some larger rooms also have their own bathroom. Beds for walk-ins are available on a first-come, first-served basis: bring ID or you'll be turned away. Free breakfast and Wi-Fi internet access.

Hostelling International runs two other hostels in San Francisco. The 75-room **HI-City Centre** (685 Ellis Street, between Larkin & Hyde Streets, Tenderloin, 474 5721) was refurbished to a good standard a few years ago, while **HI-Fisherman's Wharf** (Building 240, Fort Mason, at Bay & Franklin Streets, Marina, 771 7277) offers a wide variety of rooms (some private), free parking and outstanding views of the Bay. As with HI-Downtown, both provide free breakfast and Wi-Fi. *Photo p130.*
Internet (free Wi-Fi).

USA Hostels

711 Post Street, between Jones & Leavenworth Streets, Tenderloin, CA 94109 (440 5600, www.usahostels.com/sanfrancisco). Bus 2, 3, 4, 27, 38. **Rates** from £30 dorm bed; rooms from $80. **Credit** AmEx, Disc, MC, V. **Map** p314 L5 63
See left **Inside Track**.

CONSUME

Restaurants & Cafés

San Francisco refuses to rest on its culinary laurels.

The Bay Area's stellar reputation as a center for pioneering food movements and culinary trends is well established and well deserved. Forty years ago, when Alice Waters introduced the country to fresh California cuisine, the concept of farm-to-table dining was not yet a glimmer in the eye of the locavore movement. Today, the terms slow, sustainable, seasonal and organic are so common on menus they're almost an afterthought. In the city of San Francisco, diners will find them at either end of the price scale.

The last few years have also seen an explosion of gourmet food trucks and street vendors at spots all around town (*see p161* **Taking it to the Street**), while celebrity chefs continue to be drawn to the Bay Area for new ventures (Tyler Florence and Iron Chef Masaharu Morimoto are the latest). No matter your preference, you'll find no shortage of exciting dining options in this culinary capital.

THE LOCAL SCENE

San Francisco's come-as-you-are attitude (and dress code) basically prevails in even the most posh restaurants around town. But be warned: casual attitude doesn't mean easy access. Reservations at some of the city's 'it' spots can be as hard to come by as a warm day at Ocean Beach in July. Online reservation service Open Table (www.opentable.com) is often your best bet when it comes to snagging something on a Friday or Saturday night. Many restaurants also hold a small selection of tables for walk-ins, so it pays to call ahead. Can't decide where to go? Yelp.com offers opinions and reviews galore from local diners, though the harshest criticisms and most gushing praise should both be taken with a grain of salt.

DOWNTOWN

Union Square & Around

Bourbon Steak

335 Powell Street, between Geary and Post Streets (397 3003, www.michaelmina.net). Metro Powell/Downtown cable car Powell-Hyde or Powell-Mason/streetcar J, K, T, L, M, N. **Open** 5.30pm-10.30pm daily. **Credit** AmEx, DC, Disc, JCB, MC, V. **Map** p315 M5 ❶ American

Gotham meets SF with this outpost of celeb chef Michael Mina's steak and whisky-themed powerhouse. Looking to turn the tables on your cardiologist? Decadent is the only way to describe the steaks, and that's not because of the portion size or cost – though both are hefty – it's how the beef is cooked. Employing an elaborate process of his own devising, Mina's steaks are slowly poached in butter for an hour in thermal circulators that are precise to within a tenth of a degree, then seared for a minute on each side on a wood-fired grill. The result? Super tender, perfectly cooked steaks worth their weight in… well, butter. For lunch, choose from pizza by the slice, panini, antipasti and rich desserts.

> ❶ Blue numbers given in this chapter correspond to the location of each restaurant or café as marked on the street maps. *See pp312-319.*

INSIDE TRACK QUICK TIPS

A quick way to figure out the standard 20 per cent tip: simply double the sales tax on your bill.

★ Café Claude

7 Claude Lane, off Sutter Street, between Kearny Street & Grant Avenue (392 3505, www.cafeclaude.com). BART & Metro to Montgomery/bus 2, 3, 30, 38, 45 & Market Street routes/cable car Powell-Hyde or Powell-Mason. **Open** 11.30am-11.30pm Mon-Sat; 5.30-10.30pm Sun. **Main courses** $15. **Credit** AmEx, Disc, MC, V. **Map** p315 M5 ❷ French

Owner Stephen Decker purchased Le Barbizon café in Paris and shipped it to San Francisco one piece at a time. The result, now set in an alleyway and resplendent with French style and attitude, is as close to a true French café as can be found anywhere in America. Trad dishes include salad niçoise and steak tartare.

Café de la Presse

352 Grant Avenue, at Bush Street (398 2680, www.cafedelapresse.com). BART & Metro to Montgomery/bus 2, 3, 30, 38, 45 & Market Street routes/cable car Powell-Hyde or Powell-Mason. **Open** 7.30-10am, 11.30am-2.30pm, 5.30-9.30pm Mon-Thur; 7.30-10am, 11.30am-2.30pm, 5.30-10pm Fri; 8am-4pm, 5.30-10pm Sat, Sun. **Main courses** $25. **Credit** AmEx, Disc, MC, V. **Map** p315 M5 ❸ French

This bustling spot has become one of the most reliable in the Downtown area, with classic French-inspired fare along with café-style choices for the less committed. It also stocks a bevy of foreign newspapers and magazines for those hungry for international news.

Colibrí Mexican Bistro

438 Geary Street, between Taylor & Mason Streets (440 2737, www.colibrimexicanbistro.com). BART & Metro to Powell/bus 2, 3, 30, 38, 45 & Market Street routes/cable car Powell-Hyde or Powell-Mason. **Open** 11.30am-10pm Mon; 11.30am-11pm Tue-Thur; 11.30am-midnight Fri; 10.30am-midnight Sat; 10.30am-10pm Sun. **Main courses** $16. **Credit** AmEx, MC, V. **Map** p314 L5 ❹ Latin American

In the heart of the theater district, this unpretentious restaurant serves delicious and atypical Mexican fare. Dishes are presented tapas-style, with unfamiliar regional flavors to the fore. The selection includes brilliant tortilla soup, tamarind-sautéed shrimp served with corn cakes, and a fire-roasted *chile relleno* that will have you raving almost before you put down your fork. A different experience in Mexican eating.

Fifth Floor

Hotel Palomar, 12 4th Street, at Market Street (348 1555, www.fifthfloorrestaurant.com). BART & Metro to Powell/bus 27, 30, 38, 45 & Market Street routes/cable car Powell-Hyde or Powell-Mason. **Open** 7-10am, 5-11pm Mon-Thur; 7-10am, 5pm-midnight Fri; 8-11am, 5pm-midnight Sat; 8-11am Sun. **Main courses** $50. **Credit** AmEx, Disc, MC, V. **Map** p315 M6 ❺ French

Since its start-of-the-century debut, this chic and reliable high-dollar restaurant (and lounge and bar) has become established as one of the best places in the city to find a five-star French experience. The dining room is sophisticated and stylish, and the daily changing menu is among the city's best. Preparations are unfussy, and service is top-notch. The wine list, administered by one of the area's top sommeliers, is among the best in the region.

Kuleto's & Bar Norcini

Villa Florence Hotel, 221 Powell Street, at Geary Street (397 7720, www.kuletos.com). BART & Metro to Powell/bus 2, 3, 30, 38, 45 & Market Street routes/cable car Powell-Hyde or Powell-Mason. **Open** 7-10.30am, 11.30am-10.30pm Mon-Thur; 7-10.30am, 11.30am-11pm Fri; 8-10.30am, 11.30am-11pm Sat; 8-10.30am, 11.30am-10.30pm Sun. **Main courses** $27. **Credit** AmEx, Disc, MC, V. **Map** p315 M6 ❻ Italian & pizza

Located near Union Square, this sophisticated spot for authentic, seasonal, and expertly executed Italian food has been atop diners' and critics' lists for more than 20 years. Up front, Bar Norcini features house-baked pastries in the morning, pizzas and paninis at lunch, and a wine bar with housemade salumi, artisan cheeses, and 40 wines by the glass every evening.

Masa's

648 Bush Street, between Stockton & Powell Streets (989 7154, www.masasrestaurant.com). Bus 1, 2, 3, 30, 38, 45, 91/cable car Powell-Hyde or Powell-Mason. **Open** 5.30-9.30pm Tue-Sat. Set meal $95 and above. Credit AmEx, Disc, MC, V. Map p315 M5 ❼ French

Masa's was the first notable restaurant to combine SF haute cuisine with a French dining aesthetic. The kitchen has seen many talented chefs at the stoves, but each has maintained the high level of care taken by his predecessor, ensuring the Masa's experience remains one worth having (and paying for). The French-inspired fare is typically as mouthwatering as it is eye-popping.

Scala's Bistro

Sir Francis Drake Hotel, 432 Powell Street, between Post & Sutter Streets (395 8555, www.scalasbistro.com). BART & Metro to Powell/bus 2, 3, 30, 38, 45 & Market Street routes/cable car Powell-Hyde or Powell-Mason. **Open** 7-10.30am, 11.30am-4pm, 5.15-11pm Mon-Wed; 7-10.30am, 11.30-4pm, 5.15pm-midnight

CONSUME

Thur, Fri; 8am-4pm, 5.15pm-midnight Sat; 8am-4pm, 5.15-11pm Sun. **Main courses** $25. **Credit** AmEx, Disc, MC, V. **Map** p315 M5 ❽ Italian & pizza

Recently refurbished to fine effect, this bustling bistro is frequented by tourists staying in Union Square and locals attracted by robust, reasonably priced Cal-Mediterranean food. Reliable choices range from the daily risotto to fresh-made pasta. Meal-size salads are a hit during lunch.

The Financial District

Kokkari Estiatorio

200 Jackson Street, at Front Street (981 0983, www.kokkari.com). BART & Metro to Embarcadero/bus 1, 10, 12, 41. **Open** 11.30am-2.30pm, 5.30-10pm Mon-Thur; 11.30am-2.30pm, 5.30-11pm Fri; 5-11pm Sat; 5-10pm Sun. **Main courses** $20. **Credit** AmEx, Disc, MC, V. **Map** p315 N4 ❾ Greek

Kokkari serves what it describes as 'Hellenic cuisine'. It's outstanding, although highly priced, and unlike what most people think of when it comes to Greek food. The *pikilia*, an appetizer plate featuring three traditional Greek dips with fresh pittas, is a good place to start. Grilled lamb chops, pan-roasted fish and traditional dishes like moussaka are main-course highlights.

Michael Mina

252 California Street, between Front & Battery Streets (397 9222, www.michaelmina.net). BART to Embarcadero/streetcar & bus all Market Street routes. **Open** 11.30am-2pm, 5.30pm-10pm Mon-Thur, Sun; 11.30am-2pm, 5.30pm-10.30pm Fri-Sat. **Mains** $40. **Credit** AmEx, DC, Disc, MC, V. **Map** p315 N4 ❿ American

Famed chef Michael Mina created a stir when he uprooted his Union Square restaurant and relocated back to the spot in the Financial District where he got his start (the former Aqua). He hasn't

Frisco Foraging

Farmers' markets are a San Francisco specialty.

In the decades since 'California cuisine' made Northern California chefs internationally famous, their ideal of using fresh, seasonal, sustainably farmed ingredients made by local producers has migrated from the kitchens of four-star restaurants to the plates of mere mortals. Farmers' markets have exploded in neighborhoods throughout the Bay Area and it's no wonder – with the amount of food production that happens here it may be easier to eat and drink things produced within a 100-mile radius of the Bay Area than any other area of the country.

San Francisco's largest farmers' market surrounds the Ferry Building, with some 80 farm stands, as well as scores of vendors selling everything from locally made jam, cheeses, breads and baked goods to prepared snacks. At the opposite end of the spectrum, **ForageSF** (www.foragesf.com) is a 'wild foods community' geared towards, yes, foraging wild foods and educating the community about the edible goodies growing all around them. Its Wild Food Walks are a great way to see the region while learning about harvesting and cooking wild foods, and at its SF Underground Market home chefs, dedicated amateurs and a few pros serve everything from cupcakes to quinoa.

Weekly farmers' markets include:

- **Alemany Farmers Market** 100 Alemany Boulevard, near Bayshore Freeway, Mission/Bernal Heights (647 2043). **Open** 6am-3pm Sat.
- **Crocker Galleria Farmers Market** Crocker Galleria, 50 Post Street, between Kearny Street & Montgomery Street, Financial District (393 1505). **Open** 11am-3pm Thur.
- **Ferry Plaza Farmers Market** Ferry Building, 1 Ferry Plaza, Embarcadero (291 3276). **Open** 10am-2pm Tue; 8am-2pm Sat.
- **Fillmore Farmers Market** O'Farrell Street at Fillmore Street & Fillmore Center Plaza, Fillmore District. **Open** 9am-1pm Sat.
- **Heart of the City Farmers Market** Market Street, between 7th & 8th streets, Civic Center (558 9455). **Open** 7am-5.30pm Wed; 7am-5pm Sun.
- **Noe Valley Farmers Market** 3861 24th Street, between Vicksburg & Sanchez Streets, Noe Valley (248 1332). **Open** 8am-1pm Sat, live music at 10am.
- **Stonestown Farmers Market** West side parking lot near Macy's, off Buckingham Way, Sunset (564 8848). **Open** 9am-1pm Sun.
- **UCSF Farmers Market** 505 Parnassus Avenue, between Hillway Avenue & 3rd Avenue, Sunset. **Open** *May-Oct* 10am-3pm Wed.

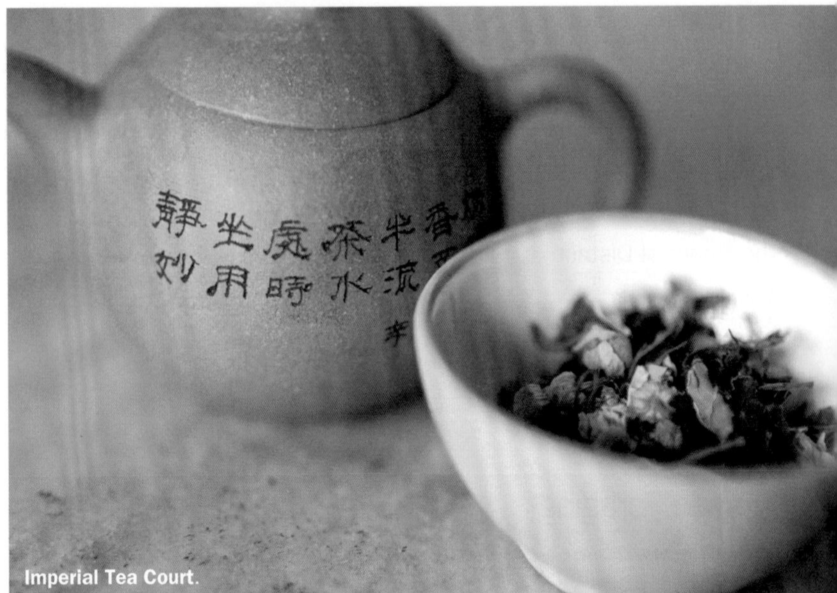

Imperial Tea Court.

lost a step. His new menu approach has scrapped the signature three-way preparations in favor of French-influenced food made with Japanese ingredients. Less frou frou than its predecessor, it's still dining on a grand scale (and at a grand price), but one taste of the *ahi* tuna tartare or Maine lobster pot pie and you'll whip out your credit card without a second thought.

Plouf

40 Belden Place, between Bush & Pine Streets (986 6491, www.ploufsf.com). BART & Metro to Montgomery/bus bus 1, 2, 3, 15, 30, 38 45 & Market Street routes/cable car California & Drumm. **Open** 11.30am-3pm, 5.30-10pm Mon-Thur; 11am-3pm, 5.30-11pm Fri; 5.30-11pm Sat. **Main courses** $20. **Credit** AmEx, MC, V. **Map** p315 M5 ⓫ French

This charming, always-packed restaurant is named after the French word for 'splash'. No dining experience here is complete without a bucket of steamed mussels, but the ever-changing array of fish is also excellent. At lunch, join the throngs at sidewalk tables in the alley for a little bit of Paris.

► *For more about the outdoor dining scene at Belden Place, see p48.*

Sam's Grill

374 Bush Street, between Montgomery & Kearny Streets (421 0594, www.belden-place/samsgrill). BART & Metro to Montgomery/bus 1, 2, 3, 15, 30, 38 45 & Market Street routes/cable car California. **Open** 11am-9pm Mon-Fri. **Main courses** $20. Credit AmEx, Disc, MC, V. **Map** p315 M5 9 ⓬ American

Sam's has been satisfying San Franciscan appetites for over 140 years. The restaurant holds fast to history, with a friendly atmosphere and a charming dining room paneled in dark wood and punctuated by bright-white tablecloths. The American menu is largely driven by seafood, but it's worth opting for such local specialties as the wonderful Hangtown Fry. At lunch, don't pass on the burgers.

★ Tadich Grill

240 California Street, between Battery and Front streets, (391 1849, www.tadichgrill.com). BART to Embarcadero/streetcar & bus all Market Street routes. **Open** 11am-9.30pm Mon-Fri, 11.30am-9.30pm Sat. Reservations not accepted. **Main courses** $20. **Credit** MC, V. **Map** p315 N4 ⓭ Fish & seafood

At 160 years, San Francisco's oldest restaurant may seem a little worn around the edges, but its clubby old-school atmosphere and classic yesteryear dishes more than make up for it. White-coated waiters usher you into private wooden booths or point to seats at the huge mahogany bar where crab Louis, shrimp à la Newburg, Hangtown Fry (oysters and eggs), and giant bowls of San Francisco *cioppino* (shellfish stew) are served – accompanied by big hunks of sourdough bread. A power-lunching spot for city politicos and financiers, Tadich is as close as you'll get in San Francisco to reliving the Barbary Coast days.

The Embarcadero

Americano

Hotel Vitale, 8 Mission Street, at the Embarcadero (278 3777, www.americanorestaurant.com). BART & Metro to Embarcadero/streetcar F/bus 2, 14, 31, 41 & Market Street routes. **Open** 6.30-10.30am, 11.30am-2.30pm, 5.30-10pm Mon-Fri; 7.30-11am, 5.30-10pm Sat; 7.30-11am, 4-10pm Sun. **Main courses** $26. **Credit** AmEx, Disc, MC, V. **Map** p315 O4 ⑭ American

This sleek, understatedly elegant restaurant in the Hotel Vitale offers seasonally fresh, Italian-inspired food, with many ingredients sourced from the Ferry Plaza Farmers' Market across the street. Try panini at lunch, grilled ribeye at dinner, and the restaurant's own-made gelato for dessert. Much attention is also paid to the breakfasts.

Boulevard

1 Mission Street, at Steuart Street (543 6084, www.boulevardrestaurant.com). BART & Metro to Embarcadero/streetcar F/ bus 2, 14, 31, 41 & Market Street routes. **Open** 11.30am-2pm, 5.30-10pm Mon-Thur; 11.30am-2pm, 5.30-10.30pm Fri; 5.30-10.30pm Sat; 5.30-10pm Sun. **Main courses** $35. **Credit** AmEx, Disc, MC, V. **Map** p315 O4 ⑮ American

Since 1993, this classic-looking restaurant has been one of San Francisco's most consistently reliable: from the service to the cooking, there's seldom a misstep. Always busy, it attracts locals and visitors with waterfront views and hearty food. Self-taught chef Nancy Oakes specializes in elaborate New American dishes – pork chops, steaks and risottos – although wood-roasted dishes are another strength.

Café de Stijl

1 Union Street, at Front Street (291 0808, www.destijl.com). Bus 10, 12. **Open** 7am-5pm Mon-Fri. **Main courses** $9.50. **Credit** AmEx, Disc, MC, V. **Map** p315 N3 ⑯ International

Named after the Dutch art movement, de Stijl is a small but lively café with sleek decor, pleasant ambience and a wide-ranging menu. Middle Eastern dishes are a specialty, as are Tuscan-style roast chicken and bowl-sized lattes.

Epic Roasthouse

369 Embarcadero between Harrison & Folsom Streets (369 9955, www.epicroasthousesf.com). BART & Metro to Embarcadero/streetcar F/bus 2, 14, 31, 41 & Market Street routes. **Open** 5-9.30pm Mon-Thur, Sun; 5pm-10pm Fri; 11am-3pm Sun. **Main courses** $39. **Credit** AmEx, DC, MC, V. **Map** p315 P5 ⑰ American

The first destination waterfront restaurant to be built on the Embarcadero in decades, Epic Roasthouse and its adjoining sister, Waterbar (*see p139*) co-opted a pristine piece of waterfront real estate with spectacular views of the Bay Bridge. Chef Jan Birnbaum goes far beyond the standard steakhouse, with wood-fired oven offerings that include aged Kobe beef, rib eye, pork and lamb, and tableside prime rib – all presented bone-in. For the less carnivorous, there's also poultry and seafood. If you don't have a reservation, try upstairs at Quiver Bar.

Fog City Diner

1300 Battery Street, at Greenwich Street (982 2000, www.fogcitydiner.com). Bus 39. **Open** 11.30am-10pm Mon-Thur; 11.30am-11pm Fri; 10.30am-11pm Sat; 10.30am-10pm Sun. **Main courses** $20. **Credit** AmEx, DC, MC, V. **Map** p315 N2 ⑱ American

From the outside, this looks like a modern update of a classic 1950s diner. Inside, the decor is swankier, and the menu lurches from burgers and steaks to crab cakes and grilled salmon. The menu is too long for its own good, and prices are higher than they should be, but you can still eat well here.

Globe Restaurant

290 Pacific Avenue, at Battery Street (391 4132, www.globerestaurant.com). Bus 1, 10, 12, 41. **Open** 11.30am-3pm, 6pm-1am Mon-Fri; 6pm-1am Sat; 6pm-midnight Sun. **Main courses** $22. **Credit** AmEx, Disc, MC, V. **Map** p315 N3 ⑲ American

A popular hangout for off-duty chefs, this dining room has an exposed-brick look that imparts an urban, New York feel to it. The menu offers such standards as wood-oven pizzas, braised short ribs and grilled salmon, prepared with fresh ingredients and without complications.

Gott's Roadside

1 Ferry Building, at the Embarcadero (1-866 328 3663, www.gottsroadside.com). BART & Metro to Embarcadero/streetcar F/bus 2, 14, 31 & Market Street routes. **Open** 10.30am-10pm daily. **Main courses** $11. **Credit** AmEx, MC, V. **Map** p315 O4 ⑳ American

Some 50 years after the original opened its drive-thru window in the Napa Valley, the second branch of Gott's Roadside (formerly Taylor's Refresher) set up shop in the Ferry Building. The decor is rather more modern than at the original, and the menu a little posher in parts, but the basics – burgers, fries, malts and shakes – remain peerless.

Imperial Tea Court

27 Ferry Market Place, Ferry Building, at the Embarcadero (544 9830, www.imperialtea.com). BART & Metro to Embarcadero/streetcar F/bus 2, 14, 31 & Market Street routes. **Open** 10am-6pm Mon-Fri; 9am-6.30pm Sat; 10.30am-6pm Sun. **Main courses** $10. **Credit** AmEx, MC, V. **Map** p315 O4 ㉑ Café

There are few better places in the city of San Francisco for tea. This serene tea house, an offshoot of the original Chinatown shop, offers a vast array of teas, served to the accompaniment of birds chirping in cages. Presented in the traditional Chinese *gaiwan* (covered cup), the teas include Fancy Dragon Well, Silver Needle and Snow Water; they're all available to take away too, along with teapots, teacups and other accessories. Traditional nibbles – dim sum to noodles – are served as an accompaniment.

Market Bar

1 Ferry Building, at the Embarcadero (434 1100, www.marketbar.com). BART & Metro to Embarcadero/streetcar F/bus 2, 14, 31 & Market Street routes. **Open** 11.30am-9pm Mon-Fri; 9am-8pm Sat, Sun. **Main courses** $22. **Credit** AmEx, MC, V. **Map** p315 O4 ㉒ American

This casual brasserie at the waterfront features hearty California cuisine and some Italian fare. The catch here is the excellent seafood: soul-warming bouillabaisse and *cioppino*. Dinner begins with fresh bread, and typically finishes with a lovely dessert, such as chocolate croissant pudding.

Ozumo

161 Steuart Street, at Mission Street (882 1333, www.ozumo.com). BART & Metro to Embarcadero/streetcar F/bus 2, 14, 31, 41 & Market Street routes. **Open** 11.30am-2pm, 5.30-10pm Mon-Wed; 11.30am-2pm, 5.30-10.30pm Thur; 11.30am-2.30pm, 5.30-11pm Fri; 5.30-11pm Sat; 5.30-10pm Sun. **Main courses** $25. **Credit** AmEx, DC, MC, V. **Map** p315 O4 ㉓ Asian

A beautiful contemporary Japanese restaurant where some 6,000sq ft (560sq m) of design panache swaddle an equally chic crowd. The front dining room holds a bar and lounge serving an exhaustive menu of sakés and rare teas. Amble past the *robata* grill – the meat, fish and vegetables from the *robata* menu are the real attractions – and you'll come to an enormous main dining room, with a sushi bar and Bay Bridge views.

Grounds Control

The coffee culture pioneers.

Seattle may lay claim to the first Starbucks, but more than a century before the first vente latte, San Francisco was already steeped in coffee culture. Pioneer Steam Coffee and Spice Mills was founded in San Francisco in 1850, but it became better known after James A Folger acquired it and renamed it in 1872. Folger's Coffee went on to become the largest coffee company in the world and the building at 101 Howard Street (now on the National Register of History Places) still has its name emblazoned on the side. The building at 2 Harrison Street was headquarters to another coffee pioneer, Hills Brothers. Founded in 1878 by brothers Austin and RW Hills, the company began as a market stall and exploded in 1900 after RW invented vacuum packing – a method still widely used today.

The beans were firmly planted, but it wasn't until 1966, when Alfred Peet opened Peet's Coffee, Tea & Spices at 2124 Vine Street in Berkeley, that the modern-day coffee revolution began. What distinguished Peet's coffee was the insistence on high-quality beans, fresh roasted in small batches and, crucially, much darker than was the norm at the time. The founders of Starbucks, Gordon Bowker, Zev Siegl and Jerry Baldwin, who met while students at the University of San Francisco, got their start researching roasters when Siegl got a job at Peet's. Later, they sourced their beans from Peet's when they created Starbucks in 1971. Peet's focused on tea and coffee sales; Starbucks on coffee bars – and the rest is history. (The ultimate irony may still yet unfold: as the guide goes to press, rumors are circulating that Starbucks is in discussions to purchase Peet's.)

Today, San Francisco coffee culture has undergone a renaissance, with small-batch, single-origin artisanal roasters popping up all over town. The most well known, **Blue Bottle Coffee** (*see p141*), created the market for the trend and now boasts several outlets throughout the region. Other notable roasters include **Caffè Roma** (*see p146*) and **Graffeo Coffee** (735 Columbus Avenue, between Mason & Powell Streets, 986 2420, www.graffeo.com) in North Beach; **Ritual Roasters** (*see p152*), **Four Barrel** (375 Valencia Street, between 14th & 15th Streets, 252 0800, www.fourbarrelcoffee.com), **De la Paz** (933 Treat Avenue, between 22nd & 23rd Street, 525 4344, www.delapazcoffee.com) and **Philz** (3101 24th Street, at Folsom Street, 875 9370, www.philzcoffee.com) in the Mission; and SoMa's **Sightglass Coffee** (270 7th Street, between Howard & Folsom Streets, 861 1313, www.sightglasscoffee.com).

For addled coffee obsessives, there's also the coffee-themed Java Walk tour (http://www.zerve.com/JavaWalk/Coffee), which covers the history of San Francisco coffee culture and visits some of the city's best coffeehouses (samples included).

Slanted Door

1 Ferry Building, at the Embarcadero (861 8032, www.slanteddoor.com). BART & Metro to Embarcadero/streetcar F/bus 2, 14, 31 & Market Street routes. **Open** 11am-2.30pm, 5.30-10pm Mon-Thur, Sun; 11am-2.30pm, 5.30-10.30pm Fri, Sat. **Main courses** $30. **Credit** AmEx, DC, MC, V. **Map** p315 O4 ㉔ Asian

The sleek lines and Bay views of Charles Phan's popular restaurant are alluring, but the attraction remains Phan's incredible, inventive Vietnamese-inspired food. There isn't a bad choice on the menu, although the shaking beef, the spicy short ribs and the shrimp and crab spring rolls continue to stand out.

Waterbar

399 Embarcadero at Harrison Street (284 9922, www.waterbarsf.com). BART & Metro to Embarcadero/streetcar F/ bus 2, 14, 31, 41 & Market Street routes. **Open** 11.30am-2pm, 5.30-9.30pm Mon-Thur, Sun; 11.30am-2pm, 5.30-10pm Tue-Sat; 11.30am-2.45pm Sat, Sun. **Main courses** $34. **Credit** AmEx, DC, Disc, MC, V. **Map** p315 N5 ㉕ Fish & seafood

Sister to Epic Roasthouse (*see p137*), Waterbar takes full advantage of its Embarcadero waterfront location with panoramic views of the Bay from both inside and the outdoor patio. A pair of massive, 19-foot circular aquariums anchors the main floor, filled with all-manner of fish and marine creatures. A glass "caviar" chandelier and a horseshoe-shaped raw bar offers dramatic seating for the sustainably harvested seafood menu, which might include oak-roasted wild striped bass with chick pea falafel, grilled Serrano ham-wrapped sturgeon, or chili-roasted steelhead.

Yank Sing

Rincon Center, 101 Spear Street, at Mission Street (781 1111, www.yanksing.com). BART & Metro

Blue Bottle Coffee.

CONSUME

to Montgomery/bus 2, 31, 38, 108 & Market Street routes. **Open** 11am-3pm Mon-Fri; 10am-4pm Sat, Sun. **Main courses** dim sum $6. **Credit** AmEx, DC, MC, V. **Map** p315 O4 ㉖ Asian

The quality of Yank Sing's dim sum explains how it manages to thrive in the corner of a massive office complex. Non-English-speaking waitresses roll out an endless array of steaming dumplings; a loyal, on-the-go business crowd snaps them up with speed.

Other locations 29 Stevenson Street, SoMa, 541 4949.

The Tenderloin

Dottie's True Blue Café

522 Jones Street, at O'Farrell Street (885 2767). BART & Metro to Powell/bus 2, 3, 27, 31, 38/cable car Powell-Hyde or Powell-Mason. **Open** 7.30am-3pm Mon, Wed-Sun. **Main courses** $10. **Credit** Disc, MC, V. **Map** p314 L6 ㉗ Café

Be prepared to wait a little to be seated for your breakfast: maybe *huevos rancheros* or pancakes, possibly a funky omelet or huge scramble of cheese and veggies. When it arrives, it may well be one of the best breakfasts you've ever tasted. A quintessential piece of West Coast Americana.

Fish & Farm

339 Taylor Street, at Ellis Street (474 3474, www.fishandfarmsf.com). BART & Metro to Powell/bus 2, 3, 27, 31, 38 & Market Street routes/cable car Powell-Hyde or Powell-Mason. **Open** 5-10pm Mon-Wed, Sun; 5-11pm Thur-Sat. **Main courses** $25. **Credit** AmEx, Disc, MC, V. **Map** p314 L6 ㉘ American

Building on the city's claim to embrace sustainability in all facets of life, this chic, intimate restaurant endeavors to source items on its menu from no more than 100 miles away, and makes ingredients for the all-organic cocktail list in-house. Dishes are simple, tasty and elegantly plated, and include many familiar but inventively interpreted American favorites – Liberty Ale-battered fish and chips to Niman Ranch country pork chops. The wine list consists of varietals from small organic and biodynamic producers.

Millennium

580 Geary Street (in Hotel California), at Jones Street (345 3900, www.millenniumrestaurant.com). BART & Metro to Powell/bus 2, 3, 27, 31, 38/cable car Powell-Hyde or Powell-Mason. **Open** 5.30-9.30pm Mon-Thur, Sun; 5.30-10.30pm Fri, Sat. **Main courses** $25. **Credit** AmEx, Disc, MC, V. **Map** p314 L6 ㉙ International

Casual, elegant Millennium is still setting the pace when it comes to vegetarian and vegan cooking in San Francisco, doing things with vegetables that you'd never dream possible. The food, both the carte and the tasting menu, changes frequently, driven by the freshest available ingredients; it's accompanied by one of the best all-organic wine lists in the US.

$ Shalimar

532 Jones Street, at O'Farrell Street (928 0333, www.shalimarsf.com). BART & Metro to Powell/bus 2, 3, 27, 31, 38/cable car Powell-Hyde or Powell-Mason. **Open** noon-midnight daily. **Main courses** $7. **No credit cards. Map** p314 L6 ㉚ Indian

Locals have other favorites, but this is some of the best Indian and Pakistani cuisine you'll find in the city – never mind the nonexistent decor and the grubby corner of the Tenderloin it's located on. Dishes here are fairly spicy, turned out at speed and at predictably keen prices.

Other locations 1409 Polk Street, Polk Gulch (776 4642).

Civic Center

Jardinière

300 Grove Street, at Franklin Street (861 5555, www.jardiniere.com). BART & Metro to Civic Center Metro to Van Ness/bus 5, 21, 47, 49, 90. **Open** 5-10pm (last orders) Mon, Sun; 5-10.30pm (last orders) Tue-Sat. **Main courses** $30. **Credit** AmEx, Disc, MC, V. **Map** p318 K7 ㉛ French

This beautiful, whimsically shaped (meant to resemble an overturned champagne glass) restaurant is one of the best high-dollar special-occasion eateries in the state. Chef Traci Des Jardins continues to seek out the best and most environmentally friendly local ingredients. Starters can be a meal in themselves,

INSIDE TRACK OUTDOOR DINING

Sunshine in the summer is a rarity in Fog City, but when the rays come out to play, expect hordes of San Franciscans to head alfresco. Located bayside in the industrial China Basin neighborhood, the **Ramp** (855 China Basin Street, at Illinois Street, 621 2378, www.ramprestaurant.com) is a boozy SF brunch institution on sunny days. Head here for eggs benedict and burgers and fries served up with margaritas and bloody marys. Across from the AT&T ballpark, more upscale **MoMo's** (760 2nd Street at King Street, 227 8660, www.sfmomos.com) boasts large front decks where the pre-game crowd sips pints of beer and martinis and chows down on excellent burgers and sausages. At the other end of town, where Golden Gate Park meets Ocean Beach, the **Park Chalet** and **Beach Chalet** (*see p93*) are perfect for both sunny days and foggy weather, with big brunches (upstairs) and seafood-heavy lunches next to a roaring fire (downstairs).

but save room for the stellar mains (or try the $125 tasting menu). The wine list has pages of sparklers.
▶ *Traci Des Jardins also runs Public House at AT&T Park, see p144.*

$ Saigon Sandwich Café

560 Larkin Street, between Turk & Eddy Streets (474 5698). BART & Metro to Civic Center/bus 5, 19, 27, 31, 38, 47, 49, 90. **Open** 6am-6pm Mon-Sat; 7.30am-5pm Sun. **Main courses** $3. **No credit cards. Map** p314 K6 ㉜ Café

Still the Civic Center's best unsung spot, this tiny, dingy room is typically jammed with foodies and federal workers who file in for huge sandwiches at rock-bottom prices. The bare-bones menu is made up almost entirely of Vietnamese *banh mi* sandwiches, which are prepared with such ingredients as roast pork with a chili sauce.

$ Tu Lan

8 6th Street, at Market Street (626 0927, http://tulansf.blogspot.com). BART & Metro to Powell/streetcar F/bus 5, 14, 27 & Market Street routes. **Open** 11am-9.30pm Mon-Sat. **Main courses** $6.75. **No credit cards. Map** p318 L7 ㉝ Asian

Other restaurants around town put a modern American spin on Vietnamese cuisine, serving the food in chic surroundings and upping the charges in the process. Tulan, however, keeps things authentic, scruffy and cheap: the menu sticks to Vietnamese basics, the room hasn't been decorated in decades (in a neighborhood that could generously be described as downtrodden) and the prices are gloriously low.

★ Zuni Café

1658 Market Street, between Franklin & Gough Streets (552 2522, www.zunicafe.com). Metro to Van Ness/streetcar F/bus 6, 9, 14, 47, 49, 71, 90. **Open** 11.30am-11pm Tue-Thur, Sun; 11.30am-midnight Fri, Sat. **Main courses** $25. **Credit** AmEx, MC, V. **Map** p318 K8 ㉞ American

After more than 30 years, Zuni has developed a dedicated following as a destination restaurant that's on a par with Berkeley's Chez Panisse. Chef Judy Rodgers's Cal-Ital food manages to be both memorable and transparently simple. The art-filled setting, comprising four separate dining rooms, can be quite a scene before and after cultural events in the vicinity, but the sourdough bread and oysters on an iced platter, the roast chicken for two and the wood-fired pizzettas are attractions in themselves.

SOMA & SOUTH BEACH

Yerba Buena Gardens & Around

Ame

689 Mission Street, at 3rd Street (284 4040, www.amerestaurant.com). BART & Metro to Montgomery/bus 12, 14, 30, 45 & Market Street routes. **Open** 6-9.30pm Mon-Thur; 5.30-10pm Fri, Sat; 5.30-9.50pm Sun. **Main courses** $28-$38. **Credit** AmEx, Disc, MC, V. **Map** p315 N6 ㉟ International

Hiro Sone and Lissa Doumani, the team behind Terra in Napa Valley, have brought its Japonesque sensibilities to this stylish and intimate dining room in the St Regis Hotel. The menu emphasizes raw – sashimi, *crudo*, tartare, carpaccio – and southern France: grilled duck with a *ragût* of wild mushrooms, confit of giblets and bok choy. The bar features limited-edition sakés and small-lot wines.

★ Bar Agricole

355 11th St. at Harrison Street (355 9400, www.baragricole.com). Bus 9, 12, 27, 47. **Open** 6-10pm Sun-Wed, 6-11pm Thur-Sat. *Bar* 6pm until customers leave daily. **Main courses** $22. **Credit** AmEx, MC, V. **Map** p318 L9 ㊱ American

With an artisanal cocktail list that's as extensive as the food menu, you'll be hardpressed to choose between another Monkey's Gland or another order of the sheep's milk ricotta dumplings with fiddlehead ferns. Go for both—and while you're at it, try the chopped liver on toast and any other of the exquisitely seasonal, impeccably fresh plates, as you sip your slavishly crafted cocktail (even the ice is tailor-made for each drink). Undoubtedly the biggest thing to splash down on the 11th Street club corridor in recent years, Bar Agricole feels at once earthy and ethereal – with walls made from old barrel staves and light fixtures made from hundreds of glass tubes that look like windswept waves. Belly up to the bar (getting a sit-down reservation can be challenging) or try brunch on the sunny, enclosed front patio.
▶ *After dinner, head next door to Slim's for some of the city's best live music; see p240.*

★ Blue Bottle Coffee

66 Mint Street, at Jessie Street (495 3394, www.bluebottlecoffee.net). BART & Metro to Powell/streetcar F/bus 5, 14, 27 & Market Street routes. **Open** 7am-7pm Mon-Fri; 8am-6pm Sat; 8am-4pm Sun. Mains $6. Credit MC, V. **Map** p315 M6 ㊲ Café

Grounds zero for the city's coffee-obsessed, Blue Bottle opened a full-service café in 2008, so now loyal fans can temper caffeine highs with breakfast and lunch snacks (frittatas, soups, salads, and sandwiches). The main draw though is still single-origin small-batch and ridiculously fresh coffee (nothing is more than 48 hours out of the roaster), and the fascinatingly complicated coffee-making equipment: A five-light siphon bar is the first of its kind in the United States; the beakers and flasks that drip Kyoto-style iced-coffee are something out of a mad scientist's lab. Order a Gibraltar (you have to ask; it's not on the menu)—the perfect blend of espresso and foam, served in a short glass.

$ Bossa Nova

139 8th Street, at Minna Street (558 8004, www.bossahome.com). BART & Metro to Civic Center/bus 12, 14, 19 & Market Street routes. **Open** 11am-2.30pm, 5-10pm Tue-Thur, Sun; 11am-2.30pm, 5-11pm Fri, Sat. *Bar* until 2am daily. **Main courses** $15. **Credit** AmEx, Disc, MC, V. **Map** p318 L7 J 38 International

Although Bossa Nova is off the beaten track and lacks a sign, locals have found their way to this very hip, eclectically appointed and quite tasty bit of Rio in the city. It's popular for its nightly namesake music as well as for its refreshing take on Brazilian food. Plantain chips and salsa verde get things started while you sip a caipirinha and await the soccer uniform-clad waitstaff to usher out such delicacies as shellfish stew with coconut milk, seasoned lamb tenderloin, and grilled T-bone big enough for two.

Brainwash

1122 Folsom Street, between 7th & 8th Streets (861 3663, www.brainwash.com). Bus 12, 14, 19, 47. **Open** *Café* 8am-9pm daily. *Laundromat* 7am-10pm Mon-Thur; 7am-11pm Fri, Sat; 8am-10pm Sun. **Main courses** $10. **Credit** DC, MC, V. **Map** p319 M8 39 Café

Part laundromat, part bar/café and part performance space, this popular spot remains one of the premier singles hangouts in town. People bring along their dirty linens and a wandering eye as they peruse the array of potential mates and the menu of soups, salads and burgers. On most evenings, the atmosphere is brightened by live music, poetry readings or improv comedy (all ages, no cover).

$ Le Charm

315 5th Street, at Folsom Street (546 6128, www.lecharm.com). Bus 12, 14, 27, 30, 45, 47, 91. **Open** 11.30am-2pm, 5.30-9.30pm Tue-Thur; 11.30am-2pm, 5.30-10pm Fri; 5.30-10pm Sat; 5-8.30pm Sun. **Main courses** $25. **Credit** AmEx, MC, V. **Map** p319 N7 40 French

One of the few places in town where you can enjoy eating your way through an authentic French bistro menu without having to make a massive cash outlay. Alongside an excellent standard carte, Le Charm has a three-course prix fixe menu ($30) that includes main courses such as pan-roasted calf's liver and steak-frites. The pick of the desserts is the tarte tatin.

LuLu

816 Folsom Street, between 4th & 5th Streets (495 5775, www.restaurantlulu.com). BART & Metro to Powell/bus 12, 14, 27, 30, 45, 47, 91. **Open** 11.30am-11pm daily. **Main courses** $25. **Credit** AmEx, MC, V. **Map** p319 N7 41 Italian & pizza

LuLu majors in delicious, rustic, Italian-influenced cuisine, including specialties from the wood-fired oven, rotisserie and grill. Pizzas, pasta and shellfish come on large platters, designed to be shared. LuLu's wine bar next door offers a more intimate alternative; and the LuLu Petite deli in the Ferry Building (362 7019) features gourmet products and take-out.

Salt House

545 Mission Street, between 1st & 2nd Streets (543 8900, www.salthousesf.com). BART & Metro to Montgomery/bus 10, 12, 14 & Market Street routes. **Open** 11.30am-5pm, 5.30-10pm Mon-Wed; 11.30am-5pm, 5.30-11pm Fri; 5.30-10pm Sat; 5.30-9pm Sun. **Main courses** $27. **Credit** AmEx, Disc, MC, V. **Map** p315 N5 42 American

Built into a loft-style space in a small brick building quickly being overshadowed by new neighboring skyscrapers, this downtown hotspot (from the people behind Town Hall; *see below*) offers inventive contemporary American cuisine that changes seasonally. Standouts include roasted lamb loin and dry-aged rib-eye grilled to perfection. At lunch, don't miss the Cuban pork sandwich and housemade chips.

Town Hall Restaurant

342 Howard Street, at Fremont Street (908 3900, www.townhallsf.com). BART & Metro to Embarcadero/bus 5, 9, 14, 38, 41, 71, 108. **Open** 11.30am-2.30pm, 5.30-10pm Mon-Thur; 11.30am-2.30pm, 5.30-11pm Fri; 5.30-11pm Sat; 5.30-10pm Sun. **Main courses** $27. **Credit** AmEx, MC, V. **Map** p315 O5 43 American

A little slice of New England, chefs Mitchell and Steven Rosenthal, and legendary front-of-house man Doug Washington cultivate a chummy loyal crowd for their American and southern classics. Highlights might include sautéed dayboat scallops or Chimay-seasoned short ribs. The bar is known for its specialty cocktails, including an excellent *sazerac*.

XYZ

W Hotel, 181 3rd Street, at Howard Street (817 7836, www.xyz-sf.com). BART & Metro to Montgomery/bus 10, 12, 14, 30, 45 & Market Street routes. **Open** 6.30-10.30am, 11.30am-2pm, 6-10pm Mon-Thur; 6.30-10.30am, 11.30am-2pm, 6-11pm Fri; 7am-2pm, 6-11pm Sat; 6am-2pm Sun. **Main courses** $26. **Credit** AmEx, Disc, MC, V. **Map** p315 N6 44 American

Adjacent to the lobby of the W, XYZ holds fast to its austere decor and sophisticated clientele. Although the parade of chefs who have worked here is long, the kitchen has been re-energized more recently with a tempting choice of modern California fare with Provençal touches. The seasonally changing menu might include the likes of seared Sonoma duck breast or rabbit ravioli. The wine list is excellent.

South Park & South Beach

$ ★ The American

1 South Park Avenue at 2nd Street (243 0107, www.theamericansf.com). Metro to 2nd & King/bus 10, 12, 30, 45, 91. **Open** 8am-3pm

CONSUME

Mon-Fri; 10am-4pm Sat, Sun; 10am-7pm on Giants game nights. **Main courses** $8. Disc, MC, V. **Map** p315 O6 ㊺ Diner

If your idea of perfection looks like melted cheese oozing from between two slices of grilled sourdough bread and a bowl of smoky roasted-tomato soup, then your life is now complete. On a corner of hip South Park, the American offers a brief, but satisfying menu of gourmet grilled-cheese sandwiches (think sharp cheddar, gruyere, fontina, havarti), augmented by things like applewood smoked bacon, kalamata olive tapenade, and roasted wild mushrooms. Seasonal soups, salads, and housemade desserts round out the lunch menu. They also serve egg and cheese combos for breakfast, and – in a nice mash-up of low- and high-brow, afternoon wine and grilled-cheese pairings.

Butler & the Chef

155 South Park, at 3rd Street (896 2075, www.thebutlerandthechef.com). Metro to 2nd & King/bus 10, 12, 30, 45, 91. **Open** 8am-3pm Tue-Sat; 10am-3pm Sun. **Main courses** $12. **Credit** AmEx, Disc, MC, V. **Map** p319 O7 ㊻ Café

Marlowe.

This *très* French little café is always crowded with locals who queue for the fresh-made breakfast pastries and wonderful breads. Tuck into pain au chocolat or sip a Pernod while chatting with Pierre, the amiable owner. The Butler & the Chef also runs a warehouse of French antiques (290 Utah Street, at 16th Street, Potrero Hill, 626 9600).

Coco 500

500 Brannan Street, at 4th Street (543 2222, www.coco500.com). Metro to 4th & King/bus 10, 12, 30, 45, 47, 91. **Open** 11.30am-10pm Mon-Thur; 11.30am-11pm Fri; 5.30-11pm Sat. **Main courses** $21. **Credit** AmEx, Disc, MC, V. **Map** p319 N7 ㊼ International

This SoMa restaurant is a reinvention of sorts for its popular proprietor, Loretta Keller, whose penchant for Parisian hospitality has given way to a small plate style. Mediterranean-influenced dishes prepared with organic, today-fresh ingredients range from light pizzas from a wood-fired oven to beef-cheek mole and whole fish with fennel saffron sauce. Seafood, steaks and poultry are also cooked *a la plancha.*

★ Marlowe

330 Townsend Street, at 4th Street (974 1836, www.marlowesf.com). **Open** 11.30am-2.30pm, 5.30-10pm Mon-Wed; 11.30am-2.30pm, 5.30-11pm Thur-Sat. **Main courses** $13-$28. **Credit** AmEx, DC, Disc, MC, V. **Map** p319 O7 ㊽ American

If you haven't tried the brussels sprout chips, burger, and poulet vert at Marlowe, you may be the only ones in town. The cozy hotspot South of Market (across from the Caltrain station and a block from AT&T ballpark) has found a winning combination both with owner Anna Weinberg and chef Jennifer Puccio, and with pairings such as toasted pistachios with bourbon, maple, and smoked salt, and pork chops with parmesan dumplings. But it's the brussels sprout chips (feathery leaves fried with meyer lemon and sea salt) and poulet vert (chicken marinated overnight in a mash of basil, parsley, tarragon, and other green herbs) that top the popularity charts. The full menu is served until late – a rarity.

Paragon

701 2nd Street, at Townsend Street (537 9020, www.paragonrestaurant.com). Metro to 2nd & King/bus 10, 30, 45, 91. **Open** 11.30am-2.30pm, 5.30pm-close Mon-Fri; 5.30pm-close Sat. Also open for lunch on Sat, Sun on Giants game days. **Main courses** $19. **Credit** AmEx, Disc, MC, V. **Map** p319 P7 ㊾ American

Before Giants games, fans press shoulder to shoulder at the huge bar here. The attractive dining room is similarly energy-charged. The classic American brasserie fare is rustic and reliable; steaks and seafood come with hearty sides such as mashed potato or vegetable gratin.

Public House

24 Willie Mays Plaza, corner of King & 3rd Streets (644 0240, www.publichouse.com). Metro to 2nd & King/bus 10, 30, 45, 47, 91. **Open** 4-10pm Mon-Thur, Sun; 4-11pm Fri, Sat. **Main courses** $15. **Credit** AmEx, DC, MC, V. **Map** p319 O7 ⑩ American

Traci Des Jardins of Jardinière (*see p140*) oversees the menu at this sports pub and grill at AT&T ballpark, with giant TVs in every room, a huge selection of draft beers and cask ales, and good comfort food, including chops, ribs, burgers, and mac and cheese.

▶ *For more on AT&T Park, see p250.*

Tres Agaves

130 Townsend Street, between 2nd & 3rd Streets, (227 0500, www.tresagaves.com). Metro to 2nd & King/bus 10, 12, 30, 45, 47, 91. **Open** 11.30am-10pm Mon-Wed, Sun; 11.30am-11pm Thur-Sat. **Main courses** $19. **Credit** AmEx, Disc, MC, V. **Map** p319 O7 ⑪ Latin American

Tequila expert Julio Bermejo teamed up with impresario Eric Rubin, chef Joseph Manzare and rocker Sammy Hagar to create this homage to the Mexican state of Jalisco, home to the town of Tequila. The cavernous brick and timber space houses ample bar space to serve a huge variety of artisan, pure-agave tequilas, while the display kitchen turns out gourmet regional Mexican cuisine around the clock.

Twenty Five Lusk

25 Lusk Street, off Townsend between 3rd & 4th Streets. (495 5875, www.25lusk.com) Metro to 2nd & King/bus 10, 12, 30, 45, 47, 91. **Open** 5.30-10pm Mon-Thur, 5.30-11pm Fri-Sun. *Lounge* 5pm-close daily. **Credit** AmEx, DC, Disc, MC, V. **Map** p319 O7 ⑫ American

Not since the giddy days of the dotcom boom has San Francisco seen anything this glamorous South of Market. The name refers to the address – tucked down an obscure alley in a 1917 meat-processing warehouse. Inside, the huge bi-level space, designed by architect Cass Calder Smith, combines original brick and exposed timbers with glass and polished metal: A slick bar and lounge with steel ski-lodge fireplaces occupies the downstairs; upstairs diners view the kitchen through glass panels, where chef Matthew Dolan crafts intricately composed plates of local, seasonal ingredients. If you can tear yourself away from all the fabulousness twittering around you, try offerings such as grilled steelhead with fennel, black garlic, Dungeness crab and lobster beignet. For dessert, the redcurrant soufflé with espresso chocolate sauce is a winner.

★ Zuppa

564 4th Street, between Bryant & Brannan Streets (777 5900, www.zuppa-sf.com). Metro to 4th & King/bus 10, 12, 30, 45, 47, 91. **Open** 11.30am-2.30pm, 5-10pm Mon-Thur; 11.30am-2.30pm, 5-11pm Fri; 5-11pm Sat; 5-9pm Sun. **Main courses** $19-$34. **Credit** AmEx, Disc, MC, V. **Map** p319 N7 ⑬ Italian & pizza

Despite the long banquettes that flank the dining room, and the post-work young professionals and Mission hipsters who sit in them, it's the rustic, fresh-made southern Italian cuisine that steals the show at Zuppa. Almost everything on the menu is excellent,

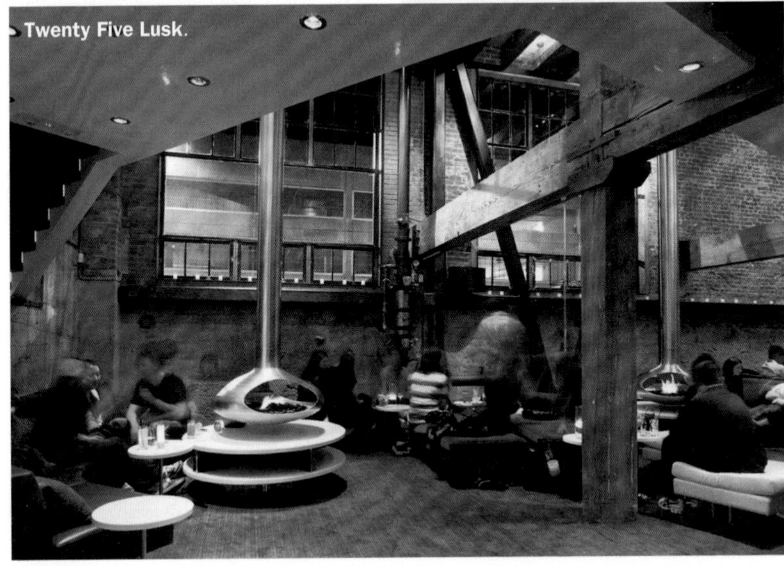
Twenty Five Lusk.

CONSUME

especially the house-cured meats offered at each table and fresh, seasonal dishes that use ingredients from the rooftop garden. The wine list is all-Italian.

NOB HILL & CHINATOWN

Nob Hill & Polk Gulch

Café Nook

1500 Hyde Street, at Jackson Street (447 4100, www.cafenook.com). Bus 1, 10, 12, 19, 27/cable car Powell-Hyde. **Open** 7am-10pm Mon-Fri; 8am-10pm Sat; 8am-9pm Sun. **Main courses** $7. **Credit** Disc, MC, V. **Map** p314 K4 54 Café

This unassuming little café is popular for its easy-going atmosphere, good prices and Monday-Friday free Wi-Fi access. The menu is an assortment of bagels, soups, salads and sandwiches, plus small-plate-style appetizers. There's a list of sakés and wines in the evening.

Dining Room

Ritz-Carlton Hotel, 600 Stockton Street, at California Street (773 6198, www.ritzcarltondiningroom.com). Bus 1, 2. 3, 30, 45, 91/cable car California. **Open** 6-9pm Tue-Thur; 5.30-9.30pm Fri, Sat. **Main courses** $30. **Credit** AmEx, Disc, MC, V. **Map** p315 M4 55 French

The Dining Room has a global reputation and a wait-staff-to-diner ratio of almost 1:1. It's opulent without being over the top, although it can feel a little serious. The modern French menu is inventive and artfully executed by chef Ron Siegel (the first non-Japanese to win the Iron Chef contest), as are the famous seasonal specialty menus, such as the annual white truffle festival. Master sommelier Stephane Lacroix will guide you to an appropriate wine, and the bar list of single malts is one of the largest in the US.

Fleur de Lys

777 Sutter Street, between Jones & Taylor Streets (673 7779, www.fleurdelyssf.com). Bus 2, 3, 27, 38/cable car California. **Open** 6-9.30pm Mon-Thur; 5.30-10.30pm Fri; 5-10.30pm Sat. **Set meals** $72 3 courses; $82 4 courses; $95 5 courses. **Credit** AmEx, Disc, MC, V. **Map** p314 L5 56 French

A fine dining experience so memorable it's been duplicated in Las Vegas. Chef Hubert Keller's cuisine is deserving of a wider audience because of his vast repertoire: his menu is lush, even exorbitant. It all plays out like a symphony, a feast for the eyes as much as the palate, enhanced by service that is attentive without being overbearing. One of the best pull-out-all-the-stops restaurants in town.

★ Swan Oyster Depot

1517 Polk Street, between California & Sacramento Streets (673 1101). Bus 1, 2, 3, 12, 19, 47, 49, 90/cable car California. **Open** 8am-5.30pm Mon-Sat. **Main courses** $25. **No credit cards**. **Map** p314 K5 57 Fish & seafood

Don't miss this Polk Gulch institution: half fish market, half counter-service hole in the wall, it has been delighting locals since 1912. The best time to visit is between November and June, when the local Dungeness crab is in season. But at any time of year, the selections are straight-from-the-water fresh. Specialties include clam chowder and an obscenely large variety of oysters, best downed with a pint of locally brewed Anchor Steam beer. You can buy shellfish to take away.

▶ *For other good Dungeness crab options, see p148* **Inside Track**.

Chinatown

San Francisco's best Chinese food is probably found in the Richmond (*see p94*), but there are still worthwhile options in Chinatown. The Chinese crowd at **Dol Ho's** (808 Pacific Avenue, at Stockton Street, 392 2828) speaks volumes about the food's authenticity, and **House of Nanking** (919 Kearny Street, at Jackson Street, 421 1429), while touristy, never disappoints with its food.

Alfred's Steakhouse

659 Merchant Street, between Kearny & Montgomery Streets (781 7058, www.alfredssteakhouse.com). Bus 1, 10, 12, 30, 41, 45, 91. **Open** 5-9.30pm Mon, Tue, Fri, Sat; 11.30am-2pm, 5.30-9.30pm Thur. **Main courses** $30. **Credit** AmEx, Disc, MC, V. **Map** p315 M4 58 American

With decades of experience as one of the city's best steakhouses, Alfred's feels like a bit of San Francisco gone by, but it continues to prove itself worthy of a fiercely loyal fanbase. The chief attractions are giant Chicago ribeyes, tender T-bones and a porterhouse that covers the plate, but the fish and pasta are also from the top drawer. The bar, which mixes superlative martinis, stocks more than 100 single malts.

R&G Lounge

631 Kearny Street, between Clay & Sacramento Streets (982 7877, www.rnglounge.com). Bus 1, 10, 12, 30, 41, 45, 91. **Open** 11am-9.30pm daily. **Main courses** $16. **Credit** AmEx, Disc, MC, V. **Map** p315 M4 59 Chinese

Always busy and often chaotic, R&G Lounge has two levels for dining, neither of them much to look at. However, the Hong Kong-style food is authentic, emphasizing seafood that's taken mainly from the in-house tanks. People come from miles around to try the deep-fried salt and pepper crab and barbecue pork.

Yuet Lee

1300 Stockton Street, at Broadway (982 6020). Bus 10, 12, 20, 30, 39, 41, 45, 91/cable car Powell-Mason. **Open** 11am-midnight Mon-Thur, Sun; 11-3am Fri, Sat. **Main courses** $12. **Credit** MC, V. **Map** p315 M3 60 Chinese

Terrific seafood and the opportunity to indulge in some small-hours dining attract sundry restaurant folk to this tiny, bright-green Chinatown eaterie. The roasted squab with fresh coriander and lemon, sautéed clams with black bean sauce, and 'eight precious noodle soup', made with eight kinds of meat, are all worth trying. Bear in mind, though, that the lighting is glaringly unflattering and the service matter-of-fact.

NORTH BEACH TO FISHERMAN'S WHARF

North Beach

Caffe Puccini

411 Columbus Avenue, at Vallejo Street (989 7033). Bus 10, 12, 30, 39, 41, 45, 91/cable car Powell-Mason. **Open** 6am-11.30pm Mon-Thur, Sun; 6am-12.30am Fri, Sat. **Main courses** $8. **Credit** Disc, MC, V. **Map** p315 M3 61 Café

Like the composer after whom the café is named, friendly owner Graziano Lucchese is from Lucca in northern Italy. His welcoming café serves vast sandwiches stuffed with salami, prosciutto and mortadella.

Caffè Roma

526 Columbus Avenue, at Union Street (296 7942, www.cafferoma.com). Bus 10, 12, 30, 39, 41, 45, 91/cable car Powell-Mason. **Open** 6am-7pm Mon-Thur; 6am-9pm Fri; 6.30am-10pm Sat; 7am-7pm Sun. **Main courses** $8. **Credit** Disc, MC, V. **Map** p315 M3 62 Café

Some say it's the strongest coffee in the city – it's certainly among the most coveted, roasted on the premises by three generations of the Azzollini family. Espressos and other coffees, and a range of pastries and gelati are served in a large, airy space, perfect for sipping, thinking and explaining your latest conspiracy theory.

Other locations 885 Bryant Street, SOMA (296 7662).

★ Caffe Trieste

601 Vallejo Street, at Grant Avenue (982 2605, www.caffetrieste.com). Bus 10, 12, 30, 39, 41, 45, 91. **Open** 6.30am-11pm Mon-Thur, Sun; 6.30am-midnight Fri, Sat. **Main courses** $8. **No credit cards**. **Map** p315 M3 63 Café

One of the city's great cafés, a former hangout for Kerouac and Ginsberg and the spot where Coppola is said to have written the screenplay for *The Godfather*. The dark walls are plastered with photos of opera singers and famous regulars. There are muffins, pastries and sandwiches to eat, and the lattes are legendary, as are the opera sessions held here on a Saturday afternoon.

Other locations 1667 Market Street, Civic Center (551 1000)

▶ *For more about SF's coffee culture, see p138* **Grounds Control**.

Boudin Sourdough Bakery & Café. *See p148.*

House

1230 Grant Avenue, at Columbus Avenue & Vallejo Street (986 8612, www.thehse.com). Bus 10, 12, 30, 39, 41, 45, 91. **Open** 11.30am-2.30pm, 5.30-10pm Mon-Thur; 11.30am-2.30pm, 5.30-11pm Fri; 11.30am-2.30pm, 5-11pm Sat; 5-10pm Sun. **Main courses** $25. **Credit** AmEx, Disc, MC, V. **Map** p315 M3 64 Asian

This no-frills (though often ear-shatteringly loud) Chinese fusion dining room works wonders with fresh, seasonal produce and East-meets-West preparations. The Chinese chicken salad with sesame soy illustrates the menu: light, tangy and big enough to be a meal on its own. The menu changes often, resisting trends while remaining decidedly sophisticated.

Mama's on Washington Square

1701 Stockton Street, at Filbert Street (362 6421, www.mamas-sf.com). Bus 10, 12, 30, 39, 41, 45, 91/cable car Powell-Mason. **Open** 8am-3pm Tue-Sun. **Main courses** $9. **No credit cards**. **Map** p315 M3 65 Café

The weekend queue is part of the fun at this wildly popular North Beach mainstay. Once seated, you'll be faced with such temptations as a giant made-to-order 'm'omelette' or the Monte Cristo sandwich on homemade bread. Service is swift and familiar.

Mario's Bohemian Cigar Store

566 Columbus Avenue, at Union Street (362 0536). Bus 10, 12, 30, 39, 41, 45, 91/cable car

CONSUME

Powell-Mason. **Open** 10am-11pm daily. **Main courses** $10. **Credit** MC, V. **Map** p315 M3 ⑯ Café

You can't buy a cigar at Mario's, nor will you be allowed to smoke one. Instead, sip a flavored Italian soda and watch the neighborhood while perusing a light menu of focaccia sandwiches (the grilled eggplant and the meatball are the best) and salads, own-made biscotti, beer and coffee. Mario's location means it's always packed, so lunch may be slow in coming, but there's no more essential North Beach café.

★ L'Osteria del Forno

519 Columbus Avenue, between Green and Union Streets (982 1124, www.losteriadelforno.com). Bus 10, 12, 30, 39, 41, 45, 91/cable car Powell-Mason. **Open** 11.30am-10pm Mon, Wed, Thur, Sun; 11.30am-10.30pm Fri, Sat. **Main courses** $14. **No credit cards. Map** p314 L3 ⑰ Italian

On a street awash in knock-offs, this tiny osteria stands out for its impeccable authenticity. In a room the size of a postage stamp, two Italian women slave over an oven that issues the best focaccia (and focaccia sandwiches) and thin-crust pizzas in North Beach. The menu also features salads, soups, and fresh pastas, plus a roast of the day (pray for the roast pork braised in milk). Small baskets of warm focaccia keep you going until the arrival of the entrees, which you should accompany with a glass of Italian red (there's a full bar, with a nice selection of grappas as well). Note that it's cash-only.

Sodini's

510 Green Street, at Grant Avenue (291 0499). Bus 10, 12, 30, 39, 41, 45, 91. **Open** 5-10pm Mon-Thur; 5-11pm Fri; 10.30am-11pm Sat; 10.30am-10pm Sun. **Main courses** $20. **Credit** AmEx, Disc, MC, V. **Map** p315 M3 ⑱ Italian

Sodini's is small and darkly romantic, in a Chianti-bottle-as-candle-holder sort of way. Patrons are jammed close together to enable the servers to squeeze past with platters of sloppy pasta and rib-sticking lasagne. The fact that it's off the beaten track doesn't dampen its popularity: be sure to arrive earlier than you intend to eat and sign the list; you can then drop over to a neighborhood bar while waiting for a table. Once inside, the wine is cheap and in plentiful supply.

Tommaso's Ristorante Italiano

1042 Kearny Street, at Pacific Avenue (398 9696, www.tommasosnorthbeach.com). Bus 1, 10, 12, 20, 30, 41, 45, 91. **Open** 5-10.30pm Tue-Sat; 4-9.30pm Sun. **Main courses** $22. **Credit** AmEx, Disc, MC, V. **Map** p315 M3 ⑲ Italian & pizza

Tommaso's is known citywide for its simple Italian food, which has been served family-style in a tiny, boisterous room since 1935. The wood-fired pizzas and calzones deserve their reps and the house red is surprisingly good. No affectations, no frills and no reservations. Join the queue and keep your eyes peeled: you never know who might walk in.

Fisherman's Wharf

Alioto's

8 Fisherman's Wharf, at Taylor & Jefferson Streets (673 0183, www.aliotos.com). Streetcar F to Pier 39/bus 39, 47/cable car Powell-Mason. **Open** 11am-11pm daily. **Main courses** $26. **Credit** AmEx, Disc, MC, V. **Map** p314 K1 ⑦⓪ Fish & seafood

Alioto's began as a sidewalk stand serving crab and shrimp cocktails to passers-by. Now more than eight decades later, the crab stand (which still offers fresh-caught Dungeness to throngs of hungry tourists) is part of a hugely popular restaurant owned by members of the same local family. The room offers amazing views of the Bay, and the kitchen manages to turn out decent (if pricey) seafood, as well as fish-centered Sicilian specialties.

Ana Mandara

981 Beach Street, at Polk Street (771 6800, www.anamandara.com). Streetcar F to Fisherman's Wharf/bus 10, 19, 20, 30, 47/cable car Powell-Hyde. **Open** 11.30am-2pm, 5.30-9.30pm Mon-Thur; 11.30am-2pm, 5.30-10.30pm Fri; 5.30-10.30pm Sat; 5.30-9.30pm Sun. **Main courses** $26. **Credit** AmEx, Disc, MC, V. **Map** p314 J2 ⑦① Asian

Although located in touristy Ghirardelli Square, this fabulous French-Vietnamese restaurant could hold its own in the foodiest of neighborhoods. The room is beautiful, with soaring ceilings and a staircase that sweeps you to a chic lounge. The sumptuous and beautifully presented specialties are enriched with the aromas and flavors of Vietnam. The Cham Bar has live jazz from Thursday to Saturday.

CONSUME

Blue Mermaid

Argonaut Hotel, 471 Jefferson Street, at Hyde Street (771 2222, www.bluemermaidsf.com). Streetcar F to Fisherman's Wharf/bus 19, 30, 47, 91/cable car Powell-Hyde. **Open** 7am-9pm Mon-Thur, Sun; 7am-10pm Fri, Sat. **Main courses** $18. **Credit** AmEx, Disc, MC, V. **Map** p314 K2 ⑦② Fish & seafood

Designed to recall the history of the working wharf (don't miss the excellent on-site museum), this rustic-looking restaurant is set into the corner of the Argonaut Hotel. The menu is perfect for San Francisco's fogged-in days, with hearty chowders spooned up from large cauldrons – the award-winning Dungeness crab and corn are winners. The Treasure Chest offers a choice of marine dishes. There's also a children's menu: this place is a top choice for families.

Beretta. *See p150*

Boudin Sourdough Bakery & Café

160 Jefferson Street, at Taylor Street (928 1849, www.boudinbakery.com). Streetcar F to Pier 39/bus 39, 47/cable car Powell-Mason. **Open** *Café* 8am-9pm Mon-Thur, Sun; 8am-10pm Fri, Sat. *Bistro* 11.30am-9pm Mon-Thur, Sun; 11.30am-10pm Fri,

Sat. **Main courses** *Bistro* $25. *Café* $9. **Credit** AmEx, Disc, MC, V. **Map** p314 L1 ⑬ Café

The city's original sourdough bread bakery, the Boudin family has been baking their bread from the same mother dough since 1849. The flagship store, a relaxing alternative to ear-busting crab and seafood stands along the Wharf, offers delights such as sourdough pizzas and clam chowder served in a hollowed-out sourdough bowl. There's a small museum upstairs, where you can also view the fascinating baking operations. *Photo p146.*

Other locations throughout the Bay Area.

Gary Danko

800 North Point Street, at Hyde Street (749 2060, www.garydanko.com). Streetcar F to Fisherman's Wharf/bus 19, 30, 47, 91/cable car Powell-Hyde. **Open** 5.30-10pm daily. **Set meals** $68 3 courses; $85 4 courses; $102 5 courses. **Credit** AmEx, Disc, MC, V. **Map** p314 K2 ⑭ American

Superstar chef Danko's fine-dining restaurant near the wharf is fabulous – and fabulously understated. The best way to experience his dexterity and genius is via the tasting menus, which change seasonally but might include seared foie gras with caramelized red onions as a starter, beef tenderloin with king trumpet mushrooms as a main, and farmhouse cheeses to finish. A more casual adventure can be had at the bar. Reservations are essential and can be hard to come by.

Russian Hill

La Boulange de Polk

2310 Polk Street, at Green Street (345 1107, www.baybread.com). Bus 12, 19, 41, 45, 47, 49, 90/cable car Powell-Hyde. **Open** 7am-7pm daily. **Main courses** $9. **Credit** AmEx, MC, V. **Map** p314 K3 ⑮ Café

In the style of a Parisian boulangerie, this café serves beautiful pastries and tasty fresh-baked bread. The best spot to watch a morning unfold is from one of the inviting pavement tables, but they can be difficult to acquire, especially at the weekend.

Other locations throughout the city.

La Folie

2316 Polk Street, between Union & Green Streets (776 5577, www.lafolie.com). Bus 12, 19, 41, 45, 47, 49, 90/cable car Powell-Hyde. **Open** 5.30-10.30pm Mon-Sat. **Set meals** $75 3 courses; $85 4 courses; $95 5 courses. **Credit** AmEx, Disc, MC, V. **Map** p314 K3 ⑯ French

If you want to find out why chef Roland Passot enjoys a passionate following, opt for the five-course discovery menu ($95) and sample his ever-changing selection of classic French fare, prepared with seasonally fresh ingredients. The Provençal decor and attentive staff add to the charm of this delightful French-Californian eaterie. The adjoining Green Room is a good option for intimate dining.

THE BEST DUNGENESS CRAB

Crab salad, Louie, and take-home.
Swan Oyster Depot. *See p145.*

Walk-away crab cocktails.
Alioto's crab stand at Fisherman's Grotto. *See p148.*

Finger-licking salt & pepper crab.
R&G Lounge. *See p145.*

Helmand Palace

2424 Van Ness Avenue, between Union & Green Streets (345 0072, www.helmandrestaurantsanfrancisco.com). Bus 12, 19, 27, 41, 45, 47, 49, 90. **Open** 5.30-10pm Mon-Thur, Sun; 5.30-11pm Fri, Sat. **Main courses** $12. **Credit** AmEx, Disc, MC, V. **Map** p314 J3 ⑰ Afghan

The Helmand – the city's only Afghan restaurant – moved from North Beach and added 'Palace' to its name, but it's still as good as it ever was. Influenced by the flavors of India, Asia and the Middle East, the food is deliciously aromatic, with marinades and fragrant spices. Specialties include leek ravioli and lamb *lawand* (leg of lamb sautéed with garlic, onion, tomatoes, mushrooms, yoghurt and spices).

Pesce

2227 Polk Street, between Green & Vallejo Streets (928 8025, www.pescebarsf.com). Bus 12, 19, 41, 45, 47, 49, 90/cable car Powell-Hyde. **Open** 5-10pm Mon-Thur, Sun; 5-11pm Fri, Sat. **Main courses** small plates $12. **Credit** AmEx, Disc, MC, V. **Map** p314 K4 ⑱ Fish & seafood

Modest and comfortable, Pesce is a great place to make a mess with your local specialty *cioppino*. This simple restaurant and bar proves that fabulous seafood doesn't have to be fancy or expensive, making it wildly popular with those lucky enough to live nearby. Starters include excellent mussels, cod cakes and calamares; main courses tend to be Italian.

Sushi Groove

1916 Hyde Street, between Union & Green Streets (440 1905, www.sushigroove.com). Bus 10, 12, 19, 41, 45/cable car Powell-Hyde. **Open** 5.30-10pm Mon-Thur; 5.30-10.30pm Fri, Sat. **Main courses** sushi $12. **Credit** AmEx, MC, V. **Map** p314 K3 ⑲ Japanese

If you don't mind sitting elbow to elbow in a dining room that's roughly the size of a walk-in closet, join the stylish clientele at this creative and highly charged Japanese sushi restaurant. The decor is postmodern, the mood music is loungy and the original rolls and salads are mostly very good. Fresh crab, sea urchin and eel join the familiar mackerel, tuna and salmon. The impressive saké selection is worth the trip alone.

Zarzuela

2000 Hyde Street, at Union Street (346 0800, www.themenupage.com/zarzuela). Bus 19, 41, 45/cable car Powell-Hyde. **Open** 5.30-10.30pm Mon-Thur; 5.30-11pm Fri, Sat. **Main courses** $14-$19. Tapas $7. **Credit** Disc, MC, V. **Map** p314 K3 ⑳ Spanish

The tapas are always spot-on at cozy Zarzuela, where the Spanish cuisine is served amid walls of bullfight posters and maps of Spain. Favourite old standbys such as grilled aubergine filled with goat's cheese, sautéed shrimps in garlic and olive oil, and fried potatoes with garlic and sherry vinegar never disappoint.

THE MISSION & THE CASTRO

The Mission

Atlas Café

3049 20th Street, at Alabama Street (648 1047, www.atlascafe.net). Bus 9, 12, 27, 33, 90. **Open** 6.30am-10pm Mon-Fri; 8am-8pm Sat, Sun. **Main courses** $7.35. **No credit cards**. **Map** p318 L11 ㉛ Café

This comfortable, popular café is one of the outer Mission's best hangouts, with people lining up for fresh breakfast pastries in the morning and settling into lattes for the afternoon and evening. A daily list of grilled sandwiches includes many vegetarian specialties (try the beet loaf), and there are also soups and salads. There's music (usually bluegrass) on Thursday evenings. On nice days, try for a sunny seat on the patio at the back (where dogs are allowed).

Beretta

1199 Valencia Street, at 23rd Street (695 1199, www.berettasf.com). BART 24th Street Mission/bus 12, 14, 48, 49, 67. **Open** 5.30pm-1am Mon-Fri; 11am-1am Sat, Sun. **Main courses** $14. **Credit** AmEx, MC, V. **Map** p318 K12 ㉜ Italian & pizza

Chef-owner Ruggero Gadaldi had an instant hit on his hands when he opened this smart, stylish southern Italian eatery and powered the bar with veteran cocktail jockeys who knew their way around a shaker. The crowds squeeze in and mingle over concoctions such as the *nuestra paloma* (tequila, elderflower, cointreau, grapefruit, and bitters) and nibble authentic appetizers that might include a delectable bruschette of *crescenza* and broccoli *rabe*, or eggplant *caponatina* with *burrata*. The anchor of the main courses are perfectly fired thin-crust pizzas topped with a variety of seasonal ingredients. *Photo p148.*

► *The same team runs Starbelly and Pesce, see p154 and p149.*

★ Delfina

3621 18th Street, between Dolores & Guerrero Streets (552 4055, www.delfinasf.com). BART 16th Street Mission/Metro to Church & 18th Street/bus 14, 22 33, 49. **Open** 5.30-10pm Mon-Thur; 5.30-11pm Fri, Sat; 5-10pm Sun.**Main courses** $20. **Credit** MC, V. **Map** p318 J10 ㉝ American

Hog & Rocks.

Chef/owner Craig Stoll favors simplicity over whimsy, and tradition over fashion. and yet his food is never ordinary: fresh pasta, fish and braised meats all burst with flavor. The menu changes daily, reflecting Stoll's desire to stay on his toes; it's a pity the staff don't always seem to share his ambition. Stoll's casual Pizzeria Delfina (437 6800) is just next door, serving some of the best thin-crust pizzas in town.

★ Flour + Water

2401 Harrison Street at 20th Street (826 7000, www.flourandwater.com). Bus 14, 14L, 27, 12. **Open** 5.30-11pm Mon-Wed, Sun; 5.30pm-midnight Thur-Sat. **Main courses** $17. **Credit** AmEx, MC, V. **Map** p318 L11 84 Italian & pizza

At the time of writing, this insanely (and deservedly) popular house of pasta and Neapolitan pizza was due to expand down the street with Central Kitchen, an all-communal-table eaterie envisioned as a 'commissary meets culinary events space' – complete with a *salumeria* for cured meats, fresh pasta, cheese, oils, and sandwiches. Good news for diners, as it's near impossible to get a seat in the original restaurant most nights. As the name indicates, flour and water are the two main ingredients here, but what they do with them is nothing short of art. Pastas are slavishly nurtured to melt-in-your-mouth perfection; supe- thin pizzas emerge exquisitely blistered from the 900-degree Italian wood-fired oven; salumi (from whole animals butchered on site) turns up in everything from pork trotters to prosciutto-wrapped petrale sole. Try for a reservation or chance it – they reserve half the dining room and bar for walk-ins.

Foreign Cinema

2534 Mission Street, between 21st & 22nd Streets (648 7600, www.foreigncinema.com). BART 24th Street Mission/bus 12, 14, 48, 49, 67. **Open** 6-10pm Mon-Thur; 5.30-11pm Fri; 11am-11pm Sat; 11am-10pm Sun. *Bar & gallery* until 2am daily. **Main courses** $25. **Credit** AmEx, Disc,MC, V. Map p318 K11 85 International

Now one of the stalwarts of Mission dining, this restaurant is dominated by the screen on one side of the outdoor courtyard dining room, on which classic foreign films are projected each night; there are speakers at each table if you want to listen. But the focus is still the food, a frequently updated list of classically rooted Mediterranean favorites and a massive range of stellar oysters. The popular adjacent bar, Laszlo, contributes to the steady stream of customers.

► *For more on outdoor cinema, see p216* **Films Alfresco**.

Hog & Rocks

3431 19th Street, at San Carlos Street (550 8627, www.hogandrocks.com). BART 16th Street Mission/Metro to Church & 18th Street/bus 14, 22, 33, 49. **Open** 5pm-1am Mon-Fri (last orders midnight); 11am-1am (last orders midnight) Sat; Sun. *Brunch* 11am-4pm Sat, Sun. **Main courses** $13. **Credit** AmEx, MC, V. **Map** p318 K11 86 American

The unlikely pairing of ham and oysters (clearly not for the kosher) has been a hit in this comfortable-chic Mission District hobnobbing spot. Neighborhood denizens belly up to the bar or tall communal tables for classic cocktails, plates of cured ham (Serrano to La Quericia Picante), and a wide variety of oysters. There are other good options as well – including a lavish brunch, and very good fish and chips and bratwurst platters – but the mingly crowd tends toward the Manhattans and miyagis.

Limón

524 Valencia Street, at 16th Street (252 0918, www.limon-sf.com). BART 16th Street Mission/bus 14, 22, 33, 49. **Open** noon-4pm, 5-10.30pm Mon-Thur; noon-4pm, 5-11pm Fri; 11.30am-4pm, 5-11pm Sat; 11.30am-4pm, 5-10pm Sun. **Main courses** $20. **Credit** AmEx, MC, V. **Map** p318 K10 87 International

One of a handful of SF eateries glamorizing Peruvian food, this chic, packed, low-lit hotspot serves the traditional dishes of this South American country inventively infused with Chinese and Japanese influences. There are few misses on the menu. The popular dishes such as *lomo saltado*, beef stir-fried with french fries, tomatoes and onions, and grilled lamb served with crispy plantains are easily paired with zesty sangria and other Latin-inspired cocktails.

★ Mission Pie

2901 Mission Street at 25th Street (282 4743, www.missionpie.com). BART to 24th Street Mission/bus 14, 49. **Open** 7am-9pm Mon-Thur; 7am-10pm Fri; 8am-10pm Sat; 9am-9pm Sun. **Pies** $4 slice, $22 whole. **Credit** MC, V. **Map** p318 K13 88 Café

Wholesome, handmade pies – strawberry-rhubarb to banana cream – and fresh-brewed fair-trade coffee are turned out by local youth, who gain valuable work skills at both the pie shop and its partner, Pie Ranch, south of the city, where much of the produce is cultivated. The feel-good atmosphere seems to be baked right into the sweet and savory treats, making this homey coffee shop a place that will tempt you to linger for hours.

Nihon

1779 Folsom Street, at 14th Street (552 4400, www.nihon-sf.com). BART 16th Street/bus 9, 12, 22, 33, 47, 90. **Open** 5.30pm-1.30am Tue-Sat. **Main courses** $15. **Credit** AmEx, Disc, MC, V. **Map** p318 L9 89 Japanese

With its emphasis on scene and style, this sushi lounge has given this out-of-the-way location a bit of life. The space features edgy design, with conversation-starters in each of three areas: a bar, a lounge and a bottle-service room. The menu has nicely presented renditions of Japanese small plates, as well as fresh sushi and sashimi. At the bar, a menu of more than 400 whiskies – the largest single malt whisky collection on the West Coast – is a big plus.

Pauline's Pizza

260 Valencia Street, between Brosnan & 14th Streets (552 2050, www.paulinespizza.com). BART 16th Street Mission/bus 14, 49. **Open** 5-10pm Tue-Sat. **Main courses** $18. **Credit** MC, V. **Map** p318 J9 90 Italian & pizza

Pauline's inventive thin-crust pies all come with top-quality ingredients: roasted peppers, perhaps, or goat's cheese, edible flowers or exotic vegetables. The pesto pizza (basil and pesto are baked into the crust) is justly renowned.

Range

842 Valencia Street, at 22nd Street (282 8283, www.rangesf.com). BART 24th Street Mission/ Metro to Church & 24th Street/bus 14, 33, 49. **Open** 6.30pm-close (last reservation 9pm) Mon-Thur; 5.30pm-close (last reservation 9.30pm) Fri-Sun. **Main courses** $24. **Credit** AmEx, MC, V. **Map** p314 K11 91 American

The concise and constantly changing menu at this Mission eatery never fails to have something on it that you want to eat – wild-nettle stuffed pasta with lemon and goat cheese, or slow-cooked lamb shoulder with parsnip purée. The meyer lemon pudding cake will make you weep.

Ritual Roasters

1026 Valencia Street, between 21st & 22nd Streets (641 1024, www.ritualroasters.com). BART to 24th Street Mission/bus 14, 49. **Open** 6am-10pm Mon-Fri; 7am-10pm Sat; 7am-9pm Sun. **Credit** MC, V. **Map** p318 K11 92 Café

In the Bay Area, where coffee is regarded with religious concern, it's not surprising that folks talk about this place with zealot-like rapture. The beans, formerly from Portland's Stumptown roasters, are now roasted in-house. The room itself is a fairly standard café; some are here to talk, but most to surf.

St Francis Fountain

2801 24th Street, at York Street (826 4200, www.stfrancisfountainsf.com). Bus 9, 10, 27, 33, 48, 90. **Open** 8am-10pm Mon-Sat; 8am-9pm Sun. **Main courses** $7.75. **Credit** MC, V. **Map** p319 M12 93 Café

An almost classical link from old Mission to new, this ancient soda fountain has been given a new lease of life in recent years thanks to the attention lavished on it by new owners a few years back. The menu offers a few nods to the 21st century, but it's mainly a wonderfully retro experience, from the Formica tabletops to the magnificent mac and cheese and ice-cream sodas.

★ Saison

2124 Folsom Street at 17th Street, (828 7990, www.saisonsf.com). BART 16th Street/bus 9, 12, 22, 33, 47, 90. **Open** 6-9pm Tue-Sat. *Seatings* 7pm Fri; 5pm, 8pm Sat, Sun. **Set meal** 7 courses $118; wine pairings $78. **Credit** AmEx, MC, V. **Map** p318 L10 94 American

There's something at once disconcerting and reassuring about a restaurant that crafts arguably the most exquisite and intricate farm-to-table cuisine in the city and accompanies it with a soundtrack that veers from Allman Brothers to Tom Petty. That hard-to-peg sensibility matches its setting – tucked in a rustic carriage house behind the Saddle Café, at the end of a gravel courtyard. Committed diners settle in for a three-hour, intensely personal fine-dining extravaganza from chef Joshua Skenes that begins with champagne, and unfolds with seven courses that may include anything and everything fresh, local, and hand-foraged – from a layered epiphany of wafer-thin nasturtium leaves, beets, shaved radishes, oxalis, ice plant, and greens, to wild sea bream with river vegetables. If you want to try San Francisco cuisine at its most exciting and inventive, the pretty penny you'll spend here is likely worth it. *Photo p154.*

Slow Club

2501 Mariposa Street, at Hampshire Street (241 9390, www.slowclub.com). Bus 9, 22, 27, 33, 90. **Open** 8am-2.30pm, 6.30-10pm Mon-Thur; 8am-2.30pm, 6.30-11pm Fri; 10am-2.30pm, 6.30-11pm Sat; 10am-2.30pm Sun. **Main courses** $24. **Credit** AmEx, MC, V. **Map** p319 M10 95 American

With its remote location and hideaway vibe, this is a true locals' hangout. Slow Club's understated charm makes it one of the coolest restaurants in town. Typical mains include pan-roasted chicken and braised beef shank. There are no reservations, but you can wait in the cozy bar area.

★ Tartine Bakery

600 Guerrero Street at 18th Street (487 2600, www.tartinebakery.com). BART 16th Street Mission/Metro to Church & 18th Street/bus 14, 22, 33, 49. **Open** 8am-7pm, Mon; 7:30am-7pm Tue-Wed; 7:30am-8pm Thur-Fri; 8am-8pm Sat; 9am-8pm Sun. **Main items** $10. **Credit** AmEx, MC, V. **Map** p118 J10 96 Café

Locals line up around the block when Tartine's crusty, chewy country bread loaves come out of the oven after 5pm. The smell alone will make you weep. Once inside though, you'll be tormented by other mouthwatering temptations, including heavenly croque monsieurs, hot-pressed sopressata, fontina, and brocolli rabe pesto sandwiches, fresh fruit bread puddings, frangipane tarts, and lemon meringue cakes. Almost everything here is made using local, organic ingredients, including espresso from Four Barrel Coffee.

Tartine Bakery.

The Castro

For other good Castro eateries, *see pp225-27.*

Chow

215 Church Street, at Market Street (552 2469, www.chowfoodbar.com). Metro to Church/ streetcar F/bus 22, 37. **Open** 8am-11pm Mon-Thur, Sun; 8am-midnight Fri, Sat. **Main courses** $12. **Credit** AmEx, Disc, MC, V. **Map** p318 J9 97 American

Chow's hugely popular, well-priced, straight-ahead American fare ranges widely from roast chicken and burgers to Asian noodles, and the kitchen succeeds at most things it tries. Staff are pally, and the portions huge.

Other locations Park Chow, 1240 9th Avenue, Sunset (665 9912).

Home

2100 Market Street, at Church Street (503 0333, www.home-sf.com). Metro to Church/streetcar F/bus 22, 37. **Open** 5-10pm Mon-Thur; 5-midnight Fri; 10am-midnight Sat; 10am-10pm Sun. **Main courses** $17. **Credit** AmEx, Disc, MC, V. **Map** p318 H9 98 American

One of the Castro's can't-go-wrong options, this sceney restaurant has big-city atmosphere but small-town comfort. The crowd tends to be on the make, but that doesn't interfere with good conversation and generous portions of well-prepared classic American fare. Roast chicken and meatloaf are right at home alongside seafood specialties and vegetable spring rolls. At weekend brunch, there's a make-your-own bloody mary bar.

Starbelly

3583 16th Street, at Market Street (252 7500, www.starbellysf.com). Metro to Castro/streetcar F/bus 22, 35, 37. **Open** 11.30am-11pm Mon-Thur; 11.30am-midnight Fri, Sat; 10.30am-3pm Sat, Sun. **Main courses** $16. **Credit** AmEx, Disc, MC, V. **Map** p318 H10 99 American

In a neighborhood not traditionally known for its cuisine, Starbelly is among a handful of restaurants setting about to change that. Chef Adam Timney turns out top-notch comfort food with California spin: chicken liver pâté, to-die-for housemade salumi platter, rotisserie chicken with butternut squash bread pudding. The relaxed setting – with communal tables and a large outdoor patio – adds to the enjoyment. *Photo p157.*

Noe Valley

$ Alice's

1599 Sanchez Street, at 29th Street (282 8999). Metro to Church & 29th/bus 24. **Open** 11am-9.30pm

Saison. *See p152.*

Mon-Thur; 11am-10pm Fri, Sat; noon-9.30pm Sun. **Main courses** $9. **Credit** MC, V. Chinese

Banish any thought of Arlo Guthrie from your mind: it's worth trekking to Alice's restaurant for the spicy Hunan and Mandarin cooking. The clean and spare setting enhances such dishes as asparagus salmon in black bean sauce or delicate orange beef; and the spicy fried string beans will remain in your memory for all the right reasons.

★ Firefly

4288 24th Street, at Douglass Street (821 7652, www.fireflyrestaurant.com). Metro to Church & 24th/bus 24, 35, 48. **Open** 5.30-9pm Mon-Thur, Sun; 5.30-10pm Fri, Sat. **Main courses** $22. **Credit** AmEx, MC, V. **Map** p317 G12 100 American

White-topped tables aglow with soft lights and a room buzzing with good conversation are hallmarks of this neighborhood restaurant. The eclectic menu might feature fried chicken (among the best in town), honey-braised lamb shoulder or rib-sticking chicken and dumplings. There are always a number of inventive seasonal vegetarian selections, and special menus for the Jewish holiday. Warm, romantic and utterly charming.

★ Incanto

1550 Church Street, at DuncanStreet (641 4500, www.incanto.biz). Metro to Church & 24th/bus 48. **Open** 5.30-9.30pm Mon, Sun; 5.30-10pm Wed-Sat. **Main courses** $24. **Credit** AmEx, MC, V. Italian

Chris Cosentino's highly regarded restaurant is known for championing sustainably harvested produce, meat and seafood, and for the frequent appearance of offal on the daily changing menu (part of Cosentino's commitment to snout-to-tail no-waste cooking). Typically robust dishes might include milk-braised pork with braising greens and polenta. Italian wines are a very big deal here.

Lovejoy's Tea Room

1351 Church Street, at Clipper Street (648 5895, www.lovejoystearoom.com). Metro to Church & 24th/bus 48. **Open** 11am-6pm Wed-Sun. **Main courses** $13. **Credit** MC, V. Café

Select from Lovejoy's six different teas, including the Queen's Tea ($24.95) and the Wee Tea ($13.95) for children. They're all served in a room furnished with a jumble of antiques and knick-knacks.

THE HAIGHT & AROUND

Cole Valley

Eos Restaurant

901 Cole Street, at Carl Street (566 3063, www.eossf.com). Metro to Carl & Cole/bus 6, 37, 43, 66, 71. **Open** 5.30-10pm Mon-Thur, Sun; 5.30-11pm Fri, Sat. **Main courses** $17. **Credit** AmEx, MC, V. **Map** p317 E10 101 Asian

The best of East-West fusion, served in a comfortably spare, highly designed restaurant. The kitchen produces unique dishes such as tea-smoked Muscovy duck breast and fermented black bean-braised short-rib timbale. The same menu is served in the cozy wine bar next door (101 Carl Street).

★ Zazie

941 Cole Street, at Parnassus Street (564 5332, www.zaziesf.com). Metro to Carl & Cole/bus 6, 37, 43, 66, 71. **Open** 8am-2.30pm, 5.30-9.30pm Mon-Thur; 8am-2.30pm, 5.30-10pm Fri; 9am-3pm, 5.30-10pm Sat; 9am-3pm, 5.30-9.30pm Sun. **Main courses** $18. **Set meal** $23.50 3 courses. **Credit** MC, V. **Map** p317 E10 102 French

This delightful spot oozes bonhomie and serves up gentle breakfasts (don't miss the lemon-ricotta pancakes), a small variety of lunch dishes (pasta, sandwiches), a more French menu for dinner and a fabulous weekend brunch. Some see Zazie as a café, others a bistro, but it manages to pull off both.

Haight-Ashbury

Alembic

1725 Haight Street, between Cole & Shrader Streets (666 0822, www.alembicbar.com). Metro to Cole & Carl/bus 33, 37, 43, 66, 71. **Open** noon-1am daily. *Bar* until 2am daily. **Main courses** $18. **Credit** AmEx, Disc, MC, V. **Map** p317 E9 103 International

The Haight has no shortage of excellent drinking holes, but few possess the panache of this whisky-fueled destination in the heart of the neighborhood. The food menu is spare but pretty good, consisting of hits like the house made saké gravlax, *spätzle* and spiced lamb burger. Everything is designed as accompaniment to the main attraction: booze. A head-spinning array of boutique beers, Scottish single malts, American whiskies and even rare ryes ensures the trendy clientele is always kept happily buzzing along.

► *For a rundown of the city's artisan cocktail spots, see p175* **California Cuisine by the Glass**.

THE BEST MODERN MEXICAN FOOD

Elegant cantina, family recipes, killer guacamole.
Colibrí Mexican Bistro. *See p134.*

Glorious ceviches & handmade corn-masa tortillas near the ballpark.
Maya (303 2nd Street, 543 2928, www.mayasf.com).

Two-dozen pure agave tequilas; fantastic taco platters.
Tres Agaves. *See p144.*

Grind Café

783 Haight Street, at Scott Street (864 0955, www.thegrindcafe.com). Bus 6, 22, 24, 71. **Open** 7am-9pm Mon-Fri; 7am-7pm Sat; 8am-7pm Sun. **Main courses** $9. **Credit** AmEx, Disc, MC, V. **Map** p317 H9 (104) Café

This casual café is populated by too-cool-for-school denizens of the Lower Haight, probably spending the morning leafing through Sartre or sweating off a hangover, or both. The best eats are the vegetable-packed omelets and stacks of pancakes. The open-air patio welcomes dog owners and the occasional cigarette.

Kate's Kitchen

471 Haight Street, between Fillmore & Webster Streets (626 3984, www.kates-kitchensf.com). Bus 6, 22, 71. **Open** 8am-2.45pm Mon-Fri; 8.30am-3.45pm Sat, Sun. **Main courses** $7.50 **No credit cards**. **Map** p317 H8 (105) Café

A buzzing spot that's an excellent choice when you've got a mountain of Sunday papers to wade through at your leisure. Ease into the day with the assistance of a giant bowl of granola, a huge omelette or the signature dish of hush puppies (drop pancakes made of cornmeal). Lower Haight's unofficial brunch HQ.

$ Thep Phanom

400 Waller Street, at Fillmore Street (431 2526, www.thepphanom.com). Bus 6, 22, 71. **Open** 5.30-10.30pm daily. **Main courses** $15. **Credit** AmEx, Disc, MC, V. **Map** p317 H9 (106) Thai

Be sure to book in advance at Thep Phanom – and once you're there, be sure to order the *tom ka gai* (coconut chicken soup) as a starter. The 'angel wings' – fried chicken wings stuffed with glass noodles – are another universally popular choice. This place is often hailed as the best Thai restaurant in San Francisco.

The Western Addition

1300 On Fillmore

1300 Fillmore Street, at Eddy Street (771 7100, www.1300fillmore.com). Bus 5, 22, 31, 38. **Open** 4.30-10pm Mon-Thur; 4.30pm-midnight Fri, Sat; 10.30am-2.30pm, 5.30-10pm Sun. **Main courses** $24. **Credit** AmEx, MC, V. **Map** p317 H7 (107) American

Part of the long-overdue and much-anticipated revitalization of the historic Fillmore Jazz District, this soul-food eatery is, along with Yoshi's (see below), a welcome addition to the area. The Southern-influenced fare is anchored in classics: fried chicken, barbecued shrimp with grits, and mac and cheese. The room has a lounge-club atmosphere, with big leather chairs and endless classic jazz streaming through the air. Don't miss the Heritage Wall in the lounge, with a collection of historic photos and TV screens scrolling through images of jazz greats who once played in the area.

$ Café Abir

1300 Fulton Street, at Divisadero Street (567 6503, www.dajanigroup.net/establishments/cafe-abir/). Bus 5, 21, 24. **Open** 6am-11pm Mon-Sat, 6.30am-9pm Sun. **Main courses** $10. **No credit cards**. **Map** p317 G7 (108) Café

This hip, laid-back café is one of the most popular options in the Western Addition area, and the friendly staff and well-chosen house music mean it's as much about nightlife as morning life. An organic grocery store, a bar, a coffee roastery and an international newsstand supplement the large café. Choose from the freshly made sandwiches and deli salads, or just get a bagel to accompany your latte and newspaper.

★ Nopa

560 Divisadero Street, at Hayes Street (864 8643, www.nopasf.com). Bus 5, 21, 24. **Open** 6pm-1am Mon-Fri; 11am-2.30pm, 6pm-1am Sat, Sun. **Main courses** $24. **Credit** AmEx, Disc, MC, V. **Map** p317 G8 (109) Italian & pizza

One of the hottest restaurants in town, Nopa's attractions include the wood-fired oven, and the late hours – unusual in a city where many kitchens pack up at 10pm. Italian- and Med-inspired ('urban rustic') dishes can show an inventive use of ingredients – like pasta with home-smoked bacon, Brussels sprouts and goat's cheese. Others are more classic – the likes of pork chop with cannellini beans, wilted greens and salsa verde.

Yoshi's

1330 Fillmore Street, at Eddy Street (655 5600, www.yoshis.com/sf). Bus 5, 22, 31, 38. **Open** 5.30-9pm Mon-Wed; 5.30-10pm Thur; 5.30-10.30pm Fri, Sat; 5-9pm Sun. *Bar & lounge* 5pm-2am daily. **Main courses** $30. **Credit** AmEx, MC, V. **Map** p317 H7 (110) Japanese

The San Francisco branch of the legendary East Bay jazz club and sushi restaurant has infused the Fillmore Heritage Center with a vibrancy not seen since the area served as a West Coast jazz mecca. The calendar of jazz performers, both well known and up-and-coming, is the main attraction, but the extensive menu of sushi and other Japanese specialties doesn't disappoint. Book in advance and arrive early to enjoy dinner before moving in to the theater for the show.

► *For more on Yoshi's as a music venue, see p238.*

Japantown

$ Mifune

Japan Center, 1737 Post Street, between Webster & Buchanan Streets (922 0337, www.mifune.com). Bus 2, 3, 22, 38. **Open** 11am-9.30pm daily. **Main courses** $14. **Credit** AmEx, MC, V. **Map** p314 H6 (111) Asian

Mifune's motto is 'It's okay to slurp your noodles', which gives you an idea of the atmosphere and focus of this place. Good for kids and vegetarians, here

Starbelly. *See p154.*

you'll find the lowly noodle prepared in at least 30 different ways. Orders come quickly, and the food is that appealing combination: inexpensive and delicious.

O Izakaya Lounge

Hotel Kabuki, 1625 Post Street, at Laguna Street (614 5431, www.jdvhotels.com/dining). Bus 2, 3, 38. **Open** 6.30-10.30am Mon, Tue; 6.30-10.30am, 5-10pm Wed-Fri; 7-11am, 5-10pm Sat, Sun. **Main courses** *small plates* $15. **Credit** AmEx, Disc, MC, V. **Map** p314 J6 112 Japanese

Situated in the Hotel Kabuki, this combination izakaya house and Japanese sports bar is a bit oddball, but that's part of the charm. The menu features small plates of traditional Japanese cuisine prepared with fresh local ingredients, which diners can consume at the bar watching Japanese baseball. Menu specialties include the likes of pork belly braised with house-made *kimchee*, and seaweed salad with mustard greens and *umeboshi*. There are more than 20 different sakés on offer, which can be sampled by the flight or in one of the signature saké cocktails.

Seoul Garden

22 Peace Plaza, Geary Boulevard, at Laguna Street (563 7664, www.seoulgardenbbq.com). Bus 2, 3, 38. **Open** 11am-midnight daily. **Main courses** $20. **Credit** AmEx, MC, V. **Map** p314 H6 113 Korean

A good choice when all the Japanese eateries are too crowded (which is often the case). Here you grill marinated beef at your table while nibbling at the myriad little dishes that make up Korean cuisine.

CONSUME

Hayes Valley

Absinthe

398 Hayes Street, at Gough Street (551 1590, www.absinthe.com). Metro to Van Ness/bus 5, 21, 47, 49, 90 & Market Street routes. **Open** 11.30am-midnight Tue-Fri; 11am-midnight Sat; 11am-10.30pm Sun. *Bar* until 2am Thur-Sat. **Main courses** $26. **Credit** AmEx, Disc, MC, V. **Map** p318 J7 114 French

The spirit of bohemian France is reborn in San Francisco at this boisterous brasserie. The French menu lists reliable favorites, including excellent coq au vin and cassoulet. Try the seafood platter to start. The bar – thanks to a change in the law – now offers genuine absinthe too.

Destino

1815 Market Street, between Guerrero & Valencia Streets (552 4451, www.destinosf.com). Metro to Van Ness/streetcar F/bus 6, 71. **Open** 5-10pm Mon-Thur, Sun; 5-11pm Fri-Sat. **Main courses** $16. **Credit** AmEx, MC, V. **Map** p318 J9 115 Latin American

This casual, fun restaurant serves specialties from Central and South America in a lively neighborhood setting. The theme is small plates meant for sharing, but à la carte options are also available. Empanadas, ceviches and other indigenous dishes are all given a robust, flavorful treatment. From seafood to meat, it all works well and is always unique. Try the three-course prix fixe menu ($35) to take the guesswork out of ordering.

Suppenküche

601 Hayes Street, at Laguna Street (252 9289, www.suppenkuche.com). Bus 5, 21. **Open** 5-10pm Mon-Sat; 10am-2.30pm, 5-10pm Sun. **Main courses** $16. **Credit** AmEx, Disc, MC, V. **Map** p318 J8 116 German

If you're hungry for something that's going to last you all day, then Suppenküche is a good bet. Its menu, which covers *spätzle*, schnitzels and dense, dark breads, is authentically German, and not for the faint of belly. An impressive array of flavorsome German beers is served in tall steins; seating is on benches.

¡Viva la Tortilla!

Mission burritos are simply the best.

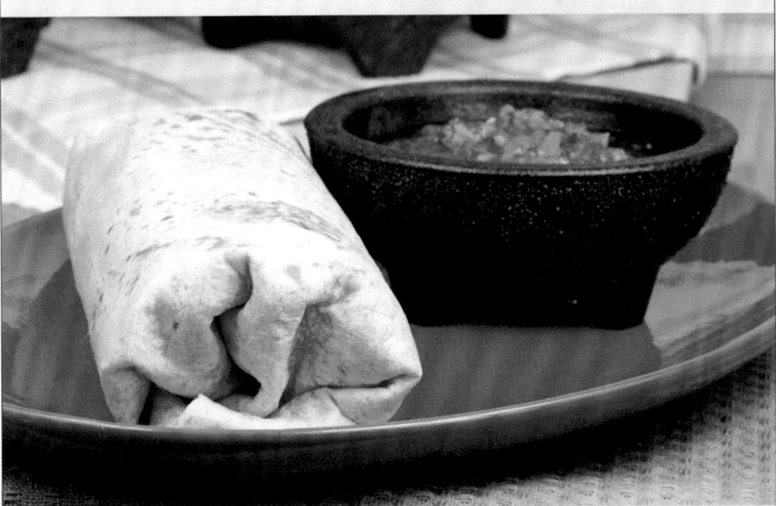

Evidence of San Francisco's supremacy in the realm of the burrito can be found in New York City, where an Upper West Side Mexican eaterie has a sign in its window boasting that it serves 'San Francisco Mission District-Style' burritos. Imitators are everywhere, but while the real thing can be found throughout SF, the epicenter for the glorious steamed tortillas packed with meat (optional), cheese, rice, beans, guacamole and spicy salsa is undoubtedly the Mission.

On September 29, 1969, the first Mission burrito was sold at the still-extant **La Cumbre Taqueria** (515 Valencia Street, at 16th Street, 863 8205). Today, the Mission is packed with burrito joints, walk-up counters dishing up immense hunks of food for a meager few bucks. Mainstream mega-taquería **Pancho Villa** (3071 16th Street, at Valencia Street, 864 8840, www.panchovillasf.com) and the respected **El Toro** (598 Valencia Street, at 17th Street, 431 3351), are both good and authentic. However, the best places are a bit further afield. Consistent champion **Taqueria San Francisco** (2794 24th Street, at York Avenue, 641 1770) slings exquisite *carne asada* (grilled beef) into lightly grilled, warm and flaky tortillas, while **Taqueria Cancun** (2288 Mission Street, near 19th Street, 252 9560) does a particularly fine vegetarian burrito. Pair the slabs at **El Farolito** (2777 Mission Street, at 24th Street, 826 4870) with refreshing cantaloupe *agua fresca* – 'fresh water' flavored with fruit. At **Papalote** (3409 24th Street, at Valencia Street, 970 8815, www.papalote-sf.com), the ingredients are fresher and the decor is more colorful, but the price is still right.

SUNSET, GOLDEN GATE PARK & RICHMOND

Sunset

Ebisu

1283 9th Avenue, between Irving Street & Lincoln Way (566 1770, www.ebisusushi.com). Metro to Judah & 9th/bus 6, 43, 44, 66, 71. **Open** 11.30am-2pm, 5-10pm Tue-Fri; noon-2.30pm, 5-11pm Sat; noon-2.30pm, 5-10pm Sun. **Main courses** $20. **Credit** AmEx, MC, V. **Map** p316 C10 117 Japanese

Many locals agree that this is the best sushi in town – and so there's often a wait for a table. Put your name on the list and get a drink at the bar with a light heart, because you're going to enjoy house specialties like the 'pink Cadillac' (salmon sushi roll) and seafood salad. Good as the sushi is, you can happily forgo it for the traditional Japanese cooked food.

Java Beach Café

1396 La Playa Boulevard, at Judah Street (665 5282, www.javabeachcafe.com). Metro to Ocean Beach/bus 18. **Open** 5.30am-11pm Mon-Fri; 6am-11pm Sat, Sun. **Main courses** $7. **Credit** MC, V. Café

Java Beach is funky and civilized, with the wetsuits and grand Pacific views making it feel a bit like Hermosa Beach in Los Angeles – minus the perma-tans, of course. Surfers, cyclists and ordinary passers-by pop in for a basic sandwich, some soup or maybe a pastry.

★ Outerlands

4001 Judah Street, at 45th Avenue (661 6140, www.outerlandssf.com). Metro N Judah. **Open** 11am-3pm, 6-10pm Tue-Sat; 10am-2.30pm Sun. No reservations. **Main courses** $19. **Credit** MC, V. American

It's perhaps only a bit of an exaggeration to say that Outerlands may be the restaurant that rescues the foggy Outer Sunset from wallowing endlessly as a culinary backwater. Salvaged barn-wood fence and arty sculptures speak to the surfer crowd that gathers here for the short, simple and delectable locally harvested menu – seasonal soups, house-baked breads, and mains that range from California yellowtail with grilled favas and nasturtium-potato purée to savory bread pudding. On weekends, brunch of Dutch pancakes, French toast, and 'eggs in jail' served with a side of Zoe's bacon is among the best in town.

Tart to Tart

641 Irving Street, between 7th & 8th Avenues (504 7068). Metro to Judah & 9th/bus 6, 43, 44, 66, 71. **Open** 6am-1am Mon-Thur, Sun; 6am-2am Fri, Sat. **Main courses** $6. **Credit** MC, V. **Map** p316 C10 118 Café

There are few late-night options in the Inner Sunset, perhaps because residents are mainly families. No matter: at Tart to Tart you can get freshly made cookies and cakes, above-average salads and sandwiches, and more tarts than you could comfortably sample over the course of a month.

Golden Gate Park

Park Chow, sister restaurant to **Chow** *(see p154)*, is handy for Golden Gate Park, as are the **Beach Chalet** and **Park Chalet** *(see p93)*.

Richmond

Bistro Chapeau!

126 Clement Street, between 2nd & 3rd Avenues (750 9787, www.chapeausf.com). Bus 1, 2, 33, 38, 44. **Open** 5-10pm Mon-Thur, Sun; 5-10.30pm Fri, Sat. **Main courses** $22. **Credit** AmEx, Disc, MC, V. **Map** p312 A6 119 French

Bistro Chapeau! is a proper little French charmer, with cozy bistro decor and friendly staff. The Provençal fare is just as comforting, with excellent trad dishes like coq au vin, onion soup and duck à l'orange. There's a fine brunch on Sundays, which makes an ideal opportunity for exploring the bubbly list. 'Hat!', appropriately enough, is more or less French for 'Wow!'.

Blue Danube Coffee House

306 Clement Street, at 4th Avenue (221 9041). Bus 1, 2, 33, 38, 44. **Open** 7am-10pm Mon-Thur, Sun; 7am-11pm Fri, Sat. **Main courses** $8. **No credit cards**. **Map** p312 C6 120 Café

One of San Francisco's first hip coffee houses, the Blue Danube still enjoys a loyal following after more than a quarter century in business: grab a latte or a pint, and sit watching passers-by from the large streetside windows.

Khan Toke Thai House

5937 Geary Boulevard, between 23rd & 24th Avenues (668 6654). Bus 29, 38. **Open** 5-10pm daily. **Main courses** $12. **Credit** AmEx, MC, V. Thai

Locals often overlook one of the city's most attractive Thai restaurants, Khan Toke. But it should be considered by anyone looking for an authentic experience. Slip off your shoes, sit on a low chair (with a padded back support) and enjoy fiery, colorful curries with excellent noodles.

★ Mayflower

6255 Geary Boulevard, at 27th Avenue (387 8338, www.mayflower-seafood.com). Bus 29, 38. **Open** 11am-2.30pm, 5-9.30pm Mon-Fri; 10am-2.30pm, 5-10pm Sat, Sun. **Main courses** $20. *Dim sum* $3-$7. **Credit** AmEx, Disc, MC, V. Chinese

Best known for its terrific mid-morning dim sum, the Mayflower also serves good seafood, fine claypot dishes and superb roast chicken and duck. Alongside the broad range of typical Cantonese options you'll find Mongolian beef, another favorite. The restaurant is large, noisy and family-oriented; arrive after 8pm if you want to avoid the dinner hordes.

Q Restaurant

225 Clement Street, at 3rd Avenue (752 2298, www.qrestaurant.com). Bus 1, 2, 33, 38, 44. **Open** 11am-3pm, 5-11pm Mon-Fri; 10am-11pm Sat; 10am-10pm Sun. **Main courses** $13. **Credit** MC, V. **Map** p312 C6 121 American

A delightful restaurant, serving top-notch comfort food. The name comes from its earlier ambitions as a barbecue joint, but the kitchen now runs to grilled steaks and seafood, pasta and some of the city's top fried chicken. A good wine list and eclectic decor make Q one of a kind.

Ton Kiang

5821 Geary Boulevard, between 22nd & 23rd Avenues (387 8273, www.tonkiang.net). Bus 29, 38. **Open** 10am-9pm Mon-Thur; 10am-9.30pm Fri; 9.30am-9.30pm Sat; 9am-9pm Sun. **Main courses** $15. **Credit** AmEx, Disc, MC, V. Chinese

This large restaurant's stock-in-trade is quality *hakka* cuisine, a style of Chinese gypsy cooking. Favorite dishes include the authentic salt-baked chicken served with a ground garlic and ginger paste. It's also an all-day spot for excellent dim sum – very popular on weekend mornings.

CONSUME

PACIFIC HEIGHTS TO THE GOLDEN GATE BRIDGE

Pacific Heights

Citizen Cake

2125 Fillmore Street, at Sacramento Street (861 2228, www.citizencake.com). Bus 1, 2, 3, 10, 22, 24. **Open** 10am-10pm Mon-Sat; 10am-9pm Sun. **Main courses** $18. **Credit** AmEx, MC, V. **Map** p313 H5 122 Café

Quite possibly the trendiest place for dessert in town, chef Elizabeth Falkner's iconic restaurant and pâtisserie sells gorgeous sweet things to a crowd of well-dressed and good-looking patrons. Lunch and dinner menus, with offerings such as pot roast stroganoff and Moroccan spiced meatballs, are also worth exploring.

Ella's

500 Presidio Avenue, at California Street (441 5669, www.ellassanfrancisco.com). Bus 1, 2, 3, 43. **Open** 7am-3pm Mon-Fri; 8.30am-2pm Sat, Sun. **Main courses** $12. **Credit** AmEx, Disc, MC, V. **Map** p313 F5 123 Café

This stylish, neighborly corner restaurant is famed for its weekend brunch. The wait can be long, but it's worth it. Favorites include the chicken hash with eggs and toast, and the potato scramble, prepared with a frequently changing list of fresh ingredients. The thick, perfectly crisped French toast is superb.

Florio

1915 Fillmore Street, between Bush & Pine Streets (775 4300, www.floriosf.com). Bus 1, 2, 3, 22, 24. **Open** 5.30-10pm daily. **Main courses** $20. **Credit** AmEx, MC, V. **Map** p313 H5 124 French

A quintessential local bistro, Florio is warm and welcoming, with just the right degree of refinement. Dark wood and white tablecloths set the tone for the French-inspired rural cooking. The ribeye steak-frites and the Tuscan seafood stew are always soul-warming. Service is swift and friendly.

Fresca

2114 Fillmore Street, at California Street (447 2668, www.frescasf.com). Bus 1, 2, 3, 10, 22, 24. **Open** 11am-3pm, 5-10pm Mon-Thur; 11am-3pm, 5-11pm Fri; 10am-3pm, 5-11pm Sat; 11am-3pm, 5-9pm Sun. **Main courses** $26. **Credit** AmEx, Disc, MC, V. **Map** p313 H5 125 Latin American

Fresca claims to have San Francisco's only ceviche bar, but has a broader menu than you might expect. Try tangy halibut ceviche or flambéed pisco prawns to start, followed by grilled ribeye with fries and plantains or sweet soy-roasted trout. The space can be very loud and tables are crammed together, but the quality of the Peruvian food makes up for any discomfort.

Other locations 3945 24th Street, Noe Valley (695 0549); 24 West Portal Avenue, Sunset (759 8087).

Harris'

2100 Van Ness Avenue, at Pacific Avenue (673 1888, www.harrisrestaurant.com). Bus 1, 10, 12, 19, 27, 47, 49, 90. **Open** 5.30-9.30pm Mon-Fri; 5-10pm Sat; 5-9pm Sun. **Main courses** $45. **Credit** AmEx, Disc, MC, V. **Map** p314 J4 126 American

One of San Francisco's steakhouse veterans, Harris' offers classy old-style dining, with big steaks, big martinis, and big bills at meal's end. Sink into your booth, start with a strong cocktail, then proceed with a textbook caesar salad (put together at your table), a prime piece of carefully aged steak (from the restaurant's own ranch) and a baked potato with all the trimmings. Hefty desserts follow.

SPQR

1911 Fillmore Street, between Bush & Pine Streets (771 7779, www.spqrsf.com). Bus 1, 2, 3, 22, 24. **Open** 5.30-10pm Mon-Fri; 11am-2.30pm, 5.30-10.30pm Sat; 11am-2.30pm, 5.30-10pm Sun. **Main courses** $20. **Credit** AmEx, MC, V. **Map** p313 H5 127 Italian

In this small, spare, one-room dining space, the spirit of Roman cuisine shines through. Dishes are rustic, unadorned and incredibly flavorful, the best in straightforward Italian cooking. Pork *saltimbocca* with carrots and pickled peppers, calamares with ceci beans, and beef brisket with pancetta, red wine and tomato are specialties. The toughest part is getting a table – reservations aren't accepted, but browsing the excellent by-the-glass wine list will help pass the time.

Spruce

3640 Sacramento Street, at Spruce Street (931 5100, www.sprucesf.com). Bus 1, 2, 3, 33. **Open** 11.30am-11pm Mon-Fri; 5-11pm Sat, Sun. **Main courses** $35. **Credit** AmEx, MC, V. **Map** p313 E5 128 American

In the sleepy but upscale Presidio Heights neighborhood, this posh, handsome restaurant has managed to set the city abuzz, and the scarcity of reservations shouldn't put you off. Once you're in, you're part of the scene, a locals-only feel where a lounge, a takeout area and a formal dining room all exist peacefully. Specialties of Chef Mark Sullivan's fresh, inventive menu include butter-poached lobster and grilled steak, and other extravagances.

Cow Hollow

Betelnut

2030 Union Street, between Webster & Buchanan Streets (929 8855, www.betelnutrestaurant.com). Bus 22, 41, 45. **Open** 11.30am-11pm Mon-Thur,

Taking it to the Street

How to track down the best food trucks.

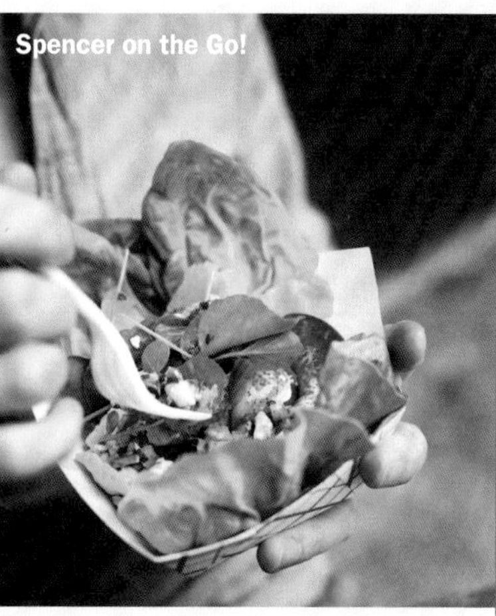

The Rib Whip. Gobba Gobba Hey. The Creme Brulee Man. Adobo Hobo. Evil Jerk Cart. Curry Up Now. Gourmet urban food trucks with hip street names line the parking lots and alleyways of San Francisco these days. Given the generally astronomical costs associated with starting a restaurant in the city, many aspiring chefs have taken a cue from taco trucks and staked out prime locations around town. While entire websites have been devoted to taco trucks alone, the best way to get a handle on the SF street food scene as a whole is to do a crawl on your own. Guided by **Roaming Hunger** (www.roaminghunger.com/sf), a website dedicated to tracking US street food, users can find the precise, real-time locations of everything from the Belgian waffle guy to the dude with the killer curry, or a French food truck (like Spencer on the Go!, *pictured*). Alternatively, drop into **Off the Grid** (www.offthegridsf.com), a roving gathering of multiple food trucks at locations throughout the city – some complete with live music, craft vendors and entertainment (currently operating Wed-Sat). Today's food trucks are far from the roach coaches of yesteryear, and today's street vendors are inventive, creative and quality-driven. The new truck stop, in fact, may be some of the finest dining you do in SF.

Sun; 11.30am-midnight Fri, Sat. **Main courses** $17. **Credit** AmEx, Disc, MC, V. **Map** p313 H4 ⓬⓽ Asian
This cool-looking restaurant has managed to retain its popularity by combining a relatively exotic South Pacific concept and consistent execution. Sidestep the sometimes-can't-be-bothered attitude up front, join the crowd at the bar and peruse a menu that's made for grazing. The best bet is to keep ordering small plates (tea-smoked duck, braised short ribs, papaya salad) until either your waistline or your credit card goes pop.

Presidio Social Club
563 Ruger Street, Building 563, at Lombard Street (885 1888, www.presidiosocialclub.com). Bus 41, 43, 45. **Open** 11.30am-10pm Mon-Fri; 10am-10pm Sat, Sun. **Main courses** $25. **Credit** AmEx, Disc, MC, V. **Map** p313 F4 130 American
Housed in a historic building in the verdant Presidio, this rambling wooden structure – a former army barracks – is an ideal setting for the charm within. The intimate setting gives way to a lively crowd as the evening progresses and the foghorn moans outside. The menu features unfussy classics of the comforting steaks and chops variety, simply prepared using local ingredients. With its large communal table, the bar is perfect for soaking up the atmosphere on misty evenings.

The Marina & the Waterfront

$ Bin 38
3232 Scott Street, between Lombard & Chestnut Streets (567 3838, www.bin38.com). Bus 28, 30, 43, 91. **Open** 5pm-midnight Mon-Thur; 4pm-1.30am Fri; 2pm-1.30am Sat; 2pm-midnight Sun. **Main courses** $16. **Credit** AmEx, Disc, MC, V. **Map** p313 G3 131 American
A surprisingly sophisticated find among the collection of after-work destinations, this wine bar and small-plates restaurant is as big on atmosphere as it is on choice of tipple. The menu of Wine Country-inspired American fare is designed to easily pair with selections from the wine and beer list. Indeed, suggestions are offered on the page – so you needn't worry if your grilled grass-fed beef tenderloin kebabs will go well with the cabernet from Napa's Spring Mountain.

THE BEST BRILLIANT BRUNCHES

Enormous American breakfasts worth the wait.
Dottie's True Blue Café. *See p140.*

Lavish brunch with equally lavish views of the Pacific.
Beach Chalet. *See p93.*

Bonhomie and lemon-ricotta pancakes.
Zazie. *See p155.*

★ Greens
Building A, Fort Mason Center, Marina Boulevard, at Buchanan Street (771 6222, www.greensrestaurant.com). Bus 22, 28. **Open** 5.30-9pm Mon; 11.45am-2.30pm, 5.30-9pm Tue-Sat; 10.30am-2pm Sun. **Main courses** $19. **Credit** AmEx, Disc, MC, V. **Map** p313 H2 132 American
Vegans and carnivores alike extol the virtues of venerable Greens, with its waterfront views of the Golden Gate Bridge and award-winning, all-vegetarian menu. An extensive wine list complements mesquite-grilled vegetables and wood-fired pizzas topped with wild mushrooms. If you don't fancy queuing, pick up sandwiches or soups from the takeaway counter.

Grove
2250 Chestnut Street, at Avila Street (474 4843). Bus 28, 30, 43, 91. **Open** 7am-11pm Mon-Fri; 8am-11pm Sat, Sun. **Main courses** $10. **Credit** AmEx, Disc, MC, V. **Map** p313 G3 133 Café
This happening place is a true outpost of Marina café culture. As well as coffee, beer, wine and comfort food (the likes of lasagne or chicken pot pie), patrons can enjoy chess and backgammon. The Fillmore Street location offers the same kind of woodsy interior and big cappuccinos, but for a less trend-conscious clientele.
Other locations 2016 Fillmore Street, Pacific Heights (474 1419).

Isa
3324 Steiner Street, between Chestnut & Lombard Streets (567 9588, www.isarestaurant.com). Bus 22, 28, 30, 43, 45, 91. **Open** 5.30-10pm Mon-Thur; 5.30-10.30pm Fri, Sat; 5.30-9pm Sun. **Main courses** $20. **Credit** AmEx, Disc, MC, V. **Map** p313 G3 134 International
Expect such interesting fare as roast mussels with shallots and white wine, or hanger steak with tarragon mustard and roast garlic potatoes from the tapas-like menu at Isa. Cozy, with a secluded back patio, it is winningly free of Marina affectations.

Tipsy Pig
2231 Chestnut Street, at Pierce Street (292-2300, www.thetipsypigsf.com). Bus 28, 30, 43, 76. **Open** 5pm-2am Mon-Fri (last dinner seating 10-11pm); 11am-2am Sat, Sun. **Main courses** $18. **Credit** AmEx, MC, V. **Map** p313 G3 135 American
Riding the crest of the current wave of gastropubs, the popular Tipsy Pig strikes a happy balance between the boisterous Marina singles who pack the bar, and the neighborhood regulars and families who dine on upscale comfort food in the cozy

CONSUME

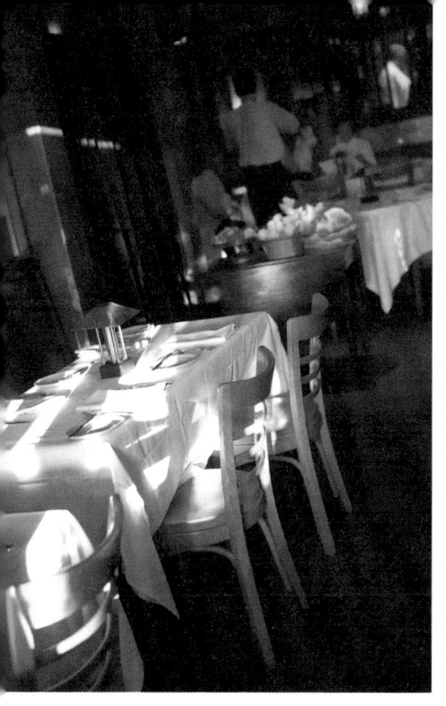

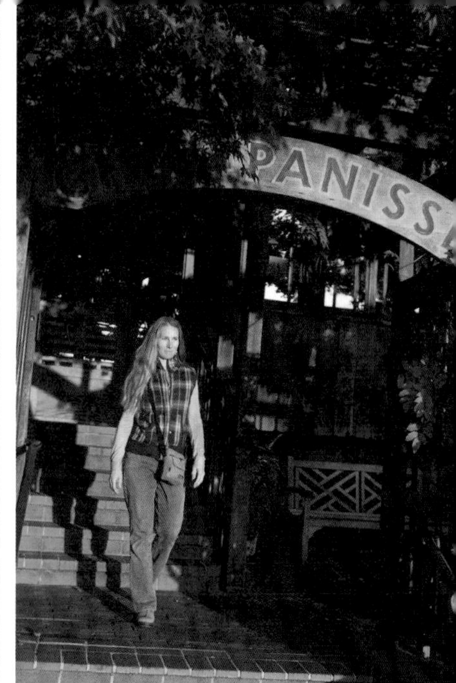

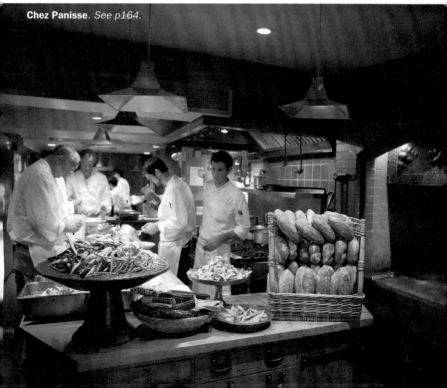

Chez Panisse. *See p164*.

English library or on the heated deck out back. Don't-miss signature dishes include Tipsy sliders (that's chimay-braised pulled pork with red cabbage slaw), chicken pot pie, a sublime burger on house-made bun, and the near-legendary smoked-bacon mac and cheese. Wash it down with an artisanal cocktail or one of 40 or so premium and craft beer selections.

The East Bay

A solid case can be made that the roots of San Francisco's current high culinary standing are grounded across the Bay. **Chez Panisse** (*see right*) is the headline-maker, but there are other dining options that make a jaunt over the bridge a powerful temptation. For more on the Oakland restaurant renaissance, *see p107* **Oakland on the Front Burner**.

OAKLAND

American

Bay Wolf

3853 Piedmont Avenue, between 40th Street & MacArthur Boulevard (1-510 655 6004, www.baywolf.com). BART to MacArthur/bus 51, 57, 59, 851. **Open** 11.30am-1.45pm, 5.30-9pm Mon-Thur; 11.30am-1.45pm, 5.30-10pm Fri; 5.30-10pm Sat; 5.30-9pm Sun. **Main courses** $12.50-$28. **Credit** AmEx, DC, MC, V.

Opened by Michael Wild in 1975, this comfortable East Bay staple is housed in a beautifully revamped Craftsman-style house. Wild is renowned for his duck specialities, which form part of a seaonal blend of California and Mediterranean fare. In nice weather, the best seats are on the enclosed redwood deck out front.

Italian & pizza

Oliveto

5655 College Avenue, at Shafter Avenue (1-510 547 5356, www.oliveto.com). BART Rockridge/bus 7, 51, 59, 851. **Open** *Café* 7am-9pm Mon; 7am-10pm Tue-Fri; 8am-10pm Sat; 8am-9pm Sun. *Restaurant* 11.30am-2pm, 5.30-9pm Mon; 11.30am-2pm, 5.30-9.30pm Tue, Wed; 11.30am-2pm, 5.30-10pm Thur, Fri; 5.30-10pm Sat, 5-9pm Sun. **Main courses** *Café* $6-$13. *Restaurant* $27-$32. **Credit** AmEx, DC, MC, V.

One of Oakland's true destination restaurants, this Rockridge area hotspot features soul-warming northern Italian fare that is almost entirely handmade. The specialty is house-cured, grilled and spit-roasted meat, and handmade pastas, but menus change daily to showcase the freshest available ingredients. The downstairs café features pizzas and baked goods from the wood-fired oven.

BERKELEY

American

Chez Panisse

1517 Shattuck Avenue, between Cedar & Vine Streets (restaurant 1-510 548 5525, café 1-510 548 5049, www.chezpanisse.com). BART Downtown Berkeley. **Open** *Restaurant sittings* (reservations required) 6-8.30pm, 8.30-9.30pm Mon-Sat. *Café* 11.30am-3pm, 5-10.30pm Mon-Thur; 11.30am-3.30pm, 5-11.30pm Fri, Sat. **Set meal** *Restaurant* $55-$85. **Main courses** *Café* $18-$24. **Credit** AmEx, DC, Disc, MC, V.

This is where chef/owner Alice Waters created California cuisine some 40 years ago. Her modest, wood-framed restaurant still reigns supreme, serving impeccable prix fixe dinners downstairs in the restaurant and more casual à la carte meals in the upstairs café. Ingredients are always fresh, local, organic and of impeccable quality. The excellent wine list combines French and Californian options, but you can also bring your own if you're prepared to pay the $25 corkage fee. You can (and should) book up to one month in advance for both the restaurant and café. *Photo p163.*

Italian

Rivoli

1539 Solano Avenue, between Neilson Street & Peralta Avenue (1-510 526 2542, www.rivoli restaurant.com). Bus 18, G. **Open** 5.30-9.30pm Mon-Thur; 5.30-10pm Fri; 5-10pm Sat; 5-9pm Sun. **Main courses** $19-$26. **Credit** AmEx, DC, Disc, MC, V.

Rivoli is a charming, intimate and neighbourly Italian-inspired restaurant, run by talented chef Wendy Brucker. The menu offers simple versions of classic dishes, made with seasonal organic produce; although it changes every three weeks, the portobello mushroom fritters (a signature dish), caesar salad and excellent hot fudge sundae are a constant presence.

Spanish

César

1515 Shattuck Avenue, between Cedar & Vine Streets (1-510 883 0222/www.barcesar.com). BART Downtown Berkeley. **Open** noon-11pm Mon-Thur, Sun; noon-11.30pm Fri, Sat. *Bar* until midnight daily. **Main courses** *Tapas* $6-$17. **Credit** AmEx, DC, MC, V.

It was pretty daring to locate César right next door to Chez Panisse (*see above*), but it has more than held its own, despite the competition. It no doubt helps that the ambience here is very different (lively, thanks in part to the presence of a bar area and open-air patio), but the food, a collection of Spanish-influenced tapas made from high-quality ingredients, also impresses. **Other locations** 4039 Piedmont Avenue, Oakland (1-510 985 1200).

Bars

San Francisco: the best place on earth to drink?

If a dedicated drinker were forced to choose the best cities in which to be confined for the rest of tippling time, San Francisco should be at the top of the list. Its proximity to one of the largest wine-growing regions in the world, dozens of top-ranked microbreweries and brewpubs, numerous craft distilleries, and a cutting-edge cocktail culture mean that San Francisco potentially offers the greatest variety of alcohol within a 100-mile radius of any city on the planet. That's saying something for a town that is home to only 815,000 people. What San Francisco lacks in size, it more than makes up for in moxie – San Franciscans spend more on booze and books than the citizens of any other American city. As a result, they are educated consumers in every sense, and those who hope to win their business or sway their palates need to stay one step ahead.

WHERE TO DRINK

Generalists will delight in the number and variety of drinking holes here, but each locale has bars that fit its personality. The hangouts in the **Financial District** suit the suits that frequent them, while those around the **Tenderloin** and the **Civic Center** tend towards the earthy (and, sometimes, seedy). **North Beach**, the place to drink back in the days of the Beats, is perhaps best avoided on weekends, when the bridge-and-tunnel crowd invades. The scene is smart, sometimes even chi-chi, in **Nob Hill** and **Pacific Heights**. **Haight-Ashbury** draws a down-to-earth, occasionally crunchy crowd; denizens of the **Lower Haight** may have more ink on their skin, but they're a friendly bunch.

The **Mission**, home to artists, musicians »and much of the city's Latin population, is powered by a bohemian energy that also drives its nightlife. Choose from Czech-style beer gardens, Moroccan-themed cocktails on roof decks, Mexican *cervecerías*, chic Euro-style bars, and a host of dives that are pure Americana. More intrepid drinkers, meanwhile, should make the trek to the **East Bay**, home to some of the region's best beer pubs. For information on how to navigate between venues by train, check out **www.beerbybart.com**, a blog that lists the best places to drink beer based on their proximity to BART stations. Note that BART shuts down at midnight, however.

About the author

Matt Markovich is a writer, photographer and communications consultant. He has written about wine, beer and spirits for the San Francisco Chronicle, San Francisco Bay Guardian and Napa Sonoma magazine.

BOOZE AND THE LAW

You have to be 21 or over to buy and consume alcohol in the US, and it can only be sold between 6am and 2am. Smoking is illegal in bars, restaurants and cafés.

DOWNTOWN

Union Square & around

Burritt Room

417 Stockton Street, at Sutter Street (400 0500, www.crescentsf.com). Bus 2, 3, 4, 30, 45, 76/ cable car Powell-Hyde or Powell-Mason. **Open** 5pm-midnight Mon-Thur, Sun; 5pm-2am Fri, Sat. **Credit** AmEx, Disc, MC, V. **Map** p315 M5 ❶

With an adventurous variety of classic, modern and seasonal cocktails along with a canned beer

❶ Green numbers given in this chapter correspond to the location of each bar as marked on the street maps. *See pp312-19.*

Rickhouse.

selection, the Burritt's decidedly noir feel does justice to the fact that it was named for Burritt Alley – the spot where Sam Spade's partner, Miles Archer, got filled with lead in Dashiell Hammett's *The Maltese Falcon*.

★ Rickhouse

246 Kearny Street, at Bush Street (398 2827, www.rickhousebar.com). BART & Metro to Montgomery/bus 5, 6, 9, 21, 31, 38. **Open** 5pm-2am Mon, Sat; 3pm-2am Tue-Fri. **Credit** AmEx, DC, Disc, MC, V. **Map** p315 M5 ❷

Rickhouse is named for the warehouses that store and age bourbon in barrels. Aptly enough, the expansive interior of the multi-room multistory bar is entirely paneled in barrel staves. And, once cozily marooned inside a bourbon cask, the staggering spirits selection and encyclopaedic cocktail menu will keep you happy until you float through the doors and evaporate into the evening air like the angel's share.

Slide

430 Mason Street, between Geary & Post Streets (421 1916, www.slidesf.com). BART Powell Street. **Open** 9pm-2am Wed-Sun. **Credit** AmEx, Disc, MC, V. **Map** p316 L5 ❸

This posh basement bar was once home to Coffee Dan's, a notorious speakeasy that patrons accessed by riding down a 15-foot slide. Featured in the 1927 Al Jolson movie, *The Jazz Singer*, it was also a gambling den and cabaret that played host to the likes of clarinetist Artie Shaw. As the current name suggests, guests once again enter the bar via a long slide that launches them into an elegant interior with plush booths, bottle service (for a hefty premium, starting at $250 per bottle), a striking backlit honey-onyx bar, acres of mahogany panelling, and a DJ booth housed in a grand piano. Despite its unbeatable provenance, the contemporary crowd is heavily South Bay-meets-LA. At the very least, it's worth sliding in to sample some of the many martinis or champagne cocktails.

Tunnel Top

601 Bush Street, at Stockton Street (986 8900, www.tunneltop.com). Bus 2, 3, 4, 30, 45, 76/ cable car Powell-Hyde or Powell-Mason. **Open** 5pm-2am Mon-Sat. **No credit cards. Map** p315 M5 ❹

The two-story Tunnel Top is perched above the Stockton Tunnel, between Chinatown and Union Square, and looks a little shabby from the outside. Inside, however, the decor is urban-decay cool; films are projected against rust-colored walls, while a DJ soundtracks the conversation. Just across the street at No.608 is the place where Robert Louis Stevenson lived.

The Financial District

★ Bix

56 Gold Street, between Montgomery & Sansome Streets (433 6300, www.bixrestaurant.com). Bus 9X, 10, 12, 20, 41. **Open** *Bar* 4.30-10pm Mon-Thur; 11.30am-midnight Fri; 5.30pm-midnight Sat; 5.30-10pm Sun. **Credit** AmEx, DC, Disc, MC, V. **Map** p315 N4 ❺

With a secretive locale and supper-club menu, Bix (named for owner Doug 'Bix' Biederbeck, who was 'very vaguely related' to 1930s jazz cornet legend Bix Beiderbecke) evokes the opulence of the Jazz Age. The room effectively combines the glamor of Harlem's Cotton Club with the splendor of a cruise liner dining room – you half expect to spy Rita Hayworth sipping a martini in a booth.

Bubble Lounge

714 Montgomery Street, between Washington & Jackson Streets (434 4204, www.sanfrancisco.bubblelounge.com). Bus 1, 9X, 10, 12, 20, 41. **Open** 5.30pm-1am Tue-Thur; 5pm-2am Fri; 6.30pm-2am Sat. **Credit** AmEx, DC, Disc, MC, V. **Map** p315 N4 ❻

After the stock market closes, stockbrokers and short-skirted executives tickle their noses with an incredible selection of sparkling wines and champagnes at this upscale hangout. The booze is paired with fine pâté, salads and caviar for a top-drawer taste of the Wall Street of the West.

The Tenderloin

Also in this part of town is the **Hemlock Tavern** (*see p242*), best known as a music venue but with a fine bar.

Bourbon and Branch

501 Jones Street, between O'Farrell and Geary Streets (931 7292, www.bourbonandbranch.com). Bus 2, 3, 4, 19, 38, 47. **Open** 6pm-2am Mon-Sat. **Credit** AmEx, DC, MC, V. **Map** p314 L6 ❼

Bourbon and Branch has one of the best selections of artisanal and rare spirits in San Francisco; and these spirits are often mixed into the bar's signature cocktails. In speakeasy tradition, reservations and a daily password are required for entry, so be sure to call or email ahead. Run by a group that either owns or advises virtually every top cocktail bar in the city, B&B also offers classes at its Beverage Academy (www.beverageacademy.com).

★ Edinburgh Castle

950 Geary Street, between Larkin & Polk Streets (885 4074, www.castlenews.com). Bus 2, 3, 4, 19, 38, 47. **Open** 5pm-2am daily. **Credit** DC, MC, V. **Map** p314 K6 ❽

Once through the humble entranceway of what appears to be a small, dark dive, the adventurous are rewarded with a raffish, capacious booze hall with 30ft vaulted ceilings. Upstairs is a small cultural venue, playing host to local bands, DJ nights, literary readings and even the odd play that suit the salty tastes of its Scottish owner. Downstairs, the jukebox cranks favorite obscurities while patrons order fish and chips and settle in with the other unpretentious patrons. The highlight of the drinks selection is a vast and affordable range of single malt whiskies. It may not be on the Spey, but it'll do for a day.

Bourbon and Branch.

One More for the Road

When Jack Kerouac nearly *met Henry Miller.*

It was a classic 'what if?' moment in Beat lore. In July 1960, the poet and owner of City Lights Books, Lawrence Ferlinghetti, had invited famed Beat writer Jack Kerouac to convalesce at his cabin in Big Sur. Kerouac had reported being 'at the end of his nerves', following the publicity blitz surrounding the film version of his novel, *The Subterraneans*, and it's likely that living in New York City hadn't helped the author's well-documented drinking problem either. The two made plans to have dinner with Henry Miller on the evening of Kerouac's arrival.

Miller, an admirer of Kerouac's writing, had recently written a truly glowing preface to the paperback edition of *The Subterraneans* and wanted to meet the author. But, once back in San Francisco, Jack made a beeline for his favorite stool at Vesuvio (*see p171*), just across a small alley from Ferlinghetti's bookstore. Kerouac set to drinking in the early afternoon and never stopped, calling Miller periodically to assure him he was on his way. Whether he really intended to leave, or was merely stringing Miller along, is anyone's guess, but an exasperated Ferlinghetti eventually left without him. Kerouac never made it.

Kerouac later confessed to being racked with guilt for avoiding Miller and chalked it up as 'an example of how really psychotically suspicious and loco I was getting' at the time – a mindset brutally evident in his grim autobiographical novel, *Big Sur*.

Some time late that night, Kerouac was poured into a cab for the 150-mile trip to Big Sur, where he was found 'sleeping heavily' in a meadow near Ferlinghetti's cabin the following morning. He and Miller never met.

CONSUME

Redwood Room

Clift Hotel, 495 Geary Street, at Taylor Street (929 2372, www.clifthotel.com). BART & Metro to Powell/bus 2, 3, 4, 27, 38, 76/cable car Powell-Hyde or Powell-Mason. **Open** 5pm-2am Mon-Thur, Sun; 4pm-2am Fri, Sat. **Credit** AmEx, DC, Disc, MC, V. **Map** p314 L6 ❾

No time was wasted in adding a bar to the Clift after the repeal of Prohibition in 1933, and the magnificent result has been a fixture for high-end cocktailing ever since. Although the decor shifted from art deco to postmodern under Ian Schrager, the bar is neither tacky nor too flamboyant – its towering walls still paneled in redwood thought to have come from a single tree. A DJ spins four nights a week for a well-dressed and moneyed crew.

Rye

688 Geary Street at Leavenworth Street (474 4448/www.ryesf.com). Bus 2, 3, 4, 19, 38, 47. **Open** 5.30-2am Mon-Fri; 7pm-2am Sat, Sun. **Credit** AmEx, Disc, MC, V. **Map** p314 L6 ❿

Rye justly holds a place in the city's craft cocktail canon, yet the vibe is less mahogany paneling and traditional glassware than concrete floors and a pool table. The happy hour and weekend crowd can mean standing room only at peak times – but who'd want to give up the pool table for extra seating, anyway? While the decor may be no-nonsense, Rye's drinks are potent, carefully crafted and relatively affordable. Add an enclosed smoking area and bartenders with good attitudes, and you have a legit, unpretentious spot to savor top cocktails.

SOMA & SOUTH BEACH

Close by AT&T Park is the **Hotel Utah** (*see venue index*), a good music venue with a great old bar.

Butter

354 11th Street, between Folsom & Harrison Streets (863 5964, www.smoothasbutter.com). Bus 9, 12, 27, 47. **Open** 6pm-2am Wed-Sun. **Credit** AmEx, DC, Disc, MC, V. **Map** p318 L9 ⓫

Butter combines chill-room vibe (complete with DJ) with trailer-trash kitsch and food. After several years on the scene, it still packs people in, and its magic formula repast of a corn dog, Twinkie and can of Pabst Blue Ribbon may just prove to be the elixir of life.

City Beer Store

1168 Folsom Street, between 7th & 8th Streets (503 1033, www.citybeerstore.com). Bus 9X, 12, 19, 27, 47. **Open** noon-9pm Tue-Sat; noon-6pm Sun. **Credit** AmEx, DC, Disc, MC, V. **Map** p318 L8 ⓬

This modest storefront operation consists of four tables and floor-to-ceiling refrigerators packed with over 300 kinds of bottled beers and six on draught. Grab a beer from the cooler, order a small plate of regional cheeses and *salametto*, and banter with the other beer-o-philes. When it's time to head out, the owners encourage patrons to mix and match a six-pack to take away.

Hi Dive

Pier 28½, Embarcadero, at Bryant Street (977 0170, www.hidive.net). Metro to Folsom/bus 12. **Open** 11.30am-late Mon-Fri; 10am-late Sat, Sun. **Credit** AmEx, DC, MC, V. **Map** p315 P5 ⓭

Once patronized by dock workers and sailors on shore leave, the Hi Dive was renovated a while back, but still draws a low-key crowd. A fine pit stop during a walk down the Embarcadero, it's right on the water, and gets lively – or, depending on your mood, crowded – before and after Giants games.

★ House of Shields

39 New Montgomery Street, at Market Street (975 8651, www.houseofshields.com). BART & Metro to Montgomery/bus 9X, 12, 30, 45, 76 and Market Street routes. **Open** 2pm-2am Mon-Fri; 7pm-2am Sat. **Credit** DC, MC, V. **Map** p315 N5 ⓮

One of the oldest and most storied bars in San Francisco, HoS was started by one Eddie Shields in 1908 and is said to house a subterranean network of tunnels once frequented by surreptitious tipplers during the dark days of Prohibition. Its carved, redwood bar was originally intended for the Palace Hotel across the street, but was moved here after it wouldn't accommodate the Maxfield Parrish painting in the hotel's Pied Piper bar. Purchased by local chef/restaurateur Dennis Leary (not that one), it's been lovingly restored to its former glory, including the original mosaic floors. And – odd observation though this may be – it has to have the biggest urinals in the world.

21st Amendment

563 2nd Street, between Bryant & Brannan Streets (369 0900, www.21st-amendment.com). Metro to 2nd & King/bus 9X, 10, 12, 30, 45, 76. **Open** 11.30am-midnight daily. **Credit** AmEx, DC, Disc, MC, V. **Map** p315 O6 ⓯

Named in honor of the constitutional diktat repealing Prohibition, this brewpub gets packed with Giants fans looking to load up on good, nicely priced booze (a mix of own-label beers and guests) before getting soaked by the exorbitant beer prices inside the stadium. At other times, it's a standard brewpub, with decent food and a convivial atmosphere.

W Hotel

181 3rd Street, at Howard Street (817 7836, www.starwoodhotels.com). BART & Metro to Montgomery/bus 9X, 12, 30, 45, 76 & Market Street routes. **Open** 7pm-2am Tue-Sat. **Credit** AmEx, DC, Disc, MC, V. **Map** p315 N6 ⓰

The two bars at this fashionable hotel (*see p124*) are filled with beautiful people. The first bar is a circular affair in the lobby, while the main room lies behind a beaded curtain above. Some may find the atmosphere a bit competitive, but the scene shifts nightly and banquettes upstairs encourage an intimate vibe.

NOB HILL & CHINATOWN

Nob Hill & Polk Gulch

Hidden Vine

1/2 Cosmo Place, at Taylor & Post Streets (674 3567, www.thehiddenvine.com). Bus 2, 3, 4, 27, 38, 76. **Open** 5pm-midnight Tue-Thur; 5pm-2am Fri, Sat. **Credit** DC, MC, V. **Map** p314 L5 ⓱

Hidden is the operative word for this extremely cozy husband-and-wife-owned wine bar that offers over 30 wines by the glass and 100 by the bottle. The thoughtfully conceived menu features numerous flights, allowing wine lovers to explore various varietals and regions. It's a great little sitting room atmosphere that encourages hushed conversation; those looking for a snack will be happy to find cheese, crackers and charcuterie to complement their fruit of the vine.

Le Colonial

20 Cosmo Place, between Jones & Taylor Streets (931 3600, www.lecolonialsf.com). Bus 2, 3, 4, 27, 38, 76. **Open** 4.30-10pm Mon-Wed, Sun; 4.30-11pm Thur-Sat. **Credit** AmEx, DC, MC, V. **Map** p314 L5 ⓲

Designed to approximate Vietnam c1920, when the country was still a French colony, this elegant hideaway has a sizeable dining room, while the stylish upstairs lounge serves tropical drinks, exotic teas and a menu highlighting Vietnamese fusion cuisine. The comfortable couches invite cocktailing and more in a lush environment of palm trees, rattan furniture and shuttered windows.

★ Tonga Room & Hurricane Bar

Fairmont Hotel, 950 Mason Street, between California & Sacramento Streets (772 5278, www.fairmont.com). Bus 1/cable car California,

THE BEST OUTDOOR DRINKING

An alfresco terrace
Jupiter (*see p177*).

A deck with a view
Medjool Sky Terrace (*see p173*).

A rockabilly beer garden
Zeitgeist (*see p173*).

A lovely lawn
Park Chalet (*see p174*).

THE BEST UPSCALE COCKTAILING

Evoking Jazz Age opulence
Bix (*see p166*).

The choice of fashionistas and financiers
MatrixFillmore (*see p176*).

With towering walls paneled in redwood
Redwood Room (*see p168*).

With panoramic views
Top of the Mark (*see p170*).

Powell-Hyde or Powell-Mason. **Open** 5pm-midnight Mon-Thur, Sun; 5pm-1am Fri, Sat. **Credit** AmEx, DC, Disc, MC, V. **Map** p314 L4 ⑲
Visit while you can, as there is an ongoing battle to save this historic gem from the wrecking ball. Despite the all-you-can-eat happy-hour dim sum, the sarong-clad waitresses and the enormous exotic cocktails, the real attraction at this long-lived tiki bar is the spectacle of house musicians performing off-key covers of cheesy pop songs while afloat on a raft on the Tonga's indoor 'lagoon'. There's even an indoor thunderstorm every 20 minutes, complete with rain.

Top of the Mark

Inter-Continental Hotel Mark Hopkins, 1 Nob Hill, at California & Mason Streets (392 3434, www.topofthemark.com). Bus 1/cable car California, Powell-Hyde or Powell-Mason. **Open** 5pm-midnight Mon-Thur, Sun; 4pm-1am Fri, Sat. **Admission** $10 after 8pm Fri, Sat. **Credit** AmEx, DC, Disc, MC, V. **Map** p314 L5 ⑳
Neatly named for its location at the summit of the InterContinental Mark Hopkins Hotel, Top of the Mark has spectacular panoramic views of the city. It's worth a quick visit just to check the view and sip a cocktail from the extensive martini menu, but arrive early in the evening to avoid the cover charge and the dress code (look smart or drink elsewhere).

Chinatown

Li Po

916 Grant Avenue, at Washington Street (982 0072). Bus 1, 9X, 12, 20, 30, 41, 45. **Open** 2pm-2am daily. **No credit cards. Map** p315 M4 ㉑
A fun spot for a pick-me-up when you're done with the junk shops on Grant Avenue. Li Po is basically a dive, but the cave façade and giant, tattered Chinese lantern inside set it nicely apart from its neighbors. It'll take you back to Barbary Coast-era San Francisco with no risk of being shanghaied by anything except the potent cocktails.

Mr Bing's

201 Columbus Avenue, at Pacific Avenue (362 1545). Bus 9X, 12, 20, 30, 41, 45. **Open** noon-2am daily. **No credit cards. Map** p315 M4 ㉒
This shambles of a bar doesn't look like much from the outside, and looks like even less once you're inside. But, thanks partly to its highly conspicuous location, it's a prince among dives, frequented by a mix of idling Chinese, haggard North Beach bums, and those who are simply, plainly desperate for a drink. For dive bar devotees, Mr Bing's is rarely less than entertaining.

NORTH BEACH TO FISHERMAN'S WHARF

North Beach

★ Comstock Saloon

155 Columbus Avenue, at Pacific Aveneu (617 0071, www.comstocksaloon.com). Bus 9X, 12, 20, 30, 41, 45. **Open** 11.30am-2am Mon-Fri; 2pm-2am Sat. **Credit** AmEx, MC, V. **Map** p315 M4 ㉓
The owners of Hayes Valley's Absinthe continue their tradition of offering beautifully prepared cocktails and gourmet fare in their latest outpost in North Beach, in a location that has been home to some of the city's most historically significant bars.
▶ *For a review of Absinthe, see p157.*

Rogue Ale's Public House

673 Union Street, between Powell Street & Columbus Avenue (362 7880, www.rogue.com). Bus 9X, 20, 30, 39, 41, 45. **Open** 3pm-midnight Mon-Thur; noon-2am Fri, Sat; noon-midnight Sun. **Credit** AmEx, DC, Disc, MC, V. **Map** p314 L3 ㉔
Oregon microbrewery Rogue Ale's bold land grab is evidenced by this ale house, devoted to its staggering array of brews. The standard selection of ambers and lagers is supplemented by such gems as chilli-pepper-tinged Chipotle Ale, Smoke Ale (with strong flavors of smokehouse almonds), Coffee Stout, and Iron Chef Morimoto's Black Obi Soba Ale.

Savoy Tivoli

1434 Grant Avenue, between Green & Union Streets (362 7023, www.savoy-tivoli.netfirms.com). Bus 9X, 12, 20, 30, 39, 41, 45. **Open** 6pm-2am Tue-Thur; 5pm-2am Fri; 3pm-2am Sat. **No credit cards. Map** p315 M3 ㉕
Opened in 1906, this long-established bar tends to get packed with preppies on warm, weekend nights due to the expanse of outdoor seating out front, but when things are a bit slower it's a perfect place to grab a beer and people-watch, or enjoy a few games of pool. Cocktails are a bit on the pricey side, but they'll do.

Spec's

12 William Saroyan Place, at Broadway & Columbus Avenue (421 4112). Bus 9X, 12, 20, 30, 41, 45. **Open** 4.30pm-2am Mon-Fri; 5pm-2am Sat, Sun. **No credit cards. Map** p315 M3 ㉖

Spec's.

Spec's really is the quintessential old-school San Francisco bar: one part North Beach bohemian and one part Wild West saloon, with a dash of weirdness thrown in for good measure. It's tucked away in a false alley (you'll see what we mean), with nearly every inch covered with dusty detritus from around the world. If you're feeling peckish, a basket of saltines and a wedge of gouda can be had for a mere four bucks.

Tony Nik's

1524 Stockton Street, at Green Street (693 0990). Bus 9X, 12, 20, 30, 39, 41, 45. **Open** 4pm-2am daily. **Credit** DC, MC, V. **Map** p315 M3 27

This venerable lounge, which is essentially a long bar with a few extra seats, opened the day after Prohibition was repealed in 1933, and keeps the old-time vibe alive thanks to Atomic Age decor and comfortably hip and friendly environs. Cocktails are a serious business here: there's always a surprise lurking behind the bar if the right mixologist is on duty.

★ Tosca Café

242 Columbus Avenue, between Broadway & Pacific Avenue (986 9651). Bus 9X, 12, 20, 30, 41, 45. **Open** 5pm-2am Mon-Sat; 7pm-2am Sun. **No credit cards**. **Map** p315 M3 28

Formica-topped tables, massive copper espresso machine, Caruso warbling from an ancient jukebox… Bars with interiors this lush deserve to double as movie sets. The house specialty, a blend of coffee, steamed milk and brandy, really packs a punch. The bada bing Italian ambience and Hollywood-connected owner have drawn the likes of Bono and Sean Penn.

★ Vesuvio

255 Columbus Avenue, between Broadway & Pacific Avenue (362 3370, www.vesuvio.com). Bus 9X, 12, 20, 30, 41, 45. **Open** 6am-2am daily. **Credit** AmEx, DC, MC, V. **Map** p315 M4 29

A funky old saloon with a stained-glass façade, Vesuvio preserves the flavor of the bars of an earlier era. It's next to the famous City Lights bookshop (*see p181*), just across Jack Kerouac Alley (the writer was a regular here), and its walls are covered with Beat memorabilia. Sit on the narrow balcony and check out the scene downstairs and on the street.

THE MISSION & THE CASTRO

The Mission

500 Club

500 Guerrero Street, at 17th Street (861 2500). BART 16th Street Mission/bus 14, 22, 26, 33, 49. **Open** 3pm-2am Mon-Fri; 1pm-2am Sat, Sun. **No credit cards**. **Map** p318 J10 30

Vying with Doc's Clock (*see p172*) for the title of the Mission's best marquee, the 'Five Hunge' is everybody's favorite dive. Cavernous booths, a punk jukebox, a pool table and cheap, stiff drinks keep the place

CONSUME

Magnolia. *See p174.*

brimming with an incredibly random crowd. Pull up a stool at the long bar and don't make plans to leave.

Argus Lounge

3187 Mission Street, at Valencia Street (824 1447, www.arguslounge.com). BART 24th Street Mission/bus 12, 14, 26, 27, 49, 67. **Open** 4pm-2am daily. **No credit cards.**

Known by some as the Peacock because of the illuminated feather out front (the only sign), the Argus is far enough down Mission to escape the gentrifying masses. A clean, simple hangout, it draws a happy crowd, including local indie-rock heroes. A great jukebox and back-room pool table add to quirky touches such as a working 1950s exercise belt. Shake it, baby.

Beauty Bar

2299 Mission Street, at 19th Street (285 0323, www.thebeautybar.com). BART 16th Street/bus 14, 22, 26, 33, 49. **Open** 5pm-2am Mon-Fri; 7pm-2am Sat, Sun. **Credit** DC, MC, V. **Map** p318 K11 ㉛

This little cocktail bar, modeled after its sister in New York (and now other locations), is decorated with bric-a-brac salvaged from a Long Island hair salon. Instead of a couch, curl up on a Naugahyde salon chair, with hairdryer still attached. A manicurist is on duty from 7.30pm to midnight, Thursday to Saturday. Seriously.

Dalva

3121 16th Street, between Mission & Guerrero Streets (252 7740). BART 16th Street/bus 14, 22, 26, 33, 49. **Open** 4pm-2am daily. **No credit cards. Map** p318 J10 ㉜

An unspoiled oasis of cool in the manic Mission bar scene, Dalva worships good music. The jukebox, named Orpheus, carries a wonderfully diverse array of sounds, from Cuban music to tiki kitsch. When it's not on, DJs spin drum 'n' bass, jazz, soul, funk, salsa and other odds and sods.

★ Doc's Clock

2575 Mission Street, at 22nd Street (824 3627). BART 24th Street Mission/bus 12, 14, 26, 48, 49, 67. **Open** 6pm-2am Mon-Sat; 8pm-2am Sun. **No credit cards. Map** p318 K12 ㉝

This place was once a total dive but, in common with many nearby bars, it had a kindly refit a while back. The mahogany bar was buffed up, the booze selection expanded, and the CD-changer now spits out anything from Air to Sufjan Stevens. Just down the road is the similarly revamped Mission Bar (2695 Mission Street, 647 2300), which lacks the shuffleboard table and magnificent neon sign of Doc's Clock, but has a great jukebox and adds some of the area's strongest drinks.

Kilowatt

3160 16th Street, between Valencia & Guerrero Streets (861 2595, www.barbell.com/kilowatt). BART 16th Street/bus 14, 22, 26, 33, 49. **Open** 4.30pm-2am Mon-Fri; 1pm-2am Sat, Sun. **No credit cards. Map** p318 J10 ㉞

Does what a solid bar should. With reasonable prices, generous drink pours, a good selection of beers, a top-notch jukebox, pool tables, dartboards and comfortable booths, this no-nonsense joint is a great option. Add in an excellent location near Dalva (*see left*), the 500 Club (*see p171*) and a number of restaurants, and it just gets better. For a meal of champions, grab a lamb shawarma from Truly Mediterranean across the street, return to the bar and order one of its mean bloody marys.

Knockout

3223 Mission Street, at Valencia Street (550 6994, www.theknockoutsf.com). BART 24th Street Mission/bus 12, 14, 26, 27, 49, 67.
Open 5pm-2am daily. **No credit cards**.
This divey old hangout takes on all challengers, hosting diverse live acts as well as DJs spinning sounds from reggae to rockabilly. Thursday night bingo sessions are a lot of fun, and happy hour karaoke is a hit too.

Medjool Sky Terrace

2522 Mission Street, between 21st & 22nd Streets (550 9055, www.medjoolsf.com). BART 24th Street Mission/bus 12, 14, 26, 48, 49, 67.
Open 5-10pm Mon-Wed; 4pm-midnight Thur; 4pm-1.30am Fri; 2pm-1.30am Sat; noon-10pm Sun. **Credit** AmEx, DC, Disc, MC, V. **Map** p318 K11 35
This two-building complex, topped by a massive roof deck, contains a restaurant, a café and an excellent hostel. However, weather permitting, the deck is the primary draw. Sip cocktails, draft beer or wine, and scoff scaled-down, lighter fare from the restaurant's menu while taking in some of the Mission street scene.

★ Zeitgeist

199 Valencia Street, at Duboce Avenue (255 7505). BART to 16th Street Mission/Metro to Van Ness/streetcar F/bus 26, 49. **Open** 9am-2am daily. **No credit cards**. **Map** p318 K9 36
Sited on the border between SoMa and the Mission, Zeitgeist is one of the hippest and most mellow bars in town, popular with bikers (Hondas over Harleys), bike messengers and people from every walk of alternative life. On sunny evenings, it's hard to find a seat at the benches and tables in the giant beer-garden-meets-junkyard back patio. The jukebox places special emphasis on underground punk.

The Castro

The majority of decent bars in the Castro are gay-oriented, although a number do draw a mixed crowd. For a full list of gay and lesbian hangouts in the area, *see p227-29*; for the **Café du Nord**, which serves double-duty as both bar and music venue, *see p241*.

Lucky 13

2140 Market Street, between Church & Sanchez Streets (487 1313). Metro to Church/streetcar F/bus 22, 37. **Open** 4pm-2am Mon-Thur; 2pm-2am Fri-Sun. **No credit cards**. **Map** p318 H9 37
Dark, spacious a[...]
been a favorite wi[...]
punk/biker bar witho[...]
pinball, pool and foosb[...]
ments are people-watching[...]
of the best German beer sele[...]

THE HAIGHT & AROU[...]

Haight-Ashbury

Hobson's Choice

1601 Haight Street, at Clayton Street (621 5859, www.hobsonschoice.com). Metro to Carl & Cole/bus 6, 7, 33, 37, 43, 71. **Open** 2pm-2am Mon-Fri; noon-2am Sat, Sun. **Credit** DC, MC, V. **Map** p317 E9 38
At this 'Victorian punch bar' (the owners' description), bartenders ladle out tall glasses of tasty rum punch; there are more than 70 varieties of rum. Fresh, grilled kebabs from the neighboring Asqew Grill soak up the booze as it settles in the bellies of the collegiate-cum-jam-band set that fills the place.

Madrone Lounge

500 Divisadero Street, at Fell Street (241 0202, www.madronelounge.com). Bus 21, 24. **Open** 2pm-midnight Mon, Sun; 2pm-2am Tue-Sat. **Credit** DC, MC, V. **Map** p317 G8 39
A funky lounge and gallery whose beautifully restored Victorian exterior brought joy to the neighbors when it was revived from almost total dilapidation. Inside, draught beers and a specialty

> **INSIDE TRACK**
> **SAN FRANCISCO BREWS**
>
> A recent study determined that the majority of Americans now live within ten miles of a microbrewery or brewpub and NorCal didn't get so much as a thank-you card. In fact, the craft brew movement started right here when Fritz Maytag bought San Francisco's Anchor Brewing in 1969 and started producing seasonal beers. In 1985, the now-defunct aSan Francisco Brewing Company (Comstock Saloon currently occupies the space) set up shop in a former Barbary Coast bar and the first American brewpub was born. To sample San Francisco's best home brews, head to microbreweries **Magnolia** (*see p174*) and **21st Amendment** (*see p169*). Other temples of beer geekery include Lower Haight's **Toronado** (*see p174*), **Lucky 13** (*see left*) in the Castro, Inner Sunset's **Social** (1326 9th Avenue, 681 0330, www.socialbrewsf.com), and Oakland's **Trappist** (*see p177*) and **Beer Revolution** (*see p177*).

Zam Zam

1633 Haight Street, between Clayton & Belvedere Streets (861 2545). Metro to Carl & Cole/bus 6, 7, 33, 37, 43, 71. **Open** 3pm-2am Mon-Fri; 1pm-2am Sat, Sun. **No credit cards. Map** p317 E9 41

This tiny bar became famous under notoriously cantankerous owner Bruno Mooshei, who waged a one-man campaign to keep it exactly as it must have been circa World War II. Mooshei died in 2000, but the place was bought by long-time patrons devoted to keeping its *Casablanca* aura intact, and they've done an excellent job.

Lower Haight

Mad Dog in the Fog

530 Haight Street, between Fillmore & Steiner Streets (626 7279). Metro to Duboce & Church/ bus 6, 7, 22, 71. **Open** 3pm-midnight Mon; 11am-2am Tue; 3pm-2am Wed-Fri; 10am-2pm Sat; 10am-midnight Sun. **No credit cards. Map** p318 H8 42

Anglophiles and expats pack the Mad Dog for pub quizzes and soccer broadcasts (it opens early at weekends for English Premier League matches). Strong selections of 20 beers on tap and another 30 in bottles back up the menu of pub grub.

Noc Noc

557 Haight Street, between Fillmore & Steiner Streets (861 5811, www.nocnocs.com). Metro to Duboce & Church/bus 6, 7, 22, 71. **Open** 5pm-2am daily. **Credit** DC, MC, V. **Map** p318 H8 43

If Dr Seuss and Trent Reznor had gone into the bar business together, this is what they'd have come up with. The decor is described as post-apocalyptic industrial, and the whole place has a peculiarly organic Gaudí feel. Always plunged in near darkness and with a mellow chill-room vibe, Noc Noc attracts a multiethnic lot.

★ Toronado

547 Haight Street, between Fillmore & Steiner Streets (863 2276, www.toronado.com). Bus 6, 7, 22, 66, 71. **Open** 11.30am-2am daily. **No credit cards. Map** p318 H8 44

This noisy hangout is a beer drinker's delight. A board posted on the wall shows the massive, ever-changing selection of draughts (which includes local brews and Belgian imports), while the blackboard behind the bar highlights bottled beer and non-alco options. Patrons are encouraged to bring in fresh sausages from Rosamunde Sausage Grill next door.

Hayes Valley

Hotel Biron

45 Rose Street, between Market & Gough Streets (703 0403, www.hotelbiron.com). Metro to Van Ness/streetcar F/bus 6, 7, 26, 71. **Open** 5pm-2am daily. **Credit** AmEx, DC, MC, V. **Map** p318 K8 45

This stylish yet unpretentious wine bar and gallery is named after the Hôtel Biron in Paris, which houses the Rodin Museum. The walls showcase the work of local artists; the impressive wine list boasts 80 wines by the bottle and 35 or so by the glass, plus a selection of beers and a small but appealing menu of cheeses, caviar and olives. A great low-key place for drinkers who like to talk.

Smuggler's Cove

650 Gough Street, between Ash & McCallister Streets (869 1900, www.smugglerscovesf.com). Bus 6, 47, 49, 71, 90. **Open** 5pm-2am daily. **Credit** AmEx, MC, V. **Map** p318 J7 46

Founder Martin Cate jumped the Bay from the now-legendary Forbidden Island (on the island of Alameda) – a place he made into one of the pre-eminent contemporary tiki bars in the US. The relatively compact space has three floors and from the top of its painted palm-thatch ceiling to the bottom of the pool into which a waterfall cascades, it is packed with nautical and rum-related bric-a-brac. Dedicated to cataloging the global history of rum, the Cove offers 70 cocktails and over 200 rums by the glass.

SUNSET, GOLDEN GATE PARK & RICHMOND

In addition to the bars listed below, the Richmond and the Sunset are characterized by a profusion of Irish joints; in the Sunset, head to the historic **Little Shamrock** (807 Lincoln Way, at 9th Avenue, 661 0060). For something a bit grander, try the **Beach Chalet** (*see p93*) for cocktails or the **Cliff House** (*see p96*) for views.

Richmond

Park Chalet

1000 Great Highway, at Fulton Street (386 8439, www.parkchalet.com). Bus 5, 18, 31, 38. **Open** noon-10.30pm daily. **Credit** AmEx, DC, MC, V.

California Cuisine by the Glass

Bars that excel in the craft of cocktail-making.

Just as famed Bay Area chefs Alice Waters and Thomas Keller focused the world on fresh, local, seasonal, organic and sustainably harvested ingredients, so San Francisco's bar managers, craft bartenders and journeyman cocktail consultants (yes, you read that correctly) have turned the mixed drink into an art form. From hardcore, vintage cocktails brimming with bitters to hand-juiced seasonal citrus, judiciously muddled fresh herbs and house-made syrups, tinctures and essences, the dedicated cocktail menus at the city's bars and restaurants look more like a product list at a natural foods store. And then there's the booze. Almost always utilizing premium spirits, many from local microdistilleries, these drinks have a personality, depth and complexity that put them on a par with the efforts of the chef de cuisine.

On the second floor of the Crescent Hotel, the **Burritt Room** (*see p165*) offers a variety of classic, modern and seasonal drinks in a decidedly noir setting that does justice to its namesake, Burritt Alley – the spot where Sam Spade's partner, Miles Archer, is shot in *The Maltese Falcon*. In the Tenderloin, the much-admired cocktail list of speakeasy **Bourbon and Branch** (*see p167*) complements one of the city's more impressive walls of spirits, packed with rare and vintage Scotch, rum and bourbon. Entry requires reservations and the evening's secret password, so be sure to call ahead. The same owners started downtown's **Rickhouse** (*see p166*). Its truly daunting, hide-bound drinks menu covers the full history of the cocktail.

It is said that the oldest tiki bar in the US is in San Francisco (the Richmond District's **Trad'r Sam's**, *see p176*), but the city's newest is also home to one of its top craft bartenders. A visit to **Smuggler's Cove** (*see left*) is like stepping into the hold of a pirate ship that has just captured a massive shipment of rare rums from around the world. The crew can whip up over 70 cocktails made with fresh juices and housemade ingredients. Grab a cocktail and relax by the indoor waterfall while pondering a list of some 200 rums. The cocktails can keep flowing during dinner at SoMa's **Bar Agricole** (*see p141*), a chic outpost in a neighborhood of dance clubs. The restaurant offers equal parts food and beverage – their cocktail selection so carefully constructed it includes unique ice for each drink. Tucked into an alley near the ballpark, SoMa's über-swank **Twenty Five Lusk** (*see p144*) is so smooth you'd almost expect to see George Clooney descending the stairs, highball in hand. And across in the Mission District's stylish **Beretta** (*see p150*), pizzas prepared in a wood-fired brick oven and Italian comfort food bolster a roster of well-shaken exotic-sounding libations such as Nuestra Paloma – a concoction of tequila, elderflower, cointreau, grapefruit, and bitters.

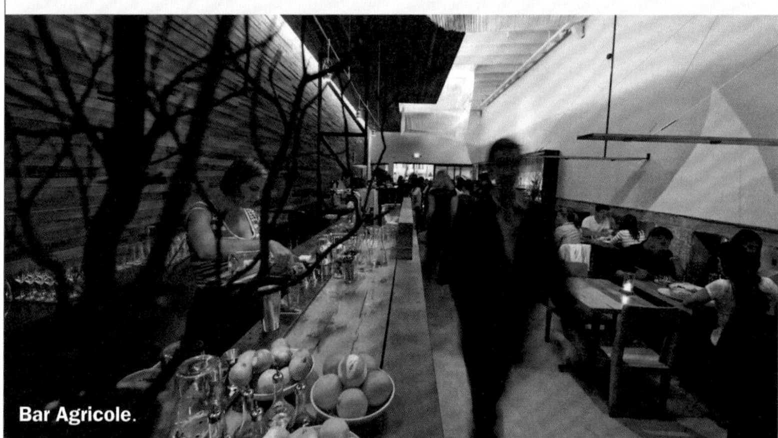

Bar Agricole.

Younger sibling of the well-known Beach Chalet, the Park Chalet doesn't have the same views of Ocean Beach (it backs on to Golden Gate Park), but it does have a gorgeous expanse of lush lawn and beautifully landscaped local flora. On sunny days, it's great to lounge in one of its Adirondack chairs while enjoying a pint (or several) of the house-brewed beer.

★ Tommy's Mexican Restaurant

5929 Geary Boulevard, between 23rd & 24th Avenues (387 4747, www.tommysmexican.com). Bus 1, 2, 29, 31, 38. **Open** noon-11pm Mon, Wed-Sun. **Credit** AmEx, DC, MC, V.

Although there is a restaurant attached to the bar, it's all about the tequila, on which Julio Bermejo, son of late founder Tommy, is a legitimate and recognized global authority. Ask him for advice on which of the 240-plus varieties to sample; then sip, don't shoot. The house margarita, made with fresh Peruvian limes, agave nectar and top-shelf tequila, is a doozy; order it 'Rocks, no salt'.

Trad'r Sam

6150 Geary Boulevard, between 25th & 26th Avenues (221 0773). Bus 1, 2, 29, 31, 38. **Open** 10am-2am daily. **No credit cards**.

A local favorite since 1939, this unabashedly traditional tiki bar serves the kind of cocktails that can only be described as dangerous. Planter's punch, mai tais, singapore slings, the ever-popular Volcano & Goldfish Bowl… There's a guaranteed hangover under every tiny umbrella.

INSIDE TRACK FRISCO FIRSTS

A hard drinking town since the Gold Rush days, San Francisco lays claim to the invention of several popular cocktails, among them **Pisco Punch**, a potent concoction of fresh pineapple, gum syrup, lemon juice and Peruvian brandy created by Duncan J Nichol, aka 'Pisco John', at a bar called the Bank Exchange. While there are many who dispute the tale, the **martini** is said to have originated with San Francisco bartender Professor Jerry Thomas in 1850. The story goes that a miner on his way to the town of Martinez across the Bay placed a gold nugget on the bar and demanded Thomas make him something special. The result – a mix of sweet vermouth, gin, bitters, and maraschino – was dubbed the 'Martinez'. Though undeniably a Dublin invention, it was Jack Koeppler, owner of the Buena Vista Café, and a San Francisco newspaper columnist who first brought **Irish coffee** to the US in 1952. Today, the BV serves some 2,000 Irish coffees a day.

PACIFIC HEIGHTS TO THE GOLDEN GATE BRIDGE

Pacific Heights

Swank Bar

Laurel Inn, 488 Presidio Avenue, between Sacramento & California Streets (346 7431, www.gbarsf.com). Bus 1, 2, 3, 4, 43. **Open** 6pm-midnight Mon, Tue; 6pm-2am Wed-Fri; 7pm-2am Sat. **Credit** AmEx, DC, Disc, MC, V. **Map** p313 F5 47

Ever wished you could have a cocktail on the set of *Mad Men*? Swank's midcentury modern decor invites patrons to enjoy period cocktails with a decidedly contemporary attention to top-shelf spirits and ingredients. Spread out on the settee in front of the fireplace and enjoy a selection of small plates from the limited bar menu. One of the few spots to find a drink – at any time of day or night – in this largely residential, upscale 'hood.

Cow Hollow

For weekend partiers in Cow Hollow and the Marina, life is unchanged since their frat and sorority house days. Located on Fillmore Street around the junction with Greenwich Street, the **City Tavern** (no.3200, 567 0918), **Balboa Café** (no.3199, 921 3944) and **Eastside West** (no.3154, 885 4000) are collectively known as the Triangle, and get packed on weekends with yuppies performing the mating ritual.

Liverpool Lil's

2942 Lyon Street, between Lombard & Greenwich Streets (921 6664, www.liverpoollils.com). Bus 28, 41, 43, 45, 76. **Open** 11am-1am Mon; 11am-2am Tue-Fri; 10am-2am Sat; 10am-1am Sun. **Credit** AmEx, DC, MC, V. **Map** p313 F3 48

A relic from 1970s fern bar days, the façade looks like it's made out of driftwood, and the main decorative touches are old sports photos and paintings of jazz greats. No matter: this is the Marina's least pretentious bar. The crowd ranges from old-timers having their morning Scotch to well-heeled new comers nipping in for a pint. There's a considerable pub menu too.

MatrixFillmore

3138 Fillmore Street, between Filbert & Greenwich Streets (563 4180, www.matrixfillmore.com). Bus 22, 28, 43, 76. **Open** 5.30pm-2am daily. **Credit** AmEx, DC, Disc, MC, V. **Map** p313 G3 49

At the original Matrix, you might have seen Hunter S Thompson in the bathroom sucking LSD off a stranger's sleeve, or the Grateful Dead playing an impromptu set. These days, however, the Matrix draws label-conscious fashionistas and financiers who sip from the pricey cocktail menu at what is really a high-style pick-up joint.

Swank Bar.

Mauna Loa

3009 Fillmore Street, at Union Street (563 5137). Bus 22, 28, 41, 43, 45, 76. **Open** 2pm-2am Mon-Fri; noon-2am Sat, Sun. **No credit cards. Map** p313 G4 ⑤⓪

Originally opened by a Hawaiian in the late 1950s, Mauna Loa has morphed into perhaps the only bar in the Marina that could be considered divey; the crowd, at least, is far more down to earth than you'll find at the Triangle. A pool table, foosball and Pop-A-Shot entertain patrons, but on weekends it's tough to maneuver through the crush.

THE EAST BAY

Oakland

Alley

3325 Grand Avenue, between Elwood & Lake Park Avenues (1-510 444 8505). BART 19th Street, then bus 12. **Open** 4.30pm-2am Tue-Sat. **No credit cards**

The Alley is designed to look like a shantytown street, complete with underwear strung between building façades and jagged fences separating the booths. At the end of the bar is a piano surrounded by bar stools, each with a mic. Anyone is free to take a seat and join the singalong that takes place Thursday through Saturday nights. And don't worry if you're not sure of all the words – neither is the pianist.

Beer Revolution

464 Third Street, between Washington & Broadway Streets (1-510 452 2337, www.beer-revolution.com). BART 12th Street, then bus 72. **Open** noon-10pm Tue-Thur; noon-11pm Fri, Sat; noon-9pm Sun. **Credit** MC, V.

Forty-four beers on tap. More than 500 bottled beers on the shelves. Enough said.

Heinold's First & Last Chance

48 Webster Street, at Jack London Square (1-510 839 6761, www.heinoldsfirstandlastchance.com). BART Oakland City Center/12th Street, then bus 58, 72L, 301. **Open** noon-1am daily. **No credit cards.**

One of California's – if not America's – most historic bars is still going strong, 125 years later. The positively Melvillian structure was built from the salvaged timbers of a whaling ship right on the Oakland docks. It was at these same tables that a young Jack London did his homework. The entire room dips in the middle and the bar (still the original, made in 1883 by a ship's carpenter) is canted at a sharp grade as the foundation settled after the Great Earthquake of 1906. As evening descends, the barman ignites the original gas lamps – the only gas lighting still in use in a commercial enterprise in California.

★ Trappist

460 8th Street, between Broadway & Washington Street (1-510 238 8900, www.thetrappist.com). BART Oakland City Center/12th Street. **Open** 4pm-midnight Wed-Fri; 2pm-midnight Sat, Sun. **Credit** DC, MC, V.

Beer lovers beware: although the Trappist can hold a mere 46 patrons, it's easy to get lost in this place for days. Working with a small group of distributors, proprietors Chuck Stilphen and Aaron Porter have created a fitting tribute to the Belgian beer bars they love so much. There's a staggering selection of Belgian and specialty beers on offer: 15 on draught and more than 120 bottled. Even better, they refuse to stock beer from major breweries. Luckily, their knowledge and informative beer menu mean that even neophytes won't be daunted.

Berkeley

Jupiter

2181 Shattuck Avenue, between Allston Way & Center Street (1-510 843 8277, www.jupiterbeer.com). BART Downtown Berkeley. **Open** 11.30am-1am Mon-Thur; 11.30am-1.30am Fri; noon-1.30am Sat; 1pm-midnight Sun. **Credit** DC, MC, V.

The copper bar, the interior walls clad in patterned tin siding, the pews (rescued from a local church), the two-story outdoor beer garden... there's much to love about this pub even before you've thought about which of the 34 locally brewed draft beers to drink, and whether to supplement it with a pizza from the wood-fired oven. Jupiter is the creation of one of the founders of the hallowed Triple Rock (1920 Shattuck Avenue, at Hearst Avenue, 1-510 843 2739, www.triplerock.com), which claims to be one of the first brewpubs in the US and is still worth a look.

Shops & Services

Independent shops for a city with an independent spirit.

San Francisco's famously diverse shopping scene continues to withstand the threat of retail boredom. Impossibly edgy thrift-chic boutiques exist within shouting distance of department store behemoths, international couture and the ever-present Gap. The local fashion scene has also felt the impact of out-of-towners such as Barneys New York and Bloomingdale's, as well as trend-driven low-price women's fashion emporiums such as H&M and Forever 21.

But the city continues to rise above it, welcoming a stream of new designers and other fun outlets. When scouring the city for the latest It bag, It coat or iPad accessory, don't be afraid to travel around town. Along with Union Square, posh neighborhoods such as Cow Hollow and Pacific Heights are great for high-end designer chic. If your tastes extend to independent designers or vintage tracksuits, head for hip residential areas such as the Mission, the Haight and Hayes Valley.

TAX & DUTY

Local sales tax, currently 9.5 per cent, will be added to all purchases. You can avoid paying this if you live out of state and either arrange shipment by US mail or courier or get the shop to do it for you. If you are taking goods out of the country, remember you'll be liable for duty and tax on goods worth more than a certain amount (£145 for the UK).

General

DEPARTMENT STORES

Barneys New York

77 O'Farrell Street, at Stockton Street, Union Square & Around (268 3500, www.barneys.com). BART & Metro to Powell/bus 2, 3, 5, 6, 9, 14, 21, 27, 30, 31, 38, 45, 71, 76, 91 & Market Street routes/cable car Powell-Hyde or Powell-Mason. **Open** 10am-7pm Mon-Wed, Fri, Sat; 10am-8pm Thur; 11am-6pm Sun. **Credit** AmEx, DC, MC, V. **Map** p315 M6.

Every fashionista's best friend, Barneys arrived in San Francisco in 2007 in a low-key manner in keeping with its tasteful style, and quickly made its presence known among San Francisco followers of fashion with its spare modernist decor and laid-back sell. The men's departments are probably the best in the city, while the women's clothing and shoes are equally well edited, with everything from Chloé and Balenciaga to Barneys' own youthful Co-Op separates.

Bloomingdale's

Westfield San Francisco Centre, 845 Market Street, between 4th & 5th Streets, Union Square & Around (856 5300, www.bloomingdales.com). BART & Metro to Powell/bus 5, 6, 9, 14, 21, 27, 30, 38, 45, 71, 91 & Market Street routes/cable car Powell-Hyde or Powell-Mason. **Open** 10am-9pm Mon-Sat; 10am-7pm Sun. **Credit** AmEx, Disc, MC, V. **Map** p315 M6.

Filling the retail gap between Macy's and Neiman Marcus, the Little Brown Bag's temple to luxury wares fills the cavernous space that once housed the stodgy Emporium department store. Of note here are the lavish fragrance section and the sparkling array of fine china and glassware to be found on the ground floor.

★ Gump's

135 Post Street, between Grant Avenue & Kearny Street, Union Square & Around (984 9439 www.gumps.com). BART & Metro to Montgomery/bus 2, 3, 5, 6, 9, 12, 14, 21, 30, 38, 45, 71, 76, 91 & Market Street routes/cable car Powell-Hyde or Powell-Mason. **Open** 10am-6pm Mon-Sat; noon-5pm Sun. **Credit** AmEx, Disc, MC, V. **Map** p315 M5.

Established in 1861, Gump's is the place where moneyed San Franciscans buy their wedding presents, china and a variety of baubles, from black pearls to custom green peridot necklaces. It's a thoroughly elegant shopping experience for those who think a silver service for less than 12 is simply out of the question.

Macy's

170 O'Farrell Street, between Powell & Stockton Streets, Union Square & Around (397 3333, www.macys.com). BART & Metro to Powell/ bus 2, 3, 5, 6, 9, 14, 21, 27, 30, 31, 38, 45, 71, 76, 91 & Market Street routes/cable car Powell-Hyde or Powell-Mason. **Open** 10am-9pm Mon-Sat; 11am-7pm Sun. **Credit** AmEx, Disc, MC, V. **Map** p315 M6.

The definitive department store: what Macy's lacks in grace, it more than makes up for in discounts. Join the fray and pick up shoes, home furnishings, and accessibly luxurious women's fashions care of DKNY, Theory, Calvin Klein and Michael Kors.

Neiman Marcus

150 Stockton Street, between Geary & O'Farrell Streets, Union Square & Around (362 3900, www.neimanmarcus.com). BART & Metro to Powell/bus 2, 3, 5, 6, 9, 14, 21, 27, 30, 31, 38, 45, 71, 76, 91 & Market Street routes/cable car Powell-Hyde or Powell-Mason. **Open** 10am-7pm Mon-Wed, Fri, Sat; 10am-8pm Thur; noon-6pm Sun. **Credit** AmEx. **Map** p315 M5.

Now commonly referred to as 'Needless Markup', Neiman Marcus was revered by old San Francisco society back in the day – when labels said 'Exclusively for Neiman Marcus'. Today, luxury of the mink-covered coat-hanger variety can still be yours, along with new designer and diffusion labels (from Prada to Blahnik).

Nordstrom

Westfield San Francisco Centre, 865 Market Street, at 5th Street, Union Square & Around (243 8500, www.nordstrom.com). BART & Metro to Powell/bus 5, 6, 9, 14, 27, 30, 45, 71 & Market Street routes/cable car Powell-Hyde or Powell-Mason. **Open** 10am-9pm Mon-Sat; 10am-7pm Sun. **Credit** AmEx, DC, Disc, MC, V. **Map** p315 M6.

Bourgeois old Nordstrom has something for everyone – there's even a spa on the top floor. The expansive men's section includes labels such as Ben Sherman and Ted Baker, while the vast women's department features silk camisoles, designer handbags, swish maternity wear and, most notably, a majestic shoe section.

Saks Fifth Avenue

384 Post Street, at Powell Street, Union Square & Around (986 4300, www.saksfifthavenue.com). BART & Metro to Powell/bus 2, 3, 5, 21, 27, 30, 31, 38, 45, 76, 91 & Market Street routes/cable car Powell-Hyde or Powell-Mason. **Open** 10am-7pm Mon-Wed; 10am-8pm Thur-Sat; 11am-6pm Sun. **Credit** AmEx, DC, MC, V. **Map** p315 M5.

The San Francisco branch of this upmarket store is less claustrophobic than most of its ilk. The second floor offers designers such as Marc Jacobs, Moschino and Gucci, but several floors up you'll find less pricey, but just as trendy, labels like Temperley London, Tory Burch and Diane von Furstenberg. At the menswear store (220 Post Street, 986 4300), the more cutting-edge creations are to be found on the fifth floor.

MALLS

If you're after tourist tat, look no further than the inexplicably popular **Fisherman's Wharf** (Jefferson Street, between Hyde & Powell Streets, 674 7503, www.fishermanswharf.org) or nearby **Pier 39** (Beach Street & Embarcadero, 705 5500, www.pier39.com). Note that the opening times for individual shops and restaurants within the malls listed below may vary.

Embarcadero Center

Sacramento Street, between Battery & Drumm Streets, Financial District (772 0700, www.embarcaderocenter.com). BART & Metro to Embarcadero/bus 1, 5, 6, 10, 12, 21, 31, 41 & Market Street routes/cable car California. **Open** 10am-7pm Mon-Fri; 10am-6pm Sat; noon-5pm Sun. **Map** p315 N4.

Major chains (Banana Republic, Gap, Victoria's Secret, Nine West) sit comfortably ensconced in the Embarcadero towers, which also host the bulk of the city's lawyers and financiers.

Ghirardelli Square

Beach Street, between Larkin & Polk Streets, Fisherman's Wharf (775 5500, www.ghirardellisq.com). Metro F to Fisherman's Wharf/bus 19, 30, 47, 49, 90, 91/cable car Powell-Hyde or Powell-Mason. **Open** 10am-6pm Mon-Thur, Sun; 10am-9pm Fri, Sat. **Map** p314 J2.

THE BEST SHOPPING APPS

For maps and directions for local shopping malls
Compasso www.apptism.com/apps/compasso.

For deals & promotions at local stores
Slifter www.slifter.com/pc/mobile.

For local garage & rummage sales
iGaragesale www.igaragesaleapp.com.

At the home of the Ghirardelli chocolate company, you can gorge yourself on ice-cream drizzled with chocolate made on the premises, and then wander around the square, which is home to a variety of retail outposts such as Ghirardelli Ts (souvenirs), Kara's Cupcakes, ElizabethW perfumery, and Lola card shop.

Westfield San Francisco Centre

865 Market Street, at 5th Street, Union Square & Around (512 6776, http://westfield.com/san francisco). BART & Metro to Powell/bus 5, 6, 9, 14, 21, 27, 30, 38, 45, 71, 91 & Market Street routes/cable car Powell-Hyde or Powell-Mason. **Open** 10am-8.30pm Mon-Sat; 10am-7pm Sun. **Map** p315 M6.

Spiral escalators wind slowly up this vast mall, enticing shoppers with mid-priced chain stores including J Crew, Abercrombie & Fitch and Club Monaco. Department store Nordstrom (*see p179*) resides on top like a society matron; express elevators whiz you straight there. On the vast east side, further draws include names such as H&M, Zara, Juicy Couture, Guess, and a nine-theater cineplex. You won't go hungry, either, with eateries such as Out the Door, the spin-off of Vietnamese celeb-stop Slanted Door (*see p139*), and a sprawling gourmet food court.

CONSUME

INSIDE TRACK
NO NICHE TOO NARROW

With books and film, San Francisco's motto is 'no niche too narrow'. Specialty bookstores run the gamut from the political to the smutty, with tomes for just about every collection and fetish imaginable. Architecture and design fiends should head to **William Stout Architectural Books** (804 Montgomery Street, Financial District, 391 6757, www.stoutbooks.com). For lefty literature, try the **Socialist Action Bookstore** (298 Valencia Street, Mission, 255 1081) or **Bound Together Anarchist Collective** (1369 Haight Street, Haight-Ashbury, 431-8355, www.boundtogetherbookstore.com). **A Different Light** (489 Castro Street, Castro, 431 0891, www.adlbooks.com) is devoted to gay, lesbian, bi-sexual and transgender literature, while **Good Vibrations** (603 Valencia Street, Mission, 522 5460, www.goodvibes.com) is 'a clean, well-lighted place' for sex toys and erotica. Sci-Fi and Stephen King fans will find plenty to occupy them at **Borderlands Books** (866 Valencia Street, Mission, 824 8203, www.borderlands-books.com), where the staff know all.

Specialist

BOOKS & MAGAZINES

San Francisco has such a strong literary history that it's no wonder bookstores are in high demand. Many antiquarian booksellers are clustered at 49 Geary Street, near Union Square, but the heaviest concentration of used bookshops is in the Mission, including the politically minded **Modern Times Bookstore** (888 Valencia Street, between19th & 20th Streets, 282 9246, www.mtbs.com) and the fiercely independent and well-edited **Dog-Eared Books** (900 Valencia Street at 20th Street, 282 1901, www.dogearedbooks.com), which features both new and used. For more specialty bookstores, *see below* **Inside Track**.

Adobe Bookshop

3166 16th Street, at Albion Street, Mission (864 3936). BART 16th Street/bus 14, 22, 33, 49. **Open** 11am-10pm Mon-Thur, Sun; 11am-11pm Fri, Sat. **Credit** MC, V. **Map** p318 J10.

Woe is the book buyer hoping to find exactly what he or she is looking for at Adobe. But those itching for a genuine taste of today's SF bohemia must stop by. Survey the hopelessly chaotic shelves, make yourself comfortable in an ancient armchair to talk to a random poet or painter, check out the artwork in the tiny exhibit space, or stay for a free performance by a local musician.

Alexander Book Co

50 2nd Street, between Market & Mission Streets, Downtown/SoMa (495 2992, www.alexander book.com). BART & Metro to Montgomery/bus 2, 3, 4, 31 & Market Street routes. **Open** 9am-6pm Mon-Fri. **Credit** MC, V. **Map** p315 N5.

One of the last of Downtown's independent bookshops, Alexander spreads over three floors with extensive selections of African-American, children's, design and fiction books.

Books Inc

2275 Market Street, at 16th Street, Castro (864 6777, www.booksinc.net). Metro to Church/ bus 24, 33, 35, 37. **Open** 10am-10pm daily. **Credit** AmEx, Disc, MC, V. **Map** p317 H10.

A huge selection of fiction and non-fiction, a lively atmosphere and a wide range of authors' readings, discussions and other events.

Other locations Opera Plaza, 601 Van Ness Avenue, Civic Center (776 1111); Laurel Village, 3515 California Street, Presidio Heights (221 3666); 2251 Chestnut Street, Marina (931 3633).

The Booksmith

1644 Haight Street, between Clayton & Belvedere Streets, Haight-Ashbury (1-800 493 7323/863 8688/www.booksmith.com). Metro to Carl &

City Lights.

Cole/bus 6, 33, 37, 43, 66, 71. **Open** 10am-10pm Mon-Sat; 10am-8pm Sun. **Credit** AmEx, Disc, MC, V. **Map** p317 E9.
The Haight's best bookshop hosts many authors' readings and events, and stocks a decent selection of magazines, both literary and obscure.

★ City Lights
261 Columbus Avenue, at Jack Kerouac Alley, between Broadway & Pacific Avenue, North Beach (362 8193/www.citylights.com). Bus 1, 10, 12, 30, 41, 45, 91. **Open** 10am-midnight daily. **Credit** AmEx, Disc, MC, V. **Map** p315 M3.
The legacy of Beat anti-authoritarianism lives on in this publishing company and bookshop, co-founded by poet Lawrence Ferlinghetti in 1953. Head upstairs to the Poetry Annex, where books by the Beats sit beside contemporary small-press works and the photocopied ravings of 'shroom-addled hippies, punks and DIY indie voices. Readings here are real events.

★ Green Apple Books & Music
506 Clement Street, at 6th Avenue, Richmond (387 2272/www.greenapplebooks.com). Bus 1, 2, 38, 44. **Open** 10am-10.30pm Mon-Thur, Sun; 10am-11.30pm Fri, Sat. **Credit** Disc, MC, V. **Map** p312 C6.
This long-standing Inner Richmond store has a staggering selection of new and used titles, crammed together in glorious disarray (don't miss the fiction and music annex a couple doors down, with its enormous record and DVD collections). For bargains on everything from graphic novels to coffee table art books, this is the place.

Kayo Books
814 Post Street, between Hyde & Leavenworth Streets, Tenderloin (749 0554, 269 6286, www.kayobooks.com). Bus 2, 3, 19, 27, 38. **Open** 11am-6pm Thur-Sat, or by appointment. **Credit** AmEx, Disc, MC, V. **Map** p314 L5.
This emporium of pulp delivers the goods for those who like their mysteries hard-boiled, their juveniles delinquent and their porn quaintly smutty. Specialties include vintage paperbacks and dime-store novels from the 1940s to the '70s, and exploitation ephemera of all levels of debasement.

Smoke Signals
2223 Polk Street, between Vallejo & Green Streets, Polk Gulch (292 6025). Bus 12, 19, 27, 41, 45, 47, 49, 90/cable car Powell-Hyde. **Open** 8am-7.30pm Mon-Sat; 8am-6pm Sun. **Credit** AmEx, Disc, MC, V. **Map** p314 K4.
You can find the latest *Le Monde* or Italian *Vogue* at this international newsstand. It also has a comprehensive selection of national and local papers, design annuals and obscure literary journals.

CHILDREN

Fashion

Cotton Sheep
573 Hayes Street, between Laguna & Octavia Streets, Hayes Valley (621 5546). Bus 5, 6, 21, 71. **Open** 11am-6pm daily. **Credit** AmEx, MC, V. **Map** p318 J8.
Organic cotton garments, designed and manufactured in Japan, rule the roost here. Check out utterly sweet children's hoodies or the truly unusual toddlers' socks shaped like Godzilla heads.

Fiddlesticks
508 Hayes Street, between Laguna & Octavia Streets, Hayes Valley (565 0508, www.shopfiddlesticks.com). Bus 5, 6, 21, 71.

Open 11am-7pm Mon-Sat; 11am-6pm Sun. **Credit** AmEx, MC, V. **Map** p318 J8.
The prices are steep, but the clothing is astonishingly stylish at this shop helmed by the owners of Lavish, a few doors down (*see p195*). Look for Livie and Luca animal motif shoes and Luna pointelle sweaters.

Kids Only

1608 Haight Street, at Clayton Street, Haight-Ashbury (552 5445). Metro to Carl & Cole/bus 7, 33, 43, 66, 71. **Open** 10.30am-6.30pm Mon-Fri; 10am-6pm Sat; 11am-5pm Sun. **Credit** AmEx, DC, Disc, MC, V. **Map** p317 E9.
Why should adults have all the fun? Here's where kids can get tooled up with leopard-print blankets, hand-made caps and tie-dye worthy of the Grateful Dead.

Laku

1089 Valencia Street, between 21st & 22nd Streets, Mission (695 1462, www.lakuyaeko.com). BART 24th Street/bus 12, 14, 48, 49. **Open** 11.30am-6.30pm Tue-Sat; noon-5pm Sun. **Credit** MC, V. **Map** p318 K11.
Exquisite, intricate little slippers and coats, sewn by Laku's owner from velvet and shantung silk on a machine in the back of the shop. For baby royalty.

Murik

73 Geary Street, at Grant Avenue, Union Square & Around (395 9200, www.murikwebstore.com). BART & Metro to Powell/bus 2, 3, 5, 6, 9, 14, 21, 30, 31, 38, 45, 71, 91 & Market routes/cable car Powell-Hyde or Powell-Mason. **Open** 10am-6pm daily. **Credit** AmEx, MC, V. **Map** p315 M5.
Sweet, affordable togs by European makers such as Joha, Juttum, Filou & Friends and Micro Bulle, using simple, whimsical motifs and tasteful, muted colors.

Toys

Ambassador Toys

2 Embarcadero Center, Financial District (345 8697, www.ambassadortoys.com). BART & Metro to Embarcadero/bus 1, 5, 6, 10, 12, 21, 31, 41/ cable car California. **Open** 9am-7pm Mon-Fri; 10am-6pm Sat, Sun. **Credit** AmEx, MC, V. **Map** p315 N4.
Does the thought of Toys R Us drive you to the brink of insanity? This straightforward store, which specializes in toys from around the world, has a charming selection of dolls, books, games and wooden animals.
Other locations 186 W Portal Avenue, Sunset (759 8697).

Chinatown Kite Shop

717 Grant Avenue, at Sacramento Street, Chinatown (989 5182, www.chinatownkite.com). Bus 1, 10, 12, 30, 41, 45, 91/cable car California. **Open** 10am-8:30pm daily. **Credit** AmEx, Disc, MC, V. **Map** p315 M4.
It only stands to reason that hilly, windy SF should have an excellent kite shop. Stocked with hundreds of different kites in every imaginable shape and color, the shop is perfectly situated for you to get kitted out before heading on to Marina Green.

ELECTRONICS & PHOTOGRAPHY

Locals love the low prices at **Best Buy** (1717 Harrison Street, at 14th Street, Upper Market, 626 9682, www.bestbuy.com). But it's left rather left in the shade by the sleek **Apple Store** (1 Stockton Street, at Ellis Street, Union Square & Around, 392 0202, www.apple.com). Authentic geeks will also hanker for a pilgrimage out of the city to superstore **Fry's Electronics** (closest location is 340 Portage Avenue, at Ash Street, Palo Alto, 1-650 496 6000, www.frys.com).

Specialist

Adolph Gasser

181 2nd Street, between Natoma & Howard Streets, SoMa (495 385, www.gassers.com). BART & Metro to Montgomery/bus 2, 4, 8, 18, 24, 27, 70, 76, 101 & Market Street routes. **Open** 9am-6pm Mon-Fri; 10am-5pm Sat. **Credit** AmEx, Disc, JCB, MC, V. **Map** p315 N6.
This justly famous photographic shop has clued-up staff and the largest inventory of photo and video equipment in northern California. There's also a good selection of scanners and digital cameras.

Discount Camera

33 Kearny Street, between Post & Market Streets, Union Square & Around (392 1103, www.discountcamera.com). BART & Metro to Montgomery/bus 2, 3, 5, 6, 9, 15, 21, 30, 31, 45, 71, 91 & Market Street routes/cable car Powell-Hyde or Powell-Mason. **Open** 8.30am-6.30pm Mon-Sat; 9.30am-6pm Sun. **Credit** AmEx, Disc, JCB, MC, V. **Map** p315 M5.
More than 45 years old, Discount Camera is recommended by concierges anxious to steer their guests away from Downtown's unscrupulous tourist traps. New and second-hand models are sold, and there's on-site camera repair.

FASHION

Designer

Unsurprisingly, San Francisco is home to branches of more or less all the major high-end labels, with many ensconced on or near Union Square. Among them are ever-elegant **Prada** (140 Geary Street, between Grant Avenue & Stockton Street, 391 8844, www.prada.com), chi-chi **Chanel** (156 Geary Street, between Grant Avenue & Stockton Street, 981 1550, www.chanel.com), and smooth **Armani**

(278 Post Street, at Stockton Street, 434 2500, www.armani.com), plus extravagant **Gucci** (240 Stockton Street, at Geary Street, 392 2808, www.gucci.com).

★ AB Fits

1519 Grant Avenue, between Union & Filbert Streets, North Beach (982 5726, www.abfits.com). Bus 10, 12, 30, 39, 41, 45, 91. **Open** 11.30am-6.30pm Tue-Sat; noon-5pm Sun. **Credit** AmEx, Disc, MC, V. **Map** p315 M3.

The jean-ius of Howard Gee and Christopher Louie is to mix familiar brands (Raleigh Denim, Notify, Tellason, LAMB, Earnest Sewn, Edun) with ones that are more rarefied (vintage denim by Nudie) or just plain fabulous. You'll also find separates and accessories by designers like Jill Platner, dePalma, and Antipast.

Dema

1038 Valencia Street, at 21st Street, Mission (206 0500, www.godemago.com). BART 24th Street/bus 14, 33, 49. **Open** 11am-7 pm Mon-Fri; noon-7pm Sat; noon-6pm Sun. **Credit** MC, V. **Map** p318 K11.

Local designer Dema Grim specializes in blouses, skirts, dresses and sheaths in gloriously fun prints. Her modern interpretations of vintage classics are timeless and very wearable.

Diana Slavin

3 Claude Lane, between Sutter & Bush Streets, Union Square & Around (677 9939, www.dianaslavin.com). BART & Metro to Montgomery/bus 2, 3, 5, 6, 9, 10, 12, 21, 30, 38, 45, 71, 91/cable car Powell-Hyde or Powell-Mason. **Open** 11am-6pm Tue-Fri; noon-5pm Sat. **Credit** AmEx, Disc, MC, V. **Map** p315 M5.

In this haberdasher's for women, Slavin designs and displays her trademark fashions: menswear-inspired clothing in rich, subtle colours and lush fabrics. Vintage Vuarnet shades and Martin Margiela shoes complete the look.

Erica Tanov

2408 Fillmore Street, between Jackson & Washington Streets, Pacific Heights (674 1228, www.ericatanov.com). Bus 1, 3, 10, 22, 24. **Open** 11am-6pm Mon-Sat; 11am-5pm Sun. **Credit** AmEx, MC, V. **Map** p313 H5.

Antique fabrics are the highlight at Erica Tanov – and they're multitasking in the form of gossamer party dresses, bed linens, delicate lingerie and imported sweaters.

★ MAC (Modern Appealing Clothing)

387 Grove Street, between Franklin & Gough Streets, Hayes Valley (863 3011, http://modernappealingclothing.com). Bus 5, 21, 47, 49, 90. **Open** 11am-7pm Mon-Sat; noon-6pm Sun. **Credit** AmEx, MC, V. **Map** p318 J7.

Belgian designers as well as local creatives get the treatment they deserve in this brother- and sister-owned boutique that resembles a chic pied-à-terre. Men, in particular, who are willing to open their wallets wide will discover great items by Martin Margiela, Dries Van Noten and Comme Des Garçons, in addition to Raf Simons for Jil Sander.

★ Margaret O'Leary

1 Claude Lane, between Kearny, Grant, Sutter & Bush Streets, Downtown (391 1010, www.margaretoleary.com). BART & Metro to Montgomery/bus 2, 3, 5, 6, 9, 10, 12, 30, 31, 38, 45, 71, 91/cable car Powell-Hyde or Powell-Mason. **Open** 10am-5pm Tue-Sat. **Credit** AmEx, MC, V. **Map** p315 M5.

Irish-born O'Leary is one of San Francisco's designer treasures. Her exquisite hand-loomed sweaters, dresses, tunics, and sets are very familiar to buyers at Neiman Marcus and Saks, but her namesake boutiques feature the full line – knitwear and sportswear made with eco-friendly yarns and fabrics, ultra-feminine and accented with perfect details.

Other locations 2400 Fillmore Street, Pacific Heights (771 9982).

Metier

355 Sutter Street, between Stockton Street & Grant Avenue, Union Square & Around (989 5395, www.metiersf.com). BART & Metro to Powell/bus 2, 3, 5, 6, 9, 21, 30, 38, 45, 71/cable car Powell-Hyde or Powell-Mason. **Open** 10am-6pm Mon-Sat. **Credit** AmEx, MC, V. **Map** p315 M5.

Touted as a 'premier Downtown design boutique', Metier is indeed Serious Fashion. From slouchy sophistication care of Cathy Waterman, the glamorous detailing of Isabel Marant and the bohemian chic of Inhabit, to lingerie by Cosabella and contemporary sterling silver jewelry from Ten Thousand Things, the 'hot mom' set at last has a place to call home.

Sunhee Moon

3167 16th Street, at Guerrero Street, Mission (355 1800, www.sunheemoon.com). BART 16th Street/bus 14, 33, 49. **Open** noon-7pm Mon-Fri; noon-6pm Sat, Sun. **Credit** MC, V. **Map** p318 K11.

SF minimalist maven Sunhee Moon is known for her way with a sash and for subtly retro-tinged modernist separates marked by clean, crisp lines and rich jewel-like hues.

Other locations 1833 Fillmore Street (928 1800).

Susan

3685 Sacramento Street, between Locust & Spruce Streets, Presidio Heights (922 3685). Bus 1, 3, 12, 22, 24. **Open** 10.30am-6.30pm Mon-Fri; 10.30am-6pm Sat. **Credit** AmEx, MC, V. **Map** p313 E5.

This retail legend celebrating its 28th year is renowned for championing fashion's avant-garde

Knocked Down & Up Again

Hayes Valley has risen from the ashes.

It's a familiar urban planning nightmare – build a freeway in the middle of a city and it completely rips apart the community fabric, not to mention creating a hulking eyesore. But in Hayes Valley, a small neighborhood just west of Civic Center, which for decades sat under the shadow of the now-defunct Central Freeway, the story has reversed itself into a happy ending. Since the 1989 earthquake all but destroyed the Central Freeway, its demolition has transformed Hayes Valley from a gritty red-light district to possibly the chicest shopping neighborhood in the city. (It perhaps proved prescient that director Erich von Stroheim filmed part his 1924 classic, *Greed*, in the neighborhood.) Streets that once sat forlornly under a tangle of concrete overpasses now boast sidewalk cafés, hipster boutiques, art galleries, and even the country's first dedicated saké shop (*see p194*). It's a great neighborhood for strolling during the day, not just for window-shopping, but for its gorgeous Victorians and tiny alleys of shotgun cottages.

A hub for local designers and craftspeople, boutiques have flourished here in large part due to an active neighborhood association that has fought to keep out chains and has encouraged open spaces. The unveiling of a tree-lined boulevard and greenway along Octavia Street in 2005 was another boon for gentrification: the rotating, often enormous art installations are among the most provocative in the city.

These days, residents come from all over town to shop for modernist home furnishings at **Propellor** (555 Hayes Street, 701 7767); peruse for couture lingerie at **Alla Prima** (*see p191*); try on Italian shoes at **Bulo** (*see p191*); and fill out their wardrobes with all manner of designer fashion at places like **Cary Lane** (560 Laguna Street, 896 4210), **Azalea** (411 Hayes Street, 861 9888), and **Ver Unica** (*see p189*).

Hayes Street.

Propellor

before they succumb to mass production for department stores. Just read the labels: Comme des Garçons, Junya Watanabi, Peter Pilotto, Lanvin, Mary Katrantzou, and Meadham Kirchhoff. Sister shop the Grocery Store (3625 Sacramento Street, 928 3615) sells diffusion lines and other designer lifestyle collections, such as The Row and J Brand.

Discount

The Bay Area has several sizeable outlet malls, but they're well outside town. An hour north on Highway 101, **Petaluma Village Premium Outlets** (2200 Petaluma Boulevard N, 1-707 778 9300, www.premiumoutlets.com) has 60 shops, including **Gap Outlet**, **Off 5th-Saks Fifth Avenue** and **Brooks Brothers**, while **Napa Premium Outlets** (Highway 29 to 1st Street exit, 629 Factory Stores Drive, 1-707 226 9876, www.premiumoutlets.com), about 90 minutes from the city, has 50 stores, among them **Barneys**, **Tommy Hilfiger**, **J Crew**, **Calvin Klein**, **Banana Republic** and **Kenneth Cole**.

★ Isda & Co.

21 South Park, off 2nd Street, between Bryant & Brannan Streets, SoMa (512 1610, www.isda-and-co.com). Bus 10, 15. **Open** 10am-6pm Tue-Sat. **Credit** AmEx, MC, V. **Map** p315 Q6.
The outlet for San Francisco designer Isda Funari, this tidy little South Park boutique features overruns and end-of-season styles at good discounts. Funari's fashions tend to the practical-chic, with long, drapey sweaters and tunics, smart urban jackets, and flirty layered skirts.

★ Jeremy's

2 South Park, off 2nd Street, between Bryant & Brannan Streets, SoMa (882 4929, www.jeremys.com). Bus 10, 15. **Open** 11am-6pm Mon-Wed, Fri, Sat; 11am-8pm Thur; noon-6pm Sun. **Credit** AmEx, MC, V. **Map** p315 O6.
Jeremy's sits on a sunny corner of South Park, hawking designer wares at discount store prices. It's a label-whore's dream come true, especially the satchels in front and the shoes at the back: if you're lucky, you just might find Jimmy Choo pumps, Prada slides and Dolce & Gabbana boots. There's also excellent menswear, ties and accessories. The Berkeley location sells more casual clothing.
Other locations 2967 College Avenue, Berkeley (1-510 849 0701).

Loehmann's

222 Sutter Street, between Grant Avenue & Kearny Street, Union Square & Around (982 3215, www.loehmanns.com). BART & Metro to Montgomery/bus 2, 3, 5, 6, 9, 10, 12, 30, 31, 38, 45, 71, 91/cable car Powell-Hyde or Powell-Mason. **Open** 9am-8pm Mon-Fri; 9.30am-8pm Sat; 11am-7pm Sun. **Credit** AmEx, Disc, MC, V. **Map** p315 M5.
Communal dressing rooms, eh? Don't be put off: the prices make Loehmann's worth a look. Designer clothes Prada, Marc by Marc Jacobs, Diane von Furstenberg, Philosophy di Alberta Ferretti, Michael Kors, and Moschino hang from the rafters; you can get more than 50% off activewear. There's a separate Loehmann's shoe store at 211 Sutter Street (395 0983).

General

Posh, preppy **Banana Republic** rules almost a full city block (256 Grant Avenue, at Sutter Street, 788 3087, www.bananarepublic.com); cheap and casual **Old Navy** has a vast store on Market Street (No.801, at 4th Street, 344 0375, www.oldnavy.com); and **Gap** is ubiquitous (890 Market Street, at 5th Street, 788 5909, www.gap.com). Other familiar brands include sexy **Bebe** (Westfield San Francisco Centre, 865 Market Street, at 5th Street, 543 2323, www.bebe.com), long-standing **Guess** (90 Grant Avenue, at Geary Street, 781 1589, www.guess.com), Brit import **French Connection** (101 Powell Street, at Ellis Street, 677 4317, www.frenchconnection.com), girly **Betsey Johnson** (160 Geary Street, at Stockton Street, 398 2516, www.betseyjohnson.com), and slick women's label **BCBG Max Azria** (331 Powell Street, at Union Square, 362 7360, www.bcbg.com).

★ Ambiance

1458 Haight Street, between Masonic Avenue & Ashbury Street, Haight-Ashbury (552 5095, www.ambiancesf.com). Metro to Carl & Cole/bus 6, 33, 37, 43, 66, 71. **Open** 10am-7pm Mon-Sat; 11am-7pm Sun. **Credit** AmEx, MC, V. **Map** p317 F9.
If you've got an occasion, Ambiance has the perfect ensemble for it: its glowing collection of retro-style dresses and saucy skirts is even arranged by color for your convenience. The sales staff here are beyond friendly.
Other locations 1864 & 1858 Union Street, Cow Hollow (923 9797, 932 9796); 3985 & 3989 24th Street, Noe Valley (647 7144, 647 5800).

American Apparel

1615 Haight Street, between Belvedere & Clayton Streets, Haight-Ashbury (431 4038, www.americanapparel.net). Bus 6, 33, 43, 71. **Open** 11am-9pm Mon-Thur; 11am-10pm Fri, Sat; noon-7pm Sun. **Credit** AmEx, Disc, MC, V. **Map** p317 E9.
This Los Angeles-founded clothing maker boasts that its T-shirts, jersey minis, hoodies, undies and bikinis are sweatshop labor-free, which makes it even harder to resist the designs, in tasty hues and desirable cuts.
Other locations 2174 Union Street, Cow Hollow (440 3220).

Anthropologie

880 Market Street, between Powell & Stockton Streets, Union Square & Around (434 2210, www.anthropologie.com). BART & Metro to Powell/bus 5, 6, 9, 14, 21, 30, 31, 38, 45, 71, 91 & Market Street routes/cable car Powell-Hyde or Powell-Mason. **Open** 10am-8pm Mon-Sat; 11am-7pm Sun. **Credit** AmEx, Disc, MC, V. **Map** p315 M6.

Indulge your desire for beaded and appliqued cardigans, patterned and floral A-line skirts and romantic, swingy jackets, plus home furnishings, decadent scented candles, cute pajamas and coquettish lingerie. The sale racks are at the back.

Other locations 750 Hearst Avenue, Berkeley (1-510 486 0705).

Behind the Post Office

1510 Haight Street, between Ashbury & Clayton Streets, Haight-Ashbury (861 2507, www.behindthepostoffice.com). Metro to Carl & Cole/bus 6, 33, 37, 43, 66, 71. **Open** 11am-7pm Mon, Thur-Sat; noon-6pm Tue, Sat; 11am-6pm Sun. **Credit** AmEx, MC, V. **Map** p317 F9.

Space is at a premium here, but this tiny boutique packs in the style with vibrant T-shirts and edgy new designers, all at moderate prices. Even better, the expert opinions of the owners are worth their weight in (carefully fitted) denim.

Candystore

3153 16th Street, between Albion & Guerrero Streets, Mission (887 7637, www.candystorecollective.com). BART 16th Street/bus 14, 22, 33, 49. **Open** 11am-6.30pm Mon-Sat; 11.30am-6pm Sun. **Credit** AmEx, Disc, MC, V. **Map** p318 J10.

Sweet stuff for trendy young women with an eye for whimsy: patterned wallets, new-wave slingbacks and gold danglers brush up against puffed sleeve hoodie-jackets, airy dresses and striped separates.

Citizen Clothing

536 Castro Street, between 18th & 19th Streets, Castro (575 3560, www.citizenbody.com). Metro to Castro/bus 24, 33, 35, 37. **Open** 10am-7pm Mon-Thur, Sun; 11am-8pm Fri; 10am-8pm Sat. **Credit** AmEx, Disc, MC, V. **Map** p317 H11.

Citizen is all about upscale utilitarian chic, meaning Scotch & Soda, Ben Sherman and Fred Perry appear alongside Penguin, Ted Baker, Jack Spade and Lacoste. Boys seeking something a bit more sporty head up the street to sibling establishment Body (450 Castro Street, 575 3562).

Diesel

101 Post Street, at Kearny Street, Union Square & Around (982 7077, www.diesel.com). BART & Metro to Montgomery/bus 2, 3, 5, 21, 30, 31, 38, 45, 91/cable car Powell-Hyde or Powell-Mason. **Open** 10am-9pm Mon-Sat; 11am-8pm Sun. **Credit** AmEx, Disc, MC, V. **Map** p315 M5.

Not just a zillion styles of jeans, retro sneakers and edgy separates, spread over three floors, but also the StyleLab line for those extra-experimental types who covet jeans made out of astronaut suits.

Dylan

2146 Chestnut Street, at Pierce Street, Marina (409 4444, www.dylanboutique.com). Bus 22, 28, 30, 43. **Open** 11am-7.30pm Mon-Sat; 11.30am-5.30pm Sun. **Credit** AmEx, MC, V. **Map** p314 K4.

This locale showcases a dizzying spread of boutique designers: clothing and jewelry by Alexander Wang, Charlotte Ronson, and J Brand, plus shoes.

Forever 21

7 Powell Street, at Market Street, Union Square & Around (984 0380, www.forever21.com). BART & Metro to Powell/bus 2, 3, 5, 6, 9, 14, 21, 30, 31, 38, 45, 71, 91 & Market Street routes/cable car Powell-Hyde or Powell-Mason. **Open** 9.30am-10pm Mon-Sat; 10am-9.30pm Sun. **Credit** AmEx, Disc, MC, V. **Map** p315 M6.

Juniors will go knock-off crazy for this rock-bottom priced mecca of flirty dresses, skimpy club-kid gear and skinny jeans. Larger sizes will have to content themselves with the glitzy jewelry, fun shoes, heaps of hip hats and adorable bags.

H&M

150 Powell Street, at O'Farrell Street, Union Square & Around (986 4215, www.hm.com). BART & Metro to Powell/bus 2, 3, 5, 6, 9, 21, 30, 38, 45, 71, 91 & Market Street routes/cable car Powell-Hyde or Powell-Mason. **Open** 10am-9pm Mon-Sat; 10am-8pm Sun. **Credit** AmEx, Disc, JCB, MC, V. **Map** p315 M6.

Dare any fashion follower to not snap up a glossy handbag, a pair of over-the-top earrings, or a lacy frock at this trend-driven giant. Stella McCartney and Viktor & Rolf designs have triggered sprees at this flagship jammed with affordable cool for men and women.

Other locations 150 Post Street, Union Square & Around (986 0156); Westfield San Francisco Centre, 845 Market Street, Union Square & Around (543 1430); Stonestown Galleria, 3251 20th Avenue, Sunset & Further South (242 1459).

Ooma

1422 Grant Avenue, between Green & Union Streets, North Beach (627 6963, www.ooma.net). Bus 12, 30, 39, 41, 45, 91. **Open** 11am-7pm Tue-Sat; noon-5pm Sun. **Credit** AmEx, MC, V. **Map** p315 M3.

The name stands for 'Objects of My Affection'; owners Glenda and Jessica have a fine eye for the latest local designer threads, making it all but impossible to leave empty-handed. 'Flirty' pretty much sums up the whimsical fashions on offer.

Rabat

4001 24th Street, at Noe Street, Noe Valley (282 7861, www.rabatshoes.com). Bus 24, 35, 48. **Open** 10.30am-7pm Mon-Fri; 10am-7pm Sat; 11am-6pm Sun. **Credit** AmEx, Disc, MC, V. **Map** p317 H12.

Down-to-earth chic is what Rabat's about. A huge variety of shoes, accessories and women's clothing provides reams of material for you to work with, and the staff are happy to suggest ways to co-ordinate it all.

Other locations 2080 Chestnut Street, Marina (929 8688).

Urban Outfitters

80 Powell Street, at Ellis Street, Union Square & Around (989 1515, www.urbanoutfitters.com). BART & Metro to Powell/bus 2, 3, 5, 6, 9, 14, 21, 30, 31, 38, 45, 71, 91 & Market Street routes/cable car Powell-Hyde or Powell-Mason. **Open** 9am-11pm Mon-Sat; 10am-10pm Sun. **Credit** AmEx, Disc, MC, V. **Map** p315 M6.

Sturdy Ben Sherman trousers, adorable Free People cardigans, old-school T-shirts, funky jewelry and tons of jeans at seriously affordable prices. Perfect for those just out of college – or those who wish they were.

Other locations 2590 Bancroft Way, Berkeley (1-510 486 1300).

Villains

1672 Haight Street, between Clayton & Cole Streets, Haight-Ashbury (626 5939, www.villainssf.com). Metro to Carl & Cole/bus 6, 33, 37, 43, 66, 71. **Open** 11am-7pm daily. **Credit** AmEx, Disc, MC, V. **Map** p317 E9.

Villains sells a mix of cropped trousers, experimental fabrics and trendy ensembles for men and women that scream 'I party!'. Next door is a great selection of covetable shoes, from Schmoove to spiked heels straight out of a Joan Jett video.

Zara

250 Post Street, at Stockton Street, Union Square & Around (399 6930, www.zara.com). BART & Metro to Powell/bus 2, 3, 5, 6, 9, 21, 30, 31, 38, 45, 71, 76, 91 & Market Street routes/cable car Powell-Hyde or Powell-Mason. **Open** 10am-8pm Mon-Sat; 10am-6pm Sun. **Credit** AmEx, Disc, MC, V. **Map** p315 M5.

Count on this sophisticated, appealing Spanish chain for low-priced, on-trend looks for both men and women. It's just the spot for a classic yet eye-catching coat, silky party halter or tissue-weight T with a deco graphic.

Used & vintage

Also check out **Urban Outfitters** (*see above*) for vintage wear mixed with new and retro-inspired styles.

INSIDE TRACK LOCAL STYLE

Founded in 2002 by Blakely Bass, **Residents Apparel Gallery** (541 Octavia Street, Hayes Valley, 621 7718, www.ragsf.com) is a clothing cooperative that showcases more than 70 local designers and artists, who rent rack space. Curator Bass limits her selection to San Francisco residents to reduce her carbon footprint, and promotes each collection with a biography of the designer. A one-stop shop for browsing the best of local fashion, clothing collections include men's, women's, and children's, as well as accessories and home decor.

Residents Apparel Gallery.

CONSUME

Buffalo Exchange
1555 Haight Street, at Clayton Street, Haight-Ashbury (431 7733, www.buffaloexchange.com). Metro to Carl & Cole/bus 6, 33, 37, 43, 66, 71. **Open** 11am-7pm Mon-Thur, Sun; 11am-8pm Fri-Sat. **Credit** MC, V. **Map** p317 F9.
Buffalo Exchange didn't achieve its lofty station as a national trade-in chain by its gentle touch: locals are used to looks of near-contempt when trying to get rid of those stone-washed Gap reverse-cut jeans. Still, the range is vast.
Other locations 1210 Valencia Street, Mission (647 8332).

Crossroads Trading Co
2123 Market Street, at Church Streets, Castro (552 8740, www.crossroadstrading.com). Metro to Church/bus 22, 37. **Open** 11am-7pm Mon-Thur, Sun; 11am-8pm Fri, Sat. **Credit** DC, MC, V. **Map** p318 H10.
People who still haven't got over that 1980s retro thing should pop into the Market and Haight Street branches of this favorite local chain; the Fillmore location (1901 Fillmore Street, 775 8885) is best for jeans, dresses and designer and vintage pieces.
Other locations throughout the city.

★ GoodByes
3483 Sacramento Street, between Laurel & Walnut Streets, Presidio Heights (674 0151, http://goodbyessf.com). Bus 1, 2, 3, 43. **Open** 10am-6pm Mon-Wed, Fri, Sat; 10am-8pm Thur; 11am-5pm Sun. **Credit** Disc, MC, V. **Map** p313 E5.
For rich pickings, take advantage of this consignment boutique's Pacific Heights proximity. Cast-offs from some of the town's most upscale closets might include a barely worn Miu Miu sweater or a classic Chanel suit.
Other locations *Menswear* 3464 Sacramento Street, Presidio Heights (346 6388).

Painted Bird
1201A Guerrero Street, at 24th Street, Mission (401 7027, www.paintedbird.org). BART 24th Street/bus 12, 14, 48, 49, 67. **Open** 11am-8pm daily. **Credit** MC, V. **Map** p318 J12.
Cooler than cool and extremely well priced, this brilliantly edited vintage outpost has become a must-shop for hipsters in search of granny sundresses, glam disco bags, flash but cute jewelry and styling shoes and boots from the 1980s, '70s and earlier eras.

Schauplatz
791 Valencia Street, between 18th & 19th Streets, Mission (864 5665). BART 16th Street/bus 14, 33, 49. **Open** 1-7pm Mon-Sat; 1-6pm Sun. **Credit** MC, V. **Map** p318 K11.
The second-hand gear on offer here, mixed with new clothing, is more artfully collated than elsewhere in the Mission. In German, Schauplatz means 'show-place'; the name makes sense when you spy Italian sunglasses, intricately beaded Moroccan mules or a Swedish policeman's leather jacket.

Static
1764 Haight Street, between Shrader & Cole Streets, Haight-Ashbury (422 0046, www.staticvintage.com). Metro to Carl & Cole/bus 6, 33, 37, 43, 66, 71. **Open** noon-7pm Mon-Thur, Sun; noon-8pm Fri, Sat. **Credit** MC, V. **Map** p317 E9.
'Vintage for the modern' is the hallmark of this Haight boutique with a distinct high-'70s, rocker-tough and California-cool sensibility. Read: used denim and leather, Gucci bags, worn-soft T-shirts and boots.

Ver Unica
526 & 437B Hayes Street, between Gough & Octavia Streets, Hayes Valley (431 0688, http://verunicasf.com). Bus 5, 6, 21, 47, 49, 71. **Open** 11am-7pm Mon-Sat; noon-6pm Sun. **Credit** AmEx, Disc, MC, V. **Map** p318 J8.
Ver Unica is where people with a proper paycheck go to buy second-hand: it sells unique retro finds, not cast-offs crammed together on dusty shelves. Stocks men's clothing, too.

★ Wasteland
1660 Haight Street, between Clayton & Cole Streets, Haight-Ashbury (863 3150, www.wastelandclothing.com). Metro to Carl & Cole/bus 6, 33, 37, 43, 66, 71. **Open** 11am-8pm Mon-Sat; noon-7pm Sun. **Credit** AmEx, MC, V. **Map** p317 E9.
Possibly the most popular used clothier in town, Wasteland sells second-hand clothing with history, including a rich supply of vintage costume jewelry, fancy gowns and worn-in leather jackets.

FASHION ACCESSORIES & SERVICES

Handbags

Coach
190 Post Street, at Grant Avenue, Union Square & Around (392 1772, www.coach.com). BART & Metro to Powell/bus 2, 3, 5, 21, 30, 31, 38, 45, 91 & Market Street routes/cable car Powell-Hyde or Powell-Mason. **Open** 10am-8pm Mon-Sat; 11am-6pm Sun. **Credit** AmEx, Disc, MC, V. **Map** p315 M5.
The logo fabric in the window of this pristine designer outlet gives no sense of the high-quality leather or suede totes, satchels and accessories within. The returns policy is incredible: staff will hand you a new bag if but a single stitch comes out of your purchase.
Other locations 1 Embarcadero Center, Financial District (362 2518); Westfield San Francisco Centre, 865 Market Street, Union Square & Around (543 7152).

Kate Spade

227 Grant Avenue, between Post & Sutter Streets, Union Square & Around (216 0880, www.katespade.com). BART & Metro to Powell/bus 2, 3, 5, 6, 21, 30, 31, 38, 45, 71, 91/cable car Powell-Hyde or Powell-Mason. **Open** 10am-6pm Mon-Sat; noon-5pm Sun. **Credit** AmEx, Disc, MC, V. **Map** p315 M5.

Once a neatly sewn label on a simple black nylon handbag, Kate Spade is now a full-blown lifestyle, with luggage, shoes, fragrances and jewelry. The bags, of course, remain exemplary.

Marc Jacobs

125 Maiden Lane, between Stockton Street & Grant Avenue, Union Square & Around (362 6500, www.marcjacobs.com). BART & Metro to Powell/bus 2, 3, 4, 15, 30, 38, 45, 76 & Market Street routes/cable car Powell-Hyde or Powell-Mason. **Open** 10am-6pm Mon-Wed, Fri, Sat; 10am-7pm Thur; noon-5pm Sun. **Credit** AmEx, Disc, MC, V. **Map** p315 M5.

Terminally cool Marc Jacobs keeps lines fresh and just affordable enough for the under-thirties. The bags sit on glowing shelves, drawing you in with their utilitarian glamor. The Marc by Marc Jacobs branch has cheeky window displays, great low-priced five-and-dime gifts and, of course, cool men's and women's clothing.

Other locations Marc by Marc Jacobs, 2142 Fillmore Street, Pacific Heights (447 9322).

Jewelry

Metier (*see p184*) also has a divine selection of contemporary and vintage jewelry.

Five & Diamond

510 Valencia Street, at 16th Street, Mission (255 9747, www.fiveanddiamond.com). BART 16th Street/bus 14, 22, 33, 49. **Open** noon-8pm Mon-Thur; noon-9pm Fri-Sat; noon-7pm Sun. **Credit** MC, V. **Map** p318 K10.

This could be rocker LA, by way of a *Mad Max* meets *Deadwood* cowboy apocalypse, if it wasn't fixed in the grungy heart of the Mission. Phoebe Minona Durland and Leighton Kelly – 'Nomadic artists', Yard Dogs Road Show burlesque/vaudeville performers, and designers – showcase their upscale piercing line here, along with wild and stunning jewelry. When you've wearied of shopping, you can hop in the chair and acquire some skin art from award-winning tattoo artist Phil Milic.

Gallery of Jewels

2115 Fillmore Street, between California & Sacramento Streets, Pacific Heights (771 5099, www.galleryofjewels.com). Bus 1, 2, 3, 4, 12, 24. **Open** 10.30am-6.30pm Mon-Sat; 11am-6pm Sun. **Credit** AmEx, Disc, MC, V. **Map** p313 H5.

Peruse local creations of silver and semi-precious stones, as well as funky beads and antique bracelets. Designs run from fresh and modern to mumsy.

Other locations 4089 24th Street, Noe Valley (285 0626); 2101 Union Street, Cow Hollow (929 0259).

★ Jeanine Payer

762 Market Street, at Grant Avenue, Downtown (788 2417, www.jeaninepayer.com). BART & Metro to Powell/bus 2, 3, 5, 6, 9, 21, 30, 38, 45, 71, 91 & Market Street routes/cable car Powell-Hyde or Powell-Mason. **Open** 11am-6pm Mon-Sat; 11am-7pm Thur. **Credit** AmEx, MC, V

Artisan metalsmith Jeanine Payer hand-engraves poetry – Emily Dickinson to Rumi – on to bracelets, rings, earrings and necklaces, creating unique talismans that are coveted by the likes of Susan Sarandon, Johnny Depp and Mick Jagger.

Launderettes

Don't miss **BrainWash** (*see p142*), SoMa's still-popular café/bar/launderette.

Star Wash

392 Dolores Street, at 17th Street, Mission (431 2443). Metro to Church & 18th/bus 22, 33. **Open** 7am-10pm daily. **No credit cards**. **Map** p318 J10.

If you don't mind having your underwear scrutinized by Bogey and Bacall (in poster form only, more's the pity), this is a great place to get your laundry done.

Leather goods & luggage

Edwards Luggage

3 Embarcadero Center, between Davis & Drumm Streets, Financial District (981 7047, www.edwardsluggage.com). BART & Metro to Embarcadero/bus 1, 2, 10, 14, 15, 31, 66, 71/cable car California. **Open** 10am-7pm Mon-Fri; 10am-6pm Sat; noon-5pm Sun. **Credit** AmEx, Disc, MC, V. **Map** p315 N4.

Since 1946, Edwards Luggage has been kitting people out with everything they need to hit the road, or the skies, from trim carry-ons to duffle bags and voltage converters.

Other locations throughout the Bay Area.

Flight 001

525 Hayes Street, between Laguna & Octavia Streets, Hayes Valley (487 1001, www.flight001.com). Bus 5, 6, 21, 71. **Open** 11am-7pm Mon-Sat; 11am-6pm Sun. **Credit** AmEx, DC, Disc, MC, V. **Map** p318 J8.

If it's important that you travel in style, Flight 001 is the place to go. Streamlined like a jet airliner, the store sells beautiful modern designs, from Japanese metal suitcases to gorgeous accessories.

Flight 001.

Hideo Wakamatsu
1980 Union Street, at Buchanan Street, Cow Hollow (255 3029, www.hideowakamatsu.com). bus 22, 41, 45. **Open** 11am-7pm Mon-Sat; 11am-6pm Sun. **Credit** AmEx, MC, V.
The designs are extremely well considered, the construction and materials are impeccable, and the prices are, well, up there in the sky with the planes. Still, it's no wonder Hideo Wakamatsu has gone from a cult name at Flight 001 to a stand-alone boutique.

Johnson Leathers
1833 Polk Street, between Jackson & Washington Streets, Polk Gulch (775 7392, www.johnson leather.com). Bus 1, 10, 12, 19, 27, 47, 49, 90/ cable car Powell-Hyde. **Open** 10.30am-6.30pm Mon-Sat; noon-5pm Sun. **Credit** AmEx, Disc, MC, V. **Map** p314 K4.
Both a factory and a shop, Johnson Leathers makes and sells jackets and motorbike racing suits, as well as vests, trousers and chaps, all at reasonable prices.

Lingerie & underwear

★ Alla Prima Fine Lingerie
539 Hayes Street, between Laguna & Octavia Streets, Hayes Valley (864 8180, www.alla primalingerie.com). Bus 5, 6, 21, 71. **Open** 11am-7pm Mon-Sat; noon-5pm Sun. **Credit** AmEx, Disc, MC, V. **Map** p318 J8.
Known for its thorough fittings and sky-high designer offerings, Alla Prima specializes in everything from Eres, Andres Sarda, Wolford and La Perla delicacies to sublime swimsuits and thigh-high fishnets.
Other locations 1420 Grant Avenue, North Beach (397 4077).

Belle Cose & Molte Cose
2036-2044 Polk Street, between Broadway & Pacific Avenue, Polk Gulch (474 3494, http:// bellecosesf.com). Bus 10, 12, 27, 49, 90. **Open** 11am-6.30pm Mon-Fri; 11am-6pm Sat; noon-5pm Sun. **Credit** MC, V. **Map** p314 K4.
'Vintage lingerie' sounds pretty scary, but here it's all about the 1920s boudoir theming. While there is the odd second-hand slip, nightie or corset for sale, the shop majors in new designer lingerie.

Dark Garden
321 Linden Street, between Octavia & Gough Streets, Hayes Valley (431 7684, www.dark garden.net). Bus 5, 6, 21, 71. **Open** 11am-5pm Mon-Wed, Sun; 11am-7pm Thur-Sat. **Credit** AmEx, Disc, MC, V. **Map** p318 J8.
Autumn Carey-Adamme's *métier* is bespoke corsets. The customer selects style, fabric and color and, by the magic of 12 individual measurements, she'll create a custom-fit garment. The off-the-rack models are seductive, and the bridal corsets remain hugely popular.

Shoes

For non-specialists with great selections, try **Barneys New York** (*see p178*), **Rabat** (*see p188*), **Nordstrom** (*see p179*) or the cut-price range at **Jeremy's** (*see p186*).

★ Bulo
418 Hayes Street, at Gough Street, Hayes Valley (255 4939/www.buloshoes.com). Bus 5, 6, 21, 71. **Open** 11am-7pm Mon-Sat; noon-6pm Sun. **Credit** AmEx, Disc, MC, V. **Map** p318 J8.

Two shops in Hayes Valley (the men's store is at No.437A, 864 3244) sell a handsome array of shoes by European designers. On big sale days, expect to queue for those Cydwoq knee-high boots.

Gimme Shoes

416 & 381 Hayes Street, at Gough Street, Hayes Valley (864 0691-800 8992, www.gimmeshoes.com). Bus 21, 47, 49. **Open** 11am-7pm Mon-Sat; noon-6pm Sun. **Credit** AmEx, Disc, MC, V. **Map** p315 M5.

The richer fare at this fashion-forward, gender-neutral shoe salon includes Paul Smith, Costume National and Fiorentini + Baker. An impressive cache of trainers and casual shoes, from Adidas to Vivienne Westwood, tempts locals out of their flip-flops.

Other locations 2358 Fillmore Street, Pacific Heights (441 3040).

Huf

516 Hayes Street, between Laguna & Octavia Streets, Hayes Valley (552 3820/www.hufsf.com). Bus 5, 6, 21, 71. **Open** 11am-7pm Mon-Sat; noon-6pm Sun. **Credit** AmEx, Disc, MC, V. **Map** p315 M5.

Sneaker demons will love the limited-edition Adidas, Nike and New Balance rarities sold at this streamlined, personable shoe shop. Be sure to check out the skull-bedecked Vans for your budding baby skater.

Other locations 808 Sutter Street, Nob Hill (614 9414).

Shoe Biz

1446 Haight Street, between Ashbury Street & Masonic Avenue, Haight-Ashbury (864 0990, www.shoebizsf.com). Metro to Carl & Cole/bus 6, 33, 43, 66, 71. **Open** 11am-7pm Mon-Sat; 11am-6pm Sun. **Credit** AmEx, Disc, MC, V. **Map** p317 F9.

Whether you need a spike heel or a hot-pink pointy-toed flat, Shoe Biz adds a bit of punky glamour to current trends. Trainer addicts should head for Shoe Biz II at No.1553 for racks of rare Pumas, Adidas and New Balance.

Other locations throughout the city.

Shoe repair

Anthony's Shoe Service

340 Kearny Street, between Pine & Bush Streets, Union Square & Around (781 1338, http://anthonysshoeservice.com). BART & Metro to Montgomery/bus 1, 2, 3, 5, 6, 9, 10, 12, 21, 30, 31, 38, 45, 71, 91 & Market Street routes/cable car Powell-Hyde or Powell-Mason. **Open** 8.30am-5.30pm Mon-Fri; 9am-5pm Sat. **Credit** AmEx, Disc, MC, V. **Map** p315 M5.

If you're down at heel, let Anthony's minister to you. Staff will undertake any kind of shoe repair, as well as handbags and other leather goods, but the work doesn't come cheap.

FOOD & DRINK

Bi-Rite Market

3639 18th Street, between Guerrero & Dolores Streets, Mission (241 9773, www.biritemarket.com). Metro to Church & 18th/bus 33. **Open** 9am-9pm daily. **Credit** AmEx, MC, V. **Map** p318 J10.

Bi-Rite is the Mission's gourmet grocery, with everything from fresh breads and organic produce to house-smoked salmon, own-made sausages, salads, cakes, an olive bar, and more than 100 cheeses. Don't miss the Bi-Rite creamery/bakery up the street at no.3692 (626 5600) for the city's most heavenly artisan ice-cream.

★ Ferry Plaza Farmers' Market

Ferry Building, Embarcadero, at Market Street. BART & Metro to Montgomery/bus 2, 6, 9, 14, 21, 31 & Market Street routes (291 3276, www.ferrybuildingmarketplace.com). **Open** *Farmers' Market* 10am-2pm Tue, Thur; 8am-2pm Sat. *Ferry Building Marketplace* 10am-6pm Mon-Fri; 9am-6pm Sat; 11am-5pm Sun. **Credit** (Marketplace only) DC, MC, V. **Map** p315 O4.

The glorious Ferry Plaza farmers' market is a sightseeing attraction in its own right, with local farmers' white tents spilling out into the open air from both the north and south arcades, and the city's best artisanal products and gourmet take-out counters lining the nave. Locals and tourists graze at stalls of aged goat's cheese, freshly baked bread slathered in cold-press olive oil, organic microgreens, pasta, chocolate, local oysters, and gourmet sausages. There's lots of bustle, especially on a Saturday: agoraphobics should visit on a non-market day to check out the excellent food shops and restaurants inside.

★ Molinari Delicatessen

373 Columbus Avenue, at Vallejo Street, North Beach (421 2337). Bus 10, 12, 30, 39. 41, 45, 91. **Open** 9am-5.30pm Mon-Sat. **Credit** MC, V. **Map** p315 M3.

Since the turn of the 20th century, Molinari's has been scratching the Italian deli itch for San Franciscans, with legendary salami and proscuitto sandwiches on hard rolls (try the Joe's Special: mozzarella, just-sliced prosciutto and pesto), own-made gnocchi and meatballs. They're so good that it's worth tolerating the huge crowds and chaotic deli-style ordering system.

Rainbow Grocery

1745 Folsom Street, at 14th Street, Mission (863 0621, www.rainbowgrocery.org). BART 16th Street/bus 9, 12, 22, 26, 33, 47, 90. **Open** 9am-9pm daily. **Credit** MC, V. **Map** p318 L9.

This worker-owned organic co-op qualifies as an SF institution for its comprehensive bulk food bins, vitamin and supplement aisles, and employees – many of whom are musicians and artists.

Ferry Plaza Farmers Market.

★ Tartine Bakery

600 Guerrero Street, between 18th & 19th Streets, Mission (487 2600, www.tartinebakery.com). Metro to Church & 18th/bus 14, 22, 33. **Open** 8am-7pm Mon; 7.30am-7pm Tue, Wed; 7.30am-8pm Thur, Fri; 8am-8pm Sat; 9am-8pm Sun. **Credit** MC, V.

Probably the best bakery in San Francisco, Tartine causes queues and makes foodies swoon over their dark-bake French breads (available after 5pm), hot-pressed sandwiches, brioche bread pudding, pastries, cakes and croissants.

Trader Joe's

3 Masonic Avenue, at Geary Boulevard, Western Addition (346 9964, www.traderjoes.com). Bus 2, 38, 43. **Open** 8am-9pm daily. **Credit** AmEx, Disc, MC, V. **Map** p313 F6.

With over 2,000 unique grocery items on its label, Trader Joe's is tough to beat for variety, quality and price. Expect organic, veggie and kosher products, cut-rate wines (yes, the $1.99 Charles Shaw Cabernet, aka Two-Buck Chuck, is still available) and affable staff.

Other locations 555 9th Street, SoMa (863 1292); 401 Bay Street, Fisherman's Wharf (351 1013).

Whole Foods Market

1765 California Street, between Franklin Street & Van Ness Avenue, Pacific Heights (674 0500, www.wholefoodsmarket.com). Bus 1. **Open** 8am-10pm daily. **Credit** AmEx, Disc, MC, V. **Map** p314 J5.

This monolithic organic foods chain can overwhelm: the cheese, meats, seafood and produce sections are

sumptuous altars to high-minded consumption. Add in the delightful hot food, deli, salad and soup take-out bars, and there's no denying the allure.
Other locations 399 4th Street, SoMa (618 0066); 450 Rhode Island Street, Potrero Hill (552 1155)

Alcohol

Arlequin Wine Merchant

384 Hayes Street, between Franklin & Gough Streets, Hayes Valley (863 1104, www.arlequinwinemerchant.com). Bus 5, 6, 21, 71. **Open** 11am-7pm Mon; 11am-8pm Tue-Sat; noon-6pm Sun. **Credit** AmEx, MC, V. **Map** p318 J8.
The owners are thoroughly unpretentious, yet savvy enough in their choice to satisfy any armchair quaffer. Taste (and then, most likely, buy) elusive domestic bottles and coveted imports, ranging from under $10 to over $200.

K&L Wine Merchants

638 4th Street, between Brannan & Townsend Streets, SoMa (896 1734, www.klwines.com). Metro 2nd & King/bus 12, 15, 30, 45, 76. **Open** 10am-7pm Mon-Fri; 9am-6pm Sat; 11am-6pm Sun. **Credit** AmEx, Disc, MC, V. **Map** p319 O7.
The SF branch of California-focused K&L is a modest warehouse, filled with carefully selected wines and spirits. Most of the staff claim specializations in particular regions and/or varietals.

PlumpJack Wines

4011 24th Street, at Noe Street, Noe Valley (282 3841, www.plumpjack.com). Bus 24, 35, 48. **Open** 11am-9pm Mon-Sat; noon-6pm Sun. **Credit** AmEx, Disc, MC, V. **Map** p317 H12.
A great selection of world wines for under $10, as well as grower-produced champagne, premium saké, vintage port, Madeira and microbrews.
Other locations 3201 Fillmore Street, Cow Hollow (346 9870).

True Sake

560 Hayes Street, between Laguna & Octavia Streets, Hayes Valley (355 9555, www.truesake.com). Bus 5, 6, 21, 71. **Open** noon-7pm Mon-Sat; 11am-6pm Sun. **Credit** AmEx, MC, V. **Map** p318 J8.
A beautiful and elegant place, this is the first US shop devoted entirely to saké. Owner Beau Timken is every bit as helpful and knowledgeable about the rice-fermented beverage as you might hope, even suggesting food pairings for your purchase.

Tea & coffee

★ Blue Bottle Café

66 Mint Street, between Jessie & Mission Streets, SoMa (495 3394, www.bluebottlecoffee.net). BART & Metro to Powell/bus 5, 6, 9, 14, 21, 27, 30, 38, 45, 71, 91 & Market Street routes/cable car Powell-Hyde or Powell-Mason. **Open** 7am-7pm Mon-Fri; 8am-6pm Sat; 8am-4pm Sun. **Map** p315 M6.
These socially conscious and obsessive coffee fiends have taken SF by storm with their perfectly roasted (on vintage 1950s German roasters), perfectly brewed coffee. Java junkies from all over drool over the five-light siphon bar, aromatic single-origin coffees and New Orleans-style iced coffee.
Other locations 315 Linden Street, at Gough Street, Hayes Valley (252 7535), & Ferry Building Marketplace (*see p192*).

Graffeo Coffee Roasting Company

735 Columbus Avenue, at Filbert Street, North Beach (1-800 222 6250, 986 2429, www.graffeo.com). Bus 30, 39, 41, 45, 91/cable car Powell-Mason. **Open** 9am-6pm Mon-Fri; 9am-5pm Sat. **Credit** MC, V. **Map** p314 L3.
If you're awake, you'll smell it. This San Francisco institution stocks fresh coffee from various plantations around the world, roasting its beans right on the premises.

Red Blossom Tea Co

831 Grant Avenue, between Washington & Clay Streets, Chinatown (395 0868, www.redblossomtea.com). Bus 1, 10, 12, 30, 41, 91/cable car California. **Open** 10am-6.30pm Mon-Sat; 10am-6pm Sun. **Credit** AmEx, MC, V. **Map** p315 M4.
Renamed and expanded in 2005, Red Blossom has been in the tea business for more than two decades – and it shows. Not only is there a selection of more than 100 teas (black and green? Pshaw! Get into pu-erh and white), but you can also get advice on the art of proper brewing.

GIFTS & SOUVENIRS

Museum gift stores are lovely places to shop. The **California Palace of the Legion of Honor** shop (*see p96*) has rare photography books, prints and offbeat jewelry from local designers, while the **Exploratorium** store (*see p208*) has science toys to spark young imaginations. The warm, welcoming shop of the **Asian Art Museum** (*see p56*) has re-creations of artifacts among its unique and pricey mementos, and the wares at the **SFMOMA MuseumStore** (*see p60*) are sometimes more of a draw than the museum.

African Outlet

524 Octavia Street, between Hayes & Grove Streets, Hayes Valley (864 3576). Bus 5, 6, 21, 71. **Open** 10.30am-7pm daily. **Credit** AmEx, MC, V. **Map** p318 J7.
This gorgeous jumble of tribal artifacts and antiques – brilliantly colored textiles, jewelry and beads, sculpture, fetishes, and ceremonial masks – has been

gathered by the owners, a Nigerian expat and his wife, who take delight in explaining their pieces to interested customers.

Curiosity Shoppe

855 Valencia Street, at 20th Street, Mission (839 6404, www.curiosityshoppeonline.com). BART 16th Street/bus 14, 33, 49. **Open** noon-7pm Tue-Sat; noon-6pm Sun. **Credit** AmEx, Disc, MC, V. **Map** p318 K11.

Owners Lauren Smith and Derek Fagerstrom set up the Curiosity Shoppe to showcase their obsession with the gorgeous and strange. Pick up a kit to make a duct tape wallet or radio receiver for that crafty chum – or simply buy a sweet charm necklace for yourself.

SFMOMA Museum Store.

Flax Art & Design

1699 Market Street, between Gough & Valencia Streets, Upper Market (552 2355, www.flaxart.com). Metro F to Valencia Street/bus 6, 14, 47, 49, 71, 90. **Open** 9.30am-7pm Mon-Sat. **Credit** AmEx, Disc, MC, V. **Map** p318 K8.

So much more than an art supply store, this Bay Area landmark teems with papers, fine pens, children's toys, blank books, timepieces, lighting, portfolios – everything you could possibly desire for the boho live/work space of your dreams.

Lavish

540 Hayes Street, at Octavia Street, Hayes Valley (565 0540, www.shoplavish.com). Bus 21, 47, 49. **Open** 11am-7pm Mon-Sat; 11am-6pm Sun. **Credit** MC, V. **Map** p318 J8.

Gorgeous letterpress cards, charming print bags, delicate jewelry and oodles of whimsical baby clothes make this a must-stop on the way to a girlie soirée or baby shower.

Little Otsu

849 Valencia Street, between 19th & 20th Streets, Mission (255 7900, www.littleotsu.com). BART 16th Street/bus 14, 33, 49. **Open** 11.30am-7.30pm Wed-Sun. **Credit** DC, MC, V. **Map** p318 K11.

Vegan principles at this artful, airy space translate as cute, recycled-paper cards (as well as diaries, calendars and books) printed with soy-based inks.

Needles & Pens

3253 16th Street, at Guerrero Street, Mission (255 1534, www.needles-pens.com). BART 16th Street/bus 14, 33, 49. **Open** noon-7pm daily. **Credit** AmEx, Disc, MC, V. **Map** p318 J10.

This epicenter of DIY culture in Mission combined with gallery space trades in 'zines, bric-a-brac and hand-embellished T-shirts. A great place to pick up a polemical print by your local anarchist.

Nest

2300 Fillmore Street, at Clay Street, Pacific Heights (292 6199, www.nestsf.com). Bus 1, 3, 10, 22, 24. **Open** 10.30am-6.30pm Mon-Fri; 10am-6pm Sat; 11am-6pm Sun. **Credit** AmEx, V. **Map** p313 H5.

A nest in the magpie sense, this Parisian bohemia-inspired shop is a beguiling compilation of tin jack-in-the-boxes, gauzy Chinese lanterns, woodcuts, glassware, French jewelry and a selection of adorable kids' clothes.

New Sam Bo Trading Co

51 Ross Aly, between Jackson & Washington Streets, Chinatown (397 2998). Bus 1, 10, 12, 30, 41, 45, 91/cable car Powell-Hyde or Powell-Mason. **Open** 10am-6pm daily. **Credit** MC, V. **Map** p315 M4.

The best things in Chinatown are found down the area's sidestreets, and this tiny shop of Buddhist

Paxton Gate.

and Taoist religious items is a prime example. New Sam Bo sells Buddhas, ceremonial candles and incense, along with intriguing paper goods that are to be burned in honor of ancestors or to request a favor of the gods.

★ Paxton Gate

824 Valencia Street, between 19th & 20th Streets, Mission (824 1872, www.paxtongate.com). BART 16th Street/bus 14, 33, 49. **Open** noon-7pm Mon-Fri; 11am-7pm Sat, Sun. **Credit** AmEx, Disc, MC, V. **Map** p318 K11.

That kneeling cushion may be more practical, but the gardener in your life is likely to find something from this deeply bizarre shop that is rather more fun that that. Alongside strange and ghoulish pieces of taxidermy – mice in anthropomorphic poses, say – sits an array of traditional, hand-crafted Japanese garden knives.

Therapy

545 Valencia Street, between 16th & 17th Streets, Mission (865 0981, www.shopatt herapy.com). BART 16th Street/bus 14, 33, 49. **Open** 11.30am-9.30pm Mon-Thur, Sun; 10.30am-10pm Fri, Sat. **Credit** AmEx, MC, V. **Map** p318 K10.

This hipster central stocks cute earrings and hair clips, stationery and undefinable gifts, as well as women's and men's clothing. For furniture and homewares, check out the other shop just a few doors down.

HEALTH & BEAUTY

Complementary medicine

Scarlet Sage Herb Co

1173 Valencia Street, between 22nd & 23rd Streets, Mission (821 0997, www.scarletsage herb.com). BART 24th Street/bus 12, 14, 48, 49, 67. **Open** 11am-6.30pm daily. **Credit** AmEx, Disc, MC, V. **Map** p318 K12.

The owners of this Mission apothecary focus on organic Native American and more familiar European herbs, essential oils, tinctures and plant essences, with a section dedicated to homeopathy. There's also a good choice of books for sale on alternative healing.

Vinh Khang Herbs & Ginsengs

512 Clement Street, between 6th & 7th Avenues, Richmond (752 8336). Bus 1, 2, 38, 44. **Open** 10.30am-7pm daily. **No credit cards. Map** p312 C6.

Feel the strength of San Francisco Chinese traditions at Vinh Khang, where herbal specialists can create a customised concoction for your ailment while you wait on the premises.

Hairdressers & barbers

Backstage Salon

2134 Polk Street, between Broadway & Vallejo Street, Polk Gulch (775 1440, www.backstagesf.com).

Bus 12, 27, 49, 76. **Open** 11am-7pm Mon-Fri, Sun; 11am-6pm Sat. **Credit** MC, V. **Map** p314 K4.
This salon and gallery showcases the work of local artists while providing intense color treatments and innovative haircuts from a rotating fleet of international stylists.

Hair Play

211 Church St, at Market Street, Noe Valley (863 0703). Metro to Church & Market/bus 22, 37. **Open** noon-6pm Mon, Sun; 10am-6pm Tue, Wed, Sat; noon-8pm Thur, Fri. **Credit** MC, V.
Hair Play's earthy interior calms, while seasoned stylists whip your hair into shape without the diva-ish attitude. Lauded by many as the best salon in San Francisco, it's popular with those who suffer the blessing of curly hair.

Opticians

City Optix

2154 Chestnut Street, between Pierce & Steiner Streets, Marina (921 1188, www.cityoptix.com). Bus 2, 4, 8, 10, 18, 24, 44. **Open** 10am-6pm Mon-Wed, Fri, Sat; 10am-8pm Thur; noon-5pm Sun. **Credit** AmEx, Disc, MC, V. **Map** p313 G3.
Alain Mikli, Oliver Peoples and LA Eyeworks frames are all sold here, and helpful staff will sift through the entire collection to find you the ideal pair.
Other locations 1685 Haight Street, Haight-Ashbury (626 1188).

Pharmacies

Walgreens Drugstore

3201 Divisadero Street, at Lombard Street, Marina (931 6417, www.walgreens.com). Bus 28, 30, 43, 76. **Open** 24hrs daily. **Credit** AmEx, Disc, MC, V. **Map** p313 F3.
Prescriptions and general drugstore purchases are available at this pharmacy around the clock.
Other 24hr locations 459 Powell Street, Union Square & Around (984 0793); 498 Castro Street, Castro (861 6276); 1189 Potrero Avenue, Mission (647 1397); 5411 Geary Boulevard, Richmond (752 8370).

Spas & salons

International Orange

2044 Fillmore Street, between Pine & California Streets, Pacific Heights (563 5000, www.internationalorange.com). Bus 1, 2, 3, 10, 22, 38. **Open** 11am-9pm Mon-Fri; 9am-7pm Sat, Sun. **Credit** AmEx, MC, V. **Map** p313 H5.
Be sure you get an appointment: the secret is out about the refined treatments and professional facials here. Try the Red Flower Japan massage, a soothing mix of botanicals that awakens your senses (or, at least, leaves you smelling decent for a good 48 hours).

★ Kabuki Springs & Spa

Japan Center, 1750 Geary Boulevard, at Fillmore Street, Western Addition (922 6000, www.kabukisprings.com). Bus 2, 3, 22, 38. **Open** 10am-10pm daily. *Men only* Mon, Thur, Sat. *Women only* Wed, Fri, Sun. *Mixed* Tue. **Admission** *Day pass* $22-$25. **Credit** AmEx, Disc, MC, V. **Map** p314 H6.
This traditional Japanese bathhouse has communal tubs, a steam room, saunas, a cold plunge pool and a restful tatami room. Shiatsu, Swedish and prenatal massages, body wraps and scrubs, and other soothing services are available by appointment.

SenSpa

1161 Gorgas Avenue, off Presidio/Crissy Field exit, Presidio (441 1777, www.senspa.com). Bus 28, 29, 43, 76/PresidiGo shuttle. **Open** 10am-9pm Tue-Fri; 9am-7pm Sat, Sun. **Credit** AmEx, MC, V. **Map** p313 E3.
Far from the madding crowd of Downtown – and somewhat challenging to locate – is this relatively new addition to the San Francisco spa scene. But what an addition: the early 20th-century storage barracks that once catered to Letterman Hospital (now George Lucas's Digital Arts campus) has been transformed into a peaceful Asian-inspired oasis with walls of falling water, plants and skylights. The holistic treatments, massages and facials are delivered by expert aestheticians; lymphatic detoxes, Ayurvedic facials and deep-tissue massages are among the specialties.

Flea Finds

Bay Area markets can turn up treasure.

Bargains are plentiful and rarities scream out to be fondled and haggled over at the Bay Area's flea markets. Come prepared: bring plenty of cash, as well as sturdy bags or a shopping cart. The earlier you arrive the better the buys, although at the end of the day, you just might score an art deco nightstand with Bakelite handles for $5 from that weary peddler who simply doesn't want to pack it up again.

The finest of all local flea markets – showcasing everything from Victorian lace and Depression-era dishware to 1950s Formica kitchen tables and 1970s stacked Superfly boots – is **Alameda Point Antiques & Collectibles Faire**, at the former Alameda Point Naval Air Station (6am-3pm, first Sun of mth, 1-510 522 7500, www.antiquesbybay.com). Touted as Northern California's largest antiques and collectibles show, with more than 800 dealers, the event takes about half a day to cover and entry costs $5-$15 (it's cheapest after 9am). No vendors of cheap socks or sellers of fallen-off-the-truck food here – everything sold at the Alameda market must be at least 20 years old, and no reproductions are permitted.

The folks behind Alameda also recently started the **Candlestick Park Antiques & Collectible Faire** (6am-3pm third Sun of mth, $5-$10, www.candlestickantiques.com) at San Francisco's football stadium on the Bay. Though similar in style to Alameda, Candlestick Park is more for bargain hunters and those in search of the intriguing one-off. Also worth a peek is San Francisco's **Alemany Flea Market** (8am-3pm Wed-Sun, 647 2043), held in the concrete freeway nexus of Highways 101 and 280, at 100 Alemany Boulevard. This smaller market highlights a less refined and varied array of goods but can yield unexpected treasures in used furniture, homewares, paper ephemera and vintage jewelry, as well as random booty culled from estate sales.

For a taste of incense-burning, multiculti Berkeley grit, stop at the **Berkeley Flea Market** (7am-6pm Sat & Sun, 1-510 644 0744), conveniently located at the Ashby BART station parking lot, at Ashby and Martin Luther King Streets. Here you'll find new and used wares, African art, jewelry, handicrafts, books, antiques, furniture, clothing and music.

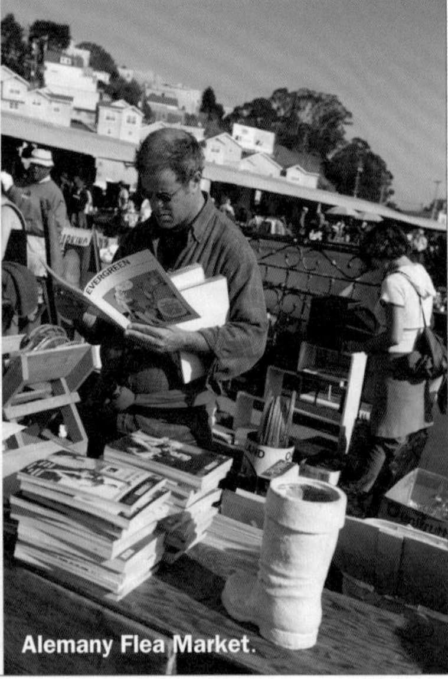

Alemany Flea Market.

CONSUME

Shops

Fresh

301 Sutter Street, at Grant Avenue, Union Square & Around (248 0210, www.fresh.com). BART & Metro to Montgomery/bus 2, 3, 6, 9, 21, 30, 31, 38, 45, 71, 91/cable car Powell-Hyde or Powell-Mason. **Open** 10am-7pm Mon-Wed, Sat; 10am-8pm Thur; 10am-6pm Sun. **Credit** AmEx, MC, V. **Map** p315 M5.

Ensconced in a Victorian corner spot, Fresh purveys its own inimitable soaps, perfumes, lotions, shower gels and make-up. As well as smelling good enough to eat (soy shampoo, pomegranate conditioner, brown sugar scrub), the products are excellent performers.

Kiehl's

2360 Fillmore Street, between Washington & Clay Streets, Pacific Heights (359 9260, www.kiehls.com). Bus 1, 3, 10, 22. **Open** 11am-7pm Mon-Sat; 10am-6pm Sun. **Credit** AmEx, MC, V. **Map** p313 H5.

The first Kiehl's botanical apothecary opened in New York's East Village in 1851; 150 years later the second opened in Pacific Heights. The products are gentle and include such perennial faves as the Creme de Corps.

Other locations Westfield San Francisco Centre, 865 Market Street, Union Square & Around (644 0112).

Sephora

33 Powell Street, at Market Street, Union Square & Around (362 9360, www.sephora.com). BART & Metro to Powell/bus 2, 3, 5, 6, 9, 14, 21, 27, 30, 31, 45, 71, 91 & Market Street routes/cable car Powell-Hyde or Powell-Mason. **Open** 10am-9pm Mon-Sat; 11am-7pm Sun. **Credit** AmEx, Disc, MC, V. **Map** p315 M6.

Sephora's USP is its interactive floor plan: you can touch, smell and try on most of the premier perfumes and make-up brands without suffering the hard sell.

Other locations 2083 Union Street, Cow Hollow (614 2704).

HOUSE & HOME

Jonathan Adler

2133 Fillmore Street, at Sacramento Street, Pacific Heights (563 9500, www.jonathanadler.com). Bus 1, 3, 10, 22, 24. **Open** 11am-6pm Mon-Sat; noon-5pm Sun. **Credit** AmEx, MC, V. **Map** p313 H5.

Everything NYC designer Jonathan Adler touches becomes utterly groovy in a very *Ice Storm* kind of way: his animal figurines, pillows, pottery and furnishings scream 'Let the key party begin!'

Monument

572 Valencia Street, at 19th Street, Mission (861 9800, www.monument.1stdibs.com). BART 16th Street/bus 14, 22, 33, 49. **Open** noon-6pm Mon-Thur, Sun; noon-7pm Fri, Sat. **Credit** AmEx, MC, V. **Map** p318 K11.

Mad glam mid-century modern makes its last glittery stand here. Take in the sensual lines of the sofas and the high drama of the mirrored cabinets.

Other Shop

327 Divisadero Street, between Oak & Page Streets, Lower Haight (621 5424, www.othershopsf.com). Bus 6, 21, 24, 71. **Open** noon-6pm daily. **Credit** MC, V. **Map** p317 G8.

Come here for retro-mod home furnishings that revitalize the Space Age – or at least remind you why it was short-lived. Primary colors, burnished chrome and a plethora of cocktail accessories.

Sur La Table

77 Maiden Lane, at Stockton Street, Union Square & Around (732 7900, www.surlatable.com). BART & Metro to Powell/bus 2, 3, 5, 6, 9, 14, 21, 27, 30, 31, 45, 71, 91 & Market Street routes/cable car Powell-Hyde or Powell-Mason. **Open** 10am-6pm Mon-Fri; 10am-7pm Sat; 11am-6pm Sun. **Credit** AmEx, Disc, MC, V. **Map** p315 M5.

Nearly everything the passionate cook might desire can be found under these eaves, including high-end single-cup espresso makers and gingerbread house-making kits.

Other locations Ferry Building Marketplace No.37, Embarcadero (262 9970); 1806 4th Street, Berkeley (1-510 849 2252).

Zinc Details

1905 Fillmore Street, between Bush & Pine Streets, Pacific Heights (776 2100, www.zincdetails.com). Bus 1, 2, 3, 22, 38. **Open** 11am-7pm Mon-Sat; noon-6pm Sun. **Credit** AmEx, Disc, MC, V. **Map** p314 H5.

Fun, funky and often fabulous contemporary design by Artemide, Le Klint, Marimekko, Vitra and other European and Japanese makers can be found in this forward-thinking, jam-packed emporium of rugs, lighting, tables, glassware, furniture, textiles and vases. Furniture is the focus of the branch at 2410 California Street (776 9002), just up Fillmore Street.

MUSIC & ENTERTAINMENT

CDs, DVDs & records

The quality and variety of independent music shops means you needn't trouble yourself with the chain stores, unless that's your preference.

On Lower Haight Street, **Groove Merchant** (No.687, at Pierce Street, 252 5766) has bins of hard-to-find jazz, funk, soul and other dusty 12-inch delights. There are soul and funk 45s at chaotic **Rooky Ricardo's** (No.448, at Fillmore Street, 864 7526), but **Jack's Record Cellar** (254 Scott Street, between Haight & Page Streets, 431 3047) has the edge for hard-to-find jazz, R&B, pop and country.

Amoeba Music

1855 Haight Street, between Shrader & Stanyan Streets, Haight-Ashbury (831 1200, www.amoeba.com). Metro to Carl & Cole/bus 6, 33, 37, 43, 66, 71. **Open** 10.30am-10pm Mon-Sat; 11am-9pm Sun. **Credit** Disc, MC, V. **Map** p317 E9.

Amoeba Music remains a mighty presence. It's partly a matter of scale – 25,000sq ft (2,325sq m) of former bowling alley, to be exact – but mainly a matter of breadth: there's every imaginable type of music, both new and second-hand, the vast majority priced very fairly, as well as a massive DVD selection. The Berkeley branch used to be the stronger of the two, but the SF store now pips it. There are free gigs, too, with some surprisingly big names. The store also launched its own imprint: one of its first releases was a 1969 concert by Gram Parsons and the Flying Burrito Brothers at SF's Avalon Ballroom.

Aquarius Records

1055 Valencia Street, between 21st & 22nd Streets, Mission (647 2272, www.aquariusrecords.org). BART 24th Street/bus 14, 49. **Open** 10am-9pm Mon-Wed, Sun; 10am-10pm Thur-Sat. **Credit** AmEx, Disc, MC, V. **Map** p318 K12.

This splendid little neighborhood record store could be classed as a boutique, were the staff not so wonderfully lacking in pretension (tiny handwritten notes attached to numerous CD covers reveal their enthusiasm). Expect carefully curated selections and rarities in everything from art rock to sludge metal.

Grooves Vinyl Attractions

1797 Market Street, between Pearl & McCoppin Streets, Hayes Valley (436 9933). Metro to Van Ness/bus 6, 71. **Open** 11.30am-7pm daily. **Credit** AmEx, Disc, MC, V. **Map** p318 J9.

Vinyl heaven – at least if your tastes don't run far beyond the 1970s. The store is packed with oddities and curios, including tons of old soundtracks, comedy records and sets by forgotten '70s crooners.

Instruments & sheet music

Clarion Music

816 Sacramento Street, at Grant Avenue, Chinatown (391 1317, www.clarionmusic.com). Bus 1, 30, 45, 91/cable car California. **Open** 11am-6pm Mon-Fri; 9am-5pm Sat. **Credit** AmEx, Disc, MC, V. **Map** p315 M4.

It stocks didgeridoos and African drums, sure, but Clarion takes them as a starting point before heading into truly exotic waters: affordable H'mong jaw harps, say, or an impressively costly deluxe pipa.

Haight-Ashbury Music Center

1540 Haight Street, at Ashbury Street, Haight-Ashbury (863 7327, www.haight-ashbury-music.com). Metro to Carl & Cole/bus 6, 33, 37, 43, 66, 71. **Open** 11am-7pm Mon-Fri; 10am-6pm Sat; noon-6pm Sun. **Credit** AmEx, MC, V. **Map** p317 F9.

A stop-off for local musos and visiting musicians, this shop sells new and second-hand instruments, microphones, mixers, amps and sheet music.

SPORTS & FITNESS

For ski, snowboard, surf and in-line skate rentals, *see p249-56.*

Lombardi Sports

1600 Jackson Street, at Polk Street, Polk Gulch (771 0600, www.lombardisports.com). Bus 1, 10, 12, 19, 27, 47, 49, 90. **Open** 10am-7pm Mon-Wed; 10am-8pm Thur, Fri; 10am-6pm Sat; 11am-6pm Sun. **Credit** AmEx, Disc, MC, V. **Map** p314 K4.

Although it does sell proper wilderness gear, affable Lombardi Sports also caters to those who weren't suckled by wolves. There's equipment and accessories for cycling, running, climbing and hiking, as well as snow-, water- and team sports, plus some fashion. The staff are knowledgeable.

See Jane Run Sports

3910 24th Street, at Sanchez Street, Noe Valley (401 8338, www.seejanerun.com). Metro to Church & 24th/bus 48. **Open** 11am-7pm Mon-Fri; 10am-6pm Sat; 11am-6pm Sun. **Credit** AmEx, Disc, MC, V. **Map** p317 H12.

A shop for women who run, cycle, swim, hike or do yoga, with staff who are more than happy to spend time matching you to the right shoes.

Sports Basement

610 Mason Street, at Crissy Field, Presidio (437 0100, www.sportsbasement.com). Bus 23, 30, 43, 91. **Open** 9am-9pm Mon-Fri; 8am-8pm Sat, Sun. **Credit** AmEx, Disc, MC, V. **Map** p312 D2.

Size is everything at Sports Basement: this large branch includes end-of-line goods from top-tier brands (North Face, Teva, Pearl Izumi), offered at reductions of 30% to 60%.

Other locations 1590 Bryant Street, Potrero Hill (575 3000).

TICKETS

While it's cheaper to buy tickets for performances directly from the venue, many don't offer this option, especially for booking online. The main booking agencies for concerts and other events are **Ticketmaster** (1-800 745 3000, www.ticketmaster.com), **TicketWeb** (1-866 468 7619, www.ticketweb.com), **StubHub** (www.stubhub.com) and **Mr Ticket** (1-800 424 7328, www.mrticket.com).

TRAVELERS' NEEDS

For luggage, *see p190-91*. For cellphones and computer repairs, *see p183.*

Arts & Entertainment

Calendar

The fun never stops.

Events in a city as extroverted and dramatic as San Francisco are bound to be colorful, and sometimes a little fruity. Spring and summer are peppered with weekly neighborhood fairs and parades, the only drawback being the accompanying street closures and driving detours. When autumn and winter roll around, most events move indoors, but the activity barely lets up. There's always something going on here, whether it's a family fun run through the city or a transvestite beauty contest.

The dates listed below are as accurate as possible, but check before you make plans: festivals do occasionally shift dates. For up-to-date information, consult the San Francisco Visitor Information Center (*see p295*) or local papers, including the free alternative press.

ARTS & ENTERTAINMENT

SPRING

St Patrick's Day Parade

From 2nd & Market Streets to Civic Center. **Date** Sun before 17 Mar. **Map** p314, p315 & p318.

The city has a sizeable Irish-American population, but everyone gets smiling Irish eyes in time for St Patrick's Day. The parade heads from 2nd and Market Streets to the Civic Center.

St Stupid's Day Parade

Transamerica Pyramid, 600 Montgomery Street, between Washington & Clay Streets, Financial District (www.saintstupid.com). Bus 1, 10, 12, 30, 41, 45, 91/cable car California. **Date** 1 Apr. **Map** p315 O4.

The silly and fun costumed procession winds its way through the Financial District every 1 April, stopping off at various 'Stations of the Stupid' (aka noted financial institutions) to pay tribute to the gods of commerce, and concluding with everyone throwing their socks on the steps of the Pacific Stock Exchange.

THE BEST OFFBEAT EVENTS

Roadworks Street Fair
Steamrollers make art prints by rolling over linoleum blocks (Sept; www.sfcb.org.)

Bring your Big Wheel Race
Crazy parents (and kids) careen down Vermont Street on Big Wheel trikes. (Easter Sun; http://bringyourownbigwheel.com.)

Poetry Grand Slam
Month-long teen poetry competition culminates with a Grand Slam at Davies Symphony Hall. (May; www.youthspeaks.org)

Cherry Blossom Festival

Japan Center, Geary Boulevard, between Fillmore & Laguna Streets, Japantown (563 2313, www.nccbf.org). Bus 2, 3, 22, 31, 38. **Date** Apr. **Map** p314 H6.

A joyous whirlwind engulfs the usually sleepy Japantown for two weekends in April. The Cherry Blossom Festival is a splendid celebration of Japanese cuisine, traditional arts and crafts, dance and martial arts. The Grand Parade starts at Civic Center and goes up Polk to Post ending in Japantown.

Cinco de Mayo

Around the city & Mission Dolores Park, Dolores & 18th Streets, Mission (www.sfcincodemayo.com). BART 16th Street/Metro to Church or Castro/bus 22. **Date** weekend before 5 May. **Map** p318 K7.

San Francisco's Latino residents and their friends celebrate General Ignacio Zaragoza's defeat of the French army at Puebla in 1862 with this raucous weekend of parades, fireworks and music. There is also a free all-day festival in Dolores Park celebrating Mexican culture on the closest Saturday.

AIDS Candlelight Memorial March & Vigil

Castro & Market Streets, Castro (331 1500, www.candlelightmemorial.org). Metro K, L, M to Castro/streetcar F/bus 24, 33, 35, 37. **Date** 3rd Sun in May. **Map** p317 H10.

This annual candlelit vigil begins at 8pm with a solemn procession from the Castro along Market Street, ending on the steps of the Main Library. There, crowds gather for speeches, an awards ceremony, celebrations and remembrances.

Bay to Breakers Foot Race

From Howard & Spear Streets, SoMa, to Ocean Beach, Golden Gate Park (359 2800, http://zazzle baytobreakers.com). **Date** 3rd Sun in May.

In an effort to raise spirits during the arduous and lengthy rebuilding process that followed the 1906 earthquake and fire, William Randolph Hearst's *San Francisco Examiner* started this grandaddy of all San Francisco events in 1912. At the height of its popularity, the race attracted more than 110,000 participants. These days, weekend warriors dressed as salmon, jog-walkers pushing kegs of beer in shopping carts, and footloose nude zanies run, walk or stumble from the foot of Howard Street (bay), a distance of about 7.5 miles to Ocean Beach (breakers).

Carnaval

Harrison Street, between 16th & 23rd Streets, Mission (920 0125, www.carnavalsf.com). BART to 16th or 24th Streets/bus 12, 22, 27, 33, 67. **Admission** $5. **Date** Memorial Day weekend. **Map** p318 L10/L11.

Organizers call it 'California's largest annual multicultural festival'. Locals call it the best place to eyeball a dazzling parade of skimpily costumed samba dancers gyrating foxily to fizzing Latin music. The street food at this Rio-style event is pretty hot too.

SUMMER

Union Street Festival

Union Street, between Gough & Steiner Streets, Cow Hollow (1-800 310 6563, www.unionstreet festival.com). Bus 41, 45, 47, 49, 90. **Date** early June. **Map** p313 H4.

This weekend-long street fair draws big crowds each June, with its artists' stands, food stalls, bands and assorted other entertainments. Don't miss the annual waiter's race, when the city's best servers race up and down a hill trying not to spill a tray of wine glasses.

Haight Ashbury Street Fair

Haight Street, between Masonic Avenue & Stanyan Street, Haight-Ashbury (www.haight ashburystreetfair.org). Metro N to Cole/bus 6, 33, 43, 66, 71. **Date** early June. **Map** p317 E9/F9.

It's the Summer of Love all over again, with more than 200 booths of greasy food, hippie craftwork and enough roach-clips, skins, bongs and hash pipes to fill out a Cheech and Chong script. Live music comes courtesy of local acts.

► *For more on the Summer of Love, see p86* **Streets of San Francisco**.

North Beach Festival

Grant Avenue, Green Street, Stockton Street & Washington Square, North Beach (989 2220, www.sfnorthbeach.org). Bus 10, 12, 30, 39, 41, 45, 91/cable car Powell-Mason. **Date** June. **Map** p315 M3.

Whip out the beret and bang out a rhythm on the bongos, daddio – it's San Francisco's oldest street

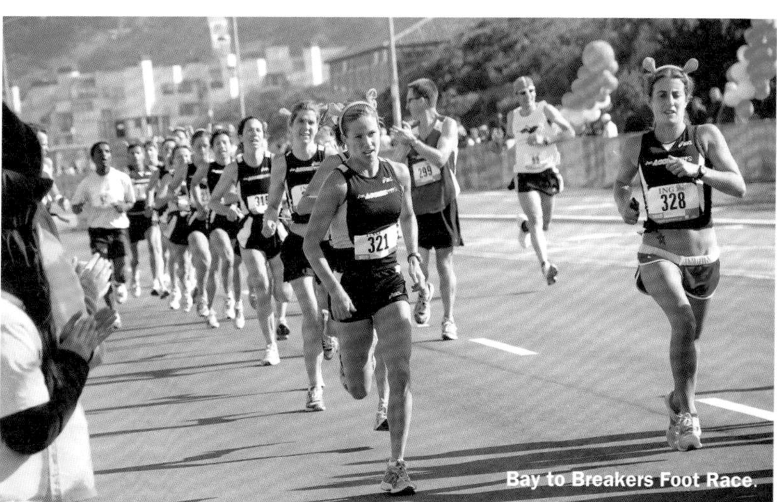

Bay to Breakers Foot Race.

party, held in the birthplace of the beatniks. The North Beach Festival is heavy on art and crafts – including an Italian chalk-art street painting competition – but there's also live music, wine and, inevitably, plenty of top-notch Italian food.

Summer Solstice

Around the city. **Date** 21 June.

San Francisco's pagans meet on the year's longest day to drum, dance and celebrate. At sunset, pound along with a drum circle in Justin Herman Plaza at the Embarcadero or join the Baker Beach bonfires.

San Francisco LGBT Pride Celebration Parade

Market Street, between Embarcadero & 8th Street, Downtown (864 3733, www.sfpride.org). **Date** last Sun in June. **Map** p314, p315 & p318.

A San Francisco institution – but a bit of a mouthful to say – the Lesbian, Gay, Bisexual and Transgender Pride Parade is every bit as campy as you'd expect. Local politicians cruising for the rainbow vote share the route with drag queens, leather daddies and dykes on bikes. It's the wildest, friendliest parade you'll ever witness. Arrive at least an hour early to see, well, anything. The parade is the culmination of a weekend of Pride, with a festival at Civic Center from noon until 6pm on Saturday.

▶ *For more on Pride Week, including the LGBT Film Festival, see p227.*

Fourth of July Waterfront Festival

Between Aquatic Park & Pier 39, Fisherman's Wharf (San Francisco Visitor Information Center 981 1280). Streetcar F/bus 39, 47/cable car Powell-Hyde or Powell-Mason. **Date** July 4. **Map** p314 K2.

You'll find plenty of live entertainment and food stalls here on the waterfront during the day, but be sure to stay for the spectacular fireworks display that gets under way after dark around 9pm (note: summer fog often makes viewing fireworks more of a theoretical event).

America's Cup

Piers 27-29 & 30-32, Embarcadero. **Admission** free. **Date** Aug 2012, July 13-Sept 1 2013. **Map** p315 M2, p315 N2.

The World Series of sailing comes to San Francisco Bay in 2012-2013, when the city hosts the 34th America's Cup Finals and the Challenger Series for the Louis Vuitton Cup, as well as an America's Cup World Series event. The Race Village will be on Pier 29, and the team bases at Pier 30-32, but viewing of events will be visible from all around the Bay – Sausalito to Fisherman's Wharf. With the Golden Gate Bridge as backdrop, it promises to be one of the most spectacular Cups in memory.

San Francisco Marathon

Around the city (1-888 958 6668, www.runsfm.com). **Date** usually 1st Sun in Aug.

The younger and more athletic cousin of Bay to Breakers Foot Race (*see p203*) has grown every year since its inception in 1977. The course starts at the Embarcadero and then heads round the entire city, through the Mission, the Haight, Fisherman's Wharf and the Marina.

AUTUMN

Ghirardelli Square Chocolate Festival

Ghirardelli Square, between North Point, Beach, Larkin & Polk Streets, Fisherman's Wharf (775 5500, www.ghirardellisq.com). Streetcar F/bus 19, 28, 30, 47, 90, 91/cable car Powell-Hyde or Powell-Mason. **Date** early Sept. **Map** p314 J2.

Keep reminding yourself that doctors say a little chocolate is good for you, as you sample chocolate-covered strawberries, decadent mousses, brownies, and all manner of over-the-top indulgences. Proceeds go to charity.

Folsom Street Fair

Folsom Street, between 7th & 12th Streets, SoMa (www.folsomstreetfair.org). Bus 12, 14, 19, 47. **Date** last Sun in Sept. **Map** p318 L8.

The Queen Mother of all leather street fairs, the Folsom Street Fair is a veritable gawkfest for visitors. Don your studded jockstrap and be prepared for masks, whips, chains and – that old favorite – public fellatio. Needless to say, this might not be suitable for the whole family.

ArtSpan Open Studios

SOMArts Gallery, 934 Brannan Street, SoMa & various other venues (861 9838, www.artspan.org). **Date** Oct.

Get up close to San Francisco's creative visionaries throughout the month of October. More than 900 artists' studios open up to the public, with a different neighborhood getting to show off its work every weekend. You'll find a free map detailing participating venues and the Directory of San Francisco Artists at SOMAarts Gallery, which also hosts the opening exhibition.

Castro Street Fair

Market & Castro Streets, from 16th to 19th Streets, Castro (841 1824, www.castrostreetfair.org). Metro K, L, M to Castro/streetcar F/bus 24, 33, 35, 37. **Date** early Oct. **Map** p317 H10.

A taste of the softer side of gay life in San Francisco, this one-day fair – started in 1974 by gay city official Harvey Milk – features food, crafts and community activists' stalls, along with plenty of rainbow merchandise.

Fleet Week

Fisherman's Wharf & Piers 30-32, Embarcadero (705 5500, www.military.com/fleetweek). Streetcar F/bus 19, 39, 44, 47/cable car Powell-Hyde or Powell-Mason. **Date** Oct. **Map** p314 & p315.

Burn, Baby, Burn

Nothing on earth is quite like Burning Man.

Even if they aren't 'burners', most San Franciscans know about Burning Man. The festival has become a part of Bay Area culture – hardly surprising as this is where it all began.

In 1986, Larry Harvey and 20 friends burned an eight-foot wooden man at Baker Beach. The event caught people's imagination and as the annual beach party grew, the size of the man grew too. By 1990, with the man standing at 40 feet and the party 800-strong, local police intervened and put a stop to the revels. Determined that Burning Man shouldn't die, Harvey and 80 others trekked to an ancient lake bed or playa in Nevada's Black Rock desert, 90 miles north of Reno. A new festival was born, its location as remote as it is stunning, with seemingly endless salt plains framed by mountains. Attendance doubled annually over the first few years in Nevada. By 2007, around 40,000 people made what became known as Black Rock City the third-largest city in the state for one week.

The early '90s pioneers were armed with little more than camping gear and high spirits, but over the years Burning Man has evolved into a highly organized event with daily newspapers, radio stations, and an airport. From oyster shacks and whisky bars to steam baths and circus rings, burners set up theme camps offering everything imaginable and unimaginable. And it's all free: the only things you can officially buy are coffee and ice. Another principle is 'leave no trace' or 'pack it in, pack it out'. The level of eco-consciousness is cheering: you won't see people littering. But, of course, the festival does leave a trace: it takes a lot of energy to power the generators for a week, and 40,000 people consume a lot when they're partying in the desert.

Those thinking of attending should remember that for all its beauty, the desert can be unforgiving. Some years have seen white-outs (dust storms) with winds that blow tents away, freezing cold nights and blistering hot days. The elements make burners earn their good time. Participants are required to bring everything they could possibly need for a week in hardcore desert conditions: food and enough water (a gallon a day); a bicycle (preferably adorned with lights and decorations); and dust masks and goggles to brave the intense storms. Lavish costumes, ingenious interactive sculptures and 'art cars' are optional. Theme camps spend weeks planning, days building, and many hands working to craft their art in their little section of the city for the entertainment of their fellow burners – just to take it apart a week later.

So why do people go to so much effort? According to burners, its down to the spirit of the occasion, which is unique and makes Burning Man far more than just a festival; many express an enthusiasm that verges on the religious. It's partly about a sense of belonging. Burners feel like a social group in West Coast society, if not across the US; the group Burners without Borders works year round on projects like reconstruction of housing after natural disasters. What started as a renegade beach party has developed into a community ethos and culture that extends well beyond that week in the desert. Of course, it's not everyone's cup of tea. Assuming you can handle the weather, if you don't love being surrounded by masses of dusty, costumed merrymakers off their heads after a week of excessive drug use, it might not be your scene. But whether you love it or hate it, it will certainly make an impression. The only way to find out is to go and see for yourself.

For almost everything you need to know, go to www.burningman.com.

Since the early 1980s, the US Navy's acrobatic Blue Angels have rattled nerves and torn up the skies over San Francisco on Columbus Day weekend. The fleet sails into San Francisco Bay on Saturday morning; a spectacular air show and free battleship tours follow. A noisy couple of days.

Halloween San Francisco

Market Street, from 15th to Castro Streets; Castro Street, from Market to 19th Streets, Castro. Metro K, L, M to Castro/streetcar F/bus 24, 33, 35, 37. **Date** 31 Oct. **Map** p317 H10.

City Hall has effectively shut down the riotous festivities that used to take in the Castro over Halloween, but you'll still find a healthy helping of drag queens, pagans, and Sarah Palin lookalikes strutting their stuff in the neighborhood. Always entertaining.

Día de los Muertos

24th & Bryant Streets, Mission (826 8009, www.dayofthedeadsf.org). Bus 27, 33, 48. **Date** Nov 2. **Map** p319 M12.

Marchers gather at 24th and Bryant Streets to celebrate the Mexican Day of the Dead. After a traditional blessing, the music starts and the procession begins: Aztec dancers, children in papier-mâché skeleton masks and women clutching bouquets of dead flowers. Things wind up in Garfield Square, where people leave candles at a huge community altar. Dress code: dark but showy. If you really want to blend in, paint your face a ghoulish white and bring a noise-maker.

Holiday Lighting Festivities

Union Square, between Geary, Powell, Post & Stockton Streets, Downtown; Ghirardelli Square, 900 North Point Street, at Polk Street, Fisherman's Wharf (http://gosanfrancisco.about.com). **Date** late Nov. **Map** p315 M5; p314 K2.

The lights go on all over town as the holidays approach, including at the above locations. At Union Square, a 67ft (20m) living white-fir Christmas tree is decorated with 2,000 lights, 400 ornaments and 500 bows. A 22ft wooden menorah is also lit as part of Hanukkah celebrations.

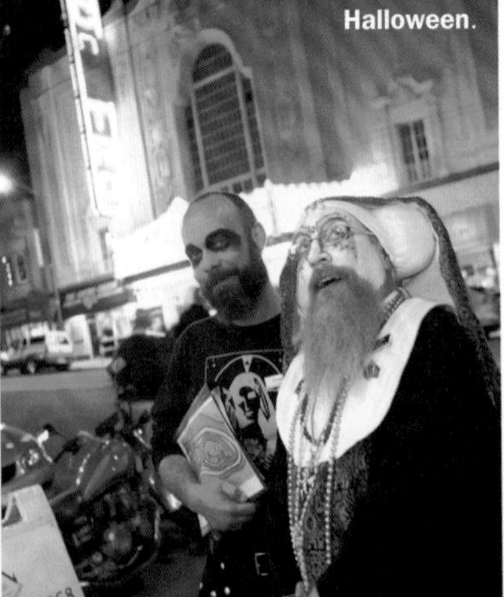
Halloween.

WINTER

New Year's Eve

Around the city. **Date** Dec 31.

For many years, San Franciscans have been gathering at Union Square or Ocean Beach to ring in the New Year. In recent years, the city fathers have sponsored free midnight fireworks along the Embarcadero, usually preceded by a cavalcade of bands performing in tents.

Martin Luther King Jr Birthday Celebration

1-510 268 3777, www.norcalmlk.org.
Date Mon after Jan 15. **Map** p315 N6.

The parade celebrating Martin Luther King's birthday started off at 4th Street and Townsend Avenue, and ended with a rally at the Yerba Buena Center for the Arts in 2011. Check the website for the route for other years.

Tet Festival

Around Civic Center & the Tenderloin (885 2743, www.vietccsf.org). **Date** Jan-Feb.

San Francisco has a large population of Vietnamese-Americans who, along with Cambodian, Latino and African-American families, transform the city center into a multicultural carnival.

San Francisco Tribal, Folk & Textile Arts Show

Fort Mason Center, Marina Boulevard, at Laguna Street, Marina (1-310 455 2886, www.caskeylees.com/SF_Tribal/SF_Tribal). Bus 22, 28. **Date** early Feb. **Map** p314 H2.

Part-show, part-sale: upwards of 100 folk and ethnic-art dealers sell all manner of pottery, baskets, textiles and jewelry.

► *For more on Fort Mason, the site of various theaters, small museums, and festivals, see p101.*

Chinese New Year

Market Street, at 2nd Street, & around Chinatown (982 3071, www.chineseparade.com). Metro or Bart to Montgomery/bus Market Street routes. **Date** Feb. **Map** p311 H3.

The start of the Chinese New Year offers the city's best parade that doesn't involve public nudity. The Miss Chinatown USA pageant, drumming, martial arts competitions, mountains of food on every street corner, firework displays and a huge procession of dancing dragons, acrobats and stilt-walkers are highlights of the party turns the city jubilant and upside down. It's also the occasion of the enormously popular annual Treasure Hunt (www.sftreasurehunts.com), which gets nearly 1,600 people scurrying round Chinatown.

Children

There are plenty of thrills in them there hills.

Having a *tête-à-tête* with belching sea lions, watching whales spout off the coast, running wild in Golden Gate Park, driving down crazy, twisting Lombard Street – the City by the Bay is like a 49-square-mile amusement park. Luckily, not only are there are enough attractions to keep children of all ages amused for weeks, but many of them will appeal to parents, too.

Details of most special events and festivals can be found in the Sunday pink section of the *San Francisco Chronicle* (www.sfgate.com) or in *SF Weekly* (www.sfweekly.com). If you're itching to escape the city, hire a car or hop on a BART train and find a whole new range of activities and attractions over in the East Bay (*see p105-09*), the best of which we also list in this chapter.

SAN FRANCISCO ATTRACTIONS & MUSEUMS

In addition to the places reviewed below, San Francisco's gorgeous **Main Library** (100 Larkin Street, between Grove & Hyde Streets) has a Children's Center, which includes a storytelling room, a creative area for crafts and performances, and even a teenagers' drop-in section. If you're stuck for something to do, it's always worth contacting one of the 30 local libraries to see what events are being put on that week; full contact details can be found at www.sfpl.org. San Francisco museums of equal interest to kids and grown-ups include the **Cable Car Museum** (*see p62*) and the ships at Maritime National Historical Park at Fisherman's Wharf.

Aquarium of the Bay

Pier 39, Embarcadero at Beach Street, Fisherman's Wharf (1-888 732 3483, www.aquariumofthebay.com). Metro F to Pier 39/bus 39, 47/cable car Powell-Mason. **Open** *May-Sept* 9am-8pm daily. *Oct-Apr* 10am-6pm Mon-Thur; 10am-7pm Fri-Sun. **Admission** $16.95; $8 3-11s & seniors; free under-3s; $39.95 family. **Credit** AmEx, Disc, MC, V. **Map** p314 L1.

Clear, acrylic underwater tunnels give visitors a diver's-eye view of the Bay, while moving walkways take you through 300ft (91m) of water, past more than 23,000 aquatic creatures. Upstairs, there are several touch tidepools with urchins and bat rays. If you've got time, combine your visit with an island hop or Bay cruise. Blue & Gold Fleet (705 5555, www.blueandgoldfleet.com) offers hour-long Bay cruises, as well as trips to Angel Island, departing from Pier 39. Alcatraz Island Cruises (981 7625, www.alcatrazcruises.com) does two-and-a-half-hour and half-day tours of Alcatraz and Angel Islands, departing from nearby Pier 33; for details, *see p73.*

★ California Academy of Sciences

55 Concourse Drive, Golden Gate Park (379 8000, www.calacademy.org). Bus 5, 16AX, 16BX, 21, 44, or 71. **Open** 9.30am-5pm Mon-Sat; 11am-5pm Sun. **Admission** $29.95 adults; $24.95 seniors, 12-17s; $19.95 4-11s; free under-4s. Free to all 3rd Wed each mth. **Credit** AmEx, MC, V. **Map** p316 C9.

The opening of the new Academy in 2008, the world's 'greenest' museum, has put San Francisco firmly on the science museum map – the only such institution to combine an aquarium, planetarium, natural history museum, and scientific research program under one roof. The complex is a sight to behold, anchored by a four-story living rainforest dome that's home to flitting butterflies and birds, and a 'living roof' that features some 1.7 million native plant species. Interspersed between is the Steinhart Aquarium, with the world's deepest living coral reef display; an Amazonian 'flooded forest' viewed via an acrylic tunnel; the all-digital Morrison Planetarium; a live penguin habitat; an African Hall with lifesize dioramas of lions and gazelles, and an alligator swamp. As opposed to most museum fare, the Academy's dining options are also first-rate: the Academy Cafe offers a half-dozen organic, sustainable ethnic food stations; the Moss Room is a proper, fancy sit-down restaurant with a dripping moss wall.

Children's Creativity Museum (Zeum)

221 4th Street, at Howard Street in Yerba Buena Gardens, SoMa (777 2800, www.zeum.org). BART or Metro to Powell/bus 12, 14, 30, 45, 91 & Market Street routes. **Open** 11am-5pm Wed-Sun. **Admission** $10; $8 discounts. **Credit** AmEx, Disc, MC, V. **Map** p315 N6.

As this guide went to press, this high-tech museum was poised to be renamed and recast with a local focus and a permanent exhibit featuring holograms of city landmarks, and activities that include make-your-own smart phone walking tours. In the same complex, you'll also find a bowling alley, a great children's playground, an ice rink, a garden and a vintage carousel.

Exploratorium

3601 Lyon Street, at Marina Boulevard, Marina (563 7337, www.exploratorium.edu). Bus 28, 30, 76. **Open** 10am-5pm Tue-Sun. **Admission** $15; $10-$12 discounts; free 1st Wed of mth. **Credit** AmEx, Disc, MC, V. **Map** p313 E2.

Housed in the historic Palace of Fine Arts, the Exploratorium has over 600 interactive exhibits about science, art and human perception. Highlights include the Tactile Dome, a geodesic hemisphere of total blackness in which you try to identify various objects – book in advance (561 0362, $20), and the giant spirograph machine, where you can make enormous spiral drawings with a pen that hangs from a pendulum. *Photo p210.*

Jeremiah O'Brien Liberty Ship

Pier 45, Embarcadero, at Taylor Street, Fisherman's Wharf (544 0100, www.ssjeremiahobrien.org). Metro to Fisherman's Wharf/bus 39, 47/cable car Powell-Mason. **Open** 10am-4pm daily. **Admission** $10; $5 discounts; $4 6-14s; free under-6s; $25 family. **Credit** MC, V. **Map** p314 K1.

There's plenty for history buffs big and small to explore aboard the *Jeremiah O'Brien*, a veteran of D-Day and the only original ship to sail under its own steam to the 50th anniversary of the Allied invasion at Normandy. From the faithfully restored engine room to the officers' bunk rooms, it's a fascinating bit of World War II arcana. At nearby Hyde Street Pier, you'll also find a flotilla of turn-of-the-19th-century ships, including the three-mast, square-rigged *Balclutha*.

► *For more about Hyde Street Pier and the Balclutha, see p73.*

FREE Randall Museum

199 Museum Street, off Roosevelt Way, Buena Vista (554 9600, www.randallmuseum.org). Bus 24, 37. **Open** 10am-5pm Tue-Sat. **Admission** free.

This small museum offers panoramic views of the city and hands-on fun for pre-teens, including an exhibit where they can create their own earthquake. Otherwise, visit the animal corral or drop in for Saturday arts-and-crafts classes.

San Francisco Zoo

Sloat Boulevard, at 47th Avenue, Sunset (753 7080, www.sfzoo.org). Metro to SF Zoo/bus 18, 23. **Open** *Memorial Day-Labor Day* Main zoo 10am-5pm daily. Children's zoo 10am-4pm daily. *Labor Day-Memorial Day* 11am-4pm daily. **Admission** $15; discounts $9, 12. **Credit** AmEx, Disc, MC, V.

The three-acre African Savanna, Grizzly Gulch, and the expansive Lemur Forest are highlights of the zoo, where more than 1,000 species of mammals and birds make their home. Combine your visit with a walk along Ocean Beach and maybe lunch at the Beach Chalet or Louis' Diner. You can look out for whales in January and February.

★ Walt Disney Family Museum

Presidio Main Post, 104 Montgomery Street at Sheridan Avenue (345 6800, www.waltdisney.org). Bus 28 or 43. **Open** 10am-6pm Mon, Wed-Sun. **Admission** $20 adults; $12-$15 reductions; free under-6s (with adult admission). **Map** p312 D3.

Opened in 2009 by a foundation headed by Walt Disney's oldest daughter, Diane, the museum is not geared full-throttle to kids, but still offers enough entertaining fare – including classic cartoons and listening stations – to ensure that young 'uns won't get bored. Housed in repurposed brick army barracks, its galleries take a chronological look at Walt's life and work, from his early cartoons to his revolutionary innovations in dimensional animation and sound. Don't miss the gallery where children get to add sound effects to Disney's classic *Steamboat Willie*.

PARKS & BEACHES

There are many child-friendly attractions near **Fisherman's Wharf** (*see p70-73*). The best are the historic ships at Hyde Street Pier and, at Pier 45, the wonderful **Musée Mécanique**, the submarine *USS Pampanito* and the *Jeremiah O'Brien*. There's a pack of rather boisterous sea lions in permanent residence on the docks at Pier 39, where you'll also find a carousel, a games arcade and street performers. The wharf is also the departure point for trips to **Angel Island** and **Alcatraz Island**. Organized outings from here include the excellent Fire Engine Tour (333 7077, www.fireenginetours.com).

Golden Gate Park attracts flocks of families at weekends, especially Sundays, when the main drive is closed to cars. Kids will want to head straight for Stow Lake, where they can

Story Time with a Twist

Once upon a time in San Francisco.

California Academy of Sciences.

While much of the lure of San Francisco appears to be geared toward adult indulgences, San Francisco is actually a kid-friendly town, too. Granted, recent census data revealed there were more dogs than children in the city, but dogs don't enjoy a good story – that's where kids have the upper hand. Luckily, San Francisco is a town known for its storytellers and if your tyke can't take another bridge or museum, settle in for a story session at one of these great venues:

Every Sunday at 1pm staff at the **Asian Art Museum** (*see p56*) lead a story time tailored to the contents of its galleries – Indian myths to Chinese folktales.

As if the **California Academy of Sciences** (*see p207*) wasn't enough of a children's wonderland, the museum has story time on Thursdays and Saturdays at 11am featuring tales about animals, usually accompanied by an actual critter that kids can touch when the story's over.

Just across the Music Concourse from the Academy of Sciences, the **De Young Museum** (*see p207*) offers a range of fun and educational activities for children, including stories and free classes on Saturdays taught by 'artist-teachers'.

Paxton Gate's Curiosities for Kids (766 Valencia Street, between 18th & 19th Streets, Mission, 252 9990, www.paxtongate.com), features a trove of toys – mostly handmade or non-plastic, and hosts a story time every Thursday from 11am until noon. The shop is just down the street from Paxton's main store (*see p196*), which offers such kid-appealing items as giant framed scarab beetles and taxidermied mice.

In addition to the wide range of classes, workshops, and speakers offered at **826 Valencia** (*see p211*), this young people's writing center is also home to San Francisco's only independent pirate supply store. Sort through mysterious drawers and bins containing baubles, flags, eye patches, glass eyes, and assorted ephemera; pull a trap-door lever to drop a chest full of scarves on your unsuspecting mom.

Last but certainly not least, branches of **San Francisco Public Library** (557 4400, www.sfpl.org) host their own story times, so one is never far away. Check online or call for the most current schedule.

hike out to Strawberry Hill or rent bicycles, paddle- and rowboats. Visit Spreckels Lake to marvel at the model boats (at Kennedy Drive & 35th Avenue), then wander down to the buffalo paddock to see the small herd of bison that have been residents in the park since 1892.

The younger set will enjoy the Koret Children's Quarter playground, built in 1887 as America's first municipal playground, featuring a huge climbing net, old-school cement slides, and the nearby historic Herschell-Spillman Carousel. For more on Golden Gate Park, *see p92-93*.

For a walk on the wilder side, head over to Ocean Beach (*see p102* **Life's a Beach**).

OTHER BAY AREA ATTRACTIONS & MUSEUMS

In addition to the places featured below, several other East Bay attractions are great for kids. The **Chabot Space & Science Museum** (*see p108*) in Oakland is possibly the next best thing to space travel; Berkeley's **Lawrence Hall of Science** (*see p110*) is also terrific

Exploratorium. *See p208.*

and very hands-on. **Oakland Zoo** (*see p108*) is well worth a visit. And if you're heading south, don't miss the world-renowned **Monterey Bay Aquarium** (*see p275*).

Bay Area Discovery Museum

East Fort Baker, 557 McReynolds Road, Sausalito (339 3900, www.baykidsmuseum.org). Blue & Gold Fleet ferry from Pier 41, or Golden Gate ferry from Ferry Building. **Open** 9am-4pm Tue-Fri; 10am-5pm Sat, Sun. **Admission** $8.50 adults; $7.50 children; free under-1s. Free 2nd Sat of mth after 1pm. **No credit cards**.

This hands-on museum, located just below the north ramp of the Golden Gate Bridge and boasting spectacular skyline views, offers a load of hands-on activities for kids of ten and under. There's Lookout Cove, an expansive outdoor area with a sea cave, climbable shipwreck and miniature Golden Gate Bridge. Discovery Bay features hands-on rotating exhibits – Sesame Street to space travel. Tot Spot gives toddlers their own indoor/outdoor nirvana, with a plastic trout-packed waterway, climbing structures and animal costumes.

FREE Marine Mammal Center

2000 Bunker Road, Fort Chronkhite, Sausalito (289 7325, www.tmmc.org). Visitor center 1049 Fort Cronkhite. Blue & Gold Fleet ferry from Pier 41, or Golden Gate ferry from Ferry Building. **Open** 10am-4pm daily. **Admission** free.

Visit the sea lions and sea otters at this recently remodeled non-profit center. The center rescues sick or stranded animals, nurtures them back to health and returns them to the Pacific. Spring is pupping season, and also the period when you can see most animals. There are self-guided audio tours, and docent-led tours are available with reservations.

Pier 39.

SHOPS & ENTERTAINMENT

FREE 826 Valencia

826 Valencia Street, between 19th & 20th Streets, Mission (642 5905, www.826valencia.org). BART 24th Street/bus 14, 26, 48, 49, 67. **Open** *Drop-in tutoring* 2.30-5.30pm Mon-Thur, Sun. *Pirate store* noon-6pm daily. **Admission** free. **Map** p318 K11.

Local literary lion Dave Eggers opened this non-profit kids' writing center in 2002, and it's become an essential destination for those traveling with young aspiring scribes. In addition to offering workshops and free drop-in tutoring for children aged eight to 18, 826 is the Bay Area's only independent pirate supply store.

FREE Metreon

4th Street, at Mission Street, SoMa (369 6000, www.metreon.com). BART or Metro to Powell/bus 12, 14, 30, 45, 91 & Market Street routes. **Open** 10.30am-8.30pm Mon-Thur, Sun; 10.30am-9.30pm Fri, Sat. **Map** p315 N6.

This mixed bag of shopping and entertainment appeals mostly to pre-teens and teens. There's the Games Workshop, a high-tech arcade (complete with virtual bowling), and a 15-screen Loews movie complex with an IMAX theater.

FREE Pier 39

Beach Street & the Embarcadero, Fisherman's Wharf (705 5500, www.pier39.com). Metro to Pier 39/bus 39, 47/cable car Powell-Mason. **Open** *Jan-mid Feb* 10am-7pm Mon-Thur, Sun; 10am-9pm Fri, Sat. *Mid Feb-mid Apr, Nov-Jan* 10am-8pm Mon-Thur, Sun; 10am-9pm Fri, Sat. *Mid Apr-Nov* 10am-9pm Mon-Thur, Sun; 10am-10pm Fri, Sat. **Map** p314 L1.

Pier 39 is a bustling tourist trap with mediocre chain restaurants. However, it's popular with younger visitors as you'll also find a potpourri of fairly decent street performers, a games arcade, a bungie jump, a carousel and kayak rentals. If you can handle the schlock, you might enjoy the beautiful views and playful (or bickering) sea lions.

Film

San Francisco: dramatic backdrop and creative hothouse.

With its distinctive neighborhoods, impossibly steep streets and picture-postcard backdrop, San Francisco has long attracted film directors. But the city's long-standing love affair with the movies goes far beyond its reputation as one of the world's finest locations. Its citizens' passion for cinema and its fertile creative environment have combined to foster everything from the digital-effects revolution at George Lucas's Industrial Light & Magic and Pixar Studios to the birth of the Asian-American and gay and lesbian film movements in the Bay Area.

INFORMATION AND TICKETS

For local listings, check the main print media outlets: the *Chronicle*, *SF Weekly* and the *Bay Guardian* all carry film listings, and the *Chronicle*'s website, www.sfgate.com, lists all local films online. Showtimes, locations and tickets are also available by phone from Fandango (1-800 326 3264, www.fandango.com), but there's a surcharge per ticket.

MAINSTREAM CINEMAS

As elsewhere, the steady decline of San Francisco's movie palaces was hastened by the rise of the massive modern multiplexes. One notable exception is the **Sundance Kabuki** (1881 Post Street, at Fillmore Street, 929 4650, www.sundancecinemas.com) in Japantown. Run by Robert Redford's Sundance Cinemas, the complex contains cafés, a full bar and the ability to enjoy beer, wine and cocktails during certain screenings. It also serves as the main venue for the San Francisco International Film Festival (*see p214* **Festivals**). The 14-screen **AMC 1000 Van Ness** (1000 Van Ness Avenue, at O'Farrell Street, 1-800 231 3307, www.amctheaters.com) on the edge of the Tenderloin, SoMa's 15-screen **AMC Metreon** (4th Street, at Mission Street, 369 6201, www.metreon.com) and the nine-screen **Century San Francisco Centre** (835 Market Street, between 4th & 5th Streets, 538 8422, www.cinemark.com) have all the ambience and individuality of an airport lobby. Still, the screens are state of the art, the seats are very comfortable and the sound systems are beyond reproach.

Other movie houses that lie within easy reach of the center of town include the Marina's funky **Presidio** (2340 Chestnut Street, between Scott & Divisadero Streets, 776 2388), the small **Opera Plaza Cinema** (601 Van Ness Avenue, at Golden Gate Avenue, 267 4893) and the **Embarcadero Cinema** (Building 1, Embarcadero Center, Battery Street, between Sacramento & Clay Streets, 352 0835).

The screening of movies isn't just limited to conventional cinemas, however. There's a lot more than just popcorn served at **Foreign Cinema** restaurant (*see p151*), which features films screened in an outdoor courtyard. Or you can catch a flick while working up a sweat on the treadmill at the **Alhambra Crunch** gym (2330 Polk Street, between Green & Union Streets, Russian Hill, 292 5444, www.crunch.com). Housed in what was once an art deco picture palace, films play on a big screen in the main exercise area. You can even get a cinematic fix while washing your clothes: gaze upon stills of screen idols during the rinse cycle at **Star Wash** (*see p190*).

REPERTORY CINEMAS

San Francisco's neighborhood theaters are a big draw. Built mostly between 1910 and 1930, the city's single-screen cinemas flourished through World War II, but many have been lost in recent years to land developers and multi-screen complexes. The **San Francisco Cinematheque** (*see p213*) is renowned for putting on avant-garde screenings at a variety of other venues. A repertory film scene also thrives in the East Bay.

★ Castro Theatre

429 Castro Street, at Market Street, Castro (621 6120, www.thecastrotheatre.com). Metro to Castro/streetcar F/bus 24, 33, 35, 37. **Tickets** $10; $7.50 reductions. **No credit cards**. **Map** p317 H10.

One of San Francisco's finest and best-loved repertory cinemas, this glorious movie palace was built in 1922 by famed Deco architect Timothy Pflueger. It became a registered landmark 55 years later, affording it proper protection. These days it's a dream space of classical murals and rare old film posters, ceilings that shimmer with gold, and films introduced to the strains of a Mighty Wurlitzer organ. *Photo p214.*

▶ *For special-event gay and camp screenings at the Castro, see p232.*

★ Red Vic

1727 Haight Street, at Cole Street, Haight-Ashbury (668 3994, www.redvicmoviehouse.com). Bus 6, 7, 33, 43, 66, 71. **Tickets** $9; $6-$7 reductions. **No credit cards**. **Map** p317 E9.

A worker-owned co-op, the Red Vic's old sofas, pop-corn in wooden bowls with butter and brewer's yeast, films ranging from revivals to the best current movies make you feel right at home. Tickets on Tuesday nights and for matinées are $7, a 'punch card' buys four pairs of tickets and costs $30.

Roxie New College Film Center & Little Roxie

3117 16th Street, between Valencia & Guerrero Streets, Mission (863 1087, www.roxie.com). BART 16th Street/bus 14, 22, 26, 33, 49, 53. **Tickets** $9.75; $5-$6 reductions. **No credit cards**. **Map** p318 J10.

A theater with non-profit status, the Roxie's range is amazing: world premières of cutting-edge documentaries, classic *films noir* and '60s horror flicks are only a taste of the adventurous programming. Next door, Little Roxie has a great projection set-up, a terrific sound system, and a program of stuff too weird even for its wacky parent. The gritty atmosphere just adds to the funkiness. Tickets are just $5 on Mondays, and cost $6 for the first show on Saturday or Sunday.

OFF-MAINSTREAM CINEMAS

Other venues to look out for include the 278-seat cinema in **SFMOMA** (*see p60*) and the 96-seat screening room in the **Yerba Buena Center for the Arts** (*see p61*), where the programs are often themed to dovetail with exhibitions. However, it's the **San Francisco Cinematheque** (*see below*) that remains the major driving force for innovative film in the city.

Artists' Television Access

992 Valencia Street, at 21st Street, Mission (824 3890, www.atasite.org). BART 24th Street Mission/Metro to Church & 18th Street/bus 14, 26, 48, 49, 67. **Tickets** $5-$20. **No credit cards**. **Map** p318 K11.

Experimental and unusual programming, including open screenings, usually Thursday to Sunday.

Ninth Street Independent Film Center

145 Ninth Street, between Mission & Howard Streets, SoMa (625 6100/www.ninthstreet.org). Bus 14, 19. **Tickets** vary. **No credit cards**. **Map** p318 L8.

Look out for screenings from San Francisco Cinematheque (*see below*), city-wide filmmakers group the Film Arts Foundation, LGBT film group Frameline, the Center for Asian American Media, and more at this state-of-the-art facility.

★ San Francisco Cinematheque

Various venues (522 1990, www.sfcinematheque.org). **Tickets** $7-$10. **Credit** varies.

Foreign Cinema.

Film Festivals

The city celebrates cinema throughout the year.

The Bay Area's love affair with film is amply demonstrated by the volume and variety of its film festivals, many of which are both the longest-running and largest of their kind in the nation – or the world. Works by local movie-makers mingle with international productions, and the quality varies from high to horrific. Below are some of the major festivals, but several smaller festivals, such as the Anti-Corporate Film Festival (www.countercorp.org), run throughout the year. For a complete listing, visit the website of the San Francisco Film Commission (www.filmsf.org).

Castro Theatre. *See p213.*

Berlin & Beyond
263 8760, www.goethe.de/ins/us/saf/prj/bby/enindex.htm. **Venues** Castro Theater. **Date** late Oct.
Presented by the Goethe-Institut San Francisco, B&B focuses on the films of Germany, Austria and Switzerland. Celebrating its 15th anniversary in 2010, it recently partnered with German Currents in Los Angeles to create a united West Coast German Film Event, sharing programming and personnel.

Film Arts Festival of Independent Cinema
552 8760, www.filmarts.org. **Venues** various theaters. **Date** early Nov.
A real snapshot of NorCal independents. Programming for the six-day fest is drawn from Bay Area filmmakers, featuring documentary, experimental and traditional narrative pieces in formats that range from Super-8 shorts to high-end DV.

IndieFest
820 3907, www.sfindie.com. **Venues** various theaters. **Date** Early-mid Feb.
The 2011 event was the 13th IndieFest. The first showed 85 films over 14 days and prompted organizer Jeff Ross to create three more festivals: **Another Hole in the Head** highlighting the horror genre, **DocFest** in fall, and the **Winter Music Festival**. IndieFest now runs concurrently with the Winter Music Festival, and with more music-themed films added to the schedule, there's always a lively crowd for screenings.

Jewish Film Festival
621 0556, www.sfjff.org. **Venues** various theaters. **Date** late July-early Aug.
The world's largest Jewish film festival, the SFJFF spends two weeks presenting contemporary (and some archival) films on Jewish culture.

MadCat Women's International Film Festival
436 9523, www.madcatfilmfestival.org. **Venues** various theaters. **Date** mid Sept & early Oct.
This radical, alternative women's film festival takes place over three weeks, squeezing in pioneering films that range from earnest feminist polemics to raunchy sexploitation.

Mill Valley Film Festival
383 5256, www.mvff.org. Venues Cine Arts Sequoia, Mill Valley; Rafael Film Center, San Rafael. **Date** early Oct.
One of California's most influential film events, the MVFF offers 11 days of films and sells over 40,000 tickets. Galas, tributes to actors and filmmakers, panels,

workshops and seminars make the 33 year-old MVFF the real deal – and the top choice in the Bay Area for those hoping to get a glimpse of celebrities.

Noir City
www.noircity.com. **Venues** Palace of Fine Arts; Balboa Theatre. **Date** Jan.
With 24 films shown over ten days, the Noir City festival now packs the lavish, historic Castro Theatre with noir devotees from around the world. Presented by the Film Noir Foundation (www.filmnoir foundation.org), which counts author James Ellroy among its board members, Noir City is the highlight of the foundation's public exhibitions. Noir fans take note: FNF also restores original prints of classics, rarities and lost noir films and reissues numerous titles on DVD.

Ocean Film Festival
561 6251, http://oceanfilmfest.org. **Venues** Theater 39. **Date** mid March.
The Ocean Film Festival was launched in 2004 'to increase public understanding of the environmental, social and cultural importance of marine ecosystems and foster a spirit of ocean stewardship'. It is one of only two such festivals in the world and screens more than 40 films, ranging from wildlife and adventure films to conservation documentaries.

Oakland Underground Film Festival
www.oakruff.org. **Venues** Grand Lake Theater; Pavilion Theater, Jack London Square; various others. **Date** late Sept.
Just two years old, the OUFF has begun to make a name for itself with carefully selected films emphasizing the work of local filmmakers with themes of social justice, urban life, and the environment. Venues have included the classic Grand Lake Theater and a local brewery; events include screenings, performances and art installations.

San Francisco International Asian American Film Festival
863 0814, www.festival.asianamerican media.org. **Venues** various theaters. **Date** mid Mar.
The largest and longest-running Asian-American filmmaking showcase in the US, the SFIAAFF presents over 120 works at venues throughout the Bay Area. A production of the Center for Asian American Media (CAMM), the festival has become the premiere event for Asian films in America and a significant launching pad for Asian American filmmakers.

San Francisco International Film Festival
561 5000, www.sfiff.org. **Venues** various theaters. **Date** mid Apr-early May.
North America's longest-running film festival (it turned 50 in 2007), and one of its best. Held over two weeks, the festival screens more than 150 films and events and sells over 80,000 tickets. As *Variety* editor Alex Romanelli put it, 'Few festivals are more suited to their city than the International. It's clearly a festival programmed by those who love film for people who love film.' Amen to that.

San Francisco International Lesbian & Gay Film Festival
703 8650, www.frameline.org. **Venues** various theaters. **Date** late June.
An integral part of the month-long Gay Pride festivities, the SFILGFF seriously parties and parties seriously: both a potent political statement and an unbridled celebration, with features, shorts, docs and experimental works.

San Francisco Silent Film Festival
777 4908, www.silentfilm.org. **Venue** Castro Theatre, Castro. **Date** early-mid July.
Screenings at this three-day event have musical accompaniment by a pianist, a Wurlitzer organist, or anything from Indian duos to avant-garde chamber groups.

Spike & Mike's Festival of Animation
1-858 459 8707, www.spikeandmike.com. **Venues** Victoria Theatre, Mission. **Date** late Feb-Apr.
Mainstream animators such as Nick Park (*Wallace & Gromit*), Pixar's John Lasseter (*Toy Story*, *Cars*), and Tim Burton, have shown early works at Spike & Mike's cult festival, but its Sick and Twisted segment has also launched the likes of Mike Judge (*Beavis and Butt-head*), Matt Stone and Trey Parker (*South Park*), Pete Docter (*Up*; *Monsters, Inc.*) and many, many more.

For the stuff you simply can't see anywhere else, be it documentary, feature film, animation or whatever, this is the name to look for. The Cinematheque offers 50 events a year from October to December and February to June at venues including the Yerba Buena Center (*see p61*), the Roxie New College Film Center (*see p213*) and the Ninth Street Independent Film Center (*see p213*).

EAST BAY CINEMAS

In addition to the venues listed, the historic, lavishly restored art deco gem, the **Paramount Theatre** (2025 Broadway, at 20th Street, Oakland, 1-510 465 6400, www.paramount theatre.com), shows classic movies preceded by music from its massive Mighty Wurlitzer organ.

★ Grand Lake Theater

3200 Grand Avenue, Oakland (1-510 452 3556, www.renaissancerialto.com). AC Transit NL/ BART MacArthur Station, then AC Transit bus 57/19th Street Station then AC Transit bus 12. **Credit** MC, V.

The Grand Lake was originally constructed in 1926, but lost its mojo in recent decades. A loving restoration has restored it to its former glory, complete with a Wurlitzer organ played on select nights. The owner, noted leftist curmudgeon Allen Michaan, also uses the marquee as a low-tech Twitter feed to vent his political convictions. One large main theater and two elegant small theaters, with Egyptian and Moorish motifs, show everything from first-run blockbusters to film festivals and live opera and ballet simulcast from around the globe.

★ Pacific Film Archive

2575 Bancroft Way, between Telegraph Avenue & Bowditch Street, Berkeley (1-510 642 1124, www.bampfa.berkeley.edu). BART Downtown Berkeley, then AC Transit bus 7, 51. **Tickets** $9.50; $5.50-$6.50 reductions. **Credit** AmEx, DC, MC, V.

The PFA has a collection of more than 7,000 titles, including Soviet, US avant-garde and Japanese cinema. Some 650 of them are screened annually to a clued-up audience.

FOREIGN-LANGUAGE FILMS

Venues offering screenings of European films in their original languages include the **Alliance Française** (1345 Bush Street, between Polk & Larkin Streets, 775 7755, www.afsf.com) in Polk Gulch; the **Goethe Institut** (530 Bush Street, between Grant Avenue & Stockton Street, 263 8760, www.goethe.de/ins/us), which sponsors the annual Berlin & Beyond Festival (*see p214* **Film Festivals**; and the **Instituto Italiano di Cultura** (814 Montgomery Street, between Pacific Avenue & Jackson Streets, 788 7142, www.iicsanfrancisco.esteri.it) in the Jackson Square district.

Films alfresco

Where to find that special experience of cinema in the open air.

San Francisco's outdoor film fests offer a rare chance to grab a picnic basket, a blanket, and a bottle of wine and enjoy film in the great (sometimes chilly) outdoors.

The largest is **Film Night in the Park** (453 4333, www.filmnight.org), which features classics and family-friendly fare from *Casablanca* to *Cars* on Friday and Saturday evenings from June to October, with screenings taking place in Marin County's public parks, Downtown's Union Square, the Mission's Dolores Park and North Beach's Washington Square Park throughout the summer and early autumn.

The neighbourhood-focused **Bernal Heights Outdoor Cinema** (641 8417, www.bhoutdoorcine.org) showcases the work of indie filmmakers living in and around this most bohemian of locales, with featured screenings ranging from arty animated shorts to cutting-edge documentaries. Films, most of them no more than half an hour long, are shown for free in local parks throughout September, with various meet-the-filmmaker events after the show.

More subversive fare is on offer at the **Overcooked Cinema/Zeitgeist International Film Festival** (www.overcookedcinema.com, $5), featuring short films and videos (9pm, all under 15 minutes) every second Monday in June, July and August, with screenings taking place at beloved biker bar Zeitgeist (199 Valencia Street, at Duboce Avenue, Mission, 255 7505), which has a huge outdoor patio. The annual, free **Film in the Fog Night**, presented by the San Francisco Film Society (www.sffs.org) in early October, screens classic sci-fi flicks in the Presidio. Across the Bay, **Old Oakland Outdoor Cinema** (1-510 238 4734, www.film oakland.com) screens four mainstream classics between July and October on a closed-off block of 9th Street between Broadway and Washington (chairs provided).

Galleries

Heart and soul drive the local art scene.

Thanks to its general climate of open-mindedness and innovation, all forms of art, high and low, have always found a welcome home in San Francisco. The city of San Francisco actually sponsors a significant amount of art, both as a way of supporting local artists and of beautifying the urban landscape. Witness the Art in Storefronts initiative, a project of the San Francisco Arts Commission (www.sfartscommission.org) that places art installations in vacant storefronts.

The best way to tour the gallery scene is by neighborhood. A number of downtown galleries are grouped in single buildings, so you can hit many venues in one go. Others coordinate their openings, with cheap wine flowing on either the first Thursday or last Saturday of each month.

DOWNTOWN

Most of San Francisco's upscale commercial galleries can be found in the Union Square district. Two buildings, just doors apart on Geary Street, house a few dozen galleries between them, and provide a quick way to survey the scene.

49 Geary Street

49 Geary Street, between Kearny Street & Grant Avenue, Union Square. BART & Metro to Powell/ bus 2, 3, 30, 38, 45 & Market Street routes/cable car Powell-Hyde or Powell-Mason. **Map** p315 M5.

Art Exchange *4th floor (956 5750).* **Open** 11.30am-5.30pm Tue-Sat. **No credit cards.**
The Art Exchange specializes in secondary market art, meaning that it handles the resale of artworks from private collections. The gallery is wide open, with works large and small covering every square inch of wall space. If you're looking to learn more about purchasing art as an investment, the Art Exchange's Claire Carlevaro is the person to talk to.

Fraenkel Gallery *4th floor (981 2661, www.fraenkelgallery.com).* **Open** 10.30am-5.30pm Tue-Fri; 11am-5pm Sat. **Credit** (books only) MC, V.
There is a whiff of the official about the Fraenkel, a photography gallery established in 1979. Is it the warm space, inspiring quiet contemplation, or the gallery's impressive roster of photographers (Diane Arbus, Richard Avedon, Nan Goldin, Robert Frank) that elicits such reverence? You decide.

Jack Fischer Gallery *Suite 440 (956 1178, www.jackfischergallery.com).* **Open** 11am-5.30pm Tue-Sat; also by appointment. **Credit** MC, V.
Fischer says that the work he exhibits is 'from the heart and the gut'. His tiny gallery is devoted to 'outsider' and self-taught artists, and is so intelligently curated, stuffed with passionate work full of raw energy and surprise, that one hardly notices the confines of the space itself.

★ **Mark Wolfe Contemporary Art** *Suite 202 (369 9404, www.wolfecontemporary.com).* **Open** 11am-5pm Tue-Fri; Sat by appointment. **Credit** AmEx, MC, V.
Mark Wolfe moved his former Urbis Artium Gallery here in 2005 and began pursuing a more formal direction. The large space is impressive; the art runs from high-tech and conceptual to crafty and fun.

Robert Koch Gallery *5th floor (421 0122, www.kochgallery.com).* **Open** 10.30am-5.30pm Tue-Sat. **Credit** MC, V.
Representing contemporary giants like Edward Burtynsky, Sally Mann, David Parker and Bill Owens, Robert Koch's gallery has a bit of a museum feel. Specializing in modernist and experimental photography from the early to mid-20th century, Koch's shows can feel revelatory.

★ **Stephen Wirtz Gallery** *3rd floor (433 6879, www.wirtzgallery.com).* **Open** 9.30am-5.30pm Tue-Fri; 10.30am-5.30pm Sat. **No credit cards.**

From Todd Hido's spooky suburban landscapes to Melanie Pullen's fashion victims and the Starn Twins' multimedia extravaganzas, Stephen Wirtz's exhibitions invariably prompt discussion. The large gallery boasts five distinct spaces where any number of provocative works might be on display. The gallery often launches young artists.

Toomey Tourell *Suite 417 (989 6444, www.toomey-tourell.com).* **Open** 11am-5.30pm Tue-Fri; 11am-5pm Sat. **Credit** AmEx, MC, V.
If you like your art big, shiny and a bit in your face, then stop here. Featuring the likes of map artist Matthew Picton and 'book coroner' Brian Dettmer, the gallery has a playful side beneath all the polish.

Open Studios.

77 Geary Street

77 Geary Street, between Kearny Street & Grant Avenue, Union Square. BART & Metro to Powell/bus 2, 3, 30, 38, 45 & Market Street routes/cable car Powell-Hyde or Powell-Mason. **Map** p315 M5.

Marx & Zavettero Gallery *2nd floor (627 9111, www.marxzav.com).* **Open** 10.30am-5.30pm Tue-Fri; 11am-5pm Sat. **Credit** AmEx, MC, V.
Whether it is exhibiting David Hevel's pop icon animal sculptures, Michael Arcega's conceptual constructions or Yoon Lee's fierce paintings, this gallery feels like it must have access to an extra dimension, expanding its frontiers to accommodate each new artist's vision.

Patricia Sweetow Gallery *Mezzanine (788 5126, www.patriciasweetowgallery.com).* **Open** 10.30am-5.30pm Tue-Fri; 10.30am-5pm Sat. **No credit cards**.
Sweetow recently relocated to 77 Geary, where she shows painting, photography and sculpture from both established and emerging artists. To get a feel for the gallery, check out Jamie Vasta's glitter paintings, Jonathan Burstein's collage portraits or Christian Nguyen's architectural charcoals.

Rena Bransten Gallery
2nd floor (982 3292, www.renabranstengallery.com). **Open** 10.30am-5.30pm Tue-Fri; 11am-5pm Sat. **Credit** MC, V.
In business since 1974, Rena Bransten originally focused on ceramic sculpture. Today the gallery's stable is more diverse, including sculptor Ruth Asawa, conceptual artist Vik Muniz, photographer Rebeca Bollinger, and the late ceramicist Viola Frey.

UNION SQUARE & AROUND

Dolby Chadwick

Suite 205, 210 Post Street, between Stockton Street & Grant Avenue (956 3560, www.dolbychadwickgallery.com). BART & Metro to Montgomery or Powell/bus 2, 3, 30, 38, 91 & Market Street routes/cable car Powell-Hyde or Powell-Mason. **Open** 10am-6pm Tue-Fri; 11am-5pm Sat. **Credit** MC, V. **Map** p315 M5.
Don't be intimidated by the creaky ride up in the old lift; this gallery couldn't be friendlier. Tall windows frame a view as compelling as the art.

Gallery Paule Anglim

14 Geary Street, at Market Street (433 2710, www.gallerypauleanglim.com). BART & Metro to Powell/bus 2, 3, 30, 38, 91 & Market Street routes/cable car Powell-Hyde or Powell-Mason. **Open** 10am-5.30pm Tue-Fri; 10am-5pm Sat. **No credit cards**. **Map** p315 M5.
An unimpressive façade gives no indication of the airy, light-filled interior, which hosts two shows – a major and a minor one – at any given time. Expect everything from Bay Area innovators such as David Ireland and Barry McGee to international superstars like Louise Bourgeois and Robert Bechtle.

★ John Berggruen Gallery

228 Grant Avenue, between Post & Sutter Streets (781 4629, www.berggruen.com). BART & Metro to Montgomery/bus 2, 3, 30, 38, 91 & Market Street routes/cable car Powell-Hyde or Powell-Mason. **Open** 9.30am-5.30pm Mon-Fri; 10.30am-5pm Sat. **No credit cards**. **Map** p315 M5.
Founded in the mid 1970s, Berggruen, with its smooth white walls and sleek blond floors, has played host to some of the biggest names in contemporary art, including Ellsworth Kelly, Alexander Calder, Robert Rauschenberg, Brice Marden and Frank Stella.

John Pence

750 Post Street, between Jones & Leavenworth Streets (441 1138, www.johnpence.com). Bus 2, 3, 27, 38. **Open** 10am-6pm Mon-Fri; 10am-5pm Sat. **Credit** AmEx, MC, V. **Map** p314 L5.
John Pence is the largest gallery in San Francisco, established in 1974 and offering an impressive 8,000 sq ft (750 sq m) of exhibition space. It is home to a

diverse stable of academic realists and features a rotating series of themed group exhibitions.

SOMA & SOUTH BEACH

★ 111 Minna Gallery

111 Minna Street, between 2nd & New Montgomery Streets (974 1719, www.111 minnagallery.com). BART & Metro to Montgomery/bus 2, 12, 14, 30, 91 & Market Street routes. **Open** *Gallery* noon-5pm Wed-Sat. *Bar* 5-9pm Wed-Sat. **Admission** *Events* $5-$20. **Credit** AmEx, MC, V. **Map** p315 N5.

Smartly morphing into a happening hotspot most nights, 111 Minna is a laid-back urban hangout that features great art, drinking, dancing and a monthly indie film series. The gallery is home to an impressive roster of local and international artists, with tunes spun by a peerless collection of jet-set DJs. Check the website for special late-night events.

Andrea Schwartz Gallery

525 2nd Street, between Bryant & Brannan Streets (495 2090, www.asgallery.com). Metro to 2nd & King/bus 2, 10. **Open** 9am-5pm Mon-Fri; 1-5pm Sat. **Credit** AmEx, MC, V. **Map** p315 O6.

This large space is aggressively modern, with steel girders, concrete floors and two walls of plate glass. The work is equally contemporary, featuring artists along the lines of Tracy Krumm and Seamus Conley.

Braunstein/Quay

430 Clementina Street, between 5th & 6th Streets (278 9850, www.braunsteinquay.com). Bus 12, 14, 27, 47. **Open** 11am-5.30pm Tue-Sat. **No credit cards**. **Map** p319 M7.

Founded in the early 1960s, Braunstein/Quay made its reputation promoting Bay Area talent and launching several influential artists, among them the late ceramics master Peter Voulkos. Braunstein likes to mix things up, presenting various forms of sculpture, glass, furniture and fiber in a fine-arts setting.

Catherine Clark Gallery

150 Minna Street, between 3rd & New Montgomery Streets (399 1439, www.cclark gallery.com). BART & Metro to Montgomery/ bus 2, 12, 14, 30, 91 & Market Street routes. **Open** 11am-6pm Tue-Sat. **Credit** AmEx, MC, V. **Map** p315 M5.

Clark has a keen eye for modern art with legs: many works by her stable of sculptors, painters and mixed-media artists walk straight into regional museums. She recently moved to these premises, behind SFMOMA, where she continues to provoke with a fun, slightly political bent. The gallery is one of few in town specializing in video art.

★ Crown Point Press

20 Hawthorne Street, between Howard & Folsom Streets, SoMa (974 6273, www.crownpoint.com). BART & Metro to Montgomery/bus 10, 12, 14, 30, 45, 91. **Open** 10am-6pm Tue-Sat. **Credit** MC, V. **Map** p315 N6.

Crown Point is the world's leading publisher of prints. Laura Owens and other established artists work in print studios on the premises; their works are then shown in the gallery's large, airy and inviting space.

Gallery 16

501 3rd Street, at Bryant Street (626 7495, www. gallery16.com). Metro to 2nd & King/bus 12, 30, 45, 47, 91. **Open** 10am-5pm Mon-Fri; 11am-5pm Sat. **Credit** AmEx, Disc, MC, V. **Map** p319 O7.

Gallery 16 publishes limited edition artist prints and books through its collaboration with Urban Digital Color. The gallery relocated to a huge space that features a wall of windows looking out on to 3rd Street, filling it with light.

MM Galleries

101 Townsend Street, Suite 207, at 2nd Street (543 1550, www.mmgalleries.com). Metro to 2nd & King/bus 10, 30, 45, 91. **Open** 11am-5pm Tue-Sat; also by appointment. **Credit** Disc, MC, V. **Map** p319 O7.

Marina and Kit, MM's co-owners and co-curators, may be more aptly described as co-conspirators. Seeing art as play, they bring a sense of mischief to every show. MM is a comfortable space, and each exhibition has a casual, accessible feel that belies the gallery's acumen for recognizing serious talent.

Modernism

685 Market Street, between 3rd & New Montgomery Streets (541 0461, www.modernism inc.com). BART & Metro to Montgomery/bus 2, 3, 31 & Market Street routes. **Open** 10am-5.30pm Tue-Sat. **Credit** AmEx, MC, V. **Map** p315 N5.

INSIDE TRACK CREATION THEORY

It could be said that making art is much like childbirth: it's one thing to see the end result, another thing entirely to witness the act of creation. That's the idea behind ArtSpan's **SF Open Studios** (www.artspan.org/sf-open-studios, *pictured*). The first and largest open studio program in the US, the event occurs each October and May and involves an opening exhibition followed by four successive weekends of open studio events arranged by neighborhood throughout the city. An online guide allows visitors to search by artist's name, location, medium and style. A unique chance to tear down the wall between artist and audience, it's also a great way to purchase affordable art.

Modernism grapples with the age-old conundrum of how to show fine art that attracts high prices while at the same time maintaining a hospitable atmosphere. And it loses the battle. If you're not rich and conservatively dressed, there's a good chance you won't feel comfortable. A shame, as the art is amazing.

SF Camerawork

2nd floor, 657 Mission Street, between New Montgomery & 3rd Streets (512 2020, www.sfcamerawork.org). BART & Metro to Montgomery/streetcar F/bus 10, 14, 30, 91 & Market Street routes. **Open** noon-5pm Tue-Sat. **Admission** *Suggested donation* $5; $2 reductions. **Credit** MC, V. **Map** p315 N6.

This nonprofit institution is devoted to supporting photographers. Founded in 1974, it's now in a huge space around the corner from SFMOMA. The gallery still focuses on photography but has expanded its remit to include film, video, installation art and other related media.

★ Varnish Fine Art

77 Natoma Street, between 1st & 2nd Streets (222 6131, www.varnishfineart.com). BART & Metro to Montgomery/bus 10, 12, 14, 30, 91 & Market Street routes. **Open** 11am-11pm Tue-Fri; 1-5pm Sat. **Credit** AmEx, MC, V. **Map** p315 N5.

Specializing in cast metal sculpture – and excellent wine – Varnish's core belief is that viewing art should be fun. This combination art gallery, library and wine bar is a great spot to meet for drinks before dinner and a good place to find new works by emerging artists.

NORTH BEACH

A Aversano Galleria

850 Greenwich Street, at Jansen Street (400 5072, www.aaversano.com). Metro F Line Castro Station. **Open** hours vary, phone for details. **No credit cards**. **Map** p314 L3.

This one-room gallery on a North Beach corner shows eclectic works in a variety of genres ranging from outsider and folk art to contemporary painters and photography.

THE MISSION & THE CASTRO

Adobe Books

3166 16th Street, between Guerrero & Valencia Streets (864 3936). BART to 16th Street Mission/bus 14, 22, 33, 49. **Open** 11am-10pm Mon-Thur, Sun; 11am-11pm Fri, Sat. **Credit** MC, V. **Map** p318 J10.

It may look like a used bookstore – which it is – but in the back of Adobe lies a tiny yet influential gallery run by a collective of Mission artists. Openings often feature in-store musical performances.

★ Creativity Explored

3245 16th Street, between Dolores & Guerrero Streets (863 2108, www.creativityexplored.org). BART to 16th Street Mission/Metro to Church/bus 14, 22, 33, 49. **Open** 10am-3pm Mon-Wed, Fri; 10am-7pm Thur; 1-6pm Sat. **Credit** AmEx MC, V. **Map** p318 J10.

The gallery at this nonprofit space features the art of developmentally disabled artists who create, exhibit and sell their work on the premises. Be careful with your wallet, especially at the annual Halloween show, where some of the coolest portraits and abstracts in the city can be yours for under $100.

Eleanor Harwood Gallery

1295 Alabama Street, at 25th Street (867 7770, www.eleanorharwood.com). BART 24th Street Mission/bus 9, 10, 12, 27, 33, 48. **Open** 11am-6pm Wed-Sat; also by appointment. **Credit** AmEx, Disc, MC, V. **Map** p318 L12.

The Eleanor Harwood Gallery, established in 2006 by one of the former curators at Adobe Books (*see p180*), is devoted to young locals such as James Chronister, Francesca Pastine and Jill Sylvia.

Galeria de la Raza

2857 24th Street, at Bryant Street (826 8009, www.galeriadelaraza.org). BART to 24th Street/bus 9, 27, 33, 48. **Open** 1-7pm Tue; noon-6pm Wed-Sat. **Credit** MC, V. **Map** p319 M12.

This storefront gallery has celebrated contemporary Chicano/Latino culture since 1970 with bi-monthly exhibitions and the ongoing (Re)Generation project, designed to support young Latino artists.

Lab

2948 16th Street, at Capp Street (864 8855, www.thelab.org). BART to 16th Street Mission/

INSIDE TRACK PARTY ARTY

For almost two decades, the **San Francisco Art Dealers Association** (49 Geary Street, 788 9818, www.firstthursdayart.com) has encouraged its members to host informal open house events on the first Thursday of every month from 5.30pm to 7.30pm. While not all galleries in the city participate, the majority of those around Union Square do, making for a lively scene at 49 Geary as gawkers, buyers, sellers and artists wander through enjoying snacks and wine. A great opportunity to check out both established artists and up-and-comers, First Thursdays allow casual lurkers to feel less conspicuous than during solo weekday visits when the spaces tend to seem bigger and painfully hushed.

bus 9, 12, 14, 27, 33, 48, 67. **Open** *Exhibitions* 1-6pm Thur-Sat. **Credit** MC, V. **Map** p318 K10.
Located on a seedy corner, the Lab favors political and subversive photography, paintings and multimedia works. The gallery's auctions, held several times a year, can be counted on for edgy pieces at decent prices.

Little Tree
3412 22nd Street, at Guerrero Street (643 4929, www.littletreegallery.com). BART to 24th Street Mission/Metro to Church & 24th Street/bus 48. **Open** 3-6pm Wed-Fri; noon-6pm Sat; also by appointment. **Credit** AmEx, MC, V. **Map** p318 J12.
This intimate gallery mounts gorgeous, affordable art in a laid-back yet professional setting. Featuring witty and accomplished emerging artists, Little Tree crams a great deal of fun into its small space.

★ Needles & Pens
3523 16th Street, between Guerrero & Dolores Streets (255 1534, www.needles-pens.com). BART to 16th Street Mission/Metro to Church/bus 22, 24, 33, 35, 37. **Open** noon-7pm daily. **Credit** AmEx, DC, MC, V. **Map** p318 J10.
Needles stocks a huge range of handmade gifts by local artists, including clothes, along with the latest in self-published 'zines and arty periodicals.

Receiver Gallery
1415 Valencia Street, at 25th Street (550 7287, www.receivergallery.com). BART 24th Street Mission/Metro to Church & 24th Street/bus 12, 27, 36, 48, 67. **Open** 10am-6pm Mon-Fri; also by appointment. **Credit** AmEx, Disc, MC, V. **Map** p318 K12.
Receiver is a combination interactive design studio and art gallery that also sells limited edition T-shirts. The emphasis is on graphics, cartoons and illustrations, and the roster features artists like Matt Furie, Jake Watling and Hannah Stouffer.

★ Southern Exposure
417 14th Street, at Valencia Street (863 2141, www.soex.org). BART to 16th Street Mission/ Metro to Church/bus 14, 22, 49. **Open** noon-6pm Tue-Sat. **Credit** MC, V. **Map** p318 L10.
Large and inclusive, SoEx is the best not-for-profit gallery in the city – and many a young artist has been discovered here. The group exhibitions and parties are legendary; the juried art shows draw respected curators.

THE HAIGHT & AROUND

Giant Robot
618 Shrader Street, at Haight Street (876 4773, www.giantrobot.com). Metro to Carl & Cole/bus 33, 37, 43, 66, 71. **Open** 11.30am-8pm Mon-Sat; noon-6pm Sun. **Credit** MC, V. **Map** p317 E9.
It's a quarterly 'zine inspired by anime, punk rock and kung fu. It's also a shop at the far end of Haight that sells indie comics, Japanese goods and artist-designed T-shirts, and regularly hosts small exhibitions by a local or international artist.

★ Park Life
220 Clement Street, at 3rd Avenue (386 7275, www.parklifestore.com). Bus 1, 2, 4, 33, 38. **Open** noon-8pm Mon-Thur; 11am-9pm Sat; 11am-7pm Sun. **Credit** AmEx, MC, V. **Map** p312 D6.
Park Life is a store stocking all kinds of intriguing design items, many of them handmade by locals. The schedule of monthly art exhibitions is a bonus. When sued by pop art multimillionaire Jeff Koons for selling balloon animal paperweights that looked like his balloon animal sculpture, the store's lawyer replied, 'As virtually any clown can attest, no one owns the idea of making a balloon dog, and the shape created by twisting a balloon into a dog-like form is part of the public domain.' Advantage: Park Life.

Upper Playground
220 Fillmore Street, at Haight Street (861 1960, www.fifty24sf.com). Metro to Duboce & Church/ bus 6, 22, 71. **Open** noon-7pm daily. **Credit** AmEx, Disc, MC, V. **Map** p317 H8.
The art gallery here, Fifty24SF, shares space with a clothing and record store (used soul and jazz vinyl a specialty). Monthly exhibits have a strong sense of the fantastic and a deep connection to pop culture.

HAYES VALLEY

San Francisco Arts Commission
401 Van Ness Avenue, at McAllister Street (554 6080, www.sfacgallery.org). Bus 5, 6, 19, 21, 47, 49, 71. **Open** noon-5pm Wed-Sat; sometimes open later, phone for details. **Credit** AmEx, Disc, MC, V. **Map** p318 K7.
This nonprofit space focuses on contemporary art and the Bay Area's place in that field. In addition to regular programming at the War Memorial Building, SFAC maintains Grove Street Windows (155 Grove Street), where you can watch projections and other site-specific installations, and runs the Art at City Hall program, a quarterly exhibition often curated in collaboration with local organizations.

ON THE STREET

You can find works of art all over the city without entering a gallery. San Francisco's well-established public art program is one of the most respected in the country. Additionally, locals have covered the walls of Balmy Alley (at 24th Street) and Clarion Alley (at Valencia) in the Mission district with some of the best murals you're likely to see anywhere; *see p78* **Mission Murals**.

Gay & Lesbian

Always in the vanguard.

According to the Advocate.com's list of the Gayest Cities in America, San Francisco doesn't even crack the top ten, which may come as a surprise considering its reputation as the gay capital of the US. There is little quarrel that the city is the center of the gay universe in the larger public consciousness, and that it continues to be at the forefront of the struggle for gay rights.

In February 2004, more than 4,000 lesbian and gay couples made a dash for City Hall after new mayor Gavin Newsom directed officials to issue marriage licenses to same-sex couples. But the Winter of Love – as it became known – was shortlived. A California Supreme Court ruling nullifying the marriages touched off a rollercoaster of legislation and legal battles, the final outcome of which is yet to be determined (*see p228* **'I Do' Blues**).

It's nothing new for San Francisco. From the excoriating energy of Ginsberg's *Howl* and the revolutionary Daughters of Bilitis to the pre-Pride days of gay liberation and the election of Harvey Milk, California's first openly gay politician in 1977, the city has long been a lightning rod for the upheavals associated with queer rights.

NEIGHBORHOODS

Polk Street, the Tenderloin, North Beach, Haight-Ashbury and SoMa were the neighborhoods of choice for gays and lesbians back in the 1970s, but the **Castro** – with its street fair, flourishing restaurants and bars, and talismanic **Castro Theatre** (*see p213*) – soon took over. Today, the area remains vibrant, with trendy, expensive houses and streets brimming with Pride flags, bars, eateries and shops.

Middle-class lesbians with kids and dogs have settled in cheery residential neighborhoods such as **Bernal Heights** and the **Outer Mission**. Affluent queers thrive in villagey and ultra-gentrified **Noe Valley**, filled with chic shops and cozy cafes, and in **Hayes Valley**, home to trendy restaurants, wine bars, and **Marlena's** (*see p230*), one of the city's oldest drag bars. Gay men still gravitate towards **SoMa**, which is home to almost all of the gay clubs and many good gay bars, sex clubs and dance joints frequented by the brawny, bear-like and well-toned. **Duboce Triangle** (between Market, Waller and Castro Streets) and **Potrero Hill** both also draw queer folk.

RESOURCES & INFORMATION

Queer San Francisco past and present can be explored at the Reading Room in the **Center** (1800 Market Street, at Octavia Boulevard, 865 5555, www.sfcenter.org), the **Eureka Valley/Harvey Milk Memorial Branch Library** in the Castro (1 José Sarria Court, 16th Street, at Market Street, 355 5616, www.sfpl.org), and at the James C Hormel Gay & Lesbian Center at the **Main Library** (*see p56*). **Cruisin' the Castro** (255 1821, www.webcastro.com) is a mazy walking tour, hosted by 'Leader of the Pack' Kathy Amendola that covers the history of SF's famous gay neighborhood. SoMa is home to the **GLBT Historical Society** (Suite 300, 657 Mission Street, between New Montgomery & 3rd Streets, 777 5455, www.glbthistory.org, $4 suggested donation, closed Mon & Sun), which has riveting historical and cultural exhibits. They are also behind the new **GLBT History Museum** in the Castro (4127 18th Street, between Castro & Collingwood Street, 621 1107, www.glbthistory.org/museum, $5 admission, closed Mon & Tue, *see also right* **Inside Track**), the first of its kind in the US.

The best resources for up-to-date information are the free newspapers, notably the *San*

Francisco Bay Times and the BAR (*Bay Area Reporter*). You'll find them in cafés, bookstores and street corner boxes. The Center (*see left*) organizes meetings and events, as well as gathering information. The **Women's Building** (*see p79*) is a hub of resources and services. Queer-about-town Larry-bob Roberts regularly updates his voluminous website listings at www.sfqueer.com. The non gay-specific *Bay Guardian*, *SF Weekly* and *San Francisco Chronicle* are also worth a look.

WHERE TO STAY

For accommodation across the city, *see p121-32*. Noteworthy gay-owned, gay-friendly or simply delightful places are listed below; another particular favorite of ours is **Parker Guest House** (*see p129*), a lovely mini-mansion dating back to 1909.

Castro

Beck's Motor Lodge

2222 Market Street, at 15th Street, CA 94114 (621 8212, www.becksmotorlodgesf.com). Metro to Castro/streetcar F/bus 22, 24, 37. **Rates** $120-$185 double. **Credit** AmEx, Disc, MC, V. **Map** p318 H10.

Relatively cheap rates, a sun deck, private baths and, above all, a prime Castro location, help Beck's retain its popularity. Inside, the tacky carpets and garish soft furnishings offer a glimpse of quintessential motel Americana. Beware – or not – its reputation for being a very cruisey place to stay.

Inn on Castro

321 Castro Street, at Market Street, CA 94114 (861 0321, www.innoncastro.com). Metro to Castro/streetcar F/bus 24, 33, 35, 37. **Rates** $125-$185 double. **Credit** AmEx, Disc, MC, V. **Map** p318 H10.

A beautifully restored Edwardian, with eight rooms and four apartments decorated with contemporary furnishings, original modern art and elaborate flower arrangements. The sumptuous breakfast includes delicious own-made muffins and fresh fruit.

24 Henry Guesthouse & Village House

24 Henry Street, between Sanchez & Noe Streets, CA 94114 (1-800 900 5686/864 5686, www.24henry.com). Metro to Church & 18th or Castro/streetcar F/bus 22, 24, 37. **Rates** $85-$149 double. **Credit** AmEx, MC, V. **Map** p318 H9.

All are welcome to this B&B, a handsome Victorian in the heart of the Castro. Of five furnished rooms, one has an en suite bathroom; the others share a double shower room with separate toilet. The Village House (4080 18th Street, between Castro & Hartford Streets), another Victorian, has five beautiful rooms.

INSIDE TRACK
QUEERS MAKE HISTORY

With more than a modicum of pride, 2011 saw the opening of the **GLBT History Museum** (*see left*), the first of its kind in the US. Located in the Castro, on the site of assassinated supervisor Harvey Milk's old camera shop, the small, but dense museum features 1,600 square feet of gallery and program space. Exhibits include letters, manuscripts, photos, memorabilia and items like Harvey Milk's kitchen table and sunglasses. Rotating exhibits focus on gay, lesbian, bisexual, and transgender culture and issues. The inaugural show, Our Vast Queer Past: Celebrating San Francisco's GLBT History will be on view through 2011.

GLBT History Museum.

Willows Inn

710 14th Street, at Church Streets, CA 94114 (431 4770, www.willowssf.com). Metro to Castro/streetcar F/bus 22, 37. **Rates** $109-$140 double. **Credit** AmEx, Disc, MC, V. **Map** p318 H9.

This converted Edwardian has 12 comfy rooms with bentwood willow and antique furnishings. Baths are shared, but all rooms have vanity sinks. Soft kimono bathrobes are provided, and complimentary breakfast and cocktails are served daily.

Other neighborhoods

★ Hayes Valley Inn

417 Gough Street, at Hayes Street, Hayes Valley, CA 94102 (431 9131, www.hayesvalleyinn.com). Bus 5, 21, 47, 49, 90. **Rates** $72-$112 double. **Credit** AmEx, Disc, MC, V. **Map** p318 J8.

A European-style, 28-room pension in the center of lively and lovely Hayes Valley, adjacent to the Crepe House restaurant. There's a bar here, and pets are welcome too. A kitchen and parlor are available to guests, but bathrooms are shared (although rooms have their own sinks).

Metro

319 Divisadero Street, at Page Street, Haight, CA 94117 (861 5364, www.metrohotelsf.com). Bus 6, 21, 24, 71. **Rates** $76-$130 double. **Credit** AmEx, Disc, MC, V. **Map** p317 G8.

The Metro is a gay-friendly establishment with a large patio and 24 well-appointed rooms with private baths in up-and-coming NoPa (North of Panhandle). Hip boutique shopping and unique eateries are little more than a stone's throw away.

RESTAURANTS & CAFÉS

GLBT diners are welcome throughout the city, but the following is a selection of our favorite places, some of which have a determinedly queer milieu. For the main restaurants and cafés section, *see p137-641.*

The Castro

2223 Restaurant & Bar

2223 Market Street, between Noe & Sanchez Streets (431 0692, www.2223restaurant.com). Metro to Castro/streetcar F/bus 22, 24, 37. **Open** 5-9pm Mon-Thur; 5-10.30pm Fri; 11am-2pm, 5-10.30pm Sat; 10am-2.30pm, 5-9.30pm Sun. **Main courses** $22. **Credit** AmEx, MC, V. **Map** p318 H10.

Expect vibrant dishes that awaken the senses at this sleek restaurant. There are Med, Mexican and Caribbean influences on the menu, and excellent pizza, pasta and fish. It's one of the area's more popular places for the queer crowd, so the din may intrude on romantic tête-à-têtes. Sunday brunch is a definite winner.

Bagdad Café

2295 Market Street, at Noe Street (621 4434, www.bagdadcafesf.com). Metro to Castro/streetcar F/bus 24, 33, 35, 37. **Open** 24hrs daily. **Main courses** $12-$23. **Credit** AmEx, Disc, MC, V. **Map** p318 H10.

This bustling diner has a bird's-eye view of the busy Market-Noe intersection. As well as good views, it's a decent option for a sandwich, vegetarian lasagne or post-bar breakfast.

★ Café Flore

2298 Market Street, at Noe Street (621 8579, www.cafeflore.com). Metro to Castro/streetcar F/bus 24, 33, 35, 37. **Open** 7am-1am Mon-Thur, Sun; 7am-2am Fri, Sat. **Main courses** $13. **Credit** AmEx, MC, V. **Map** p317 H10.

Fresh-faced boys and girls crowd Flore's gorgeous patio day and night to check each other out, sip coffee and feast on local favorites (brunch is a must). Deep house and lounge tunes pump from the DJ booth. *Photos p226.*

Castro Country Club

4058 18th Street, at Hartford Street (552 6102, www.castrocountryclub.org). Metro to Castro/streetcar F/bus 24, 33, 35, 37. **Open** 7am-11pm Mon-Thur; 7am-midnight Fri; 9am-midnight Sat; 9am-10pm Sun. **Credit** MC, V. **Map** p318 H11.

A great alternative to boozy nights, this club is home to clean and sober queers. There's a sitting room, a coffee bar and café, a room for board games, a video theater and a backyard patio. The front steps are Castro's central gossip parlor and cruise lookout.

Catch

2362 Market Street, at Castro Street (431 5000, www.catchsf.com). Metro to Castro/streetcar F/bus 24, 33, 35, 37. **Open** 11.30am-2.30pm, 5.30-9pm Mon, Tue; 11.30am-2.30pm, 5.30-10pm Wed, Thur; 11.30am-2.30pm, 5.30-11pm Fri; 11am-3.30pm, 5.30-11pm Sat; 11am-3.30pm, 5.30-9.30pm Sun. **Main courses** $16. **Credit** AmEx, Disc, MC, V. **Map** p318 H10.

This seafood restaurant has an enclosed heated outdoor deck and live piano music. Dishes are well turned out, but not exceptional. No one seems to mind, though: the bar fills up with local yuppies on a date (or looking for one) and a broad selection of gym rats. You'll need to book at weekends.

Firewood Café

4248 18th Street, between Collingwood & Diamond Streets (252 0999, www.firewoodcafe.com). Metro to Castro/streetcar F/bus 24, 33, 35, 37. **Open** 11am-10pm Mon-Thur, Sun; 11am-11pm Fri, Sat. **Main courses** $12. **Credit** AmEx, MC, V. **Map** p317 G11.

There's sometimes a queue outside the door for evening meals here, but the loyal customers are willing to wait. Menu standouts include melt-in-the-mouth roast chicken, pasta dishes and thin-crust pizzas. Eat in or phone to take out. Queer heaven.

★ Home

2100 Market Street, at Church Street (503 0333, www.home-sf.com). Metro to Church/streetcar F/bus 22, 37. **Open** 5-10pm Mon-Thur; 5pm-midnight Fri; 10am-midnight Sat; 10am-10pm Sun. **Main courses** $17. **Credit** AmEx, Disc, MC, V. **Map** p318 H9.

True American comfort food – think meatloaf, collard greens, pot roast and banana bread pudding – is served (sometimes by drag queens) in a lively atmosphere accompanied by an impressive list of specialty cocktails. Sunday brunch is lavish and loud, with a build-your-own-Bloody-Mary bar.

La Mediterranée

288 Noe Street, between Market & 16th Streets (431 7210, www.cafelamed.com). Metro to Castro/streetcar F/bus 24, 33, 35, 37. **Open** 11am-10pm Mon-Thur, Sun; 11am-11pm Fri, Sat. **Main courses** $12. **Credit** AmEx, Disc, MC, V. **Map** p318 H10.

A well-established success, due in no small part to the owners' brilliant use of fresh ingredients. Everything is keenly priced, with terrific houmous and baba ganoush, plus an excellent filo pastry combination plate. Feels like a genuine Mediterranean escape.

Other locations 2210 Fillmore Street, Pacific Heights (921 2956).

Lime

2247 Market Street, between Noe and Sanchez Streets (621 5256, www.lime-sf.com). Metro to Castro/streetcar F/bus 24, 33, 35, 37. **Open** 5pm-midnight Sun-Thur; 5pm-1am Fri-Sat. **Credit** AmEx, Disc, MC, V. **Map** p318 H10.

An upscale combo of bar and restaurant, the kitchen here turns out globally inspired small plates that are great for nibbling while sipping expertly prepared mojitos and martinis. The look is minimalist modern, with saturated pink lighting on white furnishings; the crowd is mixed with a nod to smartly dressed lesbians. During the day, wildly popular sandwich shop, Ike's Place, serves from here.

Samovar

498 Sanchez Street, at 18th Street (626 4700, http://samovarlife.com). Metro to Castro/streetcar F/bus 24, 33, 35. **Open** 10am-10pm daily. **Main courses** $22. **Credit** AmEx, Disc, MC, V. **Map** p318 H10.

The Castro's only tearoom, this tranquil spot is a hit with locals searching out a Zen-like refuge. There are more than 100 teas, including Russian zavarka served from a samovar. If you're peckish, try the healthy small plates paired with their tea country of origin.

Other locations Yerba Buena Gardens, Upper Terrace, 730 Howard Street, SoMa (227 9400).

Café Flore. *See p225.*

Other neighborhoods

★ Asia SF

201 9th Street, at Howard Street, SoMa (255 2742, www.asiasf.com). Bart & Metro to Civic Center/streetcar F/bus 6, 9, 12, 14, 19, 27, 47, 71, 90. **Open** *Restaurant* 6.30-10pm Tue, Wed; 6-10.30pm Thur, Sun; 7-11pm Fri; 5-11.15pm Sat. *Club* 7pm-3am Fri, Sat. **Set meals** $44.95-$49. **Credit** AmEx, Disc, MC, V. **Map** p318 L8.

Those lovely ladies who serve you? They're not. Not women, that is, nor drag queens. The sexy creatures who bring the food and dance seductively atop the long red bar are 'gender illusionists'. The food is inventive Cal-Asian, with small plates and shareable portions. A restaurant, lounge and club all in one, Asia SF's crowd is a compelling mix of local party-goers and wide-eyed businessmen. Reservations essential.

Emma's Coffee House

1901 Hayes Street, at Ashbury Street, Haight (221 3378). Bus 5, 21, 43. **Open** 6.30am-8pm Mon-Fri; 7am-8pm Sat, Sun. **No credit cards**. **Map** p317 F8.

Emma's is the real deal when it comes to the mighty bean, serving robustly strong Italian-style coffee made the right way. Two iMacs are available for customer use (first 15mins free with purchase). Saunter upstairs for a read in the tranquil lounge.

Liberty Café

410 Cortland Avenue, between Bennington & Wool Streets, Bernal Heights (695 8777, www.thelibertycafe.com). Bus 24, 67. **Open** 11.30am-3pm, 5.30-10pm Tue-Fri; 9am-3pm, 5.30-10pm Sat, Sun. **Main courses** $22. **Credit** AmEx, Disc, MC, V.

A neighborhood gem that serves exquisite home-style American food. The chicken pot pie is a delight, while the desserts are among the best in the city, from the voluptuous banana cream pie to a luscious strawberry shortcake topped with whipped cream.

★ Mabel's Just for You Café

732 22nd Street, at 3rd Street, Potrero Hill (647 3033/www.justforyoucafe.com). Metro to 20th Street/bus 22, 48, 91. **Open** 7.30am-3pm Mon-Fri; 8am-3pm Sat, Sun. **Main courses** $11. **Credit** MC, V. **Map** p319 P11.

The popularity of the original version of this dyke-run café prompted the owners to move to these bigger quarters in Dogpatch, close to the Bay. The house speciality is a Cajun-style breakfast, with superb grits and fluffy pancakes.

Regalito Rosticeria

3481 18th Street, at Valencia Street, Mission (503 0650, www.regalitosf.com). BART to 16th Street/bus 14, 22, 33, 49. **Open** 5-10pm Mon-Fri; 11am-10pm Sat, Sun. **Main courses** $15. **Credit** AmEx, Disc, MC, V. **Map** p318 K10.

Opened in 2006 by chef Thomas Peña and his partner, Regalito offers Mexican-style cooking at its best. Hearty enchiladas verdes, delicately spiced chilli relleno, and the pollo regalito – roast chicken marinated in lemon or chilli-garlic sauce – represent an authentic taste of California's other native cuisine.

Restaurant Paul K

199 Gough Street, at Oak Street, Hayes Valley (552 7132, www.paulkrestaurant.com). Bus 6, 21, 71. **Open** 5-10pm Tue-Thur; 5-11pm Fri, Sat; 5-9:30pm Sun. **Credit** AmEx, Disc, MC, V. **Map** p318 J8.

This elegant yet cozy spot is popular with opera and symphony-goers and the neighborhood crowd. The menu reflects owner Paul Kavouksorian's Armenian heritage, as well as Greek and North African influences. Mezza platters are perfect for pre-show sharing; eggs benedict are the ticket for weekend brunch.

BARS

The Castro

Badlands

4121 18th Street, at Castro Street (626 9320, www.sfbadlands.com). Metro to Castro/streetcar F/bus 24, 33, 35, 37. **Open** 3pm-2am daily. **No credit cards**. **Map** p318 H11.

Young suburbanites drenched in scent and sporting the latest in designer label knock-offs flock to this flashy video bar, which boasts one of the few dance floors in the Castro. The music ranges from popular hip hop to early 1990s diva favourites, and the queue outside on weekends is often a scene of its own.

440 Castro

440 Castro Street, at 18th Street (621 8732, www.the440.com). Metro to Castro/streetcar F/bus 24, 33, 35, 37. **Open** noon-2am daily. **No credit cards**. **Map** p318 H11.

Festivals Gay

The gay calendar.

June's month-long **Gay Pride**, the largest gay carnival in the world, is the highlight of the year. It includes the spirit-buoying Trans March on Friday (www.transmarch.org), the boisterous Saturday night women-only Dyke March (241 8882,www.dykemarch.org), both with onlookers of any gender cheering from the sidelines, and Sunday's Pride Parade (*see p204*). The crowds stream up Market Street to Civic Center Plaza to watch the leather-and-lace Dykes on Bikes leading the parade with their full-throttled Harley power and roar. The centerpiece of Pride is Frameline's **San Francisco International Lesbian & Gay Film Festival** (*see p215*), a two-week festival of shorts, documentaries and features.

Still racy, September's leather-besotted **Folsom Street Fair** (www.folsomstreetfair.com, *see p204*) is the second largest gay event in SF; the **Up Your Alley Fair** (www.folsomstreetfair.com/alley), a cruisey and risqué S&M festival in late July in SoMa, and the bear-oriented **Hairrison Street Fair** (summer dates vary, www.hairrison.org) also attract crowds. The Castro's other major street celebration, Halloween, has been all but shut down in recent years due to dangerous overcrowding and an unsavory atmosphere.

On a more somber note, there's the AIDS **Candlelight Vigil** in May with a walk along Market Street to the Main Library; the **AIDS Walk San Francisco** (www.aidswalk.net/sanfran) in July; and **World AIDS Day** on 1 December, which sees events throughout the city. You can also view portions of the AIDS Memorial Quilt (www.aidsquilt.org), founded in 1987.

'I Do' Blues

Will Proposition 8 succeed in stopping gay Californians from tying the knot?

The staggeringly convoluted history of gay marriage in California added another layer of controversy in November 2008, when voters narrowly passed Proposition 8, a state constitutional amendment dubbed the 'California Marriage Protection Act', which deemed only marriage between a man and a woman legitimate. With wording identical to a Proposition 22 passed in 2000 that was ruled unconstitutional by the California Supreme Court, it is not clear voters understood which way they voted. A 'Yes' vote would add the words 'only marriage between a man and a woman is valid or recognized in California'. A 'No' vote would mean that the then-current language, stating that marriage was 'between any two people' would remain.

With the exception of the presidential contest that year, the massive campaigns for and against Prop 8 generated the most money spent on any campaign in the country. Civil rights groups and gay marriage advocates were stunned by the sheer amount of cash raised by the opposition, primarily several large, out-of-state religious organizations, which donated millions in support of the initiative. Legal battles ensued, and continue. Courts have since ruled that marriages performed during the window when same-sex marriages were legal could not be annulled retroactively. Also, same-sex couples wed during that period in other jurisdictions outside the state of California would retain their marriage rights.

Most recently, the American Foundation for Equal Rights challenged the validity of Prop 8 and found a number of powerful backers, including the ACLU, Lambda Legal, and the City of San Francisco itself. Both Attorney General Jerry Brown (now California's Governor) and then-Governor Arnold Schwarzenegger, who had waffled in previous challenges, refused to defend the constitutional amendment – a first in the state's history. Even the original judge in the case was somewhat out of the ordinary. US District Court Judge Vaughn Walker was considered conservative, if not libertarian, in his leanings. He is also gay – a fact that generated protests from Prop 8 supporters.

As this guide goes to press, the California Supreme Court is considering who has standing, or the right to defend Prop 8. The Ninth Circuit Court of Appeals is deciding whether Prop 8 is constitutional, and requests have been issued to expedite oral arguments in the Supreme Court. Meanwhile, Senator Dianne Feinstein, who represents the San Francisco region in Washington DC, has introduced legislation to repeal the federal Defense of Marriage Act (DOMA) and states around the country continue their own battles for and against same-sex marriage.

To keep abreast of developments, Prop 8 supporters can visit www.protectmarriage.com, while opponents – those who support the right for same-sex couples to wed – can peruse www.stop8.org. Everything clear now?

Formerly Daddy's, the Castro's reigning leather bar, 440 Castro has reinvented itself as a moderately swanky lounge but hasn't quite managed to shake off its preening he-man past. The crowd is an odd mix of old-school cruisers and youthful fans of hard techno, but the drinks specials are just right to smooth out the rougher edges.

★ Harvey's

500 Castro Street, at 18th Street (431 4278, www.harveyssf.com). Metro to Castro/streetcar F/bus 24, 33, 35, 37. **Open** 11am-11pm Mon-Fri; 9am-2am Sat, Sun. **Credit** AmEx, MC, V. **Map** p318 H11.

The site of an infamous brawl with cops during the 1979 White Night riot that followed the lenient sentencing of Dan White, Harvey Milk's assassin, this bar-restaurant – itself named after Harvey Milk – is usually pervaded by a spirit of bonhomie. Saturday nights host a mixed bag of drag and musical performances, and the décor highlights the colorful clientele.

► *For more on the Harvey Milk story, see p25.*

Midnight Sun

4067 18th Street, at Hartford Street (861 4186, www.midnightsunsf.com). Metro to Castro/ streetcar F/bus 24, 33, 35, 37. **Open** 2pm-2am Mon-Fri; 1pm-2am Sat, Sun. **No credit cards. Map** p318 H11.

The big draw at Midnight Sun is video – that is, classic and contemporary music cross-cut with comedy clips, *The Sopranos* or *Sex and the City*. Two-for-one cocktails are on offer during the week (2-7pm), and weekends are a boy fest.

Mix

4086 18th Street, at Hartford Street (431 8616, www.sfmixbar.com). Metro to Castro/streetcar F/bus 24, 33, 35, 37. **Open** 6am-2am daily. **No credit cards. Map** p318 H11.

This rough-and-ready sports bar is a haven for queer jocks and those who adore them. Fervent fans pack the place to root for the San Francisco 49ers, and sunny weekends see the back patio grilling up burgers and hot dogs. The windows face 18th Street, which is perfect for ogling.

Moby Dick's

4049 18th Street, at Hartford Street (861 1199, www.mobydicksf.com). Metro to Castro/streetcar F/bus 24, 33, 35, 37. **Open** 2pm-2am Mon-Fri; noon-2am Sat, Sun. **No credit cards. Map** p318 H11.

A true neighborhood bar, Moby Dick's is exactly as it has been since the 1980s. It's popular with pool players (despite the fact that there's only one table) and pinball addicts (there are four machines at the back), but big windows and a prime Castro location afford ample cruising potential too. Daily drinks specials add to the attraction.

★ Orbit Room

1900 Market Street, at Laguna Street (252 9525, www.orbitroomcafe.com). Metro to Van Ness or Church/streetcar F/bus 6, 71. **Open** 5pm-2am Mon-Wed; 4pm-2am Thur, Fri; 2pm-2am Sat, Sun. **No credit cards. Map** p318 J9.

This high-ceilinged art deco retreat with pedestal tables is a coffeehouse by day and a cocktail bar by night. The crowd is quite young, a mix of straights and queers, with some uptown lesbians thrown into the mix. Good music, café food and the city's best cocktail mixologist make it a relaxing place to flutter away a gentle evening.

Pilsner Inn

225 Church Street, at Market Street (621 7058, www.pilsnerinn.com). Metro to Church/streetcar F/bus 22. **Open** noon-2am Mon-Fri; 10-2am Sat, Sun. **No credit cards. Map** p318 J9.

It all happens here, especially on the heated patio at the back. The Pilsner is a local favorite among youngish beauty boys, who play pool, pinball and computer games, or chat over the sounds of the retro jukebox. There's a wide choice of draft beers, and customers can wait at the front for opening tables at ever-popular Chow (*see p154*), serving American staples.

Twin Peaks Tavern

401 Castro Street, at Market Street (864 9470, www.twinpeakstavern.com). Metro to Castro/ streetcar F/bus 24, 33, 35, 37. **Open** noon-2am Mon-Wed; 8am-2am Thur-Sat; 10am-2am Sun. **No credit cards. Map** p318 H10.

Billing itself as 'the Gateway to the Castro', the snug Twin Peaks Tavern was one of the first gay bars in the US to brave the public gaze with street-level windows. Nowadays, habitués are mostly older, enjoying a quiet chat, good music and even a game of cards. The lovely antique bar serves everything except bottled beer.

The Mission

Although it's not strictly a gay bar, **El Rio** (3158 Mission Street, at Cesar Chavez Street, 282 3325, www.elriosf.com) draws queers to its riotous music nights. Among them are Mango, the monthly lesbian Saturday party, which has a huge following, and Sunday Salsa, also very queer.

Esta Noche

3079 16th Street, at Mission Street (861 5757). BART to 16th Street Mission/bus 14, 22, 33, 49. **Open** noon-2am daily. **No credit cards. Map** p318 K10.

In business for decades, this gay-Latino-drag-sports bar attracts a gregarious, diverse clientele. There's a pool table for the daytime and animated drag shows and rousing lip-synching at night. Music mixes US and Latino pop, cumbia and merengue (DJs play nightly), and the place doubles as a welcome mat for Latino queens who are new to town. A word of warning, however: the street outside can be a bit on the menacing side.

★ Lexington Club

3464 19th Street, at Lexington Street (863 2052, www.lexingtonclub.com). BART to 16th Street Mission/bus 14, 26, 33, 49. **Open** 5pm-2am Mon-Thur; 3pm-2am Fri-Sun. **No credit cards. Map** p318 K11.

A legendary lesbian-owned, lesbian-operated bar, where 'every night is ladies' night'. Primarily for the younger set, the Lexington has a pool table (free on Mondays) and a full bar; crimson walls and church-pew seating give the place a ready-for-anything atmosphere. There's no dancing, but theme nights include Sister Spit's rowdy performances, and Sunday L Word parties. There are frequent drinks specials too.

SoMa

★ Eagle Tavern

398 12th Street, at Harrison Street (626 0880, www.sfeagle.com). Bus 9, 12, 27, 47, 90. **Open** noon-2am daily. **No credit cards. Map** p318 L9.

A venerable gay bar offering all-male leather action, random mud-wrestling, goings-on in the beer garden and a chance to cozy up to gay (and straight) indie rockers and punk outfits, including Pansy Division, Erase Errata and Enorchestra. Sunday afternoon beer busts (between 3.30pm and 5.30pm) are ground zero for local alternaqueers.

Hole in the Wall

289 8th Street, between Howard & Folsom Streets (431 4695, www.holeinthewallsaloon.com). Bus 12, 14, 19, 27, 47. **Open** noon-2am daily. **No credit cards. Map** p318 L8.

This self-proclaimed 'nasty little biker bar', a veritable SoMa institution, is a magnet for the biker crowd, although gay locals and tourists seem to love it too. There's a beautifully re-felted pool table, video games, pinball, rock 'n' roll oldies playing on repeat and a bewildering array of gay memorabilia covering the walls and ceiling.

Lone Star Saloon

1354 Harrison Street, between 9th & 10th Streets (863 9999, www.lonestarsf.com). Bus 12, 19, 27, 47, 90. **Open** 4pm-2am Mon-Thur; 2pm-2am Fri; noon-2am Sat, Sun. **No credit cards. Map** p318 L8.

Once unabashed 'bear country', the Lone Star has of late become more of a fashion show for beauty bears. That said, it's still a jolly enough place, with pinball machines, a pool table and a rear patio for smoking, and authentic bear types can still be hunted here.

Powerhouse

1347 Folsom Street, between 9th & 10th Streets (552 8689, www.powerhouse-sf.com). Bus 9, 12, 14, 19, 27, 47, 90. **Open** 4pm-2am daily. **No credit cards. Map** p318 L8.

White-hot and cruisey as hell, Powerhouse is one of the city's most popular gay bars. Entertainment includes buzz-cut nights, underwear or bare-chest parties, wrestling, leather nights and S&M lessons.

Other neighborhoods

Aunt Charlie's Lounge

133 Turk Street, at Taylor Street, Tenderloin (441 2922, www.auntcharlieslounge.com). BART & Metro to Powell/streetcar F/bus 27, 31, 45 & Market Street routes/cable car Powell-Hyde or Powell-Mason. **Open** noon-2am Mon-Fri; 10-2am Sat; 10am-midnight Sun. **No credit cards. Map** p314 L6.

Sports nights, stiff drinks, old-fashioned drag shows and lip-synching on weekends, plus a long-standing Tenderloin location all combine to make this a popular spot with loyal attendees.

Cinch

1723 Polk Street, between Clay & Washington Streets, Polk Gulch (776 4162). Bus 1, 12, 19, 27, 47, 49, 90/cable car California. **Open** 9am-2am Mon-Fri; 6am-2am Sat, Sun. **No credit cards. Map** p314 K4.

A double-shot of old-school San Francisco gay bar, circa 1979. With an ostensible Western theme, this comfortably ramshackle haunt harks back to the days when this stretch of Polk Street was a more rough-and-tumble area of hustlers, chasers and drag queens with a broken heel or two. A tiered smoking patio out back is perfect for slurred conversation.

Deco Lounge

510 Larkin Street, at Turk Street, Tenderloin (346 2025, http://decosf.com). Bus 5, 19, 31, 38, 47, 49, 90. **Open** 4pm-2am Mon-Fri; 1pm-2am Sat, Sun. **No credit cards. Map** p314 K6.

Laid out like a spacious 1940s piano bar, complete with plush decor and classic movie posters framed and artfully lit on the walls, Deco somewhat incongruously hosts many of the wildest gay parties in the Tenderloin. Wet jockstrap contests, offbeat drag shows and techno-driven bear parties can be found here on many weekend nights; weekdays host a crew of seen-it-all regulars.

★ Marlena's

488 Hayes Street, at Octavia Street, Hayes Valley (864 6672, www.marlenasbarsf.com). Bus 6, 21, 71. **Open** noon-2am daily. **No credit cards. Map** p318 J8.

An eclectic crowd (including drag queens on the weekends) shows up for the superb martinis at this treasured former speakeasy – one of San Francisco's

The Café.

oldest drag bars. A fold-down Murphy stage lends an eccentric, cozy ambience. Drag shows second and fourth Saturday of the month.

Martuni's

4 Valencia Street, at Market Street, Hayes Valley (241 0205, http://martunis.ypguides.net/). BART or Metro to Van Ness/streetcar F/bus 6, 14, 49, 71. **Open** 2pm-2am daily. **Credit** MC, V. **Map** p318 J8.

Martuni's is a warm, inviting piano bar with an open mic. The martinis are enormous, the music mostly show tunes, and the clientele extremely diverse.

Stray Bar

309 Cortland Avenue, at Bocana Street, Bernal Heights (821 9263, www.straybarsf.com). Bus 24. **Open** 4pm-2am Mon-Wed; 3pm-2am Thur, Fri; 1pm-2am Sat, Sun. **Credit** Disc, MC, V.

Recently opened and beautifully renovated, this girl bar attracts a heterogeneous clientele. The nightly entertainment varies from live blues and jazz singers to DJs spinning every kind of music. Weekday happy hours from 5pm to 8pm are another draw.

Wild Side West

424 Cortland Avenue, at Wool Street, Bernal Heights (647 3099). Bus 14, 24, 49. **Open** 2pm-2am daily. **No credit cards.**

Probably the longest-lived lesbian hotspot in the city, Wild Side West really sees itself as just another neighborhood bar. The walls are a shifting art installation, the patio is perfect for live music or poetry, and the clientele is happily mixed. The ace jukebox plays Janis Joplin, Patsy Cline and – naturally – 'Walk on the Wild Side'.

NIGHTCLUBS

The dance scene changes with bewildering rapidity, so call ahead, check websites or get club-scene mags *Odyssey* and *Gloss* to make sure a particular night is happening. Most clubs are 21 and over, so bring valid photo ID. For more nightclubs, *see p244-48.*

The Castro

The Café

2369 Market Street, at Castro Street (861 3846, www.cafesf.com). Metro to Castro/streetcar F/bus 24, 33, 35, 37. **Open** 5pm-2am Mon-Fri; 3pm-2am Sat, Sun. **Admission** varies. **No credit cards. Map** p318 H10.

There's dancing every night at the Café, the Castro's largest and most popular club. Once the area's only women's bar, it now mainly attracts boys from outlying areas, but lasses show up during the day, on weeknights and (especially) on Sunday afternoons. The music blends house, hip hop and salsa. There are two bars, a dancefloor and a patio, plus pinball, pool and computer games.

SoMa

Mezzanine (444 Jessie Street, at 6th Street, *see p246*) is also a big hit with the boys.

Eight

1151 Folsom Street, between 7th & 8th Streets (431 1151, www.eightsf.com). BART or Metro to Civic Center/streetcar F/bus 12, 19, 47. **Open** 9pm-3am Fri; varies Thur, Sat, Sun. **No credit cards. Map** p319 M8.

A solid, bi-level (two floors, that is) nightclub with a lovely lounge at the top and a rolling program of themed events, Eight is also known for its attractive staff. Fridays host Dragon, a high-energy party for Asians and friends; other nights, disco, techno and even Middle Eastern tunes pack the dancefloor.

★ Endup

401 6th Street, at Harrison Street (646 0999, www.theendup.com). Bus 12, 27, 47. **Open** 10pm-4am Mon, Thur; 11pm-11am Fri; 6am-1pm, 10pm-6am Sat; 6am-4am Sun. **Admission** free-$20. **No credit cards.** Map p319 M7.

A fixture since 1973, the Endup boasts all-night house and techno madness at weekends, plus a Saturday morning club from 6am and the legendary T-Dance from 6am on Sundays, which sees drag queens and straight ravers reveling together.

★ Stud

399 9th Street, at Harrison Street (252 7883, www.studsf.com). Bus 12, 19, 27, 47. **Open** from 5pm daily, closing varies. **Admission** free-$15. **No credit cards. Map** p318 L8.

Now more than 40 years old, the Stud still has dancing all week. The crowd is mainly gay and male, but the club prides itself on being 'omnisexual'. Nights range from queer punk and '80s disco to house.

ENTERTAINMENT & CULTURE

The Castro

The **Castro Theatre** (*see p213*) hosts gay and camp screenings: you haven't lived until you've seen *Valley of the Dolls* or *All About Eve* here. There are frequent *Sound of Music* singalongs and, on Christmas Eve, the SF Gay Men's Chorus singing 'Home for the Holidays'.

The Mission

Brava! For Women in the Arts

Theatre Center, 2789 24th Street, at York Street (641 7657, box office 647 2822, www.brava.org). BART 24th Street/bus 9, 27, 33, 48. **Tickets** vary. **Credit** Disc, MC, V. **Map** p319 M12.

Brava is one of few theaters that specialize in work by women of color and lesbian playwrights.

QComedy Showcase

Locations vary (533 9133, www.qcomedy.com).

What's so funny about queers? QComedy Showcase will tell you at its many shows about town. The ebullient Nick Leonard hosts and performs regularly; top-flight comics Heather Gold, Charlie Ballard and Aundré the Wonderwoman also appear.

★ Theatre Rhinoceros

2926 16th Street, between Mission Street & South Van Ness Avenue (861 5079, www.therhino.org). BART to 16th Street Mission/bus 14, 22, 26, 33, 49, 53. **Tickets** $15-$35. **Credit** AmEx, MC, V. **Map** p318 K10.

Billing itself as the 'world's oldest continually producing, professional queer theatre', Rhino creates theater that is genuinely inviting rather than self-segregating. Its productions comprise comedy, reinterpreted classics, original drama and the occasional musical.

Other neighborhoods

The **Magic Theatre** (*see p258*) hosts a lesbian playwright festival every January and showcases queer plays through the year. Groundbreaking gay theater is staged at the **New Conservatory Theatre** (25 Van Ness Avenue, between Fell & Oak Streets, Hayes Valley).

SPORTS, HEALTH & FITNESS

All of San Francisco's workout spaces (*see p253*) are queer-friendly, but those listed below are especially gay-oriented. All offer daily (around $12-$20) and weekly ($40-$50) gym memberships.

Gold's Gym Castro

2301 Market Street, at Noe Street, Castro (626 4488, www.goldsgym.com). Metro to Castro/streetcar F/bus 24, 33, 35, 37. **Open** 5am-midnight Mon-Thur; 5am-11pm Fri; 7am-9pm Sat; 7am-8pm Sun. **Credit** AmEx, Disc, MC, V. **Map** p318 H10.

Cruisey, with a steam room that can only be described as steamy. Friendly staff and a fierce sound system make Gold's popular with both gay boys and lesbians.

Gym SF

2275 Market Street, between Sanchez & Noe Streets, Castro (863 4700, www.thegymsf.com). Metro to Castro/streetcar F/bus 24, 33, 35, 37. **Open** 5am-11pm Mon-Fri; 7am-10pm Sat; 8am-8pm Sun. **Credit** MC, V. **Map** p318 H10.

The Castro's most notorious men-only sweat palace, well laid-out, seriously steamy and with enough weights for even the most ardent muscle man.

Magnet

4122 18th Street, at Castro Street, Castro (581 1600, www.magnetsf.org). Metro to Castro/streetcar F/bus 24, 33, 35, 37. **Open** 11am-6pm Mon, Tue, Sat; 11am-9pm Wed-Fri. **Map** p317 G11.

In response to rising HIV and STD rates among the city's queer men, local community health groups have rallied to create Magnet. This welcoming space looks more like an upscale café than a health clinic. There are hangout areas here, as well as internet access, and free, anonymous HIV and STD testing and counseling.

World Gym

290 De Haro Street, at 16th Street, Potrero Hill (703 9650, www.worldgym.com). Bus 10, 19, 22. **Open** 5am-midnight Mon-Thur; 5am-11pm Fri; 6am-9pm Sat; 7am-8pm Sun. **Credit** AmEx, Disc, MC, V. **Map** p319 M10.

The gym of gyms, where serious work is done. There are classes in almost everything, including yoga, boxing, Thai boxing, kickboxing and spin. The clientele takes in the whole of hetero San Francisco. Fabulous.

Music

SF pushes musical borders and boundaries.

It could be said that San Francisco is the wild-eyed love child of 1,000 bands. Artists, writers and musicians have been coming here for decades, melding their sounds, styles, and sensibilities into a freewheeling musical panoply whose outsized cultural impact is staggering for a city this small. Both the rock and classical scenes reflect this: they are among the most forward thinking – and well-funded and attended – in the US.

The revival of the tech economy in the last few years means that once again there's money to power the innovative musical climate. From opera and symphony world premières, to annual festivals ranging from Noise Pop to bluegrass and jazz, the musically inclined won't lack for top-notch entertainment.

Classical & Opera

The exploratory impulse that courses through much of the city's cultural landscape extends to its classical music scene. San Francisco's major orchestra and opera company are both renowned for their challenging projects, and a number of the city's smaller ensembles have built their reputations on contemporary music. However, there's plenty of familiar repertoire on offer at venues large and small. Area ensembles have also been making a concerted effort to reach new audiences, which means virtuosic performances are presented at fair prices in venues ranging from the modern (**Louise M Davies Symphony Hall**, *see p234*) to the historic (**St Patrick's Church**, *see p59*). Ticketing can be complicated. Several of the larger ensembles sell tickets via subscription packages, and the most popular shows do sell out. However, individual tickets are available for most concerts; even on nights listed as sell-outs, there are usually a few seats available on the evening.

INFORMATION & TICKETS

The best overall sources of music information are the *San Francisco Bay Guardian* (www.sfbg.com) and *SF Weekly* (www.sfweekly.com), both of which carry extensive listings. San Francisco Opera and Symphony tickets can be purchased directly at venues, online at www.sfopera.com and www.sfsymphony.org, or at StubHub's (www.stubhub.com) Union Square kiosk

MAJOR COMPANIES & VENUES

San Francisco Opera

War Memorial Opera House, 301 Van Ness Avenue, at Grove Street, Civic Center (864 3330, www.sfopera.com). BART & Metro to Civic Center, Metro to Van Ness/bus 5, 19, 21, 47, 49 & Market Street routes. **Box office** 10am-5pm Mon; 10am-6pm Tue-Fri; 10am-6pm Sat during performance season. **Tickets** $25-$360. **Credit** AmEx, MC, V. **Map** p318 K7.

Inaugurated in 1923, the SF Opera is currently under the direction of David Gockley, who's gained acclaim with commissions such as Appomattox, from composer Philip Glass and librettist Christopher Hampton, and more recently with Heart of a Soldier an opera by Christopher Theofanidis to commemorate the 10th anniversary of the 9/11 attacks, with renowned baritone Thomas Hampson leading the cast. The ambitious Wagner's Ring cycle culminates with three entire cycles in the 2011-12 season, including the production-première performances of Siegfried and Götterdämmerung. In addition, such crowd-pleasers as *Turandot*, *The Magic Flute*, *Don Giovanni* and *Carmen* complement more contemporary fare such as *Nixon in China*. Future seasons include composer Mark Adamo's première of *The Gospel of Mary Magdalene* and the Bay Area première of Jake Heggie's *Moby Dick* in autumn 2012. The fall season runs early September to December; the summer season from May to July.

The SF Opera is based in the War Memorial Opera House, a grand Beaux Arts building designed

INSIDE TRACK CLASSICAL ON THE CHEAP

If the steep price of opera tickets makes you want to wail like a diva, head to the **War Memorial Opera House** box office (301 Van Ness Avenue, across from City Hall) at 11am on the day of the performance, when a small number of student rush tickets go on sale; they remain on sale until 30 minutes before showtime and cost just $15. There's also a limited number of standing-room-only spots available behind the orchestra section for $10, but you'll have to get to the box office by 10am to secure one. For symphony tickets, you can queue up for $15-$20 Center Terrace seats two hours before curtain time (two tickets per person, cash only). The seats are located on the stage, directly behind and to the side of the orchestra – so close you can practically read the brass section's scores.

by City Hall architect Arthur Brown Jr. and built in 1932 as a memorial to the soldiers who fought in World War I. The 3,176-seat auditorium is modeled on European opera houses, with a vaulted ceiling, a huge art deco metal chandelier and a marble foyer. An $84-million revamp in 1997 not only restored the elegant building (restorers found clouds painted on the ceiling when they scraped away the grime), but installed up-to-date electronics and stage gear. The San Francisco Ballet (*see p262*) also performs here.

San Francisco Performances

Various venues (392 2545, www.performances.org). **Box office** (180 Redwood Street, Suite 100) 9.30am-5pm Mon-Fri; 10am-4pm Sat. **Tickets** vary. **Credit** MC, V.

Directed with imagination and enthusiasm by Ruth Felt, this independent promoter puts on a program of over 200 concerts each year in a wide variety of styles: the 2010-11 season included concerts by Philip Glass and Yo-Yo Ma. Most performances are held at the Herbst Theatre (*see p257*), the Yerba Buena Center for the Arts Theater (*see p260*), the Florence Gould Theater in the California Palace of the Legion of Honor (*see p96*), and Koret Auditorium at the de Young Museum (*see p94*), but there are also events at the likes of St John's Presbyterian Church in Berkeley (*see p236*) and the Hotel Rex (*see p115*).

★ San Francisco Symphony

Louise M Davies Symphony Hall, 201 Van Ness Avenue, at Hayes Street, Civic Center (864 6000, www.sfsymphony.org). BART & Metro to Civic Center, Metro to Van Ness/bus 5, 19, 21, 47, 49 & Market Street routes. **Box office** 10am-6pm Mon-Fri; noon-6pm Sat; 2hrs before concert Sun. **Tickets** $15-$140. **Credit** MC, V. **Map** p318 K7.

Formed to boost public morale shortly after the 1906 earthquake and fire, the San Francisco Symphony performed its first concert in 1911. Today, under the dynamic direction of Michael Tilson Thomas, the orchestra is internationally recognized for its innovative work, winning several Grammy awards in the process. The symphony's indepth study of Mahler has garnered the ensemble particular acclaim.

The Symphony is based at the Louise M Davies Symphony Hall. Commonly known as Davies, the striking, multi-tiered, curved-glass edifice has flawless acoustics and clear sightlines. There isn't a bad seat in the house, and that includes the 40 in the center terrace section behind the orchestra that sell for just $20 and go on sale two hours before most performances (call for details). In addition to SF Symphony concerts, look out for events in the Great Performers series, which imports world-renowned soloists, conductors and ensembles for one-nighters.

Yerba Buena Center for the Arts Theater

701 Mission Street, at 3rd Street, SoMa (978 2787, www.ybca.org). BART & Metro to Montgomery/bus 10, 12, 14, 30, 45 & Market Street routes. **Box office** noon-6pm Tue, Wed, Sun; noon-8pm Thur-Sat. **Tickets** $10-$60. **Credit** AmEx, MC, V. **Map** p319 N6.

This 757-seat auditorium plays host to some of the most exciting contemporary music and dance companies in the country, among them Kronos Quartet, Smuin Ballets, and the San Francisco Contemporary Music Players. Designed by modernist architect James Stewart Polshek, the exterior of the cube-shaped theater is covered in aluminium panels that catch the sparkling San Francisco light.

► *From May to October, you can catch free music and dance performances and lunchtime concerts at Yerba Buena Gardens as part of the Yerba Buena Gardens Festival (www.ybgf.org).*

CHURCH VENUES

A number of the city's churches host recitals and chamber concerts, often featuring local young musicians and often free of charge. Among them are the **Old First Presbyterian Church** (1751 Sacramento Street, between Polk Street & Van Ness Avenue, 776 5552, www.oldfirst.org) on the edge of Pacific Heights; the **First Unitarian Universalist Church** (1187 Franklin Street, at Geary Street, 776 4580, www.uusf.org) near the Civic Center, famous for its Bartok birthday concert on the third Sunday in March; and Nob Hill's **Grace Cathedral** (*see p65*). **St Patrick's Church** (*see p59*) hosts concerts at 12.30pm every Wednesday, and **St Mary's Cathedral**

(660 California Street) at 12.30pm every Tuesday (www.noontimeconcerts.org).

For a very different kind of devotional music and an 'only in San Francisco' experience, one church venue stands out: **St John Coltrane African Orthodox Church** (1286 Fillmore Street, 673 7144, www.coltranechurch.org). Dedicated to the belief that the divine spoke through jazz saxophone legend John Coltrane and, in particular, his composition *A Love Supreme*, the church holds a mass/jam session on Sundays from 11.45am-2.30pm.

OTHER ENSEMBLES & VENUES

Aside from the players listed above, a number of groups call the city home. Among them the **Philharmonia Baroque Orchestra** (252 1288, www.philharmonia.org) performs baroque and classical repertoire on original instruments. The orchestra's season consists of about six programs a year (September to April), which they 'tour' to the **Herbst Theatre** (*see p257*) and Berkeley's **First Congregational Church** (2345 Channing Way, 1-510 848 3696, www.fccb.org), plus locations in Palo

San Francisco Symphony.

Alto and Contra Costa County. The **New Century Chamber Orchestra** (357 1111, www.ncco.org) has a similar set-up, playing roughly six times a year at the Florence Gould Theater in the **California Palace of the Legion of Honor** (*see p96*) and at **St John's Presbyterian Church** in Berkeley (2727 College Avenue, between 1st & Garber Streets, 1-510 845 6830, www.stjohnsberkeley.org).

A few local ensembles are in demand across the world. The **Kronos Quartet** (731 3533, www.kronosquartet.org) focuses on new works, many of them composed for the group. Founded in 1970, the **San Francisco Contemporary Music Players** (278 9566, www.sfcmp.org) is also in the vanguard of modern music, and commissions new works from both young and more established composers. The music performed by the all-male, Grammy-winning a cappella group **Chanticleer** (252 8589, www.chanticleer.org) is less challenging, but performed with no less skill. All three ensembles tour for much of the year but play in the Bay Area regularly: Kronos and the SFCMP at the **Yerba Buena Center** (*see p61*), and Chanticleer, whose Christmas program is terrific, at a wide variety of local venues.

Two groups give the SF Opera some small measure of competition. Donald Pippin's **Pocket Opera** (972 8930, www.pocketopera.org) presents operas in English; performances are generally held at the Florence Gould Theater in the **California Palace of the Legion of Honor** (*see p96*). The **Lamplighters Musical Theatre** (227 4797, www.lamplighters.org) has been presenting lighter works, including more Gilbert and Sullivan than strictly necessary, for half a century. The company performs at the **Yerba Buena Center** (*see p61*) and the **Herbst Theatre** (*see p257*). Finally, look out for the **San Francisco Conservatory of Music** (864 7326, www.sfcm.edu), which showcases its student talent at a relatively new 400-seat Civic Center concert hall.

Jazz & blues

San Francisco's love of jazz goes back to the days when its bustling Fillmore District was considered a West Coast counterpart to the Harlem Renaissance. Jazz legend Dave Brubeck was born in nearby Concord, lived in Berkeley for many years and enjoyed a long residency at the Blackhawk, a now-defunct jazz club in the Tenderloin District. Several classic albums were recorded here ranging from Miles Davis' *Live at the Blackhawk* and Thelonius Monk's *Alone in San Francisco* to *Friday Night in San Francisco*, a three-way throwdown between guitar virtuosos Al Di Meola, Paco De Lucia and John McLaughlin. And jazz history continues to be made as the Bay Area continues to turn out musicians: the Berkeley High Jazz Ensemble, a high-school program, has spawned the likes of Joshua Redman, David Murray and eight-string guitar master Charlie Hunter. The year 2007 saw the consolidation of the Fillmore Jazz Preservation District as Oakland's famed **Yoshi's** (*see p238*) opened a San Francisco flagship venue on Fillmore Street.

In addition, the **Fillmore Auditorium** (*see p239*), the **Hemlock Tavern** (*see p242*), the **Great American Music Hall** (*see p240*) and the **Intersection for the Arts** (*see p259*) stage sporadic jazz shows. In the Mission District, **Savanna Jazz** (2937 Mission Street, between 25th & 26th Streets, 285-3369, www.savannajazz.com) has won accolades for its lively and eclectic calendar. In the Haight, jazzy jam sessions accompany Neapolitan pizza at **Club Deluxe** (1511 Haight Street, between Ashbury and Clayton, 552 6949, www.sfclubdeluxe.com); and in North Beach, live jazz is the perfect backdrop to cocktails on the outdoor patio at **Savoy Tivoli** (*see p170*).

TICKETS

Booking ahead isn't always necessary at San Francisco's jazz and blues venues. However, at weekends and for big names, an advance reservation is always a good idea; Yoshi's is frequently busy, even during the week.

FESTIVALS

From June to October, **SF Jazz Summerfest** (www.sfjazz.org) runs around 25 free early evening and lunchtime shows in outdoor locations inside and outside the city. Now year-round, the big guns at the **San Francisco Jazz Festival** (www.sfjazz.org) sponsors a series of shows at venues throughout town. The free **Fillmore Street Jazz Festival** (1-800 731 0003, www.fillmorejazzfestival.com) in early July consists of two days of local acts.

VENUES

Biscuits & Blues

401 Mason Street, at Geary Street, Union Square (292 2583, www.biscuitsandblues.com). Bus 2, 3, 4, 27, 30, 31, 38, 45, 91/cable car Powell-Hyde or Powell-Mason. **Open** 6pm-midnight daily. **Shows** 8pm and/or 10pm. **Admission** $30 and under. **Credit** AmEx, MC, V. **Map** p318 L5.

This subterranean nightclub/restaurant is a pretty basic affair. Partly due to its location, it attracts a portion of middle-aged tourists and suburbanites, and can get fairly stuffy when crowded. However, it's still the best place in town to catch mainstream blues, played for genuinely excited crowds. The American food has a Southern accent.

★ Boom Boom Room

1601 Fillmore Street, at Geary Boulevard, Fillmore (673 8000, www.boomboomblues.com). Bus 2, 3, 22, 31, 38. **Open** 4pm-2am Tue-Sun. **Shows** 9pm Tue-Sun. **Admission** $5-$20. Credit MC, V. **Map** p314 H6.

Around for more than 50 years, the Boom Boom Room has been remade as a classy version of a blues joint: John Lee Hooker named it after his signature song and, until his death in 2001, held court up front. These days, the venue attracts solid blues, roots, funk, R&B and groove-oriented acts, with an occasional surprise rock star dropping in. *See also p242* **Historic venues**.

Elbo Room

647 Valencia Street, between 17th & 18th Streets, Mission (552 7788, www.elbo.com). BART 16th Street Mission/bus 14, 22, 33, 49. **Open** 5pm-2am daily. **Shows** 9pm or 10pm daily. **Admission** free-$12. **No credit cards**. **Map** p318 K10.

The Throne Room of West Coast Jazz

Yoshi's has breathed new life into the Fillmore District.

Throughout the middle 20th century San Francisco's Fillmore District was synonymous with jazz. Known as the 'Harlem of the West', this outpost of cool drew the top performers of its day – Ella Fitzgerald, Louis Armstrong, Miles Davis, Thelonious Monk and Duke Ellington headlined the more than two-dozen clubs, and many performers, including Dave Brubeck, launched their careers here. But following the disastrous process of 'urban renewal' in the '60s, '70s and '80s, the once-vibrant neighborhood became a poster child for urban decay, with only the Fillmore Auditorium remaining as a reminder of its golden era.

Decades of ill-conceived, poorly funded and flat-out mismanaged attempts to revitalize the area followed, until a major new project, the **Fillmore Jazz Heritage Center**, took root. The $72 million multi-use development now houses a museum, 1300 On Fillmore, an upscale soul food restaurant, screening rooms, 80 condominiums and its centerpiece: **Yoshi's San Francisco** (*see p238*), a 28,000 square foot jazz venue that includes a state-of-the-art 470-seat club and 370-seat Japanese restaurant

The almost miraculous evolution of Yoshi's began in 1973 when three friends, Yoshie Akiba (for whom the club was named), Kaz Kajimura and Hiroyuki Hora opened a 25-seat Japanese restaurant in Berkeley. Wildly successful, Yoshi's moved to bigger digs in 1977 and over the next two decades built a reputation for being one of the premiere jazz venues in the Bay Area. In 1997 the owners constructed a purpose-built, 330-seat jazz club in Oakland's Jack London Square that quickly became the top jazz venue in the region, attracting top names such as Diana Krall, Branford Marsalis, Dizzy Gillespie, Harry Connick Jr, McCoy Tyner and Pat Metheny.

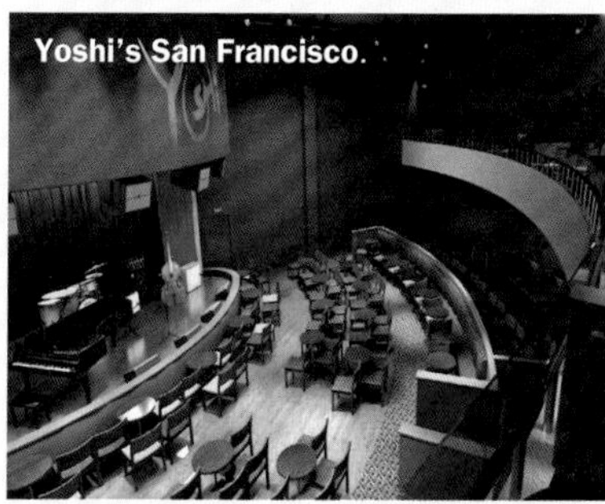
Yoshi's San Francisco.

When the Fillmore Jazz Preservation District took shape, Yoshi's seemed the clear choice to anchor the revitalization effort. But it was a serious gamble. Could the region support another high-end jazz venue? Would Yoshi's SF cannibalize the Oakland audience?

When Yoshi's San Francisco opened in 2007, it immediately drew praise from press, fans and artists alike. But when the economic downturn gripped the city, the club began to lose money. Thanks to creative programming, including late-night DJ sets and a new program featuring noted hip hop acts backed by live bands such as Public Enemy, De La Soul, and Mos Def, the San Francisco flagship made it into the black in 2010.

Today, Yoshi's SF appears to be reviving the Fillmore District, with sellout shows and truly inspired bookings. Above all, Yoshi's SF has continued to build on its legacy and win the hearts and minds of artists who often have the option of playing larger venues, but prefer the passionate audiences Yoshi's has always drawn. As nine-time Grammy winner Wynton Marsalis tells it, 'Yoshi's has tremendous integrity. Its presentation and booking is right on.'

Although the Elbo has been commandeered by yuppies, it continues to be a place to hear good music on a lively stretch of Valencia Street. You're likely to hear jazz (usually with a beat-driven edge), pure funk, soul or Latin jazz in the open-raftered space upstairs, but also hip hop, hard rock, metal and random whacked-out experimentalism. On Sundays, it's the legendary Dub Mission DJ night, a reggae revival that just celebrated its 15th anniversary.

Rasselas Jazz

1534 Fillmore Street, at Geary Boulevard, Fillmore (346 8696, www.rasselasjazzclub.com). Bus 2, 3, 22, 31, 38. **Open** 5pm-1am daily. **Shows** usually 9pm Mon-Thur, Sun; 6pm, 9pm Fri, Sat. **Admission** usually 2 drink minimum. **Credit** AmEx, MC, V. **Map** p314 H6.

Designed to be an anchor of the Fillmore Jazz Preservation District, Rasselas suffers from unadventurous programming, yet still manages to draw lively crowds at weekends. The decor – high ceilings, bachelor-pad furniture and a crackling fireplace behind the band – is suggestive of a 1960s playboy den; combos and old R&B acts usually get the weekend crowds of African-American revelers and white yuppies up on to their feet.

Saloon

1232 Grant Avenue, at Columbus Avenue, North Beach (989 7666, www.sfblues.net/Saloon.html). Bus 10, 12, 30, 39, 41, 45, 91. **Open** noon-2am daily. **Shows** 9pm Mon-Thur; 4pm Fri-Sun. **Admission** free-$5. **No credit cards. Map** p315 M3.

A beer hall that scandalized the neighborhood when it was established back in 1861 (it's now the oldest continuously operating bar in all of San Francisco), the Saloon has survived earthquakes and shifting musical tastes, and still remains a no-nonsense, rough-edged joint with a busy, bluesy calendar. Psychedelic-era rockers gracing the stage might include former members of Jefferson Airplane and Country Joe & the Fish.

★ Yoshi's

1330 Fillmore Street, at Eddy Street, Western Addition (655 5600, www.yoshis.com/san francisco). Bus 5, 22, 31, 38. **Open** *Box office* noon-8.30pm daily. *Lounge* from 5.30pm Mon-Sat, 5pm Sun. **Admission** varies. **Credit** AmEx, Disc, MC, V.

The handsome, refined Jack London Square venue established Yoshi's as the best jazz joint in the Bay Area – possibly along the entire West Coast – and founder/co-owner Kaz Kajimura has consolidated its reputation among artists and audiences alike with the Fillmore Street branch in the Jazz Preservation District, which boasts a slightly larger live room and the same excellent acoustics as its predecessor. Both locations do good business on the strength of their upmarket Japanese food, but the main attraction in both is the music, a cultured line-up of big names (working the weekend slots) and newcomers (earlier in the week). Book well in advance.

Other locations 510 Embarcadero West, Jack London Square, Oakland (510.238.9200)

▶ *For more on Yoshi's see p237* **The Throne Room of West Coast Jazz**.

Rock, pop & hip hop

Public perception of the San Francisco sound is still stuck in the 1960s, when the likes of Jefferson Airplane drew young pilgrims; later, the Dead Kennedys, Metallica and Black Rebel Motorcycle Club added to the city's reputation for noisy guitar rock. These days, however, the Bay Area also has a potent hip hop scene, while Oakland is a hotbed of electronic and improvised noise experimentation informed by punk and indie-rock aesthetics.

The scene suffered a setback with the dotcom bust. Though the city recovered, music faced a longer hangover. Clubs and rehearsal spaces bit the dust, and musicians headed to cheaper climes. In the last few years, the scene has picked up: well-renovated halls such as the **Independent** (*see p240*) sprang up; once-DJ-centered clubs such as the **Mezzanine** (*see p246* built proper live music stages; and hotspots such as the **Rickshaw Stop** (*see p243*) now draw trendies and serious listeners alike to once-quiet neighborhoods.

The scene's continued success can be chalked up to a cross-genre cadre of youthful musicians and forward-thinking bookers and promoters who continue to form bands and fill stages all over: at clubs and other music events, sure, but also at galleries and warehouses. These days, SF boasts one of the most exciting underground scenes in the US. It has spawned international names like Devendra Banhart and Joanna Newsom (both of whom have since left the city limits); kicked off the clicks, whizzes and synths of E-40, the Federation, Turf Talk and the rest of the hyphy movement; nurtured rockers such as Wooden Ships, Film School, Vetiver, Citay and Rogue Wave, who've all landed on respected indie labels; and inspired those – like hip hoppers Lyrics Born, the Coup and Blackalicious, the rap experimentalists of Anticon and electronica terrorist Kid 606 – who are making it on their own imprints. The variety on that list is indicative of the eclecticism of the city's music today.

TICKETS

For larger concerts – pretty much anything at the 'major venues' below – it's worth buying tickets in advance. Where possible, buy from the venue's own box office to avoid the booking fees levied by Ticketmaster (*see p200*). Advance purchase isn't always necessary for the venues listed under 'Bars & clubs', but it's never a bad idea if you want to be on the safe side. Always call ahead or look at venue websites before making a special trip.

FESTIVALS

Perhaps the most exciting festival to arise in years is the **Hardly Strictly Bluegrass Festival** (www.strictlybluegrass.com), a three-day long festival held in early October in San Francisco's Golden Gate Park. Entirely free (thanks to the good graces and large fortune of founder Warren Hellman), the festival drew 600,000 in 2010 with a top-flight, eclectic lineup of artists to rival New Orleans' Jazz Fest.

There's everything from rock to opera at the **Stern Grove Festival** (www.sterngrove.org), on Sundays from June to August. Performances take place in an idyllic amphitheatre set in a grove of eucalyptus trees; admission is free. Probably the biggest rock festival of the year in SF is **Noise Pop** (www.noisepop.com), a week-long, city-wide series of indie shows in February. June's similarly spreadeagled **Mission Creek Music & Arts Festival** (www.mcmf.org) likewise concentrates on alternative rock, albeit with a more local focus and a more experimental edge. And, speaking of experimental, lovers of the avant-garde ought to investigate August's **San Francisco Electronic Music Festival** (www.sfemf.org).

INSIDE TRACK HARDLY STRICTLY BLUEGRASS

When billionaire investment banker, mayonnaise heir and banjo picker Warren Hellman announced a decade ago that he was going to launch a free bluegrass festival in San Francisco's Golden Gate Park, you could almost hear the collective 'Huh?'. Originally consisting of two stages and nine bands, **Hardly Strictly Bluegrass** has since exploded into the city's biggest free musical extravaganza – a monumental event every October that stretches three full days, has six stages and features the country's biggest names in popular music. More than half a million people attended in 2010 to see emerging bands, movie star-musicians like Steve Martin, major performers such as Elvis Costello trying out new material, and an eclectic assortment of headliners ranging from Emmylou Harris and Steve Earle to Patti Smith, Rosanne Cash, and Gillian Welch.

MAJOR VENUES

The venues detailed below all host concerts on a regular basis. In addition, a handful of larger arenas stage the occasional show. In San Francisco these include **AT&T Park** (*see p250*), the **Nob Hill Masonic Center** (1111 California Street, at Taylor Street), the **Palace of Fine Arts** (*see p101*) the **Concourse at SF Design Center** (635 8th Street, at Brannan Street) and the cavernous **Bill Graham Civic Auditorium** (99 Grove Street, at Polk Street, 974 4060, www.billgrahamcivic.com). Other venues include the **Henry J Kaiser Arena** (10 10th Street) and **Oracle Arena** in Oakland (*see p250*); and the Berkeley Community Theater at **Berkeley High School and Greek Theatre** (1-510 642 9988, www.calperfs.berkeley.edu, www.anotherplanetent.com) in Berkeley. A bit further out, the **Shoreline Amphitheatre** in Mountain View (1-650 967 3000, www.shorelineamp.com), the **Sleep Train Pavilion** in Concord (1-925 363 5701, www.chroniclepavilion.com), and the **San José State University Event Center** (290 South 7th Street, San Jose, 1-408 924 6360) and **HP Pavilion** in San José (1-408 287 9200, www.hppsj.com) also stage big-name shows from time to time, especially during the summer months. Check venue websites or contact Ticketmaster (*see 200*) for tickets. *See also p235* **And the Band Played On**.

Bimbo's 365 Club

1025 Columbus Avenue, at Chestnut Street, North Beach (474 0365, www.bimbos365club.com). Bus 30, 39, 47, 91/cable car Powell-Mason. **Box office** 10am-4pm Mon-Fri. **Tickets** $18-$75. **Credit** (advance bookings only) MC, V. **Map** p314 L2.

Bimbo's began life as a Market Street speakeasy in 1931, moving to North Beach two decades later. The venue is still owned by the descendants of Agostino 'Bimbo' Giuntoli, one of its original owners, and has been nicely preserved, with a mermaid theme running throughout. Rita Hayworth once worked the boards as a dancer, but these days you're more likely to see Prefuse 73 spinning vinyl, or tribute bands such as Super Diamond working up the crowd.

★ Fillmore Auditorium

1805 Geary Boulevard, at Fillmore Street, Fillmore (24hr hotline 346 6000, www.thefillmore.com). Bus 2, 3, 22, 31, 38. **Box office** 10am-4pm Sun; also 7.30-10pm show nights. **Tickets** $20-$50. **Credit** AmEx, Disc, MC, V. **Map** p314 H6.

The 1,200-capacity Fillmore was built in 1912, but is better known as the venue in which Bill Graham launched his rock-promotion empire and became the staging ground for the 'San Francisco Sound' that

Bottom of the Hill.

included bands such as the Grateful Dead, among many, many others as well as memorable shows by the likes of the Who, Johnny Winter, Eric Clapton, Mike Bloomfield and Santana. The performers who play the gorgeous room tend to be on the verge of making it massive (or already massive and yearning for the more intimate good ole days).

★ Great American Music Hall

859 O'Farrell Street, between Polk & Larkin Streets, Tenderloin (885 0750, www.musichallsf.com). Bus 2, 3, 4, 19, 27, 31, 38, 47, 49, 90. **Box office** 10.30am-6pm Mon-Fri; 1hr before show Sat, Sun. **Tickets** $15-$40. **Credit** MC, V. **Map** p314 K6.

Originally a bordello, then a highfalutin nightclub operated by notorious fan dancer Sally Rand, the grande dame of the city's smaller venues is as beautiful today as at any point in its century-long history. The lavish room, done out with enormous mirrors, rococo woodwork and gold-leaf trim, is these days run by the owners of Slim's (*see right*), who present a cutting-edge roster of well-regarded local and touring musicians (many of the indie-rock ilk). Try to snag one of the coveted seats on the upper balcony.

Independent

628 Divisadero Street, at Hayes Street, Western Addition (771 1421, www.theindependentsf.com). Bus 5, 21, 24. **Box office** 11am-6pm Mon-Fri; 1hr before show. **Tickets** $18-$30. **Credit** MC, V. **Map** p317 G8.

New owners have given this venerable black box the makeover it deserved, with work that included the installation of a stellar sound and light system. In accordance with the varied sounds in the club's storied past, the calendar is filled with a mix of touring rock, pop, metal, rap, jazz, Americana, jam and otherwise undefinable offerings such as Madlib, Sunn 0))), the Boredoms, Fiery Furnaces, High on Fire and Lyrics Born.

The Regency Ballroom

1290 Sutter Street, at Van Ness Avenue (1-800 745 3000, www.theregencyballroom.com). Bus 2, 3, 19, 38, 47, 49, 90. **Tickets** use Ticketmaster or the Warfield box office; prices vary. **Credit** AmEx, MC, V. **Map** p314 K5.

Formerly a Masonic temple, a dance studio, a Polish arts foundation and a movie theater, this gorgeous Beaux Arts-style ballroom, with its horseshoe-shaped balcony, hardwood floors and fin-de-siècle teardrop chandeliers, now stages everything from opera to rock and jazz gigs to dance events. The landmark 1909 building incorporates the legendary Avalon Ballroom (now the Grand), which once hosted shows by the likes of Janis Joplin and Country Joe & the Fish.

Slim's

333 11th Street, between Folsom & Harrison Streets, SoMa (255 0333, www.slims-sf.com). Bus 9, 12, 27, 47, 90. **Box office** 10.30am-6pm Mon-Fri. **Tickets** $14-$24. **Credit** MC, V. **Map** p318 L9.

It might be one of San Francisco's more important music venues, but the 550-capacity Slim's isn't one of its most comfortable: most patrons have to stand, sightlines are compromised by the floor-to-ceiling pillars and, on busy nights, it gets pretty steamy. The schedule is mostly made up of rock bands, who play alongside a smattering of hip hop acts, reggae groups and rootsy singer/songwriters.

The Warfield

982 Market Street, at Mason Street, Tenderloin (775 7722, www.thewarfieldtheatre.com). BART & Metro to Powell/bus 14, 27, 31 & Market Street routes/cable car Powell-Hyde or Powell-Mason. **Box office** 10am-4pm Sun; also 7.30-10pm show nights. **Tickets** $20-$50. **Credit** AmEx, MC, V. **Map** p315 M6.

Another grand old theater, this one dating back to 1922, that has been converted into a rock and pop venue in later life. A step up from the Fillmore in terms of capacity, the ornate, 2,100-seat room hosts major national and international acts, many making their last stop on the circuit before vaulting to arena-sized venues. It's very well designed: even the rear-most balcony seats have good views of the stage.

BARS & CLUBS

Several other bars and nightclubs around the city host worthwhile music nights. Among them are a number of gay venues , including the **Eagle Tavern** (*see p230*), which hosts punk and hardcore shows, and **Kimo's** (1351 Polk Street, Nob Hill, 885 4535), a landmark gay bar where rock acts of varying quality perform in its upstairs room.

Note that for all venues listed here, opening hours and showtimes can vary: 'usually 9pm' means the occasional show may begin at 8.30pm or 10pm. Always call or check online (most venues keep their websites bang up to date) before setting out.

Bottom of the Hill

1233 17th Street, at Missouri Street, Potrero Hill (621 4455, www.bottomofthehill.com). Bus 10, 22. **Open** 8.30pm-2am Mon, Tue, Sat, Sun; 4pm-2am Wed-Fri. **Shows** usually 9pm daily. **Admission** $12-$25. **Credit** AmEx, MC, V. **Map** p319 N10.

This little club, wedged among warehouses at the base of Potrero Hill, has long been a favorite with the indie-rock crowd. It features local and touring acts most nights, as well as occasional arena acts (Mars Volta, the Beastie Boys) hankering to play an intimate show. Underground bands that play here one year may become cult sensations or even major stars the next. The decor is classic dive, with quirky touches.

Café du Nord & the Swedish American Hall

2170 Market Street, between Church & Sanchez Streets, Castro (861 5016, www.cafedunord.com). Metro to Church/streetcar F/bus 22, 37. **Open** 1hr before show-2am. **Shows** times vary, daily. **Admission** $10-$35. **Credit** (bar only) AmEx, MC, V. **Map** p318 H9.

Several SF nightspots carry the feel of a Prohibition-era speakeasy, but none captures the spirit quite as well as the Café du Nord. Mind you, it does have a head start: it actually was one. The subterranean front room, which hosts cultured alternative acts, has red velvet walls and a 40ft (12m) mahogany bar that bustles with scenesters. Owner Guy Carson also books the likes of Cat Power, Joanna Newsom, Bert Jansch and Jenny Lewis to play the quaint, larger Swedish American Hall upstairs.

Edinburgh Castle Pub

950 Geary Street, at Polk Street, Tenderloin (885 4074, www.castlenews.com). Bus 2, 3, 19, 27, 31, 38, 47, 49, 90. **Open** *Pub* 5pm-2am daily. *Venue* from 9.30pm. **Show times** vary. **Admission** *Pub* free. *Venue* $5. **Credit** MC, V. **Map** p314 K6.

This oak-clad, beer-stained ode to Highland high times offers fish 'n' chips till 11pm and plenty of booths for loud conversation, but trip upstairs, past the pool table on the mezzanine, to catch the live punk, indie and metal shows, in addition to the occasional northern soul dance party and quiz night.

El Rio

3158 Mission Street, at Cesar Chavez Street, Mission (282 3325, www.elriosf.com). BART 24th Street Mission/bus 12, 14, 27, 36, 49. **Open** 5pm-2am Mon-Thur; 4pm-2am Fri; 1pm-2am Sat, Sun (5pm-2am Sat, Sun Dec-Feb). **Shows times** vary. **Admission** free-$10. **No credit cards.**

Head to the El Rio on a Sunday afternoon and make your way to the garden, where you'll find San Francisco's most diverse and lively salsa party: a local tradition for more than 25 years and now taking place year-round. There's an outdoor barbecue, dancing lessons, decent margaritas and a friendly crowd of straights and queers. Other

Café du Nord & the Swedish American Hall.

ARTS & ENTERTAINMENT

And the Band Played On

Musical history was made at these landmark venues.

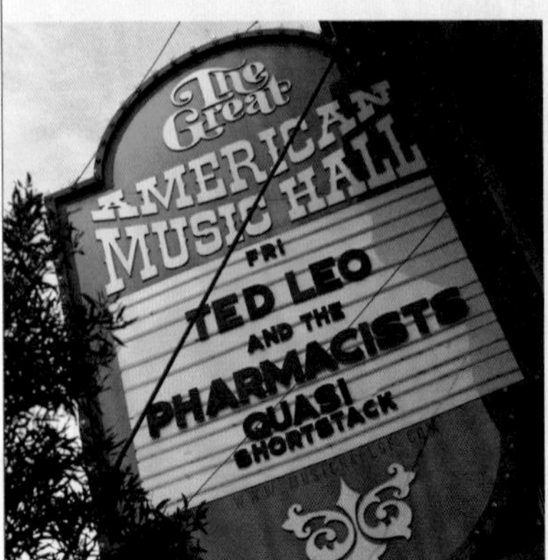

Great American Music Hall.

Some accuse San Franciscans of being mired in musical nostalgia – fixated on 1950s Beat bohemia or stuck in a Summer of Love flashback. Perhaps they have a point, but in a city with a musical history this extraordinary, it would be harsh to criticize a music-lover for wanting to explore the iconic, still-raging hotspots where it all happened.

The town's grandest beauty – the **Great American Music Hall** (*see p240*) – is the perfect place to start: constructed in 1907, this erstwhile bordello has maintained its baroque, gilded beauty, supported by marble columns and lined with ornate Barbary Coast-era mirrors. In the 1930s, it was owned by renowned fan-dancer/stripper Sally Rand, said to still haunt its corridors. Now the former jazz joint is known for its diverse rock and pop shows.

Further east on Geary is the **Fillmore** (*see p239*), once a jazz-era big-band venue that went by the moniker the Majestic Ballroom. The elegant, chandeliered auditorium where rock impresario Bill Graham made his name has since ushered in memorable shows by the likes of the Who, Johnny Winter, Eric Clapton, Mike Bloomfield and Santana, as the posters lining the walls of the upstairs bar attest.

Just across the street lies the **Boom Boom Room** (*see p237*), in the same space that housed the once-jumping jazz joint Jack's, a linchpin of the district's lively African-American nightlife scene in the 1940s and '50s. John Lee Hooker gave the place its name and held court here until his death in 2001.

Less likely to be booming with cool sounds is the stately Beaux Arts-style

nights you might encounter experimental rock, DJs or the odd home-grown film festival.

Hemlock Tavern

1131 Polk Street, at Post Street, Tenderloin (923 0923, www.hemlocktavern.com). Bus 2, 3, 19, 38, 47, 49, 90. **Open** 4pm-2am daily. **Shows** 9.30pm daily. **Admission** free-$10. **No credit cards. Map** p314 K6.

Out front, the Hemlock looks like a capacious, matey watering hole, a lively mix of young tastemakers, art snobs and yuppies playing pool, yapping at the central bar or puffing in the open-air smoking 'room'. At the back, however, an intimate live room plays host to some of the more edgy and intelligent musical programming in the city. The roster is built around hipster-friendly artists such as Deerhoof and Wolf Eyes, with no knowing who will blow up next.

Hotel Utah

500 4th Street, at Bryant Street, SoMa (546 6300, www.thehotelutahsaloon.com). Bus 10, 12, 30, 45, 47, 91. **Open** 11.30am-2am Mon-Fri; 11am-2am Sat, Sun. **Shows** usually 9pm daily. **Admission** $6-$10. **Credit** MC, V. **Map** p319 N7.

The down-and-dirty days of the Barbary Coast are ingrained in the timbers of this 1908 watering hole, which has welcomed the likes of Marilyn Monroe, Bing Crosby and an assortment of gangsters and beatniks. Now gaining a fresh lease of life, the Utah

Grand Ballroom (*see p240*), which flings open its doors on a more irregular basis. Graham's down-home competitor and hippie king Chet Helms threw trippy rock shows in the hall during the '60s, when it was dubbed the Avalon Ballroom: there he unveiled his protégé Janis Joplin in 1966 and gathered the long-haired Love Generation for Moby Grape, the Steve Miller Blues Band and Bo Diddley, among others.

Further south in Downtown stands the ex-movie palace the **Warfield** (*see p240*), where Louis Armstrong once shared the bill with the talkies. More talent came to call when Graham announced the arrival of Bob Dylan's gospel shows here in 1979. Since then the cavernous hall has played host to such draws as the Grateful Dead, Elvis Costello, Nick Cave, Neil Young and Prince.

In North Beach, check into cellar comedy club the **Purple Onion** (140 Columbus Avenue, 956 1653, www.purpleonioncomedy.com), now suffering from a sad sports bar-style renovation. Back in its '50s and '60s heyday, the Kingston Trio, the Smothers Brothers, Rod McKuen and Maya Angelou whooped it up before tourists arrived looking for beatnik caricatures. And finally, towards Fisherman's Wharf, **Bimbo's 365 Club** (*see p239*) sets the scene for early '50s supper-club glamour with a parquet dancefloor, leather booths and kitsch-cool girl-in-a-fishbowl theme. Joey Bishop, Xavier Cugat and Louis Prima serenaded here years before the Strokes, Iggy Pop and Blonde Redhead worked its stage.

is both a characterful bar and a cozy music room, hosting indie rockers, singer-songwriters and the occasional more eclectic curiosity.

Knockout

3223 Mission Street, at Valencia Street, Mission (550 6994, www.theknockoutsf.com). Bus 12, 14, 24, 27, 36, 49. **Open** 5pm-2am daily. **Shows** usually 9pm or 10pm daily. **Admission** free-$8. **No credit cards**.

Owned by 2007 mayoral candidate and Burning Man fan Chicken John back when it was called the Odeon, this shoebox of a club sports a small stage in the back, karaoke happy hours, late-night installments of beer-sodden bingo and other quirky diversions. Catch indie-rock combos like Imperial Teen spinoff Hey Willpower and Old Time Relijun.

Make-Out Room

3225 22nd Street, between Mission & Valencia Streets, Mission (647 2888, www.makeoutroom.com). BART 24th Street Mission/bus 12, 14, 48, 49, 67. **Open** 6pm-2am daily. **Shows** usually 9pm daily. **Admission** $5-$10. **No credit cards**. **Map** p318 K12.

One of the best places in town to see smallish bands, the Make-Out Room attracts a laid-back, alternative, youthful crowd on its weekend live music nights. The decor lives up to the name: there's a bearskin rug on one wall and a stag's head on another, with a rainbow of bras strung from the antlers. The atmosphere, as with many Mission bars, is that of a cheery dive.

Red Devil Lounge

1695 Polk Street, at Clay Street, Polk Gulch (921 1695, www.reddevillounge.com). Bus 1, 12, 19, 27, 47, 49, 90. **Open** usually 8pm-2am daily. **Shows** usually 9pm daily. **Admission** $3-$30. **Credit** AmEx, Disc, MC, V. **Map** p314 K4.

This corner venue, done out with Gothic touches, has recently ramped up its music offerings, which sit alongside club nights in a fairly busy calendar. The line-ups aren't often cutting edge, but the venue does stage crowd-pulling acts such as the Misfits, the English Beat and KRS-One.

★ Rickshaw Stop

155 Fell Street, at Franklin Street, Hayes Valley (861 2011, www.rickshawstop.com). Metro to Van Ness/bus 21, 47, 49 & Market Street routes. **Open** 7pm-2am Wed-Sat. **Shows** times vary. **Admission** $5-$25. **No credit cards**. **Map** p318 K8.

Doing its best to fill a sparse strip near Civic Center, the Rickshaw taps a cool collegiate/rec-room vibe with its crash-pad decor of mod plastic loungers, foosball table and odalisque-via-Target lighting. Come for the laid-back hipster ambience and low-priced snack menu, but stay for hep local and touring bands and hot, hard-edged electro and mash-up DJs.

Thee Parkside

1600 17th Street, at Wisconsin Street, Potrero Hill (252 1330, www.theeparkside.com). Bus 10, 19, 22. **Open** 2pm-2am daily. **Shows** usually 9pm, earlier during weekends. **Admission** free-$15. **No credit cards**. **Map** p319 N10.

This roadhouse started out as a lunch spot for dot-com cube farmers. When the pink slips began to flutter, Thee Parkside found new life as a rowdy joint specializing in roots, punk, country and garage rock. Things get sweaty in the main room, where the so-called 'stage' abuts the door. In the tiki patio out back, beer guzzlers heat up with a bit of ping-pong.

Nightclubs

When the lights go down the nightlife starts up.

San Francisco is a town that's unafraid to let it all hang out. When times are good, people party. When times are bad, people party. Even in the midst of the economic downturn, San Franciscans found ways to have fun, with many clubs dropping cover prices and authorities turning a blind eye to nightspots without dance licenses so folks could shake their groove thing.

These days, if you're looking to shake it, Milk, DNA Lounge and Mezzanine are all good bets, and dancing has made a comeback at many smaller venues as well. The latest round of Silicon Valley successes has again filled the city with awkward techies eager to hit the floors – but this time good vibes, not vulgar displays of wealth, seem to rule the scene.

INFORMATION

Both print and online versions of *SF Weekly* and the *San Francisco Bay Guardian* have extensive clubs listings. It's also worth visiting Amoeba Music, Tweekin Records and Aquarius Records (for all, *see p200*) to pick up flyers and magazines advertising goings-on. Check online for details of under-the-radar events. The discussion boards at Craigslist (www.craigslist.org) are useful, while Squid List (www.laughingsquid.org) is the first place techno hippies look for multimedia extravaganzas. Blasthaus (www.blasthaus.com) lists major dance music events, while SF Station (www.sfstation.com) offers well-edited, succinctly written party listings with an updated calendar. However, the daddy of them all is Flavorpill (www.flavorpill.com/sanfrancisco), its weekly dispatch outlining the best of the city's cultural happenings.

Admission prices depend on the night, but usually vary from nothing to $25. Many clubs stay open well past last orders, but by law they can't serve alcohol between 2am and 6am. Some clubs are strictly 21 and over; if you're under 21, check the club's policy before you go. All clubs are strict about not serving alcohol to under-21s.

INSIDE TRACK THE HEAT IS ON

Want to know where the 'in' crowd is heading tonight? Check out Citysense (www.sensenetworks.com/citysense.php), a mobile app that merges vast stores of historical data and mobile phone activity to generate a real-time 'heat map' – a kind of up-to-the-minute map of human traffic – showing where people are and relative levels of activity throughout the city. Linked with other data streams such as Google and Yelp, over time the app gains a 'sense' of user preferences and tailors the map to show where people with similar interests are currently congregating. Don't worry, all information is gathered anonymously and users can delete their history at any time (iPhone, Blackberry supported; Android available summer 2011).

LATE-NIGHT TRANSPORT

The Muni Owl Service operates on the Muni Metro L and N lines and on the 5, 14, 22, 24, 38, 90, 91 and 108 bus lines from 1am until 5am. All other lines stop at 12.30am. BART runs roughly until midnight. For taxi companies, *see p287.*

DOWNTOWN

Union Square & around

Harry Denton's Starlight Room
Sir Francis Drake Hotel, 450 Powell Street, between Post & Sutter Streets (395 8595, www.harrydenton.com). BART & Metro to Powell/bus 2, 3, 27, 30, 45, 76, 91/cable car

Powell-Hyde or Powell-Mason. **Open** 6pm-2am Tue-Sat; 11am-2am Sun. **Admission** free-$15 (free before 8.30pm). **Credit** AmEx, DC, Disc, MC, V. **Map** p315 M5.
Both of Harry Denton's venues are love 'em or leave 'em affairs. Block out the stunning 21st-floor view over Union Square, the multiple mirrors and the floral carpets, and you're left with a room of dressed-up social and financial climbers dancing to 'Mustang Sally'. Meanwhile, Harry Denton's Rouge (1500 Broadway, at Polk Street, 346 7683) offers the delights of Vegas-style showgirls jiggling on the bar and mingling with the starry-eyed punters.

Rrazz Room

Hotel Nikko, 222 Mason Street, between Ellis & O'Farrell Streets (394 1189, www.therraazz room.com). BART & Metro to Powell/bus 2, 3, 4, 30, 45, 76 & Market Street routes/cable car Powell-Hyde or Powell-Mason. **Open** 2pm-1.30am daily. **Admission** $30-$55. **Credit** AmEx, DC, Disc, MC, V. **Map** p315 M6.
Australian beefcake revue *Thunder from Down Under*; '80s teen star Tiffany; television's Wonder Woman, Lynda Carter, reinventing herself as a chanteuse; drag queen revues; Motown legends. What do they have in common? The Rrazz Room at the Hotel Nikko. Cheesy? Likely. Surreal? Absolutely. But rest assured that the shows will be professionally produced and there's not an obstructed view in the room.

Ruby Skye

420 Mason Street, between Geary & Post Streets (693 0777, www.rubyskye.com). BART & Metro to Powell/bus 2, 3, 27, 30, 31, 38, 45, 76, 91/cable car Powell-Hyde or Powell-Mason. **Open** 7pm-2am Thur; 7pm-4am Fri, Sat. **Admission** $10-$30. **Credit** AmEx, Disc, MC, V. **Map** p314 L5.
Converted from an elegant 1890s theater, Ruby Skye has retained a good many of its ornate Victorian touches, while gaining thoroughly modern sound and lighting systems in the translation. But with its huge dancefloor and parade of surgically enhanced women, the whole scene feels like it's been imported from LA. Not surprisingly, it's a second home for rave-circuit big names like Sasha and Digweed. *Photo p247.*

Vessel

85 Campton Place, off Stockton Street, between Sutter & Post Streets (433 8585, www.vessel sf.com). Bart & Metro to Montgomery/bus 2, 3, 30, 38, 45, 76, 91/cable car Powell-Hyde or Powell-Mason. **Open** 10pm-2am Wed, Thur, Sat; 9.30pm-2am Fri. **Admission** free-$20. **Credit** AmEx, MC, V. **Map** p315 M5.
A blast from the city's ostentatious dotcom past – a person could easily spend upwards of $1,000 here on fancy champagne service to impress his or her other half. Still, cruising through this incredibly well-appointed bar early in the evening can be fun (you're guaranteed a long wait in line and the often disapproving scrutiny of the bouncers if you arrive after 10pm), if only to revel in the screeching decadence of San Francisco's monied class.

Ruby Skye.

The Tenderloin

★ 222 Hyde

222 Hyde Street, at Turk Street (440 0222, http://222hyde.net). BART & Metro to Civic Center/bus 5, 19, 27, 31, 38. **Open** 6pm-2am Tue-Sun. **Admission** varies. **Credit** AmEx, Disc, MC, V. **Map** p314 K6.
One of the funkiest little clubs in San Francisco, the 222 Hyde hosts hip hop, house, techno and electro nights, alongside a smattering of experimental live performances, in a hipper-than-hip yet nonetheless eminently friendly atmosphere. This is the place to scope out the upper crust of the city's underground as they munch away on gourmet pizzas or sip their moderately priced cocktails. Originally the basement was the sound booth for the neighboring Blackhawk jazz club, where jazz giants like Miles Davis, Thelonious Monk, and Dave Brubeck cut live albums.

Temple.

Suite One8one

181 Eddy Street, at Taylor Street (345 9900, www.suite181.com). BART & Metro to Powell/bus 27, 31, 38 & Market Street routes. **Open** 9pm-4am Thur-Sat. **Admission** $20. **Credit** AmEx, Disc, MC, V. **Map** p314 L6.

The ultra-swank Suite One8one is one of SF's hottest spots, but it's not for everyone. Some cologne-soaked folks are suckers for a $20 cover, and that's potentially the appeal. Past the rather surly doormen, three floors boast a series of plush rooms and VIP areas. However, the pedestrian music, not to mention the rather snooty crowd, can leave one feeling a bit empty.

SOMA & SOUTH BEACH

For gay and lesbian bars and nightclubs in SoMa, among them the **Stud**, *see pp231-32.*

★ 111 Minna

111 Minna Street, between 2nd & New Montgomery Streets (974 1719, www.111minnagallery.com). BART & Metro to Montgomery/bus 9, 12, 14, 30, 31, 38, 45, 76 & Market Street routes. **Open** *Gallery* noon-5pmWed-Sat. *Bar* 5-10pm Tue; 5pm-2am Wed-Sat. **Admission** free-$15. **Credit** AmEx, DC, MC, V. **Map** p315 N5.

This concrete box, located down an alley just south of Market Street, is an art gallery by day, but morphs into a truly happening dance club by night. It draws an unusual hybrid clientele – serious rave yuppies – but is popular with all kinds of dance-music freaks thanks to a music policy that travels from garage to Afrobeat, stopping at all stations in between.

▶ *For more on San Francisco's hybrid club-galleries, see p248* **Art & Cocktails**.

330 Ritch

330 Ritch Street, between Brannan & Townsend Streets (541 9574, www.330ritch.com). Metro N to 2nd & King/bus 10, 30, 45, 47, 76, 91. **Open** 5pm-2am Wed-Fri; 10pm-2am Sat, Sun. **Admission** free-$10. **Credit** AmEx, MC, V. **Map** p319 O7.

The young crowd seems right at home in this spacious yet intimate spot, tucked away down a SoMa alley. The sounds include hip hop and classic soul, but an increasingly interesting smattering of up-and-coming European acts and DJs have made their way on to the calendar making the overall vibe a bit more Continental.

DNA Lounge

375 11th Street, between Folson & Harrison Streets (626 1409, www.dnalounge.com). Bus 9, 12, 27, 47, 90. **Open** 9pm-2am Mon-Thur; 9pm-4am Fri, Sat; hours vary Sun. **Admission** $5-$25. **No credit cards**. **Map** p318 L9.

Goth kids flock to SoMa for all manner of musical fetishes and countercultural indulgences. But none of their nights is complete without a stop at the DNA Lounge. This long-time fixture has undergone massive remodeling over the years and now hosts DJ nights and concerts by the likes of Laibach. However, the wonderful stage set-up, viewable from both the dancefloor and the recessed mezzanine, has turned even hip hop acts on to this gem of a nightspot.

Mezzanine

444 Jessie Street, at 6th Street (820 9669, www.mezzaninesf.com). BART & Metro to Powell/bus 14, 27 & Market Street routes. **Open** 9pm-2am Fri; 9pm-7am Sat; other nights vary. **Admission** free-$30. **No credit cards**. **Map** p319 M7.

This 900-capacity club and art gallery has two long bars bordering the ample dancefloor and lofty space upstairs. Local DJs and even some live acts hold court on the weekends, while touring techno acts such as Richie Hawtin and Miss Kittin make it their sole stop in SF. Could it be that massive sound system, often thought of as the city's best?

Roe

651 Howard Street, between 3rd and Hawthorne Streets (227 0288, www.roe-sf.com). BART & Metro to Montgomery/bus 10, 14, 76 & Market Street routes. **Open** 5am-midnight Mon-Thur; 5pm-2am Fri; 9pm-3am Sat. **Credit** AmEx, DC, Disc, MC, V. **Map** p315 N6.

With a main floor and private lounge, Roe is a swank, sceney, bottle service kind of joint. With themed happy hours, pan American and Asian small-plate menu and late-night DJ sets, it's a little slice of LA right in San Francisco. If you're into that kind of thing.

6ix

60 6th Street, at Jessie Street (863 1221, www.clubsix1.com). BART & Metro to Powell/ bus 14, 27 & Market Street routes. **Open** 9pm-2am Tue-Sat. **Admission** $5-$20. **Credit** AmEx, MC, V. **Map** p318 L7.

Behind the doors of this venue, located on one of the city's grubbiest blocks (go in a group or avoid looking rich and/or touristy), you'll find a high-ceilinged chill-out room and bar with a low-ceilinged dancefloor below. DJs have been known to spin house, dub, dancehall and whatever else may be filling floors at the moment. The upstairs space features paintings and photography by local and international artists.

Temple

540 Howard Street, between 1st & 2nd Streets (978 9942, www.templesf.com). BART & Metro to Montgomery/bus 10, 12, 14, 76, 108. **Open** 10pm-4am Fri, Sat; other nights vary. **Admission** $20-$30 **Credit** AmEx, Disc, MC, V. **Map** p315 N5.

After a turn toward smaller clubs (and less expensive entry fees), many of the city's scenesters bemoaned a lack of larger venues that weren't overrun by obnoxious singles and clueless DJs. Enter Temple, a three-story behemoth featuring an in-house Thai restaurant and several VIP enclaves, which opened some years ago to great acclaim. After-hours music programming includes some of the hottest house, techno and hip hop acts performing in a supperclub environment. *Photo p245.*

Amnesia.

1015 Folsom

1015 Folsom Street, at 6th Street (431 7444, www.1015.com). Bus 12, 19, 27, 47. **Open** 10pm-5am Fri, Sat; other nights vary. **Admission** $15-$25. **No credit cards. Map** p319 M7.

San Francisco's meat-and-potatoes dance club, 1015 is always a safe bet, whether you want to go dancing before, during or after hours. The three rooms each have their own vibe – move through space and time without changing venues. You'll find the same suburban crowd of pick-up artists and bimbos as in any big club, but they don't overwhelm the place.

Wish

1539 Folsom Street, between 11th & 12th Streets (431 1661, www.wishsf.com). Metro to Van Ness/bus 9, 12, 27, 47, 90. **Open** 5pm-2am Mon-Fri; 7pm-2am Sat. **Admission** varies. **Credit** AmEx, MC, V. **Map** p318 L9.

A meat market on most nights, albeit a comfortable one, boasting some of the best down-tempo and lounge music in the city and incredibly friendly staff. This is the place to hit on weeknights for a fancy cocktail with friends or to flirt with hot San Fran citizens while soaking up the bubbly tunes on tap. On weekends, Wish is swarming with tipsy lookers eager to suck face and talk your ear off – perfect if that's what you're looking for.

THE MISSION & THE CASTRO

For gay and lesbian bars and nightclubs in the Castro, *see pp227-31.*

The Mission

Amnesia

853 Valencia Street, between 19th & 20th Streets (970 0012, http://amnesiathebar.com). Bus 14, 33, 49. **Open** 6pm-2am daily. **Admission** free-$10. **No credit cards. Map** p318 K11.

Amnesia is still resisting the party-hearty armies that take over most of this stretch of the Mission at weekends. Instead, it draws a diverse, friendly, multi-ethnic crowd, and the DJ spins suitably eclectic sounds. With a nice selection of Belgian brews and friendly staff to boot, the patrons at the bar are as likely to be neighborhood regulars as they are curious tourists checking out the action.

★ Mighty

119 Utah Street, at 15th Street (626 7001, www.mighty119.com). Bus 9, 10, 19, 22, 27, 33,

90. **Open** 10pm-4am Thur-Sat; other nights vary. **Admission** free-$20. **No credit cards**. **Map** p319 M9.

The slick interior and flawless sound system led *URB* magazine to name Mighty the 'Best New Club in America' when it first opened, and the place has continued to receive plenty of accolades from San Franciscans. Rave it up at the main stage or take it easy in the chill-out room at the back.

THE HAIGHT & AROUND

Haight-Ashbury

Milk DJ Bar & Lounge

1840 Haight Street, between Shrader & Stanyan Streets (387 6455, www.milksf.com). Bus 6, 7, 33, 43, 71. **Open** 9pm-2am daily. **Admission** free-$10. **Credit** (no credit cards at door) AmEx, Disc, MC, V. **Map** p317 E9.

For years, the Haight-Ashbury district was ground zero for the city's rock scene, but these days hip hop is creeping in and proving itself a Haight Street mainstay, due in no small part to Milk's hip hop- and R&B-friendly bookers. Flash modern decor and a decent-sized dancefloor characterize the space, while big-name guests such as DJ Shadow have been known to drop in.

Lower Haight

Underground SF

424 Haight Street, between Fillmore & Webster Streets (864 7386). Bus 33, 37, 43, 71. **Open** 9pm-2am daily. **Admission** free-$10. **Credit** MC, V. **Map** p318 H8.

On a somewhat sketchy stretch of Lower Haight, this club is little more than a converted dive with a smallish dancefloor. But set the Underground's looks aside and pay attention with your ears instead: it has a deserved reputation as a center for turntable culture, and is a favorite spot with more discerning queers who love disco-funk but hate ABBA.

The Western Addition

Madrone Art Bar

500 Divisadero Street, at Fell Street (241 0202, www.madronelounge.com). Bus 21, 24, 71. **Open** 2pm-2am daily. **Admission** free-$5. **Credit** DC, MC, V. **Map** p317 G8.

This cozy room on the edge of the Lower Haight, which also functions as a cutting-edge art gallery, draws its share of students from the nearby USF and UCSF campuses for its regular happy hours and laid-back vibe. It's tiny, so when local bands notify USF's college radio station (KUSF 90.3 FM) of their concerts here, they have little trouble filling the joint.

Hayes Valley

The best bet for lively nightlife in the area is the **Rickshaw Stop** (*see p238*). On the edge of Hayes Valley, it supplements programs of live music with hot club gatherings that draw a heavy hipster contingent; the venue always throws a great party. Arrive early for the authentic rickshaw-cart seating.

Art & Cocktails

What could be a better combination?

Want to get a drink, but need to rationalize your consumption with the veneer of being engaged in some larger cultural activity? Appreciate art, but also have a thirst? Luckily for you, the propitious pairing of art and artisanal booze is an institution in San Francisco.

Painting, sculpture, DJ nights and a full bar keep Downtown's **111 Minna** (*see p219*) going strong, while rotating shows, theme nights, and a broad cocktail and beer list make **Madrone Lounge** (*see p174*) a great place to grab a drink in NoPa (North of the Panhandle). Just up the street, the aptly named **Mini Bar** (837 Divisadero Street, between Fulton & McAllister Streets, 525-3565) may be small in stature, but it curates its wall space – and cocktail list – with great care. In Hayes Valley, cozy wine bar **Hotel Biron** (*see p174*) has charcuterie, and fruit and cheese plates to complement the art on its walls. Potrero Hill's **Project One Cafe & Gallery** (251 Rhode Island Street, between 15th & 16th Streets, 938 7173, www.p1sf.com) offers coffee, pastries and free WiFi during the day, and beer when it morphs into a bar at night. Dance club **Mighty** (*see p247*) has a deep connection with the SF art scene – its owners provide studio and exhibition space to local artists through a nonprofit they run.

Across the Bay and steps from BART, **Era Art Bar & Lounge** (19 Grand Avenue, at Broadway, Oakland, 1-510 832 4400, www.oaklandera.com) is a perfect base for checking out Oakland Art Murmur (www.oaklandartmurmur), a monthly gallery and bar crawl exploring The Town's booming art scene.

Sport & Fitness

The mountains and ocean beckon. Get out and play – or watch.

In a city where restaurant hopping and cocktail quaffing are considered sports, you might not expect folks to understand the comparatively pedestrian pleasures of beer and a ballgame. Yet despite their well-earned reputation for culture and sophistication, San Franciscans are not above donning face paint and foam fingers and packing a stadium to cheer on their team.

Mountain biking, hiking, trail running, all surf sports (board surfing, kite surfing, windsurfing) are more than just hobbies or diversions for many San Franciscans: they're a reason to live here. With access to literally thousands of miles of trails, stunning vistas and pristine wilderness ten minutes from virtually any point in the city, San Francisco is an outdoor lovers' paradise.

SPECTATOR SPORTS

The Bay Area is home to several professional sports teams, all of which inspire ferocious loyalty. San Francisco has the marquee teams – football's **49ers** and baseball's **Giants** (for both, *see p250*). Across the Bay Bridge are their more hardcore Oakland counterparts, football's **Raiders** (*see p253*) and baseball's **Athletics** (*see below*). Also in Oakland are basketball team the **Golden State Warriors** (*see p250*). An hour's drive south in San Jose are the **Sharks** (*see p250*), who have the loudest and most devoted fan base in the National Hockey League.

For information on local events, head to the *San Francisco Chronicle*'s website at www.sfgate.com/sports, or check the paper's 'Sporting Green' section, which has a calendar of local sporting events and media broadcasts. If you can stomach the phone-ins, KNBR (680 or 1050 AM, www.knbr.com) is good for news and sports gossip. If it's convenient, buy tickets in person from the team's stadium to avoid booking fees and surcharges. If that's not possible, call the team direct or buy tickets from its website. If they're sold out, try StubHub (www.stubhub.com) or Tickets.com (www.tickets.com), both of which work with the major teams. Other brokers include Premier Tickets (1-800 376 6876, www.premiertickets.com), Entertainment Ticketfinder (1-800 523 1515, www.ticketfinder.com) and Mr Tickets (1-877 678 4253, www.mrtickets.com). Be warned, though: scams abound, especially with ticket touts (scalpers).

Auto racing

Infineon Raceway

Intersection of Highways 37 & 121, Sonoma (1-800 870 7223, www.infineonraceway.com). **Open** *Box office* 8am-5pm Mon-Fri & race days. **Tickets** $20-$65. **Credit** AmEx, Disc, MC, V.

Home to everything from NASCAR to monster-truck rallies, Infineon is a fun slice of Americana located just an hour away from the city.

Baseball

Housed in a waterfront stadium that's arguably the best, if not the most beautiful in the country, the National League's **San Francisco Giants** are still floating on the euphoria of winning the 2010 World Series Championship. Across the Bay, the American League's **Oakland Athletics** play in a concrete shell in the middle of nowhere, but have the advantage of cheaper ticket prices and no freezing fog. After several losing seasons, they're hoping to come back with some promising recruits in 2011. Baseball season runs April to September, play-offs in October.

Oakland Athletics

McAfee Coliseum, 7000 Coliseum Way, Nimitz Freeway, at Hegenberger Road, Oakland (1-510 568 5600, www.oaklandathletics.com). BART

Coliseum/Oakland Airport. **Open** *Box office* 10am-6pm Mon-Fri; 10am-4pm Sat; 2hrs before game. **Tickets** $10-$71. **Credit** AmEx, Disc, MC, V.

San Francisco Giants

AT&T Park, 24 Willie Mays Plaza, at 3rd & King Streets, South Beach (972 2000, www.sfgiants.com). Metro to 2nd & King/bus 10, 30, 45. **Open** *Box office* 8.30am-5.30pm Mon-Fri; 2hrs before game Sat, Sun. **Tickets** $25-$150. **Credit** AmEx, Disc, MC, V. **Map** p319 P7.
See p251 **Freaks & Geeks**.

Basketball

The ever-struggling **Golden State Warriors**, play in the Oakland Arena behind the Coliseum. The NBA season runs November until mid April, with play-offs in May. The college teams usually offer a more exciting season, which runs from December through the 'March Madness' of the NCAA tournament. **Stanford** (1-800 782 6367, www.gostanford.com) and the University of California at **Berkeley** (1-800 462 3277, www.calbears.com) are both members of the Pac-10 and can usually be relied on to produce competitive teams while the Stanford women's team went undefeated in 2010, finally losing in a nail-biter in the Final Four.

In the summer, **Kezar Pavilion** (Waller & Stanyan Streets, Haight) hosts a free Pro-Am league that showcases top local college talent and the occasional NBA star. If you think you've got game, check out the pick-up contests across the city: the best hoops are at **James Lick Middle School** (Clipper & Castro Streets, Noe Valley).

Golden State Warriors

Oracle Arena, 7000 Coliseum Way, Nimitz Freeway, at Hegenberger Road, Oakland (1-888 479 4667, www.warriors.com). BART Coliseum/Oakland Airport. **Open** *Box office* 10am-6pm Mon-Fri; 10am-4pm Sat. **Tickets** $10-$1,200. **Credit** AmEx, Disc, MC, V.

Football

The Bay separates the NFL's **San Francisco 49ers** from the **Oakland Raiders**, and their supporters remain fanatically opposed. The 49ers' record of selling out home games for nearly 25 years (single-game seats are available if you're quick) has been brought under threat in recent years: political power plays have upstaged anything on the field as owners and city politicos wrangle for a new stadium with owners looking to make good on their threat to move the team south to Santa Clara.

Despite being a marginally more successful team in recent years (though it's all relative when you're this bad), the Raiders rarely sell out their home games in advance, and tickets can usually be obtained even minutes prior to kick-off. If you happen to find yourself in the 'Black Hole', home to Oakland's most rabid and creatively outfitted fans (think Darth Vader on a bad day), you'll likely be terrified or possibly amused. Beware the Raider Nation. In college football, legendary rivalry between **Stanford** and **Cal** (Berkeley) peaks at 'Big Game' in November, a highlight of the football season.

Oakland Raiders

McAfee Coliseum, 7000 Coliseum Way, Nimitz Freeway, at Hegenberger Road, Oakland (1-800 724 3377, www.raiders.com). BART Coliseum/Oakland Airport. **Open** *Box office* 10am-5pm Mon-Fri; 10am-2pm Sat; 2hrs before game Sun. **Tickets** $36-$161. **Credit** AmEx, Disc, MC, V.

San Francisco 49ers

Monster Park, 490 Jamestown Avenue, at Giants Drive, Bayview (656 4900, www.sf49ers.com). BART & Metro to Montgomery, then bus 78X/ Bart & Metro to Balboa Park, then bus 76X/Metro to Giman/Paul station, then bus 86. **Open** *Box office* 9am-5pm Mon-Fri. **Tickets** $29-$295. **Credit** AmEx, Disc, MC, V.

Horse racing

Golden Gate Fields

1100 Eastshore Highway, Albany (1-510 559 7300, www.goldengatefields.com). BART North Berkeley, then AC Transit shuttle bus. **Open** race days, times vary. **Box office** varies. **Tickets** $6-$15. **Credit** AmEx, Disc, MC, V.

GGF boasts spectacular views of the Golden Gate Bridge – from the parking lot. Old-time racetrack vibes coupled with wine festivals, in-field concerts or '$1 admission, $1 hot dog' days make a trip to the track all the more enjoyable, if gastronomically unadvisable.

Ice hockey

Ice hockey came to the Bay Area more than a decade ago, courtesy of the National Hockey League's **San Jose Sharks**. Hockey is still a minority taste in the Bay Area compared to the other three major sports, but the Sharks are a perennial play-off contender and routinely sell out the 'Shark Tank'. The season runs October to April, followed by two months of play-offs.

San Jose Sharks

HP Pavilion, 525 West Santa Clara Street, at Autumn Street, San Jose (ticketmaster 421 8497, box office 1-408 287 9200, www.sj-sharks.com). CalTrain to San Jose Diridon Station. **Open** *Box office* 9.30am-5.30pm Mon-Fri; from 3hrs before game Sat, Sun. **Tickets** $23-$192. **Credit** AmEx, Disc, MC, V.

Freaks & Geeks: the 2010 World Champions

How the Giants trounced the Texas Rangers to win the World Series.

It's hard to imagine a better match-up than the 2010 World Series: the freaks and geeks from Babylon by the Bay vs the Texas Rangers – a team named for frontier lawmen and once co-owned by President George W Bush. Just how freaky were the Giants? Team member Brian Wilson sported a mohawk haircut and a massive beard – dyed jet black. Once, while being interviewed on television in his apartment, a man walked by in the background clad only in a leather mask and thong. In 2009, star pitcher Tim Lincecum was arrested for possession of marijuana, prompting t-shirt vendors to print 'Let Timmy Smoke' shirts for the series. It may fairly be said that the Giants stomped the Rangers, outscoring them more than 2 to 1 over the series and, as a scowling former President Bush looked on, the Giants clinched the final game in Texas.

Given that the Giants had not won the World Series since 1954, you can imagine the euphoric welcome that awaited the team when they brought the trophy home. A week-long party ensued, followed by a tickertape parade with the team riding down Market Street surrounded by adoring fans holding up signs and cheering like it was VE Day. For longtime beleagured Giants fans, one sign said it all: 'The World Can End Now.'

ACTIVE SPORTS & FITNESS

Every Thursday, the *Chronicle* publishes a supplement called 'Outdoors', full of listings and information on open-air activities. For special events, it's also worth trying the **Visitor Information Center** (*see p294*). *Competitor Nor Cal* magazine (www.citysportsmag.com), available in gyms and sports shops, carries information on participatory sports. Note: if you're hiring expensive equipment, photo ID or a credit card is usually required for the deposit. *See also p254* **Unusual Sports**.

Bowling

Presidio Bowling Center

Building 93, at Montgomery Street & Moraga Avenue, Presidio (561 2695, www.presidiobowl.com). Bus 28, 41, 43, 45, 91. **Open** 9am-midnight Mon-Thur, Sun; 9am-2am Fri, Sat. **Rates** $4.75-$7.25/game. *Shoe rental* $4. **Credit** AmEx, Disc, MC, V. **Map** p312 D3.

Yerba Buena Bowling Center

750 Folsom Street, between 3rd & 4th Streets, SoMa (820 3532, www.skatebowl.com). BART & Metro to Montgomery/bus 9X, 12, 30, 45, 76. **Open** noon-10pm Mon-Thur; noon-midnight Fri; 10am-midnight Sat; noon-9pm Sun. **Rates** $5-$6/game. *Shoe rental* $4. **Credit** AmEx, MC, V. **Map** p315 N6.

Cycling

If you're looking to get around San Francisco quickly, hop on a bike. Hemmed in by water, the city is unable to sprawl, and while it's certainly hilly, the steepest inclines are easily avoided.

Bike stores dot the center of town, and bike lanes are widespread. Bicycles can be taken free of charge on BART, except for peak hours (7-9am and 4-6pm weekdays), as well as on Muni buses (which have bike racks mounted on the front of most vehicles); the ferries will also take you and your bike. All major outdoor public events in San Francisco are required by law to offer free and secure bike parking.

The only downers are those typical of most major urban areas: theft, which is common, and traffic, which can be nasty. Always secure your bike with a U-lock when parking it, and don't leave it outside overnight (many hotels will be able to store it if you ask nicely). Back on the roads, SUVs, Hummers and other such monstrosities are notorious for disregarding anything smaller than they are; take care.

Many tourists head to Fisherman's Wharf and rent bikes for day-rides across the **Golden Gate Bridge**, but there's even more entrancing biking elsewhere in the Bay Area. The endless trails in the **Marin Headlands** (*see p264-66*) offer unmatched sights and pulmonary exertions. For more information, telephone the Marin Headlands Visitor Center (331 1540) or the Pantoll Ranger Station (388 2070).

For more on cycling in the city, contact the terrific **San Francisco Bicycle Coalition** (www.sfbike.org). Among other resources, it publishes an immeasurably useful map of the city with all gradients marked on it, so you can avoid the worst of the hills and traffic. You can download a PDF from its website, or purchase a printed copy online or from any bike store around town. Ray Hosler's *Bay Area Bike Rides* is another very worthwhile read.

★ Bike Hut

Pier 40, Embarcadero, at 1st Street, SoMa (543 4335, www.thebikehut.com). Metro to Brannan/ bus 10. **Open** (unless raining) 10am-6pm Wed-Sun. **Rates** (incl lock & helmet) $6/hr or $22/day. **Map** p319 P7.

This excellent little enterprise, staffed by volunteers (who train kids from deprived backgrounds in bike mechanics while on the job), rents and repairs bicycles from a location just south of the Bay Bridge.

Blazing Saddles

2715 Hyde Street, at North Point Street, Fisherman's Wharf (202 8888, www.blazing saddles.com). Metro F to Fisherman's Wharf/ bus 19, 30, 47/cable car Powell-Hyde. **Open** 8am-7.30pm daily. **Rates** $7-$9/hr; $30-$88/ day. **Credit** AmEx, Disc, MC, V. **Map** p314 K2.

Bikes are rented to those with a yen for cycling the eight miles from Fisherman's Wharf over the Golden Gate Bridge to Sausalito. Guided tours are also offered, and there's a 24-hour drop-off site.

Other locations throughout the city.

Golden Gate Park Bike & Skate

3038 Fulton Street, between 6th & 7th Avenues, Richmond (668 1117, www.goldengateparkbike andskate.com). Bus 5, 21. **Open** 10am-6pm Mon-Fri; 10am-7pm Sat, Sun. **Rates** *Bikes* $5/hr or $25/day. *Skates* $5/hr or $20/day. **Credit** MC, V. **Map** p316 C8.

Bikes, rollerskates and in-line skates are all available for rent (helmet and knee and elbow pads included), and you can take skateboarding lessons.

Mike's Bikes

1233 Howard Street, between 8th & 9th Streets, SoMa (241 2453, www.mikesbikes.com). Bus 9, 12, 27, 47. **Open** 11am-7pm Mon-Fri; 10am-6pm Sat, Sun. **Credit** AmEx, Disc, MC, V. **Map** p318 L8.

Mike's doesn't offer rentals, but is an excellent one-stop shop for bikes, clothing and other accessories.

Golf

★ Gleneagles Golf Course

2100 Sunnydale Avenue, At McLaren Park, San Francisco (587 2425/http://www.gleneaglesgolf sf.com/). Bus 29, 52, 54. **Open** 7.30am-2hrs before dusk Mon-Fri; dawn-dusk Sat, Sun. **Rates** $17-$32.50. **Credit** MC, V

This nine-hole municipal course is virtually unknown to outsiders. Located deep within McLaren Park on the city's southern edge, it is a rarity in golf courses: inexpensive, beautifully maintained, challenging and laid back. *Golf* magazine named Gleneagles one of the top 20 nine-hole courses in the US. The scotch selection in the clubhouse alone is worth a visit, with some of the best price-for-age deals in the Bay Area.

Golden Gate Park Course

John F Kennedy Drive, at 47th Avenue, Golden Gate Park (751 8987, www.goldengatepark golf.com). Bus 5, 29. **Open** dawn-dusk daily. **Rates** non-residents $15-$19. **Credit** MC, V.

A handsome little nine-hole par-three municipal number, reasonably priced, great for beginners, and located at the edge of Ocean Beach.

★ Harding Park Golf Course

99 Harding Road, at Skyline Boulevard, Lake Merced (information 664 4690, reservations 750 4653, www.harding-park.com). Bus 18. **Open** dawn-dusk daily. **Rates** non-residents $45-$170. **Credit** AmEx, Disc, MC, V.

Arguably one of the best municipal courses in the country, it was completely overhauled by Arnold Palmer Golf Management and now hosts PGA Tournaments. Tee times are available up to 30 days ahead with a $10 surcharge. Also here is the nine-hole, par-30 Fleming Course (non-residents $26-$31).

Lincoln Park Golf Course

300 34th Avenue, at Clement Street, Lincoln Park (information 221 9911, reservations 750 4653, www.lincolnparkgc.com). Bus 1, 18, 38. **Open** dawn-dusk daily. **Rates** phone for information.

The wonderful view of the Golden Gate Bridge from the 17th hole has made Lincoln Park one of the most photographed courses in the US.

★ Presidio Golf Course

300 Finley Road, at Arguello Gate, Presidio (561 4653/www.presidiogolf.com). Bus 1, 2, 33. **Open** dawn-dusk daily. **Rates** *Non-residents* $49-$145. **Credit** AmEx, Disc, MC, V. **Map** p312 C5.
Former presidents Roosevelt and Eisenhower both played this 18-holer – the second oldest course west of the Mississippi – when it was owned by the Army. Built in 1885, it finally opened to the public in 1995 following a makeover by Arnold Palmer and co.

Gyms

San Franciscans love their neighborhood gyms every bit as much as their corner cafés and bars.

24 Hour Fitness Center

1200 Van Ness Avenue, at Post Street, Cathedral Hill (776 2200, www.24hourfitness.com). Bus 2, 3, 19, 31, 38, 47, 49, 90. **Open** 24hrs daily. **Rates** $15/day. **Credit** AmEx, Disc, MC, V. **Map** p314 K6.
This chain has branches all around the city, offering a variety of facilities and classes. For other locations, check online or call 1-800 249 6756.

★ Embarcadero YMCA

169 Steuart Street, between Mission & Howard Streets, Financial District (957 9622, www.ymcasf.org). BART & Metro to Embarcadero/streetcar F/bus 2, 9, 14, 21, 31, 41 & Market Street routes. **Open** 5.30am-9.45pm Mon-Fri; 8am-7.45pm Sat; 9am-5.45pm Sun. **Rates** $15/day. **Credit** MC, V. **Map** p315 O4.
San Francisco has plenty of YMCAs, but this is the only one that boasts a waterfront view. A day pass will give you access to aerobics classes, free weights, Cybex and Nautilus machines, racquetball and basketball courts, and the 25m swimming pool. For the pass, you'll need photo ID.

Koret Health & Recreation Center

University of San Francisco, Parker Avenue & Turk Boulevard, Richmond (422 6821, www.usfca.edu/koret). Bus 5, 21, 31. **Open** 6am-10pm (pool closes at 9pm) Mon-Fri; 8am-8pm (pool closes at 6pm) Sat, Sun. **Rates** $15/day. **Credit** MC, V. **Map** p317 E8.
Koret has an Olympic-sized pool, a gym and six racquetball courts, though for the latter you'll need to bring your own equipment.

Hiking

Walking San Francisco's splendid hills is a delight, and both the **Presidio** and **Golden Gate Park** offer decent walking. Less than a half-hour outside the city lie trails with stunning views and fragrant paths. Just across the Golden Gate Bridge, the short and easy **Morning Sun Trail** rises from a parking lot at Spencer Avenue (exit off US 101 north) and offers lovely views east towards the city over the Bay and Angel Island, and west to the thundering Pacific. Alternatively, take Golden Gate Transit bus 10 to Mill Valley for the day-long **Dipsea Trail** to Stinson Beach. The **Bootjack Trail** to the summit of Mount Tamalpais is popular too. Call the Pantoll Ranger Station (388 2070) for trail information or visit www.mttam.net. The **Bay Area Sierra Club** (1-510 848 0800, www.sanfranciscobay.sierraclub.org) has a wealth of hiking knowledge and internet searches yield a wealth of trail information.

Horse riding

Horses and tours are offered at the **Sea Horse & Friendly Acres Ranch** (1-650 726 2362, www.horserentals.com/seahorse.html), near Half Moon Bay, and **Chanslor Stables** (1-707 875 3333, www.chanslor.com) next to Bodega Bay.

In-line skating

Sunday skating in Golden Gate Park is hard to beat: the beach at one end, sunny meadows along the way and no motor vehicles anywhere to be seen. For wide smiles – without the wide polyester collars – join the mix of in-line skating, disco twirling and breakdancing near 6th Avenue on JFK Drive. Skates are available for rent at **Golden Gate Park Skate & Bike** (*see left*), or for purchase from Skates on Haight. On Fridays, join the Midnight Rollers night-time skate, which leaves Ferry Plaza opposite the Ferry Building at 9.15pm sharp; see www.cora.org.

Skates on Haight

1818 Haight Street, at Stanyan Street, Haight-Ashbury (752 8375, www.skatesonhaight.com). Metro to Cole & Carl/bus 7, 33, 66, 71. **Open** 10am-6pm daily. **Credit** AmEx, Disc, MC, V. **Map** p317 E9.
Skates on Haight was at least partly responsible for launching the worldwide skateboarding craze during the 1970s. Stock these days includes in-line skates, roller skates and snowboards.

Rock climbing

Devoted climbers travel to **Lake Tahoe** and **Mount Shasta**, but **Yosemite** is the state's climbing mecca, with lessons available year-round. While you're still in the city, warm up at **Mission Cliffs** or **Planet Granite**.

Mission Cliffs

2295 Harrison Street, at 19th Street, Mission (550 0515, www.mission-cliffs.com). Bus 12, 27. **Open** 6.30am-10pm Mon, Wed, Fri; 6.30am-11pm Tue, Thur; 9am-7pm Sat, Sun. **Rates** $12-$18/day. **Credit** AmEx, DC, Disc, MC, V. **Map** p318 L11.

This 14,000sq ft (4,300sq m) of urban wilderness and polished jungle gym runs beginner's lessons from noon until 7.30pm on weekdays.

Planet Granite

924 Mason Street, at Crissy Field, Presidio (692 3434, www.planetgranite.com). Bus 28, 30, 43.
Open 6am-11pm Mon-Fri; 8am-8pm Sat; 8am-6pm Sun. **Rates** $10-$18/day. **Credit** AmEx, DC, MC, V. **Map** p312 B2.
With spectacular views of the Golden Gate and the downtown skyline,this place has 25,000 sq ft of climbing, a gym, two yoga studios and top-out boldering.

Running

Crissy Field is highly popular with runners, and each step of the route from Fort Mason past Marina Green along the Golden Gate Promenade is a postcard, leading all the way to historic Fort Point beneath the bridge. The **Embarcadero** offers another lovely path beneath the Bay Bridge, and **Golden Gate Park** offers a third option, with the track at Kezar Stadium on the eastern edge providing a good spot for sprints.

For something more sociable, the **San Francisco Dolphin South End Runners** has group runs at 8.15am every Saturday, free. Check out www.dserunners.com for more details. Annual races include the **Bay to Breakers** (*see p203*) in May and the **San Francisco Marathon** (*see p204*) in July.

Sailing, kayaking & rowing

There are numerous boating and kayaking outfits in the Bay Area and along the Pacific coastline; all offer equipment, lessons and trips. For details call **Open Water Rowing** (332 1091, www.owrc.com) in Sausalito or **South End Rowing Club** (776 7372, www.south-end.org) in San Francisco. Pedalos and rowing boats are available for rent at Stow Lake in Golden Gate Park.

★ California Canoe & Kayak

409 Water Street, at Franklin Street, Jack London Square, Oakland (1-510 893 7833, www.cal kayak.com). BART 12th Street Oakland/Alameda-Oakland ferry to Oakland from Embarcadero.

Offbeat Sports

This is San Francisco: of course you'll find out-of-the-ordinary sports here.

To the mainstream sports go the stadiums, for everyone else, there's Golden Gate Park. On any given day, you'll find a contingent of offbeat and oddball sports enthusiasts looking to kick it, toss it, cast it, and roll it. Here's just a small sampling:

Archery Yes, those are indeed the slings of bows and arrows sailing into hay bales at the far western end of the park (Fulton Street & 47th Avenue). Rentals and lessons are available from the San Francisco Archery Shop (www.bysel.com/sfarch/main.html).

Fly casting.

Disc golf Golden Gate Park boasts the city's first disc golf course, an 18-hole circuit that's good course for beginners and experts alike. Head to Marx Meadow between 25th and 30th Avenues. You can also download a scorecard at www.sfdiscgolf.org.

Fly casting Perfect the art of the four-count fly cast at the WPA-built Angler's Lodge and Casting Pools, located at the west end of the park off John F Kennedy Drive and 38th Avenue (www.ggacc.org).

Kickball The children's schoolyard sport has made a huge comeback with grown-ups. Watch them in action at Little Rec Field on the southeast side of the park, near Stanyan Street (www.kickball.com/sanfrancisco).

Lawn Bowling America's oldest municipal lawn bowling club (www.sflbc.org) plays on courts near Sharon Meadow, off Stanyan Street and Middle Drive East.

Model yacht sailing Model yacht enthusiasts strut their stuff on a small dedicated lake with a boathouse at 36th Avenue and Fulton Streets. It's the only remaining venue in the US for wind-powered racing freesail yachts.

Running and cycling at **Marina Green**.

Open 10am-6pm Mon-Sat; 10am-5pm Sun. **Rates** *Kayaks* $15/hr. *Canoes* $25/hr. **Credit** AmEx, Disc, MC, V.

One of the Bay Area's best locations for hiring and buying kayaks and seagoing gear. Lessons and day trips navigate the nearby Oakland Estuary.

★ Sea Trek

Schoonmaker Point Marina, at Libertyship Way, Sausalito (weekdays 332 8494, weekends 332 4465, www.seatrek.com). Blue & Gold Fleet ferry from Pier 41, or Golden Gate ferry from Ferry Building. **Open** 9am-5pm daily. **Rates** *kayak rental* $20/hr. **Credit** AmEx, Disc, MC, V.

Sea Trek hosts summer camps for kids, books expeditions to Alaska and Baja, and supports waterway conservation. Beginners' classes in kayaking, guided tours and moonlight paddles are available; rental covers everything from pro gear to wave-rider kayaks suitable for novices.

Spinnaker Sailing

Pier 40, South Beach Harbor, Embarcadero, at Townsend Street, South Beach (543 7333, www.spinnaker-sailing.com). Metro to Brannan/ bus 10. **Open** *Summer* 9am-5pm daily. *Winter* 10am-4pm Wed-Sun. **Rates** Boat rental $382-$865/day. **Credit** AmEx, MC, V. **Map** p319 P7.

Professional instruction, boats from 22ft (7m) to 80ft (24m), and a great location near the ballpark.

► *San Francisco plays host to the America's Cup in 2013, with competitions starting in 2012; for locations and information, see p204.*

Skateboarding

The police have done a pretty thorough job of eliminating skate rats from once-favorite sites such as Justin Herman Plaza and Pier 7 on the Embarcadero, though you'll be able to sniff out a Safeway parking lot or two and any number of downtown concrete ramps. If you're posing or want to learn, invest in helmet, gloves, knee and elbow pads at DLX.

DLX

1831 Market Street, between Guerrero & Octavia Streets, Upper Market (626 5588, www.dlxsf.com). Metro to Church or Van Ness/streetcar F/bus 6, 7, 26, 66. **Open** 11am-7pm Mon-Sat; 11am-6pm Sun. **Credit** AmEx, Disc, MC, V. **Map** p318 J9.

DLX is the mother of all skateboarding shops in SF, and has a comprehensive range of clothes, boards, accessories and stickers.

Skiing & snowboarding

You can hit the slopes on a day trip, but most people prefer to spend at least a weekend in the Sierras. During the season (Nov-Apr), most ski shops offer package deals. Check www.goski.com for listings of all the major California resorts.

SFO Snowboarding

1630 Haight Street, at Ashbury Street, Haight-Ashbury (626 1141, www.sfosnow.com). Bus 6, 33, 43, 66, 71. **Open** 11am-7pm daily. **Credit** AmEx, Disc, MC, V. **Map** p317 E9.

Boards, boots, bindings and more for rent, plus an array of cold-weather clothes for sale.

Mountain West

290 Division Street, Suite 101, between 10th & Brannan Streets, SoMa (552 7055, www. mountainwestonline.com). Bus 27, 47. **Open** 10am-7pm Mon-Fri; 10am-6pm Sat; 11am-5pm Sun. **Credit** Disc, MC, V. **Map** p319 M9.

Staffed by knowledgeable enthusiasts, Mountain West is the place to buy or rent the latest skiing and snowboarding equipment with brand names like Nordica and Burton. Boot fitting, and ski and snowboard tuning and repairs are also offered.

Surfing

Here are the facts: the waves around San Francisco are dangerous and shark infested – not a good place to learn. An hour north of San Francisco on Highway 1, **Stinson Beach** has gentler waves and fewer surfers, while the experts head to **Mavericks** in Santa Cruz. But whether you're a pro headed to Ocean Beach and beyond or a newbie boogie-boarding the black-sand beaches of Marin County, there are several good options for equipment purchase and rental.

★ Aqua Surf Shop

2830 Sloat Boulevard at 46th Avenue, Ocean Beach (242 9283, www.aquasurfshop.com Metro to 46th Ave and Vincente/bus 18, 23. **Open** 10.30am-5.30pm Mon-Tue, Sun; 10am-7pm Wed-Sat. **Credit** AmEx, Disc, MC, V.

Couldn't fit your board on the plane? This local institution rents them by the day – pick up your board in the afternoon and hit the waves that evening and the following morning before returning. All sizes of wetsuits and bodyboards are also available, as are classes.

Wise Surfboards

800 Great Highway, at Cabrillo Street, Ocean Beach (750 9473, www.wisesurfboards.com). Bus 5, 18. **Open** 11am-6pm Mon-Fri; 9am-6pm Sat, Sun. **Credit** AmEx, MC, V.

Right on Ocean Beach, this shop sells boards, wetsuits and various accessories, and hosts a 24-hour surf report phoneline (273 1618).

Swimming

The ocean is usually too chilly and turbulent for a proper swim, but there are plenty of pools in town, including those at the **Embarcadero YMCA** and the **Koret Center** (for both, *see p253*). The most central pools can be found at **Hamilton Recreation Center** (Geary Boulevard & Steiner Street, 292 2001) and the **North Beach Pool** (661 Lombard Street, at Mason Street, 391 0407). For your nearest municipal pool, check the *White Pages* under 'City Government Offices: Recreation and Parks'.

Tennis

Indoor tennis is almost exclusively a members-only affair, but there are plenty of outdoor courts. **Golden Gate Park** has several (near the Stanyan Street entrance, 753 7001), and there are busy courts at **Mission Dolores Park** (*see p79*). Both locations are free and open from sunrise to sunset. You can find a full list of tennis facilities in the *SBC Yellow Pages* under 'Neighborhood Parks'.

Whale-watching

Whale-watching happens during the migration season (Nov-Dec and late Mar/early Apr), and occurs primarily just north and south of San Francisco. On occasion, it can be as easy as taking a pair of binoculars to the shore and having a look. Mendocino and Monterey are popular viewing spots, but we recommend the tip of **Point Reyes** (*see p268*), an hour's drive north of the city. You might see glorious humpback and blue whales, as well as sea lions.

Oceanic Society Expeditions

Quarters 35N, Fort Mason, at Franklin & Bay Streets, Marina (474 3385, 1-800 326 7491, www.oceanic-society.org). Bus 22, 28. **Open** 8.30am-5pm Mon-Fri. **Rates** Voyages (reservations required) $89-$120. **Credit** AmEx, Disc, MC, V. **Map** p314 H2.

A cut above most tourist trips – the staff are experts in natural history and marine life. At weekends from June to November, a full-day trip heads 26 miles west to the Farallon Islands, home of the largest seabird colony in the continental US. Along the way, humpback whales can often be seen. Trips to see grey whales take place the rest of the year.

Windsurfing

San Francisco is a popular windsurfing center; the 30-plus launch sites include Candlestick and Coyote Points, as well as Crissy Field, the site of several international competitions.

Yoga

The city's myriad yoga schools offer a variety of styles for students of all levels.

Bikram's Yoga College of India

910 Columbus Avenue, at Lombard Street, North Beach (346 5400, www.bikramyoga.com). Bus 30, 39, 41, 45, 91/cable car Powell-Mason. **Open** *Classes* 9am, 4.30pm, 6.30pm Mon-Fri; 9am, 4.30pm Sat, Sun. **Rates** $15/class. **Credit** MC, V. **Map** p314 L2.

Yogic exercises based on the 'hot yoga' techniques of Bikram Choudhury. Bring a towel, though: the classes take place in a sweltering room.

Mindful Body

2876 California Street, at Broderick Street, Pacific Heights (931 2639, www.themindfulbody.com). Bus 1, 2, 24. **Open** check website for class schedule. **Rates** $12-$16/class. **Credit** MC, V. **Map** p313 G5.

The popular Ashtanga class here builds endurance, strength and flexibility.

Yoga Tree

1234 Valencia Street, between 23rd & 24th Streets, Mission (647 9707, www.yogatreesf.com). BART 24th Street/bus 12, 14, 48, 49, 67. **Open** check website for class schedule. **Rates** $16/class. **Credit** AmEx, MC, V. **Map** p318 K12.

Popular with beginners and good for drop-ins, Yoga Tree has four locations around town and offers daily classes as well as workshops, massage and retreats. **Other locations** throughout the city.

Theater & Dance

Drama, ballet or burlesque: the many faces of SF performing arts.

Though small in size, San Francisco's theater and dance scenes prove time and again they can deliver as much cultural capital as the biggest and best of 'em. Broadway-bound mega-budget musicals such as *Wicked* flourish alongside extraordinary solo works from emerging actor-playwrights and avant-garde amalgamations of music, poetry and performance. San Francisco's discriminating audiences, excellent venues and fine pool of artistic talent make it an ideal launch pad for the rest of the country.

Meanwhile, the city's vibrant and eclectic modern dance scene takes in the entire spectrum, from the world-class **San Francisco Ballet** (*see p262*) to ethnic dance ensembles and a thriving hybrid dance-theater movement.

INFORMATION AND TICKETS

The *Chronicle*'s Sunday 'Datebook' section, accessible online at www.sfgate.com, has extensive listings. *San Francisco Weekly* and the *San Francisco Bay Guardian*, two weekly free sheets, also run reviews and listings. For online listings, check www.bayinsider.com, www.sfarts.org and www.laughingsquid.org.

Prices vary wildly: tickets for some leftfield shows are just $5, but you could pay 30 times that for a blockbuster. To avoid booking fees, call the theater's own box office or book online at its website. If you're willing to take a chance, the **TIX Bay Area** booth in Union Square (433 7827, www.tixbayarea.org) sells half-price tickets for many shows on the day of the performance. It opens at 11am from Tuesday to Friday, and at 10am on weekends. Some venues also sell through ticket agencies such as City Box Office (392 4400, www.citybox office.com). For other ticket agencies, *see p200*. Some theaters run 'pay what you can' schemes on Thursdays (or, at the Magic Theatre, Tuesdays).

MAINSTREAM THEATERS

A handful of San Francisco's theaters host major touring shows. Best of Broadway (www.shnsf.com) offers imports from the Great White Way in three beautiful old houses: the grand **Orpheum** (1192 Market Street, at Hyde Street, Civic Center) and the 2,300-seat art deco **Golden Gate Theatre** (1 Taylor Street, at Golden Gate Avenue, Tenderloin), which both specialize in musicals, and the elegant, intimate **Curran Theatre** (445 Geary Street, between Mason & Taylor Streets, Tenderloin), which stages both non-musical Broadway and pre-Broadway fare. For further information on all three, call 551 2000; to purchase tickets, which typically run from $35 to up to $200, use Ticketmaster (*see p200*).

The **Herbst Theatre** (401 Van Ness Avenue, at Grove Street, Civic Center, 392 4400) hosts local and out-of-town guests, many as part of the San Francisco Performances series (*see p234*). Finally, both the 80-year-old **Marines' Memorial Theatre** (609 Sutter Street, at Mason Street, Tenderloin, 771 6900, www.marinesmemorialtheatre.com) and the **Post Street Theatre** (450 Post Street, between Powell & Mason Streets, Union Square & Around, 321 2900, http://poststreet theatre-sf.org) present off-Broadway, regional and local productions.

REGIONAL THEATERS

★ American Conservatory Theater

Geary Theater, 415 Geary Street, between Mason & Taylor Streets, Tenderloin (information 834 3200, box office 749 2228, www.act-sfbay.org). Bus 2, 3, 27, 30, 31, 38, 45, 91/cable car Powell-Hyde or Powell-Mason. **Tickets** $10-$90. **Credit** AmEx, DC, MC, V. **Map** p314 L6.

Magic Theatre.

Since opening in 1967, ACT has been staging modern classics and new works by the likes of David Mamet and Tom Stoppard, earning it a solid reputation. It is also known for its fine conservatory, whose alumni include Annette Bening, Denzel Washington, Nicolas Cage and Danny Glover. In addition to ACT shows, the exquisite Geary Theater usually hosts one or two touring productions per season and stages its ever-popular *A Christmas Carol* every year.

Magic Theatre

Building D, Fort Mason, Marina Boulevard, at Buchanan Street, Marina (441 8822, www.magictheatre.org). Bus 22, 28/cable car Powell-Hyde. **Tickets** $30-$60. **Credit** AmEx, DC, MC, V. **Map** p314 H2.

Drawing its name from a line in Herman Hesse's *Steppenwolf*, the Magic Theatre has impressed locals throughout its 40-year history with stagings of groundbreaking works by the likes of former resident playwright Sam Shepard. The two 150-seat houses, in premises overlooking the Golden Gate Bridge, offer an intriguing mix of new works by both emerging playwrights and leading lights.

FRINGE THEATERS & COMPANIES

For gay theater and cabaret, *see p232*.

Asian American Theater Company

Various venues (tickets 1-800 838 3006, www.asianamericantheater.org). **Tickets** $10-$25. **Credit** AmEx, DC, MC, V. **Map** p318 L8.

Started by ACT (*see p257*) in 1973, the AATC fosters work that speaks to the experience of Americans of Asian and Pacific Island descent. Phillip Kan Gotanda and David Henry Hwang are among the exceptional talents nurtured in its first 30 years; both have recently returned to collaborate with the next generation. The emphasis is on new work, and the quality can vary wildly.

★ Beach Blanket Babylon

Club Fugazi, 678 Green Street, between Columbus Avenue & Powell Street, North Beach (421 4222, www.beachblanketbabylon.com). Bus 10, 12, 30, 39, 41, 45, 91/cable car Powell-Mason. **Tickets** $25-$78. **Credit** Disc, MC, V. **Map** p314 L3.

The longest-running musical revue in theatrical history, *Beach Blanket Babylon* sells its blend of parody songs, puns and outrageous headgear with such irresistible conviction that it's become an institution. Featuring an array of tabloid-friendly 'guest stars' from popular culture and the news, this queer eye on the straight world celebrates its 37th year in 2011. Evening performances are for over-21s only.

Custom Made Theatre Company

1620 Gough Street, at Austin Street (262 0477, www.custommade.org). Bus 1, 2,3, 38, 47, 49, 90. **Tickets** $20-$28 **Credit** Disc, MC, V. **Map** p314 J5.

The company produces five full-length shows each year, as well as additional performances and workshops. Recent productions include the world premiere of *Candide of California* by Brian Katz and a play by David and Amy Sedaris, *The Book of Liz*.

Dark Room

2263 Mission Street, between 18th & 19th Streets, Mission (401 7987, tickets 1-800 838 3006, www.darkroomsf.com). BART 16th Street Mission/bus 14, 22, 33, 49. **Tickets** $5-$20. **Credit** MC, V. **Map** p318 K11.

Operated by the buoyant team of Jim Fourniadis and Erin Ohanneson, this funky black box theater space in the heart of the Mission knows what it likes. And if you revel in an unabashed embrace of pop culture detritus, you'll like it too. Recent programming included *James Bond in Ladykiller: Live*. Also a comedy showcase and music venue, the Dark Room has a Sunday Bad Movie Night featuring a carefully selected cinematic stinker (free popcorn provided), with audiences encouraged to yell back at the screen.

EXIT Theatre

156 Eddy Street, between Mason & Taylor Streets, Tenderloin (673 3847, tickets 1-800 838 3006, www.theexit.org). BART & Metro to Powell/bus 27, 31, 38, 45 & Market Street routes/cable car Powell-Hyde or Powell-Mason. **Tickets** $15-$25. **Credit** AmEx, Disc, MC, V. **Map** p314 L6.

This three-stage set-up offers eclectic, provocative shows, from new one-acts to work by well-known authors. The Exit also hosts the annual San Francisco Fringe Festival every autumn, the largest in the US. The main location has the added attraction of a refreshment lounge; a fourth stage (Exit on Taylor) lies just around the corner at 277 Taylor Street.

Intersection for the Arts

446 Valencia Street, between 15th & 16th Streets, Mission (information 626 2787, box office 626 3311, www.theintersection.org). BART 16th Street/bus 14, 22, 33, 49. **Tickets** $20-35. **Credit** MC, V. **Map** p318 K10.

The oldest alternative space in San Francisco, Intersection offers a community-conscious array of artistic undertakings, including powerhouse theatre that combines the talents of resident company Campo Santo with visiting playwrights such as Naomi Iizuka and John Steppling. One can't escape the fact that the small theater isn't hugely comfortable – there are only folding chairs – but the intense performances compensate for this. There's also a great art gallery upstairs.

Leela

Multiple venues (information 820 1699, www.leela-sf.com).

All improv, all the time, Leela was named for a Sanskrit word meaning 'divine play'. Beyond performance, Leela offers improv classes. The ambience is often upbeat but the quality is erratic.

Lorraine Hansberry Theatre

Multiple venues (information 345 3980, www.lorrainehansberrytheatre.com). **Tickets** $16-$35. **Credit** AmEx, Disc, MC, V.

The foremost African-American theater in the Bay Area produces four or five plays each year, by black playwrights or dealing with issues affecting African Americans. They usually include a musical Christmas offering, such as Langston Hughes's *Black Nativity*.

★ Marsh

1062 Valencia Street, at 22nd Street, Mission (information 826 5750, tickets 1-800 838 3006, www.themarsh.org). BART 24th Street/bus 14, 49. **Tickets** $8-$35. **Credit** (advance bookings only) AmEx, Disc, MC, V. **Map** p318 K12.

The Marsh works hard to present new works, especially solo fare, priding itself on allowing performers to take risks. At the same time, the atmosphere around its two stages and adjacent café is mellow and inviting. Locally acclaimed acts such as Josh Kornbluth and Geoff Hoyle often move on to larger venues in the Bay Area or countrywide, while seasoned pros like Merle Kessler (aka Ian Shoales) and John O'Keefe alight here as well.

Project Artaud Theater

450 Florida Street, between 17th & Mariposa Streets, Mission (626 4370, www.artaud.org). Bus 9, 12, 22, 27, 33, 90. **Tickets** $5-$30. **Credit** MC, V. **Map** p318 L10.

The non-profit Project Artaud Theater offers a variety of new works, often boundary-pushing and hybrid in character, and including everything from one-person plays and modern dance to outspoken aerial circus theater. Two other member theaters share parts of the block-long structure: the Traveling Jewish Theatre (*see p260*) and the Theatre of Yugen/Noh Space (www.theatreofyugen.org), which specializes in Eastern-influenced theater, Butoh and performance art.

Pretty Sketchy

Sketchfest has become US comedy central.

From its relatively humble origins of six sketch comedy groups performing in an 80-seat theater, **SF Sketchfest** (www.sfsketchfest.com) has grown to become one of the premier comedy festivals in the US. Drawing hundreds of the top names in comedy and thousands of fans to fill halls throughout the city, Sketchfest is a comedy geek's dream come true. Featuring everything from performances to screenings, awards ceremonies to re-enactments to tribute nights, the love-fest atmosphere often makes it tough to separate fans from people 'in the business'. You may just find yourself seated next to Neil Patrick Harris watching a Zucker Bros tribute screening of *Airplane!* with a special appearance by Robert Hays, or spy David Cross catching a discussion with Monty Python member Terry Jones on the occasion of the 35th anniversary of *Life of Brian*. The month-long event is packed with huge names in intimate venues doing crazy and/or interesting things or simply waxing nostalgic about great comedy moments. What's not to like?

FREE SF Mime Troupe

Various venues (285 1717, www.sfmt.org).
No, it's not that kind of mime. These are the city's premier political satirists, who have offered free summer shows in various Bay Area parks for the past 40-plus years and count counterculture icon Peter Coyote among their alums. Decidedly left wing and always painfully contemporary, the SF Mime Troupe is a constant source of wonder and a perennial thorn in the side of the civic authorities.

SF Playhouse

533 Sutter Street, between Powell & Mason Streets, Nob Hill (677 9596, www.sfplayhouse.org). Bus 2, 3, 27, 30, 38, 45, 91/cable car Powell-Hyde or Powell-Mason. **Tickets** $20-$50. **Credit** AmEx, MC, V. **Map** p315 M5.
A modest-sized repertory house known for its sophistication, the Playhouse consistently attracts prime local talent for its mix of revivals and edgy premières (such as a recent West Coast premiere of Cormac McCarthy's *Sunset Limited*). There's also an end-of-season musical.

Thick House

1695 18th Street, at Carolina Street, Potrero Hill (401 8081, www.thickhouse.org). Bus 10, 19, 22. **Tickets** vary. **No credit cards. Map** p319 N10.
Home of Thick Description, a leading producer of multiracial theater, this black box theater also hosts other worthwhile companies, with an output geared towards contemporary and cutting-edge drama.

Traveling Jewish Theatre

Various venues (522 0786, www.tjt-sf.org).
Aesthetically sophisticated and ensemble-driven, TJT's work ranges from the classics (recently, *Death of a Salesman*) to boldly contemporary drama.

Word for Word

Various venues (437 6775, www.zspace.org/w4w.htm).
Well suited to a famously literary city, this professional theater company 'brings literature to its feet' by staging short stories by acclaimed authors such as Michael Chabon and Tobias Wolff. The thrilling inventiveness and talent brought to bear on such pop-up book productions has earned the company acclaim from both literature-lovers and lazy readers.

Yerba Buena Center for the Arts

701 Mission Street, at 3rd Street, SoMa (978 2787, www.ybca.org). BART & Metro to Montgomery/bus 10, 12, 14, 30, 45, 91 & Market Street routes. **Tickets** $5-$100. **Credit** AmEx, DC, MC, V. **Map** p315 N6.
This angled, blue-tiled box, one of the city's most striking performance spaces, boasts a wide variety of events, ranging from the Afro Solo Festival to holiday season must-see *The Velveteen Rabbit*.
► *For more on Yerba Buena, see p61.*

EAST BAY THEATERS & COMPANIES

Aurora Theatre Company

2081 Addison Street, at Shattuck Avenue, Berkeley (1-510 843 4822, www.auroratheatre.org). BART Downtown Berkeley. **Tickets** $28-$45. **Credit** AmEx, DC, MC, V.
Based in a custom-designed 150-seat theater, Aurora produces a top-notch five-play season running the gamut from Shakespeare to LaBute via new translations of Ibsen. Meticulously crafted small theater.

★ Berkeley Repertory Theater

2025 Addison Street, between Shattuck Avenue & Milvia Street, Berkeley (information 1-510 647 2900, tickets 1-510 647 2949, www.berkeleyrep.org). BART Downtown Berkeley. **Tickets** $22-$60. **Credit** AmEx, DC, Disc, MC, V.
Arguably the best repertory company in the Bay Area presenting original works, the acclaimed Berkeley Rep has been the launch pad for numerous Broadway-bound works, including, recently, the Tony Award-winning musical-play *Passing Strange*, and Carrie Fisher's *Wishful Drinking*. Comprised of a 400-seat thrust-stage auditorium and a 600-seat proscenium space, seasons usually cover a classic drama and several new works by contemporary writers.

California Shakespeare Theater

Bruns Amphitheatre, 100 Gateway Boulevard, off Cal State 24, Orinda (1-510 548 9666, www.calshakes.org). BART Orinda, then free shuttle bus. **Tickets** $32-$60. **Credit** AmEx, DC, MC, V.
Cal Shakes regularly draws on the best Bay Area and national talent in its inventive presentations of works by Shakespeare and other classic writers, such as Shaw and Marivaux. The superb 545-seat Bruns Amphitheatre, set amid rolling hills and the picnic-ready grounds of a eucalyptus grove, is beautiful, but be sure to pack a warm coat for the foggy night air.

DANCE

In addition to the companies listed below, there is a strong tradition of ethnic dance in SF. The **Lily Cai Chinese Dance Company** (474 4829, www.lilycaidance.org) has been blending ancient forms with modern dance since 1988; **Chitresh Das Dance Company** (333 9000, www.kathak.org) performs narrative-driven Kathak dance, one of the six main Indian classical dance forms; and Carolena Nericcio's **Fat Chance Belly Dance** (431 4322, www.fcbd.com) has been performing an 'American Tribal' style of traditional Middle Eastern dancing since 1987.

Robert Moses' Kin. See p262.

Alonzo King's Lines

Information 863 3040, tickets 978 2787. www.linesballet.org). **Tickets** $25-$65.

This fine contemporary and eclectic ballet company stages mainly new works and tours extensively, both at home and abroad. A staple of the SF dance scene, it performs twice a year at Yerba Buena (*see left*).

Cal Performances

Zellerbach Hall, UC Berkeley campus, Berkeley (1-510 642 9988, www.calperfs.berkeley.edu). BART Downtown Berkeley. **Tickets** $10-$250. **Credit** AmEx, DC, Disc, MC, V.

An adjunct of UC Berkeley, Cal Performances offers a smattering of everything: dance, music and drama. In the former category, it regularly presents companies from around the country and the globe, such as Alvin Ailey, Twyla Tharp and Mark Morris.

Capacitor

Various venues (308 1952, www.capacitor.org).

This unique company fuses modern dance with original prop designs and interactive media to produce science-themed performances, with subjects ranging from the origin of the universe to the future of our species and everything in between.

CounterPULSE

1310 Mission Street, at 9th Street, SoMa (626 2060, tickets 1-800 838 3006, www.counterpulse.org). BART or Metro to Civic Center/ bus 12, 14, 19, 90 & Market Street routes. **Tickets** free-$20. **Credit** AmEx, Disc, MC, V. **Map** p318 L8.

Experimental and innovative work in dance and performance, as well as puppet activism, pagan festivals, healing circles and more.

Erika Chong Shuch Performance (ESP) Project

626 2787, www.erikachongshuch.org.

Dancer and choreographer Erika Shuch's ESP Project is, along with artists like Deborah Slater and Jess Curtis, at the forefront of a strong dance-theater movement in the Bay Area. In residency at Intersection for the Arts (*see p259*), the ESP Project recently premiered a wonderfully intimate and idiosyncratic anthropology of UFO obsession, ORBIT (notes from the edge of forever).

Footloose

Shotwell Studios, 3252-A 19th Street, at Shotwell Street, Mission (920 2223, tickets 1-800 838 3006,

INSIDE TRACK DANCING OUTSIDE THE BOX

San Francisco is a long-standing champion of dance groups and performers who don't fit the standard mold. For a sampling of the eclectic fare on offer, check out www.dancersgroup.org, which lists all upcoming dance events in the area. Best bets also include the **WestWave Dance Festival** (www.westwavedancefestival.org, July), featuring the work of some 50 local choreographers; the **Ethnic Dance Festival** (www.sfethnicdancefestival.org, June), a showcase for ethnic, cultural, and folk dance – from Senegalese to Mexican *folkorico* – for more than 30 years; and the **Bay Area National Dance Week** (www.bayareandw.org, April), which presents 400-plus free dance events for all ages and abilities over ten days, kicking off with One Dance in Union Square – when hundreds of dance-inclined folks descend on the downtown plaza to shake their booties in a giant group performance.

www.ftloose.org). BART 16th Street/bus 12, 14, 49. **Tickets** $15-20. **Credit** (advance bookings only) AmEx, Disc, MC, V. **Map** p318 K11.

Not far from the established modern dance center at ODC (*see below*) is this eclectic mix of emerging and seasoned dancers and choreographers operating under the Footloose banner. The emphasis here is on work by women, culminating in an annual Women on the Way Festival of up-and-coming artists.

Joe Goode Performance Group

Information 561 6565, tickets 978 2787, www.joegoode.org. **Tickets** $19-$49.

The JGPG has pushed modern dance to new theatrical heights, pursuing with gusto its founder's mission to explore contemporary issues, from gender to AIDS. The company also holds workshops for community groups, including at-risk youth and battered women. It performs at the Yerba Buena Center (*see p260*) every June.

★ ODC Dance

3153 17th Street, between Shotwell Street & Van Ness Avenue, Mission (863 9834, www.odcdance.org). BART 16th Street/bus 12, 14, 22, 33, 49. **Tickets** $18-$30. **Credit** AmEx, DC, MC, V. **Map** p318 K10.

Founded in 1971, the Oberlin Dance Collective has garnered an international reputation for its physically and intellectually vigorous modern dance. It has its own school, gallery and theatre, which hosts a variety of works all year round, while ODC itself also performs twice a year at the Yerba Buena Center. ODC recently expanded into an adjacent 23,000sq ft (2,100sq m) performance space on Shotwell Street (ODC Dance Commons), and also began renovations on its 17th Street theatre in late 2007.

Robert Moses' Kin

Various venues (252 8364, www.robertmoseskin.org).

Consistently breaking new ground since it was founded in 1995, Moses' 11-person group was described in a 2011 review as, 'one of his finest companies' around. Collaborating with everyone from sculptors and poets to musicians and designers, it has an increasingly demanding touring schedule. *Photo p261.*

★ San Francisco Ballet

War Memorial Opera House, 301 Van Ness Avenue, between Grove & McAllister Streets, Civic Center (information 861 5600/tickets 865 2000, www.sfballet.org). RT & Metro to Civic Center/bus 21, 47, 49, 90 & Market Street routes. Tickets $20-$98. Credit AmEx, Disc, MC, V. **Map** p318 K7.

Founded in 1933, the San Francisco Ballet is the longest-running professional ballet company in the US. In 1939, it presented the first full-length US production of *Coppélia*, followed in 1940 by the country's first complete *Swan Lake*. The company is based in the War Memorial Opera House (*see p233*), and its annual season (Feb-May) is typically an even blend of traditional pieces and new works.

Smuin Ballet

Information 495 2234, tickets 978 2787, www.smuinballet.org. **Tickets** $20-$62.

The sudden death of dancer and choreographer Michael Smuin in 2007 left many wondering if the company he founded would carry on, but it did, to the delight of audiences in the Bay Area and beyond. A former principal dancer and director of SF Ballet, who also worked on Broadway and in film and television, Smuin left a national legacy of bold dancer-driven work melding classical and modern techniques. Often audacious, always technically rigorous and inventive, Smuin Ballet offers winter, spring and holiday programs of Smuin classics along with premieres by other choreographers influenced by his vision. In SF, the company performs at Yerba Buena (*see p260*).

San Francisco Ballet.

Escapes & Excursions

Half Moon Bay. *See p269*.

Heading North

Over the Golden Gate Bridge and into lush Marin County.

The Golden Gate Bridge sometimes seems the only link between bustling San Francisco and languid Marin County. The city's wealthy northern neighbor, Marin extends from Sausalito, a quarter-hour by car from San Francisco, to Bodega Bay and inland to Novato; the protected parkland that sprawls across the county leaves it virtually immune to overpopulation. Of the county's towns, those on the east side (Tiburon, Sausalito, Mill Valley) tend to be well heeled and staid, while those on the western coast (Stinson Beach, Point Reyes Station and, notoriously, Bolinas) are more bohemian.

SAUSALITO TO LARKSPUR

The first exit north of the Golden Gate Bridge, **Vista Point**, offers amazing views. Pull off at the following exit, Alexander Avenue, for the **Bay Area Discovery Museum** (*see p211*), an interactive museum geared towards youngsters that's snuggled in **Fort Baker**, at the northern foot of the bridge. Here you'll also find **Cavallo Point Lodge** (601 Murray Circle, Fort Baker, Sausalito, 1-888 651 2003, www.cavallopoint.com), a luxe eco-hotel, spa and restaurant housed in beautifully refurbished military barracks. Further west, the **Marin Headlands** offer plenty of opportunities for outdoor activity, as well as breathtaking views of the city and the wide-open Pacific Ocean. Here, too, is the **Marine Mammal Center** (289 7325, www.marinemammalcenter.org), a sanctuary for injured seals and sea lions.

Sausalito, the southernmost Marin County town, is not as quaint as its reputation suggests, but it is picturesque. Originally a fishing village, the town is now home to prosperous artists and yacht owners, and well-off businessfolk. The ferry from San Francisco's Pier 41 or Ferry Building, which provides great views of the Golden Gate Bridge and Alcatraz, docks downtown against a backdrop of manicured gardens and pretty bungalows. Along North Bridgeway, opposite Spring Street, is the turn-off for the **San Francisco Bay Model Visitor Center** (*see below*). Across Richardson Bay is tiny downtown **Tiburon**. Again, there are no real sights, just the temptation to enjoy a lingering meal at one of the harbor-view restaurants on Main Street. However, it's also notable as the departure point for the ferry to **Angel Island**.

While in Marin County, it's worth taking the North San Pedro Road exit off US 101 towards **San Rafael**. On the north side of the city is Frank Lloyd Wright's grand **Marin Civic Center** (Avenue of the Flags, 499 6400, www.marincenter.org), fondly nicknamed 'Big Pink', while a post-war **replica of Mission San Rafael Arcangel** sits on 5th Avenue. Smaller than the 1817 original, the mission has a cemetery that contains the mortal remains of Chief Marin, the Native American leader who waged battle against Spanish explorers.

From there, head to **Mill Valley**, at the bottom of Mount Tamalpais, home to charming boutiques and restaurants, as well as a prestigious film festival. You'll also find picnic-friendly **Tennessee Beach**, accessible from Highway 101. Take the Mill Valley/Shoreline Highway exit towards Stinson Beach, then turn left on Tennessee Valley Road, which ends in the parking area a mile from the beach. The **Miwok Livery Stables** (701 Tennessee Valley Road, 383 8048, www.miwokstables.com) are also around here, catering for riders of all levels of experience. Quaint **Larkspur** is little frequented by tourists; nearby is **San Quentin Prison**.

FREE San Francisco Bay Model Visitor Center

2100 Bridgeway, at Olive Street, Sausalito (332 3870, www.spn.usace.army.mil/bmvc). **Open** *Labor Day-Memorial Day* 9am-4pm Tue-Sat. *Memorial Day-Labor Day* 9am-4pm Tue-Fri; 10am-5pm Sat, Sun. **Admission** free.

This two-acre, 1:5-scale hydraulic model of San Francisco Bay and delta was built in 1957 as a means of demonstrating how navigation, recreation and ecology interact. As such, it prevented the construction of various dams that would have disastrously altered the Bay's tidal range. There are walkways over the model, from which you can watch a complete lunar day in under 15 minutes.

Where to eat, drink & stay

On Bridgeway, Sausalito's main drag, there is excellent regional Italian food at **Poggio** (no.777, 332 7771, www.poggiotrattoria.com, mains $20). In **Tiburon**, try Main Street: most come to eat, drink Margaritas and take in the views from **Guaymas** (no.5, 435 6300, www.guaymasrestaurant.com, mains $20), or for the excellent weekend brunch at **Sam's Anchor Café** (no.27, 435 4527, www.samscafe.com, mains $22), which invites you to bring your vodka lemonades on to the sunny waterfront deck. Larkspur's highly regarded **Lark Creek Inn** (234 Magnolia Avenue, 924 7766, www.larkcreek.com, mains $28) is a lovely Victorian house with giant sloping skylights, half hidden in a grove of redwoods. Its organic salads and vegetables come from the farmers' market. **Left Bank** (507 Magnolia Avenue, 927 3331, www.leftbank.com, mains $26) is a quasi-Parisian bistro. The first-rate **Marin Brewing Company** (1809 Larkspur Landing Circle, 461 4677, www.marinbrewing.com, mains $11) is a good spot for a brew and some bar food.

In Mill Valley, visit ski-lodge-style **Buckeye Roadhouse** (15 Shoreline Highway, 331 2600, www.buckeyeroadhouse.com, mains $22), for upscale all-American food and great martinis.

If you'd like to stay overnight, the **Inn Above Tide** in Sausalito (30 El Portal, 1-800 893 8433, 332 9535, www.innabovetide.com, $305-$585 double) has peaceful and well-appointed balcony rooms – with balconies literally over the bay – offering wonderful views of San Francisco.

Tourist information

Mill Valley *Mill Valley Chamber of Commerce, 85 Throckmorton Avenue (388 9700, www.millvalley.org).*
Sausalito *Historical Exhibit & Visitor Center, 780 Bridgeway (332 0505, www.sausalito.org).*

Getting there

By car

Take US 101 across the Golden Gate Bridge. For Sausalito (8 miles from San Francisco), take the Alexander Avenue or Spencer Avenue exit. For Mill Valley (10 miles) and Larkspur, take the East Blithedale exit; you can also reach Larkspur by the Paradise Drive or Lucky Drive exits. For Tiburon, turn off here but follow the signs to Highway 131.

By bus

Golden Gate Transit runs bus services from San Francisco to Sausalito (route 10), Tiburon and Mill Valley (routes 10, 70 or 80 to Marin City, then route 15) and for Larkspur (routes 70 or 80 to Corte Madera, then routes 18 or 22), but taking the ferry and connecting to a bus there is usually far quicker. See schedules at www.goldengate.org.

By ferry

Golden Gate Transit ferries run from the Ferry Building on the Embarcadero to Sausalito and

Sausalito.

Larkspur; the Blue & Gold Fleet sails to Tiburon from the Ferry Building, and to Sausalito and Angel Island from Pier 41, Fisherman's Wharf.

ANGEL ISLAND

The largest island in the San Francisco Bay is a delightful, wild place with a fascinating history. Camp Reynolds, in the east of the island, was established in 1863 by Union troops to protect the Bay against a Confederate attack; later, from 1910 to 1940, the west of the island became the site of a US government immigration station set to screen immigrants under the terms of the 1882 Chinese Exclusion Act. Known as 'the Ellis Island of the West', Angel Island was notorious. Boatloads of Chinese immigrants were detained for months so officials could interrogate them; many were eventually sent home, never having touched the mainland. During World War II, Angel Island was an equally unwelcome home to German and Japanese POWs. The military remained in control through the '50s, when the island served as a missile base, but in 1963 the land was ceded to the government as a state park.

Ayala Cove, where the ferry docks, has a visitors' center (435 3522) and also marks the beginning of the five-mile Perimeter Trail, which will take you past the immigration station, wooden Civil War barracks and other military remnants hidden among the trees. At 797 feet (243 meters), the peak of **Mount Livermore** affords a panoramic view of the Bay from the island's center. There's a wonderful diversity of bird and animal species on the island, from deer to seals, pelicans to hummingbirds. You'll also find **Quarry Beach**, a sheltered sunbathing strip popular with kayakers. Those who don't want to walk can take the tram tour and anyone who wants to stay overnight can pitch up at the campsite. For details of camping, guided tours, and bike or kayak rental, see http://angelisland.org; if you do want to camp, book well in advance.

Getting there

By ferry

The Angel Island ferry (435 2131, $13.50 return) runs from Tiburon, daily in summer and weekends only in winter. Schedule information can be found at www.angelislandferry.com.

MOUNT TAMALPAIS & MUIR WOODS

Mount Tamalpais State Park covers 10 square miles on the western and southern slopes of the peak. Visible from as far away as Sonoma, the mountain itself soars to nearly 2,600 feet (almost 800 meters), but its rise is so steep it seems far taller. Beautiful at any time of day, it's magnificent at sunset. The roads that snake over Mount Tam, while challenging, are great for hiking and for bicycling. There's a gorgeous, paved rim trail, a visitor center and snack bar (open weekends), and exhibits about the **Mount Tamalpais Railway at the top of** the East Peak (www.mttam.net). If you're feeling adventurous, call the **San Francisco Hanggliding Center** (1-510 528 2300, www.sfhanggliding.com).

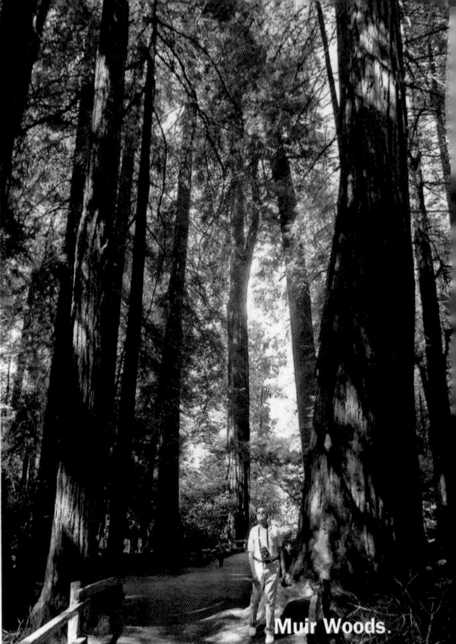
Muir Woods.

Nearby **Muir Woods National Monument** (388 2595, www.nps.gov/muwo, $5) contains majestic groves of the West Coast's tallest redwoods, many over 500 years old. You'll find several miles of trails her. Redwood Creek is lined with madrone and big-leaf maple trees, wild flowers, ferns and wild berry bushes. Deer, chipmunks and a variety of birds live peacefully among the redwoods, while the creek is a migratory route for steelhead trout and silver salmon. To avoid crowds, visit on weekday mornings and late afternoons.

Where to eat, drink & stay

The restaurant at the English-styled **Pelican Inn** (10 Pacific Way, 383 6000, www.pelican inn.com, mains $25) is not great, but it's the best eating option near the beach. It's also a fine hotel (from $200 double): quaint rooms have canopied beds, balconies and private bathrooms. Rugged travelers should try the 100-year-old **West Point Inn** (646 0702, www.westpointinn.com, $35/adult, $17.50/

child), a collection of five rustic cabins that's a two-mile hike up Mount Tam from **Pantoll Ranger Station** (388 2070). Guests bring their own sleeping bags and cook grub in a communal kitchen. There's no electricity, but nothing beats the views.

Tourist information

Mount Tamalpais *Mount Tamalpais State Park (388 2070, www.parks.ca.gov).* **Open** 7am-sunset daily.
Muir Woods *Muir Woods Visitor Center (388 2595, www.visitmuirwoods.com).* **Open** 8am-sunset daily. **Admission** $5.

Getting there

By car

Take US 101 across the Golden Gate Bridge, then turn on to Highway 1. Muir Woods is 15 miles from San Francisco.

By bus

Launched in 2005, a free shuttle bus, no.66, runs from Marin City to Muir Woods on weekends and holidays from Memorial Day to Labor Day.

STINSON BEACH & BOLINAS BEACH

The drive from Mill Valley to **Stinson Beach** along **Panoramic Highway** is long and filled with dangerous hairpin bends and sheer drops. Deer are apt to make appearances frighteningly close to the road. Nonetheless, the route is gorgeous, with spectacular views of the ocean, redwoods casting shadows on to the road and ferns dotting the ground along the way.

Stinson was only connected to Sausalito by a dirt road in 1870; prior to that, sole access was by boat, and there's still a delicious sense of isolation. A good reason to visit is the beach itself, prettier and much warmer than San Francisco's Ocean Beach. Lifeguards are on duty May through October, and there's a 50-acre park with more than 100 picnic tables. All-nude **Red Rock Beach** is a bare half mile south of downtown. Just north of Stinson Beach is the pristine **Martin Griffin Preserve,** previously known as Bolinas Lagoon Preserve (4900 Highway 1, 868 9244, www.egret.org). The Alice Kent Trail leads to an observation point, from which you can see egrets and great blue herons.

Between the lagoon and the Pacific is **Bolinas**, a beachside hamlet far enough off the beaten track for locals to find it worthwhile binning road signs to dissuade outsiders. But if you can, navigate your way into town and to the beach, which has small enough waves to be a great spot for novice surfers: try **Bolinas Surf Lessons** (2 Mile Surf Shop, 22 Brighton Avenue, 868 0264, www.surfbolinas.com). There's also kayaking and fishing; camping, campfires and dogs are allowed on the beach. The town is a haven for writers and artists, as the **Bolinas Museum** (48 Wharf Road, 868 0330, www.bolinasmuseum.org, closed Mon-Thur) makes clear. At the Palomarin field station of nearby **Point Reyes Bird Observatory** (900 Mesa Road, 868 0655, www.prbo.org), you can watch biologists catch and release birds, using special 'mist' nets, every day except Monday from May to late November, and on Wednesday, Saturday and Sunday mornings in winter.

A Whale of a Time

Nature at close quarters.

The California grey whale makes an exhausting 13,000-mile journey between Mexico and Alaska each season to mate in the warm waters of Baja California. The whales journey for three months in each direction and spend several months languishing in warm lagoons, fattening up their calves for the cold journey north. Mothers and calves like to stay close to shore, and display a clockwork-regular pattern of coming up for air, spouting like a geyser and gracefully submerging again: usually for three minutes, though they can stay under for as many as 15.

Every year orcas (killer whales) circle certain whales for attack, particularly vulnerable calves; despite the efforts of their mothers, a number of youngsters are lost each season. Yet this is nothing in comparison to the damage that has been wrought by human beings: the grey whale was hunted to virtual extinction in the late 1800s. Fortunately, the population has recovered remarkably well since the whales received full protection from the International Whaling Commission in 1947; in 1994 the California grey whale was removed from the Federal list of endangered species.

It's easy to watch the whales in action as they cruise along. From January to early May, you should be able to catch the annual spectacle from coastal vantage points such as Point Reyes or Mendocino. Better still, go on a whale-watching boat tour: **Oceanic Society Expeditions** (1-800 326 7491, 1-415 474 3385, www.oceanic-society.org) runs great trips from San Francisco ($60-$63), with a naturalist on board ready to answer your questions.

Where to eat, drink & stay

The thing to eat in Stinson is, of course, seafood: try the **Sand Dollar Restaurant** (3458 Shoreline Highway, 868 0434, www.stinsonbeachrestaurant.com, mains $21). A pleasant, casual, rather pricey beachside restaurant.

Bolinas has only a few choice spots: on Wharf Road, try the **Coast Café** (no.46, 868 2298, www.bolinashotel.com, closed Mon, mains $18). For a pint, the **Saloon at Smiley's** (41 Wharf Road, 868 1311) has been in the business for more than 150 years, and claims to be the second oldest bar in California.

Accommodation-wise, Stinson's cute and simple **Sandpiper** (1 Marine Way, 1-877 557 4737, 868 1632, www.sandpiperstinsonbeach.com, $140-$210 double) has rooms and cabins within walking distance of the waves.

Getting there

By car

Take US 101 across the Golden Gate Bridge and then, at Marin City, pick up Highway 1. This will lead you to Stinson Beach and (follow the signs) to Bolinas.

By bus

Golden Gate Transit's 63 service runs from Marin City to Stinson Beach. The West Marin Stagecoach (www.marintransit.org/stage.html) operates four buses a day from Marin City to Stinson Beach and Bolinas.

POINT REYES NATIONAL SEASHORE

If you head north from Stinson Beach on Highway 1, you'll come to the **Bear Valley Visitor Center** (*see below*) near Olema. The center acts as the entry point for the most famous parcel of land in these parts: the vast wilderness of **Point Reyes National Seashore**. This protected peninsula is an extraordinary wildlife refuge, with sea mammals, waterfalls and miles of unspoilt beaches. From the visitor center, you can either head west towards the coast for **Drake's Beach**, or go north via Inverness to the tip of the peninsula: **Point Reyes Lighthouse** (669 1534, closed Tue & Wed) is a perfect lookout for whale-watching. Several trails also start here, including the popular **Chimney Rock**. Nearby **Inverness** is picturesque, with many homes still owned by the families that built them, while tiny **Point Reyes Station** bustles with energy along its three-block Downtown; both are hubs for organic farmers and ranchers, as well as artisanal cheesemakers. Make a note to check in at the **Cowgirl Creamery** (80 4th Street, 663 9335, www.cowgirlcreamery.com), where you can try a bounty of fine local cheeses.

Further along Highway 1 is **Tomales Bay**. There, **Blue Waters Kayaking** (12938 Sir Francis Drake Boulevard, at the Golden Hinde Inn, 669 2600, www.bwkayak.com) offers half- or full-day paddle trips, and (by appointment) romantic full-moon tours.

Where to eat, drink & stay

In Point Reyes Station, the **Station House Café** (Main Street, 663 1515, www.stationhousecafe.com, closed Wed, mains $15) is a mellow place that serves California cuisine, while the **Pine Cone Diner** (60 4th Street, 663 1536, www.pineconediner.com, mains $10) is a much-treasured retro spot for breakfast or lunch.

In Inverness, **Manka's Inverness Lodge** (30 Callender Way, 669 1034, www.mankas.com, $315-$715 double) has eight rooms, a suite, two cabins and a 1911 boathouse over the water; the famed sustainable, local, organic restaurant served Prince Charles and Camilla (set menu $58).

In nearby Marshall is **Nick's Cove** (23240 State Route 1, 663 1033, www.nickscove.com, mains $18, $225-$695 double). Here, former fishing cabins built over Tomales Bay have been transformed into rustic but luxurious cottages. The restaurant is top-notch, with locally sourced seafood, meat and produce.

Since 1876, Olema has been home to the charming **Olema Inn** (10000 Sir Francis Drake Boulevard, 663 9559, www.theolemainn.com, $145-$185 double). In Point Reyes, try art-heavy **Abalone Inn** (12355 Sir Francis Drake Boulevard, 663 9149, 1-877 416 0458, www.abaloneinn.com, $110-$150 double) or **Knob Hill** (40 Knob Hill Road, 663 1784, www.knobhill.com, $80-$160 double).

Getting there

By car

Take US 101 across the Golden Gate Bridge, then Highway 1. Point Reyes is 32 miles from SF.

By bus

The West Marin Stagecoach (www.marintransit.org/stage.html) operates four buses (Mon, Wed, Fri, Sun) or five (Tue, Thur, Sat) from San Rafael Transit Center to Point Reyes.

Tourist information

Point Reyes *National Seashore Bear Valley Visitor Center (464 5100/www.nps.gov/pore).* **Open** 9am-5pm Mon-Fri; 8am-5pm Sat, Sun. *Point Reyes Lighthouse Visitor Center (669 1534/www.nps.gov/pore).* **Open** 10am-4.30pm Mon, Thur-Sun, weather permitting.

Heading South

Miles of gorgeous golden California coast.

The San Francisco peninsula stretches 42 miles (68 kilometres) south until it merges with the mainland near San Jose. On the Pacific side, you'll notice a change of scenery as well as a change of pace: from the bustling city to rolling hills, miles of beautiful rugged beaches and sleepy towns.

South of San Francisco Bay is the tech hub of Silicon Valley, with some pleasant towns. Further south is the laid-back beach town of Santa Cruz, while to the east is one of the US's crowning natural glories: Yosemite National Park.

HALF MOON BAY & THE COAST

Half Moon Bay is a small, easygoing seaside town with a rural feelt. Quaint Main Street is good for a wander, with bookstores, antiques shops, cafés and restaurants, and inns, but the town is most famous for its pumpkins at Halloween and fresh seafood.

At Half Moon Bay and Highway 1, the **Sea Horse & Friendly Acres Ranch** (1-650 726 2362, www.horserentals.com/seahorse.html) offers beach horseback rides for a range of levels. Then there's **Mavericks**: right in the middle of Half Moon Bay and about half a mile offshore, it's one of the gnarliest big-wave surf spots in the world, home every January to the Mavericks Surfing Contest, when the world's best wave riders converge to battle it out against huge Pacific swells.

Travel eight miles further down Highway 1 where it crosses Highway 84 and drop in on the **San Gregorio General Store** (1-650 726 0565, www.sangregoriostore.com). Serving the local community since 1889, it's a hybrid bar, music hall, all-purpose store and gathering place.

Continuing south from San Gregorio, you'll find probably the best of the region's beaches: **San Gregorio State Beach**, a strip of white sand distinguished by sedimentary cliffs. Another 15 miles down the coast are the historic buildings and rolling farmlands of **Pescadero**, with locals still tending their artichoke fields and strawberry patches.

Where to eat, drink & stay

In Half Moon Bay, cozy **Pasta Moon** (315 Main Street, 1-650 726 5126, www.pastamoon.com, mains $18-$23) serves elegant housemade pasta dishes. Old-school **Main Street Grill** (547 Main Street, 1-650 726 5300, www.mainstgrill hmb.com, closed dinner, mains $6.25-$9.50) offers hearty breakfast and lunch. **Half Moon Bay Brewing Company** (390 Capistrano Avenue, Princeton-by-the-Sea, 1-650 728 2739, www.hmb brewingco.com, mains $10-$21) boasts views of the harbor, plus excellent burgers. With spectacular ocean views and an outdoor deck, **Sam's Chowder House** (4210 North Cabrillo Highway, 1-650 712 0245, www.samschowder house.com, mains $15-$28) delivers platters of fresh seafood. If the line is too long, head to local favorite **Barbara's Fishtrap** (281 Capistrano Road, 1-650 728 7049) for the coast's best clam

INSIDE TRACK
PUMPKIN POWER

Every fall, Half Moon Bay turns orange with pumpkins, with prime patches lining the coastal route, Highway 1. Many of the farms here also sell other produce, including prize strawberries and artichokes, and a few double as Christmas tree farms. Head to **Farmer John's** (850 North Cabrillo Highway) to see 250-500lb Atlantic Giant pumpkins. Or, in October, hit the annual **Half Moon Bay Art & Pumpkin Festival** (www.miramarevents.com/pumpkinfest) for the World Championship Pumpkin Weigh-Off, when growers compete to see who's grown the largest gourd (the current world record is 1,725lb).

chowder. For excellent Mediterranean cuisine try **Cetrella** (845 Main Street, 1-650-726-4090, www.cetrella.com, closed Mon and lunch except Sun, mains $18-$35).

There's no shortage of places to stay in and around Half Moon Bay. The grandest is the **Ritz-Carlton** (1 Miramontes Point Road, 1-800 241 3333, 1-650 712 7000, www.ritzcarlton.com, $335-$895 double), set on a spectacular bluff overlooking the rugged coastline with two golf courses and a spa. About 25 miles south of here, **Costanoa** (2001 Rossi Road, 1-877 262 7848, 1-650 879 1100, www.costanoa.com) is part rustic resort, part campground; there are wooden cabins and a 40-room lodge ($119-$379 double), but you can also pitch a tent ($40-$65).

Getting there

By car

Half Moon Bay is 30 miles south of San Francisco on Highway 1, about a 45min drive.

By train & bus

Take a BART train to Daly City (journey time 15mins), pick up SamTrans bus 110 to Linda Mar and transfer to bus 294 for Half Moon Bay.

Tourist information

Half Moon Bay *Coastside Chamber of Commerce, 235 Main Street (1-650 726 8380, www.hmbchamber.com).* **Open** 9am-5pm Mon-Fri.

SILICON VALLEY

Silicon Valley runs south from the base of San Francisco Bay. Routinely dismissed as mere sprawl, it actually offers fine strolling in the pretty downtowns of upscale **Los Gatos** and **Saratoga**. More substantial pleasures are found in **Palo Alto**, the site of Stanford University. Here the 20 bronzes that comprise the on-campus **Rodin Sculpture Garden**, associated with the Cantor Arts Center (328 Lomita Drive, 1-650 723 3469, tours 2pm Wed, 11.30am Sat, 2pm Sun), make a neat diversion.

Despite all the concrete, **San Jose** is the most appealing Silicon Valley town for visitors. Attractions include the interactive **Children's Discovery Museum** (180 Woz Way, 1-408 298 5437, www.cdm.org, closed Mon, $10); the **Tech Museum of Innovation** (201 South Market Street, 1-408 795 6105, www.thetech.org, $10), a new interactive science and technology center and IMAX theater, and nearby **Monopoly in the Park** (Guadalupe River Park, West Fernando Street, 1-408 995 6487, www.monopolyinthepark.com). The latter, a 930-square-foot (86-square-meter) board game, is the closest ordinary people get to buying property in Silicon Valley; you'll have to reserve a game in advance. The **San Jose Museum of Art** (110 S Market Street, 1-408 271 6840, http://sjmusart.org, closed Mon, $8) has a collection of nearly 1,400 pieces, most from the latter part of the 20th century. There's good shopping, too, with S Bascom Avenue boasting **Streetlight Records** (No.980, 1-888 330 7776) and, for pop-culture collectibles, **Time Tunnel Toys** (No.532, 1-408 298 1709, closed Mon & Sun).

Rosicrucian Egyptian Museum & Planetarium

1342 Naglee Avenue, at Park Avenue, San Jose (1-408 947 3636, www.egyptianmuseum.org). **Open** 10am-5pm Mon-Fri; 11am-6pm Sat, Sun. *Planetarium shows* 2pm Mon-Fri; 2pm, 3.30pm Sat, Sun. **Admission** $9; $5-$7 reductions. **Credit** AmEx, MC, V.

Located in Rosicrucian Park, this museum is home to six real mummies, more than 4,000 ancient artifacts and full-scale replica tombs. The planetarium's free 35-minute show explores 'The Mithraic Mysteries', connecting the obscure Roman cult to modern astronomy.

Half Moon Bay. *See p269.*

ESCAPES & EXCURSIONS

Winchester Mystery House
525 South Winchester Boulevard, San Jose (1-408 247 2101, www.winchestermysteryhouse.com). **Open** from 9am daily (8am in summer); tour times vary by season. **Tours** $20.95-$28.95; $17.95-$25.95 reductions. **Credit** Disc, MC, V.
Haunted by the ghosts of those killed by the namesake rifle, widow-heiress Sarah Winchester spent 38 years continuously building this 160-room mansion to placate the malevolent spirits. Flashlight tours on Friday the 13th and Halloween are extra creepy, but at any time the oddity of the place (a staircase heads into a bare ceiling, a window is set in the floor) is impressive. Still, the small museum celebrating the gun might be seen, given the widow's fears, to be a little insensitive.

Where to eat, drink & stay

Given all the expense accounts, it's no surprise to find quality restaurants here. Just south of the airport in San Jose, **Osteria Coppa** (139 S B Street, 1-650 579 6021, www.osteria coppa.com, mains $15-$26) delivers some of the area's most authentic Italian food, with exquisite housemade pastas . Down the road on Silicon Valley's venture capital row, Menlo Park's **Madera** (2825 Sand Hill Road, 1-650 561 1540, $14-$36) offers wood-fired American cuisine and a clubby atmosphere. Neighboring Palo Alto has a variety of good ethnic restaurants, including upscale **Evvia** (420 Emerson Street, 1-650 326 0983, www.evvia.net, mains $14.50-$20), a contemporary take on Greek cuisine . In San Jose, try highly regarded chop house **AP Stumps** (163 W Santa Clara Street, 1-408 292 9928, www.apstumps.com, mains $15-$40).

If you want to stay, downtown San Jose has the **Fairmont San Jose** (170 S. Market Street, 1-408 998-1900, www.fairmont.com/sanjose, $195-$264 double) and the classy **Hotel De Anza** (233 W Santa Clara Street, 1-408 286 1000, www.hoteldeanza.com, $199-$329 double), with its Hedley Club Lounge where you can sit by the fire and take in jazz piano. If you're looking for chic luxury, try the **Hotel Valencia** on Santana Row (355 Santana Row, 1-408 551 0010, http://sanjose.hotelvalencia.com, $248-$460 double).

Getting there

By car
San Jose is about 50 miles south of San Francisco on Highway 101.

By train
CalTrain travels every 30 mins from San Francisco to San Jose, making several stops along the way, including Palo Alto. CalTrain also runs the Baby Bullet commuter train from SF to San Jose.

Tourist information

San Jose *CVB, 408 Almaden Boulevard (1-408 295 9600, 1-800 726 5673, www.sanjose.org).* **Open** 9am-5pm Mon-Fri.

SANTA CRUZ

Established as a mission at the end of the 18th century, Santa Cruz is now a beach town well known for being easygoing and politically progressive. The University of California at Santa Cruz takes the lead; its students can often be found down at robustly independent **Bookshop Santa Cruz** (1520 Pacific Avenue, 1-831 423 0900, www.bookshopsantacruz.com).

All that remains of Misión la Exaltación de la Santa Cruz is the Neary-Rodriguez Adobe in **Santa Cruz Mission State Historic Park**; commonly known as **Mission Adobe** (1-831 425 5849, closed Mon-Wed in winter, $1-$2), it once housed the mission's Native American population. Down the street is **Mission Plaza** (1-831 426 5686, closed Mon), a complete 1930s replica. The **Santa Cruz Museum of Natural History** (1305 East Cliff Drive, 1-831 420 6115, www.santacruzmuseums.org, closed Mon, $1.50-$2.50) contains information about the Ohlone people who once populated the area. The culturally inclined can visit the **Santa Cruz Museum of Art & History** (*see p273*), while pop culture fans will be unable to resist the **Mystery Spot** (465 Mystery Spot Road, 1-831 423 8897, $5), a few miles north of the city in the woods off Highway 17. It's a patch of earth 150 feet (46 meters) in diameter, which appears to confound the laws of physics and gravity. Kitsch nonsense, but fun.

Directly on the beach, the **Santa Cruz Beach Boardwalk** (400 Beach Street, 1-831 423 5590, open daily mid May-early Sept, weekends Sept-May, unlimited rides $29.95) is an amusement park that contains, among other things, a vintage carousel and a classic seaside wooden rollercoaster.

The Boardwalk's **Cocoanut Grove Ballroom** (1-831 423 2053) is another remnant, with live music on weekends and holidays bringing it back to life. Continuing the beach theme, the lighthouse contains the engaging, free **Surfing Museum** (West Cliff Drive, 1-831 420 6289, www.santacruzsurfingmuseum.org, open 10am-5pm Wed-Sun, hours vary in winter), while right outside the lighthouse is **Steamer Lane**, one of the best surfing spots in the state.

Fans of towering redwoods should head north into the Santa Cruz Mountains to **Big Basin Redwoods State Park** (21600 Big Basin Way, Boulder Creek, 1-831 338 8860, www.bigbasin.org) or **Henry Cowell Redwoods State Park** (101 North Big Trees Park Road, Felton,

1-831 335 4598), which has a tree you can drive through. Also to the north, a mile past Western Drive on Highway 1, are the 4,500 acres (1,820 hectares) of former dairy farm **Wilder Ranch State Park** (1-831 423 9703). Centered on a quaint compound of historic Victorian houses and gardens, the park also has 34 miles of trails.

Some 50 wineries are scattered across the area, most open to the public but free of the crowds that put some off the Wine Country. Two of the best are **Bonny Doon** (10 Pine Flat Road, 1-831 425 3625, www.bonnydoonvineyard.com) and the award-winning **Storrs** (303 Potrero Street, 1-831 458 5030, www.storrswine.com).

Santa Cruz Museum of Art & History

McPherson Center, 705 Front Street, at Cooper Street (1-831 429 1964, www.santacruzmah.org). **Open** 11am-5pm Tue-Sun. **Admission** $5; $2-$3 reductions; free under-12s. Free 1st Fri of mth. **Credit** MC, V.

This art museum features rotating exhibitions, as well as a permanent display of early Santa Cruz artifacts and a library.

Where to eat, drink & stay

High above Santa Cruz Yacht Harbor, the **Crow's Nest** (2218 East Cliff Drive, 1-831 476 4560, mains $14-$24) offers magnificent views and great seafood. Downtown has a whole world of options, among them the hip **Mobo Sushi** (105 S River Street, 1-831 425 1700, www.mobosushirestaurant.com, sushi $3-$6) and premier Mexican **El Palomar** (1336 Pacific Avenue, 1-831 425 7575, mains $8-$20). On the Eastside, there's fabulous wood-fired pizza to be had at **Engfer Pizza Works** (537 Seabright Avenue, 1-831 429 1856, closed Mon, pizzas $8-$15), as well as a ping pong table and an exotic array of old-time sodas.

And you're spoiled for cheap choices. One of the best is the **Saturn Café** (145 Laurel Street, 1-831 429 8505, mains $6-$8), a vegetarian diner that even meat-eaters are impressed with.

Santa Cruz has many dreary motels, but there are some charming spots too. The **Babbling Brook Inn** (1025 Laurel Street, 1-831 427 2437, www.babblingbrookinn.com, $142-$317 double) is surrounded by leafy gardens with tall redwood trees. Overlooking the sea, the **Pleasure Point Inn** (2-3665 East Cliff Drive, 1-831 469 6161, www.pleasurepointinn.com, $225-$295 double) is modern, upscale and well appointed. The Gothic Victorian **Compassion Flower Inn** (216 Laurel Street, 1-831 466 0420, www.compassionflowerinn.com, $115-$175 double) is a handsome old B&B also notable for being one of the first medical-marijuana-friendly hotels in the US.

Getting there

By car

Santa Cruz is 74 miles south of San Francisco on I-280 (take Highway 17 to I-85 to get to I-280).

By train & bus

Amtrak shuttle buses link San Jose and Santa Cruz. Greyhound buses leave San Francisco for Santa Cruz about four times a day.

Tourist information

Santa Cruz *Santa Cruz County CVB, 1211 Ocean Street, nr Washburn Avenue (1-831 425 1234/1-800 833 3494/www.scccvc.org).* **Open** 9am-5pm Mon-Fri; 10am-4pm Sat, Sun.

THE MONTEREY PENINSULA

Monterey's rise to fame was gradual. Junípero Serra set up the second of his 21 missions here, and for the Spanish, the town was a crucial settlement, and remained important when the Mexicans seceded from Spain in 1822 and assumed stewardship over California; it was at **Custom House** (*see 275*) 24 years later that the American flag was raised in California for the first time with any degree of permanency.

Monterey's unlikely journey from capital of Alta California to sardine capital of the world took several generations, during which the town and neighboring **Pacific Grove** briefly became popular resorts. The fishing industry drove the economy for the first part of the 20th century; when the fish and the money both ran out, the fishermen left the place to the tourists, and Monterey is now one of the most popular towns for visitors on the West Coast, especially during its celebrated jazz festival,

INSIDE TRACK HIGH FINANCE

Though it may appear as nothing more than a series of innocuous office buildings along a nondescript tree-lined driveway, **Sand Hill Road** in Menlo Park, 40 minutes south of San Francisco, is the Silicon Valley equivalent of Fort Knox. The suburban hilltop is home to a small, but powerful concentration of venture capital companies – the private equity firms that fund future Googles and Facebooks.
For a number of years during the dotcom boom, real estate on Sand Hill Road was among the most expensive in the world, with office space renting at around $144 a square foot in mid 2000 – higher than Manhattan or London's West End.

Bags packed, milk cancelled, house raised on stilts.

You've packed the suntan lotion, the snorkel set, the stay-pressed shirts. Just one more thing left to do – your bit for climate change. In some of the world's poorest countries, changing weather patterns are destroying lives.

You can help people to deal with the extreme effects of climate change. Raising houses in flood-prone regions is just one life-saving solution.

Climate change costs lives.
Give £5 and let's sort it *Here & Now*

www.oxfam.org.uk/climate-change

held every September (1-831 373 3366, www.montereyjazzfestival.org).

Monterey

All of downtown Monterey's low-key attractions are scattered around its fringes, meaning that **Alvarado Street**, its main drag, is populated chiefly with restaurants and shops. Stroll south and you'll come to the **Monterey Museum of Art** (559 Pacific Street, 1-831 372 5477, www.montereyart.org, closed Mon & Tue, $5), which has an august permanent collection containing photography by Ansel Adams and Edward Weston. Continuing north along Alvarado Street, meanwhile, leads you towards the water and the spreadeagled **Monterey State Historic Park** (1-831 649 7118, www.parks.ca.gov). The self-guided **Path of History tour** takes in some of the park's historic buildings (as well as others around town), including the **Custom House**, an adobe building dating back around 175 years. For further information, ask at the tourist office.

Adjoining **Fisherman's Wharf** is smaller than the version in San Francisco, but is just like it in one regard: it fails to live up to its name. The fishermen who once drove the town's economy long ago drew in their nets for the final time, leaving their former base to the tourists. Fisherman's Wharf is now merely a collection of shops and restaurants, working a tired spell on a steady stream of easily impressed visitors.

Thought Fisherman's Wharf was touristy? Wait until you see **Cannery Row**. This stretch of waterside road was once home to the robust fishing industry immortalized by John Steinbeck in his 1945 novel. Steinbeck would be appalled to see it now, its old buildings converted into bars, gift shops and hokey attractions that trade off his name in a variety of inventively crass ways. The one redeeming feature is the celebrated **Monterey Bay Aquarium**.

Monterey Bay Aquarium

886 Cannery Row (1-831 648 4800, www.mbayaq.org). **Open** *Memorial Day-Labor Day* 9.30am-6pm daily. *Labor Day-Memorial Day* 10am-6pm daily. **Admission** $29.95; $19.95-$27.95 reductions; free under-3s. **Credit** AmEx, MC, V.

The centerpiece of the museum is still the vast Kelp Forest exhibit, crammed with marine life both prosaic and exotic. Over in the Outer Bay Wing, the Outer Bay is a breathtaking collection of fish and sharks in a million-gallon tank (go during feeding time). Also in this wing is Jellies: Living Art, showcasing the staggering beauty of jellyfish. Among the other inhabitants of the building are the perennially cute sea otters (also popular at feeding time), while newer exhibits include Wild About Otters (freshwater otters), Splash Zone (penguins) and the self-explanatory Mission to the Deep. The Portola Café, with its bay views, is way above your average museum eatery, showcasing selections from the museum's nationally acclaimed Seafood Watch program, which offers a handy guide to sustainable and endangered fish.

Monterey.

Pacific Grove & Carmel

Just down the road from Monterey lies the sweet little town of **Pacific Grove**, a far less touristy settlement. Its downtown (around the junction of Lighthouse Avenue and Forest Street) is largely unencumbered by gift shops and galleries; its restaurants are no more expensive than they need to be. Pick up a walking tour leaflet from the Chamber of Commerce (*see p277*) for details on the histories of the town's century-old private residences.

The **Pacific Grove Museum of Natural History** (165 Forest Avenue, 1-831 648 5716, www.pgmuseum.org, closed Mon & Sun) is home to an interesting exhibition on the Monarch butterflies that spend winters here (ask at the visitor center for details of where to see them). The town wears its nickname, Butterfly Town USA, with pride. However, its main attraction is its craggy coastline. Catch it on a grey day, and the coast hugging **Ocean View Boulevard** is awesome, waves beating furiously against the rocks. On bluer days, it's more serene; several parks and viewpoints offer the chance to picnic while watching sea lions laze the day away.

Just south of Pacific Grove is the **17-Mile Drive**, a privately owned road, established in 1881, that takes drivers alongside some breathtaking coastal scenery. So breathtaking, in fact, that the road's owners charge drivers

Natural High

Yosemite: one of nature's peak performances.

Enchanting, intoxicating, stunning, breathtaking… that's the typical response the first time people see **Yosemite National Park**, located approximately four hours south-east of San Francisco and covering some 1,200 square miles of forest, alpine meadows, sheer granite cliffs, lush waterfalls, and undisturbed wildlife. With park elevations that range from 2,000 feet to over 13,000 feet (600 to nearly 4,000 meters), Yosemite is all about views. As you drive into the valley, the dramatic countenance of **El Capitan** greets you – a sheer rock wall 3,000 feet (914 meters) in height.

Highway 120 runs east–west for the entire length of the park, climbing to 9,945 feet (3,031 meters) at **Tioga Pass**, the highest automobile pass in California (closed in winter). Though the roads are engineered as scenic drives, the best way to experience the park and properly commune with nature is on foot. Visit in the less crowded off season, if possible, from October to May. In spring, the wildflowers are in bloom, and in winter, snowcapped peaks are majestic. If you must visit in high season, try to avoid peak times in the perpetually packed **Yosemite Valley**. You don't need reservations to visit the park (although you should certainly book lodgings in advance); the $20 entrance fee per vehicle is good for seven days. Be aware, however, that Yosemite is massive, with more than 250 miles of roads criss-crossing the park. To see even a respectable chunk, you'll need a few days.

Most people head for seven-mile-long Yosemite Valley, where most of the lodgings and services are located. Though there's plenty to do – hikes, glorious vistas, ice-skating in winter, and the park's best dining – keep in mind that the Valley makes up less than one per cent of the park. For non-Valley sites, head to **Tuolumne Meadows** (via Highway 120), stunning **Glacier Point**, the **Hetch Hetchy Reservoir** (north of Big Oak Flat) and **Tunnel View** at the eastern end of the Wawona tunnel on Highway 41.

For hiking, the Mist Trail is the most popular: three miles from **Happy Isles** to **Vernal Falls** and back, or a seven-mile round trip to Nevada Falls. The hike to **Glacier Point** is just as challenging, but you can cheat by driving there instead.

Then there's the hike to **Half Dome** (16-mile round trip), which is strictly for the hardcore, as you have to cling to cables anchored into a sheer rockface for the last half mile (reservations required). For more information on trails, see www.nps.gov/yose/planyourvisit/valley hikes.htm.

Three main areas of the Valley can satisfy your stomach's cravings: **Yosemite Lodge**, **Yosemite Village** and **Curry Village**. **Mountain Room** is the best of the handful of restaurants at Yosemite Lodge. In Yosemite Village, **Degnan's Deli** is busy at lunchtime, with sandwiches, salads and soups. Curry Village also has a variety of options, from Mexican and pizza to the grand WPA-built **Ahwahnee Hotel**, whose Sunday brunches are legendary. You'll need a reservation (1-209 372 1489).

Seven lodgings are available inside the park running the gamut from grungy to extravagant. The 260-room **Yosemite Lodge** ($218-$242 double) has all the charm of a chain motel, but is unbeatable for its central location. Those with money to blow should consider the **Ahwahnee Hotel** ($470-$525 double), a National Historic Landmark built in 1927 of huge timbers and river rock. Outside the valley, there's the whitewashed Victorian **Wawona Hotel** ($110-$191 double), and the modern, fairly upscale **Tenaya Lodge** (1-888 514 2167, www.tenayalodge.com, $135-$340 double).

Reservations for lodgings are all made at Yosemite Reservations (1-559 252 4848, www.yosemitepark.com). General information from the National Park Service (1-209 372 0200, www.nps.gov/yose).

around $9.50 just to see it. Also here is **Pebble Beach Golf Links** (1-800 654 9300, www.pebblebeach.com); regarded by many as one of the world's finest courses, it's also, at $495 a round, one of the most expensive.

The southern point of the 17-Mile Drive is the town of **Carmel-by-the-Sea**. If this cutesy idyll proves anything, it's that money doesn't buy taste. The shops hawk kitschy souvenirs and frumpy clothes; the restaurants serve average food at inflated prices; and the galleries deal mostly in art of the most preternaturally ghastly kind. Still, there's an undeniable charm to a town with cobbled streets and no mailboxes or street addresses (local mail gets delivered to the post office). And its two beaches – **Carmel Beach** at the western end of Ocean Avenue, and down the coast, the less crowded and more pleasant **Carmel River State Beach** (1-831 649 2836), which also includes a bird sanctuary – are arguably two of the most splendid on the coast. Both beaches might look idyllic, but tides can be lethal. Swimming is not recommended.

Where to eat & drink

Your best bet in downtown Monterey is chic **Montrio** (414 Calle Principal, 1-831 648 8880, www.montrio.com, closed lunch, mains $9-$30), where the California cuisine lives up to the stylish room in which it's served. **C Restaurant** (750 Cannery Row, 1-831 375 4800, www.thecrestaurant-monterey.com, open daily, mains $16.50-$45) is a sleek, modern spot directly on the bay offering spectacular views and a menu featuring local, sustainable seafood such as Dungeness crab, Monterey Bay red abalone, and diver sea scallops. **Stokes** (500 Hartnell Street, 1-831 373 1110, www.stokesrestaurant.com, closed lunch Mon-Fri, mains $15-$24) is a locals favorite for Mediterranean cuisine, housed in a gorgeous converted 170-year-old adobe house.

There's a good balance of quality to quantity in Pacific Grove. You'll find daisy-fresh fish creations at smart-casual **Passionfish** (701 Lighthouse Avenue, 1-831 655 3311, www.passionfish.net, closed lunch, mains $17-$24) and some fair Mediterranean-influenced food at **Fandango** (223 17th Street, 1-831 372 3456, www.fandangorestaurant.com, mains $17-$34). In Carmel, the best of the bunch is probably the **Flying Fish Grill** (Carmel Plaza, Mission Street, 1-831 625 1962, closed lunch, mains $18-$39).

Where to stay

There are a number of individualistic lodgings closer to downtown Monterey. The most appealing of these is the **Old Monterey Inn** (500 Martin Street, 1-800 350 2344, www.oldmontereyinn.com, $240-$480 double), an immaculate B&B set on a quiet street. Also worth a look is the elegant **Spindrift Inn** (475 Cannery Row, 1-800 841 1879, 1-831 646 8900, www.spindriftinn.com, $159-$489 double), which bears nary a trace of its former incarnation as a whorehouse. The pricey **Intercontinental Clement Monterey** (750 Cannery Row, 1-831 375 4500, $181-$526 double) is right next to the aquarium, with suites offering fireplaces and ocean-view balconies. The best bargain is likely the century-old **Monterey Hotel** (406 Alvarado Street, 1-800 966 6490, 1-831 375 3184, www.montereyhotel.com, $89-$299 double) – good value given its central location. Bear in mind that it's very difficult to find spur-of-the-moment accommodation during the annual jazz fest.

Over in Pacific Grove, try the **Martine Inn** (255 Ocean View Boulevard, 1-831 373 3388, 1-800 852 5588, www.martineinn.com, $159-$425 double). Owned by Don Martine, who spends his spare time restoring classic cars (he's happy to show them off), the hotel has 24 rooms with unique antique fixtures. Also here is the **Jabberwock Inn** (598 Laine Street, 1-888 428 7253, 1-831 372 4777, www.jabberwockinn.com, $165-$295 double), a fab B&B in a century-old mansion that's gently themed around the works of Lewis Carroll. A good bet in Carmel is the **Mission Ranch** (26270 Dolores Street, 1-800 538 8221, 1-831 624 6436, www.missionranchcarmel.com, $110-$290 double), where the tastefully decorated rustic rooms look out over handsome countryside. If money's no object, head for the award-winning **Inn at Spanish Bay** (2700 17-Mile Drive, 1-800 654 9300, www.pebblebeach.com, $565-$775 double).

Tourist information

Carmel *Chamber of Commerce, San Carlos Street, between 5th & 6th Streets (1-800 550 4333, 1-831 624 2522, www.carmelcalifornia.org).* **Open** 9am-5pm daily.

Monterey *Visitor Center, 401 Camino El Estero, at Franklin & Camino El Estero (1-888 221 1010, 1-831 649 1770, www.montereyinfo.org).* **Open** 9am-5pm daily.

Pacific Grove *Chamber of Commerce, corner of Central & Forest Avenues (1-800 656 6650, 1-831 373 3304, www.pacificgrove.org).* **Open** 9.30am-5pm Mon-Fri; 10am-3pm Sat.

Getting there

By car

Monterey is 110 miles from San Francisco if you take US 101 to CA-17 to Highway 1, and a bit further if you take Highway 1 all the way. Plan on a 2-3hr drive. It's 5 miles to Monterey from **Carmel**, and 6 miles to **Pacific Grove**.

Wine Country

Drink in the scenery.

Everything you've heard about California's Wine Country is true – rolling hills planted with lush rows of tangled vines, refreshing country air, destination restaurants, upscale resorts: the attractions are endless. It may only take an hour to drive from San Francisco to Napa and Sonoma Counties, but it really is another world.

Since pioneering Hungarian farmer Agoston Haraszthy de Mokcsa planted his 500-acre Buena Vista wine estate in the middle of the 19th century, the Wine Country has changed hugely. From modest beginnings, the area has become masterful at marketing not only its product, but itself; it has sold an image of an idyllic, cultured and romantic place – a lifestyle to which five million visitors a year aspire. Summer here is ridiculously busy, so the best times to visit are spring, when the hills are verdant and the vineyards carpeted with mustard flowers, and late autumn, when the burnished light and auburn vine leaves lend the place a calming ambience.

NAPA AND SONOMA

The region is separated into the Napa and Sonoma Valleys, located on either side of a low-lying mountain range. Of the two, Napa is the largest, the most famous and the most popular. Sonoma is far smaller and slower. No town in either valley is more than a stone's throw from countryside dotted with vines and cows. Most of the higher-priced wineries are in Napa, but alongside industry behemoths are smaller wineries, many family-owned. Even in Napa you'll find 'crossroads wineries', off the main route, that do not charge for tastings, a practice that's now pretty much standard at the majority of tasting rooms.

Dining here is as important as wining. Many wineries have picnic areas, but it's courteous to buy a bottle to enjoy with your feast. Plenty of restaurants allow BYOB: check the corkage fee when booking, and do purchase something from the wine list if you're planning to consume more than one bottle.

Most wineries are open daily. The fee, which covers tasting several wines and, in some cases, a tour, can be anything up to $10 (a few posh labels charge more), which can usually be put towards purchases.

The classic Wine Country route winds through both valleys. Drive up Highway 29 to **Calistoga**, hitting the towns of **Napa**, **Yountville**, **Oakville**, **Rutherford** and **St Helena** on the way. From Calistoga, head west on Petrified Forest Road for 12 miles towards **Fulton**, then drive a few miles south on Highway 101 to **Santa Rosa**, where you can pick up Route 12, which takes you south through the Sonoma Valley.

If you'd rather take in the scenery in a more sedate fashion, tourist offices (*see p282 & p284*) can provide information on bike hire and chauffeur-driven tours, as well as activities such as hot-air ballooning. They also distribute a booklet offering discounts at wineries.

NAPA VALLEY

The 30-mile-long Napa Valley, on the east side of the Mayacamas Mountains, was originally settled by the Wappo Indian tribe several centuries ago. The Gold Rush of the 1850s saw its population grow, with Europeans as well as Californians; Prussian immigrant Charles Krug introduced grapes here in 1861.

The valley, bisected by the Napa River, runs from the San Pablo Bay's fertile Carneros region north to Calistoga. There are now more than 250 commercial vineyards here, along with smaller boutique wineries. Many are situated on the often-busy Highway 29 (aka the St Helena Highway), which runs up the center of the valley; along the way, towns and villages have plenty of shopping and dining opportunities. Smaller wineries are found mostly on the **Silverado Trail**, a more scenic and less cramped artery to the east, or on the lanes that criss-cross the valley. Alternatively, take the **Wine Train** (1-800 427 4124, 1-707 253 2111, www.winetrain.com), which runs between Napa and St Helena or Rutherford. Rides on restored pre-1950s Pullman coaches start at $124.

Towns & attractions

Once a blue-collar town, **Napa** has grown increasingly sophisticated over the last few years, and now boasts a number of top-rated restaurants, wine shops, and theaters. Most of the changes have centered on its historic Downtown riverfront. Opened in 2008, the Oxbow Public Market (610 First Street, www.oxbowpublicmarket.com) houses gourmet food and wine vendors, as well as a farmers market, and is a great spot to pick up picnic supplies.

North of here, **Yountville** is Michelin territory, with posh restaurants, immaculate hotels and upscale shops. The tidy towns of **Rutherford** and **Oakville** are both dominated by the wineries that surround them, but **St Helena**, further north, has real charm, and can be enjoyed in a more modest way than its shiny veneer suggests. It's home to the **Robert Louis Stevenson Silverado Museum** (1490 Library Lane, 1-707 963 3757, www.silverado museum.org, noon-4pm Tue-Sun, admission free), a collection of Stevenson's manuscripts, plus his wedding ring and marriage licence. The town is best known for its slew of chic boutiques, upscale eateries and gourmet food shops: on Main Street, don't miss **Woodhouse Chocolate** (No.1367, 1-800 966 3468, 1-707 963 8413, www.woodhousechocolate.com), or, for olive oils, condiments and more, **Olivier Napa Valley** (No.1375,1-707 967 8777, www.oliviernapavalley.com). Just south of town, on Highway 29, is posh deli and wine store **Dean & Deluca**, complete with coffee and pastry bar (607 South St Helena Highway, 1-707 967 9980, www.deandeluca.com).

In **Calistoga**, it's geothermal springs and mudbaths, not wineries, that bring in the visitors. The town is awash with spas offering treatments, from dips in mineral pools to baths in volcanic ash. Among them are 60-year-old **Dr Wilkinson's Hot Springs Resort** (1507 Lincoln Avenue, 1-707 942 4102, www.drwilkinson.com, $149-$299 double) and historic **Indian Springs** (1712 Lincoln Avenue, 1-707 942 4913, www.indianspringscalistoga.com, $199-$495 double), site of town founder Sam Brannan's original hot springs resort. At the high end of the scale is the breathtaking **Calistoga Ranch**, with 46 deluxe lodges and a splendid spa (580 Lommel Road, 1-707 254 2800, www.calistogaranch.com, $565-$4,000 per lodge). The town's other draw is the

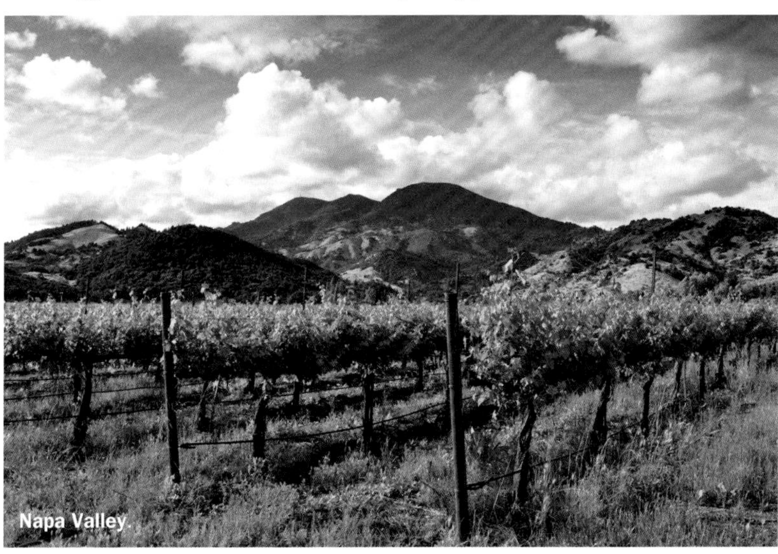
Napa Valley.

Old Faithful Geyser (www.oldfaithful geyser.com), one of only three geysers on earth that blast out water and steam at regular intervals – around every 30 to 40 minutes – to heights from 60 to 100 feet (18 to 30 meters).

Oxbow Public Market

610 & 644 First Street, Napa (1-707 259 1600, www.oxbowpublicmarket.com). **Open** daily min 9am-7pm. **Credit** AmEx, Disc, MC, V.

This upscale collection of artisan food and wine purveyors, restaurants, and farm-fresh produce is a showcase for the bounty of the Napa Valley. Worthy stops at the market include Hog Island Oyster Co., the Fatted Calf charcuterie, and Oxbow Wine Merchant, where you can sip and swirl on a lovely outdoor deck.

Wineries

Depending on the traffic, which can get pretty bad at peak times, you're rarely more than a 10-minute drive from a winery in the Napa Valley. Napa offers a number of fine tasting rooms, led by the fabulously curated selection at **Back Room Wines** (1000 Main Street, Suite 120, 1-707 226 1378, www.backroomwines.com) and the **Vintner's Collective** (1245 Main Street, 1-707 255 7150, www.vintnerscollective.com). Notable wineries southwest of town, along or off the Carneros Highway towards Sonoma, include **Domaine Carneros** (1240 Duhig Road, 1-707 257 0101, www.domaine.com), where the pinot you'll be sipping is sparkling: the winery is owned by Taittinger. The views

Grape Expectations

California wine regions.

Home to 90 per cent of the wine produced in the US, California is literally steeped in wine. Although the state only began to be taken seriously on the world wine stage in the late 1970s, wine grapes have been cultivated here since Europeans first arrived. In fact, essentially all of the vines used to start the Northern California wine industry came from Europe thanks to one man: Agoston Haraszthy.

Often called 'the Father of California Wine', Haraszthy was a Hungarian immigrant who bought a small vineyard in Sonoma in 1856 and over the next several years developed a winemaking operation that *Harper's* magazine described as 'the largest of... its kind in the world'. His winery, still in operation today, is known as Buena Vista Carneros and it is due largely to Haraszthy's efforts that so many varietals have been successfully cultivated throughout the state.

But where to find your favorite grape? The following list is a general, not definitive, guide to varietals by region. Taste around. Chances are, if you're drawn to a particular varietal, the ones being cultivated close by might interest you, too. Our list runs from north to south.

Mendocino With coastal and inland growing regions, several different varietals grow well here. By the coast, Pinot Noir, Chardonnay and Riesling are solid, while inland Zinfandel and Sauvignon Blanc do particularly well. Here, too, the Anderson Valley is noted for being climatically similar to the Champagne region in France, and produces some of America's top sparkling wines. A fifth-generation descendant of the founder of the champagne, Louis Roederer started Roederer Estates on a 580-acre vineyard here in 1982.

Sonoma One of the largest wine regions in the state (and home to the original Buena Vista vineyard), the profusion of micro-climates in the area means that on every hill and in every valley a different varietal may be under production. Cabernet Sauvignon, Pinot Noir and Zinfandel thrive here, as do Chardonnay and Sauvignon Blanc. While somewhat of a generalization, the style tends to be more Burgundy-like – a bit more mellow and understated than the massive fruit-forward wines of Napa.

Napa The name that means 'wine' to most visitors, Napa has over 35,000 acres of vines under cultivation. Known most for their big, jammy, 'fruit bomb' Cabernet Sauvignon and rich Chardonnays, varietals such as Merlot, Sauvignon Blanc and Zinfandel do equally well here, too.

Sierra Foothills Compared to Napa and Sonoma, the Sierra Foothills region is somewhat sleepy. The Gold Rush ghost towns and winding roads hold none of the Napa glitz and that's just how many visitors like it – because they know the secret of the region: Amador County turns out some of the best Zinfandels in the US. Settled by Eastern European and Italian immigrants in the 1800s, some of the varietals from their home countries thrive here on century-old vines. Try grapes you've never heard of and prepare to be surprised. If you like big reds, the Barberas are off the charts.

are spectacular, as they are from the terrace at off-the-beaten-track **Artesa Vineyards & Winery** (1345 Henry Road, 1-707 224 1668, www.artesawinery.com).

North of Napa on the Silverado Trail is **Black Stallion** (no.4089, 1-888 200 9756, www.blackstallionwinery.com), which opened in summer 2007 on the site of a former equestrian center.

Near Yountville is **Domaine Chandon** (1 California Drive, 1-888 242 6366, www.chandon.com), which offers an excellent tour ($12) introducing visitors to its interpretation of *méthode champenoise*. Oakville is home to the granddaddy of wine estates, **Robert Mondavi** (7801 St Helena Highway, 1-888 766 6328, www.robertmondavi.com, reservations recommended), a good bet for first-timers, and the unstuffy **PlumpJack** (620 Oakville Crossroad, 1-707 945 1220, www.plumpjack.com). Also here, at Oakville Cross Road and St Helena Highway, is the original, branch of the **Oakville Grocery** (*see p284*).

Another cluster of wineries draws oenophiles to Rutherford. **Mumm** (8445 Silverado Trail, 1-707 967 7700, http://mummnapa.com) has a collection of Ansel Adams photographs, while Francis Ford Coppola's **Rubicon Estate** (1991 St Helena Highway, 1-707 857 1400, www.rubiconestate.com) has cinema memorabilia. **St Supéry** (8440 St Helena Highway, 1-707 963 4507, www.stsupery.com) encourages novices with tastings suitable for first-timers.

The list of wineries in St Helena is led by historic **Beringer** (2000 Main Street, 1-707 967 4412, www.beringer.com), where events run from a $20 half-hour tour to a $110 vineyard tour with lunch. **Charles Krug** (2800 Main Street, 1-800 682 5784, www.charleskrug.com), founded in 1861, enhances its wines with summer chocolate tastings; **Burgess Cellars** (1108 Deer Park Road, 1-707 963 4766, www.burgesscellars.com, tastings by appointment only) is a beautiful mountainside winery. Two relative curiosities are **Prager** (1281 Lewelling Lane, 1-707 963 7678, www.pragerport.com), where the speciality is port, and the **Silverado Brewing Company** (3020A St Helena Highway, 1-707 967 9876, www.silveradobrewingcompany.com), for those more keen on the grain than the grape. Up the road in Calistoga, try **Clos Pegase** (1060 Dunaweal Lane, 1-707 942 4981, www.clospegase.com); for the wines, sure, but also for the architecture (by Michael Graves) and the sculpture garden.

Where to eat & drink

In recent years, celebrity-chefs have taken a shine to Napa, opening **Rotisserie & Wine** (Tyler Florence: 720 Main Street, 1-707 254 8500, www.rotisserieandwine.com) and **Morimoto Napa** (Masaharu Morimoto: 610 Main Street, 1-707 252 1600, www.morimotonapa.com). The Napa Mill complex also houses chic Napa River Inn (*see p282*), a pastry shop and a day spa, as well as several fine restaurants. 'Global comfort food' is no oxymoron at **Celadon** (500 Main Street, 1-707 254 9690, www.celadonnapa.com, mains $22), with the likes of flash-fried calamari with a spicy chipotle chili glaze, while Greg Cole's **Angèle** (540 Main Street, 1-707 252 8115, www.angelerestaurant.com, mains $25) is a favorite spot for terrace drinks and French country cooking. The river patio of the **Napa General Store** (540 Main Street, 1-707 259 0762, www.napageneralstore.com, mains $11) is good for sandwiches, salads and thin pizzas. In town, **ZuZu** (829 Main Street, 1-707 224 8555, www.zuzunapa.com, tapas $9) is a reliable tapas bar.

Yountville is renowned around the world as the home of the Michelin three-star **French Laundry** (6640 Washington Street, 1-707 944 2380/www.frenchlaundry.com, set menu $270), regularly identified as one of the world's great restaurants. Prices are high to say the least, and you'll have to book two months in advance, but you'll get a world-class meal. Thomas Keller, lord of the Laundry, also runs urbane **Bouchon** (6534 Washington Street, 1-707 944 8037, www.bouchonbistro.com, mains $27), where the French menu is priced more moderately. Its chic next-door bakery offers posh picnic fare. Philippe Jeanty is the other big name around these parts, with the casual **Bistro Jeanty** (6510 Washington Street, 1-707 944 0103, www.bistrojeanty.com, mains $25) being his signature spot.

St Helena options are plentiful: for breakfast, try the **Model Bakery** (1357 Main Street, 1-707 963 8192, www.themodelbakery.com); for lunch, there's **Ana's Cantina** (1205 Main Street, 1-707 963 4921, mains $12) or Gott's Roadside, once known as the 1949-vintage **Taylor's Refresher** (933 Main Street, 1-707 963 3486, www.gotts.com, mains $12), and still offering terrific 1950s-style burgers and shakes.

Calistoga's restaurants are concentrated mainly on Lincoln Avenue: sturdy American classics dominate at **Brannan's** (no.1374, 1-707 942 2233, www.brannansgrill.com, mains $25) and farm-to-table cuisine at **JoLe** (no.1457, 1-707 942 5938, www.jolerestaurant.com, mains $17, plus 3-, 4- and 5-course tasting menu).

Where to stay

Lodgings around Napa run the gamut from quaint Queen Anne-style B&Bs to full resorts. The sleek and luxurious **Carneros Inn**

(4048 Carneros Highway, 1-707 299 4900, www.thecarnerosinn.com, $650-$775 double), just southwest of Napa, fits into the latter category: its 86 ultra-modern cottages have fireplaces, flat-panel televisions and outdoor showers. In the Napa Mill, you'll find the deluxe, 66-room **Napa River Inn** (500 Main Street, 1-877 251 8500, 1-707 251 8500, www.napariverinn.com, $369-$735 double). **The Oak Knoll Inn** (2200 E Oak Knoll Avenue, 1-707 255 2200, www.oakknollinn.com, $350-$750 double) is one of the valley's most luxurious B&Bs; and if you've had enough of all things quaint, the **John Muir Inn** (1998 Trower Avenue, 1-800 522 8999, 1-707 257 7220, www.johnmuirnapa.com, $130-$150 double) is an above-par motel.

There are fewer budget options in Yountville; the high-class **Villagio Inn & Spa** (6481 Washington Street, 1-800 351 1133, 1-707 944 8877, www.villagio.com, $350-$675 double) is one of several deluxe hotels. In Rutherford, you'll need to spend a lot of cash for a night at the **Auberge du Soleil** (180 Rutherford Hill Road, 1-800 348 5406, 1-707 963 1211, www.aubergedusoleil.com, $550-$3,500 double/suite), one for special occasions. Along St Helena's Main Street, try the luxurious **Inn at Southbridge** (no.1020, 1-800 520 6800, 1-707 967 9400, www.innatsouthbridge.com, $350-$925 double), or the delightful **El Bonita Motel** (no.195, 1-800 541 3284, 1-707 963 3216, www.elbonita.com, $119-$179 double), an aesthetic mix of art deco and French colonial that's something of a bargain by St Helena standards. Outside town, the **Meadowood** complex (900 Meadowood Lane, 1-800 458 8080, 1-707 963 3646, www.meadowood.com, $475-$1,375 double) comprises a hotel, separate cottages and a Michelin three-star restaurant, as well as a golf course and swanky spa.

Wherever you want to stay in the area, be certain to book well in advance, especially in summer. If you do get stuck, try Napa Valley Reservations Unlimited (1-800 251 6272, www.napavalleyreservations.com).

Tourist information

Calistoga *Calistoga Chamber of Commerce & Visitor Center, 1506 Lincoln Avenue (1-707 942 6333, www.calistogachamber.com).* **Open** 8am-5pm Mon-Sat; 8am-4pm Sun.
Napa *Napa Valley Conference & Visitor Center, 1310 Napa Town Center (1-707 226 7459, www.napavalley.com).* **Open** 9am-5pm daily.
St Helena *St Helena Chamber of Commerce, 1010 Main Street (1-800 799 6456, www.sthelena.com).* **Open** 10am-5pm Mon-Fri; 11am-3pm Sat.
Yountville *Yountville Chamber of Commerce, 6484 Washington Street (1-707 944 0904, www.yountville.com).* **Open** 10am-5pm daily.

SONOMA VALLEY

The Sonoma Valley, which runs about 23 miles north from San Pablo Bay, is home to around 200 wineries. However, the main attraction of a Sonoma tour is the landscape. The county's topography is diverse, from beaches to redwood forests and rolling hills. It's also agriculturally rich, and the areas around towns such as Glen Ellen and Sebastopol brim with farms.

Towns & attractions

Although its central plaza is now ringed by restaurants, bookshops, wine tasting rooms, food shops and a cinema (the delightful 75-year-old Sebastiani Theatre), the town of **Sonoma** retains the feel of old California. The town was founded in 1823 as the **Mission San Francisco Solano** (114 East Spain Street, 1-707 938 9560, 10am-5pm daily); today, the mission is part of the loose affiliation of humbly atmospheric sites known as Sonoma State Historic Park. The town hall and Bear Flag Monument on the plaza mark the site where the Californian Bear Flag first flew: for the 25 days of the riotous Bear Flag Revolt in 1846, this was the capital of the independent Republic of California. Fast-forward more than 160 years and the plaza is home to the town's Tuesday evening farmers' market (Apr-Oct; 1-707 538 7023). Just north of Sonoma, the small town of **Glen Ellen** was once the home of Jack London, adventurer, farmer, autodidact and author; **Jack London Historic State Park** contains the charred remains of Wolf House, the author's home.

Its population is twice that of the city of Napa, but **Santa Rosa** manages to retain a low-key appeal. Historic Railroad Square is the city's busy downtown area, but the real visitor attraction is the park on the corner of Santa Rosa and Sonoma Avenues: **Luther Burbank Home & Gardens**. Also here is the **Charles M Schulz Museum** (2301 Hardies Lane, 1-707 579 4452, www.schulz museum.org), commemorating the man who created Snoopy, Charlie Brown and the whole *Peanuts* gang.

Further north is **Healdsburg**, a highfalutin boutique town where Bay Area boomers come to drop some serious cash. Gourmet food stores, artisan bakeries and sleek eateries bring in the herds – as does the annual ten-day jazz fest, held in June (1-707 433 4644) – but the **Healdsburg Museum** (221 Matheson Street, 1-707 431 3325, www.healdsburgmuseum.org), with Pomo Indian baskets and other cultural artifacts, is pretty authentic. The town's old-fashioned central square is a lovely place to stroll, and hosts a Tuesday evening farmers' market (June-Oct; 1-707 431 1956).

Luther Burbank Home & Gardens

Santa Rosa Avenue, at Sonoma Avenue (1-707 524 5445, http://lburbank.users.sonic.net). **Open** *Apr-Oct* 10am-3.30pm Tue-Sun. **Admission** $7 with tour. **No credit cards**.

America's most renowned horticulturist, Burbank developed more than 800 new varieties of plant during his life. His former house and grounds are now a national historic landmark. Guided tours (booking isn't necessary) and themed gardens explain and demonstrate this botanical pioneer's work.

Wineries

Sonoma County's quaint, family-owned wineries are more secluded than many of their Napa neighbours. Its history is intertwined with that of the California wine industry, which began at what is now the **Buena Vista Carneros Winery** (18000 Old Winery Road, 1-707 265 1472, www.buenavistacarneros.com). Of the nearly 40 wineries in the valley, several are near the city's main plaza. **Bartholomew Park Winery** (1000 Vineyard Lane, 1-707 935 9511, www.bartpark.com) is great for picnics; **Sebastiani Vineyards** (389 Fourth Street East, 1-707 933 3230, www.sebastiani.com) may not be the region's most charming winery, but it gives another perspective on the ubiquitous family.

The **Carneros** area includes southern Sonoma as well as Napa; wineries take advantage of the cooler climate to produce excellent pinot noir grapes and sparkling wines. Fans of sparkling wines should try a tasting at **Gloria Ferrer Champagne Caves** (23555 Arnold Drive, 1-707 996 7256, www.gloriaferrer.com). Further south, the **Viansa Winery** (25200 Arnold Drive, 1-800 995 4740, www.viansa.com), a Tuscan-style winery situated on a knoll, offers informal tastings, and has a large Italian-style deli.

The pick of the viticulture in and around Glen Ellen includes the **Arrowood Vineyards & Winery** (14347 Sonoma Highway, 1-800 938 5170, 1-707 935 2600, www.arrowood vineyards.com) and the **Benziger Family Winery** (1883 London Ranch Road, 1-888 490 2739, www.benziger.com), which makes its wines using bio-dynamic farming methods devised in the 1920s by Rudolf Steiner. Nearby **Kenwood** is synonymous with the **Kenwood Vineyards** (9592 Sonoma Highway, 1-707 833 5891, www.kenwoodvineyards.com), known for wine made from grapes grown on Jack London's former ranch (novelist Haruki Murakami drinks a bottle from here on his birthday each year). The original barn, now the tasting room and shop, dates from before Prohibition.

The area around Santa Rosa boasts several fine vineyards. **Kendall-Jackson Wine Center** (5007 Fulton Road, 1-866 287 9818, 1-800 769 3649, www.kj.com) has a state of the art tasting room and education center.

Where to eat & drink

In Sonoma, the **Girl & the Fig** (110 West Spain Street, 1-707 938 3634, www.thegirlandthefig.com, set menu $32), inside the landmark Sonoma Hotel (*see below*), has a reputation for garden-fresh French dishes including salads, steaks and cheese plates. Small but characterful **Café La Haye** (140 E Napa Street, 1-707 935 5994, www.cafelahaye.com, mains $21) is another winner, although it's open for dinner only (Tue-Sat). Picnickers get supplies from **Artisan Bakers** (750 W Napa Street, 1-707 939 1765, www.artisanbakers.com), the **fantastic Vella Cheese Company** (315 Second Street East, 1-707 938 3232, www.vellacheese.com) and **Sonoma Market** (500 W Napa Street, 1-707 996 3411).

In Santa Rosa, try **Willi's Wine Bar** (4404 Old Redwood Highway, 1-707 526 3096, www.starkrestaurants.com/willis_winebar.html) for superior small plates and decent wines by the glass.

Healdsburg has plenty of appealing options, from pricey to wallet-friendly. The Hotel Healdsburg (*see below*) is home to award-winning chef Charlie Palmer's **Dry Creek Kitchen** (no.317, 1-707 431 0330, www.charliepalmer.com/Properties/DryCreekKitchen, mains $32), where the changing menus are based on fresh seasonal ingredients. Within the Les Mars hotel (*see below*), Douglas Keane's Cal-French cuisine at **Cyrus** (1-707 433 3311, www.cyrusrestaurant.com, 5 courses $102, 8 courses 130) continues to make waves. DIY options include the gourmet **Oakville Grocery** (24 Matheson Street, 1-707 433 3200, www.oakvillegrocery.com), whose patio is a popular spot to eat goodies purchased inside. For a sugar rush, don't miss **Powell's**, a delightfully nostalgic sweet shop and ice-cream parlor on the corner of the main plaza (322 Center Street, 1-707 431 2784, www.powells.com).

Where to stay

In Sonoma, try the **Sonoma Hotel** (110 West Spain Street, 1-800 468 6016, 1-707 996 2996, www.sonomahotel.com, $110-$238 double) and the comfy **El Dorado Hotel** (405 First Street West, 1-707 996 3030, www.eldoradosonoma.com, $165-$225 double). To spoil yourself, the **Ledson Hotel** (480 First Street East, 1-707 996 9779, www.ledsonhotel.com, $350-$395 double) has six ultra-deluxe rooms, but for pampering to the max it has to be the stunning **Fairmont Sonoma Mission Inn & Spa** (100 Boyes Boulevard, 1-707 938 9000, www.fairmont.com/sonoma, $425-$569 double), a few miles out of town in Boyes Hot Springs.

In Kenwood, you'll likely be tempted by the historic, luxurious **Kenwood Inn & Spa** (10400 Sonoma Highway, 1-800 353 6966, 1-707 833 1293, www.kenwoodinn.com, $625-$925 double). Glen Ellen, meanwhile, is home to the **Jack London Lodge** (13740 Arnold Drive, 1-707 938 8510, www.jacklondonlodge.com, $99-$185 double), a straight-ahead motel, and **Gaige House** (13540 Arnold Drive, 1-800 935 0237, 1-707 935 0237, www.gaige.com, $259-$389 double), a luxe B&B complete with spa, pool and hot tubs.

Santa Rosa's nicest option is the 44-room **Vintners Inn** (4350 Barnes Road, 1-707 575 7350, www.vintnersinn.com, $205-$295 double), a prime place to stay for some proper Wine Country relaxation. **The Gables** (4257 Petaluma Hill Road, 1-800 422 5376, 1-707 585 7777, www.thegablesinn.com, $175-$210 double) is a lovely old Victorian Gothic inn, spread across several secluded acres.

In Healdsburg, a number of decent motels off the freeway will serve as a good base if you don't want to blow your entire budget on accommodation, but for high-flyers, the trendy **Hotel Healdsburg** (25 Matheson Street, 1-800 889 7188, 1-707 431 2800, www.hotelhealdsburg.com, $335-$450 double), and the posh French-style **Les Mars** (27 North Street, 1-877 431 1700, www.lesmarshotel.com, $575-$1,150 double), are pure luxury.

A good resource for B&B bookings is the Bed & Breakfast Association of the Sonoma Valley (1-800 969 4667, www.sonomabb.com), which shows availability and has links to the B&Bs' own websites.

Getting there

By car

Wine Country is an hour (44 miles) by car from San Francisco, over the Golden Gate along US 101. Turn east at Ignacio to Highway 37 and take Highway 121 north. From here, Highway 12 follows the Sonoma Valley, while Highway 29 leads along Napa Valley.

Tourist information

Healdsburg *Healdsburg Chamber of Commerce & Visitors Bureau, 217 Healdsburg Avenue (1-707 433 6935/www.healdsburg.org).* **Open** 9am-5pm Mon-Fri; 9am-3pm Sat; 10am-2pm Sun.
Santa Rosa *Santa Rosa CVB, 9 Fourth Street (1-800 404 7673, 1-707 577 8674, www.visitsantarosa.com).* **Open** 9am-5pm Mon-Sat; 10am-5pm Sun.
Sonoma *Sonoma Valley Visitors Bureau, 453 First Street East (1-707 996 1090, www.sonomavalley.com).* **Open** 9am-5pm Mon-Sat; 10am-5pm Sun.

Directory

Getting Around

ARRIVING & LEAVING

San Francisco International Airport (SFO) *1-650 821 8211, 1-800 435 9736, www.flysfo.com.* SFO lies 14 miles south of the city, near US101.

If you're staying Downtown, take the **train** from the BART station in the International terminal (accessible from all terminals via SFO's free Airtrain). The journey to town costs $8.10 and takes 30mins; trains leave SFO from 4am to 11.50pm. BART is a far better bet than the three SamTrans **bus** routes – the KX, the 292 and the 24-hour 397 – that serve SFO (fares vary from $2 to $5); the buses can take ages to make the journey from the airport to the city.

Shuttle vans, which hold 8-12 people and offer door-to-door service, are a more direct option. Shuttles operate on a walk-up basis at the airport, though you must book for your return journey. Firms running shuttle vans include **Bay Shuttle** (564 3400, www.bayshuttle.com), **SuperShuttle** (558 8500, www.supershuttle.com) and **American Airporter Shuttle** (202 0733, www.americanairporter.com); the airport's website has a full list. The fare into San Francisco will be around $17; ask about discounted rates for two or more travelers in the same party. Vans leave regularly from the upper level of the terminal: follow the red 'passenger vans' signs outside the baggage-claim area.

Taxis run to and from SFO, though they're pricey: expect to pay around $50 plus tip, though you might be able to haggle a flat rate. For a **limousine**, use the toll-free white courtesy phones located in the terminal to summon a car (walk-up service isn't permitted). The fare will likely be at least $60 plus tip.

Mineta San Jose International Airport (SJC)
1-408 501 7600/www.sjc.org.
SJC is the airport of choice for many Silicon Valley travelers. However, those without cars but with San Francisco lodgings face a lengthy and/or pricey journey to the city.

Without a car, the best way to get to San Francisco from SJC is by **train**. Ride the Airport Flyer bus (20mins) from the airport to Santa Clara station, then take the Caltrain service to San Francisco station (4th & King Streets, $8.50, 90mins). Door-to-door **shuttle vans,** available on a walk-up basis, are quicker, but cost up to $90. A **taxi** will set you back $130 plus tip.

Oakland International Airport (OAK) *1-510 563 3300, www.flyoakland.com.*
The ride into San Francisco from Oakland Airport is simple by train. The AirBART bus shuttle links the airport to the Coliseum/Oakland Airport BART station; the ride costs $3 and takes 15-20mins. From the station, take the next Daly City or Millbrae train to San Francisco ($3.80; about 25mins to Downtown). Note: this is not a safe option for lone passengers at night. Instead, take one of the myriad **shuttle vans**, available on a walk-up basis, or a very expensive taxi/limo ride.

Airlines

Air Canada *1-888 247 2262, www.aircanada.com.*
American Airlines *1-800 433 7300, www.aa.com.*
British Airways *1-800 247 9297, www.britishairways.com.*
Continental *domestic 1-800 523 3273, international 1-800 231 0856, www.continental.com.*
Delta *domestic 1-800 221 1212, international 1-800 241 4141, www.delta.com.*
Southwest *1-800 435 9792, www.southwest.com.*
United Airlines *domestic 1-800 864 8331, international 1-800 538 2929, www.united.com.*
US Airways *1-800 428 4322, www.usairways.com.*
Virgin Atlantic *1-800 862 8621, www.virginatlantic.com.*
Virgin America *1.877.359.8474/ www.virginamerica.com.*

PUBLIC TRANSPORT

San Francisco's mass-transit network is comprehensive and efficient. Buses, streetcars and cable cars are run by the San Francisco Municipal Railway, aka **Muni** (www.sfmta.com, 701-2311 (San Fran 3-1-1 Customer Service Center)) while the Bay Area Rapid Transit rail network, aka **BART** (989 2278, www.bart.gov) connects San Francisco to Oakland, Berkeley and beyond. Maps and timetables are available online, and free leaflets available at stations offer details on popular routes and services. However, Muni's system-wide *Street & Transit Map*, costing $3 and available from bookshops, drugstores and the SFVIC (*see p294*), is a sound investment. Further details on Bay Area transit, including route guidance, can be found at **www.transit.511.org**, or by calling 511 from a local phone.

For information about single fares on transport in San Francisco, *see right*. However, if you plan to travel often in the Bay Area, the **Clipper** card may help: the reuseable ticket is valid on all major transit networks, including Muni, BART and Caltrain. Tag the Clipper card when you start your journey (and, on BART, when you exit). The cost of the ride will be deducted, and any remaining value can be used on your next trip. When the card runs low, add funds at machines around the transit network. Clipper cards are available online and at shops displaying the Clipper logo; for more information, see www.clippercard.com.

Alternatively, the **Passport**, valid for unlimited travel on all Muni vehicles (but not BART trains), is aimed at tourists. Passports are valid for one day ($14), three days ($21) and seven days ($27), and are sold at the Visitor Center or the cable car ticket booths, both Downtown at Powell and Market, Ghirardelli Square at Hyde and Beach Streets, and in Fisherman's Wharf at Bay and Taylor Streets, Montgomery metro station, the TIX booth in Union Square, the SFMTA Customer Service Centre and SFO.

Monthly Muni passes are valid from the first of the month until three days into the following month. The A Pass ($72) is also valid on the eight BART stations within the city of SF, but not beyond (so you'll have to pay extra to get to Oakland, Berkeley and SFO). The M Pass ($62) is valid only on Muni. Monthly passes are available at the locations listed above, with the exception of TIX.

BART

Bay Area Rapid Transit is a $5-billion network of five high-speed rail lines serving San Francisco, Daly City, Colma and SFO Airport, and the East Bay. It's modern and efficient, run by computers at Oakland's Lake Merritt station, with announcements, trains, ticket dispensers, exit and entry gates all automated. BART is of minor use for getting around San Francisco – it only has eight stops in the city – four on Market Street, two on Mission Street and two further south – but it's the best way to get to Berkeley and Oakland and a convenient way to get to the airport from Downtown.

Fares vary by destination, from $1.75 to $8.10. Machines at each station dispense reusable tickets encoded with the amount of money you entered (cash and credit cards are both valid). Your fare will be deducted from this total when you end your journey, and any remaining value will be valid for future trips. You can add value to the card at all ticket machines.

Stations are marked with blue and white signs at street level. Trains run from 4am on weekdays, 6am on Saturday and 8am on Sunday, and shut down around midnight. For further information see www.bart.gov.

Buses

Muni's orange and white buses are the top mode of public transport in SF. Relatively cheap, they can get you to within a block or two of almost anywhere in town. Bus stops are marked by a large white rectangle on a street with a red kerb; a yellow marking on a telephone or lamp post; a bus shelter; and/or a brown and orange sign listing buses that serve that route.

A single journey on a Muni bus is $2; seniors, 4-17s and the disabled pay 75¢, while under-4s travel free. Exact change is required. Free transfers, which let passengers connect with a second Muni bus or streetcar route at no extra charge, are valid for 90 minutes after the original fare was paid. (The transfer tokens serve as your ticket/receipt; always ask for one when you board.)

Buses run 5am-1am during the week, 6am-1am on Saturdays and 8am-1am on Sundays. From 1am to 5am, a skeleton crew runs the Owl, eight lines on which buses run every half-hour.

Cable cars

Cable cars move at top speeds of 9.5mph on three lines: California (California Street, from the Financial District to Van Ness Avenue), Powell-Mason and Powell-Hyde (both from Market Street to Fisherman's Wharf).

Lines operate from 6am to midnight daily. If you don't have a Muni pass, buy a $5 one-way ticket from the conductor (under-5s go free). Transfers are not valid. The stops are marked by pole-mounted brown signs with a cable car symbol; routes are marked on Muni bus maps.

Ferries

Ferries are used mainly by suits during peak hours, but they double as an inexpensive tourist excursion across the Bay to Sausalito, Tiburon or Larkspur. There are also ferries from San Francisco to Alcatraz and Angel Island in San Francisco Bay.

Blue & Gold Fleet (705 8200, www.blueandgoldfleet.com) runs boats to Sausalito and Angel Island from Pier 41 at Fisherman's Wharf. Commuter services to Alameda, Oakland (both $6 one way), Tiburon and Vallejo ($9 and $12.50) leave from the Ferry Building on the Embarcadero. The competing **Golden Gate Transit Ferry Service** (455 2000, www.goldengate.org), meanwhile, runs services from the Ferry Building to Sausalito and Larkspur (both $7.10 one way).

Streetcars

The Muni Metro streetcar – or tram - is used rarely by tourists, though it's a very useful service. Five lines (J, K, L, M and N) run under Market Street in Downtown and above ground elsewhere, while the F line runs vintage streetcars on Market Street and along the Embarcadero as far as Fisherman's Wharf. The newest addition T runs along the bay front. Fares are the same as on Muni's buses, and transfers are valid.

Along Market, Muni makes the same stops as BART; past the Civic Center, routes branch out towards the Mission, the Castro, Sunset and beyond. Lines run 5am-1am Mon-Sat; 8am-1am Sun. Buses replace K, L, M, N and T for an irregular night Owl service.

Taxis

Taxi travel in San Francisco is relatively cheap, since the city is relatively small. The base fare is $3.10, with an additional charge of 45¢ per one-fifth of a mile ($2.25 a mile); there's a $2 surcharge for all rides starting at SFO. The problem is that there simply aren't enough cabs, especially during morning and evening rush hours and

MAJOR BUS ROUTES

San Francisco's bus network is comprehensive but complicated, especially to newcomers to the city. The Muni maps are very useful, but for quick reference, here are some key routes.

5, 6, 9, 21, 71 These five routes run down Market Street from the Financial District to Civic Center; for ease of use, we've used the shorthand '**Market Street routes**' for them in our Downtown listings. Route **5** continues through the Western Addition to the northern edge of Golden Gate Park; routes **6** and **71** head into the Haight, with the **6** then running into the Sunset and the **71** taking the southern edge of Golden Gate Park; route **9** runs south down Potrero Avenue in the Mission and all the way to the edge of the city; and route **21** cuts through the Hayes Valley to the northeast corner of Golden Gate Park.

14 Runs the length of Mission Street; good for riding between the Mission and Downtown.

38 Apart from a stretch in central San Francisco, where the one-way system means it's forced east down O'Farrell Street, this route runs the length of Geary Street/Boulevard.

45 After stopping at SBC Park, SFMOMA, Union Square, Chinatown and North Beach, this useful route then heads west along Union Street through Cow Hollow to the Presidio.

49 Links Fort Mason, Polk Gulch, the Tenderloin, Civic Center and the Mission along Van Ness Avenue, before heading further south.

sometimes late at night. If you're Downtown, your best bet is to head for one of the bigger hotels; or, if you're shopping or at dinner, to ask the shop or restaurant to call a cab. If you're in an outlying area, phone early to request one and ask how long you'll need to wait.

City Wide Dispatch 920 0700.
Luxor 282 4141, www.luxorcab.com.
National 648 4444.
Veteran's 552 1300.
Yellow 333 3333, www.yellowcabsf.com.

Outside San Francisco

The **CalTrain** commuter line (1-800 660 4287, www.caltrain.com) connects San Francisco with San Jose and ultimately Gilroy. Fares are calculated by the number of zones through which the train travels; fares range from $2.50 to $12.50 one way; discounts, eight-ride tickets, and daily and monthly passes are all available.

Several companies run bus services around the rest of the Bay Area. AC Transit (817 1717, quoting 'AC Transit', www.actransit.org) runs buses trans-bay and to Alameda and Contra Costa Counties; buses A to Z go across the Bay Bridge to Berkeley and Oakland. Golden Gate Transit (455 2000, www.goldengate.org) serves Marin and Sonoma Counties from Sausalito to Santa Rosa. And SamTrans (1-800 660 4287, www.samtrans.org) looks after San Mateo County, with a service to Downtown San Francisco.

DRIVING

Three words: don't do it. The traffic is no worse than in the average US city. However, the hills are hellish, the streetcars are a bitch and the parking is horrendous. There's very little street parking, and private garages charge can charge as much as $15 to $30 day.

However, if you must drive, be aware of a few things. The speed limit is 25mph; seatbelts are compulsory. Texting or talking on cell phones (unless you're hands-free) is also prohibited, and if you're caught, you'll pay a hefty fine. Cable cars always have the right of way. When parking on hills, set the handbrake and 'curb' the front wheels (towards the curb if facing downhill, away if facing uphill). Always park in the direction of the traffic, and never block driveways. Don't park at curbs colored white (passenger drop-off zones), blue (drivers with disabilities only), yellow (loading and unloading commercial vehicles only) or red (bus stops or fire hydrants). Green curbs allow only ten-minute parking. And if you venture across the water, make sure you have enough cash to pay the toll ($6 for the Golden Gate Bridge and $4 to $6 for the Bay Bridge), levied on the return trip.

For information on the latest highway conditions, call the 24-hour CalTrans Highway Information Service on 511, or check online at www.dot.ca.gov.

Parking

There are garages around town, but you'll pay for the privilege of parking in them. Inquire about discounted (or 'validated') rates, but always ask your hotel: few have their own lots, but many have an arrangement with a nearby garage.

If you're parking during the day, look out for the few large city lots where you can plug a parking meter by the hour (keep your quarters handy). Otherwise, there are garages at these locations; with the exception of the Mission garage, closed midnight-6am, all are open 24 hours.

Financial District *Between Battery, Drumm, Clay & Sacramento Streets.* **Map** p315 N4.
Union Square *333 Post Street (enter on Geary Street), between Stockton & Powell Streets.* **Map** p3315 M5.
SoMa *833 Mission Street, between 4th & 5th Streets.* **Map** p315 M6.
North Beach *735 Vallejo Street, between Stockton & Powell Streets.* **Map** p314 L3.
Chinatown *651 California Street, at Kearny Street.* **Map** p315 M4.
Mission *3255 21st Street, between Bartlett & Valencia Streets.* **Map** p318 K11.
Western Addition *1610 Geary Boulevard, between Webster & Laguna Streets.* **Map** p314 H6.
Marina *2055 Lombard Street, between Webster & Fillmore treets.* **Map** p313 H3.

Vehicle hire

Most car-hire agencies are at or near the airport, though some have satellite locations Downtown. Book well ahead if you're planning to visit at a holiday weekend. Every firm requires a credit card and matching driver's licence; few will rent to under-25s. Prices won't include tax, liability insurance or collision damage waiver (CDW); US residents may be covered on their home policy, but foreign residents will need to buy insurance.

Alamo *US: 1-877 222 9076, www.alamo.com. UK: 0871 384 1086, www.alamo.co.uk.*
Avis *US: 1-800 331 1212, www.avis.com. UK: 0844 581 0147, www.avis.co.uk.*
Budget *US: 1-800 527 0700, www.budget.com. UK: 0844 544 3470, www.budget.co.uk.*
Dollar *US: 1-800 800 3665, www.dollar.com. UK: 020 3468 7685, www.dollar.co.uk.*
Enterprise *US: 1-800 261 7331, www.enterprise.com. UK: 0800 800 277, www.enterprise.co.uk.*
Hertz *US: 1-800 654 3131, www.hertz.com. UK: 0870 844 8844, www.hertz.co.uk.*
National *US: 1-877 222 9058, www.nationalcar.com.*
Thrifty *US: 1-877 283 0898, www.thrifty.com. UK: 0203 468 7686/www.thrifty.co.uk.*

CYCLING

San Francisco is a real cycling city. A grid of major cycle routes across the town is marked by oval-shaped bike-and-bridge markers. North–south routes use odd numbers; east–west routes even; full-color signs indicate primary cross-town routes; neighborhood routes appear in green and white. The *Yellow Pages* has a map of the routes, but you can also check the **Bicycling Resource Guide** (http://bicycling.511.org) for details. Daunted by the hills? Pick up the *San Francisco Bike Map & Walking Guide*, which indicates the gradients of the city's streets. There are also two scenic cycle routes: one from Golden Gate Park south to Lake Merced, the other heading north from the southern end of Golden Gate Bridge into Marin County.

You can take bicycles on BART free of charge (except in rush hour). Bike racks on the front of certain Muni buses take up to two bikes. On CalTrain, cyclists can take their bikes on cars that display yellow bike symbols. You can also stow bikes in lockers at CalTrain stations. For more on cycling in San Francisco, including other tips for riding in town and a list of shops offering bike rentals, *see p252*.

WALKING

Exploring on foot is the most enjoyable and insightful way to see San Francisco. In a city where road rage is frequent, pedestrians walk unimpeded, often arriving sooner than their petrol-consuming counterparts.

DIRECTORY

Resources A-Z

TRAVEL ADVICE

For current information on travel to a specific country – including the latest news on health issues, safety and security, local laws and customs – contact your home country's government department of foreign affairs. Most have websites with useful advice for would-be travelers.

AUSTRALIA
www.smartraveller.gov.au

CANADA
www.voyage.gc.ca

NEW ZEALAND
www.mft.govt.nz/travel

REPUBLIC OF IRELAND
foreignaffairs.gov.ie

UK
www.fco.gov.uk/travel

USA
www.state.gov/travel

ADDRESSES

Addresses follow the standard US format. The room and/or suite number usually appears after the street address, followed on the next line by the city name and the zip code.

AGE RESTRICTIONS

Buying alcohol 21
Drinking alcohol 21
Driving 16
Sex (heterosexual couples) 18
Sex (homosexual couples) 18
Smoking 18

BUSINESS

Conventions

Big conventions are held at the **Moscone Convention Center** (747 Howard Street, between 3rd & 4th Streets, SoMa, 974 4000, www.moscone.com), situated on two SoMa blocks. The busiest times are usually mid-January (when the city hosts the MacWorld Expo), May and September.

Courier services

DHL *1-800 225 5345, www.dhl.com.* **Credit** AmEx, Disc, MC, V.
Federal Express *1-800 463 3339, www.fedex.com.* **Credit** AmEx, Disc, MC, V.
UPS *1-800 742 5877, www.ups.com.* **Credit** AmEx, Disc, MC, V.

Office services

Copy Central *22 3rd Street, at Market Street Financial District (882 7377, www.copycentral.com). BART & Metro to Montgomery/bus 2, 3, 30, 31, 38 & Market Street routes.* **Open** 8am-8pm Mon-Thur; 8am-6pm Fri; 10am-6pm Sat; noon-6pm Sun. **Credit** AmEx, Disc, MC, V. **Map** p315 M5.
Other locations 2336 Market Street, Castro, 431 6725.
FedEx Office *369 Pine Street, at Montgomery Street, Financial District (834 1053, www.fedex.com/us/office). BART & Metro to Montgomery/bus 1, 2, 3, 9, 10, 12, 31, 38, 41 & Market Street Routes/cable car California.* **Open** 7.30am-9pm Mon-Fri; 10am-6pm Sat; noon-6pm Sun. **Credit** AmEx, Disc, MC, V. **Map** p315 N5.
Other locations 1967 Market Street, Mission, 252 0864; 1 Daniel Burnham Court, Nob Hill, 292 2500 & locations throughout the city.
The UPS Store *268 Bush Street, between Montgomery & Sansome Streets, Financial District (765 1515, wwwsfmailboxes.com). BART & Metro to Montgomery/bus 1, 2, 3, 9, 10, 12, 31, 38, 41 & Market Street routes/cable car California.* **Open** 8am-5.30pm Mon-Fri. **Credit** AmEx, Disc, MC, V. **Map** p315 N5.
Office Depot *33 3rd Street, at Market Street, Financial District (777 1728, www.officedepot.com). BART & Metro to Montgomery/bus 2, 3, 30, 31, 38 & Market Street routes.* **Open** 8am-7pm Mon-Fri; 10am-5pm Sat. **Credit** AmEx, Disc, MC, V. **Map** p315 M5.
Other locations City Shopping Center, 2675 Geary Boulevard, Western Addition, 441 3044; Potrero Center, 2300 16th Street, Potrero Hill, 252 8280.

Useful organizations

The **San Francisco Main Library** (*see p56*) has access to vast amounts of business-related information. You don't need a library card for in-house print research or to read back-dated newspapers. The research desk staff are terrific; phone 557 4400 for assistance.

Law Library *401 Van Ness Avenue, at McAllister Street, Civic Center (554 6821, www.sflawlibrary.org). BART & Metro to Civic Center/bus 5, 21, 31, 47, 49, 90 & Market Street routes.* **Open** 8.30am-5pm Mon-Fri. **Map** p318 K7.
Open to the public for research, but only San Francisco-based lawyers can borrow books and materials.
Mechanic's Institute Library *57 Post Street, between Montgomery & Kearny Streets, Financial District (393 0101, www.milibrary.org). BART & Metro to Montgomery/bus 2, 3, 10, 12, 14, 30, 31, 38, 45, 91 & Market Street routes.* **Open** 9am-9pm Mon-Thur; 9am-6pm Fri; 10am-5pm Sat; 1-5pm Sun. **Admission** *Non-members* $12/day; $45/wk. *Membership* $95/yr. **Map** p315 N5.
Many of the same data sources as the Main Library but in only a fraction of the space. Its true source of fame, however, lies in its chess room (421 2258, www.chessclub.org), the best place in town for a quiet game.

CONSULATES

For a complete list, consult the *Yellow Pages.*

Australian Consulate-General *Suite 1800, 575 Market Street, at Sansome Street, CA 94105 (644 3620, www.usa.embassy.gov.au/whwh/SanFranCG.html). BART & Metro to Montgomery/bus 2,*

3, 10, 12, 14, 30, 31, 38, 45, 91 & Market Street routes. **Map** p315 N5.

British Consulate-General *Suite 850, 1 Sansome Street, at Market Street, CA 94104 (617 1300, www.britainusa.com/sf). BART & Metro to Montgomery/ bus 2, 3, 10, 12, 14, 30, 31, 38, 45, 91 & Market Street routes.* **Map** p315 N5.

Consulate-General of Canada *Suite 1288, 580 California Street, at Kearny Street, CA 94104 (834 3180, www.canada international.gc.ca/san_francisco). Bus 1, 3, 10, 12, 30, 31, 38, 45, 91/cable car California.* **Map** p314 N4.

Consulate-General of Ireland *Suite 3350, 100 Pine Street, at Front Street, CA 94111 (392 4214, www.consulateofireland sanfrancisco.org). BART & Metro to Embarcadero/bus 1, 3, 9, 10, 12, 14, 21, 31, 38, 41 & Market Street routes.* **Map** p315 N4.

New Zealand Consulate *Suite 700, 1 Maritime Plaza, Front Street, at Clay Street, CA 94111 (399 1255, www.mfat. govt.nz). BART & Metro to Embarcadero/bus 1, 10, 12, 41/cable car California.* **Map** p314 N4.

DIRECTORY

CONSUMER

Attorney General: Public Inquiry Unit *1-800 952 5225, http://ag.ca. gov/consumers/general.php.*
Call to complain about consumer law enforcement or any other agency.

Better Business Bureau *1-866 411 2221/1-510 844 2000, http://goldengate.bbb.org.*
The BBB provides information on the reliability of a company and a list of companies with good business records. It's also the place to call to file a complaint about a company.

CUSTOMS

Foreign visitors can import the following goods duty free: 200 cigarettes or 50 cigars (not Cuban; over-18s); one liter of wine or spirits (over-21s); and up to $100 in gifts ($800 for returning Americans). You must declare and maybe forfeit plants or foodstuffs. Check US Customs online for details (www.cbp.gov/xp/cgov/travel). UK Customs & Excise allows returning travelers to bring in £340 worth of goods.

DISABLED

Despite its topography, San Francisco is disabled-friendly; California is the national leader in providing facilities for the disabled. All public buildings are required by law to be wheelchair-accessible; most city buses can 'kneel' to make access easier; the majority of city street corners have ramped kerbs; and most restaurants and hotels can accommodate wheelchairs. Privileges include free parking in designated (blue) areas and in most metered spaces; display a blue and white 'parking placard' for both. Still, what a building is supposed to have and what it actually has can be different; wheelchair-bound travelers should call the **Independent Living Resource Center** (543 6222, www.ilrcsf.org).

Braille Institute *1-800 272 4553, www.brailleinstitute.org.*
Volunteers can connect anyone who has sight difficulties with services for the blind throughout the US.

California Relay Service *711 or TTY to voice 1-800 735 2929, voice to TTY 1-800 735 2922, http://ddtp.cpuc.ca.gov.* **Open** 24hrs daily.
Relays calls between TTD and voice callers.

Crisis Line for the Handicapped *1-800 426 4263. Open 24hrs daily.*
Phoneline/referral service with advice on many issues.

ELECTRICITY

US electricity voltage is 110-120V 60-cycle AC. Except for dual-voltage, flat-pin plug shavers, foreign appliances will usually need an adaptor.

EMERGENCIES

Ambulance, fire or police *911.*
Coast Guard *556 2101.*
Poison Control Center *1-800 222 1222, www.calpoison.org.*

GAY & LESBIAN

Community United Against Violence *333 4357, www.cuav.org.*
A group assisting GLBT victims of domestic violence or hate crimes.

HEALTH & MEDICAL

For **opticians** and **pharmacies**, *see p197.*

Accident & emergency

Foreign visitors should always ensure they have full travel insurance: medical treatment can be pricey. Call the emergency number on your insurance before seeking treatment; they'll direct you to a hospital that deals with your insurance company. There are 24hr emergency rooms at the locations listed below.

California Pacific Medical Center *Castro Street, at Duboce Avenue, Lower Haight (600 6000). Metro to Duboce & Church/bus 6, 24, 37, 71.* **Map** p318 H9.
For other locations, visit www.cpmc.org.

St Francis Memorial Hospital *900 Hyde Street, between Bush & Pine Streets, Nob Hill (353 6000). Bus 1, 2, 3, 19, 27, 38.* **Map** p314 K5.

San Francisco General Hospital *1001 Potrero Avenue, between 22nd & 23rd Streets, Potrero Hill (206 8000). Bus 9, 10, 27, 33, 48, 90.* **Map** p319 M12.

UCSF Medical Center *505 Parnassus Avenue, between 3rd & Hillway Avenues, Sunset (476 1000). Metro to UCSF/bus 6, 43, 66.* **Map** p316 D10.

Clinics

Haight-Ashbury Free Clinics, Inc *558 Clayton Street, at Haight Street, Haight-Ashbury (746 1950, www.hafci.org). Metro to Cole & Carl/bus 6, 33, 37, 43, 66, 71.* **Open** *Appointments* call for details. **Map** p317 E9.
Health care, including a variety of speciality clinics, is provided to the uninsured on a sliding-scale basis; most patients pay little or nothing.

Lyon-Martin Women's Health Services *1748 Market Street, between Octavia & Gough Streets, Upper Market (565 7667, www. lyon-martin.org). Metro to Van Ness/streetcar F/bus 6, 71.* **Open** *Appointments* call for details. **Credit** AmE, Disc, MC, V. **Map** p318 J8.
Named after two founders of the modern lesbian movement in the US, this clinic offers affordable health care for women and transgender patients.

St Anthony Free Medical Clinic *121 Golden Gate Avenue, at Jones Street, Tenderloin (241 8320, www.stanthonysf.org). BART & Metro to Civic Center/bus 5, 9, 19, 27, 31 & Market Street routes.* **Open** *Drop-in clinic*

8am-noon, 1-5pm Mon, Tue, Thur, Fri; 8am-noon Wed. **Map** p314 L6.
Free medical services for those with or without insurance. Arrive early.

Contraception & abortion

Planned Parenthood *1650 Valencia Street, at Mission Street, Mission (821 1282, www.plannedparenthood.org). BART to 24th Street/bus 12, 14, 27, 36, 49.* **Open** 9am-5pm Mon, Thur; 9am-12.30pm Tue. **Credit** MC, V. **Map** p314 K6.
In addition to contraception, Planned Parenthood's multilingual staff provides low-cost general health-care services, HIV testing and gynecological exams; with the exception of the morning-after pill, all are by appointment only.

Dentists

1-800 Dentist *1-800 336 8478, www.1800dentist.com.* **Open** 24hrs daily.
Provides dental referrals.
University of the Pacific School of Dentistry *2155 Webster Street, at Sacramento Street, Pacific Heights (929 6501, http://dental.pacific.edu). Bus 1, 3, 12, 22.* **Open** 8am-5pm Mon-Fri. **Map** p313 H5.
Supervised dentists-in-training provide a low-cost service.

HIV & AIDS

AIDS-HIV Nightline *434 2437/ 1-800 628 9240.* **Open** 5pm-5am daily.
Hotline offering emotional support.
California AIDS Foundation *1-800 367 2437.* **Open** 9am-5pm Mon-Fri.
Information and advice.

HELPLINES

Alcoholics Anonymous *674 1821, www.aa.org.* **Open** 24hrs daily.
Drug Crisis Information *362 3400, hearing-impaired 781 2224.* **Open** 24hrs daily.
Narcotics Anonymous *621 8600, www.na.org.* **Open** 24hrs daily.
San Francisco General Hospital Psychiatric Helpline *206 8125.* **Open** 24hrs daily.
SF Rape Treatment Center *347 3000.* **Open** 24hrs daily.
Suicide Prevention *781 0500/1-800 784 2433, www.sfsuicide.org.* **Open** 24hrs daily.
Talk Line Family Support *441 5437, www.sfcapc.org.* **Open** 24hrs daily.
Women Against Rape Crisis Hotline *647 7273.* **Open** 24hrs daily.

INSURANCE

Non-nationals should arrange comprehensive baggage, trip-cancellation and medical insurance before they leave. US citizens should consider doing the same. Read the small print: consequences of security scares, including cancelled flights, may not be covered.

INTERNET

Getting online here is very easy these days. Most hotels offer some form of in-room high-speed access for travelers with laptops; a number of hotels also provide at least one public computer.

In addition, a number of cafés and even a few bars across the city offer 'free' wireless access (you pay for your drink, but not the connection), and the city has a handful of wireless 'hotspots'; the best known is in Union Square. If you don't have a laptop, head to the **Main Library** (*see p56*), which has several terminals available for free, or an internet café. For more on getting online in the city, see www.bawug.org or www.wififreespot.com/ca.html.

LEFT LUGGAGE

Leaving luggage has got trickier since 9/11. However, larger hotels should allow you to leave bags, while at SFO, you can store everything from bags to bicycles at the Airport Travel Agency (1-650 877 0422, 7am-11pm daily), on the Departures level of the International Terminal.

LEGAL HELP

Lawyer Referral Service *989 1616, www.sfbar.org.* **Open** 8.30am-5.30pm Mon-Fri.
Callers are referred to attorneys and mediators to deal with all legal problems.

LIBRARIES

For **San Francisco Main Library**, *see p56*; for business libraries, *see p289*.

LOST PROPERTY

Property Control *850 Bryant Street, between 6th & 7th Streets, SoMa (553 1377). Bus 12, 19, 27, 47.* **Open** 8.30am-4.30pm Mon-Fri. **Map** p319 M8.
Make a police report – then hope.

Airports

For items lost en route, contact the specific airline. If you leave a bag at the airport, it may get destroyed, but it's worth calling the numbers listed below.

San Francisco International Airport *Terminal 1, 1-650 821 7014.* **Open** 8am-8pm Mon-Fri.
Mineta San Jose International Airport *Terminal A, Baggage Claim, 1-408 277 5419.* **Open** 8am-5pm Mon-Fri.
Oakland International Airport *1-510 563 3982.* **Open** 9.30am-noon Mon-Fri.

Public transport

Muni 923 6372.
BART 1-510 464 7090
AC Transit 1-510 891 4706
Golden Gate Transit 257 4476
SamTrans 1-800 660 4287.

MONEY

The US dollar ($) is divided into 100 cents (¢). Coin denominations run from the copper penny (1¢) to the silver nickel (5¢), dime (10¢), quarter (25¢) and less-common alf-dollar (50¢). There are also two $1 coins: the silver Susan B Anthony and the gold Sacagawea. Notes or 'bills' are the same green colour and size; they come in denominations of $1, $5, $10, $20, $50 and $100. The $20 and $50 have recently been redesigned with features that make them hard to forge, including, for the first time, some subtle colors other than green and black. Old-style bills remain legal currency.

ATMs

There are ATMs throughout the city: in banks, stores and even bars. ATMs accept Visa, MasterCard and American Express, as well as other cards, but almost all charge a usage fee. If you don't remember your PIN, most banks will dispense cash to cardholders. Wells Fargo offers cash advances at all of its branches.

Banks & bureaux de change

The easiest way to change money is simply use the ATM machines.

Your bank will give you the current rate of exchange and the fee is usually no more than you would pay in commission anywhere else anyway. Most banks are open from 9am to 6pm Monday to Friday and from 9amto 3pm on Saturday. Photo ID is required to cash travelers' checks. Many banks don't exchange foreign currency, so arrive with some US dollars. If you arrive after 6pm, change money at the airport. If you want to cash travelers' cheques at a shop, note that some require a minimum purchase. You can also obtain cash with a credit card from certain banks, but be prepared to pay interest rates that vary daily.

American Express Travel Services *455 Market Street, at 1st Street, Financial District (536 2600, www.americanexpress.com/travel).* BART & Metro to Montgomery/bus 1, 2, 3, 9, 10, 12, 14, 31, 38, 41 & Market Street routes. **Open** 9am-5.30pm Mon-Fri; 10am-2pm Sat. **Map** p315 N5.
AmEx will change travelers' cheques and money, and also offers (for AmEx cardholders only) poste restante.

Credit cards

Bring at least one major credit card: they are accepted – often required – at nearly all hotels, restaurants and shops. The cards most accepted in the US are American Express, Diners Club, Discover, MasterCard and Visa. Call the following numbers to report lost or stolen cards:

American Express *Cards* 1-800 992 3404. *Travellers' cheques* 1-800 221 7282.
Discover 1-800 347 2683.
MasterCard 1-800 622 7747.
Visa *Cards* 1-800 847 2911. *Travelers' checks* 1-800 227 6811.

POLICE STATIONS

Central Station *766 Vallejo Street, between Stockton & Powell Streets, North Beach (315 2400). Bus 10, 12, 30, 39, 41, 45, 91/cable car Powell-Mason.* **Map** p315 M3.
Southern Station *850 Bryant Street, between 6th & 7th Streets, SoMa (553 1373). Bus 9X, 12, 19, 27, 47.* **Map** p319 M8.

POSTAL SERVICES

Post offices are usually open 9am-5.30pm Monday to Friday, 9am to 2pm Saturday. All close on Sundays. Phone 1-800 275 8777 for information on your nearest branch. Stamps can be bought at any post office and also at some hotel receptions, vending machines and ATMs. Stamps for postcards within the US cost 44¢; for Europe, the charge is 98¢. For couriers and shippers, *see p289*.

Poste Restante *Main Post Office, 101 Hyde Street, at Golden Gate Avenue, Civic Center (1-800 275 8777). BART & Metro to Civic Center/bus 5, 6, 19, 21, 31, 71.* **Open** 10am-2pm Mon-Sat. **Map** p318 L7.
If you need to receive mail in SF and you're not sure where you'll be staying, have the envelope addressed with your name, c/o General Delivery, San Francisco, CA 94102, USA. Mail is only kept for ten days from receipt, and you must present some photo ID to retrieve it.

RELIGION

Calvary Presbyterian *2515 Fillmore Street, at Washington Street, Pacific Heights (346 3832, www.calvarypresbyterian.org). Bus 1, 3, 10, 22, 24.* **Map** p309 E3.
Cathedral of St Mary of the Assumption *1111 Gough Street, at Geary Boulevard, Western Addition (567 2020, www.stmarycathedralsf.org). Bus 2, 3, 31, 38, 47, 49, 90.* **Map** p314 J6. Catholic.
Glide Memorial *330 Ellis Street, at Taylor Street, Tenderloin (674 6000, www.glide.org). Bus 27, 31, 38/cable car Powell-Hyde & Powell-Mason.* **Map** p314 L6. Methodist.
Grace Cathedral *1100 California Street, at Taylor Street, Nob Hill (749 6300, www.gracecathedral.org). Bus 1, 2, 3, 27/cable car California.* **Map** p314 L5. Episcopalian.
Masjid Darussalam (Islamic Society of San Francisco) *20 Jones Street, at Market Street, Tenderloin (863 7997, http://islamsf.com). BART & Metro to Civic Center/streetcar F/bus 5, 31 & Market Street routes.* **Map** p318 L7.
Old St Mary's Cathedral 660 *California Street, at Grant Avenue, Chinatown (288 3800, www.oldsaintmarys.org). Bus 1, 2, 3, 10, 12, 30, 45, 91/cable car California.* **Map** p315 M5. Catholic.
St Paul's Lutheran Church *950 McAllister Street, between Buchanan & Laguna Streets, Western Addition (673 8088). Bus 5, 21,* 22, 31. **Map** p314 J6.
Temple Emanuel *2 Lake Street, at Arguello Boulevard, Presidio Heights (751 2535, www.emanuelsf.org). Bus 1, 2, 33.* **Map** p312 D6. Synagogue.
Zen Center *300 Page Street, at Laguna Street, Lower Haight (863 3136, www.sfzc.org). Bus 6, 21, 71.* **Map** p318 J8.

SAFETY & SECURITY

Crime is a reality in all big cities, but San Franciscans generally feel secure in their town. There is really just one basic rule of thumb you need to follow: use your common sense. If a neighborhood doesn't feel safe to you, it probably isn't. Only a few areas warrant caution during daylight hours and are of particular concern at night. These include the Tenderloin (north and east of Civic Center); SoMa (near the Mission/6th Street corner); Mission Street between 13th and 18th Streets; and the Hunter's Point neighbourhood near 3Com Park. Golden Gate Park should be avoided at night. Many tourist areas, most notably around Union Square, are sprinkled with homeless people who beg for change but are basically pretty harmless.

If you're unlucky enough to be mugged, your best bet is to give your attackers whatever they want, then call the police from the nearest pay phone by dialling 911. (Don't forget to get the reference number on the claim report for insurance purposes and to get travellers' cheque refunds.) If you are the victim of a sexual assault and wish to make a report, call the police, who will escort you to the hospital for treatment. For helplines that serve victims of rape or other crimes, *see p291*.

SMOKING

Smokers may rank as the only group of people who are not especially welcome in San Francisco. Smoking is banned in all public places, including banks, sporting arenas, theatres, offices, the lobbies of buildings, shops, restaurants, bars, and any and every form of public transport. There are many small hotels and B&Bs that don't allow you to light up anywhere inside. On the other hand, a select few bars cheerfully ignore the law.

STUDYING

To study in the Bay Area (or, for that matter, anywhere in the United States), exchange students should apply for a J-1 visa, while full-time students enrolled in a degree programme must apply for an F-1 visa. Both are valid for the duration of the course and for a limited period thereafter.

Foreign students need an International Student Identity Card (ISIC) as proof of student status. This can be bought from your local travel agent or student travel office.

TAX

Sales tax of 9.5 percent is added on to the label price in shops within city limits, and 9.5 to 9.75 per cent in surrounding cities. Hotels charge a 14 per cent room tax and the same percentage on hotel parking.

TELEPHONES

The phone system is reliable and, for local calls, cheap. Long-distance, particularly overseas, calls are best paid for with a rechargeable, pre-paid phonecard ($6-$35) available from vending machines and many shops. You can use your MasterCard with **AT&T** (1-800 225 5288) or **Sprint** (1-800 877 4646).

Direct dial calls

If you are dialling outside your area code, dial 1 + area code + phone number; on pay phones an operator or recording will tell you how much money to add. All phone numbers in this guide are given as if dialed from San Francisco; hence, Berkeley numbers have the 1-510 prefix, while Marin County numbers have no prefix.

Collect calls

For collect or when using a phone card, dial 0 + area code + phone number and listen for the operator/ recorded instructions. If you're completely befuddled, dial 0 and plead your case with the operator.

Area codes

San Francisco & Marin County 415
Oakland & Berkeley 510
The peninsula cities 650
San Jose 408
Napa, Sonoma & Mendocino Counties 707

International calls

Dial 011 followed by the country code. If you need operator assistance with international calls, dial 00.

Australia 61
Germany 49
Japan 81
New Zealand 64
UK 44

Public phones

Public pay phones only accept nickels, dimes and quarters, but check for a dial tone before you start feeding in your change. Local calls usually cost 50¢, though some companies operate pay phones that charge exorbitant prices, The rate also rises steeply as the distance between callers increases (an operator or recorded message will tell you how much to add).

Operator services

Operator assistance 0
Emergency (police, ambulance and fire) 911
Local & long-distance directory enquiries 411

Toll-free numbers generally start with 1-800, 1-888 or 1-877, while pricey pay-per-call lines (usually phone-sex numbers) start with 1-900.

Telephone directories

Directories in San Francisco are divided into *Yellow Pages* (classified) and *White Pages* (business and residential), and are available in hotels and at libraries around the city, and online. They contain a wealth of travel information, including area codes, event calendars, park facilities, post office addresses and city zip codes. Alternatively, dial 411 (for directory assistance) and ask for your listing by name (and, if you have it, the address).

Mobile phones

San Francisco, like most of the continental US, operates on the 1900 GSM frequency. Travelers from Europe with tri-band phones will be able to connect to one or more of the networks here with no problems, assuming their service provider at home has an arrangement with a local network; always check before traveling. European travelers with dual-band phones, however, will need to rent a handset upon arrival. Check the price of calls before you go. Rates may be hefty and, unlike in the UK, you'll probably be charged for receiving as well as making calls. It might be cheaper to rent or buy a mobile phone while you're in town – try the agency below, or check the Yellow Pages. Alternatively, you can simply get a pre-paid SIM card when you arrive.

AllCell Rentals *1-877 724 2355, www.allcellrentals. com.* **Open** 24hrs daily. **Credit** AmEx, Disc, MC, V.
Rentals of mobile, GSM and satellite phones and pagers. You pay for daily, weekly or monthly rental ($19.95/$69.95), plus the airtime (39¢ per minute). There also may be a delivery fee.

TIME & DATES

San Francisco is on Pacific Standard Time, which is three hours behind Eastern Standard Time (New York) and eight hours behind Greenwich Mean Time (UK). Daylight Savings Time, which is almost concurrent with British Summer Time, runs from the first Sunday in April, when the clocks are rolled ahead one hour, to the last Sunday in October. Going from the west to east coast, Pacific Time is one hour behind Mountain Time and two hours behind Central Time, three hours behind Eastern Time.

British readers should note that in the US, dates are written in the order month, day, year: 2.5.98 is February 5, not May 2.

TIPPING

Unlike in Europe, tipping is a way of life in the US: many locals in service industries rely on gratuities as part of their income, so you should tip accordingly. In general, tip bellhops and baggage handlers $1-$2 a bag; tip cab drivers, waiters and waitresses, hairdressers and food delivery people 15-20 per cent of the total tab; tip valets $2-$3; and tip counter staff 25¢ to 10 per cent of the order, depending on its size. In restaurants, you should tip at least 15 per cent of the total bill and usually nearer 20 per cent; most restaurants will add this to the bill automatically for a table of six or more. In bars, bank on tipping around a buck a drink, especially if you want to hang around for a while. If you look after the bartender, they'll look after you; tipping pocket change may leave you dry for a while.

TOILETS/RESTROOMS

Restrooms can be found in prime tourist areas such as Fisherman's Wharf and Golden Gate Park, as well as in shopping malls. If you're caught short, don't hesitate to enter a restaurant or a bar and ask to use its facilities.

In keeping with its cosmopolitan standing, San Francisco has installed 20 of the French-designed, self-cleaning JC Decaux lavatories throughout the high-traffic areas of the city. Keep an eye out for these forest-green commodes (they're usually plastered with high-profile advertising). Admission is 25¢ for 20min; after that, you may be fined for indecent exposure, because the door pings open automatically. Do be aware that some people use the toilets for purposes other than that for which they were designed.

TOURIST INFORMATION

One of the attractions of San Francisco is that there are many wonderful places to visit beyond the city itself. For full listings of the best of these options, including details on tourist offices, *see pp264-84*.

San Francisco Visitor Information Center *Lower level of Hallidie Plaza, 900 Market Street, at Powell Street (391 2000, www.onysanfrancisco.com). BART & Metro to Powell/bus 27, 31, 38, 45 & Market Street routes/cable car Powell-Hyde or Powell-Mason.* **Open** 9am-5pm Mon-Fri; 9am-3pm Sat, Sun. **Map** p315 M6.
Located in Downtown, this is the visitor center for the efficient and helpful San Francisco Convention & Visitor Bureau. You won't find any parking, but you will find tons of free maps, brochures, coupons and advice. The number above gives access to a 24hr recorded message listing daily events and activities; you can also use it to request free information about hotels, restaurants and shopping in the city.

VISAS & IMMIGRATION

Under the current Visa Waiver Scheme, citizens of 36 countries, including the UK, Ireland, Australia and New Zealand, do not need a visa for stays of less than 90 days (for business or pleasure). Visitors are required to have a machine-readable passport that's valid for the full 90-day period and a return or open standby ticket and authorisation through the ESTA system. Visitors must fill in the ESTA form at least 24 hours before travelling (72 hours is recommended); the form can be found on US embassy websites.

Canadians don't usually need visas but must have legal proof of their citizenship.

Citizens of other countries or people who ar staying for longer than 90 days or who are uncertain if they might need a work or study visa should contact their nearest US embassy or consulate or check its website well in advance of travel for information and application forms.

Given current security fears, it's advisable to double-check visa requirements before you set out. For more, *see p289* **Travel advice**.

For further information on visa requirements, see http://travel.state.gov. UK citizens can call the Visa Information Line: 09042 450100 (£1.23/min) or look online at www.usembassy.org.uk.

Immigration regulations apply to all visitors to the US. During the flight, you will be issued with an immigration form to present to an official on the ground. You'll have your fingerprints and photograph taken as you pass through. If you have a foreign passport, expect close questioning.

WHEN TO GO

Climate

San Francisco may be in California, but its climate, like its politics, is all its own. When planning a trip, don't anticipate the normal seasons, climatically, at least. Spring and autumn are relatively predictable, with warm days and cool nights. During the summer, however, days are often foggy and chilly, but the nights are usually mild. In midwinter, what seems like months of rain will break for a week of sun. In general, temperatures rarely stray above 80°F (27°C) or below 45°F (7°C). San Francisco is small, but the weather varies wildly between neighborhoods. The city's western terrain is flat, and so fog often covers Golden Gate Park and the Sunset and Richmond areas. However, the fog is often too heavy to climb further east, so the areas east of Twin Peaks - the Mission, the Castro, Noe Valley, Potrero Hill - are often sunny. Add in the wind that whips in to Fisherman's Wharf, and you may experience four seasons in one day.

Public holidays

New Year's Day 1 Jan
Martin Luther King Jr Day 3rd Mon in Jan
President's Day 3rd Mon in Feb
Memorial Day last Mon in May
Independence Day 4 July
Labor Day 1st Mon in Sept
Columbus Day 2nd Mon in Oct
Veterans' Day 11 Nov
Thanksgiving Day 4th Thur in Nov
Christmas Day 25 Dec

THE LOCAL CLIMATE

Average temperatures and monthly rainfall in San Francisco.

	High (°C/°F)	Low (°C/°F)	Rainfall (mm/in)
Jan	13 / 56	8 / 46	114 / 4.5
Feb	15 / 60	9 / 48	71 / 2.8
Mar	16 / 61	9 / 49	66 / 2.6
Apr	17 / 63	10 / 50	38 / 1.5
May	17 / 64	10 / 51	10 /0.4
June	19 / 66	11 / 53	5 / 0.2
July	19 / 66	12 / 54	2.5 / 0.1
Aug	19 / 66	12 / 54	2.5 / 0.1
Sept	21 / 70	13 / 56	5 / 0.2
Oct	20 / 69	13 / 55	28 / 1.1
Nov	18 / 64	10/51	64 / 2.5
Dec	14 / 57	8 / 47	89 / 3.5

Further Reference

FICTION & POETRY

Isabel Allende *Daughters of Fortune*
Delightfully written piece about one young woman's search for love during the Gold Rush.
James Dalessandro *1906: A Novel*
A fictionalized, though grippingly researched, account of San Francisco's catastrophic year of earthquake and fire.
Dave Eggers *A Heartbreaking Work of Staggering Genius*
A beautiful memoir of moving to San Francisco and raising a younger brother.
Allen Ginsberg *Howl and Other Poems*
Grab your chance to read the rant that caused all the fuss way back in the 1950s.
Glen David Gold *Carter Beats the Devil*
A sleight-of-hand comedy thriller set in 1920s San Francisco.
Dashiell Hammett *The Maltese Falcon*
One of the greatest detective writers and one of the world's best detective novels – later filmed with Humphrey Bogart – set in a dark and dangerous San Francisco.
Jack Kerouac *On the Road*; *The Subterraneans*; *Desolation Angels*; *The Dharma Bums*
Famous for a reason: bittersweet tales of drugs and sex in San Francisco and around the world, from the best-known Beat of them all.
Jack London *Tales of the Fish Patrol*; *John Barleycorn*
Early works from London, set in the writer's native city. For his musings on the Sonoma Valley, pick up *Valley of the Moon*.
Armistead Maupin *Tales of the City* (6 volumes)
This witty soap opera, later a very successful TV series, follows the lives and loves of a group of San Francisco friends starting in the 1970s.
Frank Norris *McTeague*
Working-class life and loss set in unromanticized Barbary Coast days. A cult classic of the 1890s.
Domenic Stansberry *The Last Days of Il Duce*
A fearsome, authentic piece of *noir* fiction, set in North Beach.
John Steinbeck *The Grapes of Wrath*
Grim tales of Northern California in the Great Depression by the master of American fiction.
Amy Tan *The Joy Luck Club*
A moving story of the lives and loves of two generations of Chinese-American women living in San Francisco.
Alfredo Vea *Gods Go Begging*
A San Francisco murder trial has ties to the Vietnam War.
Tom Wolfe *The Electric Kool-Aid Acid Test; The Pump House Gang*
Alternative lifestyles in trippy, hippy, 1960s California.

NON-FICTION

Walton Bean *California: An Interpretive History*
An anecdotal account of California's shady past.
Herb Caen *Baghdad by the Bay*
Local gossip and lightly poetic insight from the much-missed *Chronicle* columnist.
Carolyn Cassady *Off the Road: My Years with Cassady, Kerouac and Ginsberg*
Not enlightened feminism, but an interesting alternative examination of the Beats.
Joan Didion *Slouching Towards Bethlehem; The White Album*
Brilliant essays examining California in the past couple of decades by one of America's most respected authors.
Timothy W Drescher *San Francisco Bay Area Murals*
A well-resourced book with plenty of maps and 140 photos.
Lawrence Ferlinghetti & Nancy J Peters *Literary San Francisco*
The city's literary pedigree examined by the founder of City Lights books.
Robert Greenfield *Dark Star: An Oral Biography of Jerry Garcia*
The life and (high) times of the Grateful Dead's late frontman.
Emmett Grogan *Ringolevio: A Life Played for Keeps*
Part-memoir, part-social history, part-fable, *Ringolevio* traces the story of Grogan, one of the founders of the Diggers, from New York to 1960s Haight-Ashbury. Fantastic.
Michael Lewis *Moneyball: The Art of Winning an Unfair Game*
Oakland A's GM Billy Beane may go down as one of the most influential baseball executives of the last half-century. This vital book profiles Beane and his team.
Beth Lisick *Everybody into the Pool*
A tremendously enjoyable and occasionally laugh-out-loud funny collection of essays about Lisick's journey from child to adult in the Bay Area.
Malcolm Margolin *The Ohlone Way*
How the Bay Area's original inhabitants lived, researched from oral histories.
John Miller (ed) *San Francisco Stories: Great Writers on the City*
Contributions by Herb Caen, Anne Lamott, Amy Tan, Ishmael Reed and many others.
Ray Mungo *San Francisco Confidential*
A gossipy look behind the city's closed doors.
John Plunkett & Barbara Traub (eds) *Burning Man*
Photo-heavy manual to the the annual insanity that is the Burning Man Festival.
Marc Reisner *Cadillac Desert: A Dangerous State*
The role of water in California's history and future; a projection of apocalypse founded on shifting tectonics and hairtrigger irrigation.
Nathaniel Rich *San Francisco Noir*
San Francisco's cinematic history gets re-examined in this beautifully written piece, which falls somewhere between guidebook, cultural criticism and academic tract.
Richard Schwartz *Berkeley 1900*
An in-depth account of the early origins of complex and controversial Berkeley.
Joel Selvin *San Francisco: The Magical History*
Tour of the sights and sounds of the city's pop music history by the *Chronicle*'s music critic.
Randy Shilts *And the Band Played On*
Shilts' crucial work is still the most important account of the AIDS epidemic in San Francisco.

Gertrude Stein *The Making of Americans*
This autobiographical work includes an account of Stein's early childhood in Oakland.
Tom Stienstra & Ann Marie Brown *California Hiking*
What it says: an outstanding guide to over 1,000 hikes all over the state. Stienstra is the outdoors columnist for the *San Francisco Chronicle*. Other books in the excellent Fogohorn Outdoors series on California cover camping, hiking, biking and fishing.
Robert Louis Stevenson *An Inland Voyage; The Silverado Squatters*
Autobiographical narratives describing the journey from Europe to western America.
Bonnie Wach *San Francisco As You Like It*
City tours to suit pretty much all personalities and moods, from Ivy League shoppers to cheapskate fitness-freak vegetarians.

FILM

Birdman of Alcatraz (1961)
It's hopelessly overlong and laughably inaccurate, but, thanks largely to Burt Lancaster's likeable title turn, it's a decent film regardless.
Bullitt (1968)
This Steve McQueen film boasts the all-time greatest San Francisco car chase.
Chan Is Missing (1982)
Two cab drivers search for a man who stole their life savings in this movie, which gives an authentic, insider's look at Chinatown.
The Conversation (1974)
Gene Hackman's loner surveillance expert gets in a little deeper than he planned in Coppola's classic. The opening scene, shot in Union Square, is a cinematic *tour de force*.
Crumb (1994)
An award-winning film about the comic book master and misanthrope Robert Crumb.
Dark Passage (1947)
This classic thriller starts in Marin County, where Bogart escapes from San Quentin Prison, and ends up in Lauren Bacall's SF apartment.
Dirty Harry (1971)
Do you feel lucky?
The Graduate (1967)
Dustin Hoffman at his best, with shots of Berkeley as well as a cool wrong-direction shot on the Bay Bridge.
Harold and Maude (1971)
Bay Area scenery abounds in this bittersweet cult classic about an unbalanced boy who falls in love with an elderly woman.
Jimmy Plays Berkeley (1970)
Stirring footage of the town in its radical days, plus Hendrix at his very best
The Maltese Falcon (1941)
Hammett's classic made into a glorious 1940s thriller, full of great street scenes.
Milk (2008)
Gus Van Sant's brilliant chronicle of a of Harvey Milk, California's first openly gay elected official
The Mrs Doubtfire (1993)
Relentlessly hammy Robin Williams plays a divorcee posing as a nanny to be near his kids.
San Francisco (1936)
Ignore the first 90 minutes of moralizing and sit back to enjoy the Great Quake.
So I Married An Axe Murderer (1993)
This San Francisco-set romantic comedy features Mike Meyers giving an immensely funny send-up of 1950s beat culture.
Vertigo (1958)
A veteran cop becomes obsessed with a mysterious blonde. A die-cast San Francisco classic.
The Voyage Home: Star Trek IV (1986)
The gang come to SF to to save some whales in this flick, the best of the series.
The Wedding Planner (2000)
This update of the classic screwball comedy is a bit clunky, but J-Lo is immaculately cast.
The Wild Parrots of Telegraph Hill (2000)
A delightful documentary about Mark Bittner and the North Beach birds who love him dearly.

MUSIC

Big Brother and the Holding Company *Cheap Thrills* (1968)
Classic Janis Joplin, housed in a classic Robert Crumb sleeve. Tracks include 'Ball and Chain' and 'Piece of My Heart'.
Chris Isaak *Heart Shaped World* (1989)
What a 'Wicked Game' to be so good-looking, with a voice like that.
Creedence Clearwater Revival *Willie and the Poor Boys* (1969)
Classic southern rock with a San Francisco touch.
The Dead Kennedys *Fresh Fruit for Rotting Vegetables* (1980)
Excellent, angry San Francisco punk.
Erase Errata *At Crystal Palace* (2003)
Angular, uplifting rock from the queens of the underground.
Gold Chains *Young Miss America* (2003)
Bay Area hip hop, 21st-century style.
The Grateful Dead *Dick's Picks Vol.4* (1996)
Jerry Garcia and the boys in their 1970 prime, playing at the Fillmore East.
Jefferson Airplane *Surrealistic Pillow* (1967)
Folk, blues and psychedelia. Grace Slick helps define the San Francisco sound.
Joshua Redman *Wish* (1993)
Quality jazz from the Bay Area tenor saxophonist.
Primus *Pork Soda (1993)*
Wryly intelligent punk-funk in the Zappa tradition.
Sly and the Family Stone *Stand! (1969)*
Funk-rock masters. If you haven't heard this, you haven't really heard the 1960s.

WEBSITES

www.craigslist.org
How San Franciscans hook up. Hilarious and enlightening.
www.onlysanfrancisco.org
The CVB's site is packed with information on the town.
www.mistersf.com
A delicious collection of local oddballs, notorious history and contemporary culture.
www.sanfranciscomemories.com
Wonderful photographs of the city in days gone by.
www.sfbg.com
The online edition of the *San Francisco Bay Guardian*.
www.sfgate.com
The *San Francisco Chronicle* online.
www.sfstation.com
Upcoming events, clubs, parties, film and restaurant reviews and more.
www.sfweekly.com
Listings, reviews and features.
www.streetcar.org
The past and present of San Francisco's classic streetcars, now on the F line.
http://transit.511.org
Very useful for information on all forms of Bay Area public transport.

Content Index

Venue Index

★ **indicates a critic's choice**

INDEX

T

U

V

W

X

Y

Z

Advertisers' Index

Please refer to the relevant pages for contact details.

Maps

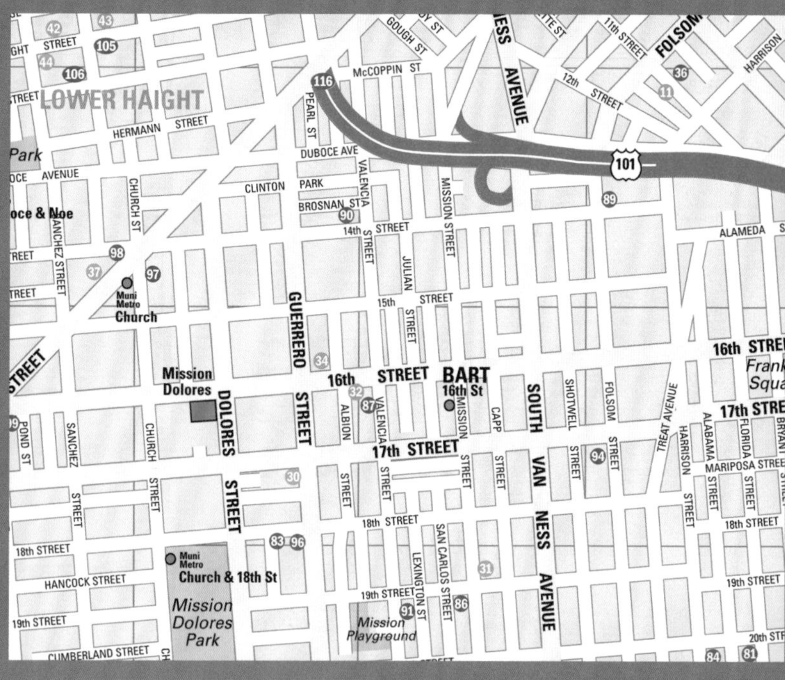

- **Major sight or landmark**
- **Hospital or college**
- **Railway station**
- **Parks**
- **River**
- **Interstate Highway** 80
- **US Highway** 101
- **State or Provincial Highway** 1
- **Main road**
- **Airport**
- **Church**
- **Area name** CASTRO

Escapes & Excursions

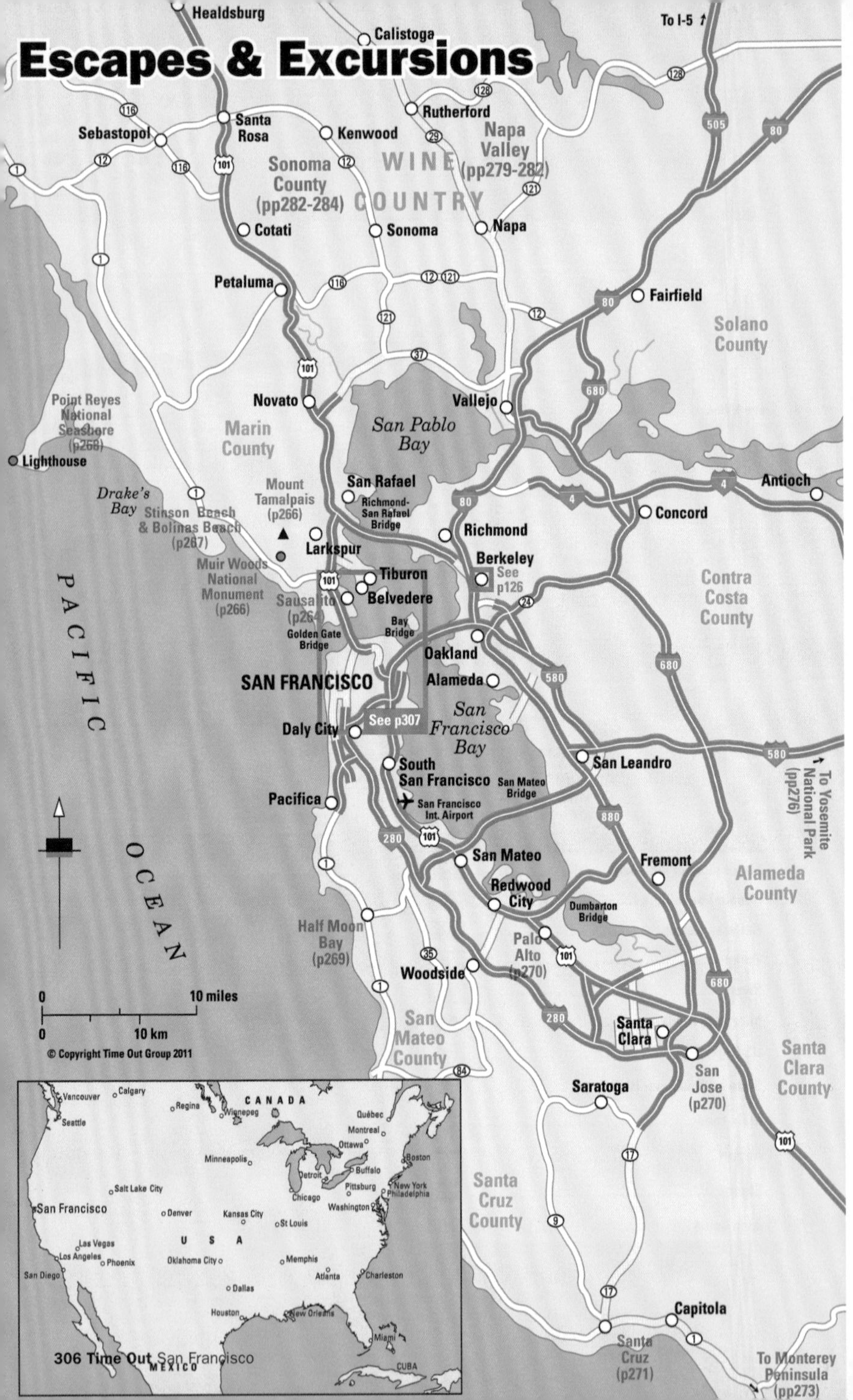

Healdsburg
Calistoga
To I-5
Santa Rosa
Sebastopol
Kenwood
Rutherford
Napa Valley (pp279-282)
Sonoma County (pp282-284)
WINE COUNTRY
Cotati
Sonoma
Napa
Petaluma
Fairfield
Solano County
Novato
Vallejo
San Pablo Bay
Point Reyes National Seashore (p268)
Lighthouse
Marin County
San Rafael
Richmond-San Rafael Bridge
Antioch
Drake's Bay
Stinson Beach & Bolinas Beach (p267)
Mount Tamalpais (p266)
Larkspur
Richmond
Concord
Berkeley
See p126
Muir Woods National Monument (p266)
Tiburon
Belvedere
Sausalito (p264)
Contra Costa County
Golden Gate Bridge
Bay Bridge
Oakland
SAN FRANCISCO
Alameda
San Francisco Bay
See p307
Daly City
PACIFIC OCEAN
South San Francisco
San Leandro
San Mateo Bridge
To Yosemite National Park (pp276)
Pacifica
San Francisco Int. Airport
San Mateo
Fremont
Alameda County
Redwood City
Dumbarton Bridge
Half Moon Bay (p269)
Palo Alto (p270)
Woodside
San Mateo County
Santa Clara
Santa Clara County
San Jose (p270)
Saratoga
Santa Cruz County
Capitola
Santa Cruz (p271)
To Monterey Peninsula (pp273)
0 10 miles
0 10 km
CANADA
Vancouver
Calgary
Seattle
Regina
Winnipeg
Québec
Montreal
Ottawa
Minneapolis
Boston
Detroit
Buffalo
New York
Chicago
Pittsburg
Philadelphia
Salt Lake City
Washington
San Francisco
Denver
Kansas City
St Louis
USA
Las Vegas
Los Angeles
Phoenix
Oklahoma City
Memphis
Atlanta
Charleston
San Diego
Dallas
Houston
New Orleans
Miami
MEXICO
CUBA

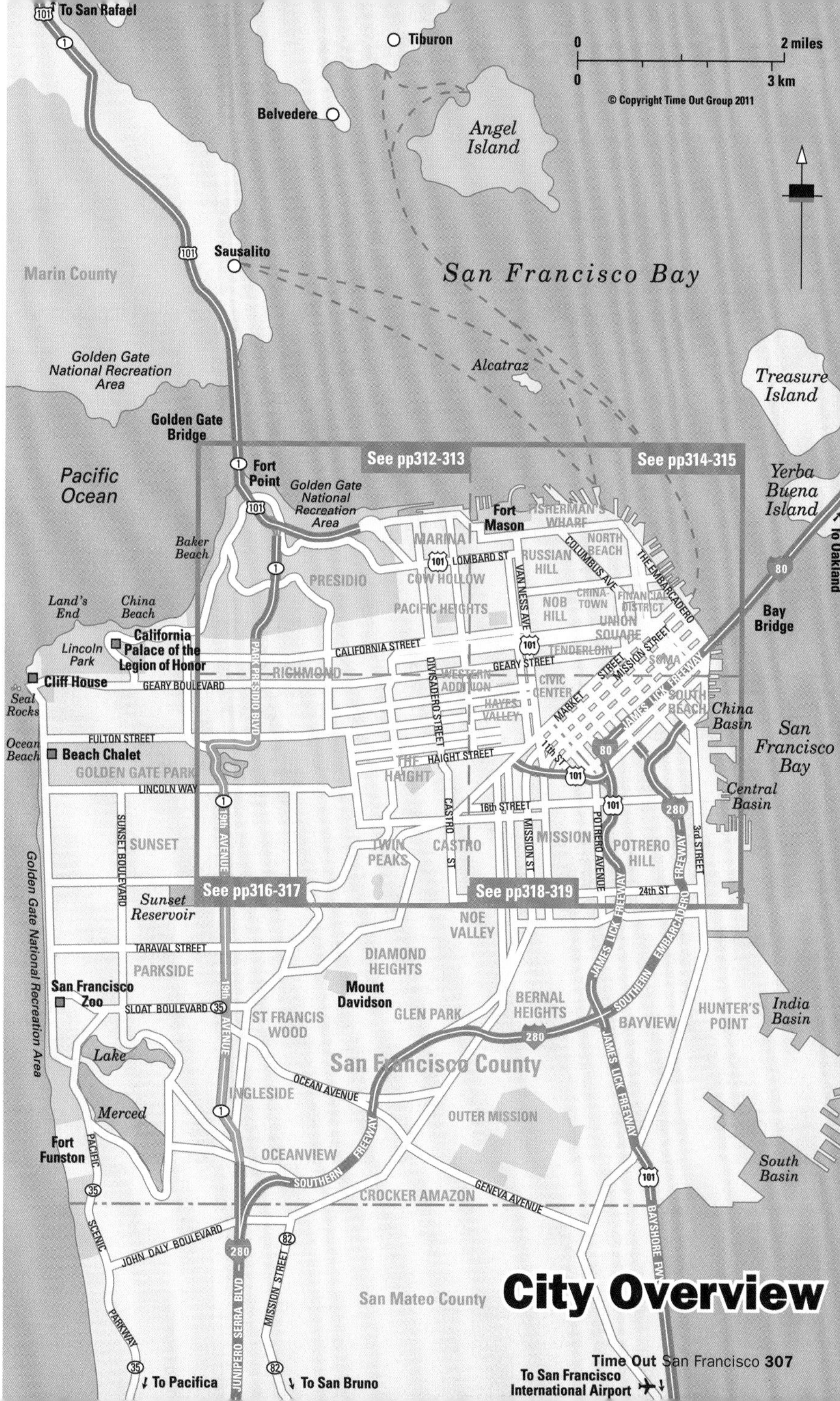

City Overview
To San Rafael
Tiburon
Belvedere
Angel Island
San Francisco Bay
Sausalito
Marin County
Golden Gate National Recreation Area
Alcatraz
Treasure Island
Golden Gate Bridge
Pacific Ocean
Fort Point
Yerba Buena Island
To Oakland
Bay Bridge
See pp312-313
See pp314-315
See pp316-317
See pp318-319
Baker Beach
Fort Mason
Fisherman's Wharf
North Beach
Marina
Russian Hill
Presidio
Cow Hollow
Lombard St
Pacific Heights
Nob Hill
Chinatown
Financial District
Union Square
Land's End
China Beach
Lincoln Park
California Palace of the Legion of Honor
California Street
Geary Street
Tenderloin
Richmond
Western Addition
Civic Center
SoMa
South Beach
Cliff House
Geary Boulevard
Seal Rocks
Hayes Valley
China Basin
Fulton Street
Ocean Beach
Beach Chalet
Golden Gate Park
The Haight
Haight Street
Lincoln Way
Park Presidio Blvd
Divisadero Street
Van Ness Ave
Columbus Ave
The Embarcadero
Market Street
Mission Street
James Lick Freeway
11th St
16th Street
Mission St
Castro St
Potrero Avenue
3rd Street
24th St
Central Basin
Sunset
Twin Peaks
Castro
Mission
Potrero Hill
19th Avenue
Sunset Boulevard
Sunset Reservoir
Noe Valley
Taraval Street
Diamond Heights
Parkside
San Francisco Zoo
Mount Davidson
Sloat Boulevard
St Francis Wood
Glen Park
Bernal Heights
Bayview
Hunter's Point
India Basin
Southern Embarcadero Freeway
San Francisco County
Lake Merced
Ocean Avenue
Ingleside
Outer Mission
Fort Funston
Oceanview
Southern Freeway
Crocker Amazon
Geneva Avenue
South Basin
Pacific Scenic Parkway
John Daly Boulevard
Junipero Serra Blvd
Mission Street
Bayshore Fwy
San Mateo County
Golden Gate National Recreation Area
To Pacifica
To San Bruno
To San Francisco International Airport
0 2 miles
0 3 km
101
1
280
80
35
82

San Francisco by Area

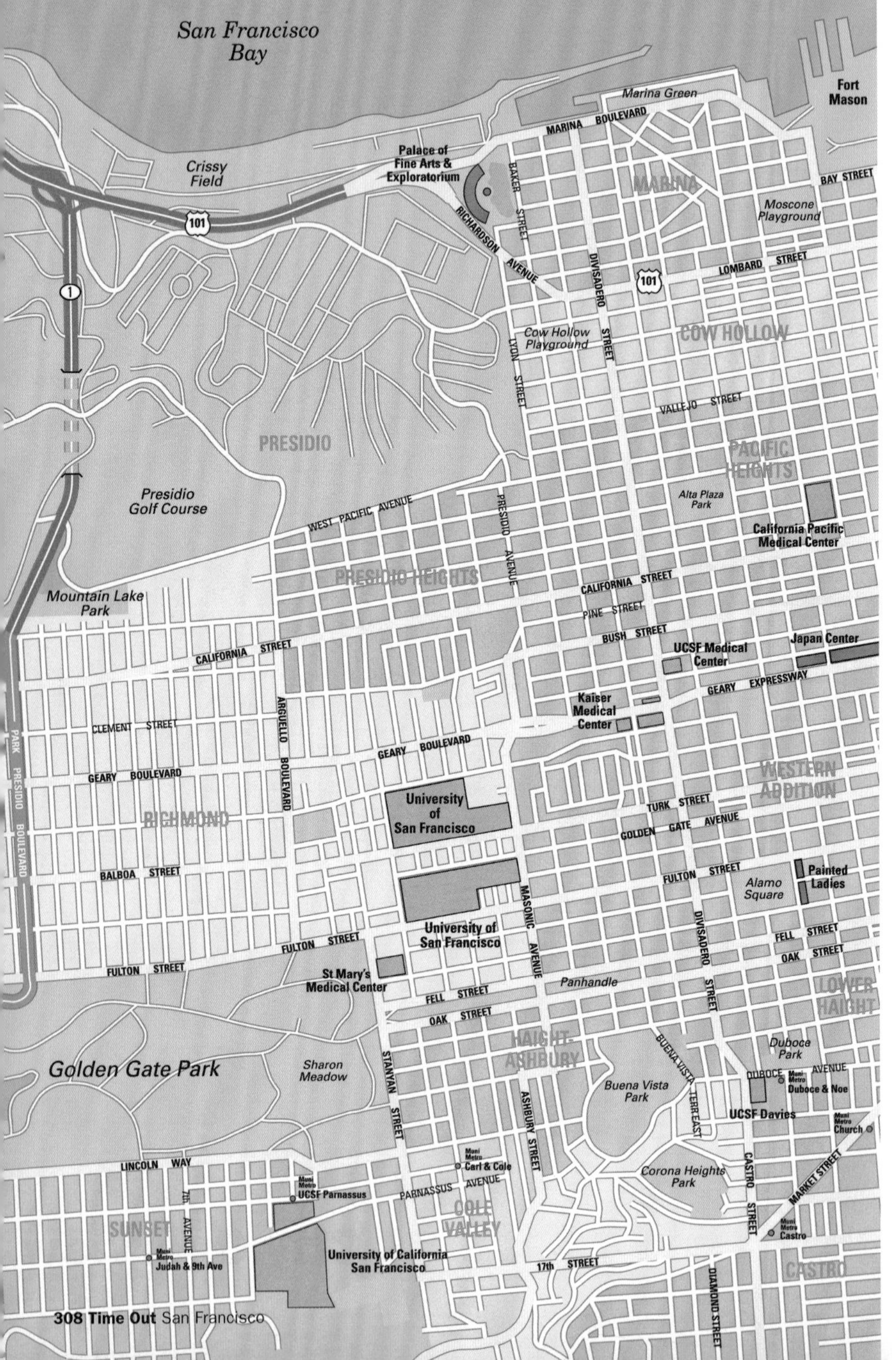

0 1/4 1/2 mile
0 1 km
© Copyright Time Out Group 2011
San Francisco Bay
Pier 39
Aquatic Park
FISHERMAN'S WHARF
JEFFERSON STREET
THE EMBARCADERO
NORTH POINT STREET
BAY STREET
Russian Hill Park
San Francisco Art Institute
NORTH BEACH
Lombard Street
Coit Tower
COLUMBUS AVENUE
BATTERY STREET
Washington Square
RUSSIAN HILL
POWELL STREET
LARKIN STREET
POLK STREET
FRANKLIN STREET
EMBARCADERO
VALLEJO STREET
BROADWAY
Jackson Square
PACIFIC AVENUE
Transamerica Pyramid
Ferry Building
JACKSON STREET
Portsmouth Square
FINANCIAL DISTRICT
101
CHINATOWN
MONTGOMERY STREET
SANSOME STREET
BART Embarcadero
STEUART STREET
NOB HILL
Huntington Park
POLK GULCH
VAN NESS AVENUE
Lafayette Park
KEARNY STREET
MARKET STREET
BEALE STREET
FREMONT STREET
Folsom
PINE STREET
St Francis Memorial Hospital
BUSH STREET
TAYLOR STREET
1st STREET
Bay Brid
SUTTER STREET
UNION SQUARE & AROUND
BART Montgomery
GEARY STREET
MASON STREET
2nd STREET
SFMOMA
HOWARD STREET
3rd STREET
TENDERLOIN
Yerba Buena Gardens
FOLSOM STREET
HARRISON STREET
BART Powell
4th STREET
Brannan
St Mary's Cathedral
GOUGH STREET
LARKIN STREET
LEAVENWORTH STREET
5th STREET
BRYANT STREET
SOMA
South Park
Jefferson Square
GOLDEN GATE AVENUE
BRANNAN STREET
80
SOUTH BEACH
Asian Art Museum
6th STREET
2nd & King
City Hall
CIVIC CENTER
BART Civic Center
7th STREET
CalTrain Depot
BERRY ST
AT & T Park
China Basin
4th & King
HAYES VALLEY
OCTAVIA STREET
8th STREET
9th STREET
10th STREET
Van Ness
3rd STREET
5th STREET
4th STREET
Mission Rock
UPPER MARKET
14th STREET
UCSF Mission Bay
GUERRERO STREET
SOUTH VAN NESS AVENUE
16th STREET
Mission Dolores
16th St BART
Franklin Square
POTRERO AVENUE
Jackson Park
280
Mariposa
Central Basin
17th STREET
MISSION
POTRERO HILL
20th St
Mission Dolores Park

Street Index

STREET INDEX

STREET INDEX

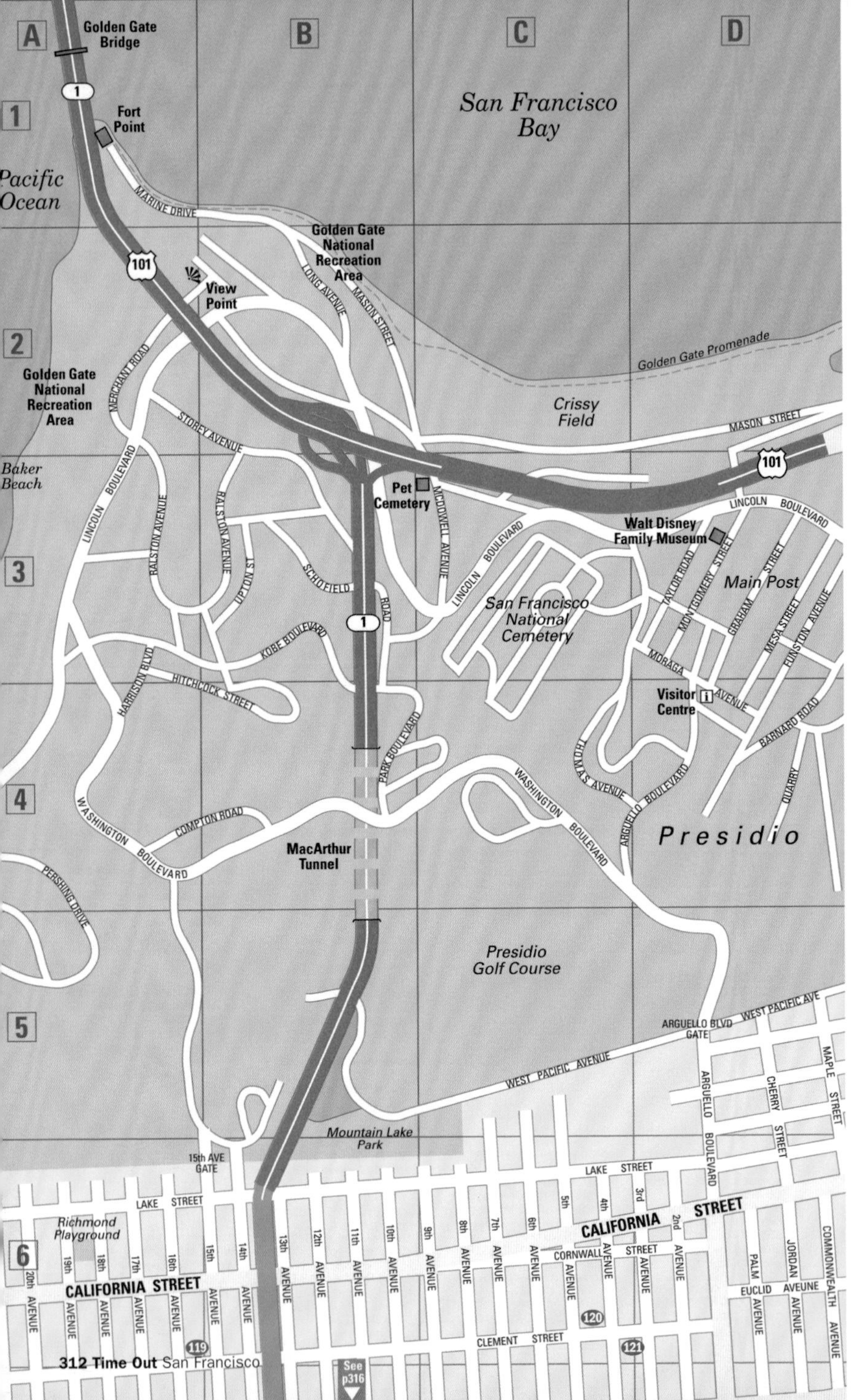

A
B
C
D
1
2
3
4
5
6
Golden Gate Bridge
Fort Point
Pacific Ocean
San Francisco Bay
Marine Drive
Golden Gate National Recreation Area
View Point
Long Avenue
Mason Street
Golden Gate Promenade
Merchant Road
Crissy Field
Mason Street
Storey Avenue
Baker Beach
Pet Cemetery
McDowell Avenue
Lincoln Boulevard
Ralston Avenue
Upton St
Schofield Road
Walt Disney Family Museum
Taylor Road
Montgomery Street
Main Post
Graham Street
San Francisco National Cemetery
Mesa Street
Funston Avenue
Kobe Boulevard
Harrison Blvd
Hitchcock Street
Moraga Avenue
Visitor Centre
Park Boulevard
Barnard Road
Thomas Avenue
Arguello Boulevard
Quarry
Washington Boulevard
Compton Road
Presidio
MacArthur Tunnel
Pershing Drive
Presidio Golf Course
West Pacific Ave
Arguello Blvd Gate
West Pacific Avenue
Maple Street
Cherry Street
Mountain Lake Park
15th Ave Gate
Lake Street
Richmond Playground
California Street
Cornwall Street
Euclid Aveune
Palm Avenue
Jordan Avenue
Commonwealth Avenue
Clement Street
20th Avenue
19th Avenue
18th Avenue
17th Avenue
16th Avenue
15th Avenue
14th Avenue
13th Avenue
12th Avenue
11th Avenue
10th Avenue
9th Avenue
8th Avenue
7th Avenue
6th Avenue
5th Avenue
4th Avenue
3rd Avenue
2nd Avenue
1
101
119
120
121

See p316

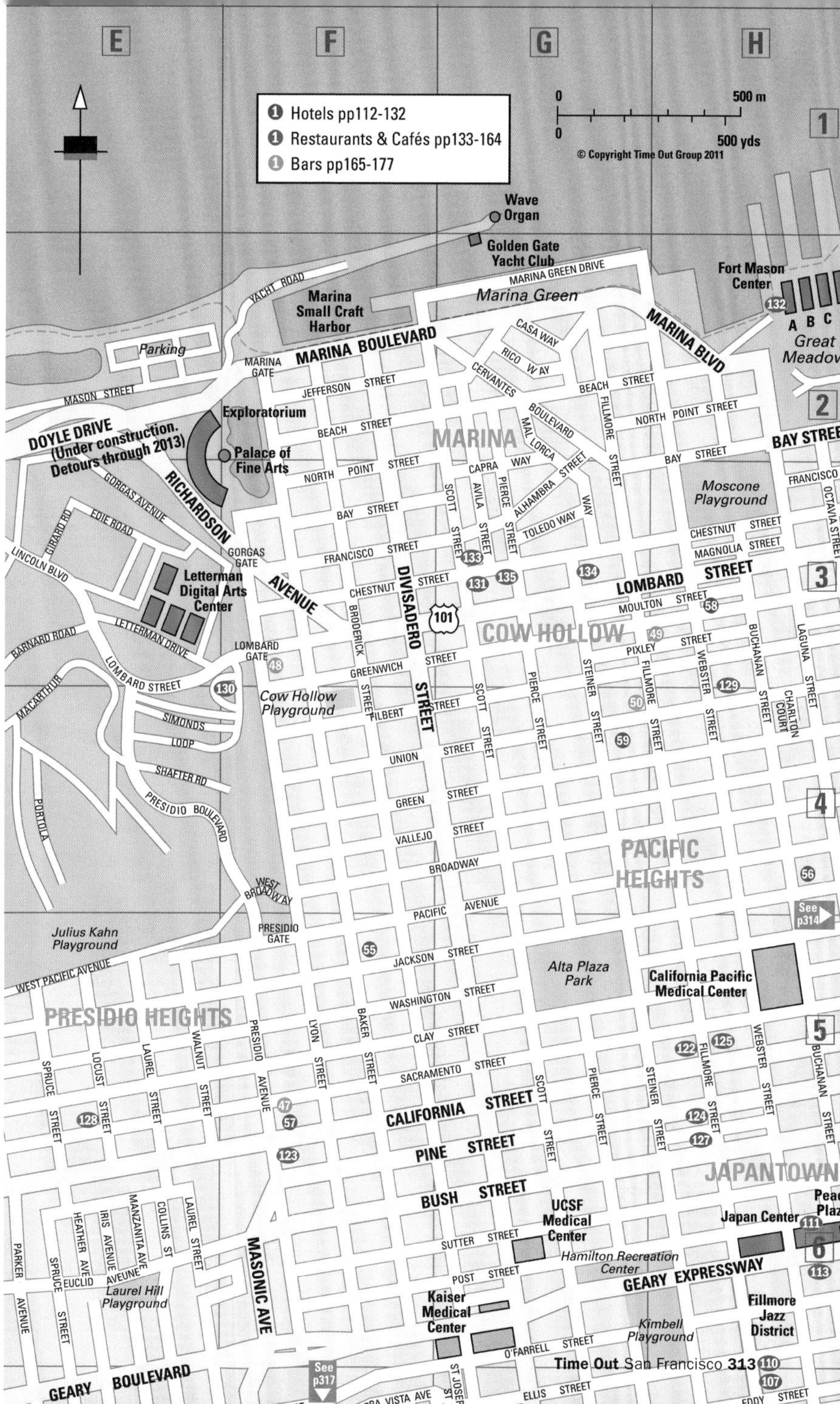
E
F
G
H
1 Hotels pp112-132
1 Restaurants & Cafés pp133-164
1 Bars pp165-177
0
500 m
0
500 yds
© Copyright Time Out Group 2011
1
2
3
4
5
6
Wave Organ
Golden Gate Yacht Club
Fort Mason Center
Marina Small Craft Harbor
Marina Green
MARINA GREEN DRIVE
YACHT ROAD
Parking
MARINA GATE
MARINA BOULEVARD
MARINA BLVD
Great Meadow
MASON STREET
DOYLE DRIVE
(Under construction. Detours through 2013)
Exploratorium
Palace of Fine Arts
RICHARDSON
AVENUE
GORGAS AVENUE
EDIE ROAD
GIRARD RD
LINCOLN BLVD
GORGAS GATE
Letterman Digital Arts Center
LETTERMAN DRIVE
BARNARD ROAD
LOMBARD GATE
LOMBARD STREET
MACARTHUR
SIMONDS LOOP
SHAFTER RD
PRESIDIO BOULEVARD
PORTOLA
WEST BROADWAY
PRESIDIO GATE
Julius Kahn Playground
WEST PACIFIC AVENUE
PRESIDIO HEIGHTS
JEFFERSON STREET
BEACH STREET
NORTH POINT STREET
BAY STREET
FRANCISCO STREET
CHESTNUT STREET
LOMBARD STREET
MOULTON STREET
GREENWICH STREET
PIXLEY STREET
FILBERT STREET
UNION STREET
GREEN STREET
VALLEJO STREET
BROADWAY
PACIFIC AVENUE
JACKSON STREET
WASHINGTON STREET
CLAY STREET
SACRAMENTO STREET
CALIFORNIA STREET
PINE STREET
BUSH STREET
SUTTER STREET
POST STREET
GEARY EXPRESSWAY
O'FARRELL STREET
ELLIS STREET
EDDY STREET
GEARY BOULEVARD
CASA WAY
RICO WAY
CERVANTES
BOULEVARD
MAL LORCA
CAPRA WAY
ALHAMBRA STREET
TOLEDO WAY
AVILA STREET
SCOTT STREET
PIERCE STREET
FILLMORE STREET
MARINA
BAY STREET
FRANCISCO STREET
OCTAVIA STREET
Moscone Playground
CHESTNUT STREET
MAGNOLIA STREET
DIVISADERO STREET
BRODERICK STREET
101
COW HOLLOW
Cow Hollow Playground
STEINER STREET
WEBSTER STREET
BUCHANAN STREET
LAGUNA STREET
CHARLTON COURT
PACIFIC HEIGHTS
See p314
Alta Plaza Park
California Pacific Medical Center
SPRUCE STREET
LOCUST STREET
LAUREL STREET
WALNUT STREET
PRESIDIO AVENUE
LYON STREET
BAKER STREET
JAPANTOWN
Peace Plaza
Japan Center
UCSF Medical Center
Hamilton Recreation Center
Kaiser Medical Center
Kimbell Playground
Fillmore Jazz District
MASONIC AVE
HEATHER AVE
IRIS AVENUE
MANZANITA AVE
COLLINS ST
LAUREL STREET
PARKER AVENUE
EUCLID AVEUNE
Laurel Hill Playground
See p317
ST JOSEPH
BUENA VISTA AVE
133
131
135
134
58
49
48
130
129
50
59
56
55
122
125
47
57
128
124
127
123
111
113
110
107
132

See p313
See p318

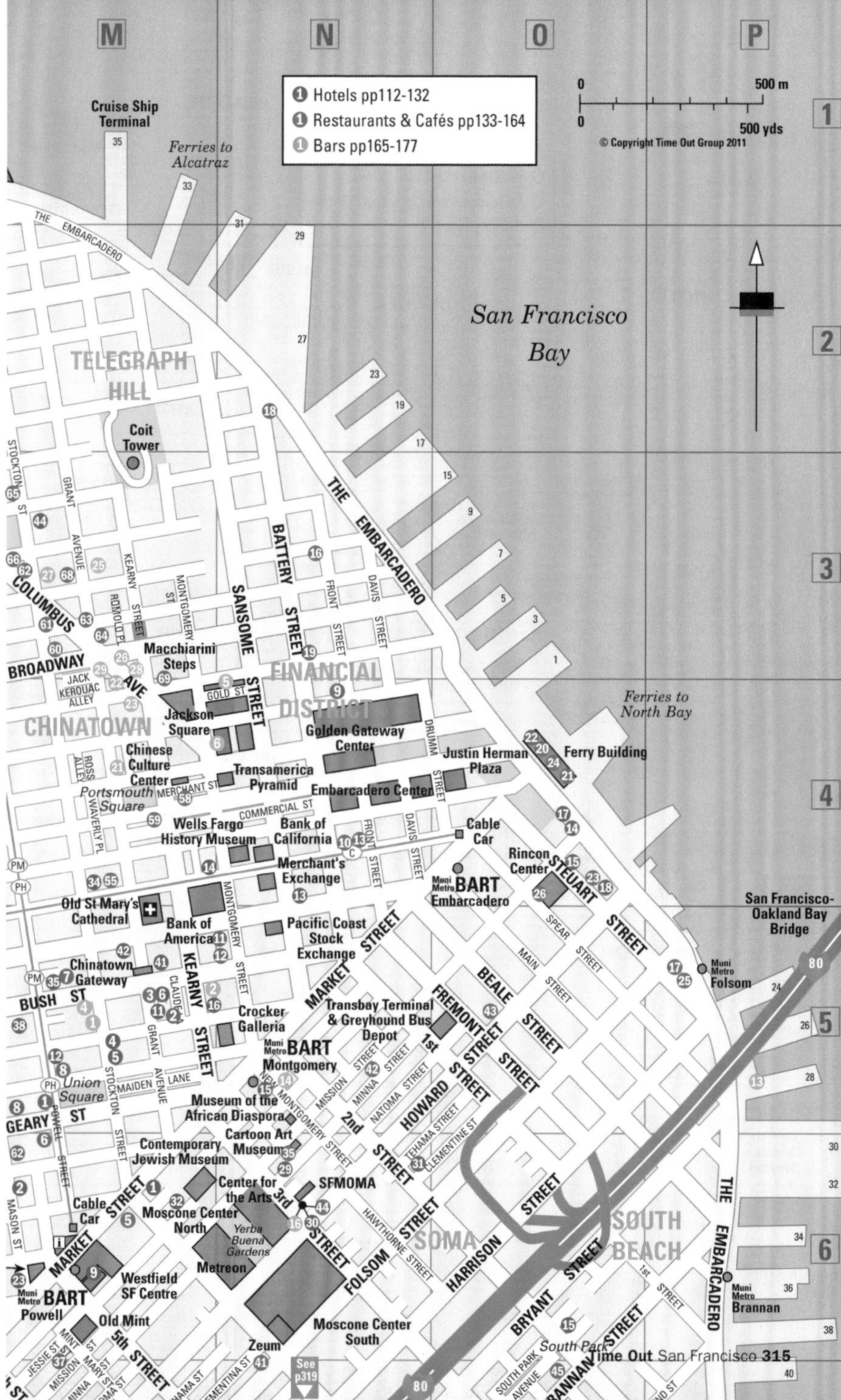
M
N
O
P
1 Hotels pp112-132
1 Restaurants & Cafés pp133-164
1 Bars pp165-177
500 m
500 yds
© Copyright Time Out Group 2011
Cruise Ship Terminal
Ferries to Alcatraz
The Embarcadero
San Francisco Bay
Telegraph Hill
Coit Tower
Financial District
Chinatown
Jackson Square
Chinese Culture Center
Portsmouth Square
Transamerica Pyramid
Golden Gateway Center
Justin Herman Plaza
Ferry Building
Ferries to North Bay
Embarcadero Center
Wells Fargo History Museum
Bank of California
Merchant's Exchange
Cable Car
Rincon Center
BART Embarcadero
Old St Mary's Cathedral
Bank of America
Pacific Coast Stock Exchange
San Francisco-Oakland Bay Bridge
Muni Metro Folsom
Chinatown Gateway
Crocker Galleria
Transbay Terminal & Greyhound Bus Depot
BART Montgomery
Union Square
Museum of the African Diaspora
Cartoon Art Museum
Contemporary Jewish Museum
Center for the Arts
SFMOMA
Moscone Center North
Yerba Buena Gardens
Metreon
SoMa
South Beach
Westfield SF Centre
BART Powell
Old Mint
Moscone Center South
Zeum
South Park
Muni Metro Brannan
See p319
Macchiarini Steps
Jack Kerouac Alley
Columbus Ave
Broadway
Bush St
Geary St
Market Street
Mission Street
Howard Street
Folsom Street
Harrison Street
Bryant Street
Brannan Street
Steuart Street
Beale Street
Fremont Street
Spear Street
Main Street
Battery Street
Sansome Street
Montgomery Street
Kearny Street
Grant Avenue
Stockton Street
Powell Street
Mason St
Drumm Street
Davis Street
Front Street
Commercial St
Merchant St
Gold St
Maiden Lane
Minna Street
Natoma Street
Tehama Street
Clementine St
Hawthorne Street
New Montgomery Street
2nd Street
3rd Street
1st Street
5th Street
Mint St
Jessie St
South Park Avenue

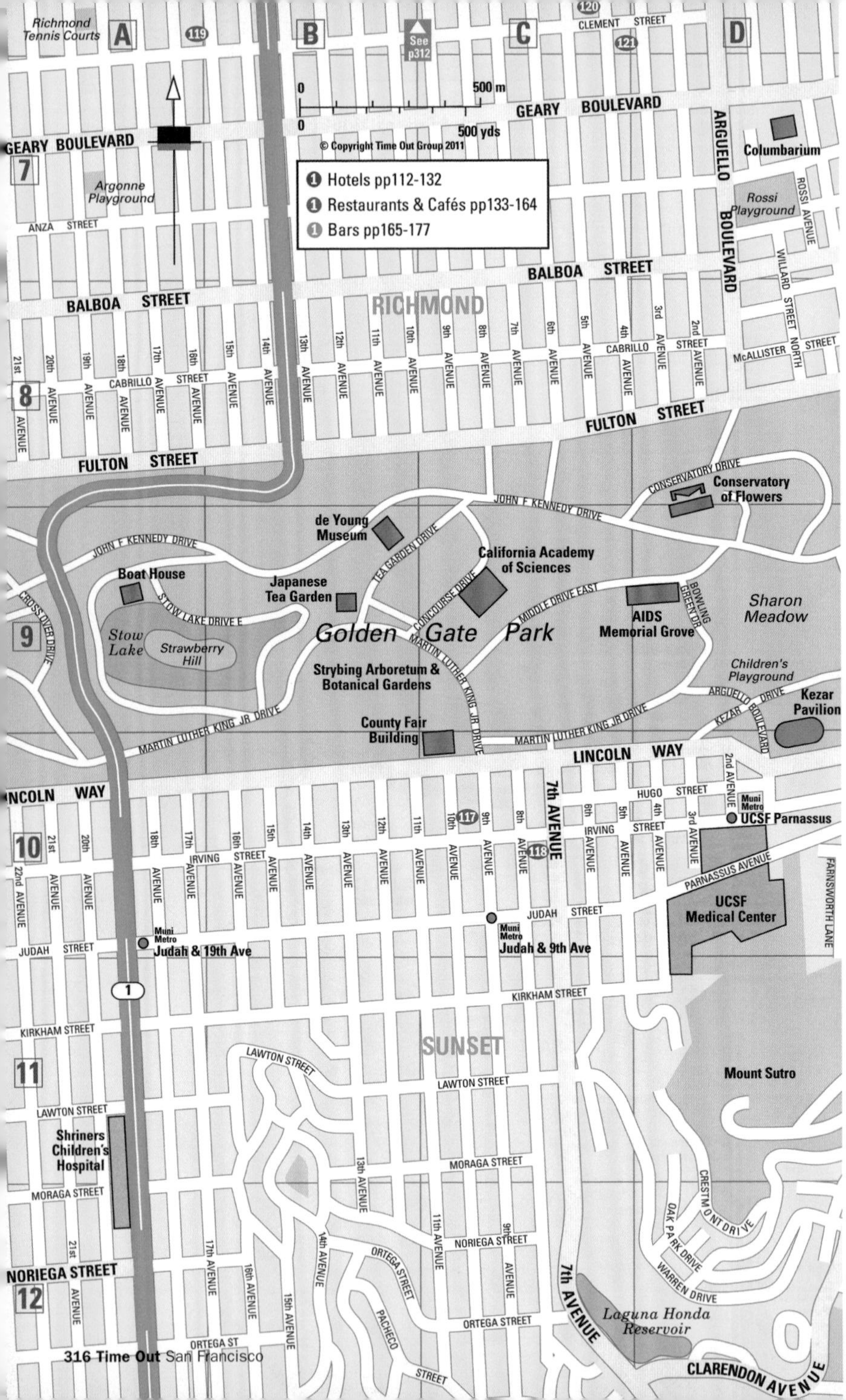

Richmond Tennis Courts
A
B
C
D
See p312
CLEMENT STREET
GEARY BOULEVARD
ARGUELLO BOULEVARD
Columbarium
0 500 m
0 500 yds
© Copyright Time Out Group 2011
Hotels pp112-132
Restaurants & Cafés pp133-164
Bars pp165-177
Argonne Playground
Rossi Playground
ANZA STREET
BALBOA STREET
RICHMOND
CABRILLO STREET
FULTON STREET
McALLISTER STREET
WILLARD STREET NORTH
ROSSI AVENUE
CONSERVATORY DRIVE
Conservatory of Flowers
JOHN F KENNEDY DRIVE
de Young Museum
TEA GARDEN DRIVE
California Academy of Sciences
Boat House
Japanese Tea Garden
CONCOURSE DRIVE
MIDDLE DRIVE EAST
BOWLING GREEN DR
Sharon Meadow
CROSSOVER DRIVE
STOW LAKE DRIVE E
Stow Lake
Strawberry Hill
Golden Gate Park
AIDS Memorial Grove
Strybing Arboretum & Botanical Gardens
Children's Playground
MARTIN LUTHER KING JR DRIVE
ARGUELLO DRIVE
KEZAR DRIVE
Kezar Pavilion
County Fair Building
LINCOLN WAY
HUGO STREET
IRVING STREET
7th AVENUE
Muni Metro
UCSF Parnassus
PARNASSUS AVENUE
UCSF Medical Center
FARNSWORTH LANE
JUDAH STREET
Judah & 19th Ave
Judah & 9th Ave
KIRKHAM STREET
SUNSET
LAWTON STREET
Mount Sutro
Shriners Children's Hospital
MORAGA STREET
NORIEGA STREET
CRESTMONT DRIVE
OAK PARK DRIVE
WARREN DRIVE
ORTEGA STREET
PACHECO STREET
Laguna Honda Reservoir
CLARENDON AVENUE
ORTEGA ST

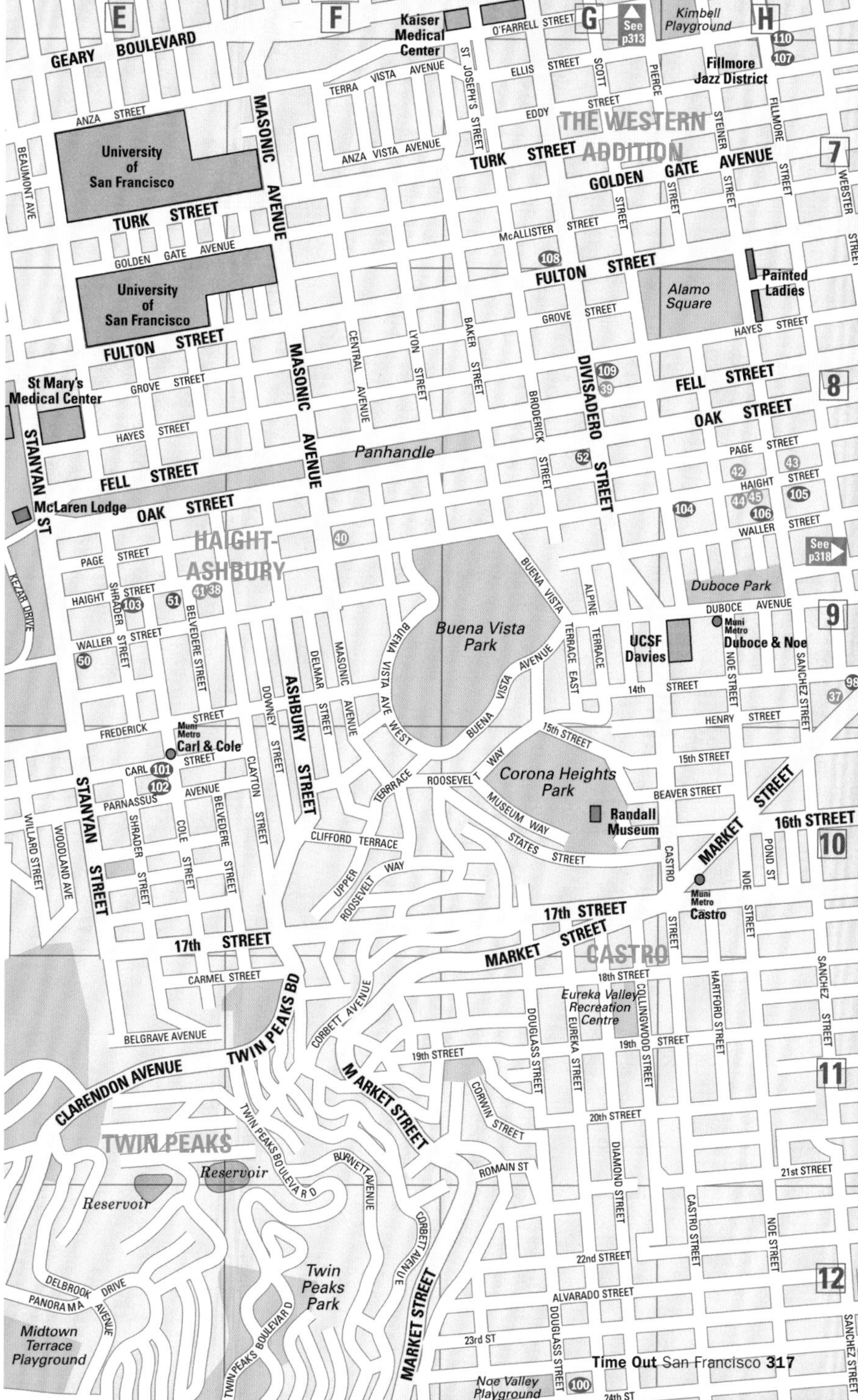

E
F
G
H
7
8
9
10
11
12
Kaiser Medical Center
Kimbell Playground
See p313
Fillmore Jazz District
THE WESTERN ADDITION
University of San Francisco
University of San Francisco
St Mary's Medical Center
McLaren Lodge
Painted Ladies
Alamo Square
Panhandle
HAIGHT-ASHBURY
Buena Vista Park
Duboce Park
See p318
UCSF Davies
Muni Metro Duboce & Noe
Muni Metro Carl & Cole
Corona Heights Park
Randall Museum
Muni Metro Castro
CASTRO
Eureka Valley Recreation Centre
TWIN PEAKS
Reservoir
Reservoir
Twin Peaks Park
Midtown Terrace Playground
Noe Valley Playground
GEARY BOULEVARD
MASONIC AVENUE
DIVISADERO STREET
MARKET STREET

THE WESTERN ADDITION
HAYES VALLEY
CIVIC CENTER
LOWER HAIGHT
SOMA
MISSION
Kimbell Playground
Fillmore Jazz District
Jefferson Square
California State Building
Veterans' Building
Asian Art Museum
St Boniface Catholic Church
City Hall
Civic Center Plaza
UN Plaza
Opera House
Symphony Hall
Main Library
Bill Graham Civic Auditorium
Muni Metro BART Civic Center
Painted Ladies
Alamo Square
Muni Metro Van Ness
Duboce Park
Muni Metro Duboce & Noe
UCSF Davies
Muni Metro Church
Mission Dolores
BART 16th St
Franklin Square
Muni Metro Castro
Muni Metro Church & 18th St
Mission Dolores Park
Mission Playground
Coronado Playground
BART 24th St
Precita Eyes Mural Arts & Visitors Center
Muni Metro Church & 24th St
See p314
See p317
101
Hotels pp112-132
Restaurants & Cafés pp133-164
Bars pp165-177
0 500 m
0 500 yds

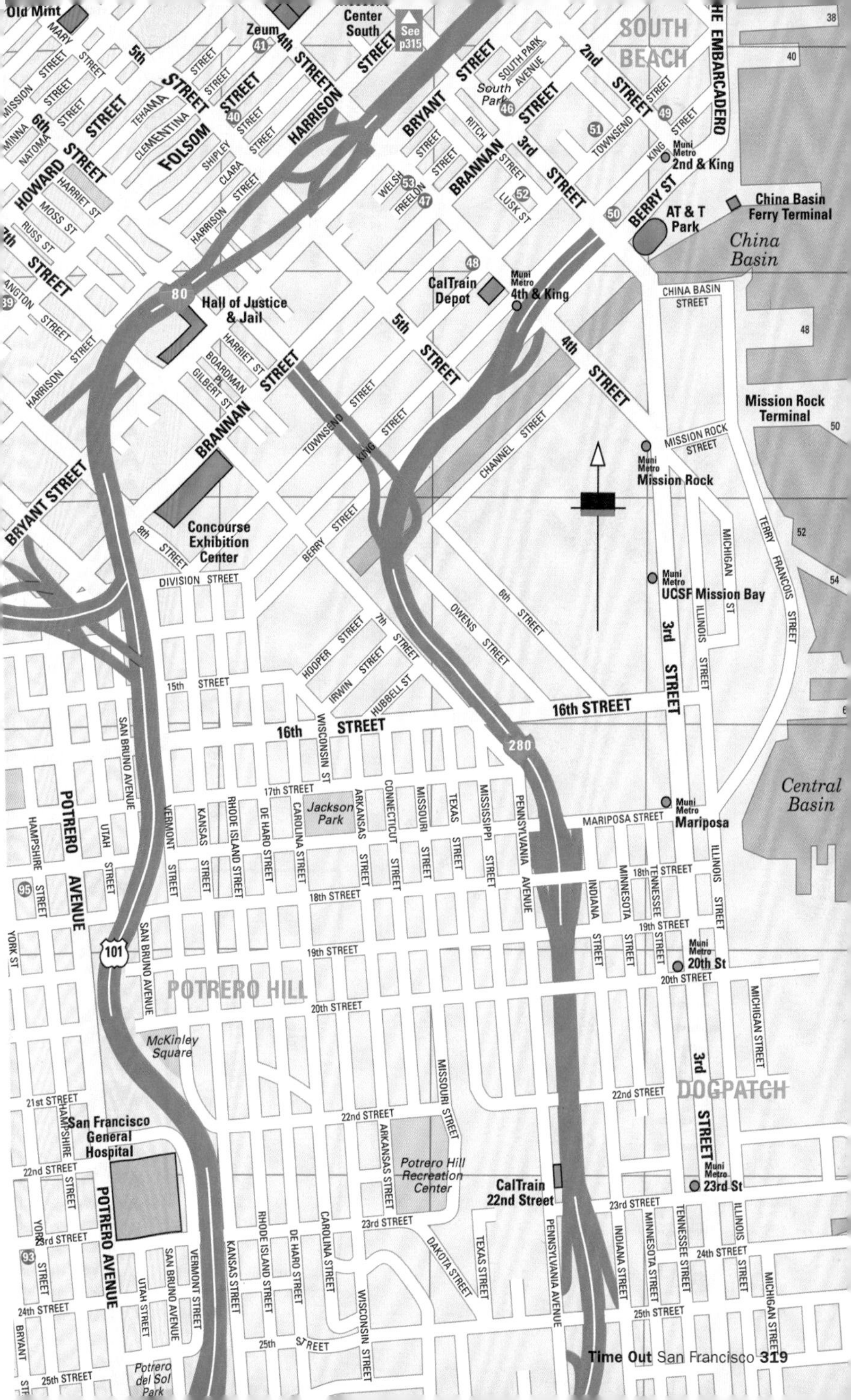
South Beach
China Basin
Central Basin
Potrero Hill
Dogpatch
AT & T Park
China Basin Ferry Terminal
Mission Rock Terminal
CalTrain Depot
Hall of Justice & Jail
Concourse Exhibition Center
Jackson Park
McKinley Square
San Francisco General Hospital
Potrero Hill Recreation Center
Potrero del Sol Park
CalTrain 22nd Street
See p315

Muni Metro

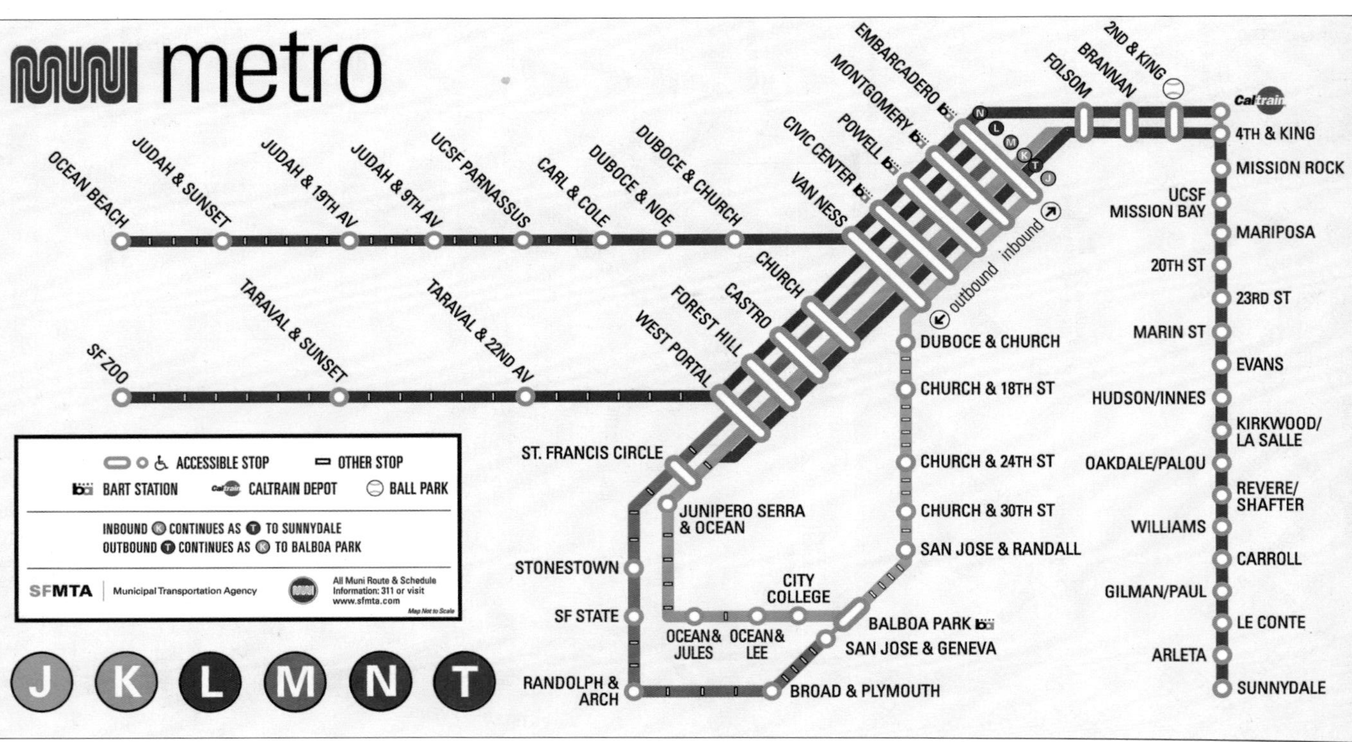

muni metro
OCEAN BEACH
JUDAH & SUNSET
JUDAH & 19TH AV
JUDAH & 9TH AV
UCSF PARNASSUS
CARL & COLE
DUBOCE & NOE
DUBOCE & CHURCH
VAN NESS
CIVIC CENTER
POWELL
MONTGOMERY
EMBARCADERO
FOLSOM
BRANNAN
2ND & KING
Caltrain
4TH & KING
MISSION ROCK
UCSF MISSION BAY
MARIPOSA
20TH ST
23RD ST
MARIN ST
EVANS
HUDSON/INNES
KIRKWOOD/ LA SALLE
OAKDALE/PALOU
REVERE/ SHAFTER
WILLIAMS
CARROLL
GILMAN/PAUL
LE CONTE
ARLETA
SUNNYDALE
inbound
outbound
DUBOCE & CHURCH
CHURCH & 18TH ST
CHURCH & 24TH ST
CHURCH & 30TH ST
SAN JOSE & RANDALL
BALBOA PARK
SAN JOSE & GENEVA
BROAD & PLYMOUTH
CITY COLLEGE
OCEAN & LEE
OCEAN & JULES
JUNIPERO SERRA & OCEAN
CHURCH
CASTRO
FOREST HILL
WEST PORTAL
TARAVAL & SUNSET
TARAVAL & 22ND AV
SF ZOO
ST. FRANCIS CIRCLE
STONESTOWN
SF STATE
RANDOLPH & ARCH
ACCESSIBLE STOP
OTHER STOP
BART STATION
CALTRAIN DEPOT
BALL PARK
INBOUND K CONTINUES AS T TO SUNNYDALE
OUTBOUND T CONTINUES AS K TO BALBOA PARK
SFMTA
Municipal Transportation Agency
All Muni Route & Schedule Information: 311 or visit www.sfmta.com
Map Not to Scale
J
K
L
M
N
T